Demographics OF THE U.S.

TRENDS AND PROJECTIONS

Demographics
OF THE U.S.
TRENDS AND PROJECTIONS
BY CHERYL RUSSELL

New Strategist Publications, Inc.

Ithaca, New York

New Strategist Publications, Inc.
P.O. Box 242, Ithaca, New York 14851
800/848-0842; 607/273-0913
www.newstrategist.com

ISBN 978-1-933588-28-5
ISBN 1-933588-28-4

Printed in the United States of America

Table of Contents

Chapter 10. Wealth

List of Tables

Chapter 3. Health

Chapter 7. Living Arrangements

Chapter 8. Population

Chapter 9. Spending

Chapter 10. Wealth

List of Illustrations

Chapter 10. Wealth

Introduction

Sometimes there is no substitute for a book. For those perusing the government's vast collection of demographic and socioeconomic statistics, the Internet is a goldmine. Yet the Internet's adoption has meant the disappearance of the government's once regular and reliable publications. Printing and distributing those trusty sources of insight into American life became too costly—and increasingly no longer cost effective. But the replacement—the vast storehouses of data on the Internet—is not the same.

Those plunging into the Internet often find themselves having a Goldilocks experience—too much of one thing, too little of another, and a lot of effort needed to find something just right. Additionally, screens of information do not allow the kind of thoughtful thumbing and reflection required for business and policy research and analysis. Especially when one tries to gain insight into ongoing trends, diving into what is available on the Internet can be an exercise in frustration. The Bureau of Labor Statistics, for example, replaces its annual labor force data with new numbers each year, making it difficult to find comparable historical labor force tables. The Census Bureau has so many areas of historical data on its web site that users almost have to don a pith helmet to find what they need.

The third edition of *Demographics of the U.S.: Trends and Projections* is the "just right" bowl of porridge, presenting the most important historical statistics and providing the kind of insight difficult to wring from screens of data. *Demographics of the U.S.* collects, in one volume, much of the demographic information that can be found only hit or miss elsewhere. New Strategist's editors scoured web sites and government reference books to locate the most revealing trend data. The result is a compilation of statistics that cannot be found in one single volume anywhere else, documenting the demographic and socioeconomic trends that have transformed the United States since 1950. *Demographics of the U.S.* is a reference book for those who want perspective on the many changes in American life—a perspective critical for understanding what the 21st century will hold.

In this edition of *Demographics of the U.S.* you will find comprehensive coverage of historical statistics, including single-year data on many topics, such as educational attainment, SAT scores, college costs, health insurance, cigarette smoking, homeownership, household income, earnings, poverty rates, labor force participation, self-employment, households by type, living arrangements of children, marital status, immigration, geographic mobility, and more. In addition, *Demographics of the U.S.* presents important trend data on race and ethnicity, homeownership, and household wealth and spending—a compilation of historical statistics and a discussion of the trends unavailable anywhere else.

How to use this book

Demographics of the U.S. is designed for easy use. It is divided into 10 chapters, organized alphabetically: Attitudes and Behavior, Education, Health, Housing, Income, Labor Force, Living Arrangements, Population, Spending, and Wealth.

Most of the tables in *Demographics of the U.S.* are based on data collected by the federal government, in particular the Census Bureau, the Bureau of Labor Statistics, the National Center for Education Statistics, the National Center for Health Statistics, and the Federal Reserve Board. The federal government continues to be the best source of up-to-date, reliable information on the changing characteristics of Americans.

To explore changes in attitudes, New Strategist extracted data from the nationally representative General Social Survey of the University of Chicago's National Opinion Research Center. NORC conducts the biennial survey through face-to-face interviews with an independently drawn, representative sample of 1,500 to 3,000 noninstitutionalized people aged 18 or older who live in the United States. The GSS is one of the best sources of attitudinal data on Americans available today. Now it is more accessible than ever, with the University of California at Berkeley putting the historical dataset online, allowing users to access this valuable resource like never before. The results are available in the Attitudes and Behavior chapter.

Several government surveys are of particular importance to *Demographics of the U.S.* Most important is the Current Population Survey. The CPS is a nationally representative survey of the civilian noninstitutionalized population aged 15 or older. The Census Bureau takes the survey each month to determine the unemployment rate, collecting information from 50,000 households. Each year, the March survey includes a demographic supplement that is the source of most national data on the characteristics of Americans, such as their incomes, educational attainment, and living arrangements. The CPS is one of the best sources of historical data, with information about various aspects of American life extending back for decades.

The American Community Survey is becoming another important source of demographic data, although it is still too new to provide much historical information. The ACS, an ongoing nationwide survey of 250,000 households per month, provides detailed demographic data at the community level since 2001. Designed to replace the census long-form questionnaire, the ACS includes more than 60 questions that formerly appeared on the long form, such as inquiries about the language spoken at home, or householders' income and education. ACS data are available for the nation, regions, states, counties, metropolitan areas, and smaller geographic units.

The Consumer Expenditure Survey is the data source for the Spending chapter. Sponsored by the Bureau of Labor Statistics, the CEX is an ongoing study of the day-to-day spending of American households. The data collected by the survey are used to update prices for the Consumer Price Index. The CEX includes an interview survey and a diary survey administered to two separate, nationally representative samples. The average spending figures shown in the Spending chapter of this book are the integrated data from both the diary and interview components of the survey. For the interview survey, about 7,500 consumer units are interviewed on a rotating panel basis each quarter for five consecutive quarters. For the diary survey, another 7,500 consumer units keep weekly diaries of spending for two consecutive weeks.

The Survey of Consumer Finances provides the data for the Wealth chapter. The SCF is a triennial survey taken by the Federal Reserve Board. The SCF collects data on the assets, debt, and net worth of American households. *Demographics of the U.S.* presents SCF data from 1989 through 2004, the latest year for which data are available.

Whenever possible, *Demographics of the U.S.* presents data from 1950 to the latest available. For most demographic and socioeconomic topics, however, it is not possible to find data going back to 1950 because many demographic concepts and classifications have emerged only in the past few decades or have changed so much that comparable historical data are nonexistent. Modern racial and ethnic classifications, for example, did not exist before the late 1970s and 1980s, and they changed again with the 2000 census, which allowed people to choose more than one racial category for the first time in modern history. Several household types now considered important received little attention until the 1960s and 1970s. The obsessive focus on generations and age groups occurred after the birth of the baby-boom generation. Analysts revised educational attainment categories in 1991, so data collected before and after that year are not strictly comparable. Important health indicators were unknown in the mid-20th century and therefore untracked. Modern-day spending and wealth data were not collected until the 1980s. Metropolitan boundaries change continuously. Occupational categories have been updated and reclassified. Despite these limitations, however, *Demographics of the U.S.* reveals much about our past and clarifies our future. It informs without overwhelming through a combination of tables, texts, and charts.

While the federal government collected most of the information published here, the tables in *Demographics of the U.S.* are not simply reprints of government spreadsheets as is the case in many other reference books. Instead, New Strategist's statisticians individually compiled and created most of the tables, adding percent change, index, and other calculations to reveal the stories behind the numbers. Each chapter of *Demographics of the U.S.* includes the demographic and lifestyle information most important to researchers. A page of text accompanies many of the tables, analyzing the data and highlighting the trends. Readers who want more statistical detail than the tables provide can plumb the original sources listed at the bottom of each table. The book contains a comprehensive table list to help researchers locate the information they need. For a more detailed search, use the index at the back of the book. Also at the back of the book is the glossary, which defines the terms commonly used in tables and text.

Demographics of the U.S.: Trends and Projections explains our complex, confusing, and ever-changing society. It makes sense of our past and sheds light on our future.

Executive Summary

The year is 1950, and you are about to be magically transported more than half a century into the future to the present time. What would you notice first? What would most surprise you? Cell phones, sure. And it would not take long before you noticed computers and the Internet. But beyond the obvious technological marvels of the day lie profound changes in our demographics and lifestyles that would be just as shocking to the 1950s time traveler as our high-tech gadgets. What are the 10 jaw-dropping demographic and socioeconomic changes that would send the time traveler's head spinning? Read on to find out.

1. We are fatter

Let's say the time traveler lands on a sidewalk outside a shopping mall. What is the first thing he would notice? Right away he would have to leap aside to make room for modern-day pedestrians. The average man and woman on the street is much heavier than those from the traveler's time. In 1960 (the earliest data available), the average woman weighed a reasonable 140 pounds. Now she weighs an oversized 164 pounds. The average man has seen his weight rise from 166 to 191 pounds. In 1950, few Americans were overweight. Today, most are overweight and nearly one-third are obese.

Most Americans are overweight

(percent of people aged 20 to 74 who are overweight, by sex, 1960–62 and 2000–04)

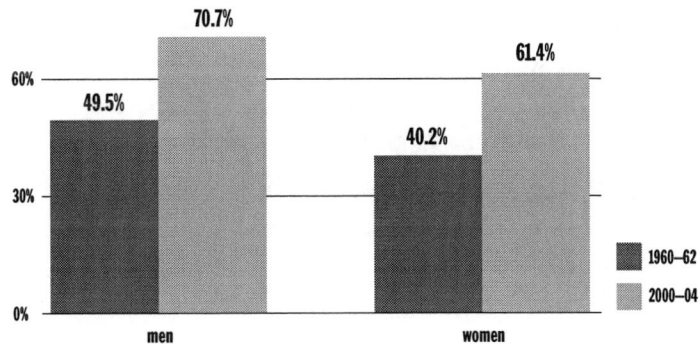

2. We are much more diverse

The traveler's second shock would be the diversity of the people around him. He would see far fewer non-Hispanic whites (in fact, he would not be familiar with the term "non-Hispanic white") and many more Asians, blacks, and Hispanics. In 1950, fully 90 percent of the population was white—and virtually all whites were non-Hispanic. Hispanics (who may be of any race) were not a part of the mix. The time traveler also would notice the much greater integration of racial and ethnic groups. During the past few decades, the percentage of Americans whose neighborhood includes blacks has grown from just 30 to fully 66 percent.

Whites account for a smaller share of Americans

(percent distribution of the population by race and Hispanic origin, 1950 and 2006)

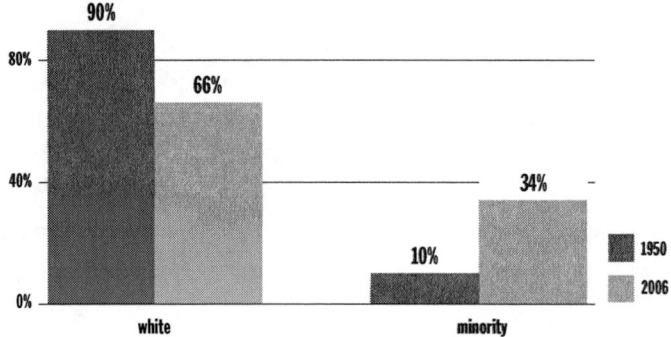

3. We are richer

Only after the traveler finished ogling the overweight and diverse crowds milling about him would he notice how much richer everyone seems compared to 1950. Not only is everyone talking on tiny, hand-held telephones, but white wires sprout from the ears of many. The parking lot is enormous and full of more cars than the traveler has ever seen at one time. The shopping mall itself is cavernous, and enclosed! The stores are air-conditioned. The traveler realizes the society in which he has landed is much more affluent than the one of 1950. In fact, the average man has seen his median income climb 77 percent since 1950, after adjusting for inflation. The traveler is intrigued. He wants to make more money too, and he goes looking for a job.

The incomes of men and women have grown

(median income of men and women aged 15 or older, 1950 and 2005; in 2005 dollars)

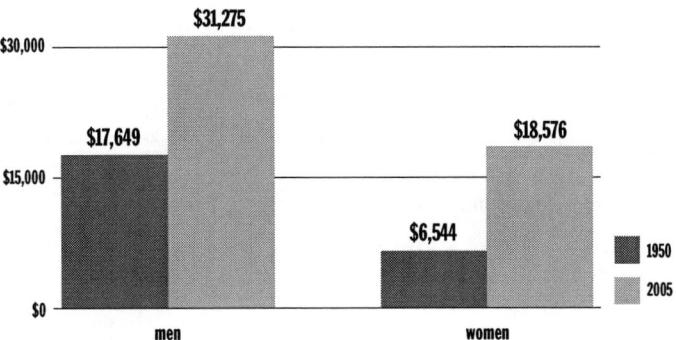

4. We are highly educated

When he applies for a job, the traveler runs into his first problem, and it is a big one. On the job application, he must report his level of educational attainment. The traveler dutifully notes that he has not completed high school. This was the norm among his peers in 1950, only 34 percent of whom had a high school diploma. Today, fully 85 percent of adults are high school graduates. Not only that, but the percentage of people with a college degree has climbed from just 6 to 28 percent. Without a high school diploma, the traveler will have a difficult time convincing anyone to hire him and an even harder time making much money.

Most people today are high school graduates and many have graduated from college

(percent of people aged 25 or older with a high school diploma or college degree, 1950 and 2006)

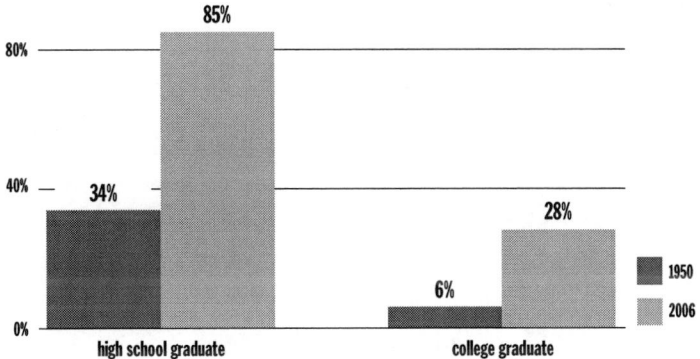

5. Spending patterns have changed

Eventually, the traveler lands a job at Wal-Mart. When he gets his first paycheck, he heads into the store to shop for food and clothes. There he experiences another shock. Food and clothing prices have plummeted. The amount of money he must spend on food is 40 percent less than it was in 1950, and his spending on clothes has decreased an even larger 51 percent. He feels almost giddy, until he tries to rent an apartment. Then he discovers the cost of housing has more than doubled. And the expense of buying and owning a car is nearly twice what it was in 1950.

Spending on some categories has plummeted

(percent change in average annual household spending on selected items, 1950 to 2005; in 2005 dollars)

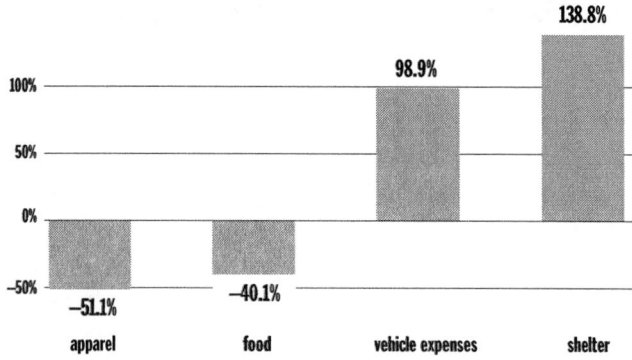

6. Working women are the norm

While at work, the traveler notices something else—women. They seem to be almost as numerous as men in the workplace. The traveler is stunned to discover that working women are now the norm. Even more surprising, two out of three married women with children are in the labor force. In 1950, few mothers worked. The traveler realizes family life must be different today. He asks his coworkers about it.

Most women, including married mothers, are in the labor force

(percent of married women with children under age 18 in the labor force, 1960 and 2005)

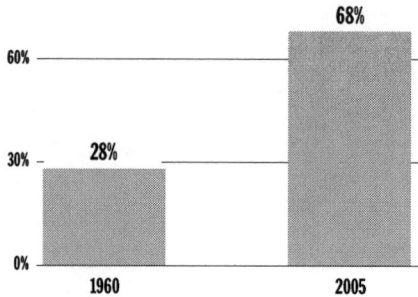

7. Fewer households are headed by nuclear families

While talking to his coworkers, the traveler discovers they are much less likely to live in a nuclear family (a married couple with children) than were his colleagues of 1950. The nuclear family share of households has plummeted from 43 to 23 percent. Many of his older coworkers live by themselves. The percentage of households headed by people living alone has climbed from 11 to 27 percent. Perhaps most surprising, many of his female colleagues head families without a husband. The traveler realizes attitudes have changed profoundly since the 1950s. He begins to ask how people feel about marriage and family.

Married couples with children account for less than one in four households today

(percent of households headed by married couples with children under age 18, 1950 and 2006)

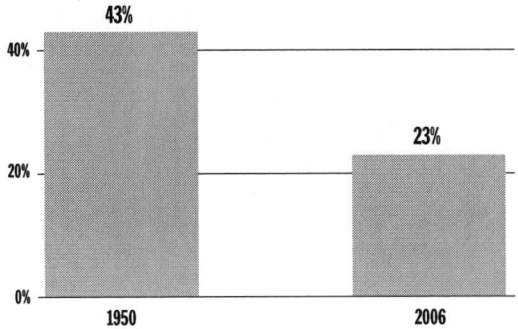

Single-person households are much more numerous

(percent of households headed by people who live alone, 1950 and 2006)

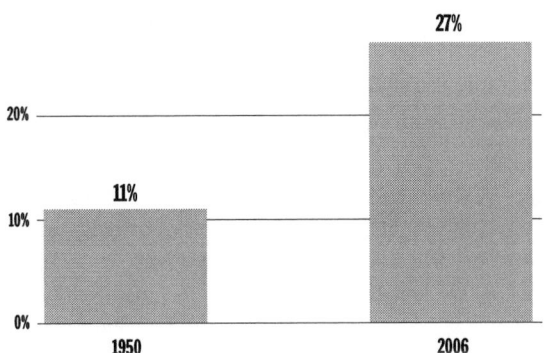

8. We are more liberal

The traveler gets an earful. His coworkers tell him the people of today no longer believe a woman's place is in the home. In fact, 62 percent disagree with the notion. Most also think a working mother can have just as warm a relationship with her children as a mother who does not work. Only one-third of the public still thinks premarital sex is always or usually wrong. And homosexuality—something no one spoke openly about in the traveler's time—is becoming accepted as well.

Most disagree that a woman's place is in the home

(percent of people aged 18 or older who disagree with the statement, "It is much better for everyone involved if the man is the achiever outside the home and the woman takes care of the home and family," 1977 and 2004)

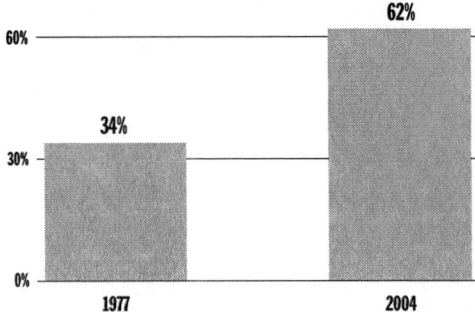

9. Out-of-wedlock childbearing is common

The traveler wonders how these more liberal attitudes toward marriage and family have changed family life. He hears more than he wants to know, with some of his coworkers revealing that their children were born out-of-wedlock. In fact, out-of-wedlock childbearing is now commonplace, with 37 percent of babies born to single mothers. In 1950, the figure was only 4 percent. The traveler is reeling at this trend. He is beginning to feel homesick and wants to return to the more strait-laced days of 1950—until he hears some good news.

More than one-third of children are born to single mothers

(percent of babies born out-of-wedlock, 1950 and 2005)

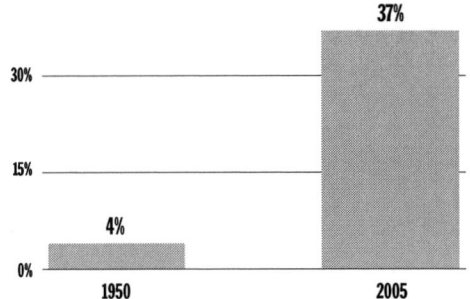

10. We are living longer

The traveler is so upset about the degree of social change since 1950 that he fears he will have a heart attack. He visits a doctor who checks his vital signs and discovers his high cholesterol and blood pressure. The doctor, prescribes several medications. He informs the traveler that the death rate from heart disease is plummeting, thanks to new drug treatments and the decline in smoking. The traveler is a smoker, as were many of his peers in 1950. The doctor advises him to quit. Now the traveler must make a decision.

Life expectancy has climbed since 1950

(number of years of life remaining at birth and at age 65, 1950 and 2004)

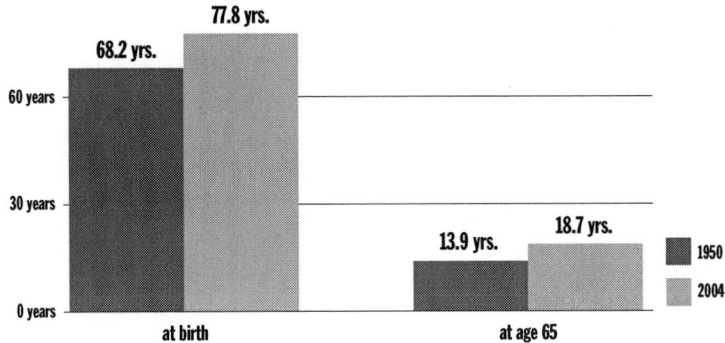

It is time for the traveler to make up his mind: remain in the present day or return to 1950. The traveler decides to stay, knowing he will enjoy a longer, healthier life. He intends to quit smoking, get his GED, and buy a cell phone.

Cheryl Russell
Editorial Director
New Strategist Publications

Attitudes and Behavior

■ The attitudes of the American public have been remarkably stable over the past three decades. The percentage of Americans who think life is exciting, for example, has grown only slightly—to 51 percent—despite dramatic change in lifestyles and technology.

■ When asked how their family's income ranks relative to the incomes of other families, fewer Americans place themselves in the middle. The percentage of those who say their incomes are in the middle fell from 57 to 47 percent between 1972 and 2004.

■ Times have changed. In 1977, two out of three Americans believed traditional sex roles—where the man is the achiever outside the home and the woman stays home and cares for the family—were best. By 2004, only 38 percent felt that way.

■ The percentage of Americans who think premarital sex is not wrong at all has grown from only 27 percent in 1972 to nearly half—46 percent—in 2004. Homosexuality is still disapproved by most Americans, but the majority is shrinking.

■ Two out of three Americans aged 18 or older believe in God and have no doubt about it, a percentage that has been fairly stable over the years. Only 3 percent do not believe in God.

■ Political views have been surprisingly stable over the decades. In 2004, the 66 percent majority of the public described its political views as moderate, only slightly liberal, or only slightly conservative—not much different from the percentage who described themselves that way more than thirty years earlier.

Americans Find Life More Exciting

But happiness has not increased.

The attitudes of the American public toward many issues have been remarkably stable over the past three decades. The percentage of Americans who think life is exciting, for example, has grown only slightly, despite dramatic change in lifestyles and technology. In 2004, 50.6 percent of the public said life was exciting, up from the 45.5 percent of 1973. There has been almost no increase in the percentage of people who say they are very happy, which stood at 31 percent in 2004. When asked whether they think people try to be helpful, a slightly larger percentage of Americans say yes (50 percent in 2004, up from 47 percent in 1972).

But some attitudes have changed. The percentage of people who say most people can be trusted has dropped by a substantial 10 percentage points over the past thirty years, from 46 to 36 percent. The percentage of Americans who agree that people will try to take advantage if they get a chance has grown from 34 to 40 percent.

■ Growing urbanization in the United States has contributed to greater distrust.

Trust in others has declined

(percent of people aged 18 or older who agree that most people can be trusted, 1973 and 2004)

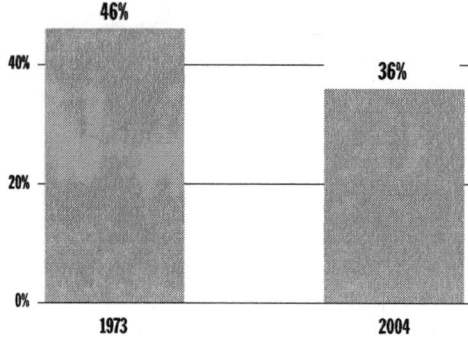

Table 1.1 General Happiness, 1972 to 2004

"Taken all together, how would you say things are these days—would you say that you are very happy, pretty happy, or not too happy?"

(percent distribution of people aged 18 or older by response, 1972 to 2004)

	total people	very happy	pretty happy	not too happy
2004	100.0%	31.3%	55.2%	13.5%
2002	100.0	30.3	57.3	12.4
2000	100.0	31.7	57.7	10.6
1998	100.0	31.8	56.1	12.1
1996	100.0	30.4	57.5	12.1
1994	100.0	28.8	59.0	12.2
1993	100.0	31.6	57.3	11.1
1991	100.0	31.1	58.0	11.0
1990	100.0	33.4	57.6	9.0
1989	100.0	32.6	57.7	9.7
1988	100.0	34.0	56.8	9.3
1987	100.0	29.1	57.5	13.4
1986	100.0	32.3	56.3	11.4
1985	100.0	28.6	60.0	11.4
1984	100.0	34.7	52.3	12.9
1983	100.0	31.2	56.1	12.8
1982	100.0	30.6	54.9	14.5
1980	100.0	33.9	52.7	13.3
1978	100.0	34.3	56.1	9.6
1977	100.0	34.8	53.2	11.9
1976	100.0	34.1	53.4	12.5
1975	100.0	32.9	54.1	13.1
1974	100.0	37.9	49.0	13.1
1973	100.0	35.9	51.1	13.1
1972	100.0	30.3	53.2	16.5

Source: Survey Documentation and Analysis, Computer-assisted Survey Methods Program, University of California, Berkeley, General Social Surveys, 1972–2004 Cumulative Data Files, Internet site http://sda.berkeley.edu/D3/GSS04/Docyr/gs04.htm

Table 1.2 Is Life Exciting? 1973 to 2004

"In general, do you find life exciting, pretty routine, or dull?"

(percent distribution of people aged 18 or older by response, 1973 to 2004)

	total people	exciting	routine	dull
2004	100.0%	50.6%	45.3%	4.1%
2002	100.0	52.1	44.2	3.7
2000	100.0	46.4	48.7	4.9
1998	100.0	45.1	49.4	5.5
1996	100.0	49.9	45.9	4.2
1994	100.0	47.4	48.4	4.1
1993	100.0	46.5	47.0	6.5
1991	100.0	44.3	51.5	4.2
1990	100.0	45.0	50.1	5.0
1989	100.0	44.5	50.1	5.3
1988	100.0	45.1	50.0	4.9
1987	100.0	44.0	51.5	4.6
1985	100.0	47.9	45.6	6.5
1984	100.0	46.8	48.2	5.0
1982	100.0	43.1	50.2	6.6
1980	100.0	46.0	48.4	5.6
1977	100.0	44.4	48.9	6.8
1976	100.0	44.7	51.6	3.7
1974	100.0	43.5	51.8	4.7
1973	100.0	45.5	49.4	5.1

Source: Survey Documentation and Analysis, Computer-assisted Survey Methods Program, University of California, Berkeley, General Social Surveys, 1973–2004 Cumulative Data Files, Internet site http://sda.berkeley.edu/D3/GSS04/Docyr/gs04.htm

Table 1.3 Helpfulness of People, 1972 to 2004

"Would you say that most of the time people try to be helpful,
or that they are mostly just looking out for themselves?"

(percent distribution of people aged 18 or older by response, 1972 to 2004)

	total people	helpful	look out for self	depends
2004	100.0%	50.2%	41.1%	8.7%
2002	100.0	47.4	43.0	9.7
2000	100.0	46.0	45.2	8.8
1998	100.0	47.9	42.8	9.3
1996	100.0	43.6	49.2	7.2
1994	100.0	46.7	46.9	6.4
1993	100.0	52.9	41.4	5.8
1991	100.0	49.4	43.4	7.2
1990	100.0	52.1	41.8	6.2
1989	100.0	50.3	44.6	5.1
1988	100.0	50.0	45.3	4.7
1987	100.0	43.6	51.9	4.5
1986	100.0	56.0	38.8	5.2
1984	100.0	52.0	44.3	3.7
1983	100.0	57.7	38.0	4.3
1980	100.0	49.0	46.6	4.4
1978	100.0	59.6	35.2	5.3
1976	100.0	43.3	50.6	6.1
1975	100.0	56.5	36.8	6.7
1973	100.0	46.9	49.4	3.7
1972	100.0	47.1	46.6	6.3

Source: Survey Documentation and Analysis, Computer-assisted Survey Methods Program, University of California, Berkeley, General Social Surveys, 1972–2004 Cumulative Data Files, Internet site http://sda.berkeley.edu/D3/GSS04/Docyr/gs04.htm

Table 1.4 Trusting in People, 1972 to 2004

"Generally speaking, would you say that most people can
be trusted or that you can't be too careful in life."

(percent distribution of people aged 18 or older by response, 1972 to 2004)

	total people	can trust	cannot trust	depends
2004	100.0%	35.9%	57.9%	6.2%
2002	100.0	34.1	58.0	7.9
2000	100.0	35.2	58.2	6.6
1998	100.0	37.6	56.5	5.8
1996	100.0	33.9	60.9	5.2
1994	100.0	34.1	61.6	4.3
1993	100.0	35.8	59.9	4.3
1991	100.0	38.5	56.6	4.9
1990	100.0	38.1	57.6	4.3
1989	100.0	41.0	55.2	3.8
1988	100.0	38.9	56.8	4.3
1987	100.0	38.6	57.8	3.7
1986	100.0	37.6	59.8	2.7
1984	100.0	47.9	49.6	2.5
1983	100.0	37.0	58.6	4.4
1980	100.0	45.5	50.7	3.8
1978	100.0	39.0	56.7	4.3
1976	100.0	44.4	51.8	3.7
1975	100.0	39.5	56.2	4.3
1973	100.0	46.0	51.0	2.9
1972	100.0	46.2	50.3	3.5

*Source: Survey Documentation and Analysis, Computer-assisted Survey Methods Program, University of California, Berkeley,
General Social Surveys, 1972–2004 Cumulative Data Files, Internet site http://sda.berkeley.edu/D3/GSS04/Docyr/gs04.htm*

Table 1.5 Fairness of People, 1972 to 2004

"Do you think most people would try to take advantage of you
if they got a chance, or would they try to be fair?"

(percent distribution of people aged 18 or older by response, 1972 to 2004)

	total people	take advantage	try to be fair	depends
2004	100.0%	39.8%	51.0%	9.2%
2002	100.0	39.7	49.6	10.7
2000	100.0	38.5	52.2	9.2
1998	100.0	38.4	52.8	8.8
1996	100.0	42.5	50.5	7.0
1994	100.0	39.6	53.6	6.7
1993	100.0	36.7	56.3	7.1
1991	100.0	36.5	57.7	5.9
1990	100.0	36.4	57.7	5.9
1989	100.0	36.5	58.2	5.2
1988	100.0	34.0	60.8	5.2
1987	100.0	41.9	53.9	4.2
1986	100.0	33.7	62.6	3.8
1984	100.0	34.6	62.2	3.2
1983	100.0	34.9	59.9	5.2
1980	100.0	34.8	60.8	4.3
1978	100.0	30.0	64.9	5.1
1976	100.0	36.4	59.5	4.2
1975	100.0	30.8	62.1	7.1
1973	100.0	37.6	57.6	4.8
1972	100.0	34.0	59.9	6.0

Source: Survey Documentation and Analysis, Computer-assisted Survey Methods Program, University of California, Berkeley, General Social Surveys, 1972–2004 Cumulative Data Files, Internet site http://sda.berkeley.edu/D3/GSS04/Docyr/gs04.htm

Americans Feel Richer and Poorer

Most are not satisfied with their financial situation.

When asked how their family's income ranks relative to the incomes of other families, fewer Americans place themselves in the middle and growing shares place themselves at the extremes. The percentage of people who say their income is above average or far above average grew from 17 to 23 percent between 1972 and 2004. The percentage of those who say they are below average grew from 26 to 30 percent during those years. The percentage of Americans who think their income is average fell from 57 to 47 percent.

Despite these shifts in perception, the proportion of people who are satisfied with their financial situation (31 percent in 2004) has not changed much in three decades, although there has been some increase in the percentage of Americans who are not at all satisfied with their finances. Job satisfaction has remained stable, as about half the public is very satisfied with the work they do. Over the decades a fairly stable 70 percent have said they would continue to work even if they had enough money to live comfortably for the rest of their life.

■ Americans sense the growing gap between rich and poor and know where they stand relative to others.

Fewer say their incomes are average

(percentage of people aged 18 or older who say their incomes are below average, average, or above average, 1972 and 2004)

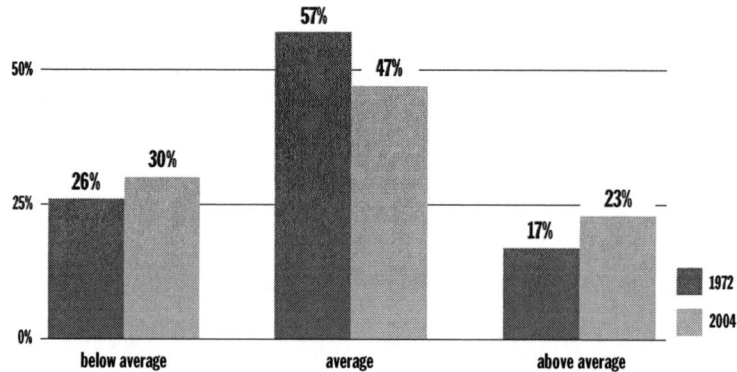

Table 1.6 Opinion of Family Income, 1972 to 2004

"Compared with American families in general, would you say
your family income is far below average, below average,
average, above average, or far above average?"

(percent distribution of people aged 18 or older by response, 1972 to 2004)

	total people	far below average	below average	average	above average	far above average
2004	100.0%	5.3%	24.3%	47.0%	20.6%	2.8%
2002	100.0	6.3	24.9	47.4	18.7	2.6
2000	100.0	5.9	22.1	48.7	20.2	3.1
1998	100.0	6.0	22.9	47.4	21.3	2.3
1996	100.0	6.2	24.4	48.3	18.6	2.5
1994	100.0	4.7	24.2	48.7	20.1	2.3
1993	100.0	6.4	23.5	48.9	19.2	2.0
1991	100.0	5.1	23.1	51.0	19.0	1.8
1990	100.0	4.9	23.5	50.1	19.5	2.0
1989	100.0	4.3	23.1	50.6	20.5	1.6
1988	100.0	4.6	23.3	51.8	18.2	2.1
1987	100.0	5.2	26.1	49.2	18.2	1.3
1986	100.0	5.7	23.9	49.8	18.5	2.1
1985	100.0	5.8	23.1	51.4	17.7	1.9
1984	100.0	5.2	23.7	51.7	17.9	1.5
1983	100.0	6.3	23.4	49.3	18.7	2.3
1982	100.0	6.2	28.4	50.6	13.7	1.1
1980	100.0	4.8	23.5	52.5	16.9	2.3
1978	100.0	4.6	22.4	53.3	18.1	1.7
1977	100.0	5.3	23.7	51.5	17.7	1.8
1976	100.0	4.1	25.1	55.2	14.8	0.9
1975	100.0	4.5	23.6	52.6	18.1	1.3
1974	100.0	3.9	20.8	55.9	18.1	1.2
1973	100.0	3.6	19.0	58.6	17.3	1.5
1972	100.0	3.6	22.0	57.4	15.9	1.1

Source: Survey Documentation and Analysis, Computer-assisted Survey Methods Program, University of California, Berkeley, General Social Surveys, 1972–2004 Cumulative Data Files, Internet site http://sda.berkeley.edu/D3/GSS04/Docyr/gs04.htm

Table 1.7 Satisfaction with Financial Situation, 1972 to 2004

"As far as you and your family are concerned, would you say that you are pretty well satisfied with your present financial situation, more or less satisfied, or not satisfied at all?"

(percent distribution of people aged 18 or older by response, 1972 to 2004)

	total people	satisfied	more or less satisfied	not at all satisfied
2004	100.0%	31.4%	42.1%	26.5%
2002	100.0	29.9	41.5	28.6
2000	100.0	29.8	45.0	25.3
1998	100.0	30.1	44.4	25.5
1996	100.0	27.7	44.4	27.8
1994	100.0	28.0	45.9	26.2
1993	100.0	26.9	44.6	28.4
1991	100.0	27.7	45.6	26.7
1990	100.0	29.7	43.2	27.1
1989	100.0	30.6	44.3	25.1
1988	100.0	30.6	45.0	24.4
1987	100.0	27.7	47.2	25.1
1986	100.0	30.4	42.7	26.9
1985	100.0	29.7	44.0	26.3
1984	100.0	28.3	45.6	26.0
1983	100.0	28.6	41.3	30.1
1982	100.0	24.6	44.1	31.3
1980	100.0	28.5	44.6	26.9
1978	100.0	33.9	42.2	23.9
1977	100.0	34.2	43.7	22.2
1976	100.0	30.7	46.0	23.3
1975	100.0	31.0	42.4	26.6
1974	100.0	31.2	45.6	23.2
1973	100.0	30.7	45.5	23.8
1972	100.0	32.5	44.8	22.8

Source: Survey Documentation and Analysis, Computer-assisted Survey Methods Program, University of California, Berkeley, General Social Surveys, 1972–2004 Cumulative Data Files, Internet site http://sda.berkeley.edu/D3/GSS04/Docyr/gs04.htm

Table 1.8 Job Satisfaction, 1972 to 2004

"On the whole, how satisfied are you with the work you do—
would you say you are very satisfied, moderately satisfied,
a little dissatisfied, or very dissatisfied?"

(percent distribution of people aged 18 or older by response, 1972 to 2004)

	total people	very satisfied	moderately satisfied	a little dissatisfied	very dissatisfied
2004	100.0%	50.3%	36.3%	8.9%	4.5%
2002	100.0	50.3	36.4	9.4	3.9
2000	100.0	45.4	42.5	8.6	3.6
1998	100.0	48.1	38.4	10.1	3.4
1996	100.0	45.0	39.7	10.9	4.4
1994	100.0	46.1	39.9	10.6	3.5
1993	100.0	43.3	41.1	10.8	4.7
1991	100.0	44.4	41.9	9.4	4.3
1990	100.0	46.2	39.7	10.5	3.7
1989	100.0	46.2	39.1	10.4	4.3
1988	100.0	46.6	39.5	10.1	3.8
1987	100.0	42.9	38.8	12.9	5.4
1986	100.0	49.1	39.4	9.0	2.6
1985	100.0	47.9	37.8	9.9	4.5
1984	100.0	45.9	35.0	12.1	7.0
1983	100.0	49.3	37.4	8.8	4.5
1982	100.0	46.0	37.7	10.7	5.6
1980	100.0	46.9	35.6	12.8	4.7
1978	100.0	50.9	36.2	8.4	4.5
1977	100.0	47.6	39.3	10.3	2.8
1976	100.0	52.1	34.3	9.1	4.5
1975	100.0	54.2	32.7	9.0	4.1
1974	100.0	47.9	37.4	10.0	4.7
1973	100.0	49.4	38.2	8.1	4.3
1972	100.0	48.5	36.8	11.2	3.5

Source: Survey Documentation and Analysis, Computer-assisted Survey Methods Program, University of California, Berkeley, General Social Surveys, 1972–2004 Cumulative Data Files, Internet site http://sda.berkeley.edu/D3/GSS04/Docyr/gs04.htm

Table 1.9 Work if Rich, 1973 to 2004

"If you were to get enough money to live as comfortably as you would like for the rest of your life, would you continue to work or would you stop working?"

(percent distribution of people aged 18 or older by response, 1973 to 2004)

	total people	continue to work	stop working
2004	100.0%	69.9%	30.1%
2002	100.0	68.8	31.2
2000	100.0	66.9	33.1
1998	100.0	69.6	30.4
1996	100.0	68.0	32.0
1994	100.0	65.8	34.2
1993	100.0	69.0	31.0
1991	100.0	66.9	33.1
1990	100.0	72.7	27.3
1989	100.0	72.2	27.8
1988	100.0	71.0	29.0
1987	100.0	75.4	24.6
1985	100.0	69.5	30.5
1984	100.0	76.0	24.0
1982	100.0	72.3	27.7
1980	100.0	76.9	23.1
1977	100.0	70.0	30.0
1976	100.0	69.0	31.0
1974	100.0	64.8	35.2
1973	100.0	69.1	30.9

Source: Survey Documentation and Analysis, Computer-assisted Survey Methods Program, University of California, Berkeley, General Social Surveys, 1973–2004 Cumulative Data Files, Internet site http://sda.berkeley.edu/D3/GSS04/Docyr/gs04.htm

Gun Ownership Has Declined

Most of the public supports gun laws.

The public has long supported gun control. In 2004, nearly 80 percent of Americans thought police permits should be required before someone could buy a gun. In 1972, a slightly smaller 72 percent felt that way. One factor behind the strong support for gun control is the decline in gun ownership. The percentage of households that own a gun has fallen from 47 percent in 1973 to just 36 percent in 2004.

Attitudes toward capital punishment have not changed much over the years. Support for the death penalty for those convicted of murder stood at about the same level in 2004 as it did in 1974—two out of three favoring capital punishment. In contrast to this stability, support for the legalization of marijuana has grown. In 1973, only 19 percent thought marijuana should be made legal. By 2004, the figure had nearly doubled to 36 percent.

■ Despite the public's strong support of gun laws, politicians have been timid about passing them.

A growing percentage favor making marijuana legal

(percentage of people aged 18 or older who think marijuana should be legalized, 1973 and 2004)

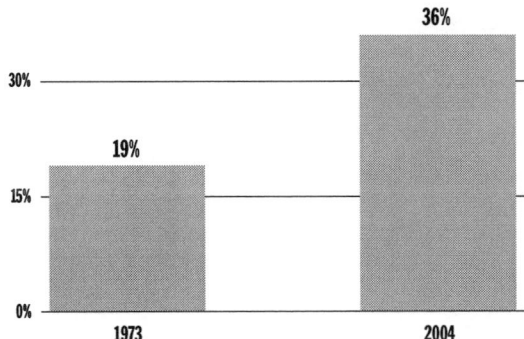

Table 1.10 Have Gun in Home, 1973 to 2004

"Do you happen to have in your home (or garage) any guns or revolvers?"

(percent distribution of people aged 18 or older by response, 1973 to 2004)

	total people	yes	no
2004	100.0%	35.7%	62.5%
2002	100.0	33.5	65.5
2000	100.0	32.5	66.3
1998	100.0	34.9	64.8
1996	100.0	40.2	59.4
1994	100.0	40.7	58.3
1993	100.0	42.1	57.2
1991	100.0	39.9	59.1
1990	100.0	42.7	57.3
1989	100.0	46.1	53.9
1988	100.0	40.1	58.9
1987	100.0	42.5	57.0
1985	100.0	44.3	55.0
1984	100.0	45.2	54.2
1982	100.0	43.8	55.1
1980	100.0	47.7	52.2
1977	100.0	50.7	49.2
1976	100.0	46.7	52.2
1974	100.0	46.2	53.1
1973	100.0	47.3	51.7

Source: Survey Documentation and Analysis, Computer-assisted Survey Methods Program, University of California, Berkeley, General Social Surveys, 1973–2004 Cumulative Data Files, Internet site http://sda.berkeley.edu/D3/GSS04/Docyr/gs04.htm

Table 1.11 Support for Gun Laws, 1972 to 2004

"Would you favor or oppose a law which would require a person
to obtain a police permit before he or she could buy a gun?"

(percent distribution of people aged 18 or older by response, 1972 to 2004)

	total people	favor	oppose
2004	100.0%	79.6%	20.4%
2002	100.0	80.5	19.5
2000	100.0	81.7	18.3
1998	100.0	83.6	16.4
1996	100.0	82.0	18.0
1994	100.0	79.3	20.7
1993	100.0	82.5	17.5
1991	100.0	82.1	17.9
1990	100.0	80.1	19.9
1989	100.0	79.1	20.9
1988	100.0	75.7	24.3
1987	100.0	73.3	26.7
1985	100.0	73.1	26.9
1984	100.0	72.3	27.7
1982	100.0	74.3	25.7
1980	100.0	70.7	29.3
1977	100.0	73.0	27.0
1976	100.0	72.6	27.4
1975	100.0	75.6	24.4
1974	100.0	76.2	23.8
1973	100.0	74.8	25.2
1972	100.0	72.4	27.6

Source: Survey Documentation and Analysis, Computer-assisted Survey Methods Program, University of California, Berkeley, General Social Surveys, 1972–2004 Cumulative Data Files, Internet site http://sda.berkeley.edu/D3/GSS04/Docyr/gs04.htm

Table 1.12 Death Penalty for Murder, 1974 to 2004

"Do you favor or oppose the death penalty for persons convicted of murder?"

(percent distribution of people aged 18 or older by response, 1974 to 2004)

	total people	favor	oppose
2004	100.0%	68.0%	32.0%
2002	100.0	68.7	31.3
2000	100.0	68.8	31.2
1998	100.0	73.3	26.7
1996	100.0	76.8	23.2
1994	100.0	79.2	20.8
1993	100.0	77.4	22.6
1991	100.0	76.2	23.8
1990	100.0	79.4	20.6
1989	100.0	78.3	21.7
1988	100.0	76.1	23.9
1987	100.0	69.2	30.8
1986	100.0	75.3	24.7
1985	100.0	79.5	20.5
1984	100.0	74.8	25.2
1983	100.0	76.8	23.2
1982	100.0	72.7	27.3
1980	100.0	71.6	28.4
1978	100.0	70.4	29.6
1977	100.0	71.8	28.2
1976	100.0	68.7	31.3
1975	100.0	64.4	35.6
1974	100.0	66.5	33.5

Source: Survey Documentation and Analysis, Computer-assisted Survey Methods Program, University of California, Berkeley, General Social Surveys, 1974–2004 Cumulative Data Files, Internet site http://sda.berkeley.edu/D3/GSS04/Docyr/gs04.htm

Table 1.13 Legalization of Marijuana, 1973 to 2004

"Do you think the use of marijuana should be made legal or not?"

(percent distribution of people aged 18 or older by response, 1973 to 2004)

	total people	made legal	not legal
2004	100.0%	36.4%	63.6%
2002	100.0	36.0	64.0
2000	100.0	33.5	66.5
1998	100.0	29.4	70.6
1996	100.0	27.0	73.0
1994	100.0	24.0	76.0
1993	100.0	23.3	76.7
1991	100.0	18.7	81.3
1990	100.0	16.8	83.2
1989	100.0	16.9	83.1
1988	100.0	17.9	82.1
1987	100.0	17.0	83.0
1986	100.0	18.3	81.7
1984	100.0	23.6	76.4
1983	100.0	21.0	79.0
1980	100.0	25.6	74.4
1978	100.0	30.5	69.5
1976	100.0	28.7	71.3
1975	100.0	21.3	78.7
1973	100.0	18.7	81.3

Source: Survey Documentation and Analysis, Computer-assisted Survey Methods Program, University of California, Berkeley, General Social Surveys, 1973–2004 Cumulative Data Files, Internet site http://sda.berkeley.edu/D3/GSS04/Docyr/gs04.htm

Americans Are Not So Mobile

But neighborhoods are changing.

The percentage of Americans who live in the same city they lived in at age 16 has barely changed over the past three decades. Despite our much-lauded mobility, most people don't move very far from home. In 2004, 40 percent of people aged 18 or older lived in the same city they lived in at age 16, down from 46 percent in 1972. The figure has bumped up and down around the 40 percent mark for decades. The percentage of Americans who live in a different state has remained stable at about one-third.

Although Americans aren't moving far from home, their neighborhoods are changing. The percentage who say blacks live in their neighborhood climbed from just 30 percent in 1972 to fully 66 percent in 2004. Integration is one factor behind this increase, as is the growing share of blacks in the population.

■ Although many Americans move each year, most moves are local.

Most people say blacks live in their neighborhood

(percentage of people aged 18 or older who say blacks live in their neighborhood, 1973 and 2004)

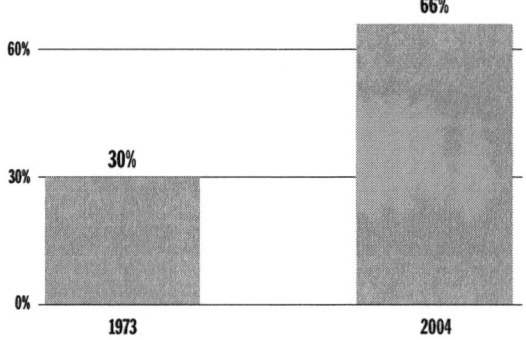

Table 1.14 Living in Same Place at Age 16, 1972 to 2004

"When you were 16 years old, were you living
in this same (city/town/county)?"

(percent distribution of people aged 18 or older by response, 1972 to 2004)

	total people	same city	same state, different city	different state
2004	100.0%	39.7%	26.3%	34.0%
2002	100.0	41.7	25.3	33.0
2000	100.0	39.3	26.1	34.6
1998	100.0	39.1	25.8	35.1
1996	100.0	37.8	24.4	37.9
1994	100.0	39.5	25.3	35.2
1993	100.0	41.3	26.6	32.1
1991	100.0	40.8	26.6	32.6
1990	100.0	39.8	28.8	31.5
1989	100.0	40.7	26.4	32.9
1988	100.0	40.7	25.4	33.9
1987	100.0	42.7	22.7	34.6
1986	100.0	42.9	25.1	32.0
1985	100.0	40.1	27.8	32.0
1984	100.0	40.0	27.1	32.9
1983	100.0	45.2	24.0	30.7
1982	100.0	47.9	22.8	29.3
1980	100.0	43.1	26.4	30.5
1978	100.0	40.7	28.5	30.8
1977	100.0	43.1	25.4	31.5
1976	100.0	43.4	25.6	31.1
1975	100.0	43.5	25.0	31.5
1974	100.0	42.8	27.4	29.8
1973	100.0	41.1	23.7	35.2
1972	100.0	46.4	20.2	33.4

Source: Survey Documentation and Analysis, Computer-assisted Survey Methods Program, University of California, Berkeley, General Social Surveys, 1972–2004 Cumulative Data Files, Internet site http://sda.berkeley.edu/D3/GSS04/Docyr/gs04.htm

Table 1.15 Integrated Neighborhoods, 1972 to 2004

"Are there any (Negroes/Blacks/African-Americans) living in this neighborhood now?"

(percent distribution of people aged 18 or older by response, 1972 to 2004)

	total people	yes	no
2004	100.0%	66.4%	33.6%
2002	100.0	71.9	28.1
2000	100.0	68.3	31.7
1998	100.0	66.4	33.6
1996	100.0	65.1	34.9
1994	100.0	64.2	35.8
1991	100.0	54.9	45.1
1990	100.0	57.5	42.5
1989	100.0	54.1	45.9
1988	100.0	56.1	43.9
1987	100.0	56.0	44.0
1986	100.0	49.1	50.9
1985	100.0	50.3	49.7
1984	100.0	53.1	46.9
1983	100.0	48.5	51.5
1982	100.0	52.4	47.6
1980	100.0	47.8	52.2
1978	100.0	50.5	49.5
1977	100.0	40.6	59.4
1976	100.0	44.0	56.0
1975	100.0	34.3	65.7
1974	100.0	43.8	56.2
1973	100.0	41.3	58.7
1972	100.0	29.8	70.2

Source: Survey Documentation and Analysis, Computer-assisted Survey Methods Program, University of California, Berkeley, General Social Surveys, 1972–2004 Cumulative Data Files, Internet site http://sda.berkeley.edu/D3/GSS04/Docyr/gs04.htm

Most People Say No to Traditional Sex Roles

Most also think working mothers are OK.

Times have changed. In 1977, two out of three Americans believed traditional sex roles—where the man is the achiever outside the home and the woman stays home and cares for the family—were best. By 2004, only 38 percent felt that way. A similar transformation occurred in attitudes toward working mothers as well. The percentage of Americans who think working mothers can have just as warm a relationship with their children as mothers who do not work climbed from 49 percent in 1977 to 66 percent in 2004.

The confusion surrounding the changing roles of husbands and wives may have contributed to the decline in marital happiness. The percentage of married people who describe their marriage as very happy fell from 68 percent in 1973 to 62 percent in 2004. At the same time, the percentage of those who describe their marriage as only pretty happy climbed from 30 to 35 percent.

■ Attitudes toward childrearing have been stable over the years. Most people still think children occasionally need to be spanked, with 73 percent saying a good, hard spanking is sometimes necessary.

Marital happiness has declined

(percentage of married people aged 18 or older who describe their marriage as very happy, 1973 and 2004)

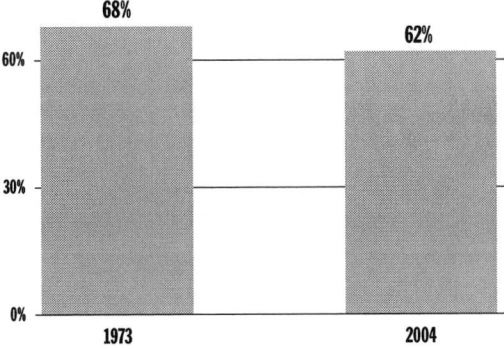

Table 1.16 Traditional Sex Roles, 1977 to 2004

"It is much better for everyone involved if the man is the achiever outside the home and the woman takes care of the home and family."

(percent distribution of people aged 18 or older by response, 1977 to 2004)

	total people	strongly agree	agree	disagree	strongly disagree
2004	100.0%	8.8%	28.7%	44.1%	18.3%
2002	100.0	10.1	28.6	42.5	18.7
2000	100.0	11.3	29.4	40.5	18.7
1998	100.0	7.2	28.0	46.0	18.9
1996	100.0	7.6	30.8	43.9	17.6
1994	100.0	6.8	28.2	46.8	18.2
1993	100.0	6.1	30.2	46.6	17.2
1991	100.0	7.6	34.5	40.7	17.2
1990	100.0	7.1	33.4	45.0	14.5
1989	100.0	9.7	31.2	42.3	16.8
1988	100.0	9.1	33.0	41.4	16.5
1986	100.0	9.1	38.6	39.9	12.4
1985	100.0	10.0	38.4	38.2	13.4
1977	100.0	18.3	47.5	28.1	6.1

Source: Survey Documentation and Analysis, Computer-assisted Survey Methods Program, University of California, Berkeley, General Social Surveys, 1977–2004 Cumulative Data Files, Internet site http://sda.berkeley.edu/D3/GSS04/Docyr/gs04.htm

Table 1.17 Working Mothers, 1977 to 2004

"A working mother can establish just as warm and secure a relationship with her children as a mother who does not work."

(percent distribution of people aged 18 or older by response, 1977 to 2004)

	total people	strongly agree	agree	disagree	strongly disagree
2004	100.0%	23.5%	42.3%	27.2%	7.0%
2002	100.0	24.2	39.4	27.1	9.3
2000	100.0	20.4	40.7	29.3	9.6
1998	100.0	22.1	45.7	25.5	6.6
1996	100.0	24.2	42.3	26.1	7.4
1994	100.0	23.4	46.3	25.5	4.9
1993	100.0	20.4	46.7	26.6	6.3
1991	100.0	20.0	45.3	28.4	6.3
1990	100.0	21.8	41.5	29.0	7.7
1989	100.0	21.6	42.4	28.9	7.1
1988	100.0	23.8	39.3	27.7	9.1
1986	100.0	22.1	40.3	29.7	7.8
1985	100.0	21.3	39.5	28.9	10.3
1977	100.0	15.7	33.3	33.6	17.5

Source: Survey Documentation and Analysis, Computer-assisted Survey Methods Program, University of California, Berkeley, General Social Surveys, 1977–2004 Cumulative Data Files, Internet site http://sda.berkeley.edu/D3/GSS04/Docyr/gs04.htm

Table 1.18 Happiness of Marriage, 1973 to 2004

"Taking things all together, how would you describe your marriage? Would you say that your marriage is very happy, pretty happy, or not too happy?"

(percent distribution of people aged 18 or older by response, 1973 to 2004)

	total people	very happy	pretty happy	not too happy
2004	100.0%	61.7%	34.6%	3.7%
2002	100.0	61.4	35.7	3.0
2000	100.0	62.4	34.3	3.2
1998	100.0	63.9	33.3	2.8
1996	100.0	61.9	35.9	2.2
1994	100.0	60.6	36.3	3.1
1993	100.0	61.8	35.3	2.9
1991	100.0	63.2	33.5	3.2
1990	100.0	64.6	33.1	2.2
1989	100.0	60.5	37.0	2.5
1988	100.0	62.5	34.1	3.4
1987	100.0	63.4	33.7	2.9
1986	100.0	63.1	33.5	3.4
1985	100.0	56.5	40.1	3.4
1984	100.0	65.6	31.4	3.0
1983	100.0	62.4	34.3	3.2
1982	100.0	63.7	33.2	3.1
1980	100.0	67.9	29.3	2.8
1978	100.0	65.2	32.2	2.6
1977	100.0	65.5	30.9	3.6
1976	100.0	66.8	30.8	2.4
1975	100.0	67.4	29.8	2.7
1974	100.0	69.1	27.4	3.5
1973	100.0	67.8	29.6	2.6

Source: Survey Documentation and Analysis, Computer-assisted Survey Methods Program, University of California, Berkeley, General Social Surveys, 1973–2004 Cumulative Data Files, Internet site http://sda.berkeley.edu/D3/GSS04/Docyr/gs04.htm

Table 1.19 Spanking, 1986 to 2004

"Do you strongly agree, agree, disagree, or strongly disagree that it is sometimes necessary to discipline a child with a good, hard spanking?"

(percent distribution of people aged 18 or older by response, 1986 to 2004)

	total people	strongly agree	agree	disagree	strongly disagree
2004	100.0%	24.7%	48.3%	20.3%	6.7%
2002	100.0	30.3	43.0	19.6	7.1
2000	100.0	32.0	42.4	17.8	7.8
1998	100.0	26.5	48.0	18.3	7.2
1996	100.0	26.6	46.3	18.6	8.5
1994	100.0	26.8	46.6	18.3	8.3
1993	100.0	22.9	50.7	19.8	6.6
1991	100.0	26.1	48.2	19.3	6.5
1990	100.0	28.5	50.8	16.8	3.9
1989	100.0	31.7	45.8	17.0	5.5
1988	100.0	30.9	48.7	14.8	5.6
1986	100.0	27.7	55.9	13.4	3.1

Source: Survey Documentation and Analysis, Computer-assisted Survey Methods Program, University of California, Berkeley, General Social Surveys, 1986–2004 Cumulative Data Files, Internet site http://sda.berkeley.edu/D3/GSS04/Docyr/gs04.htm

Sexual Attitudes Are Loosening

Most still think homosexuality is wrong, however.

The percentage of Americans who think premarital sex is not wrong at all has grown from only 27 percent in 1972 to nearly half—46 percent—in 2004. The percentage of those who think premarital sex is always wrong fell from 37 to 27 percent over the years. One factor contributing to this change is generational replacement, with younger, more tolerant generations replacing those with stricter rules regarding sexual behavior.

Homosexuality is still disapproved by most Americans, but the majority is shrinking. Between 1973 and 2004, the proportion of the public that says homosexual relations are always wrong fell from 73 to 58 percent. The percentage of Americans who say homosexuality is not wrong at all grew from 11 to 31 percent. Again, generational replacement explains much of this change.

Most Americans support legal abortion, at least in some circumstances. Attitudes toward abortion have not changed much over the past thirty years. Fully 86 percent of the public supports legal abortion if a woman's health is endangered by pregnancy, 76 percent if a woman has been raped, and 73 percent if there is a serious defect in the baby.

■ Although most people support abortion in some circumstances, only 41 percent support it for "any reason."

More think homosexuality is OK

(percentage of people aged 18 or older who think homosexuality is not wrong at all, 1973 and 2004)

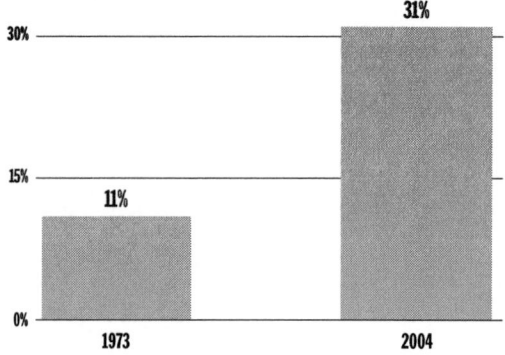

Table 1.20 Premarital Sex, 1972 to 2004

"There's been a lot of discussion about the way morals and attitudes about sex are changing in this country. If a man and woman have sex relations before marriage, do you think it is always wrong, almost always wrong, wrong only sometimes, or not wrong at all?"

(percent distribution of people aged 18 or older by response, 1972 to 2004)

	total people	always wrong	almost always wrong	sometimes wrong	not wrong at all
2004	100.0%	27.0%	8.9%	17.8%	46.3%
2002	100.0	27.3	8.2	19.9	44.5
2000	100.0	28.0	8.8	21.4	41.8
1998	100.0	26.4	9.2	21.0	43.5
1996	100.0	23.8	9.7	22.6	43.9
1994	100.0	26.0	10.1	20.4	43.5
1993	100.0	27.0	10.1	20.8	42.2
1991	100.0	27.6	9.9	18.7	43.8
1990	100.0	25.6	11.5	23.0	39.9
1989	100.0	28.0	8.7	22.8	40.6
1988	100.0	26.3	10.7	22.4	40.6
1986	100.0	27.8	8.9	23.0	40.3
1985	100.0	28.5	8.3	19.8	43.4
1983	100.0	27.4	9.9	24.2	38.5
1982	100.0	29.0	8.5	20.0	42.5
1978	100.0	29.3	11.7	20.3	38.7
1977	100.0	31.0	9.5	23.0	36.5
1975	100.0	30.9	12.3	24.0	32.8
1974	100.0	33.0	12.7	23.6	30.7
1972	100.0	36.6	11.8	24.3	27.3

Source: Survey Documentation and Analysis, Computer-assisted Survey Methods Program, University of California, Berkeley, General Social Surveys, 1972–2004 Cumulative Data Files, Internet site http://sda.berkeley.edu/D3/GSS04/Docyr/gs04.htm

Table 1.21   Homosexual Relations, 1973 to 2004

"What about sexual relations between two adults of the same sex—
do you think it is always wrong, almost always wrong,
wrong only sometimes, or not wrong at all?"

(percent distribution of people aged 18 or older by response, 1973 to 2004)

	total people	always wrong	almost always wrong	sometimes wrong	not wrong at all
2004	100.0%	57.6%	4.7%	6.9%	30.8%
2002	100.0	55.0	4.9	7.1	33.0
2000	100.0	58.8	4.5	8.0	28.8
1998	100.0	58.0	5.7	6.9	29.4
1996	100.0	60.4	5.2	6.2	28.2
1994	100.0	66.5	4.0	6.2	23.3
1993	100.0	66.3	4.3	7.3	22.0
1991	100.0	75.5	4.1	4.4	16.0
1990	100.0	76.3	4.8	6.1	12.8
1989	100.0	74.2	4.1	6.0	15.7
1988	100.0	76.8	4.7	5.7	12.8
1987	100.0	78.2	4.1	5.8	11.9
1985	100.0	75.3	4.0	7.0	13.7
1984	100.0	73.3	5.0	7.4	14.3
1982	100.0	74.8	5.3	6.5	13.4
1980	100.0	73.3	6.0	6.1	14.6
1977	100.0	71.9	5.8	7.5	14.9
1976	100.0	70.1	6.2	7.9	15.9
1974	100.0	70.5	5.0	7.9	13.0
1973	100.0	72.7	6.6	7.6	11.0

Source: Survey Documentation and Analysis, Computer-assisted Survey Methods Program, University of California, Berkeley, General Social Surveys, 1973–2004 Cumulative Data Files, Internet site http://sda.berkeley.edu/D3/GSS04/Docyr/gs04.htm

Table 1.22 Support for Legal Abortion by Reason, 1972 to 2004

"Please tell me whether or not you think it should be possible
for a pregnant woman to obtain a legal abortion if…"

(percent of respondents aged 18 or older who think it should be possible for a pregnant woman to obtain a legal abortion, by reason for abortion, 1972 to 2004)

	woman's health seriously endangered	pregnancy resulted from rape	serious defect in baby	woman is married and does not want more children	family has low income and cannot afford more children	woman is not married and does not want to marry the man	any reason
2004	86.0%	76.2%	72.9%	41.8%	41.0%	40.9%	40.6%
2002	91.6	79.7	78.5	44.8	44.4	42.0	43.0
2000	88.5	80.6	78.7	40.7	42.2	39.1	39.9
1998	87.9	80.1	78.6	42.3	44.3	42.3	40.9
1996	91.6	84.3	81.8	46.7	46.6	44.9	45.0
1994	90.6	83.6	82.3	48.3	50.4	47.6	46.3
1993	89.8	82.9	81.3	47.1	49.9	48.1	45.3
1991	91.5	86.5	83.5	44.6	48.5	44.8	42.6
1990	91.8	84.8	81.2	45.1	48.1	45.3	43.4
1989	90.1	83.2	81.3	44.5	47.7	45.4	40.3
1988	88.7	81.1	78.8	39.9	42.0	39.4	36.1
1987	87.9	79.6	78.0	41.0	44.7	40.1	39.2
1985	89.3	81.2	78.5	40.3	43.7	41.2	36.9
1984	89.5	80.4	80.2	42.7	46.3	44.2	38.6
1983	89.7	82.8	78.9	38.9	43.7	39.4	34.3
1982	90.4	83.9	82.1	45.8	49.0	45.5	38.5
1980	90.1	83.4	83.1	47.1	51.7	48.4	41.1
1978	90.6	83.2	82.0	40.3	47.4	41.1	33.3
1977	90.5	83.8	85.5	46.5	53.4	49.8	37.7
1976	90.8	83.7	83.9	46.2	53.1	50.3	–
1975	90.7	83.7	83.2	45.7	53.2	48.2	–
1974	92.4	86.5	85.1	46.9	54.8	50.1	–
1973	92.3	83.5	84.5	47.7	53.4	49.1	–
1972	86.9	79.1	78.6	39.7	48.8	43.5	–

Note: "–" means data are not available.
Source: Survey Documentation and Analysis, Computer-assisted Survey Methods Program, University of California, Berkeley, General Social Surveys, 1972–2004 Cumulative Data Files, Internet site http://sda.berkeley.edu/D3/GSS04/Docyr/gs04.htm

Americans Believe in God

Religious preferences are changing, however.

Americans rank among the most religious people in the world. Results from the General Social Survey show just how religious we are. Two out of three Americans aged 18 or older believe in God and have no doubt about it, a percentage that has been fairly stable over the years. Only 3 percent do not believe in God.

About one-third of the public believes the Bible is the actual word of God and is to be taken literally, down slightly from 38 percent who felt this way in 1984. Nearly half think the Bible was inspired by God, but is not to be taken literally. Despite these strong beliefs, fewer than half the public attends religious services at least once a month. Most attend church only several times a year at most.

Religious preferences are changing as the United States becomes more diverse. The percentage of Americans who say they are Protestant fell from 64 to 53 percent between 1972 and 2004. The percentage of people without a religion climbed from 5 to 14 percent during those years. Slightly fewer than one in four Americans is Catholic, just 2 percent are Jewish, and fewer than 1 percent are Moslem.

■ Americans' confidence in religious leaders has fallen over the decades. In 2004, only 24 percent of the public had a great deal of confidence in religious leaders, down from 36 percent in 1973.

Fewer Americans say they are Protestant

(percent distribution of Americans aged 18 or older by religious affiliation, 1972 and 2004)

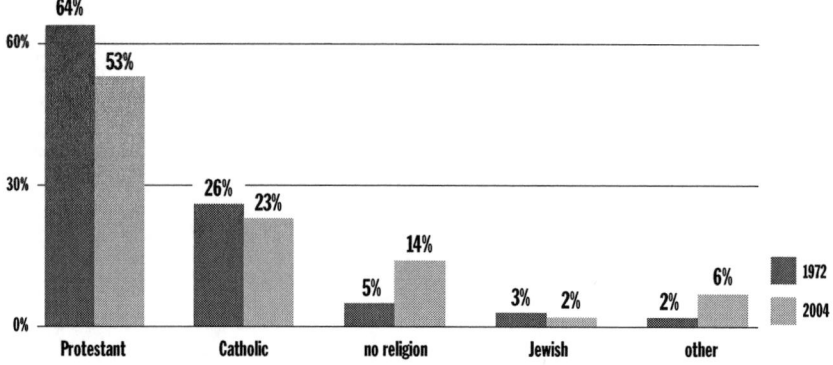

Table 1.23 Belief in God, 1988 to 2000

"Which statement comes closest to expressing what you believe about God?

1. I don't believe in God.
2. I don't know whether there is a God and I don't believe there is any way to find out.
3. I don't believe in a personal God, but I do believe in a Higher Power of some kind.
4. I find myself believing in God some of the time, but not at others.
5. While I have doubts, I feel that I do believe in God.
6. I know God really exists and I have no doubts about it."

(percent distribution of people aged 18 or older by response, 1988 to 2000)

	total people	don't believe	no way to find out	higher power	believe sometimes	believe, but doubts	know God exists
2000	100.0%	2.8%	4.2%	7.1%	3.5%	16.5%	65.8%
1998	100.0	3.2	4.9	9.8	4.7	14.7	62.8
1994	100.0	2.5	2.8	9.9	3.8	16.1	64.9
1993	100.0	2.9	4.2	8.5	3.1	15.0	66.3
1991	100.0	2.3	4.5	6.9	5.2	18.2	62.8
1988	100.0	1.5	3.8	7.9	4.4	18.9	63.5

Source: Survey Documentation and Analysis, Computer-assisted Survey Methods Program, University of California, Berkeley, General Social Surveys, 1988-2000 Cumulative Data Files, Internet site http://sda.berkeley.edu/D3/GSS04/Docyr/gs04.htm

Table 1.24 Feelings about the Bible, 1984 to 2004

"Which of these statements comes closest to describing
your feelings about the Bible?

1. The Bible is the actual word of God and is to be taken literally,
   word for word.
2. The Bible is the inspired word of God but not everything in it should be
   taken literally, word for word.
3. The Bible is an ancient book of fables, legends, history, and moral
   precepts recorded by men."

(percent distribution of people aged 18 or older by response, 1984 to 2004)

	total people	word of God	inspired word	book of fables	other
2004	100.0%	34.1%	47.5%	16.6%	1.7%
2002	100.0	29.0	54.1	14.3	2.7
2000	100.0	34.8	48.2	16.0	1.0
1998	100.0	31.5	50.7	16.7	1.1
1996	100.0	31.0	50.8	17.5	0.6
1994	100.0	32.0	52.0	15.1	0.9
1993	100.0	33.8	49.8	15.5	0.9
1991	100.0	35.4	48.7	15.1	0.8
1990	100.0	33.2	50.5	15.5	0.8
1989	100.0	32.2	50.9	16.5	0.4
1988	100.0	34.8	48.0	16.5	0.7
1987	100.0	41.3	42.7	15.4	0.5
1985	100.0	37.1	49.8	12.8	0.3
1984	100.0	38.1	47.2	13.9	0.7

Source: Survey Documentation and Analysis, Computer-assisted Survey Methods Program, University of California, Berkeley, General Social Surveys, 1984–2004 Cumulative Data Files, Internet site http://sda.berkeley.edu/D3/GSS04/Docyr/gs04.htm

Table 1.25 Attendance at Religious Services, 1972 to 2004

"How often do you attend religious services?"

(percent distribution of people aged 18 or older by response, 1972 to 2004)

	total people	more than once a week	every week	nearly every week	two to three times a month	once a month	several times a year	once a year	less than once a year	never
2004	100.0%	8.6%	18.1%	6.0%	9.1%	6.8%	13.2%	14.1%	7.1%	16.8%
2002	100.0	7.8	16.6	6.6	9.4	6.9	13.0	14.0	7.1	18.7
2000	100.0	7.1	17.8	4.8	8.1	7.2	13.5	12.2	8.0	21.3
1998	100.0	7.8	17.5	6.7	8.8	7.4	11.0	10.6	10.5	19.6
1996	100.0	7.4	17.2	5.7	9.6	6.7	14.7	14.2	9.0	15.5
1994	100.0	8.0	19.0	5.0	9.3	7.5	13.0	14.1	7.7	16.4
1993	100.0	8.6	20.5	6.3	8.7	7.1	11.2	12.3	8.7	16.5
1991	100.0	6.2	23.1	5.6	9.9	7.9	12.0	13.5	9.1	12.7
1990	100.0	7.0	23.0	5.3	9.5	7.9	13.1	12.2	8.6	13.5
1989	100.0	7.0	22.6	5.2	8.2	8.0	12.3	13.0	7.2	16.4
1988	100.0	7.4	18.7	7.4	9.7	7.8	13.1	11.4	7.3	17.2
1987	100.0	8.1	20.7	5.4	11.9	8.5	15.1	13.3	6.3	10.9
1986	100.0	9.0	22.8	4.5	10.1	8.0	11.9	12.5	7.2	14.1
1985	100.0	7.8	25.0	3.7	7.5	7.4	12.1	15.0	7.0	14.5
1984	100.0	9.3	23.6	4.9	8.4	7.5	14.1	11.8	7.3	13.0
1983	100.0	8.5	22.9	5.3	9.7	6.6	11.7	13.2	8.2	13.9
1982	100.0	8.6	19.7	6.5	9.7	7.1	14.0	14.3	7.1	13.0
1980	100.0	7.5	21.6	6.2	8.1	6.7	15.3	15.7	7.5	11.4
1978	100.0	8.1	19.6	7.0	9.5	6.7	11.5	13.2	8.8	15.7
1977	100.0	8.1	21.6	5.7	9.1	7.4	12.4	13.4	8.3	13.9
1976	100.0	8.9	20.0	6.0	6.7	7.1	15.5	13.6	9.1	13.0
1975	100.0	6.9	22.5	6.7	8.9	6.9	14.1	12.4	7.3	14.5
1974	100.0	7.9	22.5	5.8	8.7	8.0	12.7	15.3	7.0	12.2
1973	100.0	7.5	20.6	7.8	8.4	6.2	15.1	13.0	7.8	13.6
1972	100.0	6.3	28.8	6.1	8.9	6.8	14.1	11.1	8.6	9.4

Source: Survey Documentation and Analysis, Computer-assisted Survey Methods Program, University of California, Berkeley, General Social Surveys, 1972–2004 Cumulative Data Files, Internet site http://sda.berkeley.edu/D3/GSS04/Docyr/gs04.htm

Table 1.26 Religious Preferences, 1972 to 2004

"What is your religious preference? Is it Protestant,
Catholic, Jewish, some other religion, or no religion?"

(percent distribution of people aged 18 or older by response, 1972 to 2004)

	total people	Protestant	Catholic	no religion	Jewish	Moslem	Buddhism	Hinduism	other
2004	100.0%	53.0%	23.4%	14.4%	2.0%	0.6%	0.5%	0.5%	5.7%
2002	100.0	53.2	24.5	13.8	1.7	0.5	0.8	0.2	5.3
2000	100.0	54.1	24.1	14.1	2.2	0.4	0.6	0.3	4.0
1998	100.0	54.5	25.2	14.2	1.8	0.5	0.3	0.2	3.5
1996	100.0	57.4	23.6	11.7	2.3	0.0	0.0	0.0	4.9
1994	100.0	59.5	25.5	9.2	2.0	0.0	0.0	0.0	3.9
1993	100.0	64.2	22.0	9.1	2.1	0.0	0.0	0.0	2.6
1991	100.0	63.8	25.5	6.7	2.1	0.0	0.0	0.0	1.9
1990	100.0	63.1	23.9	8.0	2.0	0.0	0.0	0.0	3.1
1989	100.0	63.3	25.2	7.8	1.5	0.0	0.0	0.0	2.2
1988	100.0	61.2	25.9	8.0	2.0	0.0	0.0	0.0	2.8
1987	100.0	69.2	20.8	6.7	1.2	0.0	0.0	0.0	2.2
1986	100.0	62.8	25.8	6.7	2.6	0.0	0.0	0.0	2.1
1985	100.0	62.5	26.7	7.1	2.1	0.0	0.0	0.0	1.6
1984	100.0	63.8	25.7	7.3	1.8	0.0	0.0	0.0	1.4
1983	100.0	60.8	27.5	7.3	2.7	0.0	0.0	0.0	1.6
1982	100.0	68.1	21.6	7.1	2.1	0.0	0.0	0.0	1.1
1980	100.0	63.9	24.7	7.2	2.2	0.0	0.0	0.0	2.0
1978	100.0	64.1	25.1	7.8	1.9	0.0	0.0	0.0	1.1
1977	100.0	65.9	24.5	6.1	2.3	0.0	0.0	0.0	1.2
1976	100.0	63.5	26.1	7.6	1.8	0.0	0.0	0.0	1.0
1975	100.0	65.5	24.4	7.6	1.5	0.0	0.0	0.0	0.9
1974	100.0	64.3	25.4	6.8	3.0	0.0	0.0	0.0	0.5
1973	100.0	62.7	25.9	6.4	2.8	0.0	0.0	0.0	2.3
1972	100.0	64.1	25.7	5.2	3.4	0.0	0.0	0.0	1.7

*Source: Survey Documentation and Analysis, Computer-assisted Survey Methods Program, University of California, Berkeley,
General Social Surveys, 1972–2004 Cumulative Data Files, Internet site http://sda.berkeley.edu/D3/GSS04/Docyr/gs04.htm*

Table 1.27 Confidence in Organized Religion, 1973 to 2004

"As far as the people running these institutions are concerned,
would you say you have a great deal of confidence, only some,
or hardly any confidence at all in organized religion?"

(percent distribution of people aged 18 or older by response, 1973 to 2004)

	total people	a great deal	only some	hardly any
2004	100.0%	24.1%	51.6%	24.3%
2002	100.0	18.8	57.0	24.2
2000	100.0	28.7	51.6	19.7
1998	100.0	27.8	52.8	19.4
1996	100.0	26.3	53.7	19.9
1994	100.0	24.8	52.9	22.3
1993	100.0	23.6	51.2	25.2
1991	100.0	25.9	52.8	21.3
1990	100.0	23.7	51.6	24.7
1989	100.0	22.4	46.1	31.5
1988	100.0	20.6	47.6	31.9
1987	100.0	30.4	50.2	19.3
1986	100.0	26.0	52.2	21.7
1984	100.0	32.2	48.4	19.5
1983	100.0	29.4	52.5	18.1
1982	100.0	33.6	50.8	15.7
1980	100.0	36.7	44.8	18.5
1978	100.0	31.9	49.2	18.9
1977	100.0	41.4	46.6	12.0
1976	100.0	32.7	47.7	19.5
1975	100.0	26.0	51.2	22.8
1974	100.0	45.2	43.7	11.0
1973	100.0	36.1	47.5	16.4

Source: Survey Documentation and Analysis, Computer-assisted Survey Methods Program, University of California, Berkeley, General Social Surveys, 1972–2004 Cumulative Data Files, Internet site http://sda.berkeley.edu/D3/GSS04/Docyr/gs04.htm

Americans Are Less Confident in Leaders

The press has taken a big hit.

Whether the topic is business, education, the press, or medicine, Americans are less confident in the leaders of these institutions than they once were. The percentage of people who say they have a great deal of confidence in the leaders of major companies fell from 31 percent in 1973 to just 17 percent in 2004. Confidence in educational leaders fell from 38 to 27 percent during those years.

Confidence in the press has fallen the most. Only 9 percent of the public had a great deal of confidence in the press in 2004. The percentage of Americans who have hardly any confidence in the press climbed from 15 percent in 1973 to fully 43 percent in 2004 as the number of media outlets and criticism of the media grew.

The medical community has also seen a decline in confidence. The percentage of the public that has a great deal of confidence in the leaders of medicine fell from the 55 percent majority in 1973 to just 37 percent in 2004. One factor behind the decline may be growing problems with the health insurance system.

■ The 53 percent majority of the public thinks it is mostly the government's responsibility to help people pay for their medical bills.

Few have confidence in the press

(percent distribution of people aged 18 or older by confidence in the leaders of the press, 1973 and 2004)

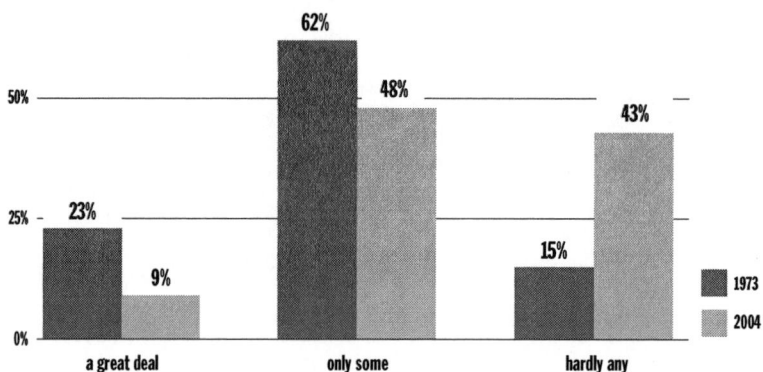

Table 1.28 Confidence in Major Companies, 1973 to 2004

"As far as the people running these institutions are concerned,
would you say you have a great deal of confidence, only some confidence,
or hardly any confidence at all in major companies?"

(percent distribution of people aged 18 or older by response, 1973 to 2004)

	total people	a great deal	only some	hardly any
2004	100.0%	17.0%	63.5%	19.5%
2002	100.0	17.7	64.1	18.3
2000	100.0	29.1	59.4	11.4
1998	100.0	27.5	59.2	13.3
1996	100.0	24.2	61.7	14.1
1994	100.0	26.3	63.5	10.3
1993	100.0	21.8	65.3	12.8
1991	100.0	21.2	65.1	13.7
1990	100.0	25.8	63.0	11.2
1989	100.0	25.1	64.0	10.9
1988	100.0	25.8	63.1	11.1
1987	100.0	29.0	60.8	10.2
1986	100.0	25.0	64.4	10.6
1984	100.0	31.8	59.2	9.0
1983	100.0	24.8	61.3	13.9
1982	100.0	22.4	61.8	15.8
1980	100.0	28.8	56.2	15.0
1978	100.0	22.7	60.6	16.8
1977	100.0	28.3	58.8	12.8
1976	100.0	23.2	54.0	22.9
1975	100.0	20.4	57.2	22.4
1974	100.0	32.5	52.4	15.0
1973	100.0	31.4	57.1	11.6

Source: Survey Documentation and Analysis, Computer-assisted Survey Methods Program, University of California, Berkeley, General Social Surveys, 1973–2004 Cumulative Data Files, Internet site http://sda.berkeley.edu/D3/GSS04/Docyr/gs04.htm

Table 1.29 Confidence in Education, 1973 to 2004

"As far as the people running these institutions are concerned,
would you say you have a great deal of confidence, only some confidence,
or hardly any confidence at all in education?"

(percent distribution of people aged 18 or older by response, 1973 to 2004)

	total people	a great deal	only some	hardly any
2004	100.0%	27.5%	58.0%	14.5%
2002	100.0	25.1	59.3	15.7
2000	100.0	27.1	57.1	15.7
1998	100.0	27.2	56.1	16.7
1996	100.0	23.2	58.4	18.4
1994	100.0	25.2	57.2	17.6
1992	100.0	22.6	58.8	18.6
1991	100.0	30.6	55.8	13.6
1990	100.0	27.4	60.1	12.5
1989	100.0	30.8	58.5	10.6
1988	100.0	30.0	61.2	8.8
1987	100.0	36.5	54.9	8.5
1986	100.0	28.0	61.1	10.8
1984	100.0	28.8	60.6	10.7
1983	100.0	29.2	57.5	13.3
1982	100.0	35.6	51.8	12.7
1980	100.0	30.5	56.8	12.7
1978	100.0	28.9	55.8	15.3
1977	100.0	41.0	50.1	8.9
1976	100.0	38.2	46.1	15.7
1975	100.0	31.5	55.5	13.0
1974	100.0	49.8	41.9	8.3
1973	100.0	37.5	54.1	8.3

Source: Survey Documentation and Analysis, Computer-assisted Survey Methods Program, University of California, Berkeley, General Social Surveys, 1973–2004 Cumulative Data Files, Internet site http://sda.berkeley.edu/D3/GSS04/Docyr/gs04.htm

Table 1.30 Confidence in the Press, 1973 to 2004

"As far as the people running these institutions are concerned,
would you say you have a great deal of confidence, only some confidence,
or hardly any confidence at all in the press?"

(percent distribution of people aged 18 or older by response, 1973 to 2004)

	total people	a great deal	only some	hardly any
2004	100.0%	9.2%	47.5%	43.3%
2002	100.0	10.2	47.3	42.5
2000	100.0	10.4	47.8	41.8
1998	100.0	9.5	47.2	43.4
1996	100.0	11.0	49.2	39.9
1994	100.0	9.9	50.4	39.7
1993	100.0	11.0	49.6	39.3
1991	100.0	16.7	54.9	28.4
1990	100.0	15.2	59.5	25.3
1989	100.0	17.1	55.5	27.4
1988	100.0	18.9	55.0	26.0
1987	100.0	19.3	57.4	23.2
1986	100.0	18.6	55.4	25.9
1984	100.0	17.3	59.9	22.8
1983	100.0	13.7	62.3	24.0
1982	100.0	18.3	61.6	20.2
1980	100.0	22.6	59.6	17.8
1978	100.0	20.5	59.5	20.1
1977	100.0	25.7	58.5	15.8
1976	100.0	29.0	53.0	18.0
1975	100.0	24.5	57.1	18.4
1974	100.0	26.2	56.1	17.7
1973	100.0	23.4	61.7	14.9

Source: Survey Documentation and Analysis, Computer-assisted Survey Methods Program, University of California, Berkeley, General Social Surveys, 1973–2004 Cumulative Data Files, Internet site http://sda.berkeley.edu/D3/GSS04/Docyr/gs04.htm

Table 1.31 Confidence in Medicine, 1973 to 2004

"As far as the people running these institutions are concerned,
would you say you have a great deal of confidence, only some confidence,
or hardly any confidence at all in medicine?"

(percent distribution of people aged 18 or older by response, 1973 to 2004)

	total people	a great deal	only some	hardly any
2004	100.0%	36.5%	49.8%	13.6%
2002	100.0	37.2	51.6	11.2
2000	100.0	44.4	46.0	9.6
1998	100.0	45.0	46.1	8.9
1996	100.0	45.1	45.9	9.0
1994	100.0	41.8	48.4	9.9
1993	100.0	39.6	51.9	8.6
1991	100.0	48.1	44.2	7.7
1990	100.0	46.1	47.0	6.9
1989	100.0	47.0	46.1	6.9
1988	100.0	51.7	42.3	6.0
1987	100.0	51.8	42.5	5.6
1986	100.0	46.5	45.9	7.6
1984	100.0	51.5	42.0	6.4
1983	100.0	52.3	41.6	6.1
1982	100.0	45.2	47.5	7.3
1980	100.0	53.1	39.3	7.5
1978	100.0	46.4	44.4	9.2
1977	100.0	52.1	41.7	6.2
1976	100.0	54.8	35.8	9.4
1975	100.0	51.3	40.8	8.0
1974	100.0	61.3	34.2	4.5
1973	100.0	54.6	39.6	5.8

Source: Survey Documentation and Analysis, Computer-assisted Survey Methods Program, University of California, Berkeley, General Social Surveys, 1973–2004 Cumulative Data Files, Internet site http://sda.berkeley.edu/D3/GSS04/Docyr/gs04.htm

Table 1.32 Should Government Help the Sick, 1975 to 2004

"In general, some people think that it is the responsibility of the government in Washington to see to it that people have help in paying for doctors and hospital bills. Others think that these matters are not the responsibility of the federal government and that people should take care of these things themselves. Where would you place yourself on this scale?"

(percent of people aged 18 or older by response, 1975 to 2004)

	total	1 government should help	2	3 agree with both	4	5 people should help themselves
2004	100.0%	32.4%	20.3%	31.7%	7.6%	8.0%
2002	100.0	32.0	19.5	34.3	7.2	7.0
2000	100.0	29.5	22.0	32.0	10.6	6.0
1998	100.0	25.6	22.9	33.0	10.0	8.5
1996	100.0	27.7	21.6	33.3	10.6	6.7
1994	100.0	25.9	21.6	31.9	11.2	9.5
1993	100.0	28.9	22.8	32.4	9.6	6.3
1991	100.0	32.3	25.2	27.3	9.4	5.8
1990	100.0	30.5	26.3	31.0	7.7	4.5
1989	100.0	31.1	22.9	30.7	7.7	7.6
1988	100.0	27.2	22.0	35.5	8.7	6.6
1987	100.0	30.9	19.9	34.4	7.9	6.8
1986	100.0	29.2	20.5	32.4	11.5	6.5
1984	100.0	24.6	19.1	35.9	12.5	7.9
1983	100.0	26.8	19.5	32.7	10.5	10.5
1975	100.0	36.6	12.9	29.1	7.9	13.4

Source: Survey Documentation and Analysis, Computer-assisted Survey Methods Program, University of California, Berkeley, General Social Surveys, 1975–2004 Cumulative Data Files, Internet site http://sda.berkeley.edu/D3/GSS04/Docyr/gs04.htm

Confidence in Political Leaders Is Low

Most Americans describe themselves as political moderates.

The public's confidence in the executive branch of government has waxed and waned over the years depending on current events and who is in the White House. Confidence in Congress has been more stable and abysmally low. In 2004, only 13 percent of the public had a great deal of confidence in Congress. The Supreme Court gets higher ratings, with 31 percent having a great deal of confidence in the nation's top court. This figure has barely changed over the decades.

Political views have been surprisingly stable over the decades. In 2004, the 66 percent majority of the public described its political views as moderate or only slightly liberal or slightly conservative. This figure was not much different from the 70 percent who placed themselves in the middle more than thirty years earlier. Only 16 percent describe themselves as strong Democrats, and 14 percent say they are strong Republicans.

Voting rates have been declining over the decades, although they bumped up in the 2004 presidential election. In 2004, 58 percent of people of voting age cast a ballot, down from 69 percent in the 1964 election. Voting rates have increased among Americans aged 65 or older, however, making older voters more important to politicians.

■ Asians and Hispanics have the lowest voting rates. In 2004, only 45 percent of Asian citizens cast a ballot. Among Hispanic citizens, the proportion was just 47 percent.

Voting rate has declined

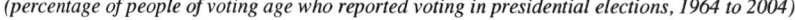

(percentage of people of voting age who reported voting in presidential elections, 1964 to 2004)

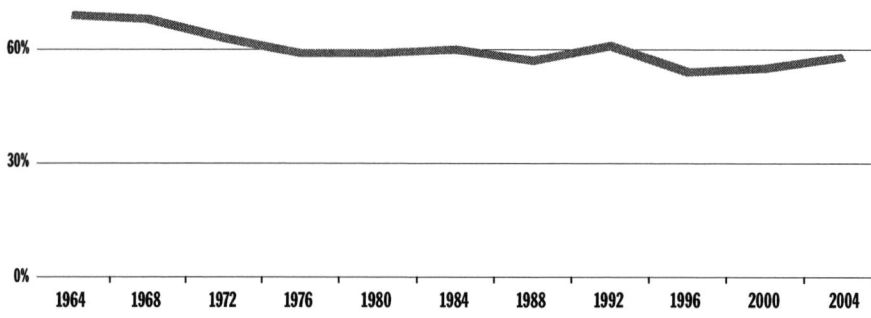

Table 1.33 Confidence in the Executive Branch of Government, 1973 to 2004

"As far as the people running these institutions are concerned, would you say you have a great deal of confidence, only some confidence, or hardly any confidence at all in the executive branch of government?"

(percent distribution of people aged 18 or older by response, 1973 to 2004)

	total people	a great deal	only some	hardly any
2004	100.0%	20.8%	47.8%	31.4%
2002	100.0	27.3	51.1	21.7
2000	100.0	13.8	51.2	35.0
1998	100.0	14.4	49.3	36.4
1996	100.0	10.5	46.4	43.1
1994	100.0	11.5	52.7	35.7
1993	100.0	12.2	54.5	33.3
1991	100.0	26.6	52.0	21.4
1990	100.0	24.2	51.9	23.9
1989	100.0	20.5	56.6	22.9
1988	100.0	17.1	55.2	27.7
1987	100.0	18.1	51.7	30.3
1986	100.0	21.2	54.6	24.2
1984	100.0	19.0	51.7	29.4
1983	100.0	13.3	56.2	30.5
1982	100.0	17.9	54.6	27.5
1980	100.0	12.5	52.0	35.5
1978	100.0	12.9	61.4	25.7
1977	100.0	28.8	56.2	15.0
1976	100.0	13.9	60.3	25.8
1975	100.0	13.7	56.1	30.3
1974	100.0	13.9	43.4	42.6
1973	100.0	29.9	51.4	18.7

Source: Survey Documentation and Analysis, Computer-assisted Survey Methods Program, University of California, Berkeley, General Social Surveys, 1973–2004 Cumulative Data Files, Internet site http://sda.berkeley.edu/D3/GSS04/Docyr/gs04.htm

Table 1.34 Confidence in Congress, 1973 to 2004

"As far as the people running these institutions are concerned,
would you say you have a great deal of confidence, only some confidence,
or hardly any confidence at all in Congress?"

(percent distribution of people aged 18 or older by response, 1973 to 2004)

	total people	a great deal	only some	hardly any
2004	100.0%	13.3%	57.6%	29.1%
2002	100.0	13.1	62.0	24.9
2000	100.0	12.6	57.9	29.5
1998	100.0	10.9	58.1	31.0
1996	100.0	7.9	48.0	44.1
1994	100.0	7.9	51.6	40.5
1993	100.0	7.1	51.3	41.6
1991	100.0	18.3	55.2	26.4
1990	100.0	15.8	60.8	23.5
1989	100.0	17.4	60.1	22.5
1988	100.0	15.9	64.0	20.1
1987	100.0	16.2	64.8	19.0
1986	100.0	16.7	62.5	20.9
1984	100.0	12.9	65.0	22.2
1983	100.0	10.2	65.8	24.0
1982	100.0	13.3	62.6	24.1
1980	100.0	9.7	55.3	35.0
1978	100.0	13.3	65.1	21.6
1977	100.0	19.7	62.7	17.6
1976	100.0	14.1	59.7	26.2
1975	100.0	13.7	60.4	25.9
1974	100.0	17.6	60.9	21.5
1973	100.0	24.1	60.6	15.3

Source: Survey Documentation and Analysis, Computer-assisted Survey Methods Program, University of California, Berkeley, General Social Surveys, 1973–2004 Cumulative Data Files, Internet site http://sda.berkeley.edu/D3/GSS04/Docyr/gs04.htm

Table 1.35 Confidence in the Supreme Court, 1973 to 2004

"As far as the people running these institutions are concerned, would you say you have a great deal of confidence, only some confidence, or hardly any confidence at all in the U.S. Supreme Court?"

(percent distribution of people aged 18 or older by response, 1973 to 2004)

	total people	a great deal	only some	hardly any
2004	100.0%	31.0%	52.6%	16.4%
2002	100.0	36.5	51.6	11.8
2000	100.0	33.9	52.6	13.5
1996	100.0	29.8	52.7	17.5
1994	100.0	31.2	51.8	17.0
1993	100.0	31.9	54.1	14.0
1991	100.0	38.6	48.6	12.8
1990	100.0	36.6	50.1	13.3
1989	100.0	36.2	52.5	11.3
1988	100.0	36.3	52.6	11.1
1987	100.0	35.8	53.2	10.9
1986	100.0	30.9	54.4	14.7
1984	100.0	34.5	52.7	12.8
1983	100.0	28.3	57.0	14.7
1982	100.0	30.5	56.3	13.3
1980	100.0	26.1	53.1	20.7
1978	100.0	29.4	55.3	15.3
1977	100.0	37.2	51.5	11.3
1976	100.0	37.5	46.2	16.3
1975	100.0	32.2	48.4	19.4
1974	100.0	34.8	50.2	15.1
1973	100.0	32.6	51.5	16.0

Source: Survey Documentation and Analysis, Computer-assisted Survey Methods Program, University of California, Berkeley, General Social Surveys, 1973–2004 Cumulative Data Files, Internet site http://sda.berkeley.edu/D3/GSS04/Docyr/gs04.htm

Table 1.36 Political Leanings, 1974 to 2004

"We hear a lot of talk these days about liberals and conservatives. Where would you place yourself on a seven-point scale on which the political views that people might hold are arranged from extremely liberal—point 1—to extremely conservative—point 7."

(percent distribution of people aged 18 or older by response, 1974 to 2004)

	total people	extremely liberal	liberal	slightly liberal	moderate	slightly conservative	conservative	extremely conservative
2004	100.0%	3.5%	9.2%	11.7%	38.0%	16.3%	17.0%	4.3%
2002	100.0	3.5	10.7	11.9	39.2	15.7	15.8	3.1
2000	100.0	4.0	11.6	10.8	39.9	14.8	15.5	3.4
1998	100.0	2.4	13.3	13.0	36.6	16.1	15.4	3.2
1996	100.0	2.2	11.0	12.2	38.1	16.4	16.7	3.4
1994	100.0	2.5	11.4	13.1	36.4	16.4	16.6	3.6
1993	100.0	1.9	11.6	13.1	37.1	17.1	16.4	2.7
1991	100.0	2.5	10.6	14.7	40.0	14.9	14.5	2.7
1990	100.0	2.7	10.7	13.6	36.2	18.3	14.6	3.9
1989	100.0	2.8	12.3	13.2	39.3	17.1	13.5	1.9
1988	100.0	2.4	12.4	13.3	36.3	17.4	15.9	2.3
1987	100.0	2.8	13.9	13.5	38.2	16.6	12.4	2.7
1986	100.0	1.8	9.4	12.6	41.3	17.3	14.9	2.7
1985	100.0	2.4	11.1	11.7	38.7	18.5	14.6	2.9
1984	100.0	2.1	9.4	12.6	40.3	19.6	13.2	2.9
1983	100.0	2.1	8.7	12.7	41.4	18.4	14.0	2.6
1982	100.0	2.8	11.4	15.4	39.9	13.5	13.2	3.9
1980	100.0	2.5	8.5	14.6	40.7	18.1	12.6	3.1
1978	100.0	1.5	9.9	16.8	38.3	18.3	13.1	2.1
1977	100.0	2.5	11.6	14.7	38.8	17.3	12.3	2.7
1976	100.0	2.2	13.3	13.3	39.9	15.8	13.6	1.9
1975	100.0	3.3	12.8	14.0	40.0	16.6	10.7	2.5
1974	100.0	1.6	14.3	14.7	40.0	15.7	11.3	2.5

Source: Survey Documentation and Analysis, Computer-assisted Survey Methods Program, University of California, Berkeley, General Social Surveys, 1974–2004 Cumulative Data Files, Internet site http://sda.berkeley.edu/D3/GSS04/Docyr/gs04.htm

Table 1.37 Political Party Affiliation, 1972 to 2004

"Generally speaking, do you usually think of yourself as a
Republican, Democrat, Independent, or what?"

(percent distribution of people aged 18 or older by response, 1972 to 2004)

	total people	strong Democrat	not strong Democrat	independent, near Democrat	independent	independent, near Republican	not strong Republican	strong Republican	other
2004	100.0%	16.2%	18.0%	10.0%	16.8%	8.5%	15.2%	14.1%	1.0%
2002	100.0	15.0	18.9	9.8	19.3	7.3	16.5	11.5	1.8
2000	100.0	14.8	18.1	11.6	20.2	9.3	14.2	10.2	1.7
1998	100.0	13.1	21.1	12.4	16.9	8.6	17.1	8.5	2.2
1996	100.0	13.8	19.9	12.3	15.8	8.9	17.3	10.6	1.5
1994	100.0	14.4	21.9	11.6	12.5	9.6	17.6	10.9	1.5
1993	100.0	14.2	20.1	11.9	12.8	9.9	18.7	11.3	1.1
1991	100.0	14.8	21.1	8.7	12.4	11.2	18.9	12.0	0.9
1990	100.0	12.4	23.0	9.7	11.3	10.5	20.5	11.7	0.9
1989	100.0	15.3	21.9	8.7	12.5	7.8	21.5	11.4	0.8
1988	100.0	15.9	21.1	12.2	12.6	9.5	18.6	9.9	0.3
1987	100.0	23.3	21.8	11.7	11.0	8.2	14.7	8.5	0.8
1986	100.0	16.7	22.9	10.8	12.7	10.2	16.4	9.6	0.6
1985	100.0	16.0	23.0	10.4	9.5	10.3	17.4	12.4	1.1
1984	100.0	18.1	19.1	14.3	11.1	10.6	16.7	8.5	1.5
1983	100.0	15.4	24.0	13.7	12.1	8.9	16.1	9.1	0.8
1982	100.0	20.6	26.1	13.1	12.2	8.2	11.6	7.4	0.7
1980	100.0	12.8	25.5	13.2	16.8	8.4	14.9	7.8	0.6
1978	100.0	14.1	25.5	13.0	14.5	8.8	16.1	7.3	0.7
1977	100.0	18.1	26.4	13.2	11.5	8.6	14.9	7.0	0.3
1976	100.0	15.1	27.0	13.8	16.1	7.0	14.3	6.4	0.3
1975	100.0	16.9	23.5	14.2	14.2	8.2	15.9	6.3	0.8
1974	100.0	16.8	25.5	14.2	9.9	7.3	14.8	7.5	4.0
1973	100.0	15.5	25.7	12.9	9.6	9.4	14.6	8.2	4.2
1972	100.0	20.3	27.1	10.0	9.9	6.2	14.4	7.8	4.3

Source: Survey Documentation and Analysis, Computer-assisted Survey Methods Program, University of California, Berkeley, General Social Surveys, 1972–2004 Cumulative Data Files, Internet site http://sda.berkeley.edu/D3/GSS04/Docyr/gs04.htm

Table 1.38 Voting Rate in Presidential Elections by Age, 1964 to 2004

(percent of people of voting age who reported voting in presidential elections by age, 1964 to 2004; percentage point change for selected years)

	total people of voting age	18 to 24	25 to 44	45 to 64	65 or older
2004	58.3%	41.9%	52.2%	66.6%	68.9%
2000	54.7	32.3	49.8	64.1	67.6
1996	54.2	32.4	49.2	64.4	67.0
1992	61.3	42.8	58.3	70.0	70.1
1988	57.4	36.2	54.0	67.9	68.8
1984	59.9	40.8	58.4	69.8	67.7
1980	59.3	39.9	58.7	69.3	65.1
1976	59.2	42.2	58.7	68.7	62.2
1972	63.0	49.6	62.7	70.8	63.5
1968	67.8	50.4	66.6	74.9	65.8
1964	69.3	50.9	69.0	75.9	66.3
Percentage point change					
2000 to 2004	3.6	9.6	2.4	2.5	1.3
1964 to 2004	−11.0	−9.0	−16.8	−9.3	2.6

Note: Before 1972, data for 18-to-24-year-olds include only 21-to-24-year-olds.
Source: Bureau of the Census, Voting and Registration, Historical Time Series Tables, Internet site http://www.census.gov/ population/www/socdemo/voting.html; calculations by New Strategist

Table 1.39 Voting Rate in Presidential Elections by Sex, 1964 to 2004

(percent of people of voting age who reported voting in presidential elections by sex, 1964 to 2004; percentage point change for selected years)

	total people of voting age	men	women
2004	58.3%	56.3%	60.1%
2000	54.7	53.1	56.2
1996	54.2	52.8	55.5
1992	61.3	60.2	62.3
1988	57.4	56.4	58.3
1984	59.9	59.0	60.8
1980	59.2	59.1	59.4
1976	59.2	59.6	58.8
1972	63.0	64.1	62.0
1968	67.8	69.8	66.0
1964	69.3	71.9	67.0
Percentage point change			
2000 to 2004	3.6	3.2	3.9
1964 to 2004	−11.0	−15.6	−6.9

Source: Bureau of the Census, Voting and Registration, Historical Time Series Tables, Internet site http://www.census.gov/ population/www/socdemo/voting.html; calculations by New Strategist

Table 1.40 Voting Rate in Presidential Elections by Race and Hispanic Origin, 1980 to 2004

(percent of total people and citizens of voting age who reported voting in presidential elections by race and Hispanic origin, 1964 to 2004; percentage point change for selected years)

	total people of voting age		Asians		blacks		Hispanics		non-Hispanic whites	
	total	citizens	total	citizens	total	citizens	total	citizens	total	citizens
2004	58.3%	63.8%	30.7%	44.6%	56.2%	59.9%	28.0%	47.2%	65.7%	67.1%
2000	54.7	59.5	25.4	43.4	53.5	56.8	27.5	45.1	60.4	61.8
1996	54.2	58.4	25.7	45.0	50.6	53.0	26.8	44.0	59.6	60.7
1992	61.3	67.7	27.3	53.9	54.1	59.2	28.9	51.6	66.9	70.2
1988	57.4	62.2	–	–	51.5	55.0	28.8	48.0	61.8	64.2
1984	59.9	64.9	–	–	55.8	60.6	32.7	50.0	63.3	66.4
1980	59.3	64.0	–	–	50.5	53.9	29.9	46.1	62.8	66.2
Percentage point change										
2000 to 2004	3.6	4.3	5.3	1.2	2.7	3.1	0.5	2.1	5.3	5.3
1980 to 2004	−1.0	−0.2	–	–	5.7	6.0	−1.9	1.1	2.9	0.9

Note: In 2004, data for Asians and blacks are for those who identify themselves as being of the respective race alone and those identifying themselves as being of the race in combination with other races; data for non-Hispanic whites is for those who identify themselves as being white alone and not Hispanic. "–" means data are not available.
Source: Bureau of the Census, Voting and Registration, Historical Time Series Tables, Internet site http://www.census.gov/population/www/socdemo/voting.html; calculations by New Strategist

Most Crime Rates Are Down, but the Murder Rate Is Rising

Americans think there is more crime in their local area.

The 51 percent majority of Americans say there is more crime in their area than there was a year ago, according to a Gallup poll. The percentage of people who feel this way has grown substantially in the past few years. In 2001, only 26 percent of the public thought crime was increasing in their local area—the lowest figure since the question was first asked in 1972.

Americans might be right about the increase in crime. The number of murders, rapes, and robberies increased between 2000 and 2005. So did burglaries and motor vehicle thefts. But the crime rate is not growing for most types of crime. The number of violent crimes per 100,000 population fell 7 percent between 2000 and 2005. The property crime rate was down 5 percent during those years. But the murder rate rose 1.8 percent between 2000 and 2005.

■ More than 16,000 Americans were murdered in 2005, a figure 7 percent greater than in 2000 and 83 percent greater than in 1960.

The majority of the public thinks local crime is increasing

(percentage of people aged 18 or older who think crime is increasing in their local area, for selected years from 1972 to 2006)

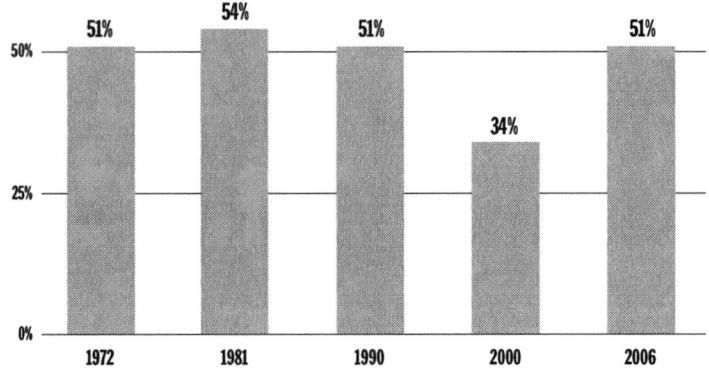

Table 1.41 **More Crime in Area, 1972 to 2006**

"Is there more crime in your area than there was a year ago, or less?"

(percent of people aged 18 or older by response, 1972 to 2006)

	total people	more	less	same
2006	100%	51%	30%	15%
2005	100	47	33	18
2004	100	37	37	22
2003	100	40	39	19
2002	100	37	34	24
2001	100	26	52	18
2000	100	34	46	15
1998	100	31	48	16
1997	100	46	32	20
1996	100	46	24	25
1992	100	54	19	23
1990	100	51	18	24
1989	100	47	21	27
1983	100	37	17	36
1981	100	54	8	29
1977	100	43	17	32
1975	100	50	12	29
1972	100	51	10	27
Percentage point change				
2000 to 2005	–	17	–16	0
1972 to 2005	–	0	20	–12

Note: Numbers will not sum to 100 because "no opinion" is not shown. "–" means not applicable.
Source: Reprinted with permission from The Gallup Organization, Internet site http://www.gallup.com

Table 1.42 Crimes Reported to Police, 1960 to 2005: Number of Crimes

(number of criminal offenses reported to police by type of crime, 1960 to 2005; percent change for selected years)

	violent crime					property crime			
	total	murder	forcible rape	robbery	aggravated assault	total	burglary	larceny-theft	motor vehicle theft
2005	1,390,695	16,692	93,934	417,122	862,947	10,166,159	2,154,126	6,776,807	1,235,226
2004	1,360,088	16,148	95,089	401,470	847,381	10,319,386	2,144,446	6,937,089	1,237,851
2003	1,383,676	16,528	93,883	414,235	859,030	10,442,862	2,154,834	7,026,802	1,261,226
2002	1,423,677	16,229	95,235	420,806	891,407	10,455,277	2,151,252	7,057,379	1,246,646
2001	1,439,480	16,037	90,863	423,557	909,023	10,437,189	2,116,531	7,092,267	1,228,391
2000	1,425,486	15,586	90,178	408,016	911,706	10,182,584	2,050,992	6,971,590	1,160,002
1999	1,426,044	15,522	89,411	409,371	911,740	10,208,334	2,100,739	6,955,520	1,152,075
1998	1,533,887	16,974	93,144	447,186	976,583	10,951,827	2,332,735	7,376,311	1,242,781
1997	1,636,096	18,208	96,153	498,534	1,023,201	11,558,475	2,460,526	7,743,760	1,354,189
1996	1,688,540	19,645	96,252	535,594	1,037,049	11,805,323	2,506,400	7,904,685	1,394,238
1995	1,798,792	21,606	97,470	580,509	1,099,207	12,063,935	2,593,784	7,997,710	1,472,441
1994	1,857,670	23,326	102,216	618,949	1,113,179	12,131,873	2,712,774	7,879,812	1,539,287
1993	1,926,017	24,526	106,014	659,870	1,135,607	12,218,777	2,834,808	7,820,909	1,563,060
1992	1,932,274	23,760	109,062	672,478	1,126,974	12,505,917	2,979,884	7,915,199	1,610,834
1991	1,911,767	24,703	106,593	687,732	1,092,739	12,961,116	3,157,150	8,142,228	1,661,738
1990	1,820,127	23,438	102,555	639,271	1,054,863	12,655,486	3,073,909	7,945,670	1,635,907
1989	1,646,037	21,500	94,504	578,326	951,707	12,605,412	3,168,170	7,872,442	1,564,800
1988	1,566,221	20,675	92,486	542,968	910,092	12,356,865	3,218,077	7,705,872	1,432,916
1987	1,483,999	20,096	91,111	517,704	855,088	12,024,709	3,236,184	7,499,851	1,288,674
1986	1,489,169	20,613	91,459	542,775	834,322	11,722,700	3,241,410	7,257,153	1,224,137
1985	1,327,767	18,976	87,671	497,874	723,246	11,102,590	3,073,348	6,926,380	1,102,862
1984	1,273,282	18,692	84,233	485,008	685,349	10,608,473	2,984,434	6,591,874	1,032,165
1983	1,258,087	19,308	78,918	506,567	653,294	10,850,543	3,129,851	6,712,759	1,007,933
1982	1,322,390	21,010	78,770	553,130	669,480	11,652,000	3,447,100	7,142,500	1,062,400
1981	1,361,820	22,520	82,500	592,910	663,900	12,061,900	3,779,700	7,194,400	1,087,800
1980	1,344,520	23,040	82,990	565,840	672,650	12,063,700	3,795,200	7,136,900	1,131,700
1979	1,208,030	21,460	76,390	480,700	629,480	11,041,500	3,327,700	6,601,000	1,112,800
1978	1,085,550	19,560	67,610	426,930	571,460	10,123,400	3,128,300	5,991,000	1,004,100
1977	1,029,580	19,120	63,500	412,610	534,350	9,955,000	3,071,500	5,905,700	977,700
1976	1,004,210	18,780	57,080	427,810	500,530	10,345,500	3,108,700	6,270,800	966,000
1975	1,039,710	20,510	56,090	470,500	492,620	10,252,700	3,265,300	5,977,700	1,009,600
1974	974,720	20,710	55,400	442,400	456,210	9,278,700	3,039,200	5,262,500	977,100
1973	875,910	19,640	51,400	384,220	420,650	7,842,200	2,565,500	4,347,900	928,800
1972	834,900	18,670	46,850	376,290	393,090	7,413,900	2,375,500	4,151,200	887,200
1971	816,500	17,780	42,260	387,700	368,760	7,771,700	2,399,300	4,424,200	948,200
1970	738,820	16,000	37,990	349,860	334,970	7,359,200	2,205,000	4,225,800	928,400
1965	387,390	9,960	23,410	138,690	215,330	4,352,000	1,282,500	2,572,600	496,900
1960	288,460	9,110	17,190	107,840	154,320	3,095,700	912,100	1,855,400	328,200

Percent change

2000 to 2005	−2.4%	7.1%	4.2%	2.2%	−5.3%	−0.2%	5.0%	−2.8%	6.5%
1960 to 2005	382.1	83.2	446.4	286.8	459.2	228.4	136.2	265.2	276.4

Source: Sourcebook of Criminal Justice Statistics Online, http://www.albany.edu/sourcebook; calculations by New Strategist

Table 1.43 Crimes Reported to Police, 1960 to 2005: Rate of Crime

(number of criminal offenses reported to police per 100,000 people by type of crime, 1960 to 2005; percent change for selected years)

	violent crime					property crime			
	total	murder	forcible rape	robbery	aggravated assault	total	burglary	larceny-theft	motor vehicle theft
2005	469.2	5.6	31.7	140.7	291.1	3,429.8	726.7	2,286.3	416.7
2004	463.2	5.5	32.4	136.7	288.6	3,514.1	730.3	2,362.3	421.5
2003	475.8	5.7	32.3	142.5	295.4	3,591.2	741.0	2,416.5	433.7
2002	494.4	5.6	33.1	146.1	309.5	3,630.6	747.0	2,450.7	432.9
2001	504.5	5.6	31.8	148.5	318.6	3,658.1	741.8	2,485.7	430.5
2000	506.5	5.5	32.0	145.0	324.0	3,618.3	728.8	2,477.3	412.2
1999	523.0	5.7	32.8	150.1	334.3	3,743.6	770.4	2,550.7	422.5
1998	567.6	6.3	34.5	165.5	361.4	4,052.5	863.2	2,729.5	459.9
1997	611.0	6.8	35.9	186.2	382.1	4,316.3	918.8	2,891.8	505.7
1996	636.6	7.4	36.3	201.9	391.0	4,451.0	945.0	2,980.3	525.7
1995	684.5	8.2	37.1	220.9	418.3	4,590.5	987.0	3,043.2	560.3
1994	713.6	9.0	39.3	237.8	427.6	4,660.2	1,042.1	3,026.9	591.3
1993	747.1	9.5	41.1	256.0	440.5	4,740.0	1,099.7	3,033.9	606.3
1992	757.7	9.3	42.8	263.7	441.9	4,903.7	1,168.4	3,103.6	631.6
1991	758.2	9.8	42.3	272.7	433.4	5,140.2	1,252.1	3,229.1	659.0
1990	729.6	9.4	41.1	256.3	422.9	5,073.1	1,232.2	3,185.1	655.8
1989	669.9	8.7	38.3	234.3	385.6	5,107.1	1,283.6	3,189.6	634.0
1988	640.6	8.5	37.8	222.1	372.2	5,054.0	1,316.2	3,151.7	586.1
1987	612.5	8.3	37.6	213.7	352.9	4,963.0	1,335.7	3,095.4	531.9
1986	620.1	8.6	38.1	226.0	347.4	4,881.8	1,349.8	3,022.1	509.8
1985	558.1	8.0	36.8	209.3	304.0	4,666.4	1,291.7	2,911.2	463.5
1984	539.9	7.9	35.7	205.7	290.6	4,498.5	1,265.5	2,795.2	437.7
1983	538.1	8.3	33.8	216.7	279.4	4,641.1	1,338.7	2,871.3	431.1
1982	570.8	9.1	34.0	238.8	289.0	5,029.7	1,488.0	3,083.1	458.6
1981	593.5	9.8	36.0	258.4	289.3	5,256.5	1,647.2	3,135.3	474.1
1980	596.6	10.2	36.8	251.1	298.5	5,353.3	1,684.1	3,167.0	502.2
1979	548.9	9.7	34.7	218.4	286.0	5,016.6	1,511.9	2,999.1	505.6
1978	497.8	9.0	31.0	195.8	262.1	4,642.5	1,434.6	2,747.4	460.5
1977	475.9	8.8	29.4	190.7	240.0	4,601.7	1,419.8	2,729.9	451.9
1976	467.8	8.8	26.6	199.3	233.2	4,819.5	1,448.2	2,921.3	450.0
1975	487.8	9.6	26.3	220.8	231.1	4,810.7	1,532.1	2,804.8	473.7
1974	461.1	9.8	26.2	209.3	215.8	4,389.3	1,437.7	2,489.5	462.2
1973	417.4	9.4	24.5	183.1	200.5	3,737.0	1,222.5	2,071.9	442.6
1972	401.0	9.0	22.5	180.7	188.8	3,560.4	1,140.8	1,993.6	426.1
1971	396.0	8.6	20.5	188.0	178.8	3,768.8	1,163.5	2,145.5	459.8
1970	363.5	7.9	18.7	172.1	164.8	3,621.0	1,084.9	2,079.3	456.8
1965	200.2	5.1	12.1	71.7	111.3	2,248.8	662.7	1,329.3	256.8
1960	160.9	5.1	9.6	60.1	86.1	1,726.3	508.6	1,034.7	183.0
Percent change									
2000 to 2005	−7.4%	1.8%	−0.9%	−3.0%	−10.2%	−5.2%	−0.3%	−7.7%	1.1%
1960 to 2005	191.6	9.8	230.2	134.1	238.1	98.7	42.9	121.0	127.7

Source: Sourcebook of Criminal Justice Statistics Online, http://www.albany.edu/sourcebook; calculations by New Strategist

2

Education

■ The educational attainment of the American population has soared over the past half-century. In 1950, only 34 percent of people aged 25 or older were high school graduates. By 2005, the figure had climbed to 85 percent.

■ Going to college is no longer an elite privilege, but the norm. Most high school graduates now continue their education on a college campus. Sixty-nine percent of high school graduates enroll in college within 12 months of graduating from high school.

■ On college campuses, women outnumber men by a wide margin, which creates a problem for college admissions officer who want to balance the student body. In 1950, women accounted for only 32 percent of college students. Today the figure is 57 percent.

■ The cost of one year of undergraduate education at a four-year college climbed from just $2,577 in 1976-77 to $17,447 in 2005–06, a 97 percent increase after adjusting for inflation.

■ Men once earned most of the degrees awarded by the nation's colleges. Today, women earn more than half of associate's, bachelor's, and master's degrees. In a few years, women will earn most doctoral and first-professional degrees as well.

Big Gains in Educational Attainment

Educational attainment is up for men and women, whites and blacks.

The educational attainment of the American population has soared since 1950. In that year, most people were high school dropouts. Only 34 percent had a high school diploma. By 2006, fully 85 percent of people aged 25 or older were high school graduates. The proportion of Americans with a college degree rose from 6 to 28 percent during those years.

Some demographic segments are better educated than others, but the gap has narrowed since 1950. Men and women are equally likely to have a high school diploma, and women are almost as likely as men to have a college degree. Women under age 55 are more likely than their male counterparts to have graduated from college.

Blacks have nearly closed the gap with whites in high school graduation rates, although whites are still much more likely to have a college degree. Asians are the best educated Americans, with half having a college degree. Hispanics have the least education. Only 59 percent have a high school diploma. Behind the lower educational attainment of Hispanics is the fact that many are immigrants who arrived in the United States as adults with little schooling.

■ The rapid rise in the cost of a college education will make it more difficult to close the educational attainment gap between blacks and whites.

Women are almost as likely as men to have a college degree

(percent of people aged 25 or older who have completed college, by sex, 1950 to 2006)

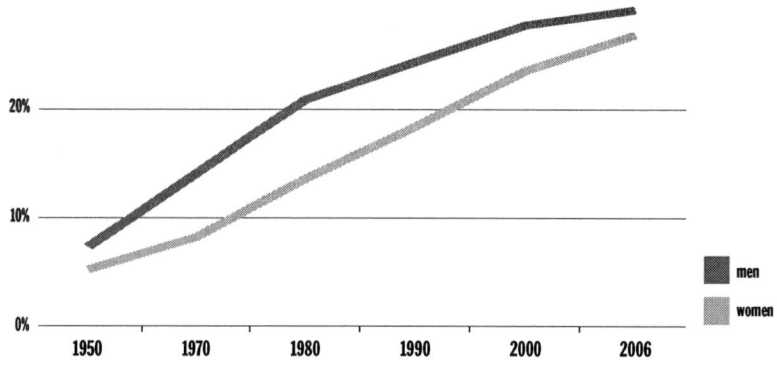

Table 2.1 High School Graduates by Sex, 1950 to 2006

(percent of people aged 25 or older who completed high school, by sex, 1950 to 2006; percentage point change for selected years)

	total	men	women
2006	85.5%	85.0%	85.9%
2005	85.2	84.9	85.5
2004	85.2	84.8	85.4
2003	84.6	84.1	85.0
2002	84.1	83.8	84.4
2001	84.1	84.1	84.2
2000	84.1	84.2	84.0
1999	83.4	83.4	83.4
1998	82.8	82.8	82.9
1997	82.1	82.0	82.2
1996	81.7	81.9	81.6
1995	81.7	81.7	81.6
1994	80.9	81.0	80.7
1993	80.2	80.5	80.0
1992	79.4	79.7	79.2
1991	78.4	78.5	78.3
1990	77.6	77.7	77.5
1989	76.9	77.2	76.6
1988	76.2	76.4	76.0
1987	75.6	76.0	75.3
1986	74.7	75.1	74.4
1985	73.9	74.4	73.5
1984	73.3	73.7	73.0
1983	72.1	72.7	71.5
1982	71.0	71.7	70.3
1981	69.7	70.3	69.1
1980	68.6	69.2	68.1
1979	67.7	68.4	67.1
1978	65.9	66.8	65.2
1977	64.9	65.6	64.4
1976	64.1	64.7	63.5
1975	62.5	63.1	62.1
1974	61.2	61.6	60.9
1973	59.8	60.0	59.6
1972	58.2	58.2	58.2
1971	56.4	56.3	56.6
1970	55.2	55.0	55.4
1969	54.0	53.6	54.4
1968	52.6	52.0	53.2
1967	51.1	50.5	51.7
1966	49.9	49.0	50.8
1965	49.0	48.0	49.9
1959	43.7	42.2	45.2
1950	34.3	32.6	36.0
Percentage point change			
2000 to 2006	1.4	0.8	1.9
1950 to 2006	51.2	52.4	49.9

Source: Bureau of the Census, Current Population Surveys, Internet site http://www.census.gov/population/www/socdemo/ educ-attn.html; calculations by New Strategist

Table 2.2 High School Graduates by Age, 1950 to 2006

(percent of people aged 25 or older who completed high school, by age, 1950 to 2006; percentage point change for selected years)

	total	25 to 34	35 to 54	55 or older
2006	85.5%	87.0%	88.4%	80.8%
2005	85.2	86.7	88.7	79.6
2004	85.2	87.1	88.8	79.1
2003	84.6	87.1	88.5	77.5
2002	84.1	86.9	88.7	75.8
2001	84.1	87.4	88.7	75.4
2000	84.1	88.2	88.8	74.6
1999	83.4	87.7	88.2	73.5
1998	82.8	87.9	87.7	72.1
1997	82.1	87.3	87.5	70.4
1996	81.7	86.9	87.3	69.9
1995	81.7	87.1	87.5	69.2
1994	80.9	86.4	87.2	67.7
1993	80.2	86.9	87.0	66.0
1992	79.4	86.5	86.0	65.2
1991	78.4	86.1	85.1	63.7
1990	77.6	86.2	84.6	61.6
1989	76.9	86.6	83.3	60.9
1988	76.2	86.4	82.7	59.8
1987	75.6	86.5	82.5	58.4
1986	74.7	86.8	81.4	57.0
1985	73.9	86.8	80.4	56.0
1984	73.3	86.5	79.3	55.8
1983	72.1	86.4	77.8	54.3
1982	71.0	86.3	76.0	53.1
1981	69.7	85.6	74.6	51.5
1980	68.6	85.4	73.5	50.1
1979	67.7	84.7	72.5	49.4
1978	65.9	84.0	70.3	47.2
1977	64.9	83.4	68.9	46.4
1976	64.1	82.7	68.3	45.2
1975	62.5	81.1	67.5	43.2
1974	61.2	80.1	66.6	41.3
1973	59.8	78.1	65.4	40.3
1972	58.2	77.2	63.2	39.1
1971	56.4	75.3	62.4	36.9
1970	55.2	73.8	61.2	35.8
1969	54.0	72.6	59.9	34.8
1968	52.6	71.1	58.6	33.3
1967	51.1	70.4	56.9	31.8
1966	49.9	69.2	55.4	30.9
1965	49.0	68.0	54.8	29.3
1959	43.7	60.5	47.0	23.9
1950	34.3	47.0	32.9	19.2
Percentage point change				
2000 to 2006	1.4	−1.2	−0.4	6.2
1950 to 2006	51.2	40.0	55.5	61.6

Source: Bureau of the Census, Current Population Surveys, Internet site http://www.census.gov/population/www/socdemo/ educ-attn.html; calculations by New Strategist

Table 2.3 High School Graduates by Age and Sex, 1950 to 2006

(percent of people aged 25 or older who completed high school, by age and sex, 1950 to 2006; percentage point change for selected years)

	25 to 34		35 to 54		55 or older	
	men	women	men	women	men	women
2006	85.4%	88.5%	87.3%	89.4%	81.6%	80.2%
2005	85.6	87.9	87.9	89.6	80.2	79.1
2004	85.7	88.4	87.8	89.7	79.8	78.4
2003	85.6	88.5	87.4	89.5	78.1	77.1
2002	85.1	88.7	88.1	89.4	76.3	75.4
2001	86.2	88.5	88.2	89.2	76.0	75.0
2000	87.1	89.2	88.5	89.0	75.1	74.2
1999	89.8	88.7	87.6	88.7	74.2	72.9
1998	86.8	89.0	86.8	88.6	73.2	71.3
1997	85.9	88.6	86.8	88.2	71.0	69.9
1996	85.9	87.9	86.9	87.7	70.7	69.3
1995	86.1	88.2	87.0	87.9	69.5	68.9
1994	85.2	87.5	87.0	87.4	68.0	67.5
1993	86.1	87.7	86.8	87.2	66.3	65.7
1992	85.9	87.0	85.9	86.0	65.0	65.3
1991	85.7	86.5	84.8	85.4	63.1	64.1
1990	85.1	87.4	84.5	84.8	61.5	61.8
1989	85.7	87.4	83.5	83.1	60.7	61.1
1988	85.4	87.5	83.0	82.5	59.3	60.2
1987	86.0	87.0	82.5	82.5	58.0	58.8
1986	86.5	87.1	81.1	81.6	56.7	57.3
1985	86.5	87.1	80.3	80.5	55.7	56.3
1984	86.5	86.6	79.0	79.7	55.1	56.3
1983	86.6	86.1	77.8	77.8	53.8	54.7
1982	86.9	85.7	75.9	76.1	52.7	53.3
1981	86.1	85.2	74.2	75.1	51.3	51.7
1980	86.0	84.8	73.1	73.8	49.6	50.6
1979	85.8	83.6	72.4	72.6	48.7	50.0
1978	85.3	82.8	70.2	70.3	46.7	47.6
1977	84.7	82.1	68.4	69.5	45.9	46.7
1976	84.1	81.4	67.8	68.8	44.5	45.8
1975	82.4	79.7	67.0	68.0	42.2	43.9
1974	81.1	79.1	66.2	67.0	40.0	42.3
1973	78.5	77.6	65.2	65.7	38.8	41.4
1972	77.9	76.4	62.4	64.0	37.6	40.3
1971	75.9	74.6	61.5	63.2	35.2	38.4
1970	74.3	73.3	60.3	62.1	34.1	37.2
1969	73.1	72.2	58.7	61.1	33.2	36.2
1968	71.3	71.0	57.5	59.7	31.4	34.9
1967	70.6	70.2	55.7	58.2	30.2	33.2
1966	69.7	68.6	53.7	56.9	28.7	32.7
1965	68.5	67.5	52.9	56.7	27.4	30.9
1959	58.8	62.1	45.0	48.9	22.1	25.6
1950	47.2	51.0	30.8	35.0	17.8	20.5
Percentage point change						
2000 to 2006	–1.7	–0.6	–1.2	0.3	6.4	6.1
1950 to 2006	38.3	37.5	56.5	54.4	63.8	59.7

Source: Bureau of the Census, Current Population Surveys, Internet site http://www.census.gov/population/www/socdemo/educ-attn.html; calculations by New Strategist

Table 2.4 High School Graduates by Race and Hispanic Origin, 1950 to 2006

(percent of people aged 25 or older who completed high school by race and Hispanic origin, 1950 to 2006; percentage point change, 2000–06)

	total	Asian	black	Hispanic	white	non-Hispanic white
2006	85.5%	87.6%	80.7%	59.3%	86.1%	90.5%
2005	85.2	87.9	81.1	58.5	85.8	90.1
2004	85.2	86.9	80.6	58.4	85.8	90.0
2003	84.6	87.8	80.0	57.0	85.1	89.4
2002	84.1	87.4	78.7	57.0	84.8	88.7
2001	84.1	87.6	78.8	56.8	84.8	88.6
2000	84.1	85.7	78.5	57.0	84.9	88.4
1999	83.4	–	77.0	56.1	84.3	87.7
1998	82.8	–	76.0	55.5	83.7	87.1
1997	82.1	–	74.9	54.7	83.0	86.3
1996	81.7	–	74.3	53.1	82.8	86.0
1995	81.7	–	73.8	53.4	83.0	85.9
1994	80.9	–	72.9	53.3	82.0	84.9
1993	80.2	–	70.4	53.1	81.5	84.1
1992	79.4	–	67.7	52.6	80.9	–
1991	78.4	–	66.7	51.3	79.9	–
1990	77.6	–	66.2	50.8	79.1	–
1989	76.9	–	64.6	50.9	78.4	–
1988	76.2	–	63.5	51.0	77.7	–
1987	75.6	–	63.4	50.9	77.0	–
1986	74.7	–	62.3	48.5	76.2	–
1985	73.9	–	59.8	47.9	75.5	–
1984	73.3	–	58.5	47.1	75.0	–
1983	72.1	–	56.8	46.2	73.8	–
1982	71.0	–	54.9	45.9	72.8	–
1981	69.7	–	52.9	44.5	71.6	–
1980	68.6	–	51.2	45.3	70.5	–
1979	67.7	–	49.4	42.0	69.7	–
1978	65.9	–	47.6	40.8	67.9	–
1977	64.9	–	45.5	39.6	67.0	–
1976	64.1	–	43.8	39.3	66.1	–
1975	62.5	–	42.5	37.9	64.5	–
1974	61.2	–	40.8	36.5	63.3	–
1973	59.8	–	39.2	–	61.9	–
1972	58.2	–	36.6	–	60.4	–
1971	56.4	–	34.7	–	58.6	–
1970	55.2	–	33.7	–	57.4	–
1969	54.0	–	32.3	–	56.3	–
1968	52.6	–	30.1	–	54.9	–
1967	51.1	–	29.5	–	53.4	–
1966	49.9	–	27.8	–	52.2	–
1965	49.0	–	27.2	–	51.3	–
1959	43.7	–	20.7	–	46.1	–
1950	34.3	–	13.7	–	–	–
Percentage point change						
2000 to 2006	1.4	1.9	2.2	2.3	1.2	2.1

Note: "–" means data are not available.
Source: Bureau of the Census, Current Population Surveys, Internet site http://www.census.gov/population/www/socdemo/educ-attn.html; calculations by New Strategist

Table 2.5 College Graduates by Sex, 1950 to 2006

(percent of people aged 25 or older who completed college by sex, 1950 to 2006; percentage point change for selected years)

	total	men	women
2006	28.0%	29.2%	26.9%
2005	27.7	28.9	26.5
2004	27.7	29.4	26.1
2003	27.2	28.9	25.7
2002	26.7	28.5	25.1
2001	26.2	28.2	24.3
2000	25.6	27.8	23.6
1999	25.2	27.5	23.1
1998	24.4	26.5	22.4
1997	23.9	26.2	21.7
1996	23.6	26.0	21.4
1995	23.0	26.0	20.2
1994	22.2	25.1	19.6
1993	21.9	24.8	19.2
1992	21.4	24.3	18.6
1991	21.4	24.3	18.8
1990	21.3	24.4	18.4
1989	21.1	24.5	18.1
1988	20.3	24.0	17.0
1987	19.9	23.6	16.5
1986	19.4	23.2	16.1
1985	19.4	23.1	16.0
1984	19.1	22.9	15.7
1983	18.8	23.0	15.1
1982	17.7	21.9	14.0
1981	17.1	21.1	13.4
1980	17.0	20.9	13.6
1979	16.4	20.4	12.9
1978	15.7	19.7	12.2
1977	15.4	19.2	12.0
1976	14.7	18.6	11.3
1975	13.9	17.6	10.6
1974	13.3	16.9	10.1
1973	12.6	16.0	9.6
1972	12.0	15.4	9.0
1971	11.4	14.6	8.5
1970	11.0	14.1	8.2
1969	10.7	13.6	8.1
1968	10.5	13.3	8.0
1967	10.1	12.8	7.6
1966	9.8	12.5	7.4
1965	9.4	12.0	7.1
1959	8.1	10.3	6.0
1950	6.2	7.3	5.2
Percentage point change			
2000 to 2006	2.4	1.1	2.9
1950 to 2006	21.8	21.6	21.3

Source: Bureau of the Census, Current Population Surveys, Internet site http://www.census.gov/population/www/socdemo/ educ-attn.html; calculations by New Strategist

Table 2.6 College Graduates by Age, 1950 to 2006

(percent of people aged 25 or older who completed college, by age, 1950 to 2006; percentage point change for selected years)

	total	25 to 34	35 to 54	55 or older
2006	28.0%	29.9%	30.2%	24.0%
2005	27.7	30.4	29.7	23.3
2004	27.7	30.2	30.0	23.0
2003	27.2	30.0	29.9	21.7
2002	26.7	30.6	29.2	20.7
2001	26.2	29.7	29.1	19.6
2000	25.6	29.3	28.5	18.9
1999	25.2	28.7	28.2	18.4
1998	24.4	27.5	27.4	17.8
1997	23.9	27.1	26.8	17.2
1996	23.6	26.5	27.0	16.5
1995	23.0	25.0	27.2	15.4
1994	22.2	23.4	26.7	15.1
1993	21.9	23.8	26.1	14.7
1992	21.4	23.2	25.7	14.2
1991	21.4	23.7	25.8	14.1
1990	21.3	23.9	25.4	13.9
1989	21.1	24.2	25.5	13.3
1988	20.3	23.6	24.5	12.5
1987	19.9	23.9	23.7	12.1
1986	19.4	24.0	22.9	11.7
1985	19.4	23.8	23.0	11.7
1984	19.1	24.3	22.0	11.6
1983	18.8	24.4	21.2	11.6
1982	17.7	23.8	19.6	10.8
1981	17.1	23.2	18.9	10.2
1980	17.0	24.1	18.3	9.9
1979	16.4	23.8	17.4	9.7
1978	15.7	23.6	16.3	8.9
1977	15.4	23.8	15.5	8.9
1976	14.7	22.6	14.6	8.9
1975	13.9	21.4	14.1	8.1
1974	13.3	20.0	13.8	7.9
1973	12.6	18.2	13.2	7.9
1972	12.0	17.9	12.2	7.9
1971	11.4	16.3	11.8	7.7
1970	11.0	15.8	11.4	7.5
1969	10.7	15.3	11.2	7.1
1968	10.5	14.7	11.2	7.0
1967	10.1	14.2	10.7	6.7
1966	9.8	13.8	10.4	6.7
1965	9.4	13.1	10.0	6.3
1959	8.1	10.8	8.4	5.1
1950	6.2	5.3	6.5	4.0
Percentage point change				
2000 to 2006	2.4	1.2	1.2	4.4
1950 to 2006	21.8	25.1	23.2	19.3

Source: Bureau of the Census, Current Population Surveys, Internet site http://www.census.gov/population/www/socdemo/ educ-attn.html; calculations by New Strategist

Table 2.7 College Graduates by Age and Sex, 1950 to 2006

(percent of people aged 25 or older who completed college, by age and sex, 1950 to 2006; percentage point change for selected years)

	25 to 34		35 to 54		55 or older	
	men	women	men	women	men	women
2006	27.1%	32.7%	30.0%	30.4%	29.4%	19.5%
2005	27.6	33.3	29.7	29.7	28.6	18.9
2004	28.0	32.4	30.5	29.6	28.8	18.2
2003	27.9	32.1	30.5	29.3	27.1	17.2
2002	28.5	32.7	30.1	28.4	26.2	16.3
2001	28.0	31.3	30.4	27.9	25.0	15.3
2000	28.6	29.9	29.6	27.4	24.3	14.6
1999	28.8	29.6	29.7	26.9	23.7	14.1
1998	26.2	28.7	29.0	25.8	22.7	13.8
1997	26.2	27.9	28.7	25.0	22.2	13.2
1996	25.9	27.1	28.8	25.3	21.6	12.3
1995	25.1	24.9	30.0	24.6	20.4	11.4
1994	23.3	23.5	29.6	23.8	19.7	11.4
1993	24.2	23.5	28.7	23.6	19.6	10.8
1992	23.3	23.1	28.8	22.8	18.9	10.5
1991	23.5	23.8	29.1	22.6	18.5	10.7
1990	24.3	23.5	29.1	22.0	18.1	10.6
1989	24.9	23.5	29.6	21.6	17.3	10.1
1988	25.0	22.3	29.1	20.2	16.4	9.4
1987	24.9	22.9	28.5	19.0	16.0	9.1
1986	25.2	22.8	27.6	18.4	15.7	8.6
1985	25.2	22.5	27.9	18.3	15.4	8.8
1984	25.9	22.8	27.2	17.0	14.9	9.0
1983	26.8	22.1	26.6	16.0	15.0	8.9
1982	26.5	21.1	24.7	14.8	14.4	8.1
1981	26.1	20.4	23.6	14.4	13.6	7.5
1980	27.5	20.9	23.0	13.9	12.6	7.9
1979	27.7	20.0	22.2	12.9	11.9	7.9
1978	27.5	19.9	21.2	11.8	11.1	7.2
1977	27.7	20.0	20.1	11.2	10.8	7.4
1976	26.8	18.6	19.3	10.3	10.9	7.3
1975	25.4	17.5	18.6	9.9	9.9	6.7
1974	23.7	16.4	18.2	9.6	9.6	6.6
1973	21.5	15.0	17.6	9.2	9.5	6.7
1972	21.6	14.3	16.4	8.2	9.4	6.6
1971	19.9	12.8	15.9	8.0	9.1	6.5
1970	19.7	12.0	15.1	8.0	8.9	6.3
1969	19.0	11.8	14.6	8.0	8.3	6.1
1968	18.8	10.7	14.5	8.1	8.0	6.1
1967	18.1	10.4	13.9	7.6	7.8	5.9
1966	17.7	10.0	13.6	7.3	7.5	5.9
1965	17.0	9.4	13.0	7.2	7.3	5.5
1959	14.8	7.0	10.5	6.5	6.0	4.2
1950	9.1	5.9	7.4	5.7	4.6	3.3
Percentage point change						
2000 to 2006	−1.6	2.8	0.4	3.1	5.1	5.0
1950 to 2006	18.0	26.9	22.6	24.7	24.8	16.2

Source: Bureau of the Census, Current Population Surveys, Internet site http://www.census.gov/population/www/socdemo/educ-attn.html; calculations by New Strategist

Table 2.8 College Graduates by Race and Hispanic Origin, 1950 to 2006

(percent of people aged 25 or older who completed college by race and Hispanic origin, 1950 to 2006; percentage point chage, 2000–06)

	total	Asian	black	Hispanic	white	non-Hispanic white
2006	28.0%	50.0%	18.5%	12.4%	28.4%	31.0%
2005	27.7	49.8	17.6	12.0	28.1	30.5
2004	27.7	48.9	17.6	12.1	28.2	30.6
2003	27.2	49.2	17.3	11.4	27.6	30.0
2002	26.7	47.2	17.0	11.1	27.2	29.4
2001	26.2	47.5	15.7	11.1	26.6	28.7
2000	25.6	43.9	16.5	10.6	26.1	28.1
1999	25.2	–	15.4	10.9	25.9	27.7
1998	24.4	–	14.7	11.0	25.0	26.6
1997	23.9	–	13.3	10.3	24.6	26.2
1996	23.6	–	13.6	9.3	24.3	25.9
1995	23.0	–	13.2	9.3	24.0	25.4
1994	22.2	–	12.9	9.1	22.9	24.3
1993	21.9	–	12.2	9.0	22.6	23.8
1992	21.4	–	11.9	9.3	22.1	–
1991	21.4	–	11.5	9.7	22.2	–
1990	21.3	–	11.3	9.2	22.0	–
1989	21.1	–	11.8	9.9	21.8	–
1988	20.3	–	11.2	10.1	20.9	–
1987	19.9	–	10.7	8.6	20.5	–
1986	19.4	–	10.9	8.4	20.1	–
1985	19.4	–	11.1	8.5	20.0	–
1984	19.1	–	10.4	8.2	19.8	–
1983	18.8	–	9.5	7.9	19.5	–
1982	17.7	–	8.8	7.8	18.5	–
1981	17.1	–	8.2	7.7	17.8	–
1980	17.0	–	7.9	7.9	17.8	–
1979	16.4	–	7.9	6.7	17.2	–
1978	15.7	–	7.2	7.0	16.4	–
1977	15.4	–	7.2	6.2	16.1	–
1976	14.7	–	6.6	6.1	15.4	–
1975	13.9	–	6.4	6.3	14.5	–
1974	13.3	–	5.5	5.5	14.0	–
1973	12.6	–	6.0	–	13.1	–
1972	12.0	–	5.1	–	12.6	–
1971	11.4	–	4.5	–	12.0	–
1970	11.0	–	4.5	–	11.6	–
1969	10.7	–	4.6	–	11.2	–
1968	10.5	–	4.3	–	11.0	–
1967	10.1	–	4.0	–	10.6	–
1966	9.8	–	3.8	–	10.4	–
1965	9.4	–	4.7	–	9.9	–
1959	8.1	–	3.3	–	8.6	–
1950	6.2	–	2.3	–	–	–
Percentage point change						
2000 to 2006	2.4	6.1	2.0	1.8	2.3	2.9

Note: "–" means data are not available.
Source: Bureau of the Census, Current Population Surveys, Internet site http://www.census.gov/population/www/socdemo/educ-attn.html; calculations by New Strategist

Most Preschoolers Are in School

The school years start earlier now that working mothers are the norm.

As mothers have gone to work, young children have gone to school. Sixty-four percent of the nation's 3-to-5-year-olds were enrolled in nursery school or kindergarten in 2005, up from just 27 percent in 1965. Most attend school all day, up from only 17 percent enrolled in full-day programs in 1970.

As the nursery school experience has become common, a shrinking share of children attends private nursery schools. The figure stood at about 46 percent in 2005, down from 76 percent forty years earlier. More than 80 percent of kindergarteners attend public programs.

The nation's elementary and secondary schools have experienced boom and bust over the past half-century. Behind the cycles of growth and decline are the baby boom, baby bust (or Generation X), and millennial generations. In 2005, the number of children in elementary and middle school (grades 1 through 8) stood at 32 million, close to the all-time high of nearly 34 million reached in 1970. The number of students in secondary school (grades 9 through 12) stood at an all-time high of 17 million in 2005. Only 8 percent of high school students attend private school, a figure that has not varied much over the decades.

More than 3 million young adults graduated from high school in 2006–07. The number of high school graduates is projected to remain above 3 million for years to come.

■ Public schools are increasingly diverse, with minorities accounting for 42 percent of students—up from 34 percent a decade earlier.

The percentage of 3-to-5-year-olds in school has more than doubled

(percent of 3-to-5-year-olds in nursery school or kindergarten, 1965 and 2005)

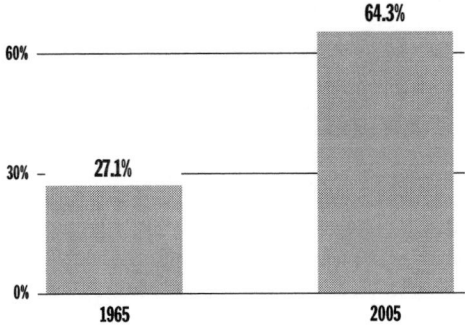

Table 2.9 Enrollment of 3-to-5-Year-Olds in Preprimary Programs, 1965 to 2005

(total number of people aged 3 to 5, and number and percent enrolled in nursery school or kindergarten, 1965 to 2005; percent and percentage point change for selected years; numbers in thousands)

	total population aged 3 to 5	enrolled in nursery school or kindergarten number	share of total	percent attending full-day
2005	12,134	7,801	64.3%	58.3%
2004	12,362	7,969	64.5	56.6
2003	12,204	7,921	64.9	55.9
2002	11,524	7,697	66.8	54.4
2001	11,899	7,602	63.9	51.8
2000	11,858	7,592	64.0	52.8
1999	11,920	7,844	65.8	53.0
1998	12,078	7,788	64.5	50.8
1997	12,121	7,860	64.8	49.9
1996	12,378	7,580	61.2	47.0
1995	12,518	7,739	61.8	47.7
1994	12,328	7,514	61.0	46.2
1993	11,954	6,581	55.1	40.1
1992	11,545	6,402	55.5	37.6
1991	11,370	6,334	55.7	38.0
1990	11,207	6,659	59.4	38.7
1989	11,039	6,026	54.6	37.1
1985	10,733	5,865	54.6	36.6
1980	9,284	4,878	52.5	31.8
1975	10,183	4,933	48.4	26.1
1970	10,949	4,104	37.5	17.0
1965	12,549	3,407	27.1	–

	percent change		percentage point change	
2000 to 2005	2.3%	2.8%	0.3	5.5
1965 to 2005	–3.5	56.0	37.2	–

Note: "–" means data are not available.
Source: National Center for Education Statistics, Digest of Education Statistics 2006, Internet site http://nces.ed.gov/programs/digest/; calculations by New Strategist

Table 2.10 Enrollment in Nursery School and Kindergarten, 1955 to 2005

(number of people enrolled in nursery school and kindergarten by control of institution, 1955 to 2005; percent and percentage point change for selected years; numbers in thousands)

	nusery school				kindergarten			
	total	public	private	private share of total	total	public	private	private share of total
2005	4,603	2,480	2,123	46.1%	3,912	3,301	552	14.1%
2004	4,739	2,487	2,252	47.5	3,992	3,417	575	14.4
2003	4,928	2,567	2,361	47.9	3,719	3,098	622	16.7
2002	4,471	2,246	2,225	49.8	3,571	2,976	594	16.6
2001	4,289	2,161	2,128	49.6	3,737	3,145	591	15.8
2000	4,401	2,217	2,184	49.6	3,832	3,173	659	17.2
1999	4,578	2,269	2,309	50.4	3,825	3,167	658	17.2
1998	4,577	2,265	2,313	50.5	3,828	3,128	700	18.3
1997	4,500	2,254	2,246	49.9	3,933	3,271	663	16.9
1996	4,212	1,868	2,344	55.7	4,034	3,353	681	16.9
1995	4,399	2,012	2,387	54.3	3,877	3,174	704	18.2
1994	4,259	1,940	2,319	54.4	3,863	3,278	585	15.1
1993	3,032	1,258	1,774	58.5	4,275	3,589	686	16.0
1992	2,899	1,098	1,801	62.1	4,130	3,507	623	15.1
1991	2,933	1,094	1,839	62.7	4,152	3,531	621	15.0
1990	3,401	1,212	2,188	64.3	3,899	3,332	567	14.5
1989	2,877	971	1,906	66.2	3,868	3,293	575	14.9
1988	2,639	838	1,770	67.1	3,958	3,420	538	13.6
1987	2,587	848	1,739	67.2	4,018	3,423	595	14.8
1986	2,554	835	1,719	67.3	3,961	3,328	633	16.0
1985	2,491	854	1,637	65.7	3,815	3,221	594	15.6
1984	2,354	761	1,593	67.7	3,484	2,953	531	15.2
1983	2,350	809	1,541	65.6	3,361	2,706	656	19.5
1982	2,153	729	1,423	66.1	3,299	2,746	553	16.8
1981	2,058	663	1,396	67.8	3,161	2,616	545	17.2
1980	1,987	633	1,354	68.1	3,176	2,690	486	15.3
1979	1,869	636	1,233	66.0	3,025	2,593	432	14.3
1978	1,824	587	1,237	67.8	2,989	2,493	496	16.6
1977	1,618	562	1,056	65.3	3,191	2,665	526	16.5
1976	1,526	476	1,050	68.8	3,490	2,962	528	15.1
1975	1,748	574	1,174	67.2	3,393	2,851	542	16.0
1974	1,607	423	1,184	73.7	3,252	2,726	526	16.2
1973	1,324	400	924	69.8	3,074	2,582	493	16.0
1972	1,283	402	881	68.7	3,135	2,636	499	15.9
1971	1,066	317	749	70.3	3,263	2,689	574	17.6
1970	1,096	333	763	69.6	3,183	2,647	536	16.8
1969	860	245	615	71.5	3,276	2,682	594	18.1
1968	816	262	554	67.9	3,268	2,709	559	17.1
1967	713	230	484	67.9	3,312	2,678	635	19.2
1966	688	215	473	68.8	3,115	2,527	588	18.9
1965	520	127	393	75.6	3,057	2,439	618	20.2
1964	471	91	380	80.7	2,830	2,349	481	17.0
1963	–	–	–	–	2,340	1,936	404	17.3
1962	–	–	–	–	2,319	1,914	405	17.5
1961	–	–	–	–	2,299	1,926	373	16.2
1960	–	–	–	–	2,092	1,691	401	19.2
1955	–	–	–	–	1,628	1,365	263	16.2

	percent change			percentage point change	percent change			percentage point change
2000 to 2005	4.6%	11.9%	-2.8%	-3.5	2.1%	4.0%	-16.2%	-3.1
1955 to 2005	–	–	–	–	140.3	141.8	109.9	-2.0

Note: "–" means data are not available.
Source: Bureau of the Census, Current Population Surveys, Internet site http://www.census.gov/population/www/socdemo/school.html; calculations by New Strategist

Table 2.11 Enrollment in Elementary and Secondary School, 1955 to 2005

(number of people enrolled in 1st through 12th grades, by control of institution, 1955 to 2005; percent and percentage point change for selected years; numbers in thousands)

	1st through 8th grade				9th through 12th grade			
	total	public	private	private share of total	total	public	private	private share of total
2005	32,408	29,048	3,360	10.4%	17,146	15,751	1,395	8.1%
2004	32,556	29,166	3,389	10.4	16,791	15,498	1,293	7.7
2003	32,565	29,204	3,361	10.3	17,062	15,785	1,276	7.5
2002	33,132	29,658	3,474	10.5	16,374	15,064	1,310	8.0
2001	33,166	29,800	3,366	10.1	16,059	14,830	1,230	7.7
2000	32,898	29,378	3,520	10.7	15,770	14,431	1,339	8.5
1999	32,873	29,264	3,609	11.0	15,916	14,638	1,278	8.0
1998	32,573	29,124	3,449	10.6	15,584	14,299	1,285	8.2
1997	32,369	29,308	3,061	9.5	15,793	14,634	1,159	7.3
1996	31,515	28,153	3,362	10.7	15,309	14,113	1,197	7.8
1995	31,815	28,384	3,431	10.8	14,963	13,750	1,213	8.1
1994	31,512	28,131	3,381	10.7	14,616	13,539	1,077	7.4
1993	31,219	28,278	2,941	9.4	13,989	12,985	1,004	7.2
1992	30,165	27,066	3,102	10.3	13,219	12,268	952	7.2
1991	29,591	26,632	2,958	10.0	13,010	12,069	945	7.3
1990	29,265	26,591	2,674	9.1	12,719	11,818	903	7.1
1989	28,637	25,897	2,740	9.6	12,786	11,980	806	6.3
1988	28,223	25,443	2,778	9.8	13,093	12,095	998	7.6
1987	27,524	24,760	2,765	10.0	13,647	12,577	1,070	7.8
1986	27,121	24,163	2,958	10.9	13,912	12,746	1,166	8.4
1985	26,866	23,803	3,063	11.4	13,979	12,764	1,215	8.7
1984	26,838	24,120	2,718	10.1	13,777	12,721	1,057	7.7
1983	27,198	24,203	2,994	11.0	14,010	12,792	1,218	8.7
1982	27,412	24,381	3,031	11.1	14,123	13,004	1,118	7.9
1981	27,795	24,758	3,037	10.9	14,642	13,523	1,119	7.6
1980	27,449	24,398	3,051	11.1	14,556	–	–	–
1979	27,865	24,756	3,109	11.2	15,116	13,994	1,122	7.4
1978	28,490	25,252	3,238	11.4	15,475	14,231	1,244	8.0
1977	29,234	25,983	3,251	11.1	15,753	14,505	1,248	7.9
1976	29,774	26,698	3,075	10.3	15,742	14,541	1,201	7.6
1975	30,446	27,166	3,279	10.8	15,683	14,503	1,180	7.5
1974	31,126	27,956	3,169	10.2	15,447	14,275	1,172	7.6
1973	31,469	28,201	3,268	10.4	15,347	14,162	1,184	7.7
1972	32,242	28,693	3,549	11.0	15,169	14,015	1,155	7.6
1971	33,507	29,829	3,678	11.0	15,183	14,057	1,126	7.4
1970	33,950	30,001	3,949	11.6	14,715	13,545	1,170	8.0
1969	33,788	29,825	3,964	11.7	14,553	13,400	1,153	7.9
1968	33,761	29,527	4,234	12.5	14,145	12,793	1,352	9.6
1967	33,440	28,877	4,562	13.6	13,790	12,498	1,292	9.4
1966	32,916	28,208	4,706	14.3	13,364	11,985	1,377	10.3
1965	32,474	27,596	4,878	15.0	12,975	11,517	1,457	11.2
1964	31,734	26,811	4,923	15.5	12,812	11,403	1,410	11.0
1963	31,245	26,502	4,742	15.2	12,438	11,186	1,251	10.1
1962	30,661	26,148	4,513	14.7	11,516	10,431	1,085	9.4
1961	30,718	26,221	4,497	14.6	10,959	9,817	1,141	10.4
1960	30,349	25,814	4,535	14.9	10,249	9,215	1,033	10.1
1955	25,458	22,078	3,379	13.3	7,961	7,181	780	9.8

	percent change			percentage point change	percent change			percentage point change
2000 to 2005	−1.5%	−1.1%	−4.5%	−0.3	8.7%	9.1%	4.2%	1.4
1955 to 2005	27.3	31.6	−0.6	−2.9	57.7	58.5	48.1	−1.7

Note: "−" means data are not available.
Source: Bureau of the Census, Current Population Surveys, Internet site http://www.census.gov/population/www/socdemo/school.html; calculations by New Strategist

Table 2.12 Minority Enrollment in the Nation's Public Elementary and Secondary Schools by State, 1993 and 2004

(percentage of students enrolled in public elementary and secondary schools who are American Indian, Asian, black, or Hispanic, by state, 1993 and 2004; percentage point change, 1993–2004)

	2004	1993	percentage point change		2004	1993	percentage point change
Total enrolled	**42.1%**	**33.9%**	**8.2**	Missouri	22.7%	17.7%	5.0
Alabama	40.3	37.6	2.7	Montana	15.5	12.2	3.3
Alaska	41.7	34.8	6.9	Nebraska	21.5	11.7	9.8
Arizona	51.7	40.4	11.3	Nevada	–	–	–
Arkansas	30.8	25.6	5.2	New Hampshire	6.2	3.1	3.1
California	68.1	57.7	10.4	New Jersey	42.9	36.6	6.3
Colorado	36.5	25.9	10.6	New Mexico	68.1	59.5	8.6
Connecticut	32.5	26.7	5.8	New York	46.9	41.8	5.1
Delaware	43.8	33.8	10.0	North Carolina	42.6	34.3	8.3
District of Columbia	95.4	96.0	–0.6	North Dakota	12.8	8.5	4.3
Florida	49.5	40.4	9.1	Ohio	20.9	17.2	3.7
Georgia	49.5	40.1	9.4	Oklahoma	39.4	28.4	11.0
Hawaii	80.0	76.3	3.7	Oregon	24.6	13.3	11.3
Idaho	16.5	10.4	6.1	Pennsylvania	24.5	18.9	5.6
Illinois	43.0	35.3	7.7	Rhode Island	29.1	18.9	10.2
Indiana	19.0	14.1	4.9	South Carolina	46.0	43.0	3.0
Iowa	12.6	6.7	5.9	South Dakota	15.4	15.1	0.3
Kansas	24.1	16.4	7.7	Tennessee	30.0	24.2	5.8
Kentucky	13.4	10.7	2.7	Texas	62.3	52.3	10.0
Louisiana	51.7	48.3	3.4	Utah	17.3	8.5	8.8
Maine	4.5	2.4	2.1	Vermont	4.2	2.5	1.7
Maryland	50.5	41.1	9.4	Virginia	39.4	32.1	7.3
Massachusetts	25.8	20.7	5.1	Washington	29.3	20.1	9.2
Michigan	27.3	22.0	5.3	West Virginia	6.1	4.6	1.5
Minnesota	20.7	11.2	9.5	Wisconsin	21.7	15.7	6.0
Mississippi	53.0	52.1	0.9	Wyoming	14.4	10.6	3.8

Note: "–" means data are not available.
Source: National Center for Education Statistics, Digest of Education Statistics 2006, Internet site http://nces.ed.gov/programs/digest/; calculations by New Strategist

Table 2.13 High School Graduates, 1949–50 to 2006–07

(number of high school graduates, 1949–50 to 2006–07; percent change for selected years; numbers in thousands)

year	high school graduates	year	high school graduates
2006–07	3,232	1981–82	2,995
2005–06	3,176	1980–81	3,020
2004–05	3,109	1979–80	3,043
2003–04	3,057	1978–79	3,101
2002–03	3,021	1977–78	3,127
2001–02	2,908	1976–77	3,152
2000–01	2,848	1975–76	3,148
1999–00	2,833	1974–75	3,133
1998–99	2,759	1973–74	3,073
1997–98	2,704	1972–73	3,035
1996–97	2,612	1971–72	3,002
1995–96	2,518	1970–71	2,938
1994–95	2,520	1969–70	2,889
1993–94	2,464	1968–69	2,822
1992–93	2,480	1967–68	2,695
1991–92	2,478	1966–67	2,672
1990–91	2,493	1965–66	2,665
1989–90	2,589	1964–65	2,658
1988–89	2,744	1963–64	2,283
1987–88	2,773	1962–63	1,943
1986–87	2,694	1961–62	1,918
1985–86	2,643	1960–61	1,964
1984–85	2,677	1959–60	1,858
1983–84	2,767	1949–50	1,200
1982–83	2,888		

Percent change

1999–00 to 2006–07	14.1%
1949–50 to 2006–07	169.3

Source: National Center for Education Statistics, Digest of Education Statistics 2006, Internet site http://nces.ed .gov/programs/digest/; calculations by New Strategist

Table 2.14 Projections of High School Graduates, 2006–07 to 2015–16

(projected number of high school graduates, 2006–07 to 2015–16; percent change 2006–07 to 2015–16; numbers in thousands)

	high school graduates
2006–07	3,232
2007–08	3,326
2008–09	3,339
2009–10	3,326
2010–11	3,301
2011–12	3,256
2012–13	3,255
2013–14	3,224
2014–15	3,241
2015–16	3,187
Percent change	
2006–07 to 2015–16	−1.4%

Source: National Center for Education Statistics, Projections of Education Statistics to 2015, Internet site http://nces.ed.gov/ programs/projections/tables.asp; calculations by New Strategist

SAT Verbal Scores Have Fallen

Math scores have increased slightly since the mid-1960s.

The number of high school students who take the Scholastic Assessment Test expanded enormously over the past few decades. Once limited to the elite, the SAT has been embraced by the masses. As growing numbers of "average" students take the test, however, some scores are declining. The average verbal score fell sharply between 1966–67 and 2005–06, down by 40 points. The average math score rose modestly-up 2 points during those years.

Most racial and ethnic groups have boosted their SAT scores since 1986–87, the first year for which racial and ethnic data are available. The increase in math scores ranged from 10 points among Mexican Americans to 37 points among Asians. The progress was not as universal on the verbal portion of the test. Verbal scores rose as much as 31 points among Asians between 1986–87 and 2005–06, but fell 3 points among Mexican Americans.

■ The new SAT, which includes a writing portion and was instituted in 2006, will make it harder to compare scores over the years.

The average SAT score fell between 1966–67 and 2004–05 because verbal scores declined

(average combined math and verbal SAT scores, 1966–67 and 2005–06)

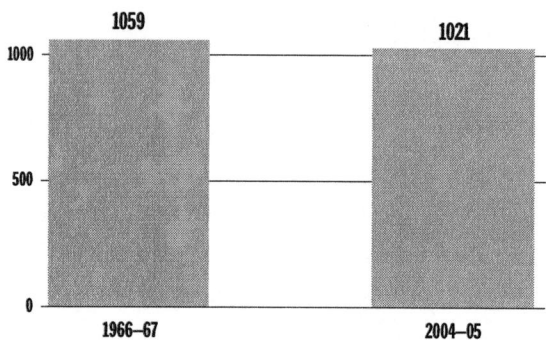

Table 2.15 Scholastic Assessment Test Scores by Sex, 1966–67 to 2005–06

(average SAT scores and change in scores, by sex, 1966–67 to 2005–06)

	math			verbal		
	total	female	male	total	female	male
2005–06	518	502	536	503	502	505
2004–05	520	504	538	508	505	513
2003–04	518	501	537	508	504	512
2002–03	519	503	537	507	503	512
2001–02	516	500	534	504	502	507
2000–01	514	498	533	506	502	509
1999–00	514	498	533	505	504	507
1998–99	511	495	531	505	502	509
1997–98	512	496	531	505	502	509
1996–97	511	494	530	505	503	507
1995–96	508	492	527	505	503	507
1994–95	506	490	525	504	502	505
1993–94	504	487	523	499	497	501
1992–93	503	484	524	500	497	504
1991–92	501	484	521	500	496	504
1990–91	500	482	520	499	495	503
1989–90	501	483	521	500	496	505
1988–89	502	482	523	504	498	510
1987–88	501	483	521	505	499	512
1986–87	501	481	523	507	502	512
1985–86	500	479	523	509	504	515
1984–85	500	480	522	509	503	514
1983–84	497	478	518	504	498	511
1982–83	494	474	516	503	498	508
1981–82	493	473	516	504	499	509
1980–81	492	473	516	502	496	508
1979–80	492	473	515	502	498	506
1978–79	493	473	516	505	501	509
1977–78	494	474	517	507	503	511
1976–77	496	474	520	507	505	509
1975–76	497	475	520	509	508	511
1974–75	498	479	518	512	509	515
1973–74	505	488	524	521	520	524
1972–73	506	489	525	523	521	523
1971–72	509	489	527	530	529	531
1970–71	513	494	529	532	534	531
1969–70	512	493	531	537	538	536
1968–69	517	498	534	540	543	536
1967–68	516	497	533	543	543	541
1966–67	516	495	535	543	545	540
Change in score						
1999–00 to 2005–06	4	4	3	−2	−2	−2
1966–67 to 2005–06	2	7	1	−40	−43	−35

Source: National Center for Education Statistics, Digest of Education Statistics 2006, Internet site http://nces.ed.gov/programs/ digest/; calculations by New Strategist

Table 2.16 Scholastic Assessment Test Scores by Race and Hispanic Origin, 1986–87 to 2005–06

(average SAT scores and change in scores by race and Hispanic origin, 1986–87 to 2005–06)

	total students	American Indian	Asian	black	Mexican American	Puerto Rican	white
Math							
2005–06	518	494	578	429	465	456	536
2004–05	520	493	580	431	463	457	536
2003–04	518	488	577	427	458	452	531
2002–03	519	482	575	426	457	453	534
2001–02	516	483	569	427	457	451	533
2000–01	514	479	566	426	458	451	531
1999–00	514	481	565	426	460	451	530
1998–99	511	481	560	422	456	448	526
1997–98	512	483	562	426	460	447	528
1996–97	511	475	560	423	458	447	526
1995–96	508	477	558	422	459	445	523
1990–91	500	468	548	419	459	439	513
1986–87	501	463	541	411	455	432	514
Change in score							
1999–00 to 2005–06	4	13	13	3	5	5	6
1986–87 to 2005–06	17	31	37	18	10	24	22
Verbal							
2005–06	503	487	510	434	454	459	527
2004–05	508	489	511	433	453	460	532
2003–04	508	483	507	430	451	457	528
2002–03	507	480	508	431	448	456	529
2001–02	504	479	501	430	446	455	527
2000–01	506	481	501	433	451	457	529
1999–00	505	482	499	434	453	456	528
1998–99	505	484	498	434	453	455	527
1997–98	505	480	498	434	453	452	526
1996–97	505	475	496	434	451	454	526
1995–96	505	483	496	434	455	452	526
1990–91	499	470	485	427	454	436	518
1986–87	507	471	479	428	457	436	524
Change in score							
1999–00 to 2005–06	–2	5	11	0	1	3	–1
1986–87 to 2005–06	–4	16	31	6	–3	23	3

Source: National Center for Education Statistics, Digest of Education Statistics 2006, Internet site http://nces.ed.gov/programs/digest/; calculations by New Strategist

Most High School Graduates Go to College

Women are more likely than men to continue their education.

Going to college is no longer an elite privilege, but the norm. Most high school graduates now continue their education on a college campus. Several decades ago, boys who graduated from high school were much more likely than girls to go to college—54.0 versus 37.9 percent in 1960. Today, the trend has reversed, with more than 70.4 percent of girls continuing their education versus 66.5 percent of boys.

Nearly half of high school graduates enroll in a four-year school within 12 months of receiving their high school diploma. Among women, the four-year school enrollment rate grew much faster than the two-year rate between 1973 and 2005. For men, the two-year rate grew faster than the four-year rate.

Not surprisingly, non-Hispanic whites are more likely than blacks or Hispanics to enroll in college. Seventy-three percent of non-Hispanic whites and a smaller 56 to 58 percent of blacks and Hispanics go to college within 12 months of graduating from high school.

College enrollment rates also vary sharply by family income. More than 80 percent of students with a family income in the top 20 percent enroll in college after graduating from high school compared with 65 percent of those with middle incomes and 52 percent of low-income students. Enrollment rates have grown at about the same rate for all income groups, meaning the enrollment rate gap has remained about the same.

■ Rapidly rising college costs threaten to lower college enrollment rates.

The college enrollment rate of women has surged during the past few decades

(percent of people aged 16 to 24 who graduated from high school in the previous 12 months and were enrolled in college as of October, by sex, 1960 and 2005)

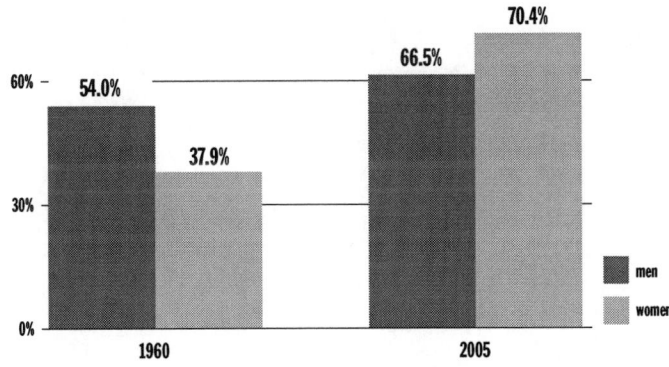

Table 2.17 College Enrollment Rate by Sex, 1960 to 2005

(percentage of people aged 16 to 24 who graduated from high school in the previous 12 months and enrolled in college as of October, by sex, and difference between men and women, 1960 to 2005; percentage point change in enrollment rate for selected years)

	total	men	women	difference between men and women
2005	68.6%	66.5%	70.4%	–3.9
2004	66.7	61.4	71.5	–10.1
2003	63.9	61.2	66.5	–5.3
2002	65.2	62.1	68.3	–6.2
2001	61.7	59.7	63.6	–3.9
2000	63.3	59.9	66.2	–6.3
1999	62.9	61.4	64.4	–3.0
1998	65.6	62.4	69.1	–6.7
1997	67.0	63.6	70.3	–6.7
1996	65.0	60.1	69.7	–9.6
1995	61.9	62.6	61.3	1.3
1994	61.9	60.6	63.2	–2.6
1993	62.6	59.9	65.2	–5.3
1992	61.9	60.0	63.8	–3.8
1991	62.5	57.9	67.1	–9.2
1990	60.1	58.0	62.2	–4.2
1989	59.6	57.6	61.6	–4.0
1988	58.9	57.1	60.7	–3.6
1987	56.8	58.3	55.3	3.0
1986	53.8	55.8	51.9	3.9
1985	57.7	58.6	56.8	1.8
1984	55.2	56.0	54.5	1.5
1983	52.7	51.9	53.4	–1.5
1982	50.6	49.1	52.0	–2.9
1981	53.9	54.8	53.1	1.7
1980	49.3	46.7	51.8	–5.1
1979	49.3	50.4	48.4	2.0
1978	50.1	51.1	49.3	1.8
1977	50.6	52.1	49.3	2.8
1976	48.8	47.2	50.3	–3.1
1975	50.7	52.6	49.0	3.6
1974	47.6	49.4	45.9	3.5
1973	46.6	50.0	43.4	6.6
1972	49.2	52.7	46.0	6.7
1971	53.5	57.6	49.8	7.8
1970	51.7	55.2	48.5	6.7
1969	53.3	60.1	47.2	12.9
1968	55.4	63.2	48.9	14.3
1967	51.9	57.6	47.2	10.4
1966	50.1	58.7	42.7	16.0
1965	50.9	57.3	45.3	12.0
1964	48.3	57.2	40.7	16.5
1963	45.0	52.3	39.0	13.3
1962	49.0	55.0	43.5	11.5
1961	48.0	56.3	41.3	15.0
1960	45.1	54.0	37.9	16.1
Percentage point change				
2000 to 2005	5.3	6.6	4.2	–
1960 to 2005	23.5	12.5	32.5	–

Note: "–" means not applicable.
Source: National Center for Education Statistics, Digest of Education Statistics 2006, Internet site http://nces.ed.gov/programs/digest/; calculations by New Strategist

Table 2.18 College Enrollment Rate by Sex and Type of Institution, 1973 to 2005

(percentage of people aged 16 to 24 who graduated from high school in the previous 12 months and were enrolled in college as of October, by sex and type of institution, 1973 to 2005; percentage point change in enrollment rate for selected years)

	men			women		
	total	two-year	four-year	total	two-year	four-year
2005	66.5%	24.7%	41.8%	70.4%	23.4%	47.0%
2004	61.4	21.8	39.6	71.5	23.1	48.5
2003	61.2	21.9	39.3	66.5	21.0	45.5
2002	62.1	20.5	41.7	68.3	23.0	45.3
2001	59.7	18.6	41.1	63.6	20.7	42.9
2000	59.9	23.1	36.8	66.2	20.0	46.2
1999	61.4	21.0	40.5	64.4	21.1	43.3
1998	62.4	24.4	38.0	69.1	24.3	44.8
1997	63.6	21.4	42.2	70.3	24.1	46.2
1996	60.1	21.5	38.5	69.7	24.6	45.1
1995	62.6	25.3	37.4	61.3	18.1	43.2
1994	60.6	23.0	37.5	63.2	19.1	44.1
1993	59.9	22.9	37.0	65.2	22.8	42.4
1992	60.0	22.1	37.8	63.8	23.9	40.0
1991	57.9	22.9	35.0	67.1	26.8	40.3
1990	58.0	19.6	38.4	62.2	20.6	41.6
1989	57.6	18.3	39.3	61.6	23.1	38.5
1988	57.1	21.3	35.8	60.7	22.4	38.3
1987	58.3	17.3	41.0	55.3	20.3	35.0
1986	55.8	21.3	34.5	51.9	17.3	34.6
1985	58.6	19.9	38.8	56.8	19.3	37.5
1984	56.0	17.7	38.4	54.5	21.0	33.5
1983	51.9	20.2	31.7	53.4	18.4	35.1
1982	49.1	17.5	31.6	52.0	20.6	31.4
1981	54.8	20.9	33.9	53.1	20.1	33.0
1980	46.7	17.1	29.7	51.8	21.6	30.2
1979	50.4	16.9	33.5	48.4	18.1	30.3
1978	51.1	15.6	35.5	49.3	18.3	31.0
1977	52.1	17.2	35.0	49.3	17.8	31.5
1976	47.2	14.5	32.7	50.3	16.6	33.8
1975	52.6	19.0	33.6	49.0	17.4	31.6
1974	49.4	16.6	32.8	45.9	13.9	32.0
1973	50.0	14.6	35.4	43.4	15.2	28.2
Percentage point change						
2000 to 2005	6.6	1.6	5.0	4.2	3.4	0.8
1973 to 2005	16.5	10.1	6.4	27.0	8.2	18.8

Source: National Center for Education Statistics, Digest of Education Statistics 2006, Internet site http://nces.ed.gov/programs/digest/; calculations by New Strategist

Table 2.19 College Enrollment Rate by Race and Hispanic Origin, 1973 to 2005

(percentage of people aged 16 to 24 who graduated from high school in the previous 12 months and were enrolled in college as of October, by race and Hispanic origin, 1973 to 2005; percentage point change in enrollment rate for selected years)

	total	non-Hispanic blacks	non-Hispanic whites	Hispanics
2005	68.6%	55.7%	73.2%	–
2004	66.7	62.5	68.8	58.1%
2003	63.9	57.5	66.2	58.0
2002	65.2	59.4	68.9	54.6
2001	61.7	54.6	64.2	52.7
2000	63.3	54.9	65.7	48.6
1999	62.9	58.9	66.3	47.4
1998	65.6	61.9	68.5	51.9
1997	67.0	58.5	68.2	55.3
1996	65.0	56.0	67.4	57.6
1995	61.9	51.2	64.3	51.6
1994	61.9	50.8	64.5	55.0
1993	62.6	55.6	62.9	55.7
1992	61.9	48.2	64.3	58.2
1991	62.5	46.4	65.4	52.6
1990	60.1	46.8	63.0	52.5
1989	59.6	53.4	60.7	52.7
1988	58.9	44.4	61.1	48.5
1987	56.8	52.2	58.6	45.0
1986	53.8	36.9	56.8	42.3
1985	57.7	42.2	60.1	46.1
1984	55.2	39.8	59.0	49.3
1983	52.7	38.2	55.0	46.7
1982	50.6	35.8	52.7	49.4
1981	53.9	42.7	54.9	48.7
1980	49.3	42.7	49.8	49.6
1979	49.3	46.7	49.9	46.3
1978	50.1	46.4	50.5	46.1
1977	50.6	49.5	50.8	48.8
1976	48.8	44.4	48.8	53.6
1975	50.7	41.7	51.1	52.7
1974	47.6	47.2	47.2	53.1
1973	46.6	32.5	47.8	48.8
Percentage point change				
2000 to 2005	5.3	0.8	7.5	9.5
1973 to 2005	22.0	23.2	25.4	9.3

Note: Hispanic enrollment rates are three-year moving averages. The 2000 to 2005 percentage point change for Hispanics is the difference between the 2000 and the 2004 moving averages.
Source: National Center for Education Statistics, Digest of Education Statistics 2006, Internet site http://nces.ed.gov/programs/digest/; calculations by New Strategist

Table 2.20 College Enrollment Rate by Family Income, 1976 to 2005

(percentage of people aged 16 to 24 who graduated from high school in the previous 12 months and were enrolled in college as of October, by family income level, 1976 to 2005; percentage point change in enrollment rate for selected years)

		family income level		
	total	low	middle	high
2005	68.6%	–	65.1%	81.2%
2004	66.7	52.0%	63.5	79.3
2003	63.9	53.1	57.6	80.1
2002	65.2	51.0	60.7	78.2
2001	61.7	50.0	56.3	79.9
2000	63.3	47.8	59.5	76.9
1999	62.9	48.5	59.4	76.1
1998	65.6	50.9	64.7	77.5
1997	67.0	50.6	60.7	82.2
1996	65.0	47.1	62.7	78.0
1995	61.9	42.1	56.0	83.5
1994	61.9	42.0	57.8	77.9
1993	62.6	44.7	56.9	79.3
1992	61.9	43.6	57.0	79.0
1991	62.5	42.2	58.4	78.2
1990	60.1	44.8	54.4	76.6
1989	59.6	45.6	55.4	70.7
1988	58.9	42.4	54.7	72.8
1987	56.8	37.6	50.0	73.8
1986	53.8	36.8	48.5	71.0
1985	57.7	35.9	50.6	74.6
1984	55.2	36.3	48.4	74.0
1983	52.7	34.0	45.2	70.3
1982	50.6	33.6	41.7	70.9
1981	53.9	32.9	49.2	67.6
1980	49.3	32.2	42.5	65.2
1979	49.3	31.6	43.2	63.2
1978	50.1	29.8	44.3	64.0
1977	50.6	32.4	44.2	66.3
1976	48.8	32.3	40.5	63.0
Percentage point change				
2000 to 2005	5.3	4.2	5.6	4.3
1976 to 2005	19.8	19.7	24.6	18.2

Note: Low income refers to the bottom 20 percent of all family incomes, high income refers to the top 20 percent of all family incomes, and middle income refers to the 60 percent in between. Low income enrollment rates are three-year moving averages. The 2000 to 2005 percentage point change for low incomes is the difference between the 2000 and the 2004 moving averages.
Source: National Center for Education Statistics, The Condition of Education, Internet site http://nces.ed.gov/programs/coe/2007/ section3/table.asp?tableID=702; calculations by New Strategist

In College, Women Outnumber Men

Women account for the 57 percent majority of college students.

In 1950, only 32 percent of students on the nation's college campuses were women. Today, women outnumber men by a growing margin, which creates problems for college admissions staff hoping to balance the campus sex ratio. It does not look like things will be getting better. The National Center for Education Statistics projects that women's share of college students will climb to 59 percent during the next few years.

The demographics of college students have changed in other ways as well. Not only are students older than they once were, but they are more racially and ethnically diverse. The number of college students aged 25 or older grew from 28 to 37 percent between 1972 and 2005. The figure is projected to rise to 41 percent during the next decade. The minority share of students has doubled since 1976, rising from 15 to 31 percent. Blacks are the largest minority on campus and account for nearly 13 percent of students. Eleven percent of college students are Hispanic, and 6.5 percent are Asian.

■ Among young adults, the educational attainment of women surpasses that of men—a trend that will grow as long as women are more likely to go to college than men.

The minority share of college students has doubled during the past three decades

(minority share of college students, 1976 and 2005)

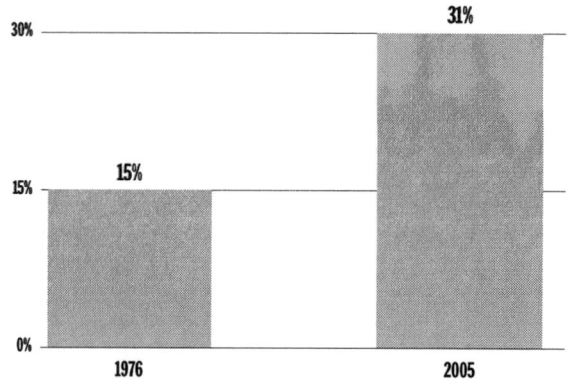

Table 2.21 College Enrollment by Sex, 1950 to 2005

(number of people aged 14 or older enrolled in college by sex, and women's share of total, 1950 to 2005; percent and percentage point change for selected years; numbers in thousands)

	total	men	women	women's share of total
2005	17,472	7,539	9,934	56.9%
2004	17,383	7,575	9,808	56.4
2003	16,638	7,318	9,319	56.0
2002	16,497	7,240	9,258	56.1
2001	15,873	6,875	8,998	56.7
2000	15,314	6,682	8,631	56.4
1999	15,203	6,956	8,247	54.2
1998	15,546	6,905	8,641	55.6
1997	15,436	6,843	8,593	55.7
1996	15,226	6,820	8,406	55.2
1995	14,715	6,703	8,013	54.5
1994	15,022	6,764	8,258	55.0
1993	14,394	6,599	7,795	54.2
1992	14,035	6,192	7,844	55.9
1991	14,057	6,439	7,618	54.2
1990	13,621	6,192	7,429	54.5
1989	13,180	5,950	7,231	54.9
1988	13,116	5,950	7,166	54.6
1987	12,719	6,030	6,689	52.6
1986	12,651	5,957	6,694	52.9
1985	12,524	5,906	6,618	52.8
1984	12,304	5,989	6,315	51.3
1983	12,320	6,010	6,310	51.2
1982	12,308	5,899	6,410	52.1
1981	12,127	5,825	6,303	52.0
1980	11,387	5,430	5,957	52.3
1979	11,380	5,480	5,900	51.8
1978	11,141	5,580	5,559	49.9
1977	11,546	5,889	5,657	49.0
1976	11,139	5,785	5,354	48.1
1975	10,880	5,911	4,969	45.7
1974	9,852	5,402	4,449	45.2
1973	8,966	5,048	3,918	43.7
1972	9,096	5,218	3,877	42.6
1971	8,087	4,850	3,236	40.0
1970	7,413	4,401	3,013	40.6
1969	7,435	4,448	2,987	40.2
1968	6,801	4,124	2,677	39.4
1967	6,401	3,841	2,560	40.0
1966	6,085	3,749	2,337	38.4
1965	5,675	3,503	2,172	38.3
1964	4,643	2,888	1,755	37.8
1963	4,336	2,742	1,594	36.8
1962	4,208	2,742	1,466	34.8
1961	3,731	2,356	1,375	36.9
1960	3,570	2,339	1,231	34.5
1955	2,379	1,579	800	33.6
1950	2,175	1,474	701	32.2

	percent change			percentage point change
2000 to 2005	14.1%	12.8%	15.1%	0.5
1950 to 2005	703.3	411.5	1,317.1	24.6

Source: Bureau of the Census, Current Population Surveys, School Enrollment, Internet site http://www.census.gov/population/www/socdemo/school.html; calculations by New Strategist

Table 2.22 Projections of College Enrollment by Sex, 2006 to 2015

(projected number of people aged 14 or older enrolled in college by sex, and women's share of total, 2006 to 2015; percent and percentage point change, 2006–15; numbers in thousands)

	total	men	women	women's share of total
2006	17,648	7,458	10,190	57.7%
2007	17,916	7,552	10,365	57.9
2008	18,202	7,657	10,545	57.9
2009	18,480	7,760	10,720	58.0
2010	18,746	7,848	10,897	58.1
2011	18,956	7,928	11,028	58.2
2012	19,182	8,000	11,182	58.3
2013	19,439	8,069	11,370	58.5
2014	19,682	8,126	11,556	58.7
2015	19,874	8,161	11,712	58.9

	percent change			percentage point change
2006 to 2015	12.6%	9.4%	14.9%	1.2

Source: National Center for Education Statistics, Projections of Education Statistics to 2015, Internet site http://nces.ed.gov/programs/projections/tables.asp; calculations by New Strategist

Table 2.23 College Enrollment by Age, 1972 to 2005

(number of people aged 14 or older enrolled in college by age; 1972 to 2005; percent change for selected years; numbers in thousands)

	total	under 20	20 to 21	22 to 24	25 to 29	30 to 34	35 or older
2005	17,472	3908	3,945	3,162	2,291	1,309	2,857
2004	17,383	3883	3,777	3,149	2,403	1,287	2,884
2003	16,638	3662	3,533	3,320	2,164	1,330	2,630
2002	16,497	3776	3,525	2,927	2,093	1,308	2,867
2001	15,873	3616	3,421	2,731	2,084	1,337	2,685
2000	15,314	3,748	3,169	2,683	1,962	1,244	2,507
1999	15,203	3,671	3,120	2,620	1,940	1,155	2,697
1998	15,546	3,793	3,092	2,561	2,148	1,266	2,685
1997	15,436	3,533	3,143	2,699	2,154	1,116	2,791
1996	15,226	3,546	2,907	2,551	2,215	1,228	2,778
1995	14,715	3,259	2,940	2,498	2,143	1,206	2,669
1994	15,022	3,201	3,028	2,650	2,026	1,393	2,725
1993	14,394	3,200	2,892	2,668	1,914	1,226	2,493
1992	14,035	3,097	2,938	2,512	1,829	1,296	2,364
1991	14,057	3,061	2,939	2,304	1,983	1,302	2,468
1990	13,621	3,197	2,767	2,178	1,927	1,235	2,319
1989	13,180	3,249	2,570	2,168	1,889	1,192	2,112
1988	13,116	3,228	2,681	2,064	1,735	1,228	2,179
1987	12,719	3,284	2,642	2,006	1,826	1,159	1,802
1986	12,651	3,168	2,374	2,136	1,860	1,245	1,867
1985	12,524	3,169	2,616	2,014	1,884	1,180	1,661
1984	12,304	3,120	2,597	2,127	1,857	1,158	1,445
1983	12,320	3,200	2,495	2,042	1,921	1,167	1,495
1982	12,308	3,183	2,689	2,060	1,859	1,129	1,389
1981	12,127	3,276	2,545	1,986	1,717	1,211	1,393
1980	11,387	3,182	2,423	1,870	1,641	1,062	1,207
1979	11,380	3,155	2,353	1,794	1,679	996	1,402
1978	11,141	3,173	2,298	1,798	1,619	950	1,303
1977	11,546	3,187	2,430	1,799	1,809	992	1,329
1976	11,139	3,218	2,398	1,846	1,686	803	1,189
1975	10,880	3,236	2,313	1,679	1,616	853	1,183
1974	9,852	2,906	2,192	1,527	1,482	720	1,025
1973	8,966	2,812	2,073	1,465	1,278	551	787
1972	9,096	2,975	2,116	1,461	1,229	531	783
Percent change							
2000 to 2005	14.1%	4.3%	24.5%	17.9%	16.8%	5.2%	14.0%
1972 to 2005	91.1	30.5	78.5	115.5	95.5	142.4	268.3

Source: Bureau of the Census, Current Population Surveys, School Enrollment, Internet site http://www.census.gov/population/www/socdemo/school.html; calculations by New Strategist

Table 2.24 Percent Distribution of College Enrollment by Age, 1972 to 2005

(percent distribution of people aged 14 or older enrolled in college by age; 1972 to 2005; percentage point change for selected years)

	total	under 20	20 to 21	22 to 24	25 to 29	30 to 34	35 or older
2005	100.0%	22.4%	22.6%	18.1%	13.1%	7.5%	16.4%
2004	100.0	22.3	21.7	18.1	13.8	7.4	16.6
2003	100.0	22.0	21.2	20.0	13.0	8.0	15.8
2002	100.0	22.9	21.4	17.7	12.7	7.9	17.4
2001	100.0	22.8	21.6	17.2	13.1	8.4	16.9
2000	100.0	24.5	20.7	17.5	12.8	8.1	16.4
1999	100.0	24.1	20.5	17.2	12.8	7.6	17.7
1998	100.0	24.4	19.9	16.5	13.8	8.1	17.3
1997	100.0	22.9	20.4	17.5	14.0	7.2	18.1
1996	100.0	23.3	19.1	16.8	14.5	8.1	18.2
1995	100.0	22.1	20.0	17.0	14.6	8.2	18.1
1994	100.0	21.3	20.2	17.6	13.5	9.3	18.1
1993	100.0	22.2	20.1	18.5	13.3	8.5	17.3
1992	100.0	22.1	20.9	17.9	13.0	9.2	16.8
1991	100.0	21.8	20.9	16.4	14.1	9.3	17.6
1990	100.0	23.5	20.3	16.0	14.1	9.1	17.0
1989	100.0	24.7	19.5	16.4	14.3	9.0	16.0
1988	100.0	24.6	20.4	15.7	13.2	9.4	16.6
1987	100.0	25.8	20.8	15.8	14.4	9.1	14.2
1986	100.0	25.0	18.8	16.9	14.7	9.8	14.8
1985	100.0	25.3	20.9	16.1	15.0	9.4	13.3
1984	100.0	25.4	21.1	17.3	15.1	9.4	11.7
1983	100.0	26.0	20.3	16.6	15.6	9.5	12.1
1982	100.0	25.9	21.8	16.7	15.1	9.2	11.3
1981	100.0	27.0	21.0	16.4	14.2	10.0	11.5
1980	100.0	27.9	21.3	16.4	14.4	9.3	10.6
1979	100.0	27.7	20.7	15.8	14.8	8.8	12.3
1978	100.0	28.5	20.6	16.1	14.5	8.5	11.7
1977	100.0	27.6	21.0	15.6	15.7	8.6	11.5
1976	100.0	28.9	21.5	16.6	15.1	7.2	10.7
1975	100.0	29.7	21.3	15.4	14.9	7.8	10.9
1974	100.0	29.5	22.2	15.5	15.0	7.3	10.4
1973	100.0	31.4	23.1	16.3	14.3	6.1	8.8
1972	100.0	32.7	23.3	16.1	13.5	5.8	8.6
Percentage point change							
2000 to 2005	–	–2.1	1.9	0.6	0.3	–0.6	0.0
1972 to 2005	–	–10.3	–0.7	2.0	–0.4	1.7	7.7

Note: "–" means not applicable.
Source: Bureau of the Census, Current Population Surveys, School Enrollment, Internet site http://www.census.gov/population/ www/socdemo/school.html; calculations by New Strategist

Table 2.25 Projections of College Enrollment by Age, 2006 to 2015

(projected number and percent distribution of people aged 14 or older enrolled in college by age, 2006 to 2015; percent change in number and percentage point change in share, 2006–15; numbers in thousands)

	total	under 20	20 to 21	22 to 24	25 to 29	30 to 34	35 or older
2006	17,648	3,881	3,780	3,049	2,538	1,294	3,105
2007	17,916	3,983	3,824	3,093	2,619	1,298	3,098
2008	18,202	4,100	3,883	3,139	2,684	1,319	3,077
2009	18,480	4,182	3,977	3,185	2,731	1,353	3,052
2010	18,746	4,178	4,107	3,249	2,769	1,398	3,045
2011	18,956	4,130	4,171	3,325	2,813	1,455	3,062
2012	19,182	4,093	4,156	3,446	2,873	1,512	3,102
2013	19,439	4,073	4,131	3,550	2,955	1,569	3,162
2014	19,682	4,068	4,099	3,613	3,054	1,618	3,229
2015	19,874	4,050	4,075	3,631	3,164	1,658	3,294

Percent change

2006 to 2015	12.6%	4.4%	7.8%	19.1%	24.7%	28.1%	6.1%

PERCENT DISTRIBUTION

2006	100.0%	22.0%	21.4%	17.3%	14.4%	7.3%	17.6%
2007	100.0	22.2	21.3	17.3	14.6	7.2	17.3
2008	100.0	22.5	21.3	17.2	14.7	7.2	16.9
2009	100.0	22.6	21.5	17.2	14.8	7.3	16.5
2010	100.0	22.3	21.9	17.3	14.8	7.5	16.2
2011	100.0	21.8	22.0	17.5	14.8	7.7	16.2
2012	100.0	21.3	21.7	18.0	15.0	7.9	16.2
2013	100.0	21.0	21.3	18.3	15.2	8.1	16.3
2014	100.0	20.7	20.8	18.4	15.5	8.2	16.4
2015	100.0	20.4	20.5	18.3	15.9	8.3	16.6

Percentage point change

2006 to 2015	–	1.6	0.9	–1.0	–1.5	–1.0	1.0

Note: "–" means not applicable.
Source: National Center for Education Statistics, Projections of Education Statistics to 2015, Internet site http://nces.ed.gov/programs/projections/tables.asp; calculations by New Strategist

Table 2.26 College Enrollment by Race and Hispanic Origin, 1994 to 2005

(number and percent distribution of people aged 15 or older enrolled in institutions of higher education by race and Hispanic origin, 1994 to 2005; percent and percentage point change for selected years; numbers in thousands)

	total	Asian	black	Hispanic	white, non-Hispanic
2005	17,472	1,184	2,298	1,942	11,715
2004	17,383	1,191	2,301	1,975	11,571
2003	16,638	1,162	2,144	1,714	11,295
2002	16,497	1,258	2,278	1,656	11,236
2001	15,873	1,280	2,230	1,700	10,602
2000	15,314	1,049	2,164	1,426	10,636
1999	15,203	1,041	1,998	1,307	10,818
1998	15,546	1,016	2,016	1,363	11,109
1997	15,436	947	1,903	1,260	11,245
1996	15,226	999	1,901	1,223	11,034
1995	14,715	617	1,772	1,207	11,024
1994	15,022	723	1,800	1,187	11,178

Percent change

2000 to 2005	14.1%	12.9%	6.2%	36.2%	10.1%
1994 to 2005	16.3	63.8	27.7	63.5	4.8

PERCENT DISTRIBUTION

2005	100.0%	6.8%	13.2%	11.1%	67.1%
2004	100.0	6.9	13.2	11.4	66.6
2003	100.0	7.0	12.9	10.3	67.9
2002	100.0	7.6	13.8	10.0	68.1
2001	100.0	8.1	14.0	10.7	66.8
2000	100.0	6.8	14.1	9.3	69.5
1999	100.0	6.8	13.1	8.6	71.2
1998	100.0	6.5	13.0	8.8	71.5
1997	100.0	6.1	12.3	8.2	72.9
1996	100.0	6.6	12.5	8.0	72.5
1995	100.0	4.2	12.0	8.2	74.9
1994	100.0	4.8	12.0	7.9	74.4

Percentage point change

2000 to 2005	–	–0.1	–1.0	1.8	–2.4
1994 to 2005	–	2.0	1.2	3.2	–7.4

Note: Enrollment figures by race and Hispanic origin in this table are based on a survey of households. They differ from race and Hispanic origin enrollment figures in the following table, which are based on surveys of institutions of higher education. Asians, blacks, and non-Hispanic whites are the race-alone population. Numbers will not add to total because Hispanics may be of any race and not all races are shown. "–" means not applicable.
Source: Bureau of the Census, Current Population Surveys, School Enrollment, Internet site http://www.census.gov/population/ www/socdemo/school.html; calculations by New Strategist

Table 2.27 College Enrollment by Race and Hispanic Origin, 1976 to 2005

(number and percent distribution of people aged 15 or older enrolled in institutions of higher education by race and Hispanic origin, 1976 to 2005; percent and percentage point change for selected years; numbers in thousands)

	total	minority					white, non-Hispanic	nonresident alien
		total minority	American Indian	Asian	black, non-Hispanic	Hispanic		
2005	17,488	5,407	176	1,134	2,215	1,882	11,495	585
2004	17,272	5,259	176	1,109	2,165	1,810	11,423	590
2003	16,901	5,033	173	1,076	2,069	1,716	11,275	592
2002	16,612	4,881	166	1,074	1,979	1,662	11,140	591
2001	15,928	4,588	158	1,019	1,850	1,561	10,775	565
2000	15,312	4,322	151	978	1,730	1,462	10,462	529
1999	14,791	4,012	145	910	1,641	1,317	10,263	516
1998	14,507	3,885	144	901	1,583	1,257	10,179	444
1997	14,502	3,771	143	859	1,551	1,219	10,266	465
1996	14,368	3,637	138	828	1,506	1,166	10,264	466
1995	14,262	3,496	131	797	1,474	1,094	10,311	454
1990	13,819	2,705	103	572	1,247	782	10,723	392
1980	12,087	1,949	84	286	1,107	472	9,833	305
1976	10,986	1,691	76	198	1,033	384	9,076	219

Percent change

2000 to 2005	14.2%	25.1%	16.6%	16.0%	28.0%	28.7%	9.9%	10.6%
1976 to 2005	59.2	219.8	131.6	472.7	114.4	390.1	26.7	167.1

PERCENT DISTRIBUTION BY RACE AND HISPANIC ORIGIN

2005	100.0%	30.9%	1.0%	6.5%	12.7%	10.8%	65.7%	3.3%
2004	100.0	30.4	1.0	6.4	12.5	10.5	66.1	3.4
2003	100.0	29.8	1.0	6.4	12.2	10.2	66.7	3.5
2002	100.0	29.4	1.0	6.5	11.9	10.0	67.1	3.6
2001	100.0	28.8	1.0	6.4	11.6	9.8	67.6	3.5
2000	100.0	28.2	1.0	6.4	11.3	9.5	68.3	3.5
1999	100.0	27.1	1.0	6.2	11.1	8.9	69.4	3.5
1998	100.0	26.8	1.0	6.2	10.9	8.7	70.2	3.1
1997	100.0	26.0	1.0	5.9	10.7	8.4	70.8	3.2
1996	100.0	25.3	1.0	5.8	10.5	8.1	71.4	3.2
1995	100.0	24.5	0.9	5.6	10.3	7.7	72.3	3.2
1990	100.0	19.6	0.7	4.1	9.0	5.7	77.6	2.8
1980	100.0	16.1	0.7	2.4	9.2	3.9	81.4	2.5
1976	100.0	15.4	0.7	1.8	9.4	3.5	82.6	2.0

Percentage point change

2000 to 2005	–	2.7	0.0	0.1	1.4	1.2	–2.6	–0.1
1976 to 2005	–	15.5	0.3	4.7	3.3	7.3	–16.9	1.4

Note: Enrollment figures by race and Hispanic origin in this table are based on a survey of institutions of higher education. They differ from race and Hispanic origin enrollment figures in the preceding table, which are based on surveys of households. "–" means not applicable.
Source: National Center for Education Statistics, Digest of Education Statistics 2006, Internet site http://nces.ed.gov/programs/ digest/; calculations by New Strategist

College Costs Are Soaring

The increase in college costs has been greater at private institutions.

A student enrolled in a four-year undergraduate program in 2005-06 was charged an average of $17,447 for tuition, fees, room, and board. The figure was just $2,577 in 1976–77, a tally that rises to $8,845 after adjusting for inflation. If you calculate the percent change between today's expense and the inflation-adjusted expense of 1976–77, you find that college costs have grown by 97 percent over the past thirty years—a near doubling even after adjusting for inflation.

The cost of attending a private institution is much greater than the cost of going to a public school, and the difference is increasing. In 1976–77, total charges at public four-year programs were 49 percent as high as those at the average private institution. By 2005–06, the public school charges were a smaller 44 percent of the private school amount.

■ Most students do not pay the full amount charged by public or private colleges, but depend on scholarships and grants to cut the costs somewhat.

Paying for college was easier on the household budget a few decades ago

(average annual tuition, fees, room, and board for undergraduate programs at four-year institutions, 1976–77 and 2005–06; in 2005 dollars)

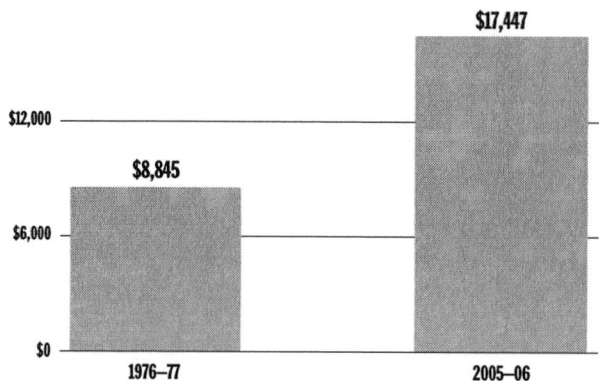

Table 2.28 College Costs, 1976–77 to 2005–06

(average annual tuition, fees, room, and board for undergraduate programs at four-year institutions, by control of school, 1976–77 to 2005–06)

	total institutions	public institution	private institution	cost of attending public institution as a percent of cost of attending private institution
2005–06	$17,447	$12,108	$27,317	44.3%
2004–05	16,465	11,441	26,489	43.2
2003–04	15,504	10,674	25,083	42.6
2002–03	14,439	9,787	23,787	41.1
2001–02	13,639	9,196	22,896	40.2
2000–01	12,922	8,653	21,856	39.6
1999–00	12,352	8,275	20,706	40.0
1998–99	11,888	8,027	19,929	40.3
1997–98	11,277	7,673	19,070	40.2
1996–97	10,841	7,334	18,442	39.8
1995–96	10,330	7,014	17,612	39.8
1994–95	9,728	6,670	16,602	40.2
1993–94	9,296	6,365	15,904	40.0
1992–93	8,758	6,020	15,009	40.1
1991–92	8,238	5,693	14,258	39.9
1990–91	7,602	5,243	13,237	39.6
1989–90	7,212	4,975	12,284	40.5
1988–89	6,725	4,678	11,474	40.8
1987–88	6,272	4,403	10,659	41.3
1986–87	5,964	4,138	10,039	41.2
1985–86	5,504	3,859	9,228	41.8
1984–85	5,160	3,682	8,451	43.6
1983–84	4,747	3,433	7,759	44.2
1982–83	4,406	3,196	7,126	44.9
1981–82	3,951	2,871	6,330	45.4
1980–81	3,499	2,550	5,594	45.6
1979–80	3,167	2,327	5,013	46.4
1978–79	2,917	2,145	4,609	46.5
1977–78	2,725	2,038	4,240	48.1
1976–77	2,577	1,935	3,977	48.7

Source: National Center for Education Statistics, Digest of Education Statistics 2006, Internet site http://nces.ed.gov/programs/ digest/; calculations by New Strategist

Women Earn Most Bachelor's and Master's Degrees

Their share of first-professional degrees is about to top 50 percent.

Before 1977, men earned most degrees on the nation's college campuses. Today, women earn 62 percent of associate's degrees, 57 percent of bachelor's degrees, and 59 percent of master's degrees. The National Center for Education Statistics projects women will earn most doctoral and first-professional degrees within the next few years.

Over the past several decades, minorities have earned an ever-larger share of degrees awarded by institutions of higher education. Among minority groups on campus, blacks earn the largest share of degrees at the associate's, bachelor's, master's and doctoral level. Blacks earned 12 percent of associate's degrees in 2004–05, up from 8 percent in 1976–77. They earned 9 percent of bachelor's and master's degrees, up from 6 and 7 percent, respectively, in 1976–77. At the first-professional level, Asians earn the largest share of degrees among minority groups—12 percent. Blacks earned 7 percent of first-professional degrees.

■ Rising college costs make it increasingly difficult for blacks, with lower than average household incomes, to afford a college education.

Women's share of bachelor's degrees has grown steadily for decades

(percent of bachelor's degrees awarded to women, 1965–66 and 2004–05)

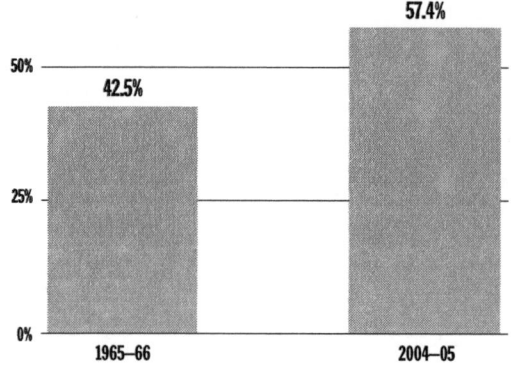

Table 2.29 Degrees Conferred by Level of Degree, 1965–66 to 2004–05

(number of degrees conferred by institutions of higher education by level of degree, 1965–66 to 2004–05; percent change for selected years)

	associate's	bachelor's	master's	doctoral	first-professional
2004–05	696,660	1,439,264	574,618	52,631	87,289
2003–04	665,301	1,399,542	558,940	48,378	83,041
2002–03	632,912	1,348,503	512,645	46,024	80,810
2001–02	595,133	1,291,900	482,118	44,160	80,698
2000–01	578,865	1,244,171	468,476	44,904	79,707
1999–00	564,933	1,237,875	457,056	44,808	80,057
1998–99	559,954	1,200,303	439,986	44,077	78,439
1997–98	558,555	1,184,406	430,164	46,010	78,598
1996–97	571,226	1,172,879	419,401	45,876	78,730
1995–96	555,216	1,164,792	406,301	44,652	76,734
1994–95	539,691	1,160,134	397,629	44,446	75,800
1993–94	530,632	1,169,275	387,070	43,185	75,418
1992–93	514,756	1,165,178	369,585	42,132	75,387
1991–92	504,231	1,136,553	352,838	40,659	74,146
1990–91	481,720	1,094,538	337,168	39,294	71,948
1989–90	455,102	1,051,344	324,301	38,371	70,988
1988–89	436,764	1,018,755	310,621	35,720	70,856
1987–88	435,085	994,829	299,317	34,870	70,735
1986–87	436,304	991,264	289,349	34,041	71,617
1985–86	446,047	987,823	288,567	33,653	73,910
1984–85	454,712	979,477	286,251	32,943	75,063
1983–84	452,240	974,309	284,263	33,209	74,468
1982–83	449,620	969,510	289,921	32,775	73,054
1981–82	434,526	952,998	295,546	32,707	72,032
1980–81	416,377	935,140	295,739	32,958	71,956
1979–80	400,910	929,417	298,081	32,615	70,131
1978–79	402,702	921,390	301,079	32,730	68,848
1977–78	412,246	921,204	311,620	32,131	66,581
1976–77	406,377	919,549	317,164	33,232	64,359
1975–76	391,454	925,746	311,771	34,064	62,649
1974–75	360,171	922,933	292,450	34,083	55,916
1973–74	343,924	945,776	277,033	33,816	53,816
1972–73	316,174	922,362	263,371	34,777	50,018
1971–72	292,014	887,273	251,633	33,363	43,411
1970–71	252,311	839,730	230,509	32,107	37,946
1969–70	206,023	792,316	208,291	29,866	34,918
1968–69	183,279	728,845	193,756	26,158	35,114
1967–68	159,441	632,289	176,749	23,089	33,939
1966–67	139,183	558,534	157,726	20,617	31,695
1965–66	111,607	520,115	140,602	18,237	30,124
Percent change					
1999–00 to 2004–05	23.3%	16.3%	25.7%	17.5%	9.0%
1965–66 to 2004–05	524.2	176.7	308.7	188.6	189.8

Source: National Center for Education Statistics, Digest of Education Statistics 2006, Internet site http://nces.ed.gov/programs/ digest/; calculations by New Strategist

Table 2.30 Projections of Degrees Conferred by Level of Degree, 2005–06 to 2015–16

(projected number of degrees conferred by institutions of higher education by level of degree, 2005–06 to 2015–16; percent change 2005–06 to 2015–16)

	associate's	bachelor's	master's	doctoral	first-professional
2005–06	682,000	1,456,000	584,000	49,500	85,100
2006–07	686,000	1,488,000	603,000	50,500	87,400
2007–08	694,000	1,523,000	619,000	50,900	89,700
2008–09	704,000	1,561,000	635,000	51,100	91,900
2009–10	714,000	1,596,000	647,000	51,200	93,400
2010–11	721,000	1,622,000	657,000	51,700	94,500
2011–12	726,000	1,645,000	670,000	52,600	95,900
2012–13	730,000	1,665,000	685,000	53,800	97,300
2013–14	735,000	1,682,000	705,000	55,300	99,200
2014–15	740,000	1,697,000	731,000	56,900	101,400
2015–16	744,000	1,705,000	757,000	58,500	103,800
Percent change					
2005–06 to 2015–16	9.1%	17.1%	29.6%	18.2%	22.0%

Source: National Center for Education Statistics, Projections of Education Statistics to 2015, Internet site http://nces.ed.gov/programs/projections/tables.asp; calculations by New Strategist

Table 2.31 Associate's Degrees Conferred by Sex, 1965–66 to 2004–05

(number of associate's degrees conferred by institutions of higher education by sex and women's share of total, 1965–66 to 2004–05; percent and percentage point change for selected years)

	total associate's degrees	men	women	women's share of total
2004–05	696,660	267,536	429,124	61.6%
2003–04	665,301	260,033	405,268	60.9
2002–03	632,912	253,060	379,852	60.0
2001–02	595,133	238,109	357,024	60.0
2000–01	578,865	231,645	347,220	60.0
1999–00	564,933	224,721	340,212	60.2
1998–99	559,954	218,417	341,537	61.0
1997–98	558,555	217,613	340,942	61.0
1996–97	571,226	223,948	347,278	60.8
1995–96	555,216	219,514	335,702	60.5
1994–95	539,691	218,352	321,339	59.5
1993–94	530,632	215,261	315,371	59.4
1992–93	514,756	211,964	302,792	58.8
1991–92	504,231	207,481	296,750	58.9
1990–91	481,720	198,634	283,086	58.8
1989–90	455,102	191,195	263,907	58.0
1988–89	436,764	186,316	250,448	57.3
1987–88	435,085	190,047	245,038	56.3
1986–87	436,304	190,839	245,465	56.3
1985–86	446,047	196,166	249,881	56.0
1984–85	454,712	202,932	251,780	55.4
1983–84	452,240	202,704	249,536	55.2
1982–83	449,620	203,991	245,629	54.6
1981–82	434,526	196,944	237,582	54.7
1980–81	416,377	188,638	227,739	54.7
1979–80	400,910	183,737	217,173	54.2
1978–79	402,702	192,091	210,611	52.3
1977–78	412,246	204,718	207,528	50.3
1976–77	406,377	210,842	195,535	48.1
1975–76	391,454	209,996	181,458	46.4
1974–75	360,171	191,017	169,154	47.0
1973–74	343,924	188,591	155,333	45.2
1972–73	316,174	175,413	140,761	44.5
1971–72	292,014	166,227	125,787	43.1
1970–71	252,311	144,144	108,167	42.9
1969–70	206,023	117,432	88,591	43.0
1968–69	183,279	105,661	77,618	42.3
1967–68	159,441	90,317	69,124	43.4
1966–67	139,183	78,356	60,827	43.7
1965–66	111,607	63,779	47,828	42.9

	percent change			percentage point change
1999–00 to 2004–05	23.3%	19.1%	26.1%	1.4
1965–66 to 2004–05	524.2	319.5	797.2	18.7

Source: National Center for Education Statistics, Digest of Education Statistics 2006, Internet site http://nces.ed.gov/programs/digest/; calculations by New Strategist

Table 2.32 Projections of Associate's Degrees Conferred by Sex, 2005–06 to 2015–16

(projected number of associate's degrees conferred by institutions of higher education by sex, and women's share of total, 2005–06 to 2015–16; percent and percentage point change 2005–06 to 2015–16)

	total associate's degrees	men	women	women's share of total
2005–06	682,000	262,000	420,000	61.6%
2006–07	686,000	263,000	423,000	61.7
2007–08	694,000	264,000	430,000	62.0
2008–09	704,000	264,000	440,000	62.5
2009–10	714,000	268,000	447,000	62.6
2010–11	721,000	270,000	451,000	62.6
2011–12	726,000	271,000	455,000	62.7
2012–13	730,000	272,000	458,000	62.7
2013–14	735,000	273,000	462,000	62.9
2014–15	740,000	273,000	467,000	63.1
2015–16	744,000	272,000	472,000	63.4
	percent change			percentage point change
2005–06 to 2015–16	9.1%	3.8%	12.4%	1.9

Source: National Center for Education Statistics, Projections of Education Statistics to 2015, Internet site http://nces.ed.gov/programs/projections/tables.asp; calculations by New Strategist

Table 2.33 Associate's Degrees Conferred by Race and Hispanic Origin, 1976–77 to 2004–05

(number and percent distribution of associate's degrees conferred by institutions of higher education, by race and Hispanic origin, 1976–77 to 2004–05; percent and percentage point change for selected years)

	total associate's degrees	American Indian	Asian	black, non-Hispanic	Hispanic	white, non-Hispanic	nonresident alien
2004–05	696,660	8,435	33,669	86,402	78,557	475,513	14,084
2003–04	665,301	8,119	33,149	81,183	72,270	456,047	14,533
2002–03	632,912	7,462	32,610	75,430	66,175	437,794	13,441
2001–02	595,133	6,832	30,945	67,343	60,003	417,733	12,277
2000–01	578,865	6,623	28,463	63,855	57,288	411,075	11,561
1999–00	564,933	6,497	27,782	60,221	51,573	408,772	10,088
1998–99	559,954	6,424	27,586	57,439	48,670	409,086	10,749
1997–98	558,555	6,246	25,196	55,314	45,876	413,561	12,362
1996–97	571,226	5,984	25,159	56,306	43,549	429,464	10,764
1995–96	555,216	5,573	23,138	52,014	38,254	426,106	10,131
1994–95	539,691	5,482	20,677	47,067	35,962	420,656	9,847
1993–94	530,632	4,876	18,444	45,523	32,118	419,694	9,977
1992–93	514,756	4,408	16,763	42,886	30,283	411,435	8,981
1991–92	504,231	4,060	15,821	40,228	27,262	408,871	7,989
1990–91	481,720	3,871	15,257	38,835	25,540	391,264	6,953
1989–90	455,102	3,430	13,066	34,326	21,504	376,816	5,960
1988–89	432,144	3,331	12,519	34,664	20,384	354,865	6,381
1984–85	429,815	2,953	9,914	35,791	19,407	355,343	6,407
1980–81	410,174	2,584	8,650	35,330	17,800	339,167	6,643
1976–77	404,956	2,498	7,044	33,159	16,636	342,290	3,329

Percent change

1999–00 to 2004–05	23.3%	29.8%	21.2%	43.5%	52.3%	16.3%	39.6%
1976–77 to 2004–05	72.0	237.7	378.0	160.6	372.2	38.9	323.1

PERCENT DISTRIBUTION BY RACE AND HISPANIC ORIGIN

2004–05	100.0%	1.2%	4.8%	12.4%	11.3%	68.3%	2.0%
2003–04	100.0	1.2	5.0	12.2	10.9	68.5	2.2
2002–03	100.0	1.2	5.2	11.9	10.5	69.2	2.1
2001–02	100.0	1.1	5.2	11.3	10.1	70.2	2.1
2000–01	100.0	1.1	4.9	11.0	9.9	71.0	2.0
1999–00	100.0	1.2	4.9	10.7	9.1	72.4	1.8
1998–99	100.0	1.1	4.9	10.3	8.7	73.1	1.9
1997–98	100.0	1.1	4.5	9.9	8.2	74.0	2.2
1996–97	100.0	1.0	4.4	9.9	7.6	75.2	1.9
1995–96	100.0	1.0	4.2	9.4	6.9	76.7	1.8
1994–95	100.0	1.0	3.8	8.7	6.7	77.9	1.8
1993–94	100.0	0.9	3.5	8.6	6.1	79.1	1.9
1992–93	100.0	0.9	3.3	8.3	5.9	79.9	1.7
1991–92	100.0	0.8	3.1	8.0	5.4	81.1	1.6
1990–91	100.0	0.8	3.2	8.1	5.3	81.2	1.4
1989–90	100.0	0.8	2.9	7.5	4.7	82.8	1.3
1988–89	100.0	0.8	2.9	8.0	4.7	82.1	1.5
1984–85	100.0	0.7	2.3	8.3	4.5	82.7	1.5
1980–81	100.0	0.6	2.1	8.6	4.3	82.7	1.6
1976–77	100.0	0.6	1.7	8.2	4.1	84.5	0.8

Percentage point change

1999–00 to 2004–05	–	0.1	–0.1	1.7	2.1	–4.1	0.2
1976–77 to 2004–05	–	0.6	3.1	4.2	7.2	–16.3	1.2

Note: "–" means not applicable.
Source: National Center for Education Statistics, Digest of Education Statistics 2006, Internet site http://nces.ed.gov/programs/digest/; calculations by New Strategist

Table 2.34 Bachelor's Degrees Conferred by Sex, 1965–66 to 2004–05

(number of bachelor's degrees conferred by institutions of higher education by sex and women's share of total, 1965–66 to 2004–05; percent and percentage point change for selected years)

	total bachelor's degrees	men	women	women's share of total
2004–05	1,439,264	613,000	826,264	57.4%
2003–04	1,399,542	595,425	804,117	57.5
2002–03	1,348,503	573,079	775,424	57.5
2001–02	1,291,900	549,816	742,084	57.4
2000–01	1,244,171	531,840	712,331	57.3
1999–00	1,237,875	530,367	707,508	57.2
1998–99	1,200,303	518,746	681,557	56.8
1997–98	1,184,406	519,956	664,450	56.1
1996–97	1,172,879	520,515	652,364	55.6
1995–96	1,164,792	522,454	642,338	55.1
1994–95	1,160,134	526,131	634,003	54.6
1993–94	1,169,275	532,422	636,853	54.5
1992–93	1,165,178	532,881	632,297	54.3
1991–92	1,136,553	520,811	615,742	54.2
1990–91	1,094,538	504,045	590,493	53.9
1989–90	1,051,344	491,696	559,648	53.2
1988–89	1,018,755	483,346	535,409	52.6
1987–88	994,829	477,203	517,626	52.0
1986–87	991,264	480,782	510,482	51.5
1985–86	987,823	485,923	501,900	50.8
1984–85	979,477	482,528	496,949	50.7
1983–84	974,309	482,319	491,990	50.5
1982–83	969,510	479,140	490,370	50.6
1981–82	952,998	473,364	479,634	50.3
1980–81	935,140	469,883	465,257	49.8
1979–80	929,417	473,611	455,806	49.0
1978–79	921,390	477,344	444,046	48.2
1977–78	921,204	487,347	433,857	47.1
1976–77	919,549	495,545	424,004	46.1
1975–76	925,746	504,925	420,821	45.5
1974–75	922,933	504,841	418,092	45.3
1973–74	945,776	527,313	418,463	44.2
1972–73	922,362	518,191	404,171	43.8
1971–72	887,273	500,590	386,683	43.6
1970–71	839,730	475,594	364,136	43.4
1969–70	792,316	451,097	341,219	43.1
1968–69	728,845	410,595	318,250	43.7
1967–68	632,289	357,682	274,607	43.4
1966–67	558,534	322,711	235,823	42.2
1965–66	520,115	299,287	220,828	42.5

	percent change			percentage point change
1999–00 to 2004–05	16.3%	15.6%	16.8%	0.3
1965–66 to 2004–05	176.7	104.8	274.2	15.0

Source: National Center for Education Statistics, Digest of Education Statistics 2006, Internet site http://nces.ed.gov/programs/digest/; calculations by New Strategist

Table 2.35 Projections of Bachelor's Degrees Conferred by Sex, 2005–06 to 2015–16

(projected number of bachelor's degrees conferred by institutions of higher education by sex, and women's share of total, 2005–06 to 2015–16; percent and percentage point change 2005–06 to 2015–16)

	total bachelor's degrees	men	women	women's share of total
2005–06	1,456,000	608,000	849,000	58.3%
2006–07	1,488,000	618,000	870,000	58.5
2007–08	1,523,000	629,000	894,000	58.7
2008–09	1,561,000	640,000	921,000	59.0
2009–10	1,596,000	651,000	945,000	59.2
2010–11	1,622,000	658,000	964,000	59.4
2011–12	1,645,000	664,000	980,000	59.6
2012–13	1,665,000	670,000	995,000	59.8
2013–14	1,682,000	674,000	1,007,000	59.9
2014–15	1,697,000	677,000	1,019,000	60.0
2015–16	1,705,000	677,000	1,028,000	60.3

	percent change			percentage point change
2005–06 to 2015–16	17.1%	11.3%	21.1%	2.0

Source: National Center for Education Statistics, Projections of Education Statistics to 2015, Internet site http://nces.ed.gov/programs/projections/tables.asp; calculations by New Strategist

Table 2.36 Bachelor's Degrees Conferred by Race and Hispanic Origin, 1976–77 to 2004–05

(number and percent distribution of bachelor's degrees conferred by institutions of higher education, by race and Hispanic origin, 1976–77 to 2004–05; percent and percentage point change for selected years)

	total bachelor's degrees	American Indian	Asian	black, non-Hispanic	Hispanic	white, non-Hispanic	nonresident alien
2004–05	1,439,264	10,307	97,209	136,122	101,124	1,049,141	45,361
2003–04	1,399,542	10,638	92,073	131,241	94,644	1,026,114	44,832
2002–03	1,348,503	9,816	87,943	124,241	89,030	994,234	43,239
2001–02	1,291,900	9,165	83,093	116,623	82,966	958,597	41,456
2000–01	1,244,171	9,049	78,902	111,307	77,745	927,357	39,811
1999–00	1,237,875	8,719	77,912	108,013	75,059	929,106	39,066
1998–99	1,200,303	8,423	74,197	102,214	70,085	907,245	38,139
1997–98	1,184,406	7,903	71,678	98,251	66,005	901,344	39,225
1996–97	1,172,879	7,425	68,859	94,349	62,509	900,809	38,928
1995–96	1,164,792	6,976	64,433	91,496	58,351	905,846	37,690
1994–95	1,160,134	6,610	60,502	87,236	54,230	914,610	36,946
1993–94	1,169,275	6,192	55,689	83,909	50,299	939,008	34,178
1992–93	1,165,178	5,683	51,481	78,099	45,417	952,194	32,304
1991–92	1,136,553	5,228	47,428	72,680	41,087	941,663	28,467
1990–91	1,094,538	4,583	42,529	66,375	37,342	914,093	29,616
1989–90	1,051,344	4,390	39,230	61,046	32,829	887,151	26,698
1988–89	1,016,350	3,951	37,674	58,078	29,918	859,703	27,026
1984–85	968,311	4,246	25,395	57,473	25,874	826,106	29,217
1980–81	934,800	3,593	18,794	60,673	21,832	807,319	22,589
1976–77	917,900	3,326	13,793	58,636	18,743	807,688	15,714

Percent change

1999–00 to 2004–05	16.3%	18.2%	24.8%	26.0%	34.7%	12.9%	16.1%
1976–77 to 2004–05	56.8	209.9	604.8	132.1	439.5	29.9	188.7

PERCENT DISTRIBUTION BY RACE AND HISPANIC ORIGIN

2004–05	100.0%	0.7%	6.8%	9.5%	7.0%	72.9%	3.2%
2003–04	100.0	0.8	6.6	9.4	6.8	73.3	3.2
2002–03	100.0	0.7	6.5	9.2	6.6	73.7	3.2
2001–02	100.0	0.7	6.4	9.0	6.4	74.2	3.2
2000–01	100.0	0.7	6.3	8.9	6.2	74.5	3.2
1999–00	100.0	0.7	6.3	8.7	6.1	75.1	3.2
1998–99	100.0	0.7	6.2	8.5	5.8	75.6	3.2
1997–98	100.0	0.7	6.1	8.3	5.6	76.1	3.3
1996–97	100.0	0.6	5.9	8.0	5.3	76.8	3.3
1995–96	100.0	0.6	5.5	7.9	5.0	77.8	3.2
1994–95	100.0	0.6	5.2	7.5	4.7	78.8	3.2
1993–94	100.0	0.5	4.8	7.2	4.3	80.3	2.9
1992–93	100.0	0.5	4.4	6.7	3.9	81.7	2.8
1991–92	100.0	0.5	4.2	6.4	3.6	82.9	2.5
1990–91	100.0	0.4	3.9	6.1	3.4	83.5	2.7
1989–90	100.0	0.4	3.7	5.8	3.1	84.4	2.5
1988–89	100.0	0.4	3.7	5.7	2.9	84.6	2.7
1984–85	100.0	0.4	2.6	5.9	2.7	85.3	3.0
1980–81	100.0	0.4	2.0	6.5	2.3	86.4	2.4
1976–77	100.0	0.4	1.5	6.4	2.0	88.0	1.7

Percentage point change

1999–00 to 2004–05	–	0.0	0.5	0.7	1.0	−2.2	0.0
1976–77 to 2004–05	–	0.4	5.3	3.1	5.0	−15.1	1.4

Note: "–" means not applicable.
Source: National Center for Education Statistics, Digest of Education Statistics 2006, Internet site http://nces.ed.gov/programs/digest/; calculations by New Strategist

Table 2.37   Master's Degrees Conferred by Sex, 1965–66 to 2004–05

(number of master's degrees conferred by institutions of higher education by sex and women's share of total, 1965–66 to 2004–05; percent and percentage point change for selected years)

	total master's degrees	men	women	women's share of total
2004–05	574,618	233,590	341,028	59.3%
2003–04	558,940	229,545	329,395	58.9
2002–03	512,645	211,381	301,264	58.8
2001–02	482,118	199,120	282,998	58.7
2000–01	468,476	194,351	274,125	58.5
1999–00	457,056	191,792	265,264	58.0
1998–99	439,986	186,148	253,838	57.7
1997–98	430,164	184,375	245,789	57.1
1996–97	419,401	180,947	238,454	56.9
1995–96	406,301	179,081	227,220	55.9
1994–95	397,629	178,598	219,031	55.1
1993–94	387,070	176,085	210,985	54.5
1992–93	369,585	169,258	200,327	54.2
1991–92	352,838	161,842	190,996	54.1
1990–91	337,168	156,482	180,686	53.6
1989–90	324,301	153,653	170,648	52.6
1988–89	310,621	149,354	161,267	51.9
1987–88	299,317	145,163	154,154	51.5
1986–87	289,349	141,269	148,080	51.2
1985–86	288,567	143,508	145,059	50.3
1984–85	286,251	143,390	142,861	49.9
1983–84	284,263	143,595	140,668	49.5
1982–83	289,921	144,697	145,224	50.1
1981–82	295,546	145,532	150,014	50.8
1980–81	295,739	147,043	148,696	50.3
1979–80	298,081	150,749	147,332	49.4
1978–79	301,079	153,370	147,709	49.1
1977–78	311,620	161,212	150,408	48.3
1976–77	317,164	167,783	149,381	47.1
1975–76	311,771	167,248	144,523	46.4
1974–75	292,450	161,570	130,880	44.8
1973–74	277,033	157,842	119,191	43.0
1972–73	263,371	154,468	108,903	41.3
1971–72	251,633	149,550	102,083	40.6
1970–71	230,509	138,146	92,363	40.1
1969–70	208,291	125,624	82,667	39.7
1968–69	193,756	121,531	72,225	37.3
1967–68	176,749	113,552	63,197	35.8
1966–67	157,726	103,109	54,617	34.6
1965–66	140,602	93,081	47,521	33.8

	percent change			percentage point change
1999–00 to 2004–05	25.7%	21.8%	28.6%	1.3
1965–66 to 2004–05	308.7	151.0	617.6	25.6

Source: National Center for Education Statistics, Digest of Education Statistics 2006, Internet site http://nces.ed.gov/programs/ digest/; calculations by New Strategist

Table 2.38 Projections of Master's Degrees Conferred by Sex, 2005–06 to 2015–16

(projected number of master's degrees conferred by institutions of higher education by sex, and women's share of total, 2005–06 to 2015–16; percent and percentage point change 2005–06 to 2015–16)

	total master's degrees	men	women	women's share of total
2005–06	584,000	228,000	356,000	61.0%
2006–07	603,000	234,000	369,000	61.2
2007–08	619,000	239,000	380,000	61.4
2008–09	635,000	245,000	390,000	61.4
2009–10	647,000	251,000	397,000	61.4
2010–11	657,000	255,000	402,000	61.2
2011–12	670,000	260,000	409,000	61.0
2012–13	685,000	267,000	418,000	61.0
2013–14	705,000	275,000	431,000	61.1
2014–15	731,000	284,000	447,000	61.1
2015–16	757,000	293,000	464,000	61.3

	percent change			percentage point change
2005–06 to 2015–16	29.6%	28.5%	30.3%	0.3

Source: National Center for Education Statistics, Projections of Education Statistics to 2015, Internet site http://nces.ed.gov/ programs/projections/tables.asp; calculations by New Strategist

Table 2.39 Master's Degrees Conferred by Race and Hispanic Origin, 1976–77 to 2004–05

(number and percent distribution of master's degrees conferred by institutions of higher education, by race and Hispanic origin, 1976–77 to 2004–05; percent and percentage point change for selected years)

	total master's degrees	American Indian	Asian	black, non-Hispanic	Hispanic	white, non-Hispanic	nonresident alien
2004–05	574,618	3,295	32,783	54,482	31,485	379,350	73,223
2003–04	558,940	3,192	30,952	50,657	29,666	369,582	74,891
2002–03	512,645	2,837	27,245	44,272	24,974	341,735	71,582
2001–02	482,118	2,624	25,411	40,370	22,385	327,645	63,683
2000–01	468,476	2,481	24,283	38,265	21,543	320,480	61,424
1999–00	457,056	2,246	23,218	35,874	19,253	320,485	55,980
1998–99	439,986	2,016	22,072	32,541	17,838	313,487	52,032
1997–98	430,164	2,053	21,133	30,155	16,248	308,196	52,379
1996–97	419,401	1,940	19,061	28,403	15,440	305,005	49,552
1995–96	406,301	1,778	18,216	25,822	14,442	298,133	47,910
1994–95	397,629	1,621	16,847	24,166	12,905	293,345	48,745
1993–94	387,070	1,699	15,411	21,986	11,933	289,536	46,505
1992–93	369,585	1,405	13,863	19,744	10,638	279,827	44,108
1991–92	352,838	1,280	12,960	18,256	9,521	271,177	39,644
1990–91	337,168	1,178	11,650	16,616	8,887	261,232	37,605
1989–90	324,301	1,090	10,439	15,336	7,892	254,299	35,245
1988–89	309,770	1,086	10,335	14,095	7,277	242,764	34,213
1984–85	280,421	1,256	7,782	13,939	6,864	223,628	26,952
1980–81	294,183	1,034	6,282	17,133	6,461	241,216	22,057
1976–77	316,602	967	5,122	21,037	6,071	266,061	17,344

Percent change

1999–00 to 2004–05	25.7%	46.7%	41.2%	51.9%	63.5%	18.4%	30.8%
1976–77 to 2004–05	81.5	240.7	540.0	159.0	418.6	42.6	322.2

PERCENT DISTRIBUTION BY RACE AND HISPANIC ORIGIN

2004–05	100.0%	0.6%	5.7%	9.5%	5.5%	66.0%	12.7%
2003–04	100.0	0.6	5.5	9.1	5.3	66.1	13.4
2002–03	100.0	0.6	5.3	8.6	4.9	66.7	14.0
2001–02	100.0	0.5	5.3	8.4	4.6	68.0	13.2
2000–01	100.0	0.5	5.2	8.2	4.6	68.4	13.1
1999–00	100.0	0.5	5.1	7.8	4.2	70.1	12.2
1998–99	100.0	0.5	5.0	7.4	4.1	71.2	11.8
1997–98	100.0	0.5	4.9	7.0	3.8	71.6	12.2
1996–97	100.0	0.5	4.5	6.8	3.7	72.7	11.8
1995–96	100.0	0.4	4.5	6.4	3.6	73.4	11.8
1994–95	100.0	0.4	4.2	6.1	3.2	73.8	12.3
1993–94	100.0	0.4	4.0	5.7	3.1	74.8	12.0
1992–93	100.0	0.4	3.8	5.3	2.9	75.7	11.9
1991–92	100.0	0.4	3.7	5.2	2.7	76.9	11.2
1990–91	100.0	0.3	3.5	4.9	2.6	77.5	11.2
1989–90	100.0	0.3	3.2	4.7	2.4	78.4	10.9
1988–89	100.0	0.4	3.3	4.6	2.3	78.4	11.0
1984–85	100.0	0.4	2.8	5.0	2.4	79.7	9.6
1980–81	100.0	0.4	2.1	5.8	2.2	82.0	7.5
1976–77	100.0	0.3	1.6	6.6	1.9	84.0	5.5

Percentage point change

1999–00 to 2004–05	–	0.1	0.6	1.6	1.3	–4.1	0.5
1976–77 to 2004–05	–	0.3	4.1	2.8	3.6	–18.0	7.3

Note: "–" means not applicable.
Source: National Center for Education Statistics, Digest of Education Statistics 2006, Internet site http://nces.ed.gov/programs/digest/; calculations by New Strategist

Table 2.40 Doctoral Degrees Conferred by Sex, 1965–66 to 2004–05

(number of doctoral degrees conferred by institutions of higher education by sex and women's share of total, 1965–66 to 2004–05; percent and percentage point change for selected years)

	total doctoral degrees	men	women	women's share of total
2004–05	52,631	26,973	25,658	48.8%
2003–04	48,378	25,323	23,055	47.7
2002–03	46,024	24,341	21,683	47.1
2001–02	44,160	23,708	20,452	46.3
2000–01	44,904	24,728	20,176	44.9
1999–00	44,808	25,028	19,780	44.1
1998–99	44,077	25,146	18,931	42.9
1997–98	46,010	26,664	19,346	42.0
1996–97	45,876	27,146	18,730	40.8
1995–96	44,652	26,841	17,811	39.9
1994–95	44,446	26,916	17,530	39.4
1993–94	43,185	26,552	16,633	38.5
1992–93	42,132	26,073	16,059	38.1
1991–92	40,659	25,557	15,102	37.1
1990–91	39,294	24,756	14,538	37.0
1989–90	38,371	24,401	13,970	36.4
1988–89	35,720	22,648	13,072	36.6
1987–88	34,870	22,615	12,255	35.1
1986–87	34,041	22,061	11,980	35.2
1985–86	33,653	21,819	11,834	35.2
1984–85	32,943	21,700	11,243	34.1
1983–84	33,209	22,064	11,145	33.6
1982–83	32,775	21,902	10,873	33.2
1981–82	32,707	22,224	10,483	32.1
1980–81	32,958	22,711	10,247	31.1
1979–80	32,615	22,943	9,672	29.7
1978–79	32,730	23,541	9,189	28.1
1977–78	32,131	23,658	8,473	26.4
1976–77	33,232	25,142	8,090	24.3
1975–76	34,064	26,267	7,797	22.9
1974–75	34,083	26,817	7,266	21.3
1973–74	33,816	27,365	6,451	19.1
1972–73	34,777	28,571	6,206	17.8
1971–72	33,363	28,090	5,273	15.8
1970–71	32,107	27,530	4,577	14.3
1969–70	29,866	25,890	3,976	13.3
1968–69	26,158	22,722	3,436	13.1
1967–68	23,089	20,183	2,906	12.6
1966–67	20,617	18,163	2,454	11.9
1965–66	18,237	16,121	2,116	11.6

	percent change			percentage point change
1999–00 to 2004–05	17.5%	7.8%	29.7%	4.6
1965–66 to 2004–05	188.6	67.3	1,112.6	37.1

Source: National Center for Education Statistics, Digest of Education Statistics 2006, Internet site http://nces.ed.gov/programs/digest/; calculations by New Strategist

Table 2.41 Projections of Doctoral Degrees Conferred by Sex, 2005–06 to 2015–16

(projected number of doctoral degrees conferred by institutions of higher education by sex, and women's share of total, 2005–06 to 2015–16; percent and percentage point change 2005–06 to 2015–16)

	total doctoral degrees	men	women	women's share of total
2005–06	49,500	25,700	23,800	48.1%
2006–07	50,500	26,100	24,400	48.3
2007–08	50,900	26,200	24,700	48.5
2008–09	51,100	26,100	24,900	48.7
2009–10	51,200	26,100	25,100	49.0
2010–11	51,700	26,300	25,500	49.3
2011–12	52,600	26,600	26,100	49.6
2012–13	53,800	27,000	26,800	49.8
2013–14	55,300	27,500	27,800	50.3
2014–15	56,900	28,000	28,900	50.8
2015–16	58,500	28,400	30,100	51.5

	percent change			percentage point change
2005–06 to 2015–16	18.2%	10.5%	26.5%	3.4

Source: National Center for Education Statistics, Projections of Education Statistics to 2015, Internet site http://nces.ed.gov/ programs/projections/tables.asp; calculations by New Strategist

Table 2.42 Doctoral Degrees Conferred by Race and Hispanic Origin, 1976–77 to 2004–05

(number and percent distribution of doctoral degrees conferred by institutions of higher education, by race and Hispanic origin, 1976–77 to 2004–05; percent and percentage point change for selected years)

	total doctoral degrees	American Indian	Asian	black, non-Hispanic	Hispanic	white, non-Hispanic	nonresident alien
2004–05	52,631	237	2,911	3,056	1,824	30,261	14,342
2003–04	48,378	217	2,632	2,900	1,662	28,214	12,753
2002–03	46,024	196	2,426	2,517	1,561	27,698	11,626
2001–02	44,160	180	2,319	2,395	1,434	26,903	10,929
2000–01	44,904	177	2,587	2,207	1,516	27,454	10,963
1999–00	44,808	160	2,420	2,246	1,305	27,843	10,834
1998–99	44,077	194	2,299	2,136	1,302	27,838	10,308
1997–98	46,010	186	2,339	2,067	1,275	28,803	11,340
1996–97	45,876	175	2,667	1,865	1,120	28,596	11,453
1995–96	44,652	159	2,641	1,632	997	27,773	11,450
1994–95	44,446	130	2,689	1,667	984	27,846	11,130
1993–94	43,185	134	2,024	1,385	900	27,212	11,530
1992–93	42,132	107	1,578	1,350	824	26,816	11,457
1991–92	40,659	120	1,598	1,239	824	26,229	10,649
1990–91	39,294	106	1,504	1,248	757	25,855	9,824
1989–90	38,371	98	1,225	1,149	780	26,221	8,898
1988–89	35,659	85	1,323	1,066	629	24,884	7,672
1984–85	32,307	119	1,106	1,154	677	23,934	5,317
1980–81	32,839	130	877	1,265	456	25,908	4,203
1976–77	33,126	95	658	1,253	522	26,851	3,747

Percent change

1999–00 to 2004–05	17.5%	48.1%	20.3%	36.1%	39.8%	8.7%	32.4%
1976–77 to 2004–05	58.9	149.5	342.4	143.9	249.4	12.7	282.8

PERCENT DISTRIBUTION BY RACE AND HISPANIC ORIGIN

2004–05	100.0%	0.5%	5.5%	5.8%	3.5%	57.5%	27.3%
2003–04	100.0	0.4	5.4	6.0	3.4	58.3	26.4
2002–03	100.0	0.4	5.3	5.5	3.4	60.2	25.3
2001–02	100.0	0.4	5.3	5.4	3.2	60.9	24.7
2000–01	100.0	0.4	5.8	4.9	3.4	61.1	24.4
1999–00	100.0	0.4	5.4	5.0	2.9	62.1	24.2
1998–99	100.0	0.4	5.2	4.8	3.0	63.2	23.4
1997–98	100.0	0.4	5.1	4.5	2.8	62.6	24.6
1996–97	100.0	0.4	5.8	4.1	2.4	62.3	25.0
1995–96	100.0	0.4	5.9	3.7	2.2	62.2	25.6
1994–95	100.0	0.3	6.1	3.8	2.2	62.7	25.0
1993–94	100.0	0.3	4.7	3.2	2.1	63.0	26.7
1992–93	100.0	0.3	3.7	3.2	2.0	63.6	27.2
1991–92	100.0	0.3	3.9	3.0	2.0	64.5	26.2
1990–91	100.0	0.3	3.8	3.2	1.9	65.8	25.0
1989–90	100.0	0.3	3.2	3.0	2.0	68.3	23.2
1988–89	100.0	0.2	3.7	3.0	1.8	69.8	21.5
1984–85	100.0	0.4	3.4	3.6	2.1	74.1	16.5
1980–81	100.0	0.4	2.7	3.9	1.4	78.9	12.8
1976–77	100.0	0.3	2.0	3.8	1.6	81.1	11.3

Percentage point change

1999–00 to 2004–05	–	0.1	0.1	0.8	0.6	–4.6	3.1
1976–77 to 2004–05	–	0.2	3.5	2.0	1.9	–23.6	15.9

Note: "–" means not applicable.
Source: National Center for Education Statistics, Digest of Education Statistics 2006, Internet site http://nces.ed.gov/programs/digest/; calculations by New Strategist

Table 2.43 First-Professional Degrees Conferred by Sex, 1965–66 to 2004–05

(number of first-professional degrees conferred by institutions of higher education by sex and women's share of total, 1965–66 to 2004–05; percent and percentage point change for selected years)

	total first-professional degrees	men	women	women's share of total
2004–05	87,289	43,849	43,440	49.8%
2003–04	83,041	42,169	40,872	49.2
2002–03	80,810	41,834	38,976	48.2
2001–02	80,698	42,507	38,191	47.3
2000–01	79,707	42,862	36,845	46.2
1999–00	80,057	44,239	35,818	44.7
1998–99	78,439	44,339	34,100	43.5
1997–98	78,598	44,911	33,687	42.9
1996–97	78,730	45,564	33,166	42.1
1995–96	76,734	44,748	31,986	41.7
1994–95	75,800	44,853	30,947	40.8
1993–94	75,418	44,707	30,711	40.7
1992–93	75,387	45,153	30,234	40.1
1991–92	74,146	45,071	29,075	39.2
1990–91	71,948	43,846	28,102	39.1
1989–90	70,988	43,961	27,027	38.1
1988–89	70,856	45,046	25,810	36.4
1987–88	70,735	45,484	25,251	35.7
1986–87	71,617	46,523	25,094	35.0
1985–86	73,910	49,261	24,649	33.4
1984–85	75,063	50,455	24,608	32.8
1983–84	74,468	51,378	23,090	31.0
1982–83	73,054	51,250	21,804	29.8
1981–82	72,032	52,223	19,809	27.5
1980–81	71,956	52,792	19,164	26.6
1979–80	70,131	52,716	17,415	24.8
1978–79	68,848	52,652	16,196	23.5
1977–78	66,581	52,270	14,311	21.5
1976–77	64,359	52,374	11,985	18.6
1975–76	62,649	52,892	9,757	15.6
1974–75	55,916	48,956	6,960	12.4
1973–74	53,816	48,530	5,286	9.8
1972–73	50,018	46,489	3,529	7.1
1971–72	43,411	40,723	2,688	6.2
1970–71	37,946	35,544	2,402	6.3
1969–70	34,918	33,077	1,841	5.3
1968–69	35,114	33,595	1,519	4.3
1967–68	33,939	32,402	1,537	4.5
1966–67	31,695	30,401	1,294	4.1
1965–66	30,124	28,982	1,142	3.8

	percent change			percentage point change
1999–00 to 2004–05	9.0%	–0.9%	21.3%	5.0
1965–66 to 2004–05	189.8	51.3	3,703.9	46.0

Source: National Center for Education Statistics, Digest of Education Statistics 2006, Internet site http://nces.ed.gov/programs/digest/; calculations by New Strategist

Table 2.44 Projections of First-Professional Degrees Conferred by Sex, 2005–06 to 2015–16

(projected number of first-professional degrees conferred by institutions of higher education by sex, and women's share of total, 2005–06 to 2015–16; percent and percentage point change 2005–06 to 2015–16)

	total first-professional degrees	men	women	women's share of total
2005–06	85,100	41,600	43,500	51.1%
2006–07	87,400	42,200	45,200	51.7
2007–08	89,700	42,800	46,900	52.3
2008–09	91,900	43,500	48,400	52.7
2009–10	93,400	44,000	49,300	52.8
2010–11	94,500	44,500	50,000	52.9
2011–12	95,900	45,000	50,900	53.1
2012–13	97,300	45,500	51,800	53.2
2013–14	99,200	46,100	53,100	53.5
2014–15	101,400	46,700	54,700	53.9
2015–16	103,800	47,200	56,500	54.4

	percent change			percentage point change
2005–06 to 2015–16	22.0%	13.5%	29.9%	3.3

Source: National Center for Education Statistics, Projections of Education Statistics to 2015, Internet site http://nces.ed.gov/ programs/projections/tables.asp; calculations by New Strategist

Table 2.45 First-Professional Degrees Conferred by Race and Hispanic Origin, 1976–77 to 2004–05

(number and percent distribution of first-professional degrees conferred by institutions of higher education, by race and Hispanic origin, 1976–77 to 2004–05; percent and percentage point change for selected years)

	total first-professional degrees	American Indian	Asian	black, non-Hispanic	Hispanic	white, non-Hispanic	nonresident alien
2004–05	87,289	564	10,501	6,313	4,445	63,429	2,037
2003–04	83,041	565	9,964	5,930	4,273	60,379	1,930
2002–03	80,810	586	9,790	5,715	4,086	58,678	1,955
2001–02	80,698	581	9,584	5,811	3,965	58,874	1,883
2000–01	79,707	543	9,261	5,416	3,806	58,598	2,083
1999–00	80,057	564	8,584	5,555	3,865	59,637	1,852
1998–99	78,439	612	8,152	5,333	3,864	58,720	1,758
1997–98	78,598	561	7,757	5,499	3,552	59,443	1,786
1996–97	78,730	514	7,374	5,301	3,615	60,280	1,646
1995–96	76,734	463	6,627	5,022	3,475	59,525	1,622
1994–95	75,800	413	6,396	4,747	3,231	59,402	1,611
1993–94	75,418	371	5,892	4,444	3,131	60,143	1,437
1992–93	75,387	370	5,176	4,132	2,996	61,165	1,548
1991–92	74,146	298	4,841	3,628	2,867	61,170	1,342
1990–91	71,948	261	3,835	3,588	2,547	60,631	1,086
1989–90	70,988	257	3,362	3,409	2,425	60,487	1,048
1988–89	70,856	264	2,976	3,148	2,269	61,214	985
1984–85	71,057	248	1,816	3,029	1,884	63,219	861
1980–81	71,340	192	1,456	2,931	1,541	64,551	669
1976–77	63,953	196	1,021	2,537	1,076	58,422	701

Percent change

1999–00 to 2004–05	9.0%	–	22.3%	13.6%	15.0%	6.4%	10.0%
1976–77 to 2004–05	36.5	187.8%	928.5	148.8	313.1	8.6	190.6

PERCENT DISTRIBUTION BY RACE AND HISPANIC ORIGIN

2004–05	100.0%	0.6%	12.0%	7.2%	5.1%	72.7%	2.3%
2003–04	100.0	0.7	12.0	7.1	5.1	72.7	2.3
2002–03	100.0	0.7	12.1	7.1	5.1	72.6	2.4
2001–02	100.0	0.7	11.9	7.2	4.9	73.0	2.3
2000–01	100.0	0.7	11.6	6.8	4.8	73.5	2.6
1999–00	100.0	0.7	10.7	6.9	4.8	74.5	2.3
1998–99	100.0	0.8	10.4	6.8	4.9	74.9	2.2
1997–98	100.0	0.7	9.9	7.0	4.5	75.6	2.3
1996–97	100.0	0.7	9.4	6.7	4.6	76.6	2.1
1995–96	100.0	0.6	8.6	6.5	4.5	77.6	2.1
1994–95	100.0	0.5	8.4	6.3	4.3	78.4	2.1
1993–94	100.0	0.5	7.8	5.9	4.2	79.7	1.9
1992–93	100.0	0.5	6.9	5.5	4.0	81.1	2.1
1991–92	100.0	0.4	6.5	4.9	3.9	82.5	1.8
1990–91	100.0	0.4	5.3	5.0	3.5	84.3	1.5
1989–90	100.0	0.4	4.7	4.8	3.4	85.2	1.5
1988–89	100.0	0.4	4.2	4.4	3.2	86.4	1.4
1984–85	100.0	0.3	2.6	4.3	2.7	89.0	1.2
1980–81	100.0	0.3	2.0	4.1	2.2	90.5	0.9
1976–77	100.0	0.3	1.6	4.0	1.7	91.4	1.1

Percentage point change

1999–00 to 2004–05	–	-0.1	1.3	0.3	0.3	-1.8	0.0
1976–77 to 2004–05	–	0.3	10.4	3.3	3.4	-18.7	1.2

Note: "–" means not applicable.
Source: National Center for Education Statistics, Digest of Education Statistics 2006, Internet site http://nces.ed.gov/programs/digest/; calculations by New Strategist

3

Health

■ Americans don't feel as good as they once did. During the past decade, the percentage of adults who rate their health as excellent or very good fell from 59 to 55 percent.

■ In 1950, 86 percent of the nation's newborns were white. Today, only 55 percent of newborns are non-Hispanic white and 24 percent are Hispanic.

■ Americans have a weight problem. Among men, the percentage of people with a healthy weight fell from 48 to 28 percent between 1960–62 and 2001–04. Among women, the figure fell from 54 to 36 percent during those years.

■ The percentage of Americans with health insurance has remained fairly stable for decades. Overall, 85 percent have health insurance, a figure that is down slightly from the 87 percent of two decades ago. Because of population growth, however, the number of uninsured Americans climbed by more than 10 million during those years.

■ Death rates are dropping, especially for heart disease. Between 1999 and 2004, the death rate due to heart disease fell 19 percent. Every demographic segment experienced a decline in the heart disease death rate.

■ Since 1950, life expectancy at birth has climbed ten years, from 68 to 78 years. Life expectancy at older ages is also up. At age 65, people can expect to live 19 more years, up from 14 more years in 1950.

Health Status Is Declining

Fewer Americans say their health is "excellent" or "very good."

During the past decade, the percentage of Americans aged 18 or older who rate their health as excellent or very good has fallen from 59 to 55 percent, according to the Center for Disease Control and Prevention's Behavioral Risk Factor Surveillance System. The decline, while not large, is pervasive. The percentage of Americans who rate their health highly fell in nearly every demographic segment between 1995 and 2006.

The biggest decline in health is being reported by Hispanics. The percentage of Hispanics saying their health is excellent or very good fell a stunning 16 percentage points between 1995 and 2006, from 53 to 36 percent. By age, 25-to-54-year-olds experienced the greatest decline in health status. Among people aged 65 or older, in contrast, health status increased slightly during the past decade.

Many researchers have noted the decline in health status, but no one can explain it. One possible cause is the growing problem of obesity, especially among the middle aged. Another factor may be the growing number of people without health insurance, especially among Hispanics.

■ The most affluent and best educated have experienced smaller declines in health status over the past decade, pointing toward a socioeconomic explanation.

The middle aged have seen the biggest declines in health status

(percent of people aged 18 or older who rate their health as excellent or very good, by age, 1995 and 2006)

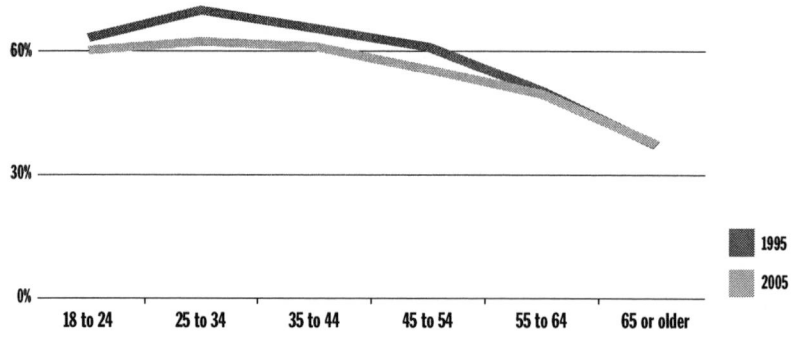

Table 3.1 Health Status, 1995 to 2006

"How is your general health?"

(percent distribution of people aged 18 or older by response, 1995 to 2006; percentage point change, 1995–2006)

	total	excellent	very good	good	fair	poor
2006	100.0%	20.7%	34.4%	30.2%	10.9%	3.7%
2005	100.0	20.3	33.9	30.7	11.1	4.0
2004	100.0	20.9	33.7	29.9	10.9	3.9
2003	100.0	21.8	33.6	29.5	10.9	3.9
2002	100.0	21.4	33.9	29.9	10.5	3.9
2001	100.0	22.0	34.4	29.2	10.5	3.6
2000	100.0	22.3	33.9	29.3	10.2	3.4
1999	100.0	22.7	34.4	28.6	9.9	3.4
1998	100.0	23.6	33.6	28.0	9.9	3.3
1997	100.0	23.6	34.1	28.1	9.6	3.3
1996	100.0	23.9	34.2	28.1	9.8	3.2
1995	100.0	24.8	34.0	27.7	9.5	3.2
Percentage point change						
1995 to 2006	–	–4.1	0.4	2.5	1.4	0.5

Note: "–" means not applicable.
Source: Centers for Disease Control and Prevention, Behavioral Risk Factor Surveillance System, Prevalence Data; Internet site http://apps.nccd.cdc.gov/brfss/index.asp; calculations by New Strategist

Table 3.2 Health Status by Selected Characteristics, 1995 and 2006

"How is your general health?"

(percent of people aged 18 or older responding "excellent" or "very good," by selected characteristics, 1995 and 2006; percentage point change, 1995–2006)

	percent responding "excellent" or "very good"		percentage point change
	2006	1995	
Total people	**55.1%**	**58.8%**	**–3.7**
Sex			
Female	54.2	57.7	–3.5
Male	56.0	59.5	–3.5
Age			
Aged 18 to 24	60.2	63.2	–3.0
Aged 25 to 34	62.3	69.9	–7.6
Aged 35 to 44	61.1	65.5	–4.4
Aged 45 to 54	55.5	61.0	–5.5
Aged 55 to 64	49.5	50.2	–0.7
Aged 65 or older	37.4	37.2	0.2
Race and Hispanic origin			
Black	44.6	48.4	–3.8
Hispanic	36.3	52.5	–16.2
White	58.6	61.2	–2.6
Household income			
Under $15,000	27.6	38.1	–10.5
$15,000 to $24,999	37.8	48.9	–11.1
$25,000 to $34,999	47.4	60.7	–13.3
$35,000 to $49,999	56.5	66.7	–10.2
$50,000 or more	69.4	75.8	–6.4
Education			
Not a high school graduate	29.2	34.1	–4.9
High school graduate only	46.3	53.9	–7.6
Some college	56.4	63.1	–6.7
College graduate	69.5	73.0	–3.5

Source: Centers for Disease Control and Prevention, Behavioral Risk Factor Surveillance System, Prevalence Data; Internet site http://apps.nccd.cdc.gov/brfss/index.asp; calculations by New Strategist

More Are Using Condoms

The pill is the most popular contraceptive.

More than 60 percent of women aged 15 to 44 use birth control, and among birth control users the pill is most popular. Overall, 31 percent of women aged 15 to 44 who use contraception were on the pill in 2002, according to the National Survey of Family Growth. This is up slightly from the 28 percent of 1982. Contracepting women under age 25 are most likely to be on the pill, with more than half using the pill as a contraceptive.

Condom use has surged over the past two decades because of the emergence of AIDS. The percentage of contracepting women aged 15 to 44 (or their partners) who use condoms climbed from 12 to 24 percent between 1982 and 2002. Teenagers are especially likely to use condoms, with 45 percent of contracepting 15-to-19-year-olds using condoms in 2002.

As women get older, they are more likely to opt for sterilization. Overall, only 27 percent of contracepting women aged 15 to 44 have been sterilized, but the figure rises to 46 percent among women aged 35 to 44. A smaller 18 percent of women aged 35 to 44 have male partners who have been sterilized.

■ The percentage of teenagers who depend on withdrawal for birth control increased substantially during the past two decades. Because withdrawal is an unreliable birth control method, its use may lead to more unwanted pregnancies in the years ahead.

Condom use increased in every age group

(percent of contracepting women aged 15 to 44 who use condoms as their method of birth control, by age, 1982 and 2002)

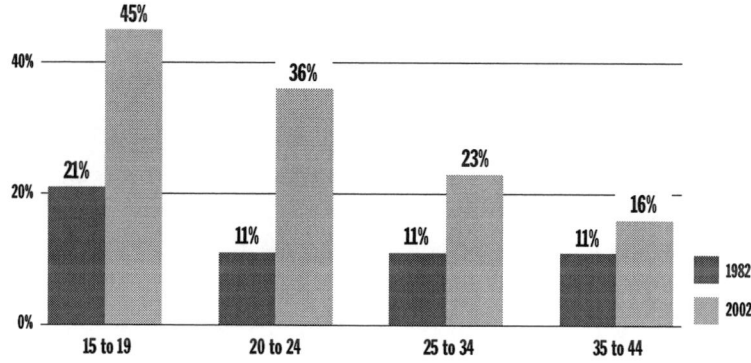

Table 3.3 Contraceptive Use by Age, 1982 to 2002

(percent of women aged 15 to 44 who use contraception, by method and age, selected years, 1982 to 2002; percentage point change, 1982–2002)

	2002	1995	1988	1982	percentage point change 1982–2002
ANY METHOD					
Total women, aged 15 to 44	**61.9%**	**64.2%**	**60.3%**	**55.7%**	**6.2**
Aged 15 to 19	31.5	29.8	32.1	24.2	7.3
Aged 20 to 24	60.7	63.5	59.0	55.8	4.9
Aged 25 to 34	68.6	71.1	66.3	66.7	1.9
Aged 35 to 44	69.9	72.3	68.3	61.6	8.3
BIRTH CONTROL PILL					
Total women, aged 15 to 44 who use contraception	**31.0**	**27.0**	**30.8**	**28.0**	**3.0**
Aged 15 to 19	53.8	43.8	58.8	63.9	−10.1
Aged 20 to 24	52.5	52.1	68.2	55.1	−2.6
Aged 25 to 34	34.8	33.4	32.6	25.7	9.1
Aged 35 to 44	15.0	8.7	4.3	3.7	11.3
CONDOM					
Total women, aged 15 to 44 who use contraception	**23.8**	**23.4**	**14.6**	**12.0**	**11.8**
Aged 15 to 19	44.6	45.8	32.8	20.8	23.8
Aged 20 to 24	36.0	33.7	14.5	10.7	25.3
Aged 25 to 34	23.1	23.7	13.7	11.4	11.7
Aged 35 to 44	15.6	15.3	11.2	11.3	4.3
STERILIZATION, FEMALE					
Total women, aged 15 to 44 who use contraception	**27.0**	**27.8**	**27.6**	**23.2**	**3.8**
Aged 15 to 19	–	–	–	–	–
Aged 20 to 24	3.6	4.0	4.6	4.5	−0.9
Aged 25 to 34	21.7	23.8	25.0	22.1	−0.4
Aged 35 to 44	45.8	45.0	47.6	43.5	2.3
STERILIZATION, MALE					
Total women, aged 15 to 44 who use contraception	**10.2**	**10.9**	**11.7**	**10.9**	**−0.7**
Aged 15 to 19	–	–	–	–	–
Aged 20 to 24	–	–	–	–	–
Aged 25 to 34	7.2	7.8	10.2	10.1	−2.9
Aged 35 to 44	18.2	19.5	20.8	19.9	−1.7
WITHDRAWAL					
Total women, aged 15 to 44 whho use contraception	**8.8**	**6.1**	**2.2**	**2.0**	**6.8**
Aged 15 to 19	15.0	13.2	3.0	2.9	12.1
Aged 20 to 24	11.9	7.1	3.4	3.0	8.9
Aged 25 to 34	10.7	6.0	2.8	1.8	8.9
Aged 35 to 44	4.7	4.5	0.8	1.3	3.4

Note: Method of contraception used in the month of interview. "–" means sample is too small to make a reliable estimate.
Source: National Center for Health Statistics, Health, United States, 2006, Internet site http://www.cdc.gov/nchs/hus.htm; calculations by New Strategist

Most Babies Are Born to Women in Their Twenties

This pattern has not changed in the past half-century.

During the past 55 years, the annual number of births has fluctuated through cycles of baby boom and baby bust. Births peaked at 4.3 million in the late 1950s and early 1960s as the last of the baby boomers were born. The number fell below 4 million in 1965 as the first baby busters (or generation X) were born. Births climbed above 4 million again in the early 1990s with the echo boom (or millennial generation) in full swing. The number fell below 4 million for a few years, between 1994 and 1999, then topped 4 million again in 2000 and has remained above that level through 2005.

Behind the rollercoaster of births is the changing role of women. As more women went to college and then to work, they postponed childbearing. In 1950, fully 59 percent of births were to women aged 20 to 29. By 2005, the figure had fallen to 52 percent. The share of births to women aged 30 or older grew from 27 to 37 percent during those years. The proportion of births to women under age 20 has barely changed since 1950.

Birth rates are lower today than they were in 1950 in every age group. Between 2000 and 2005, however, birth rates have increased in the older age groups as women who postponed having children while finishing school and starting a career finally took the plunge. Among women under age 25, however, birth rates have continued to fall.

■ The growing Hispanic population may boost birth rates among women in their early twenties because Hispanics have children at a younger age than non-Hispanic whites.

Births have been on a rollercoaster for decades

(annual number of births for selected years, 1950 to 2005; numbers in millions)

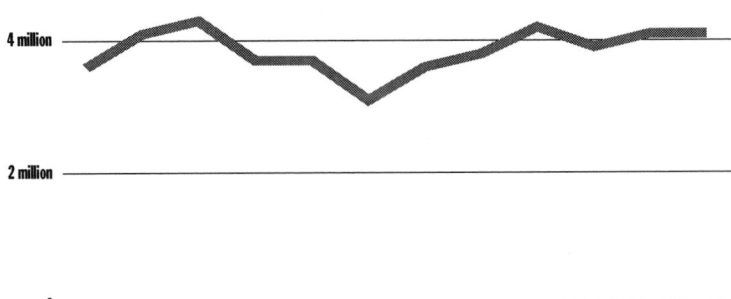

Table 3.4 Number of Births, 1950 to 2005

(number of births by year and decade, 1950 to 2005; percent change from preceding year or decade, 1950–2005; numbers in thousands)

	number	percent change from preceding year or decade		number	percent change from preceding year or decade
2005	4,140	0.7%	1977	3,327	5.0%
2004	4,112	0.5	1976	3,168	0.8
2003	4,090	1.7	1975	3,144	−0.5
2002	4,022	−0.1	1974	3,160	0.7
2001	4,026	−0.8	1973	3,137	−3.7
1991–2000	**39,760**	**4.5**	1972	3,258	−8.4
2000	4,058	2.5	1971	3,556	−4.7
1999	3,959	0.4	**1961–1970**	**38,280**	**−7.0**
1998	3,942	1.6	1970	3,731	3.6
1997	3,881	−0.3	1969	3,600	2.8
1996	3,891	−0.2	1968	3,502	−0.5
1995	3,900	−1.3	1967	3,521	−2.4
1994	3,953	−1.2	1966	3,606	−4.1
1993	4,000	−1.6	1965	3,760	−6.6
1992	4,065	−1.1	1964	4,027	−1.7
1991	4,111	−1.1	1963	4,098	−1.7
1981–1990	**38,054**	**14.7**	1962	4,167	−2.4
1990	4,158	2.9	1961	4,268	0.2
1989	4,041	3.4	**1951–1960**	**41,160**	–
1988	3,910	2.7	1960	4,258	0.3
1987	3,809	1.4	1959	4,245	−0.2
1986	3,757	−0.1	1958	4,255	−1.2
1985	3,761	2.5	1957	4,308	2.1
1984	3,669	0.8	1956	4,218	3.0
1983	3,639	−1.1	1955	4,097	0.5
1982	3,681	1.4	1954	4,078	2.8
1981	3,629	0.5	1953	3,965	1.3
1971–1980	**33,189**	**−13.3**	1952	3,913	2.4
1980	3,612	3.4	1951	3,823	5.3
1979	3,494	4.8	1950	3,632	–
1978	3,333	0.2			

Note: "–" means not applicable.
Source: National Center for Health Statistics, Births: Final Data for 2004, National Vital Statistics Report, Vol. 55, No. 1, 2006; and Births: Preliminary Data for 2005, Health E-Stats, Internet site http://www.cdc.gov/nchs/births.htm; and Bureau of the Census, Historical Statistics of the United States: Colonial Time to 1970, Part 1, 1975; calculations by New Strategist

Table 3.5 Births by Age of Mother, 1950 to 2005

(number of births by age of mother, 1950 to 2005; percent change for selected years; numbers in thousands)

	total	under 20	20 to 24	25 to 29	30 to 34	35 to 39	40 or older
2005	4,140	421	1,040	1,132	952	483	111
2004	4,112	422	1,034	1,104	966	476	110
2003	4,090	421	1,032	1,086	976	468	107
2002	4,022	433	1,022	1,060	951	454	101
2001	4,026	454	1,022	1,058	943	452	98
2000	4,059	478	1,018	1,088	929	452	94
1999	3,959	485	982	1,078	892	434	87
1998	3,942	494	965	1,083	889	425	85
1997	3,881	493	942	1,069	887	410	80
1996	3,891	503	945	1,071	898	400	75
1995	3,900	512	966	1,064	905	384	70
1994	3,953	518	1,001	1,089	906	372	66
1993	4,000	514	1,038	1,129	901	357	61
1992	4,065	517	1,070	1,179	895	345	58
1991	4,111	532	1,090	1,220	885	331	54
1990	4,158	534	1,094	1,277	886	318	50
1989	4,041	518	1,078	1,263	842	294	46
1988	3,910	489	1,067	1,239	804	270	41
1987	3,809	473	1,076	1,216	761	248	36
1986	3,757	472	1,102	1,200	721	230	31
1985	3,761	478	1,141	1,201	696	214	29
1984	3,669	480	1,142	1,166	658	196	28
1983	3,639	499	1,160	1,148	625	180	27
1982	3,681	524	1,206	1,152	605	168	26
1981	3,629	537	1,212	1,128	581	146	25
1980	3,612	562	1,226	1,108	550	141	24
1975	3,144	595	1,094	937	376	115	28
1970	3,731	656	1,419	995	428	180	53
1965	3,760	599	1,337	926	529	283	86
1960	4,258	594	1,427	1,093	688	360	97
1955	4,097	490	1,274	1,119	722	345	93
1950	3,632	425	1,131	1,022	598	293	80

Percent change

2000 to 2005	2.0%	−11.9%	2.2%	4.0%	2.5%	6.9%	18.1%
1950 to 2005	14.0	−0.9	−8.0	10.8	59.2	64.8	38.8

Note: Numbers may not add to total because "age not stated" is not shown.
Source: National Center for Health Statistics, Births: Preliminary Data for 2005, Health E-Stats, Internet site http://www.cdc
.gov/nchs/births.htm; and Bureau of the Census, Statistical Abstract of the United States 1980, 1990, 1992, and 2007, Internet site
http://www.census.gov/compendia/statab/; calculations by New Strategist

Table 3.6 Percent Distribution of Births by Age of Mother, 1950 to 2005

(percent distribution of births by age of mother, 1950 to 2005; percentage point change for selected years)

	total	under 20	20 to 24	25 to 29	30 to 34	35 to 39	40 or older
2005	100.0%	10.2%	25.1%	27.3%	23.0%	11.7%	2.7%
2004	100.0	10.3	25.1	26.8	23.5	11.6	2.7
2003	100.0	10.3	25.2	26.6	23.9	11.4	2.6
2002	100.0	10.8	25.4	26.4	23.6	11.3	2.5
2001	100.0	11.3	25.4	26.3	23.4	11.2	2.4
2000	100.0	11.8	25.1	26.8	22.9	11.1	2.3
1999	100.0	12.3	24.8	27.2	22.5	11.0	2.2
1998	100.0	12.5	24.5	27.5	22.6	10.8	2.2
1997	100.0	12.7	24.3	27.5	22.9	10.6	2.1
1996	100.0	12.9	24.3	27.5	23.1	10.3	1.9
1995	100.0	13.1	24.8	27.3	23.2	9.8	1.8
1994	100.0	13.1	25.3	27.5	22.9	9.4	1.7
1993	100.0	12.9	26.0	28.2	22.5	8.9	1.5
1992	100.0	12.7	26.3	29.0	22.0	8.5	1.4
1991	100.0	12.9	26.5	29.7	21.5	8.1	1.3
1990	100.0	12.8	26.3	30.7	21.3	7.6	1.2
1989	100.0	12.8	26.7	31.3	20.8	7.3	1.1
1988	100.0	12.5	27.3	31.7	20.6	6.9	1.0
1987	100.0	12.4	28.2	31.9	20.0	6.5	0.9
1986	100.0	12.6	29.3	31.9	19.2	6.1	0.8
1985	100.0	12.7	30.3	31.9	18.5	5.7	0.8
1984	100.0	13.1	31.1	31.8	17.9	5.3	0.8
1983	100.0	13.7	31.9	31.5	17.2	4.9	0.7
1982	100.0	14.2	32.8	31.3	16.4	4.6	0.7
1981	100.0	14.8	33.4	31.1	16.0	4.0	0.7
1980	100.0	15.6	33.9	30.7	15.2	3.9	0.7
1975	100.0	18.9	34.8	29.8	12.0	3.7	0.9
1970	100.0	17.6	38.0	26.7	11.5	4.8	1.4
1965	100.0	15.9	35.6	24.6	14.1	7.5	2.3
1960	100.0	14.0	33.5	25.7	16.2	8.5	2.3
1955	100.0	12.0	31.1	27.3	17.6	8.4	2.3
1950	100.0	11.7	31.1	28.1	16.5	8.1	2.2

Percentage point change

	total	under 20	20 to 24	25 to 29	30 to 34	35 to 39	40 or older
2000 to 2005	–	–1.6	0.0	0.5	0.1	0.5	0.4
1950 to 2005	–	–1.5	–6.0	–0.8	6.5	3.6	0.5

Note: Numbers may not add to total because "age not stated" is not shown. "–" means not applicable.
Source: National Center for Health Statistics, Births: Preliminary Data for 2005, Health E-Stats, Internet site http://www
.cdc.gov/nchs/births.htm; and Bureau of the Census, Statistical Abstract of the United States 1980, 1990, 1992, and 2007, Internet
site http://www.census.gov/compendia/statab/; calculations by New Strategist

Table 3.7 Birth Rate by Age of Mother, 1950 to 2005

(number of births per 1,000 women aged 15 to 44, and per 1,000 women in specified age group, 1950 to 2005; percent change for selected years)

	total	15 to 19	20 to 24	25 to 29	30 to 34	35 to 39	40 to 44	45 to 49
2005	66.7	40.4	102.2	115.6	95.9	46.3	9.1	0.6
2004	66.3	41.1	101.7	115.5	95.3	45.4	8.9	0.5
2003	66.1	41.6	102.6	115.6	95.1	43.8	8.7	0.5
2002	64.8	43.0	103.6	113.6	91.5	41.4	8.3	0.5
2001	65.3	45.3	106.2	113.4	91.9	40.6	8.1	0.5
2000	65.9	47.7	109.7	113.5	91.2	39.7	8.0	0.5
1999	64.4	48.8	107.9	111.2	87.1	37.8	7.4	0.4
1998	64.3	50.3	108.4	110.2	85.2	36.9	7.4	0.4
1997	63.6	51.3	107.3	108.3	83.0	35.7	7.1	0.4
1996	64.1	53.5	107.8	108.6	82.1	34.9	6.8	0.3
1995	64.6	56.0	107.5	108.8	81.1	34.0	6.6	0.3
1994	65.9	58.2	109.2	111.0	80.4	33.4	6.4	0.3
1993	67.0	59.0	111.3	113.2	79.9	32.7	6.1	0.3
1992	68.4	60.3	113.7	115.7	79.6	32.3	5.9	0.3
1991	69.3	61.8	115.3	117.2	79.2	31.9	5.5	0.2
1990	70.9	59.9	116.5	120.2	80.8	31.7	5.5	0.2
1989	69.2	57.3	113.8	117.6	77.4	29.9	5.2	0.2
1988	67.3	53.0	110.2	114.4	74.8	28.1	4.8	0.2
1987	65.8	50.6	107.9	111.6	72.1	26.3	4.4	0.2
1986	65.4	50.2	107.4	109.8	70.1	24.4	4.1	0.2
1985	66.3	51.0	108.3	111.0	69.1	24.0	4.0	0.2
1984	65.5	50.6	106.8	108.7	67.0	22.9	3.9	0.2
1983	65.7	51.4	107.8	108.5	64.9	22.0	3.9	0.2
1982	67.3	52.4	111.6	111.0	64.1	21.2	3.9	0.2
1981	67.3	52.2	112.2	111.5	61.4	20.0	3.8	0.2
1980	68.4	53.0	115.1	112.9	61.9	19.8	3.9	0.2
1975	66.0	55.6	113.0	108.2	52.3	19.5	4.6	0.3
1970	87.9	68.3	167.8	145.1	73.3	31.7	8.1	0.5
1965	96.3	70.5	195.3	161.6	94.4	46.2	12.8	0.8
1960	118.0	89.1	258.1	197.4	112.7	56.2	15.5	0.9
1955	118.3	90.5	242.0	190.5	116.2	58.7	16.1	1.0
1950	106.2	81.6	196.6	166.1	103.7	52.9	15.1	1.2

Percent change

	total	15 to 19	20 to 24	25 to 29	30 to 34	35 to 39	40 to 44	45 to 49
2000 to 2005	1.2%	−15.3%	−6.8%	1.9%	5.2%	16.6%	13.8%	20.0%
1950 to 2005	−37.2	−50.5	−48.0	−30.4	−7.5	−12.5	−39.7	−50.0

Source: National Center for Health Statistics, Births: Preliminary Data for 2005, Health E-Stats, and Births: Final Data for 2004, National Vital Statistics Reports, Vol. 55, No. 1, 2006, Internet site http://www.cdc.gov/nchs/births.htm; and Bureau of the Census, Historical Statistics of the United States: Colonial Times to 1970, Part 1, 1975; calculations by New Strategist

Hispanics Now Account for One in Four Births

A half-century ago, Hispanic births were not separately recorded in the statistics.

In 1950, the National Center for Health Statistics collected birth data for only two racial groups—blacks and whites. In that year, 86 percent of newborns were white and 14 percent were black. Times have changed. In 2005, the white share of births had fallen to 78 percent. That figure can hardly be compared to the 86 percent of 1950, however, because today (unlike 1950) it includes millions of Hispanics who may be of any race. The figure better capturing the growing diversity of the nation's newborns is the 55 percent who are born to non-Hispanic whites. Twenty-four percent of babies today are born to Hispanics, 15 percent to blacks, 6 percent to Asians, and 1 percent to American Indians.

Among babies born to Hispanics in 2004, fully 72 percent were born to Mexican Americans. The fertility rate (the number of births per 1,000 women aged 15 to 44) is higher for Mexican Americans than for any other racial or ethnic group in the U.S., at 106.8 births per 1,000 Mexican-American women aged 15 to 44 in 2004. In contrast, non-Hispanic whites have the lowest birth rate, just 58.4 births per 1,000 women aged 15 to 44. The Asian and black rates, at 66.6 and 68.9, respectively, are closer to the non-Hispanic white rate than to the 99.1 rate for all Hispanics in 2005.

The birth rate has dropped steeply for blacks since 1950. The Hispanic rate, with historical data going back only as far as 1989, bottomed out in 1999 and has increased since then. The Asian rate is also higher today than in the late 1990s.

■ The higher birth rate of Hispanics guarantees their growing power and influence in the United States.

A shrinking share of births are to non-Hispanic whites

(percent distribution of births by race and Hispanic origin, 1990 and 2005)

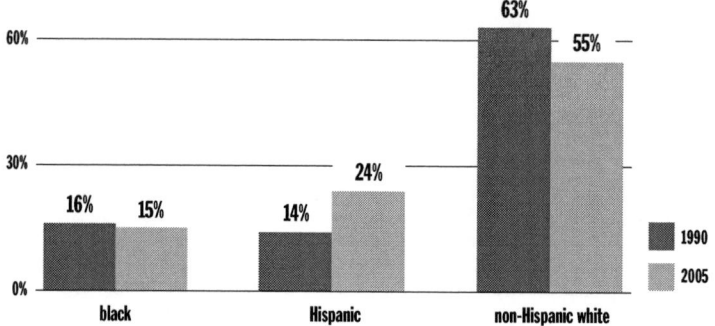

Table 3.8 Births by Race and Hispanic Origin, 1950 to 2005

(number of births by race and Hispanic origin, 1950 to 2005; percent change for selected years; numbers in thousands)

	total	American Indian	Asian	black	Hispanic	white total	white non-Hispanic
2005	4,140	45	231	633	983	3,232	2,285
2004	4,112	44	229	616	946	3,223	2,297
2003	4,090	43	221	600	912	3,226	2,322
2002	4,022	42	211	594	877	3,175	2,298
2001	4,026	42	200	606	852	3,178	2,327
2000	4,059	42	201	623	816	3,194	2,363
1999	3,959	40	181	606	764	3,133	2,346
1998	3,942	40	173	610	735	3,119	2,361
1997	3,881	39	170	600	710	3,073	2,333
1996	3,892	38	166	595	701	3,093	2,359
1995	3,900	37	160	603	680	3,099	2,383
1994	3,953	38	158	636	665	3,121	2,439
1993	4,000	39	153	659	654	3,150	2,472
1992	4,065	40	150	674	643	3,202	2,527
1991	4,111	39	145	683	623	3,241	2,590
1990	4,158	39	142	684	595	3,290	2,627
1989	4,041	39	133	673	532	3,192	2,526
1988	3,910	37	129	639	450	3,102	–
1987	3,809	35	117	611	406	3,044	–
1986	3,757	34	108	593	–	3,019	–
1985	3,761	34	105	581	373	3,038	–
1984	3,669	33	99	568	–	2,967	–
1983	3,639	33	96	563	–	2,946	–
1982	3,681	32	93	569	–	2,985	–
1981	3,629	30	85	565	–	2,948	–
1980	3,612	29	74	568	–	2,936	–
1975	3,168	28	–	512	–	2,552	–
1970	3,731	26	–	572	–	3,091	–
1965	3,760	24	–	581	–	3,124	–
1960	4,258	21	–	602	–	3,601	–
1955	4,097	–	–	613	–	3,485	–
1950	3,632	–	–	524	–	3,108	–
Percent change							
2000 to 2005	2.0%	7.1%	14.9%	1.6%	20.5%	1.2%	–3.3%
1950 to 2005	14.0	–	–	20.8	–	4.0	–

Note: Race of child before 1980, race of mother 1980 and after; blacks in 1950 and 1955 include black and other races; numbers will not add to total because Hispanics may be of any race; "–" means data are not available or not applicable.
Source: National Center for Health Statistics, Births: Preliminary Data for 2005, Health E-Stats; and Births: Final Data for 2004, National Vital Statistics Reports, Vol. 55, No. 1, 2006, Internet site http://www.cdc.gov/nchs/births.htm; and Bureau of the Census, Statistical Abstract of the United States 1990 and 1991; calculations by New Strategist

Table 3.9 Percent Distribution of Births by Race and Hispanic Origin, 1950 to 2005

(percent distribution of births by race and Hispanic origin, 1950 to 2005; percentage point change for selected years)

	total	American Indian	Asian	black	Hispanic	white total	white non-Hispanic
2005	100.0%	1.1%	5.6%	15.3%	23.7%	78.1%	55.2%
2004	100.0	1.1	5.6	15.0	23.0	78.4	55.9
2003	100.0	1.1	5.4	14.7	22.3	78.9	56.8
2002	100.0	1.0	5.2	14.8	21.8	78.9	57.1
2001	100.0	1.0	5.0	15.1	21.2	78.9	57.8
2000	100.0	1.0	5.0	15.3	20.1	78.7	58.2
1999	100.0	1.0	4.6	15.3	19.3	79.1	59.3
1998	100.0	1.0	4.4	15.5	18.6	79.1	59.9
1997	100.0	1.0	4.4	15.5	18.3	79.2	60.1
1996	100.0	1.0	4.3	15.3	18.0	79.5	60.6
1995	100.0	0.9	4.1	15.5	17.4	79.5	61.1
1994	100.0	1.0	4.0	16.1	16.8	79.0	61.7
1993	100.0	1.0	3.8	16.5	16.4	78.8	61.8
1992	100.0	1.0	3.7	16.6	15.8	78.8	62.2
1991	100.0	0.9	3.5	16.6	15.2	78.8	63.0
1990	100.0	0.9	3.4	16.5	14.3	79.1	63.2
1989	100.0	1.0	3.3	16.7	13.2	79.0	62.5
1988	100.0	0.9	3.3	16.3	11.5	79.3	–
1987	100.0	0.9	3.1	16.0	10.7	79.9	–
1986	100.0	0.9	2.9	15.8	–	80.4	–
1985	100.0	0.9	2.8	15.4	9.9	80.8	–
1984	100.0	0.9	2.7	15.5	–	80.9	–
1983	100.0	0.9	2.6	15.5	–	81.0	–
1982	100.0	0.9	2.5	15.5	–	81.1	–
1981	100.0	0.8	2.3	15.6	–	81.2	–
1980	100.0	0.8	2.0	15.7	–	81.3	–
1975	100.0	0.9	–	16.2	–	80.6	–
1970	100.0	0.7	–	15.3	–	82.8	–
1965	100.0	0.6	–	15.5	–	83.1	–
1960	100.0	0.5	–	14.1	–	84.6	–
1955	100.0	–	–	15.0	–	85.1	–
1950	100.0	–	–	14.4	–	85.6	–
Percentage point change							
2000 to 2005	–	0.1	0.6	–0.1	3.6	–0.6	–3.0
1950 to 2005	–	–	–	0.9	–	–7.5	–

Note: Race of child before 1980, race of mother 1980 and after; blacks in 1950 and 1955 include black and other races; numbers will not add to total because Hispanics may be of any race; "–" means data are not available or not applicable.
Source: National Center for Health Statistics, Births: Preliminary Data for 2005, Health E-Stats; and Births: Final Data for 2004, National Vital Statistics Reports, Vol. 55, No. 1, 2006, Internet site http://www.cdc.gov/nchs/births.htm; and Bureau of the Census, Statistical Abstract of the United States 1990 and 1991; calculations by New Strategist

Table 3.10 Births to Hispanics by Hispanic Origin, 1989 to 2004

(number of births to Hispanics by Hispanic origin, 1989 to 2004; percent change for selected years; numbers in thousands)

	total Hispanic	Mexican	Puerto Rican	Cuban	Central and South American
2004	946	678	61	15	144
2003	912	655	58	15	136
2002	877	628	58	14	126
2001	852	611	58	14	121
2000	816	582	58	13	113
1999	764	541	57	13	103
1998	735	516	57	13	98
1997	710	499	55	13	97
1996	701	490	55	13	98
1995	680	470	55	12	95
1994	665	455	57	12	93
1993	654	444	58	12	92
1992	643	432	60	11	89
1991	623	411	60	11	87
1990	595	386	59	11	83
1989	532	327	56	11	72
Percent change					
2000 to 2004	15.9%	16.5%	5.2%	15.4%	27.4%
1989 to 2004	77.8	107.3	8.9	36.4	100.0

Note: Numbers will not add to total because "other and unknown Hispanic origin" is not shown.
Source: National Center for Health Statistics, Births: Final Data for 2004, National Vital Statistics Reports, Vol. 55, No. 1, 2006, Internet site http://www.cdc.gov/nchs/births.htm; calculations by New Strategist

Table 3.11 Percent Distributon of Births to Hispanics by Hispanic Origin, 1989 to 2004

(percent distribution of births to Hispanics by Hispanic origin, 1989 to 2004; percentage point change for selected years)

	total Hispanic	Mexican	Puerto Rican	Cuban	Central and South American
2004	100.0%	71.7%	6.4%	1.6%	15.2%
2003	100.0	71.8	6.4	1.6	14.9
2002	100.0	71.6	6.6	1.6	14.4
2001	100.0	71.7	6.8	1.6	14.2
2000	100.0	71.3	7.1	1.6	13.8
1999	100.0	70.8	7.5	1.7	13.5
1998	100.0	70.2	7.8	1.8	13.3
1997	100.0	70.3	7.7	1.8	13.7
1996	100.0	69.9	7.8	1.9	14.0
1995	100.0	69.1	8.1	1.8	14.0
1994	100.0	68.4	8.6	1.8	14.0
1993	100.0	67.9	8.9	1.8	14.1
1992	100.0	67.2	9.3	1.7	13.8
1991	100.0	66.0	9.6	1.8	14.0
1990	100.0	64.9	9.9	1.8	13.9
1989	100.0	61.5	10.5	2.1	13.5
Percentage point change					
2000 to 2004	–	0.3	–0.7	0.0	1.4
1989 to 2004	–	10.2	–4.1	–0.5	1.7

*Note: Numbers will not add to total because "**other and unknown Hispanic origin**" is not shown. "–" means not applicable.*
Source: National Center for Health Statistics, Births: Final Data for 2004, National Vital Statistics Reports, Vol. 55, No. 1, 2006, Internet site http://www.cdc.gov/nchs/births.htm; calculations by New Strategist

Table 3.12 Birth Rate by Race and Hispanic Origin, 1950 to 2005

(number of live births per 1,000 women aged 15 to 44 by race and Hispanic origin, 1950 to 2005; percent change for selected years)

	total	American Indian	Asian	black	Hispanic	white	
						total	non-Hispanic
2005	66.7	58.9	66.6	68.9	99.1	66.4	58.4
2004	66.3	58.9	67.1	67.6	97.8	66.1	58.4
2003	66.1	58.4	66.3	66.3	96.9	66.1	58.5
2002	64.8	58.0	64.1	65.8	94.4	64.8	57.4
2001	65.3	58.1	64.2	67.6	96.0	65.0	57.7
2000	65.9	58.7	65.8	70.0	95.9	65.3	58.5
1999	64.4	59.0	60.9	68.5	93.0	64.0	57.7
1998	64.3	61.3	60.1	69.4	93.2	63.6	57.6
1997	63.6	60.8	61.3	69.0	94.2	62.8	56.8
1996	64.1	61.8	62.3	69.2	97.5	63.3	57.1
1995	64.6	63.0	62.6	71.0	98.8	63.6	57.5
1994	65.9	65.8	63.9	75.9	100.7	64.2	58.2
1993	67.0	69.7	64.3	79.6	103.3	64.9	58.9
1992	68.4	73.1	66.1	82.4	106.1	66.1	60.0
1991	69.3	73.9	67.1	84.8	106.9	66.7	60.9
1990	70.9	76.2	69.6	86.8	107.7	68.3	62.8
1989	69.2	79.0	68.2	86.2	104.9	66.4	60.5
1988	67.3	76.8	70.2	82.6	–	64.5	–
1987	65.8	75.6	67.1	80.1	–	63.3	–
1986	65.4	75.9	66.0	78.9	–	63.1	–
1985	66.3	78.6	68.4	78.8	–	64.1	–
1984	65.5	79.8	69.2	78.2	–	63.2	–
1983	65.7	81.8	71.7	78.7	–	63.4	–
1982	67.3	83.6	74.8	80.9	–	64.8	–
1981	67.3	79.6	73.7	82.0	–	64.8	–
1980	68.4	82.7	73.2	84.7	–	65.6	–
1975	66.0	–	–	87.9	–	62.5	–
1970	87.9	–	–	115.4	–	84.1	–
1965	96.3	–	–	133.2	–	91.3	–
1960	118.0	–	–	153.5	–	113.2	–
1955	118.3	–	–	155.3	–	113.7	–
1950	106.2	–	–	137.3	–	102.3	–
Percent change							
2000 to 2005	1.2%	0.3%	1.2%	–1.6%	3.3%	1.7%	–0.2%
1950 to 2005	–37.2	–	–	–49.8	–	–35.1	–

Note: Race of child before 1980, race of mother 1980 and after; blacks in 1950 and 1955 include black and other races; "–" means data are not available or not applicable.
Source: National Center for Health Statistics, Births: Preliminary Data for 2005, Health E-Stats; and Births: Final Data for 2004, National Vital Statistics Reports, Vol. 55, No. 1, 2006, Internet site http://www.cdc.gov/nchs/births.htm; and Bureau of the Census, Historical Statistics of the United States: Colonial Times to 1970, Part 1, 1975; calculations by New Strategist

Table 3.13 Birth Rate of Hispanics by Hispanic Origin, 1989 to 2004

(number of live births per 1,000 Hispanic women aged 15 to 44 by Hispanic origin, 1989 to 2004; percent change for selected years)

	total Hispanic	Mexican	Puerto Rican	Cuban	Central and South American
2004	97.8	106.8	68.4	53.2	89.3
2003	96.9	105.5	61.6	61.7	91.2
2002	94.4	102.8	65.4	59.0	86.1
2001	96.0	105.7	72.2	56.7	82.7
2000	95.9	105.1	73.5	49.3	85.1
1999	93.0	101.5	71.1	47.0	84.8
1998	93.2	103.2	69.7	46.5	83.5
1997	94.2	106.6	65.8	53.1	80.6
1996	97.5	110.7	66.5	55.1	84.2
1995	98.8	109.9	71.3	52.2	89.1
1994	100.7	109.9	78.2	53.6	93.2
1993	103.3	110.9	79.8	53.9	101.5
1992	106.1	113.3	87.9	49.4	104.7
1991	106.9	114.9	87.9	47.6	105.5
1990	107.7	118.9	82.9	52.6	102.7
1989	104.9	106.6	86.6	49.8	95.8
Percent change					
2000 to 2004	2.0%	1.6%	−6.9%	7.9%	4.9%
1989 to 2004	−6.8	0.2	−21.0	6.8	−6.8

Source: National Center for Health Statistics, Births: Final Data for 2004, National Vital Statistics Reports, Vol. 55, No. 1, 2006, Internet site http://www.cdc.gov/nchs/births.htm; calculations by New Strategist

Out-of-Wedlock Births Have Surged

More than two-thirds of black births are to single mothers.

More than one-third of births in 2005 were to unmarried women. The out-of-wedlock share of births has climbed steadily for decades, rising from just 4 percent in 1950 to the 37 percent of 2005.

Out-of-wedlock childbearing has increased in every racial and ethnic group over the decades. The biggest increase has been among blacks. Nearly 70 percent of black babies were born to single mothers in 2005, up from just 17 percent in 1950. Among non-Hispanic whites, the proportion of babies born out of wedlock climbed from 10 to 25 percent between 1980 and 2005. Nearly half (48 percent) of Hispanic births are out-of-wedlock, up from 24 percent in 1980. Among Asians, only 16 percent of births are to single mothers, but the figure is more than double the 7 percent of 1980.

■ Millions of children are being raised by single mothers, suggesting that the out-of-wedlock share of births will continue to rise.

More than one-third of births today are to single mothers

(percent of babies born to unmarried women, 1950 to 2005)

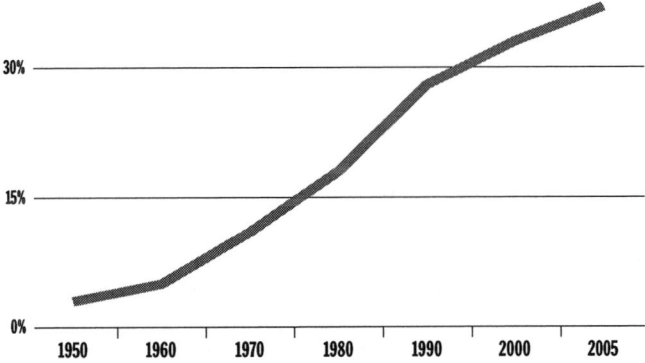

Table 3.14 Births to Unmarried Women, 1950 to 2005

(total number of births, number to unmarried women, and unmarried share of total, 1950 to 2005; percent and percentage point change for selected years; numbers in thousands)

		births to unmarried women	
	total births	number	share of total
2005	4,140	1,525	36.8%
2004	4,112	1,470	35.7
2003	4,090	1,416	34.6
2002	4,022	1,366	34.0
2001	4,026	1,349	33.5
2000	4,059	1,347	33.2
1999	3,959	1,305	33.0
1998	3,942	1,294	32.8
1997	3,881	1,257	32.4
1996	3,891	1,260	32.4
1995	3,900	1,254	32.2
1994	3,953	1,290	32.6
1993	4,000	1,240	31.0
1992	4,065	1,225	30.1
1991	4,111	1,214	29.5
1990	4,158	1,165	28.0
1989	4,041	1,094	27.1
1988	3,910	1,005	25.7
1987	3,809	933	24.5
1986	3,757	878	23.4
1985	3,761	828	22.0
1984	3,669	770	21.0
1983	3,639	738	20.3
1982	3,681	715	19.4
1981	3,629	687	18.9
1980	3,612	666	18.4
1979	3,494	598	17.1
1978	3,333	544	16.3
1977	3,327	516	15.5
1976	3,168	468	14.8
1975	3,144	448	14.2
1974	3,160	418	13.2
1973	3,137	407	13.0
1972	3,258	403	12.4
1971	3,556	401	11.3
1970	3,731	399	10.7
1969	3,600	361	10.0
1968	3,502	339	9.7
1967	3,521	318	9.0
1966	3,606	302	8.4

(continued)

	total births	births to unmarried women	
		number	share of total
1965	3,760	291	7.7%
1964	4,027	276	6.9
1963	4,098	259	6.3
1962	4,167	245	5.9
1961	4,268	240	5.6
1960	4,258	224	5.3
1959	4,245	221	5.2
1958	4,255	209	4.9
1957	4,308	202	4.7
1956	4,218	194	4.6
1955	4,097	183	4.5
1950	3,632	142	3.9

	percent change		percentage point change
2000 to 2005	2.0%	13.2%	3.7
1950 to 2005	14.0	973.9	32.9

Source: National Center for Health Statistics, Births: Final Data for 2000 through 2004; and Births, Preliminary Data for 2005; and Nonmarital Childbearing in the United States, 1940–99, Internet site http://www.cdc.gov/nchs/births.htm, calculations by New Strategist

Table 3.15 Births to Unmarried Women by Race and Hispanic Origin, 1950 to 2005

(births to unmarried women as a percent of total births by race and Hispanic origin, 1950 to 2005)

	total	American Indian	Asian	black	Hispanic	non-Hispanic white
2005	36.8%	63.3%	16.2%	69.5%	47.9%	25.4%
2004	35.7	62.3	15.5	68.8	46.4	24.5
2003	34.6	61.3	15.0	68.2	45.0	23.6
2002	34.0	59.7	14.9	68.2	43.5	23.0
2001	33.5	–	–	68.4	42.5	22.5
2000	33.2	58.4	14.8	68.5	42.7	22.1
1999	33.0	58.9	15.4	68.9	42.2	22.1
1998	32.8	59.3	15.6	69.1	41.6	21.9
1997	32.4	58.7	15.6	69.2	40.9	21.5
1996	32.4	58.0	16.7	69.8	40.7	21.5
1995	32.2	57.2	16.3	69.9	40.8	21.2
1994	32.6	57.0	16.2	70.4	43.1	20.8
1993	31.0	55.8	15.7	68.7	40.0	19.5
1992	30.1	55.3	14.7	68.1	39.1	18.5
1991	29.5	55.0	13.9	67.9	38.5	18.0
1990	28.0	53.6	13.2	66.5	36.7	16.9
1985	22.0	40.7	9.5	61.2	29.5	12.4
1980	18.4	39.2	7.3	56.1	23.6	9.6
1975	14.3	32.7	–	49.5	–	–
1970	10.7	22.4	–	37.6	–	–
1965	7.7	–	–	26.3	–	–
1960	5.3	–	–	21.6	–	–
1955	4.5	–	–	19.4	–	–
1950	4.0	–	–	16.8	–	–
Percentage point change						
2000 to 2005	3.6	4.9	1.4	1.0	5.2	3.3
1950 to 2005	32.8	–	–	52.7	–	–

Note: Births to unmarried blacks before 1970 are to black and "other" races; "–" means data not available.
Source: National Center for Health Statistics, Births: Final Data for 2000 through 2004; and Births: Preliminary Data for 2005; and Nonmarital Childbearing in the United States, 1940–99, Internet site http://www.cdc.gov/nchs/births.htm, calculations by New Strategist

Most Americans Are Overweight

The ranks of the obese are growing.

In 1960–62 the average man weighed 166 pounds. During the 40 years since then he has gained an additional 25 pounds and now weighs 191. Women gained almost as much as men, with their average weight rising from 140 to 164 pounds between 1960–62 and 1999–2002.

Because of this substantial weight gain, the percentage of Americans whose weight is defined as healthy (body mass index between 18.5 and 24.9) has dropped sharply. Among men, the percentage with a healthy weight fell from 48 to 28 percent between 1960–62 and 2001–04. Among women, the percentage with a healthy weight fell from 54 to 36 percent.

As the ranks of those with a healthy weight have declined, the percentage of Americans who are overweight (body mass index of 25 or higher) has ballooned. Between 1960–62 and 2001–04, the percentage of men classified as overweight climbed from 50 to 71 percent. Among women the figure rose from 40 to 61 percent. Even more alarming is the increase in obesity (body mass index of 30 or higher). Among men, the obesity rate rose from 11 to 30 percent during those years. Among women it increased from 16 to 34 percent.

■ The growing number of overweight Americans will mean more people with serious health problems.

Fewer men and women have a healthy weight

(percent of people aged 20 to 74 with a healthy weight, by sex, 1960–62 and 2001–04)

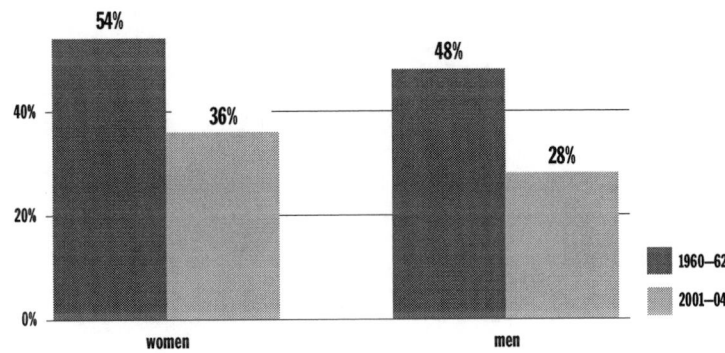

Table 3.16 Average Measured Weight by Sex and Age, 1960–62 to 1999–2002

(average weight in pounds of people aged 20 to 74, by sex and age, 1960–62 to 1999–2002; change in pounds 1960–62 to 1999–2002)

	weight in pounds					change in pounds 1960–62 to 1999–2002
	1999–2002	1988–94	1976–80	1971–74	1960–62	
Men aged 20 to 74	**191.0**	**182.4**	**173.8**	**173.4**	**166.3**	**24.7**
Aged 20 to 29	183.4	172.5	167.9	169.6	163.9	19.5
Aged 30 to 39	189.1	182.3	175.5	178.1	169.9	19.2
Aged 40 to 49	196.0	187.3	179.7	177.6	169.1	26.9
Aged 50 to 59	195.4	189.2	176.0	173.2	167.7	27.7
Aged 60 to 74	191.5	180.8	167.5	165.4	158.9	32.6
Women aged 20 to 74	**164.3**	**154.1**	**145.4**	**144.2**	**140.2**	**24.1**
Aged 20 to 29	156.5	141.7	135.7	133.9	127.7	28.8
Aged 30 to 39	163.0	154.4	145.5	144.4	138.8	24.2
Aged 40 to 49	168.2	157.5	148.8	148.7	142.8	25.4
Aged 50 to 59	169.2	163.4	150.4	148.2	146.5	22.7
Aged 60 to 74	164.7	154.2	146.9	146.3	147.3	17.4

Note: Data are based on measured weight of a sample of the civilian noninstitutionalized population.
Source: National Center for Health Statistics, Mean Body Weight, Height, and Body Mass Index, United States 1960–2002, Advance Data, No. 347, 2004, Internet site http://www.cdc.gov/nchs/pressroom/04news/americans.htm; calculations by New Strategist

Table 3.17 Adults Measured as Having a Healthy Weight by Sex and Age, 1960–62 to 2001–04

(percent of people aged 20 to 74 who have a healthy weight by sex and age, 1960–62 to 2001–04; percentage point change, 1960–62 to 2001–04)

	percent with healthy weight					percentage point change 1960–62 to 2001–04
	2001–04	1988–94	1976–80	1971–74	1960–62	
Men aged 20 to 74	**28.1%**	**37.9%**	**45.4%**	**43.0%**	**48.3%**	**–17.3**
Aged 20 to 34	38.3	51.1	57.1	54.7	55.3	–18.8
Aged 35 to 44	26.5	33.4	41.3	35.2	45.2	–14.8
Aged 45 to 54	21.2	33.6	38.7	38.5	44.8	–17.5
Aged 55 to 64	22.2	28.6	38.7	38.3	44.9	–16.5
Aged 65 to 74	23.1	30.1	42.3	42.1	46.2	–19.2
Women aged 20 to 74	**36.2**	**45.3**	**53.7**	**54.3**	**54.1**	**–17.5**
Aged 20 to 34	44.2	57.9	65.0	65.8	67.6	–20.8
Aged 35 to 44	38.3	47.1	55.6	56.7	58.4	–17.3
Aged 45 to 54	31.0	37.2	48.7	49.3	47.6	–17.7
Aged 55 to 64	29.2	31.5	43.5	41.1	38.1	–14.3
Aged 65 to 74	27.0	37.0	37.8	40.6	36.4	–10.8

Note: Healthy weight is defined as a body mass index between 18.5 and 24.9. Body mass index is calculated by dividing weight in kilograms by height in meters squared. Data are based on measured height and weight of a representative sample of the civilian noninstitutionalized population.
Source: National Center for Health Statistics, Health, United States, 2006, Internet site http://www.cdc.gov/nchs/hus.htm; calculations by New Strategist

Table 3.18 Adults Measured as Overweight by Sex and Age, 1960–62 to 2001–04

(percent of people aged 20 to 74 who are overweight by sex and age, 1960–62 to 2001–04; percentage point change, 1960–62 to 2001–04)

	percent overweight					percentage point change 1960–62 to 2001–04
	2001–04	1988–94	1976–80	1971–74	1960–62	
Men aged 20 to 74	**70.7%**	**61.0%**	**52.9%**	**54.7%**	**49.5%**	**21.2**
Aged 20 to 34	59.0	47.5	41.2	42.8	42.7	16.3
Aged 35 to 44	72.9	65.5	57.2	63.2	53.5	19.4
Aged 45 to 54	78.5	66.1	60.2	59.7	53.9	24.6
Aged 55 to 64	77.3	70.5	60.2	58.5	52.2	25.1
Aged 65 to 74	76.1	68.5	54.2	54.6	47.8	28.3
Women aged 20 to 74	**61.4**	**51.2**	**42.0**	**41.1**	**40.2**	**21.2**
Aged 20 to 34	51.6	37.0	27.9	25.8	21.2	30.4
Aged 35 to 44	60.1	49.6	40.7	40.5	37.2	22.9
Aged 45 to 54	67.4	60.3	48.7	49.0	49.3	18.1
Aged 55 to 64	69.9	66.3	53.7	54.5	59.9	10.0
Aged 65 to 74	71.5	60.3	59.5	55.9	60.9	10.6

Note: Overweight is defined as a body mass index of 25 or higher. Body mass index is calculated by dividing weight in kilograms by height in meters squared. Data are based on measured height and weight of a representative sample of the civilian noninstitutionalized population.
Source: National Center for Health Statistics, Health, United States, 2006, Internet site http://www.cdc.gov/nchs/hus.htm; calculations by New Strategist

Table 3.19 Adults Measured as Obese by Sex and Age, 1960–62 to 2001–04

(percent of people aged 20 to 74 who are obese by sex and age, 1960–62 to 2001–04; percentage point change, 1960–62 to 2001–04)

	percent who are obese					percentage point change 1960–62 to 2001–04
	2001–04	1988–94	1976–80	1971–74	1960–62	
Men aged 20 to 74	**30.2%**	**20.6%**	**12.8%**	**12.2%**	**10.7%**	**19.5**
Aged 20 to 34	23.2	14.1	8.9	9.7	9.2	14.0
Aged 35 to 44	33.8	21.5	13.5	13.5	12.1	21.7
Aged 45 to 54	31.8	23.2	16.7	13.7	12.5	19.3
Aged 55 to 64	36.0	27.2	14.1	14.1	9.2	26.8
Aged 65 to 74	32.1	24.1	13.2	10.9	10.4	21.7
Women aged 20 to 74	**34.0**	**26.0**	**17.1**	**16.8**	**15.7**	**18.3**
Aged 20 to 34	28.6	18.5	11.0	9.7	7.2	21.4
Aged 35 to 44	33.3	25.5	17.8	17.7	14.7	18.6
Aged 45 to 54	38.0	32.4	19.6	18.9	20.3	17.7
Aged 55 to 64	39.0	33.7	22.9	24.1	24.4	14.6
Aged 65 to 74	37.9	26.9	21.5	22.0	23.2	14.7

Note: Obesity is defined as a body mass index of 30 or higher. Body mass index is calculated by dividing weight in kilograms by height in meters squared. Data are based on measured height and weight of a representative sample of the civilian noninstitutionalized population.
Source: National Center for Health Statistics, Health, United States, 2006, Internet site http://www.cdc.gov/nchs/hus.htm; calculations by New Strategist

Cigarette Smoking Has Fallen Sharply

The percentage of people who smoke has been cut in half over the past forty years.

In the mid-1960s, most men smoked cigarettes. In 1965, when cigarette advertising was in full swing and before the adverse effects of smoking were well known, fully 52 percent of men aged 18 or older were smokers. Among men aged 25 to 34, the figure was an even higher 61 percent. By 2004, only 23 percent of men aged 18 or older smoked cigarettes. Among women, the percentage who smoke fell from 34 percent in 1965 to 19 percent in 2004. The decline in smoking has even influenced teenagers. In 2006, only 47 percent of high school seniors had ever smoked cigarettes, down from 74 percent in 1975.

Drug use among high school seniors was lower in 2006 than in 1975, according to the University of Michigan's Monitoring the Future survey. The percentage of high school seniors who have used any illicit drug in their lifetime fell from 55 to 48 percent during those years. The percentage of those who have ever used marijuana fell from 47 to 42 percent. In 2006, alcohol was the substance most widely used by high school seniors, with 73 percent having drunk alcohol in their lifetime. This figure was down from 90 percent in 1975, however.

■ Although Americans are much less likely to smoke cigarettes than in the past, a substantial 21 percent still smoke.

Cigarette smoking has fallen among men and women

(percent of people aged 18 or older who smoke cigarettes, by sex, 1965 and 2004)

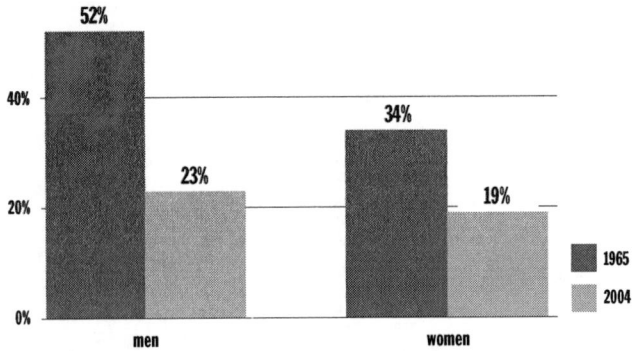

Table 3.20 Cigarette Smoking by Men, 1965 to 2004

(percent of men aged 18 or older who smoke cigarettes by age, 1965 to 2004; percentage point change for selected years)

	total, both sexes	men					
		total	18–24	25–34	35–44	45–64	65 or older
2004	20.9%	23.4%	25.6%	26.1%	26.5%	25.0%	9.8%
2003	21.6	24.1	26.3	28.7	28.1	23.9	10.1
2002	22.4	25.1	32.1	27.2	29.7	24.5	10.1
2001	22.7	25.1	30.2	26.9	27.3	26.4	11.5
2000	23.2	25.6	28.1	28.9	30.2	26.4	10.2
1999	23.5	25.7	29.5	29.1	30.0	25.8	10.5
1998	24.1	26.4	31.3	28.5	30.2	27.7	10.4
1997	24.7	27.6	31.7	30.3	32.1	27.6	12.8
1995	24.7	27.0	27.8	29.5	31.5	27.1	14.9
1994	25.5	28.2	29.8	31.4	33.2	28.3	13.2
1993	25.0	27.7	28.8	30.2	32.0	29.2	13.5
1992	26.5	28.6	28.0	32.8	32.9	28.6	16.1
1991	25.6	28.1	23.5	32.8	33.1	29.3	15.1
1990	25.5	28.4	26.6	31.6	34.5	29.3	14.6
1988	28.1	30.8	25.5	36.2	36.5	31.3	18.0
1987	28.8	31.2	28.2	34.8	36.6	33.5	17.2
1985	30.1	32.6	28.0	38.2	37.6	33.4	19.6
1983	32.1	35.1	32.9	38.8	41.0	35.9	22.0
1979	33.5	37.5	35.0	43.9	41.8	39.3	20.9
1974	37.1	43.1	42.1	50.5	51.0	42.6	24.8
1965	42.4	51.9	54.1	60.7	58.2	51.9	28.5
Percentage point change							
2000 to 2004	–2.3	–2.2	–2.5	–2.8	–3.7	–1.4	–0.4
1965 to 2004	–21.5	–28.5	–28.5	–34.6	–31.7	–26.9	–18.7

Source: National Center for Health Statistics, Health, United States, 2006, Internet site http://www.cdc.gov/nchs/hus.htm; calculations by New Strategist

Table 3.21 Cigarette Smoking by Women, 1965 to 2004

(percent of women aged 18 or older who smoke cigarettes by age, 1965 to 2004; percentage point change for selected years)

	total, both sexes	women					
		total	18–24	25–34	35–44	45–64	65 or older
2004	20.9%	18.5%	21.5%	21.0%	21.6%	19.8%	8.1%
2003	21.6	19.2	21.5	21.3	24.2	20.2	8.3
2002	22.4	19.8	24.5	21.3	23.7	21.1	8.6
2001	22.7	20.6	23.2	22.7	25.7	21.4	9.1
2000	23.2	20.9	24.9	22.3	26.2	21.7	9.3
1999	23.5	21.5	26.3	23.5	26.5	21.0	10.7
1998	24.1	22.0	24.5	24.6	26.4	22.5	11.2
1997	24.7	22.1	25.7	24.8	27.2	21.5	11.5
1995	24.7	22.6	21.8	26.4	27.1	24.0	11.5
1994	25.5	23.1	25.2	28.8	26.8	22.8	11.1
1993	25.0	22.5	22.9	27.3	27.4	23.0	10.5
1992	26.5	24.6	24.9	30.1	27.3	26.1	12.4
1991	25.6	23.5	22.4	28.4	27.6	24.6	12.0
1990	25.5	22.8	22.5	28.2	24.8	24.8	11.5
1988	28.1	25.7	26.3	31.3	27.8	27.7	12.8
1987	28.8	26.5	26.1	31.8	29.6	28.6	13.7
1985	30.1	27.9	30.4	32.0	31.5	29.9	13.5
1983	32.1	29.5	35.5	32.6	33.8	31.0	13.1
1979	33.5	29.9	33.8	33.7	37.0	30.7	13.2
1974	37.1	32.1	34.1	38.8	39.8	33.4	12.0
1965	42.4	33.9	38.1	43.7	43.7	32.0	9.6
Percentage point change							
2000 to 2004	−2.3	−2.4	−3.4	−1.3	−4.6	−1.9	−1.2
1965 to 2004	−21.5	−15.4	−16.6	−22.7	−22.1	−12.2	−1.5

Source: National Center for Health Statistics, Health, United States, 2006, Internet site http://www.cdc.gov/nchs/hus.htm; calculations by New Strategist

Table 3.22 Lifetime Drug Use by 12th Graders, 1975 to 2006

(percent of 12th graders who have ever used drugs, drunk alcohol, or smoked cigarettes, by type of substance, 1975 to 2006; percentage point change for selected years)

	any illicit drug	any illicit drug except marijuana	marijuana/ hashish	inhalants	halluci- nogens	cocaine	amphet- amines	sedatives	tranquilizers	alcohol	cigarettes
2006	48.2%	26.9%	42.3%	11.1%	8.3%	8.5%	12.4%	10.2%	10.3%	72.7%	47.1%
2005	50.4	27.4	44.8	11.4	8.8	8.0	13.1	10.5	9.9	75.1	50.0
2004	51.1	28.7	45.7	10.9	9.7	8.1	15.0	9.9	10.6	76.8	52.8
2003	51.1	27.7	46.1	11.2	10.6	7.7	14.4	8.8	10.2	76.6	63.7
2002	53.0	29.5	47.8	11.7	12.0	7.8	16.8	9.5	11.4	78.4	57.2
2001	53.9	30.7	49.0	13.0	14.7	8.2	16.2	8.7	10.3	79.7	61.0
2000	54.0	29.0	48.8	14.2	13.0	8.6	15.6	9.2	8.9	80.3	62.5
1999	54.7	29.4	49.7	15.4	13.7	9.8	16.3	8.9	9.3	80.0	64.6
1998	54.1	29.4	49.1	15.2	14.1	9.3	16.4	8.7	8.5	81.4	65.3
1997	54.3	30.0	49.6	16.1	15.1	8.7	16.5	8.1	7.8	81.7	65.4
1996	50.8	28.5	44.9	16.6	14.0	7.1	15.3	7.6	7.2	79.2	63.5
1995	48.4	28.1	41.7	17.4	12.7	6.0	15.3	7.4	7.1	80.7	64.2
1994	45.6	27.6	38.2	17.7	11.4	5.9	15.7	7.0	6.6	80.4	62.0
1993	42.9	26.7	35.3	17.4	10.9	6.1	15.1	6.3	6.4	80.0	61.9
1992	40.7	25.1	32.6	16.6	9.2	6.1	13.9	5.5	6.0	87.5	61.8
1991	44.1	26.9	36.7	17.6	9.6	7.8	15.4	6.2	7.2	88.0	63.1
1990	47.9	29.4	40.7	18.0	9.4	9.4	17.5	6.8	7.2	89.5	64.4
1989	50.9	31.4	43.7	17.6	9.4	10.3	19.1	6.5	7.6	90.7	65.7
1988	53.9	32.5	47.2	16.7	8.9	12.1	19.8	6.7	9.4	92.0	66.4
1987	56.6	35.8	50.2	17.0	10.3	15.2	21.6	7.4	10.9	92.2	67.2
1986	57.6	37.7	50.9	15.9	9.7	16.9	23.4	8.4	10.9	91.3	67.6
1985	60.6	39.7	54.2	15.4	10.3	17.3	26.2	9.2	11.9	92.2	68.8
1984	61.6	40.3	54.9	14.4	10.7	16.1	27.9	9.9	12.4	92.6	69.7
1983	62.9	40.4	57.0	13.6	11.9	16.2	26.9	9.9	13.3	92.6	70.6
1982	64.4	41.1	58.7	12.8	12.5	16.0	27.9	10.3	14.0	92.8	70.1
1981	65.6	42.8	59.5	12.3	13.3	16.5	32.2	11.3	14.7	92.6	71.0
1980	65.4	38.7	60.3	11.9	13.3	15.7	26.4	11.0	15.2	93.2	71.0
1979	65.1	37.4	60.4	12.7	14.1	15.4	24.2	11.8	16.3	93.0	74.0
1978	64.1	36.5	59.2	12.0	14.3	12.9	22.9	13.7	17.0	93.1	75.3
1977	61.6	35.8	56.4	11.1	13.9	10.8	23.0	15.6	18.0	92.5	75.7
1976	58.3	35.4	52.8	10.3	15.1	9.7	22.6	16.2	16.8	91.9	75.4
1975	55.2	36.2	47.3	–	16.3	9.0	22.3	16.9	17.0	90.4	73.6
Percentage point change											
2000 to 2006	−5.8	−2.1	−6.5	−3.1	−4.7	−0.1	−3.2	1.0	1.4	−7.6	−15.4
1975 to 2006	−7.0	−9.3	−5.0	–	−8.0	−0.5	−9.9	−6.7	−6.7	−17.7	−26.5

Note: "–" means data are not available.
Source: University of Michigan, Monitoring the Future, Internet site http://monitoringthefuture.org/data/06data
.html#2006data-drugs; calculations by New Strategist

Hypertension and High Cholesterol Are Less of a Problem

Diabetes is increasingly prevalent, however.

There has been considerable progress in alleviating many health conditions in the past few decades. Hypertension declined substantially between 1960–62 and 1999–2000. Overall, the percentage of adults with hypertension fell from 38 to 29 percent during those years.

The prevalence of high cholesterol has also been falling as Americans have become aware of the problem and changed their lifestyles accordingly. In 1960–62, one-third of adults had high cholesterol. By 2001–04 the rate had been cut in half, to just 16.5 percent.

The trend is different with diabetes. Ten percent of adults had diabetes in 2001–04, up from 8 percent in 1988–94, making it one of the nation's more important health problems.

The use of prescription drugs to treat a variety of illnesses, particularly chronic conditions, increased greatly between 1988–94 and 1999–2002. The percentage of people aged 18 or older who took at least one prescription drug in the past month rose from 38 to 45 percent during those years. The percentage of Americans who take three or more drugs climbed from 11 to 18 percent.

■ With more Americans controlling their high blood pressure, the rate of heart disease could decline in the future.

Hypertension is lower in both men and women

(percent of people aged 20 to 74 with hypertension, by sex, 1960–62 and 1999–2000)

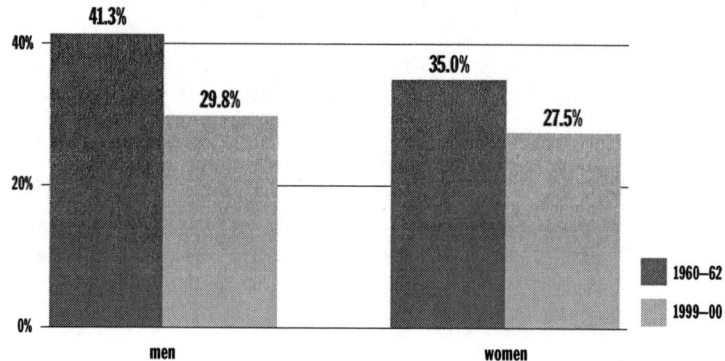

Table 3.23 Hypertension by Sex and Age, 1960–62 to 1999–2000

(percent of people aged 20 to 74 with hypertension by sex and age, 1960–62 to 1999–2000; and percentage point change, 1960–62 to 1999–00)

	1999–00	1988–94	1976–80	1971–74	1960–62	percentage point change 1960–62 to 1999–00
TOTAL AGED 20 TO 74	**28.7%**	**23.9%**	**70.4%**	**39.8%**	**38.1%**	**–9.4**
Men aged 20 to 74	**29.8**	**26.4**	**45.2**	**43.9**	**41.3**	**–11.5**
Aged 20 to 34	11.8	8.6	28.9	24.8	22.8	–11.0
Aged 35 to 44	19.2	20.8	40.5	39.1	37.7	–18.5
Aged 45 to 54	36.9	34.0	53.6	55.0	47.6	–10.7
Aged 55 to 64	50.7	42.9	61.8	62.5	60.3	–9.6
Aged 65 to 74	68.3	57.3	67.1	67.2	68.8	–0.5
Women aged 20 to 74	**27.5**	**21.4**	**35.8**	**35.8**	**35.0**	**–7.5**
Aged 20 to 34	3.1	3.3	11.1	11.2	9.3	–
Aged 35 to 44	18.6	12.6	28.8	28.2	24.0	–5.4
Aged 45 to 54	33.4	25.1	47.1	43.6	43.4	–10.0
Aged 55 to 64	57.9	44.1	61.1	62.5	66.4	–8.5
Aged 65 to 74	73.4	60.6	71.8	78.3	81.5	–8.1

Note: Hypertension is defined as a systolic pressure of at least 140 mmHg or a diastolic pressure of at least 90 mmHg; in addition, anyone who takes antihypertensive medication is considered to have hypertension. "–" means sample is too small to make a reliable estimate.
Source: National Center for Health Statistics, Health, United States, 2003, Internet site http://www.cdc.gov/nchs/hus.htm; calculations by New Strategist

Table 3.24 High Cholesterol by Sex and Age, 1960–62 to 2001–04

(percent of people aged 20 to 74 with high serum cholesterol by sex and age, 1960–62 to 2001–04; and percentage point change, 1960–62 to 2001–04)

	2001–04	1988–94	1976–80	1971–74	1960–62	percentage point change 1960–62 to 2001–04
TOTAL AGED 20 TO 74	16.5%	19.7%	27.8%	28.6%	33.3%	–16.8
Men aged 20 to 74	16.6	18.8	26.4	27.9	30.6	–14.0
Aged 20 to 34	9.0	8.2	11.9	12.4	15.1	–6.1
Aged 35 to 44	21.2	19.4	27.9	31.8	33.9	–12.7
Aged 45 to 54	23.1	26.6	36.9	37.5	39.2	–16.1
Aged 55 to 64	19.9	28.0	36.8	36.2	41.6	–21.7
Aged 65 to 74	11.0	21.9	31.7	34.7	38.0	–27.0
Women aged 20 to 74	16.2	20.5	28.8	29.1	35.6	–19.4
Aged 20 to 34	9.3	7.3	9.8	10.9	12.4	–3.1
Aged 35 to 44	11.4	12.3	20.7	19.3	23.1	–11.7
Aged 45 to 54	20.0	26.7	40.5	38.7	46.9	–26.9
Aged 55 to 64	27.6	40.9	52.9	53.1	70.1	–42.5
Aged 65 to 74	26.3	41.3	51.6	57.7	68.5	–42.2

Note: High cholesterol is defined as 240 mg/dL or more.
Source: National Center for Health Statistics, Health, United States, 2003 and 2006, Internet site http://www.cdc.gov/nchs/hus.htm; calculations by New Strategist

Table 3.25 Diabetes by Selected Characteristics, 1988–94 and 2001–04

(percent of people aged 20 or older with diabetes, by sex, race, Hispanic origin, and age, 1988–94 and 2001–04, and percentage point change 1988–94 to 2001–04)

	2001–04	1988–94	percentage point change
Total people	10.0%	7.8%	2.2
Female	8.9	7.8	1.1
Male	11.2	7.9	3.3
Black, non-Hispanic	12.7	10.4	2.3
White, non-Hispanic	9.4	7.5	1.9
Hispanic, Mexican	9.2	9.0	0.2
Aged 20 to 39	2.3	1.6	0.7
Aged 40 to 59	11.0	8.9	2.1
Aged 60 or older	22.5	18.9	3.6

Note: People with diabetes include those diagnosed by a physician and those who have not been diagnosed but who have a fasting blood glucose of at least 126 mg/dL.
Source: National Center for Health Statistics, Health, United States 2006, Internet site http://www.cdc.gov/nchs/hus.htm; calculations by New Strategist

Table 3.26 Prescription Drug Use by Sex and Age, 1988–94 and 1999–2002

(percent of people aged 18 or older taking at least one or three or more prescription drugs in the past month, by sex and age, 1988–94 and 1999–02; percentage point change, 1988–94 to 1999–2002)

	at least one			three or more		
	1999–02	1988–94	percentage point change	1999–02	1988–94	percentage point change
Total people	**45.1%**	**37.8%**	**7.3**	**17.6%**	**11.0%**	**6.6**
Under age 18	24.2	20.5	3.7	4.1	2.4	1.7
Aged 18 to 44	35.9	31.3	4.6	8.4	5.7	2.7
Aged 45 to 64	64.1	54.8	9.3	30.8	20.0	10.8
Aged 65 or older	84.7	73.6	11.1	51.6	35.3	16.3
Female	**51.2**	**44.6**	**6.6**	**21.1**	**13.6**	**7.5**
Under age 18	22.0	20.6	1.4	3.9	2.3	1.6
Aged 18 to 44	44.6	40.7	3.9	10.2	7.6	2.6
Aged 45 to 64	72.0	62.0	10.0	37.4	24.7	12.7
Aged 65 or older	88.1	78.3	9.8	55.7	38.2	17.5
Male	**38.7**	**30.6**	**8.1**	**13.9**	**8.3**	**5.6**
Under age 18	26.2	20.4	5.8	4.3	2.6	1.7
Aged 18 to 44	27.1	21.5	5.6	6.7	3.6	3.1
Aged 45 to 64	55.6	47.2	8.4	23.5	15.1	8.4
Aged 65 or older	80.1	67.2	12.9	46.0	31.3	14.7

Source: National Center for Health Statistics, Health, United States 2006, Internet site http://www.cdc.gov/nchs/hus.htm; calculations by New Strategist

Employment-Based Health Insurance Coverage Is Declining

Only 60 percent of Americans were covered by employer-provided health insurance in 2006.

The percentage of the population with health insurance has remained fairly stable since 1987. Overall, 84 percent of Americans have health insurance, a figure that is down slightly from 87 percent two decades ago. Nearly 47 million people (16 percent) do not have health insurance. Although the percentage without insurance has not increased much, the number without insurance has grown by more than 15 million in the past two decades.

The U.S. population is more likely to be covered by government health insurance today than in the past. In 2006, 27 percent of Americans were covered by Medicare (the government's health insurance program for people aged 65 or older), Medicaid (the government's health insurance program for the poor), or military health insurance. The percentage of the population covered by employer-provided health insurance fell from 62 percent in 1987 to just below 60 percent in 2006. The percentage buying health insurance directly—which can be costly—fell from 12 percent in 1994 (the earliest data available) to just 9 percent in 2006.

■ Many people with employer-provided health insurance are covered under a family member's plan.

Employer-provided health insurance is less common

(percent of people covered by employer-provided health insurance, 1987 and 2006)

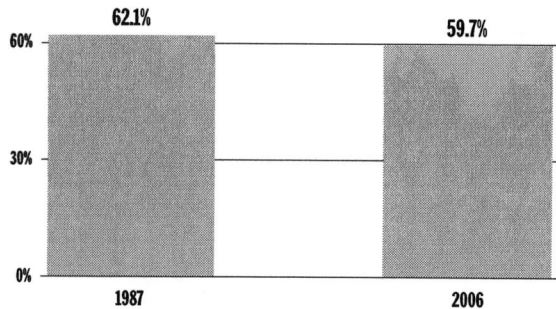

Table 3.27 Health Insurance Coverage, 1987 to 2006

(total number of people, and number and percent covered by health insurance, 1987 to 2006; numbers in thousands)

	total people	with health insurance		without health insurance	
		number	percent	number	percent
2006	296,824	249,829	84.2%	46,995	15.8%
2005	293,834	249,020	84.7	44,815	15.3
2004	291,166	247,669	85.1	43,498	14.9
2003	288,280	244,876	84.9	43,404	15.1
2002	285,933	243,914	85.3	42,019	14.7
2001	282,082	242,322	85.9	39,760	14.1
2000	279,517	241,091	86.3	38,426	13.7
1999	276,804	238,037	86.0	38,767	14.0
1998	271,743	228,800	84.2	42,943	15.8
1997	269,094	226,735	84.3	42,359	15.7
1996	266,792	225,699	84.6	41,093	15.4
1995	264,314	223,733	84.6	40,582	15.4
1994	262,105	222,387	84.8	39,718	15.2
1993	259,753	220,040	84.7	39,713	15.3
1992	256,830	218,189	85.0	38,641	15.0
1991	251,447	216,003	85.9	35,445	14.1
1990	248,886	214,167	86.1	34,719	13.9
1989	246,191	212,807	86.4	33,385	13.6
1988	243,685	211,005	86.6	32,680	13.4
1987	241,187	210,161	87.1	31,026	12.9

Source: Bureau of the Census, Historical Health Insurance Tables, http://www.census.gov/hhes/www/hlthins/historic/index.html

Table 3.28 Health Insurance Coverage by Type, 1987 to 2006

(number and percent distribution of people by health insurance coverge status, 1987 to 2006; numbers in thousands)

| | | covered by private or government health insurance | | | | | | | | not covered |
| | total people | private health insurance | | | government health insurance | | | | | |
		total	total	employment based	direct purchase	total	Medicaid	Medicare	military	
2006	296,824	249,829	201,690	177,152	27,066	80,270	38,281	40,343	10,547	46,995
2005	293,834	249,020	201,167	176,924	27,055	80,213	38,104	40,177	11,166	44,815
2004	291,166	245,860	198,658	174,186	27,193	79,392	37,963	39,708	10,660	45,306
2003	288,280	243,320	197,869	174,020	26,486	76,755	35,647	39,456	9,979	44,961
2002	285,933	242,360	198,973	175,296	26,639	73,624	33,246	38,448	10,063	43,574
2001	282,082	240,875	199,860	176,551	26,057	71,295	31,601	38,043	9,552	41,207
2000	279,517	239,714	201,060	177,848	26,524	69,037	29,533	37,740	9,099	39,804
1999	276,804	236,576	198,841	175,101	27,415	67,683	28,506	36,923	8,648	40,228
1998	271,743	227,462	190,861	168,576	25,948	66,087	27,854	35,887	8,747	44,281
1997	269,094	225,646	188,532	165,091	27,158	66,685	28,956	35,590	8,527	43,448
1996	266,792	225,077	187,395	163,221	28,335	69,000	31,451	35,227	8,712	41,716
1995	264,314	223,733	185,881	161,453	30,188	69,776	31,877	34,655	9,375	40,582
1994	262,105	222,387	184,318	159,634	31,349	70,163	31,645	33,901	11,165	39,718
1993	259,753	220,040	182,351	148,318	–	68,554	31,749	33,097	9,560	39,713
1992	256,830	218,189	181,466	148,796	–	66,244	29,416	33,230	9,510	38,641
1991	251,447	216,003	181,375	150,077	–	63,882	26,880	32,907	9,820	35,445
1990	248,886	214,167	182,135	150,215	–	60,965	24,261	32,260	9,922	34,719
1989	246,191	212,807	183,610	151,644	–	57,382	21,185	31,495	9,870	33,385
1988	243,685	211,005	182,019	150,940	–	56,850	20,728	30,925	10,105	32,680
1987	241,187	210,161	182,160	149,739	–	56,282	20,211	30,458	10,542	31,026

Percent distribution

2006	100.0%	84.2%	67.9%	59.7%	9.1%	27.0%	12.9%	13.6%	3.6%	15.8%
2005	100.0	84.7	68.5	60.2	9.2	27.3	13.0	13.7	3.8	15.3
2004	100.0	84.4	68.2	59.8	9.3	27.3	13.0	13.6	3.7	15.6
2003	100.0	84.4	68.6	60.4	9.2	26.6	12.4	13.7	3.5	15.6
2002	100.0	84.8	69.6	61.3	9.3	25.7	11.6	13.4	3.5	15.2
2001	100.0	85.4	70.9	62.6	9.2	25.3	11.2	13.5	3.4	14.6
2000	100.0	85.8	71.9	63.6	9.5	24.7	10.6	13.5	3.3	14.2
1999	100.0	85.5	71.8	63.3	9.9	24.5	10.3	13.3	3.1	14.5
1998	100.0	83.7	70.2	62.0	9.5	24.3	10.3	13.2	3.2	16.3
1997	100.0	83.9	70.1	61.4	10.1	24.8	10.8	13.2	3.2	16.1
1996	100.0	84.4	70.2	61.2	10.6	25.9	11.8	13.2	3.3	15.6
1995	100.0	84.6	70.3	61.1	11.4	26.4	12.1	13.1	3.5	15.4
1994	100.0	84.8	70.3	60.9	12.0	26.8	12.1	12.9	4.3	15.2
1993	100.0	84.7	70.2	57.1	–	26.4	12.2	12.7	3.7	15.3
1992	100.0	85.0	70.7	57.9	–	25.8	11.5	12.9	3.7	15.0
1991	100.0	85.9	72.1	59.7	–	25.4	10.7	13.1	3.9	14.1
1990	100.0	86.1	73.2	60.4	–	24.5	9.7	13.0	4.0	13.9
1989	100.0	86.4	74.6	61.6	–	23.3	8.6	12.8	4.0	13.6
1988	100.0	86.6	74.7	61.9	–	23.3	8.5	12.7	4.1	13.4
1987	100.0	87.1	75.5	62.1	–	23.3	8.4	12.6	4.4	12.9

Note: "–" means data are not available.
Source: Bureau of the Census, Historical Health Insurance Tables, Current Population Survey, Internet site http://www.census.gov/hhes/www/hlthins/historic/index.html

Hospital Outpatient Care Has Grown Rapidly

Most surgeries are now performed on outpatients.

As health care costs mount and health insurers limit medical care reimbursements, hospitals have shifted their services toward less expensive outpatient care. The number of people admitted to hospitals grew only 16 percent between 1970 and 2004, much more slowly than outpatient care. The number of outpatient visits more than doubled during those years, rising 265 percent. Hospitals cared for 662 million outpatients in 2004, up from 181 million in 1970.

Even surgery has become an outpatient service. Outpatient surgery accounted for 63 percent of all surgeries in 2004, up from just 16 percent in 1980. The length of a hospital stay reflects these trends. In 2004, the average length of a hospital stay was just 4.8 days, down from 7.3 days in 1980. Length of stay declined for almost every health condition. The length of stay following a heart attack fell from 12.6 to 5.8 days between 1980 and 2004. For childbirth, length of stay fell from 3.8 to 2.6 days.

■ The shift from inpatient to outpatient care and shorter hospital stays have not adversely affected patient health as evidenced by the continuing decline of the nation's mortality rate.

Hospital outpatients greatly outnumber inpatients and the gap is growing

(number of hospital outpatients and inpatients, 1970 and 2004; numbers in thousands)

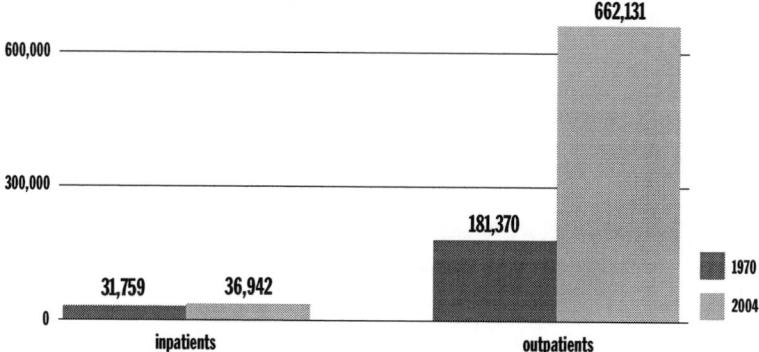

Table 3.29 Hospital Admissions, Outpatient Visits, and Outpatient Surgery, 1970 to 2004

(number of admissions to hospitals, number of outpatient visits to hospitals, and outpatient surgery as a percent of total surgery in community hospitals, 1970 to 2004; percent change in admissions and outpatient visits, and percentage point change in outpatient surgery for selected years; numbers in thousands)

	hospital admissions	outpatient visits	outpatient surgery as a percent of total surgery
2004	36,942	662,131	63.3%
2003	36,611	648,560	63.3
2002	36,326	640,515	63.4
2001	35,644	612,276	63.0
2000	34,891	592,673	62.7
1999	34,181	573,461	62.4
1998	33,766	545,481	61.6
1997	33,624	520,600	60.7
1996	33,307	505,455	59.5
1995	33,282	483,195	58.1
1994	33,125	453,584	57.2
1993	33,201	435,619	55.4
1992	33,536	417,874	53.8
1991	33,567	387,675	52.3
1990	33,774	368,184	50.6
1989	33,742	352,200	48.7
1988	34,107	336,200	46.8
1987	34,439	310,700	43.4
1986	35,219	294,600	40.3
1985	36,304	282,140	34.6
1984	37,938	276,566	27.8
1983	38,887	273,168	23.8
1982	39,095	313,667	20.8
1981	39,169	265,332	18.5
1980	38,892	262,951	16.3
1979	37,802	262,009	–
1978	37,243	263,606	–
1977	37,060	263,775	–
1976	36,776	270,951	–
1975	36,157	254,844	–
1974	35,506	250,481	–
1973	34,352	233,555	–
1972	33,265	219,182	–
1971	32,664	199,725	–
1970	31,759	181,370	–

	percent change		percentage point change
2000 to 2004	5.9%	11.7%	0.6
1970 to 2004	16.3	265.1	–

Note: Community hospitals include all short-term care, nonfederal hospitals; "–" means data are not available.
Source: Hospital Statistics 2006 edition, Health Forum LLC, An American Hospital Association Company, 2005

Table 3.30 Length of Hospital Stay by Diagnosis, 1980 and 2004

(average length of stay in days for discharges from short-stay hospitals by first-listed diagnosis, 1980 and 2004, change in days, 1980–2004; excludes newborn infants)

	number of days		change,
	2004	1980	1980–04
Total conditions	**4.8**	**7.3**	**–2.5**
Infectious and parasitic diseases	6.6	6.9	–0.3
Septicemia	8.4	14.3	–5.9
Neoplasms	5.7	10.5	–4.8
Malignant neoplasms	6.6	11.9	–5.3
Malignant neoplasm of large intestine and rectum	8.6	15.7	–7.1
Malignant neoplasm of trachea, bronchus, and lung	6.9	12.8	–5.9
Benign neoplasms	3.2	6.2	–3.7
Benign neoplasm of uterus	2.5	–	–
Endocrine, nutritional, and metabolic diseases, and immunity disorders	4.0	9.6	–5.6
Diabetes mellitus	4.7	10.5	–5.8
Volume depletion	3.3	8.9	–5.6
Diseases of the blood and blood forming organs	4.7	7.2	–2.5
Anemias	4.9	–	–
Mental disorders	7.1	11.6	–4.5
Psychoses	7.9	14.8	–6.9
Schizophrenic disorders	10.8	–	–
Major depressive disorder	6.8	–	–
Diseases of the nervous system and sense organs	5.3	5.4	–0.1
Diseases of the circulatory system	4.7	10.0	–5.3
Essential hypertension	2.3	–	–
Heart disease	4.6	9.5	–4.9
Acute myocardial infarction	5.8	12.6	–6.8
Coronary atherosclerosis	3.5	10.0	–6.5
Other ischemic heart disease	2.7	7.7	–5.0
Cardiac dysrhythmias	3.7	7.6	–3.9
Congestive heart failure	5.4	10.4	–5.0
Cerebrovascular disease	5.2	12.4	–7.2
Diseases of the respiratory system	5.2	6.3	–1.1
Acute bronchitis and bronchiolitis	3.3	4.7	–1.4
Pneumonia	5.5	8.3	–2.8
Chronic bronchitis	5.0	–	–
Asthma	3.2	6.0	–2.8
Diseases of the digestive system	4.7	7.0	–2.3
Appendicitis	3.1	5.5	–2.4
Noninfectious enteritis and colitis	4.7	5.6	–0.9
Intestinal obstruction	6.2	–	–
Diverticula of intestine	5.0	–	–
Cholelithiasis	4.0	9.3	–5.3
Acute pancreatitis	5.7	–	–

(continued)

	number of days		change,
	2004	1980	1980–2004
Diseases of the genitourinary system	3.8	5.6	−1.8
Calculus of kidney and ureter	2.4	5.0	−2.6
Urinary tract infection	4.9	–	–
Complications of pregnancy, childbirth, and the puerperium	2.7	2.5	0.2
Diseases of the skin and subcutaneous tissue	5.1	8.0	−2.9
Cellulitis and abscess	4.8	8.0	−3.2
Diseases of the musculoskeletal system and connective tissue	3.9	8.3	−4.4
Osteoarthrosis and allied disorders	3.9	–	–
Intervertebral disc disorders	2.8	9.9	−7.1
Congenital anomalies	6.8	6.6	0.2
Certain conditions originating in the perinatal period	10.7	8.7	2.0
Symptoms, signs, and ill-defined conditions	2.7	4.5	−1.8
Injury and poisoning	5.5	7.7	−2.2
Fractures, all sites	5.6	10.8	−5.2
Fracture of neck of femur	6.4	20.6	−14.2
Poisonings	3.1	–	–
Certain complications of surgical and medical care	6.2	–	–
Supplementary classifications	3.7	3.7	2.5
Females with deliveries	2.6	3.8	−1.2

Note: "–" means data are not available.
Source: National Center for Health Statistics, Trends in Hospital Utilization: United States, 1988–92, Vital and Health Statistics, Series 13, No. 124, 1996, Internet site http://www.cdc.gov/nchs/products/pubs/pubd/series/sr13/130-121/sr13_124.htm, and 2004 National Hospital Discharge Survey, Advance Data, No. 371, 2006, Internet site http://www.cdc.gov/nchs/about/major/hdasd/ listpubs.htm; calculations by New Strategist

The Heart Disease Death Rate Is Falling

The rate has declined in almost every age group.

The death rate from heart disease has been dropping for decades. The decline in recent years—since 1999—has been substantial, despite the aging of the population. Behind the falling death rate are improved drug and medical treatments, which allow people to better manage heart disease. Between 1999 and 2004, the heart disease death rate fell 19 percent.

Every demographic segment has experienced a decline in the death rate from heart disease. The decline in the heart disease death rate between 1999 and 2004 ranges from 16 percent for black males to 26 percent for Asian males. In 2004, the heart disease death rate was highest for black males at 342.1 deaths per 100,000 population. It was lowest for Asian females at 96.1 deaths per 100,000 population.

■ Because heart disease is the leading cause of death in the United States, the substantial decline in the death rate due to heart disease suggests continued gains in life expectancy.

The heart disease death rate fell 19 percent between 1999 and 2004

(number of deaths due to heart disease per 100,000 population, 1999 and 2004)

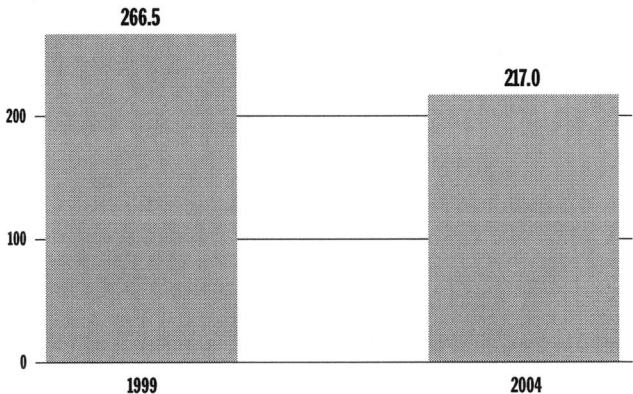

Table 3.31 Death Rate from Heart Disease by Age, 1999 to 2004

(number of deaths due to heart disease per 100,000 population by age, 1999 to 2004; percent change, 1999–2004)

	2004	2003	2002	2001	2000	1999	percent change, 1999–04
Total, age adjusted	**217.0**	**232.3**	**240.8**	**247.8**	**257.6**	**266.5**	**–18.6%**
Under age 1	10.3	11.0	12.4	11.9	13.0	13.8	–25.4
Aged 1 to 4	1.2	1.2	1.1	1.5	1.2	1.2	0.0
Aged 5 to 14	0.6	0.6	0.6	0.7	0.7	0.7	–14.3
Aged 15 to 24	2.5	2.7	2.5	2.5	2.6	2.8	–10.7
Aged 25 to 34	7.9	8.2	7.9	8.0	7.4	7.6	3.9
Aged 35 to 44	29.3	30.7	30.5	29.6	29.2	30.2	–3.0
Aged 45 to 54	90.2	92.5	93.7	92.9	94.2	95.7	–5.7
Aged 55 to 64	218.8	233.2	241.5	246.9	261.2	269.9	–18.9
Aged 65 to 74	541.6	585.0	615.9	635.1	665.6	701.7	–22.8
Aged 75 to 84	1,506.3	1,611.1	1,677.2	1,725.7	1,780.3	1,849.9	–18.6
Aged 85 or older	4,895.9	5,278.4	5,446.8	5,664.2	5,926.1	6,063.0	–19.2

Note: Age adjusted to the 2000 standard population. Age-adjusted rates are computed by applying age-specific rates to a standard age distribution. In this case, the rates for 1999 through 2004 were applied to the age distribution of the population in 2000. This is done to allow for the comparison of rates over time, absent the effect of the aging of the population.
Source: National Center for Health Statistics, Health, United States, 2006 (updated tables), Internet site http://www.cdc.gov/nchs/hus.htm; calculations by New Strategist

Table 3.32 Death Rate from Heart Disease by Sex, Race, and Hispanic Origin, 1999 to 2004

(number of age-adjusted deaths due to heart disease per 100,000 population by sex, race, and Hispanic origin, 1999 to 2004; percent change, 1999–2004)

	2004	2003	2002	2001	2000	1999	percent change, 1999–04
Total, age adjusted	**217.0**	**232.3**	**240.8**	**247.8**	**257.6**	**266.5**	**–18.6%**
Total males	**267.9**	**286.6**	**297.4**	**305.4**	**320.0**	**331.0**	**–19.1**
Asians	146.5	158.3	169.8	169.8	185.5	198.9	–26.3
Blacks	342.1	364.3	371.0	384.5	392.5	407.2	–16.0
Hispanics	193.9	206.8	219.8	232.6	238.2	249.2	–22.2
Non-Hispanic whites	268.7	286.9	297.7	304.8	319.9	330.0	–18.6
Total females	**177.3**	**190.3**	**197.2**	**203.9**	**210.9**	**218.1**	**–18.7**
Asians	96.1	104.2	108.1	112.9	115.7	124.2	–22.6
Blacks	236.5	253.8	263.2	269.8	277.6	283.7	–16.6
Hispanics	130.0	145.8	149.7	161.0	163.7	172.3	–24.6
Non-Hispanic whites	175.1	187.1	193.7	200.0	206.8	213.9	–18.1

Note: Age adjusted to the 2000 standard population. Age-adjusted rates are computed by applying age-specific rates to a standard age distribution. In this case, the rates for 1999 through 2004 were applied to the age distribution of the population in 2000. This is done to allow for the comparison of rates over time, absent the effect of the aging of the population.
Source: National Center for Health Statistics, Health, United States, 2006 (updated tables), Internet site http://www.cdc.gov/nchs/hus.htm; calculations by New Strategist

Increasingly, Cancer Is a Treatable Condition

The incidence of some types of cancer is declining and survival has become more likely.

The number of new cases of cancer being diagnosed per 100,000 population is falling, according to data collected by the National Center for Health Statistics. The overall cancer incidence rate fell 4 percent among females between 1990 and 2003 (the latest data available). It was down an even larger 10 percent among males. The only types of cancer with increasing incidence among females are lung cancer and non-Hodgkin's lymphoma. Among males, only non-Hodgkin's lymphoma saw an increase. For females, the biggest decline was in the incidence of cervical cancer. For males, the biggest decline was for lung cancer.

Cancer survival rates are increasing for most types of cancer thanks to early detection and better treatment. Survival rates are rising for males and females, whites and blacks. Males have experienced the greatest increase in five-year survival rates. Among white males, the five-year cancer survival rate climbed from 43 to 68 percent between 1975–77 and 1996–2002. The climb was even steeper for black males, for whom the cancer survival rate rose from 33 to 60 percent. For white females, the five-year cancer survival rate stood at 67 percent in 1999–2002. It was lower for black females, at 54 percent.

■ The incidence of breast cancer fell sharply between 2001 and 2003, a decline attributed to the reduction in the use of hormone replacement therapy.

Survival rate for breast cancer is improving

(ratio of the five-year survival rate for females with breast cancer to the expected five-year survival rate for females of the same age, by race, 1975–77 and 1996–2002)

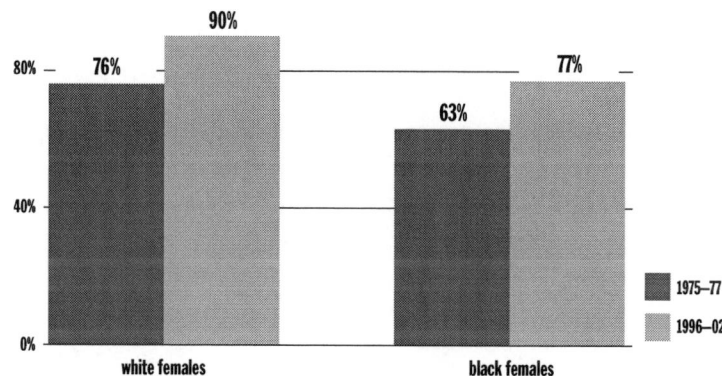

Table 3.33 Cancer Incidence Rate by Sex, 1990 to 2003

(number of new cases of cancer per 100,000 age-adjusted population by sex and selected cancer site, 1990 to 2003; percent change in rate, 1990–2003)

	2003	2002	2001	2000	1995	1990	percent change 1990–03
Female, total	**393.3**	**409.0**	**413.1**	**410.4**	**409.4**	**410.8**	**–4.3%**
Breast	121.1	130.6	134.2	133.3	130.5	129.2	–6.3
Cervix uteri	8.0	8.2	8.7	8.8	9.9	11.9	–32.8
Colon and rectum	42.4	44.5	45.0	45.8	45.8	50.2	–15.5
Corpus uteri	22.5	23.3	24.0	23.3	24.4	24.3	–7.4
Leukemia	8.8	9.2	9.8	9.8	10.0	9.8	–10.2
Lung and bronchus	48.0	48.7	48.4	48.5	49.3	47.2	1.7
Non-Hodgkin's lymphoma	16.5	16.0	15.8	15.7	15.1	14.5	13.8
Oral cavity and pharynx	5.7	6.4	6.6	6.1	7.0	7.3	–21.9
Ovary	13.0	13.5	14.0	14.0	14.5	15.5	–16.1
Pancreas	9.9	10.2	9.8	9.8	9.9	10.0	–1.0
Stomach	5.8	6.1	5.7	6.1	6.2	6.7	–13.4
Urinary bladder	8.8	9.1	9.0	9.0	9.3	9.5	–7.4
Male, total	**525.7**	**546.4**	**557.4**	**559.6**	**562.6**	**583.4**	**–9.9**
Colon and rectum	56.8	59.2	61.1	62.4	63.1	72.2	–21.3
Leukemia	15.2	15.6	16.6	16.1	17.4	17.0	–10.6
Lung and bronchus	73.0	74.7	76.5	77.4	86.8	95.0	–23.2
Non-Hodgkin's lymphoma	23.1	23.2	23.7	23.3	24.9	22.6	2.2
Oral cavity and pharynx	14.7	15.4	14.9	15.7	16.4	18.5	–20.5
Pancreas	12.1	12.6	12.7	12.8	12.7	13.0	–6.9
Prostate gland	160.4	174.3	177.2	176.6	165.6	166.6	–3.7
Stomach	11.4	11.9	11.8	12.5	13.5	14.6	–21.9
Urinary bladder	35.6	35.1	36.3	36.6	35.3	37.2	–4.3

Note: Age-adjusted incidence rates are calculated by applying age specific incidence rates in each year to a standard population with a fixed age distribution. They should be viewed as an index rather than an actual measure of cancer risk.
Source: National Center for Health Statistics, Health, United States, 2006, Internet site http://www.cdc.gov/nchs/hus.htm; calculations by New Strategist

Table 3.34 Cancer Survival Rate of Females by Race, 1975–77 to 1996–2002

(ratio of the five-year survival rate for the patient group to the expected five-year survival rate for females of that age and race, by type of cancer, 1975–77 to 1996–2002; percentage point change in rate, 1975–77 to 1996–2002)

	1996–02	1993–95	1990–92	1987–89	1984–86	1981–83	1978–80	1975–77	percentage point change 1975–77 to 1996–02
White female, total	**67.1%**	**64.4%**	**63.5%**	**62.0%**	**59.9%**	**57.5%**	**57.0%**	**57.7%**	**9.4**
Colon	64.8	61.7	63.6	60.9	59.4	56.0	54.4	52.0	12.8
Rectum	66.9	63.3	62.2	59.2	58.8	55.3	51.7	50.3	16.6
Pancreas	4.5	4.5	4.8	3.5	3.0	3.3	2.6	2.2	2.3
Lung and bronchus	18.0	17.8	16.7	15.8	16.7	17.0	16.6	16.0	2.0
Melanoma of skin	93.9	92.8	92.1	91.3	91.0	87.7	88.2	86.5	7.4
Breast	90.1	88.0	86.7	85.3	80.4	77.7	75.6	75.8	14.3
Cervix uteri	74.6	74.7	71.9	73.6	70.0	68.9	69.2	70.6	4.0
Corpus uteri	87.0	86.6	87.2	85.7	85.5	83.9	85.3	89.0	–2.0
Ovary	44.6	42.6	42.5	39.9	38.9	40.2	37.9	36.4	8.2
Non-Hodgkin's lymphoma	65.8	59.6	58.6	57.1	55.6	53.0	51.6	48.9	16.9
Black female, total	**53.9**	**51.8**	**49.2**	**48.9**	**46.3**	**45.5**	**46.6**	**47.2**	**6.7**
Colon	52.7	52.6	53.0	54.5	50.1	52.4	50.7	46.7	6.0
Rectum	59.2	57.2	49.4	58.0	48.7	43.5	34.9	47.8	11.4
Pancreas	5.8	3.8	4.0	6.1	5.3	3.2	7.4	2.0	3.8
Lung and bronchus	14.9	15.8	12.9	11.5	13.0	14.9	18.0	14.0	0.9
Melanoma of skin	75.0	–	–	90.5	–	–	–	–	–
Breast	77.3	72.9	71.6	71.2	65.1	64.0	63.9	62.5	14.8
Cervix uteri	66.3	64.3	58.6	58.4	58.4	61.6	61.7	64.8	1.5
Corpus uteri	62.2	62.3	57.1	59.3	58.4	54.4	56.3	61.8	0.4
Ovary	38.9	42.6	36.8	35.5	40.6	39.3	40.3	43.4	–4.5
Non-Hodgkin's lymphoma	60.7	54.5	47.8	53.5	51.0	51.5	57.7	56.1	4.6

Note: "–" means data are not available.
Source: National Center for Health Statistics, Health, United States, 2006, Internet site http://www.cdc.gov/nchs/hus.htm; calculations by New Strategist

Table 3.35   Cancer Survival Rate of Males by Race, 1975–77 to 1996–2002

(ratio of the five-year survival rate for the patient group to the expected five-year survival rate for males of that age and race, by type of cancer, 1975–77 to 1996–2002; percentage point change in rate, 1975–77 to 1996–2002)

	1996–02	1993–95	1990–92	1987–89	1984–86	1981–83	1978–80	1975–77	percentage point change 1975–77 to 1996–02
White male, total	**67.8%**	**63.5%**	**61.5%**	**53.3%**	**49.1%**	**47.5%**	**45.2%**	**43.2%**	**24.6**
Oral cavity and pharynx	62.0	60.8	57.2	54.3	55.0	53.8	55.1	53.9	8.1
Esophagus	16.9	14.8	12.8	11.4	9.2	6.8	5.5	5.1	11.8
Stomach	20.5	19.7	16.4	16.0	15.2	16.0	14.4	13.7	6.8
Colon	67.6	62.5	64.5	62.5	60.2	57.5	52.6	51.1	16.5
Rectum	66.0	61.6	60.6	59.8	57.2	52.3	50.6	48.3	17.7
Pancreas	5.3	4.0	4.4	3.2	2.2	2.3	2.6	2.7	2.6
Lung and bronchus	13.7	13.3	13.0	12.5	11.7	12.3	12.0	11.5	2.2
Prostate gland	99.9	98.3	95.8	85.4	77.3	75.0	73.2	69.6	30.3
Urinary bladder	84.2	85.2	84.4	83.5	79.9	80.3	77.4	75.5	8.7
Non-Hodgkin's lymphoma	62.5	51.0	48.4	49.2	51.9	52.4	48.3	47.7	14.8
Leukemia	50.5	50.5	48.0	47.4	42.6	40.0	37.6	34.8	15.7
Black male, total	**60.3**	**54.7**	**47.5**	**38.8**	**35.4**	**34.2**	**33.2**	**32.7**	**27.6**
Oral cavity and pharynx	35.1	33.4	28.6	30.4	29.7	26.3	29.8	30.2	4.9
Esophagus	10.8	8.1	9.8	5.0	7.6	3.6	3.3	1.6	9.2
Stomach	21.2	18.0	23.7	17.2	17.5	17.1	16.0	16.4	4.8
Colon	56.3	52.2	56.2	51.6	49.4	46.0	47.7	45.3	11.0
Rectum	57.9	53.7	54.2	49.0	44.0	38.2	35.0	41.6	16.3
Pancreas	3.2	3.5	3.2	5.1	4.2	4.0	4.3	2.7	0.5
Lung and bronchus	11.3	11.7	9.6	11.1	10.6	10.5	10.0	10.7	0.6
Prostate gland	98.0	93.7	85.9	72.2	66.2	63.7	62.7	61.3	36.7
Urinary bladder	68.9	70.4	67.9	68.0	63.7	65.5	64.0	56.4	12.5
Non-Hodgkin's lymphoma	52.9	35.6	38.2	42.6	44.9	49.5	48.0	41.4	11.5
Leukemia	39.4	42.0	31.3	35.0	32.3	33.7	28.3	30.4	9.0

Source: National Center for Health Statistics, Health, United States, 2006, Internet site http://www.cdc.gov/nchs/hus.htm; calculations by New Strategist

The Death Rate Is Falling

But the death rate is rising for the least-educated Americans.

As the U.S. population has grown, so has the annual number of deaths. From 1.5 million deaths per year during the 1950s, the figure climbed to 2.4 million per year by 2004. But the number of deaths is not climbing as fast as the aging population would suggest because the death rate is falling.

The death rate has dropped over the past few years for a variety of reasons. Better medical care and improved drug treatments for heart disease and cancer have lowered mortality rates for the two leading causes of death. Fewer people smoke cigarettes, lowering the death rate from smoking-related diseases. The death rate is rising for diseases associated with the very old, however. The death rate due to Alzheimer's disease climbed 32 percent between 1999 and 2004. Deaths due to Parkinson's disease were up 13 percent during those years.

One of the troubling trends in mortality statistics is the divergent direction of mortality rates by education. The death rate fell substantially between 1994 and 2003 for people aged 25 to 64 with at least some college education. But it rose substantially for high school dropouts. The death rate for high school dropouts climbed 13 percent between 1994 and 2003, while it fell 17 percent for people with at least some college education.

■ Education is having an increasingly important influence on health status, perhaps because the educated can better navigate the health care system and the complexities of drug regimens.

Death rate is rising for people without a high school diploma

(percent change in number of age-adjusted deaths per 100,000 population aged 25 to 64, by educational attainment, 1994 to 2003)

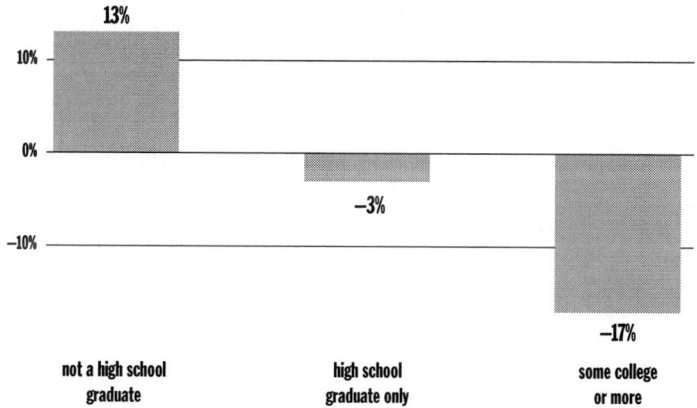

Table 3.36 Number of Deaths, 1950 to 2004

(number of deaths by year and decade, 1950 to 2004; percent change from preceding year and decade, 1950–2004; numbers in thousands)

	number	percent change from preceding year or decade		number	percent change from preceding year or decade
2004	2,398	−2.0%	1977	1,900	−0.5%
2003	2,448	0.2	1976	1,909	0.8
2002	2,443	1.1	1975	1,893	−2.1
2001	2,416	0.5	1974	1,934	−2.0
			1973	1,973	0.5
1991–2000	**22,969**	**10.5**	1972	1,964	1.1
2000	2,404	0.6	1971	1,942	1.1
1999	2,391	2.3			
1998	2,337	1.0	**1961–1970**	**18,386**	**17.0**
1997	2,314	0.0	1970	1,921	−0.1
1996	2,315	0.1	1969	1,922	−0.4
1995	2,312	1.4	1968	1,930	4.3
1994	2,279	0.4	1967	1,851	−0.6
1993	2,269	4.3	1966	1,863	1.9
1992	2,176	0.3	1965	1,828	1.7
1991	2,170	1.0	1964	1,798	−0.9
			1963	1,814	3.2
1981–1990	**20,791**	**7.5**	1962	1,757	3.2
1990	2,148	−0.1	1961	1,702	−0.6
1989	2,150	−0.8			
1988	2,168	2.1	**1951–1960**	**15,721**	–
1987	2,123	0.9	1960	1,712	3.3
1986	2,105	0.9	1959	1,657	0.5
1985	2,086	2.3	1958	1,648	0.9
1984	2,039	1.0	1957	1,633	4.4
1983	2,019	2.2	1956	1,564	2.3
1982	1,975	−0.2	1955	1,529	3.2
1981	1,978	−0.6	1954	1,481	−2.4
			1953	1,518	1.4
1971–1980	**19,347**	**5.2**	1952	1,497	1.0
1980	1,990	4.0	1951	1,482	2.1
1979	1,914	−0.7	1950	1,452	–
1978	1,928	1.5			

Note: "–" means not applicable.
Source: Bureau of the Census, Statistical Abstract of the United States: 1980; and Historical Statistics of the United States: Colonial Times to 1970, Part 1, 1975; and National Center for Health Statistics, Deaths: Final Data for 2004, National Vital Statistics Report, Vol. 55, No. 19, 2007, Internet site http://www.cdc.gov/nchs/deaths.htm; calculations by New Strategist

Table 3.37 Death Rate by Cause of Death, 1999 to 2004

(number of age-adjusted deaths per 100,000 population by selected cause of death, and percent change, 1999 to 2004)

	2004	2003	2002	2001	2000	1999	percent change 1999–04
All causes	**800.8**	**832.7**	**845.3**	**854.5**	**869.0**	**875.6**	**−8.5%**
Diseases of heart	217.0	232.3	240.8	247.8	257.6	266.5	−18.6
Malignant neoplasms	185.8	190.1	193.5	196.0	199.6	200.8	−7.5
Cerebrovascular disease	50.0	53.5	56.2	57.9	60.9	61.6	−18.8
Chronic lower respiratory diseases	41.1	43.3	43.5	43.7	44.2	45.4	−9.5
Accidents	37.7	37.3	36.9	35.7	34.9	35.3	6.8
Diabetes mellitus	24.5	25.3	25.4	25.3	25.0	25.0	−2.0
Alzheimer's disease	21.8	21.4	20.2	19.1	18.1	16.5	32.1
Influenza and pneumonia	19.8	22.0	22.6	22.0	23.7	23.5	−15.7
Nephritis, nephrotic syndrome, nephrosis	14.2	14.4	14.2	14.0	13.5	13.0	9.2
Septicemia	11.2	11.6	11.7	11.4	11.3	11.3	−0.9
Suicide	10.9	10.8	10.9	10.7	10.4	10.5	3.8
Chronic liver disease and cirrhosis	9.0	9.3	9.4	9.5	9.5	9.6	−6.3
Essential hypertension	7.7	7.4	7.0	6.8	6.5	6.2	24.2
Parkinson's disease	6.1	6.2	5.9	5.9	5.7	5.4	13.0
Homicide	5.9	6.0	6.1	7.1	5.9	6.0	−1.7

Note: Age-adjusted death rates are calculated by applying age-specific death rates in each year to the 2000 standard population. They should be viewed as an index rather than an actual measure of mortality risk. Death rates are based on the 10th Revision of the International Classification of Diseases. Earlier data are not strictly comparable.
Source: National Center for Health Statistics, Health, United States, 2006 (updated tables), Internet site http://www.cdc.gov/ nchs/hus.htm; and Deaths: Final Data for 2004, National Vital Statistics Report, Vol. 55, No. 19, 2007, Internet site http://www. cdc.gov/nchs/deaths.htm; calculations by New Strategist

Table 3.38 Death Rate by Sex and Education, 1994 to 2003

(number of age-adjusted deaths per 100,000 people aged 25 to 64 by sex and educational attainment, 1994 to 2003; percent change, 1994–2003)

	not a high school graduate	high school graduate only	some college or more
Total aged 25 to 64			
2003	669.9	490.9	211.7
2002	575.1	490.9	211.3
2001	576.6	480.9	214.6
2000	591.0	484.5	216.7
1999	585.3	474.5	219.1
1998	561.6	465.8	223.9
1997	554.1	473.4	232.7
1996	579.6	492.5	241.8
1995	604.7	512.5	251.9
1994	594.6	506.4	254.8
Percent change, 1994–03	12.7%	–3.1%	–16.9%
Men aged 25 to 64			
2003	826.8	650.9	252.5
2002	726.1	650.2	253.5
2001	745.8	631.2	257.3
2000	780.2	641.8	260.8
1999	763.7	636.7	264.2
1998	727.6	627.1	271.9
1997	719.7	634.4	283.4
1996	763.9	669.6	300.7
1995	801.1	713.2	316.8
1994	793.6	707.1	323.5
Percent change, 1994–03	4.2%	–7.9%	–21.9%
Women aged 25 to 64			
2003	496.8	349.4	171.0
2002	416.6	350.7	168.8
2001	407.1	348.6	171.5
2000	409.0	347.7	171.9
1999	409.9	337.3	172.6
1998	395.6	330.9	174.3
1997	387.2	337.5	180.2
1996	396.6	344.2	180.3
1995	408.6	348.1	183.5
1994	397.3	342.9	182.1
Percent change, 1994–03	25.0%	1.9%	–6.1%

Note: Age-adjusted to the 2000 standard population using four age groups: 25 to 34, 35 to 44, 45 to 54, and 55 to 64. Death rates are based on the 10th Revision of the International Classification of Diseases. Earlier data are not strictly comparable.
Source: National Center for Health Statistics, Health, United States, 2006 (updated tables), Internet site http://www.cdc.gov/nchs/hus.htm; calculations by New Strategist

Life Expectancy Is Growing

Life expectancy at birth is approaching 80 years.

Since 1950, life expectancy at birth has climbed by ten years, from 68 to 78. Life expectancy at age 65 has also risen from 14 years to almost 19 years. Female life expectancy continues to be considerably greater than male. At birth, females can expect to live for 80 years, males for just 75 years. Even at age 65, females have a significantly longer life expectancy than males—20 versus 17 years. What accounts for this difference? Most likely, females are biologically sturdier than males.

There is also a life expectancy gap between blacks and whites. At birth, blacks can expect to live 73 years, while white life expectancy is a longer 78 years. At age 65, the life expectancy gap between blacks and whites is much narrower. At age 65, blacks can expect to live 17 more years, while whites can expect to live an additional 19 years. Behind the life expectancy gap between blacks and whites are disparities in income and access to health care.

■ With the heart disease death rate falling rapidly, we may see significant gains in life expectancy at older ages in the years ahead.

The life expectancy of Americans has climbed ten years since 1950

(years of life remaining at birth, 1950 and 2004)

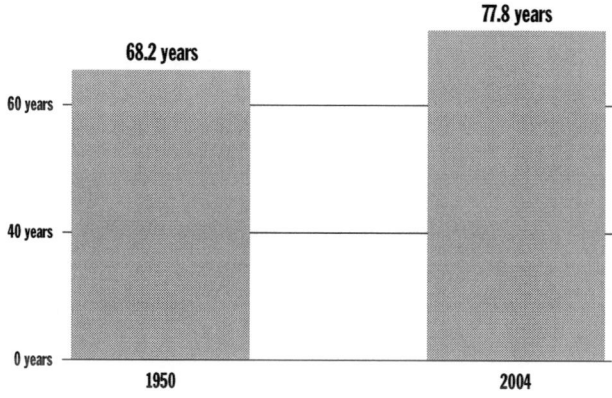

Table 3.39 Life Expectancy by Age, 1950 to 2004

(years of life remaining at birth and age 65, 1950 to 2004; change in years of life remaining for selected years)

	at birth	at age 65
2004	77.8 yrs.	18.7 yrs.
2003	77.5	18.4
2002	77.3	18.2
2001	77.2	18.1
2000	77.0	18.0
1999	76.7	17.7
1998	76.7	17.8
1997	76.5	17.7
1996	76.1	17.5
1995	75.8	17.4
1994	75.7	17.4
1993	75.5	17.3
1992	75.8	17.5
1991	75.5	17.4
1990	75.4	17.2
1980	73.7	16.4
1970	70.8	15.2
1960	69.7	14.3
1950	68.2	13.9
Change in years		
1990 to 2004	0.8	0.7
1950 to 2004	9.6	4.8

Source: National Center for Health Statistics, Health, United States, 2001 and 2006, Internet site http://www.cdc.gov/nchs/; calculations by New Strategist

Table 3.40 Life Expectancy by Sex, 1950 to 2004

(years of life remaining at birth by sex, 1950 to 2004; difference between female and male life expectancy and change in years of life remaining for selected years)

	at birth		difference at birth	at age 65		difference at age 65
	female	male		female	male	
2004	80.4 yrs.	75.2 yrs.	5.2 yrs.	20.0 yrs.	17.1 yrs.	2.9 yrs.
2003	80.1	74.8	5.3	19.8	16.8	3.0
2002	79.9	74.5	5.4	19.5	16.6	2.9
2001	79.8	74.4	5.4	19.4	16.4	3.0
2000	79.7	74.3	5.4	19.3	16.2	3.1
1999	79.4	73.9	5.5	19.1	16.1	3.0
1998	79.5	73.8	5.7	19.2	16.0	3.2
1997	79.4	73.6	5.8	19.2	15.9	3.3
1996	79.1	73.1	6.0	19.0	15.7	3.3
1995	78.9	72.5	6.4	18.9	15.6	3.3
1994	79.0	72.4	6.6	19.0	15.5	3.5
1993	78.8	72.2	6.6	18.9	15.3	3.6
1992	79.1	72.3	6.8	19.2	15.4	3.8
1991	78.9	72.0	6.9	19.1	15.3	3.8
1990	78.8	71.8	7.0	18.9	15.1	3.8
1980	77.4	70.0	7.4	18.3	14.1	4.2
1970	74.7	67.1	7.6	17.0	13.1	3.9
1960	73.1	66.6	6.5	15.8	12.8	3.0
1950	71.1	65.6	5.5	15.0	12.8	2.2
Change in years						
2000 to 2004	0.7	0.9	−0.2	0.7	0.9	−0.2
1950 to 2004	9.3	9.6	−0.3	5.0	4.3	0.7

Source: National Center for Health Statistics, Health, United States, 2001 and 2006, Internet site http://www.cdc.gov/nchs/; calculations by New Strategist

Table 3.41 Life Expectancy by Race, 1950 to 2004

(years of life remaining at birth by race, 1950 to 2004; difference between black and white life expectancy and change in years of life remaining for selected years)

	at birth		difference at birth	at age 65		difference at age 65
	black	white		black	white	
2004	73.1 yrs.	78.3 yrs.	−5.2 yrs.	17.1 yrs.	18.7 yrs.	−1.6 yrs.
2003	72.7	78.0	−5.3	17.0	18.5	−1.5
2002	72.3	77.7	−5.4	16.6	18.2	−1.6
2001	72.2	77.7	−5.5	16.4	18.2	−1.8
2000	71.9	77.6	−5.7	16.2	18.0	−1.8
1999	71.4	77.3	−5.9	16.0	17.8	−1.8
1998	71.3	77.3	−6.0	16.1	17.8	−1.7
1997	71.1	77.1	−6.0	16.1	17.8	−1.7
1996	70.2	76.8	−6.6	15.8	17.6	−1.8
1995	69.6	76.5	−6.9	15.6	17.6	−2.0
1994	69.5	76.5	−7.0	15.7	17.5	−1.8
1993	69.2	76.3	−7.1	15.5	17.4	−1.9
1992	69.6	76.5	−6.9	15.7	17.6	−1.9
1991	69.3	76.3	−7.0	15.5	17.5	−2.0
1990	69.1	76.1	−7.0	15.4	17.3	−1.9
1980	68.1	74.4	−6.3	15.1	16.5	−1.4
1970	64.1	71.7	−7.6	14.2	15.2	−1.0
1960	63.6	70.6	−7.0	13.9	14.4	−0.5
1950	60.8	69.1	−8.3	13.9	–	–
Change in years						
2000 to 2004	1.2	0.7	0.5	0.9	0.7	0.2
1950 to 2004	12.3	9.2	3.1	3.2	–	–

Note: "–" means data are not available.
Source: National Center for Health Statistics, Health, United States, 2001 and 2006, Internet site http://www.cdc.gov/nchs/; calculations by New Strategist

4

Housing

■ The proportion of American households that own their home hit an all-time high of 69.0 percent in 2004. Since then, the figure has drifted downward slightly to 68.8 percent in 2006. In 1950, just 55.0 percent of households owned their home.

■ Between 1982 and 2006, the homeownership rate increased the most for householders aged 65 or older. In contrast, the homeownership rate of householders aged 35 to 54 is lower today than in the early 1980s.

■ Fewer than half of black and Hispanic households own their home. Hispanics were slightly less likely than blacks to own a home in 1976. Thirty years later, they are slightly more likely to be homeowners.

■ The homeownership rate is higher in the Midwest than in the other regions of the country. Seventy-three percent of households in the Midwest owned their home in 2006.

■ Among the nation's 75 largest metropolitan areas, the homeownership rate is highest in Akron, Ohio, at 78 percent in 2006. It is lowest in Fresno, California, at 52 percent.

■ During the past half-century, the nation's housing improved dramatically. In 1950, one-third of housing units did not have complete plumbing facilities. By 2005, a miniscule 0.4 percent lacked complete plumbing.

Homeownership Is Close to Its Record High

The homeownership rate peaked in 2004.

The proportion of American households that own their home hit an all-time high of 69.0 percent in 2004. Since then, the figure has drifted downward slightly to 68.8 percent in 2006. In 1950, just 55.0 percent of households owned their home. Behind the increase in homeownership over the past few decades is the aging of the baby-boom generation into the peak home-owning age groups.

Homeownership rises with age, and the rate is highest among the oldest adults. More than 80 percent of householders aged 55 or older owned their home in 2006 compared with only 43 percent of householders under age 35. Between 1982 and 2006, the homeownership rate increased the most for householders aged 65 or older—up 6.5 percentage points—as a more affluent generation moved into the age group. In contrast, the homeownership rate of householders aged 35 to 54 fell slightly during those years. Householders aged 55 to 64 have seen their homeownership rate climb by less than 1 percentage point during the past two decades.

■ The homeownership rate should resume its climb as boomers age into their sixties.

Homeownership is down for the middle aged

(percentage point change in homeownership rate of householders by age, 1982 to 2006)

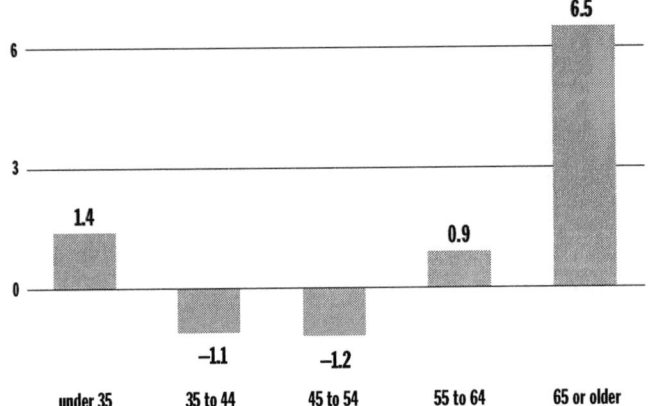

Table 4.1 Homeownership, 1950 to 2005

(total number of households, and number and percent of households that own their home, 1950 to 2005; percent and percentage point change for selected years; numbers in thousands)

	total households	homeowners	
		number	share of total
2005	111,091	74,319	66.9%
2000	105,480	69,816	66.2
1990	91,947	59,025	64.2
1980	80,390	51,795	64.4
1970	63,445	39,886	62.9
1960	53,024	32,797	61.9
1950	42,826	23,560	55.0

	percent change		percentage point change
2000 to 2005	5.3%	6.4%	0.7
1950 to 2005	159.4	215.4	11.9

Source: Bureau of the Census, 2005 American Community Survey, Internet site http://www.census.gov/acs/www/; and Census 2000, Table DP-1. Profile of General Demographic Characteristics; and Statistical Abstract of the United States 1995; calculations by New Strategist

Table 4.2 Homeowners by Age, 1982 to 2006

(number of households that own a home by age of householder, 1982 to 2006; percent change for selected years; numbers in thousands)

	total homeowners	under 35	35 to 44	45 to 54	55 to 64	65 or older
2006	75,380	10,648	15,161	17,445	14,173	17,953
2005	74,553	10,723	15,412	17,129	13,668	17,622
2004	73,574	10,726	15,370	16,905	13,108	17,465
2003	72,054	10,439	15,394	16,499	12,468	17,253
2002	71,278	10,236	15,612	16,266	11,915	17,250
2001	72,594	10,360	16,441	16,743	11,526	17,524
2000	71,249	10,161	16,429	16,058	11,100	17,501
1999	70,098	9,949	16,228	15,499	10,989	17,433
1998	68,638	9,802	16,159	14,969	10,601	17,106
1997	67,142	9,630	15,880	14,536	10,150	16,946
1996	66,042	9,793	15,534	13,996	9,850	16,869
1995	64,738	9,803	15,093	13,501	9,712	16,629
1994	63,136	9,453	14,733	12,962	9,714	16,273
1993	62,535	9,559	14,611	12,516	9,746	16,103
1992	61,823	9,480	14,223	11,977	10,031	16,106
1991	61,010	9,664	14,137	11,249	9,999	15,962
1990	60,248	9,955	13,789	10,957	10,011	15,536
1989	59,755	10,348	13,429	10,774	10,096	15,106
1988	58,700	10,038	12,905	10,440	10,146	14,888
1987	57,915	10,057	12,631	10,075	10,344	14,549
1986	56,844	10,090	12,178	9,827	10,390	14,118
1985	56,152	10,089	11,943	9,615	10,437	13,841
1984	55,671	10,150	11,516	9,580	10,487	13,676
1983	54,671	9,997	11,008	9,610	10,442	13,341
1982	54,237	10,241	10,711	9,709	10,370	12,978
Percent change						
2000 to 2006	5.8%	4.8%	−7.7%	8.6%	27.7%	2.6%
1982 to 2006	39.0	4.0	41.5	79.7	36.7	38.3

Note: Numbers may not add to total because "age not stated" is not shown.
Source: Bureau of the Census, Housing Vacancy Surveys, Internet site http://www.census.gov/hhes/www/housing/hvs/historic/histt12.html; calculations by New Strategist

Table 4.3 Percent Distribution of Homeowners by Age, 1982 to 2006

(percent distribution of households that own a home by age of householder, 1982 to 2006; percentage point change for selected years)

	total homeowners	under 35	35 to 44	45 to 54	55 to 64	65 or older
2006	100.0%	14.1%	20.1%	23.1%	18.8%	23.8%
2005	100.0	14.4	20.7	23.0	18.3	23.6
2004	100.0	14.6	20.9	23.0	17.8	23.7
2003	100.0	14.5	21.4	22.9	17.3	23.9
2002	100.0	14.4	21.9	22.8	16.7	24.2
2001	100.0	14.3	22.6	23.1	15.9	24.1
2000	100.0	14.3	23.1	22.5	15.6	24.6
1999	100.0	14.2	23.2	22.1	15.7	24.9
1998	100.0	14.3	23.5	21.8	15.4	24.9
1997	100.0	14.3	23.7	21.6	15.1	25.2
1996	100.0	14.8	23.5	21.2	14.9	25.5
1995	100.0	15.1	23.3	20.9	15.0	25.7
1994	100.0	15.0	23.3	20.5	15.4	25.8
1993	100.0	15.3	23.4	20.0	15.6	25.8
1992	100.0	15.3	23.0	19.4	16.2	26.1
1991	100.0	15.8	23.2	18.4	16.4	26.2
1990	100.0	16.5	22.9	18.2	16.6	25.8
1989	100.0	17.3	22.5	18.0	16.9	25.3
1988	100.0	17.1	22.0	17.8	17.3	25.4
1987	100.0	17.4	21.8	17.4	17.9	25.1
1986	100.0	17.8	21.4	17.3	18.3	24.8
1985	100.0	18.0	21.3	17.1	18.6	24.6
1984	100.0	18.2	20.7	17.2	18.8	24.6
1983	100.0	18.3	20.1	17.6	19.1	24.4
1982	100.0	18.9	19.7	17.9	19.1	23.9
Percentage point change						
2000 to 2006	–	–0.1	–2.9	0.6	3.2	–0.7
1982 to 2006	–	–4.8	0.4	5.2	–0.3	–0.1

Note: "–" means not applicable.
Source: Bureau of the Census, Housing Vacancy Surveys, Internet site http://www.census.gov/hhes/www/housing/hvs/historic/histt12.html; calculations by New Strategist

Table 4.4 Homeownership Rate by Age, 1982 to 2006

(percentage of households that own their home by age of householder, 1982 to 2006; percentage point change for selected years)

	total households	under 35	35 to 44	45 to 54	55 to 64	65 or older
2006	68.8%	42.6%	68.9%	76.2%	80.9%	80.9%
2005	68.9	43.0	69.3	76.6	81.2	80.6
2004	69.0	43.1	69.2	77.2	81.7	81.1
2003	68.3	42.2	68.3	76.6	81.4	80.5
2002	67.9	41.3	68.6	76.3	81.1	80.6
2001	67.8	41.2	68.2	76.7	81.3	80.3
2000	67.4	40.8	67.9	76.5	80.3	80.4
1999	66.8	39.7	67.2	76.0	81.0	80.1
1998	66.3	39.3	66.9	75.7	80.9	79.3
1997	65.7	38.7	66.1	75.8	80.1	79.1
1996	65.0	39.1	65.5	75.6	80.0	78.9
1995	64.7	38.6	65.2	75.2	79.5	78.1
1994	64.0	37.3	64.5	75.2	79.3	77.4
1993	64.0	37.3	65.1	75.3	79.9	77.3
1992	64.1	37.6	65.1	75.1	80.2	77.1
1991	64.1	37.8	65.8	74.8	80.0	77.2
1990	63.9	38.5	66.3	75.2	79.3	76.3
1989	63.9	39.1	66.6	75.5	79.6	75.8
1988	63.8	39.3	66.9	75.6	79.5	75.6
1987	64.0	39.5	67.2	76.1	80.2	75.5
1986	63.8	39.6	67.3	76.0	79.9	75.0
1985	63.9	39.9	68.1	75.9	79.5	74.8
1984	64.5	40.5	68.9	76.5	80.0	75.1
1983	64.6	40.7	69.3	77.0	79.9	75.0
1982	64.8	41.2	70.0	77.4	80.0	74.4
Percentage point change						
2000 to 2006	1.4	1.8	1.0	−0.3	0.6	0.5
1982 to 2006	4.0	1.4	−1.1	−1.2	0.9	6.5

Source: Bureau of the Census, Housing Vacancy Surveys, Internet site http://www.census.gov/hhes/www/housing/hvs/annual01/ann01t15.html; calculations by New Strategist

Married Couples Are Most Likely to Own a Home

Most female-headed families also are homeowners.

Married couples are far more likely to own a home than other household types. In 2006, fully 84 percent of married-couple households owned their home. Among male-headed families, the figure is 59 percent. Among female-headed families, 51 percent own their home. The majority of men and women who live alone are homeowners as well. Every household type has seen its homeownership rate rise over the past few decades.

Because the number of married couples is growing more slowly than other types of households, the married-couple share of homeowners is shrinking. Couples accounted for 61 percent of homeowners in 2006, down from 71 percent in 1982. A substantial 22 percent of homeowners are men or women who live alone, up from 16 percent a few decades earlier.

■ Married couples are most likely to own a home because many are dual earners and can afford the mortgage payment.

Most people who live alone own their home

(percent of households owning their home, by household type, 2006)

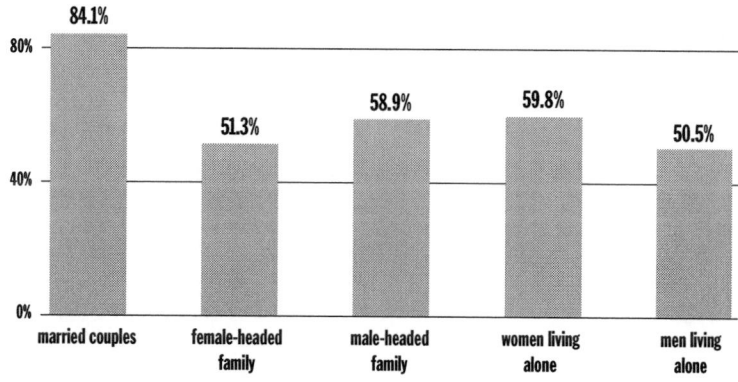

Table 4.5 Homeowners by Household Type, 1982 to 2006

(number of households that own a home by type of household, 1982 to 2006; percent change for selected years; numbers in thousands)

	total homeowners	family households			nonfamily households			
					female householder		male householder	
		married couples	female hh, no spouse present	male hh, no spouse present	living alone	other	living alone	other
2006	75,380	46,215	6,904	2,968	9,923	1,204	6,622	1,541
2005	74,553	46,010	6,779	2,943	9,784	1,141	6,361	1,535
2004	73,574	45,753	6,536	2,859	9,670	1,085	6,174	1,502
2003	72,054	45,191	6,277	2,614	9,438	1,082	6,028	1,424
2002	71,278	44,819	6,191	2,559	9,501	1,041	5,799	1,369
2001	72,594	45,792	6,429	2,576	9,548	1,047	5,774	1,425
2000	71,249	45,535	6,283	2,427	9,135	1,011	5,480	1377
1999	70,098	45,053	6,097	2,341	8,965	941	5,375	1,324
1998	68,637	44,280	5,865	2,289	8,761	922	5,248	1,270
1997	67,142	43,582	5,784	2,139	8,548	867	4,968	1,255
1996	66,042	43,222	5,661	2,075	8,313	743	4,810	1,217
1995	64,738	42,733	5,489	1,925	8,184	638	4,638	1,131
1994	63,136	41,846	5,404	1,777	7,898	676	4,432	1,102
1993	62,535	41,591	5,286	1,801	7,847	650	4,355	1,005
1992	61,823	41,417	5,105	1,743	7,701	600	4,293	958
1991	61,010	41,088	5,057	1,640	7,536	583	4,176	931
1990	60,248	40,793	4,902	1,646	7,449	546	4,016	895
1989	59,755	40,814	4,838	1,608	7,178	512	3,919	886
1988	58,700	39,927	4,929	1,830	6,849	469	3,619	798
1987	57,915	39,685	4,921	1,751	6,635	440	3,451	769
1986	56,844	39,198	4,770	1,640	6,497	427	3,365	709
1985	56,152	38,907	4,697	1,604	6,470	401	3,150	693
1984	55,671	38,722	4,702	1,555	6,413	366	3,014	631
1983	54,671	38,405	4,567	1,470	6,107	356	2,860	611
1982	54,237	38,382	4,498	1,437	5,971	346	2,804	569
Percent change								
2000 to 2006	5.8%	1.5%	9.9%	22.3%	8.6%	19.1%	20.8%	11.9%
1982 to 2006	39.0	20.4	53.5	106.5	66.2	248.0	136.2	170.8

Source: Bureau of the Census, Housing Vacancy Surveys, Internet site http://www.census.gov/hhes/www/housing/hvs/historic/histt15.html; calculations by New Strategist

Table 4.6 Percent Distribution of Homeowners by Household Type, 1982 to 2006

(percent distribution of households that own a home by type of household, 1982 to 2006; percentage point change for selected years)

| | | family households | | | nonfamily households | | | |
| | total homeowners | married couples | female hh, no spouse present | male hh, no spouse present | female householder | | male householder | |
					living alone	other	living alone	other
2006	100.0%	61.3%	9.2%	3.9%	13.2%	1.6%	8.8%	2.0%
2005	100.0	61.7	9.1	3.9	13.1	1.5	8.5	2.1
2004	100.0	62.2	8.9	3.9	13.1	1.5	8.4	2.0
2003	100.0	62.7	8.7	3.6	13.1	1.5	8.4	2.0
2002	100.0	62.9	8.7	3.6	13.3	1.5	8.1	1.9
2001	100.0	63.1	8.9	3.5	13.2	1.4	8.0	2.0
2000	100.0	63.9	8.8	3.4	12.8	1.4	7.7	1.9
1999	100.0	64.3	8.7	3.3	12.8	1.3	7.7	1.9
1998	100.0	64.5	8.5	3.3	12.8	1.3	7.6	1.9
1997	100.0	64.9	8.6	3.2	12.7	1.3	7.4	1.9
1996	100.0	65.4	8.6	3.1	12.6	1.1	7.3	1.8
1995	100.0	66.0	8.5	3.0	12.6	1.0	7.2	1.7
1994	100.0	66.3	8.6	2.8	12.5	1.1	7.0	1.7
1993	100.0	66.5	8.5	2.9	12.5	1.0	7.0	1.6
1992	100.0	67.0	8.3	2.8	12.5	1.0	6.9	1.5
1991	100.0	67.3	8.3	2.7	12.4	1.0	6.8	1.5
1990	100.0	67.7	8.1	2.7	12.4	0.9	6.7	1.5
1989	100.0	68.3	8.1	2.7	12.0	0.9	6.6	1.5
1988	100.0	68.0	8.4	3.1	11.7	0.8	6.2	1.4
1987	100.0	68.5	8.5	3.0	11.5	0.8	6.0	1.3
1986	100.0	69.0	8.4	2.9	11.4	0.8	5.9	1.2
1985	100.0	69.3	8.4	2.9	11.5	0.7	5.6	1.2
1984	100.0	69.6	8.4	2.8	11.5	0.7	5.4	1.1
1983	100.0	70.2	8.4	2.7	11.2	0.7	5.2	1.1
1982	100.0	70.8	8.3	2.6	11.0	0.6	5.2	1.0
Percentage point change								
2000 to 2006	–	–2.6	0.3	0.5	0.3	0.2	1.1	0.1
1982 to 2006	–	–9.5	0.9	1.3	2.2	1.0	3.6	1.0

Note: "–" means not applicable
Source: Bureau of the Census, Housing Vacancy Surveys, Internet site http://www.census.gov/hhes/www/housing/hvs/historic/histt15.html; calculations by New Strategist

Table 4.7 Homeownership Rate by Household Type, 1982 to 2006

(percentage of households that own a home by type of household, 1982 to 2006; percentage point change for selected years)

| | total households | family households | | | nonfamily households | | | |
| | | married couples | female hh, no spouse present | male hh, no spouse present | female householder | | male householder | |
					living alone	other	living alone	other
2006	68.8%	84.1%	51.3%	58.9%	59.8%	45.5%	50.5%	40.8%
2005	68.9	84.2	51.0	59.1	59.6	44.7	50.3	41.7
2004	69.0	84.0	50.9	59.6	59.9	43.5	50.5	41.7
2003	68.3	83.3	49.6	57.9	59.1	43.1	50.0	40.0
2002	67.9	82.9	49.2	57.3	59.6	41.9	48.6	38.7
2001	67.8	82.9	49.9	57.9	59.0	41.0	48.2	38.6
2000	67.4	82.4	49.1	57.5	58.1	40.6	47.4	38.0
1999	66.8	81.8	48.2	56.1	57.6	41.5	46.3	37.2
1998	66.3	81.5	47.0	55.7	56.9	40.3	45.7	36.7
1997	65.7	80.8	46.1	54.0	56.7	39.5	45.2	35.9
1996	65.4	80.2	46.1	55.5	56.0	35.9	44.9	35.5
1995	64.7	79.6	45.1	55.3	55.4	33.0	43.8	34.2
1994	64.0	78.8	44.2	52.8	54.5	34.3	43.1	33.6
1993	64.0	78.7	43.9	53.7	54.6	35.0	42.8	32.6
1992	64.1	78.7	43.6	53.6	54.1	34.0	43.5	32.4
1991	64.1	78.5	43.9	54.3	53.8	33.8	43.1	31.8
1990	63.9	78.1	44.0	55.2	53.6	32.5	42.4	31.7
1989	63.9	78.3	44.1	55.7	52.6	30.8	41.8	31.5
1988	63.8	78.9	45.3	56.1	51.8	30.5	39.9	31.3
1987	64.0	78.7	45.8	56.5	51.6	30.7	39.9	31.1
1986	63.8	78.4	45.3	56.8	50.9	31.4	40.0	29.8
1985	63.9	78.2	45.8	57.8	51.3	30.6	38.8	30.1
1984	64.5	78.2	46.9	59.2	52.2	30.0	38.9	28.8
1983	64.6	78.3	47.0	59.2	52.0	29.7	38.3	29.5
1982	64.8	78.5	47.1	59.3	51.2	30.1	38.0	28.3
Percentage point change								
2000 to 2006	1.4	1.7	2.2	1.4	1.7	4.9	3.1	2.8
1982 to 2006	4.0	5.6	4.2	−0.4	8.6	15.4	12.5	12.5

Source: Bureau of the Census, Housing Vacancy Surveys, Internet site http://www.census.gov/hhes/www/housing/hvs/annual01/ann01t15.html; calculations by New Strategist

Nearly Half of Blacks and Hispanics Are Homeowners

The homeownership rate is much higher for whites.

The homeownership rate of the nation's black households has been rising, but the gap in homeownership between whites and blacks is growing. In 2006, 72 percent of white households owned their home compared with a much smaller 47 percent of black households—a gap of 25 percentage points. In 1976, the gap was a slightly smaller 24 percentage points. Although black homeownership has climbed by 3 percentage points over those years, the white rate has climbed even more.

In contrast to blacks, the Hispanic homeownership rate is growing faster than the white rate, and the gap in homeownership between Hispanics and whites (a racial category that includes most Hispanics, since Hispanics may be of any race) is shrinking. Hispanics were slightly less likely than blacks to own a home in 1976. By 2006 they were slightly more likely to be homeowners.

■ With housing prices close to their record highs, it may become increasingly difficult for blacks and Hispanics to buy a home in the years ahead.

Homeownership has climbed the most for Hispanics

(percent of households that own their home, by race and Hispanic origin, 1976 and 2006)

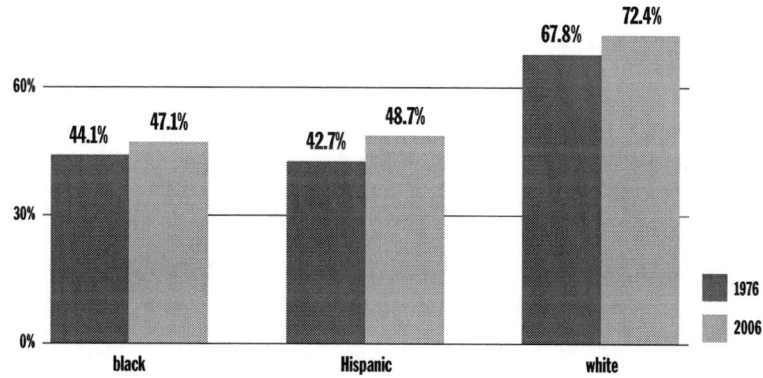

Table 4.8 Homeowners by Race and Hispanic Origin, 1976 to 2006

(number of households that own a home by race and Hispanic origin of householder, 1976 to 2006; percent change for selected years; numbers in thousands)

	total homeowners	black	Hispanic	white
2006	78,330	6,778	6,103	67,744
2005	78,539	6,932	6,003	67,838
2004	77,092	6,825	5,539	66,681
2003	75,909	6,549	5,385	66,070
2002	74,399	6,414	4,984	65,149
2001	73,319	6,282	4,574	64,353
2000	70,370	6,055	4,243	62,077
1999	69,241	5,723	4,096	61,350
1998	67,873	5,735	3,857	60,050
1997	66,356	5,510	3,543	58,826
1996	65,143	5,085	3,274	58,282
1995	64,045	4,888	3,278	57,449
1994	62,374	4,791	3,060	55,879
1993	62,220	4,726	2,654	55,915
1992	61,310	4,683	2,547	55,117
1991	60,395	4,526	2,423	54,527
1990	59,846	4,445	2,443	54,094
1989	59,419	4,417	2,457	53,737
1988	58,214	4,323	2,292	52,697
1987	57,258	4,505	2,198	51,657
1986	56,408	4,361	2,115	51,017
1985	55,845	4,185	2,007	50,661
1984	55,157	4,204	1,749	50,055
1983	54,494	4,043	1,684	49,484
1982	56,317	4,230	1,852	51,110
1981	55,881	4,230	1,822	50,737
1980	54,891	4,173	1,753	49,913
1979	52,283	3,887	1,514	47,751
1978	49,398	3,553	1,408	45,291
1977	48,083	3,431	1,302	44,148
1976	47,408	3,313	1,259	43,628
Percent change				
2000 to 2006	11.3%	11.9%	43.8%	9.1%
1976 to 2006	65.2	104.6	384.7	55.3

Note: Numbers will not add to total because Hispanics may be of any race and not all races are shown. Estimated total homeowners in this table differ slightly from those in the other tables because they are based on a different survey.
Source: Bureau of the Census, Current Population Surveys, Internet site http://www.census.gov/population/www/socdemo/hh-fam.html; calculations by New Strategist

Table 4.9 Percent Distribution of Homeowners by Race and Hispanic Origin, 1976 to 2006

(percent distribution of households that own a home by race and Hispanic origin of householder, 1976 to 2006; percentage point change for selected years)

	total homeowners	black	Hispanic	white
2006	100.0%	8.7%	7.8%	86.5%
2005	100.0	8.8	7.6	86.4
2004	100.0	8.9	7.2	86.5
2003	100.0	8.6	7.1	87.0
2002	100.0	8.6	6.7	87.6
2001	100.0	8.6	6.2	87.8
2000	100.0	8.6	6.0	88.2
1999	100.0	8.3	5.9	88.6
1998	100.0	8.4	5.7	88.5
1997	100.0	8.3	5.3	88.7
1996	100.0	7.8	5.0	89.5
1995	100.0	7.6	5.1	89.7
1994	100.0	7.7	4.9	89.6
1993	100.0	7.6	4.3	89.9
1992	100.0	7.6	4.2	89.9
1991	100.0	7.5	4.0	90.3
1990	100.0	7.4	4.1	90.4
1989	100.0	7.4	4.1	90.4
1988	100.0	7.4	3.9	90.5
1987	100.0	7.9	3.8	90.2
1986	100.0	7.7	3.7	90.4
1985	100.0	7.5	3.6	90.7
1984	100.0	7.6	3.2	90.8
1983	100.0	7.4	3.1	90.8
1982	100.0	7.5	3.3	90.8
1981	100.0	7.6	3.3	90.8
1980	100.0	7.6	3.2	90.9
1979	100.0	7.4	2.9	91.3
1978	100.0	7.2	2.9	91.7
1977	100.0	7.1	2.7	91.8
1976	100.0	7.0	2.7	92.0
Percentage point change				
2000 to 2006	–	0.1	1.8	–1.7
1976 to 2006	–	1.7	5.1	–5.5

Note: Numbers will not add to total because Hispanics may be of any race and not all races are shown. "–" means not applicable.
Source: Bureau of the Census, Current Population Surveys, Internet site http://www.census.gov/population/www/socdemo/hh-fam.html; calculations by New Strategist

Table 4.10 Homeownership Rate by Race and Hispanic Origin, 1976 to 2006

(percent of households that own a home by race and Hispanic origin of householder, 1976 to 2006; percentage point change in rate for selected years)

	total households	black	Hispanic	white
2006	68.5%	47.1%	48.7%	72.4%
2005	69.3	49.0	49.3	73.0
2004	68.8	48.9	47.4	72.5
2003	68.2	47.5	47.5	72.1
2002	68.1	48.2	47.5	71.8
2001	67.8	47.7	45.6	71.5
2000	67.2	47.1	45.5	70.8
1999	66.7	45.5	45.2	70.3
1998	66.2	46.0	44.9	69.7
1997	65.7	45.5	43.1	69.2
1996	65.4	45.5	41.2	69.0
1995	64.7	43.9	42.4	68.6
1994	64.2	41.9	41.6	67.8
1993	64.5	42.5	40.1	68.1
1992	64.1	42.2	39.9	67.5
1991	64.0	42.3	39.0	67.3
1990	64.1	42.4	41.2	67.5
1989	64.0	42.4	41.6	67.4
1988	63.9	41.8	40.2	67.2
1987	64.0	42.4	40.6	66.8
1986	63.8	45.4	40.6	66.6
1985	64.3	44.5	41.1	67.3
1984	64.6	44.1	40.4	67.3
1983	64.9	45.5	41.2	67.6
1982	67.4	45.3	46.5	70.2
1981	67.8	47.2	46.6	70.6
1980	68.0	47.8	47.6	70.5
1979	67.6	48.6	46.0	70.2
1978	65.0	48.2	42.6	67.7
1977	64.9	44.5	42.3	67.6
1976	65.1	44.1	42.7	67.8
Percentage point change				
2000 to 2006	1.3	0.0	3.2	1.6
1976 to 2006	3.4	3.0	6.0	4.6

Note: Estimated total homeownership rates in this table differ slightly from those in the other tables because they are based on a different survey.
Source: Bureau of the Census, Current Population Surveys, Internet site http://www.census.gov/population/socdemo/hh-fam/ tabHH-5.txt; calculations by New Strategist

Homeownership Is Highest in the Midwest

Among the states, West Virginia has the highest homeownership rate.

The homeownership rate is substantially higher in the Midwest than in the other regions of the country. Seventy-three percent of Midwestern households owned their home in 2006. This compares with a homeownership rate of 71 percent in the South and 65 percent in the Northeast and West. Lower housing prices in the Midwest account for the region's high homeownership rate. Between 1960 and 2006, the homeownership rate climbed the most in the Northeast (up 10 percentage points) and rose by the smallest amount in the West (only 2.5 percentage points).

By state, homeownership is highest in West Virginia (78 percent) and lowest in the District of Columbia (46 percent) and New York (56 percent). Washington, D.C., has a low rate of homeownership because it is a metropolitan area. New York has a low rate because the New York metropolitan area dominates the state's statistics. Many residents of New York City rent rather than buy because housing prices are high. Since 1984, the homeownership rate has grown the most in Alaska and Hawaii (up more than 9 percentage points). It has declined in three states: Nebraska, North Dakota, and Kansas.

■ The homeownership rate should climb in most states in the years ahead as more people enter the age groups in which homeownership peaks.

Homeownership in the West is below average

(percent of households that own their home, by region, 2006)

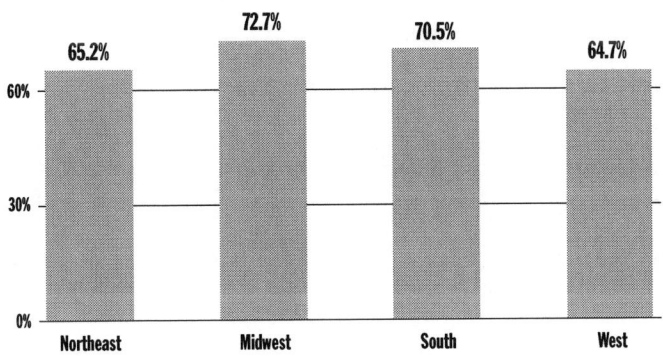

Table 4.11 Homeownership Rate by Region, 1960 to 2006

(percent of households that own a home by region, 1960 to 2006; percentage point change for selected years)

	total households	Northeast	Midwest	South	West
2006	68.8%	65.2%	72.7%	70.5%	64.7%
2005	68.9	65.2	73.1	70.8	64.4
2004	69.0	65.0	73.8	70.9	64.2
2003	68.3	64.4	73.2	70.1	63.4
2002	67.9	64.3	73.1	69.7	62.5
2001	67.8	63.7	73.1	69.8	62.6
2000	67.4	63.4	72.6	69.6	61.7
1999	66.8	63.1	71.7	69.1	60.9
1998	66.3	62.6	71.1	68.6	60.5
1997	65.7	62.4	70.5	68.0	59.6
1996	65.4	62.2	70.6	67.5	59.2
1995	64.7	62.0	69.2	66.7	59.2
1994	64.0	61.5	67.7	65.6	59.4
1993	64.0	61.8	67.1	65.7	59.9
1992	64.1	62.5	67.2	65.8	59.3
1991	64.1	62.3	67.2	66.1	58.6
1990	63.9	62.6	67.5	65.7	58.0
1989	63.9	62.0	67.7	65.9	57.8
1988	63.8	61.3	67.5	65.8	58.5
1987	64.0	61.7	67.3	66.3	58.4
1986	63.8	61.4	66.9	66.1	58.3
1985	63.9	60.8	66.9	66.4	59.0
1984	64.5	61.2	68.4	67.0	58.5
1983	64.6	61.5	69.3	67.0	58.2
1982	64.8	61.1	69.4	66.7	59.4
1981	65.4	60.8	69.7	68.2	60.2
1980	65.6	60.8	68.9	68.7	60.0
1970	64.2	58.1	69.5	66.0	60.0
1960	62.1	55.5	66.4	63.4	62.2
Percentage point change					
2000 to 2006	1.4	1.8	0.1	0.9	3.0
1960 to 2006	6.7	9.7	6.3	7.1	2.5

Source: Bureau of the Census, Housing Vacancy Surveys, Internet site http://www.census.gov/hhes/www/housing/hvs/annual06/ ann06t12.html; calculations by New Strategist

Table 4.12 Homeownership Rate by State, 1984 to 2006

(percentage of households that own a home by state, 1984 to 2006; percentage point change for selected years)

	2006	2000	1990	1984	percentage point change 2000–06	percentage point change 1984–06
Total households	**68.8%**	**67.4%**	**63.9%**	**64.5%**	**1.4**	**4.3**
Alabama	74.2	73.2	68.4	73.7	1.0	0.5
Alaska	67.2	66.4	58.4	57.6	0.8	9.6
Arizona	71.6	68.0	64.5	65.2	3.6	6.4
Arkansas	70.8	68.9	67.8	65.9	1.9	4.9
California	60.2	57.1	53.8	53.7	3.1	6.5
Colorado	70.1	68.3	59.0	64.7	1.8	5.4
Connecticut	71.1	70.0	67.9	67.8	1.1	3.3
Delaware	76.8	72.0	67.7	70.4	4.8	6.4
District of Columbia	45.9	41.9	36.4	37.3	4.0	8.6
Florida	72.4	68.4	65.1	66.5	4.0	5.9
Georgia	68.5	69.8	64.3	63.6	–1.3	4.9
Hawaii	59.9	55.2	55.5	50.7	4.7	9.2
Idaho	75.1	70.5	69.4	69.7	4.6	5.4
Illinois	70.4	67.9	63.0	62.4	2.5	8.0
Indiana	74.2	74.9	67.0	69.9	–0.7	4.3
Iowa	74.0	75.2	70.7	71.3	–1.2	2.7
Kansas	70.0	69.3	69.0	72.7	0.7	–2.7
Kentucky	71.7	73.4	65.8	70.2	–1.7	1.5
Louisiana	71.3	68.1	67.8	70.1	3.2	1.2
Maine	75.3	76.5	74.3	74.1	–1.2	1.2
Maryland	72.6	69.9	64.9	67.8	2.7	4.8
Massachusetts	65.2	59.9	58.6	61.7	5.3	3.5
Michigan	77.4	77.2	72.3	72.7	0.2	4.7
Minnesota	75.6	76.1	68.0	72.6	–0.5	3.0
Mississippi	76.2	75.2	69.4	72.3	1.0	3.9
Missouri	71.9	74.2	64.0	69.5	–2.3	2.4
Montana	69.5	70.2	69.1	66.4	–0.7	3.1
Nebraska	67.6	70.2	67.3	69.3	–2.6	–1.7
Nevada	65.7	64.0	55.8	58.9	1.7	6.8
New Hampshire	74.2	69.2	65.0	67.1	5.0	7.1
New Jersey	69.0	66.2	65.0	63.4	2.8	5.6
New Mexico	72.0	73.7	68.6	68.0	–1.7	4.0
New York	55.7	53.4	53.3	51.1	2.3	4.6
North Carolina	70.2	71.1	69.0	68.8	–0.9	1.4
North Dakota	68.3	70.7	67.2	70.1	–2.4	–1.8
Ohio	72.1	71.3	68.7	67.7	0.8	4.4
Oklahoma	71.6	72.7	70.3	71.0	–1.1	0.6
Oregon	68.1	65.3	64.4	61.9	2.8	6.2
Pennsylvania	73.2	74.7	73.8	71.1	–1.5	2.1
Rhode Island	64.6	61.5	58.5	60.9	3.1	3.7
South Carolina	74.2	76.5	71.4	69.1	–2.3	5.1
South Dakota	70.6	71.2	66.2	69.6	–0.6	1.0
Tennessee	71.3	70.9	68.3	67.6	0.4	3.7
Texas	66.0	63.8	59.7	62.5	2.2	3.5
Utah	73.5	72.7	70.1	69.9	0.8	3.6
Vermont	74.0	68.7	72.6	66.9	5.3	7.1
Virginia	71.1	73.9	69.8	68.3	–2.8	2.8
Washington	66.7	63.6	61.8	65.7	3.1	1.0
West Virginia	78.4	75.9	72.0	72.0	2.5	6.4
Wisconsin	70.2	71.8	68.3	65.2	–1.6	5.0
Wyoming	73.7	71.0	68.9	68.8	2.7	4.9

Source: Bureau of the Census, Housing Vacancy Surveys, Internet site http://www.census.gov/hhes/www/housing/hvs/annual06/ann06t13.html; calculations by New Strategist

Homeownership Is Highest in the Suburbs

It is lowest in the cities.

In the suburbs of the nation's metropolitan areas, just over 76 percent of households own their home. This homeownership rate is slightly higher than the 75.9 percent found in non-metropolitan areas. In the principal cities (formerly central cities) of metropolitan areas, only 54 percent of households own their home. Between 1965 and 2006, the homeownership rate climbed regardless of metropolitan status in the cities, suburbs, and nonmetropolitan areas.

Tracking homeownership rates by individual metropolitan area is tricky because metropolitan definitions change with every census. Among the nation's 75 largest metropolitan areas in 2006, the homeownership rate was highest in Akron, Ohio, at 78 percent. It was lowest in Fresno, California, at 52 percent. Between 1986 and 2000, the homeownership rate rose in most of the large metropolitan areas. Many metros have seen homeownership rates fall since 2000, however. Between 2005 and 2006, the biggest losers were Syracuse, New York, and Worcester, Massachusetts (down 6 percentage points). The biggest gainer was El Paso, Texas, where the homeownership rate climbed 8 percentage points between 2005 and 2006.

■ Look for the homeownership rate to rise in metropolitan areas with relatively low housing prices and growing economies.

Homeownership rate varies by metropolitan area

(percent of households that own their home in the metropolitan areas with the highest and lowest homeownership rate, among the 75 largest metropolitan areas, 2006)

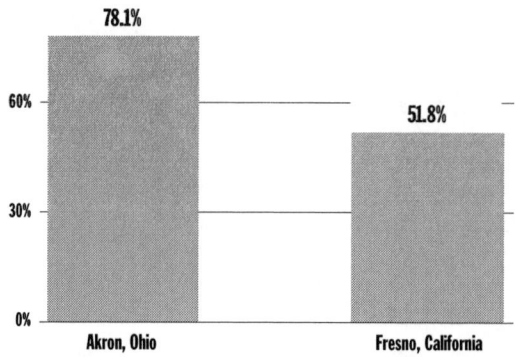

Table 4.13 Homeownership Rate by Metropolitan Status, 1965 to 2006

(percentage of households that own a home by metropolitan status, 1965 to 2006; percentage point change for selected years)

	total households	metropolitan area			nonmetro areas
		total	in principal cities	suburbs	
2006	68.8%	67.4%	54.3%	76.1%	75.9%
2005	68.9	67.4	54.2	76.4	76.3
2004	69.0	67.3	53.1	75.7	76.3
2003	68.3	66.5	52.3	75.0	75.6
2002	67.9	66.1	51.7	74.7	75.4
2001	67.8	66.1	51.9	74.6	75.0
2000	67.4	65.5	51.4	74.0	75.2
1999	66.8	64.7	50.4	73.6	75.4
1998	66.3	64.2	50.0	73.2	74.7
1997	65.7	63.7	49.9	72.5	73.7
1996	65.4	63.4	49.7	72.2	73.5
1995	64.7	62.7	49.5	71.2	72.7
1994	64.0	61.7	48.5	70.3	72.0
1993	64.0	61.5	48.6	70.3	72.6
1992	64.1	61.6	49.3	70.1	72.8
1991	64.1	61.4	48.7	70.2	73.2
1990	63.9	61.3	48.7	70.1	73.2
1989	63.9	61.3	48.7	70.2	72.8
1988	63.8	61.3	48.3	70.6	72.6
1987	64.0	61.4	48.7	70.8	72.8
1986	63.8	61.2	48.5	70.8	72.3
1985	63.9	60.2	47.7	69.1	71.9
1984	64.5	60.8	49.0	69.7	72.3
1983	64.6	60.9	49.2	69.8	72.9
1982	64.8	61.0	49.1	70.0	73.0
1981	65.4	61.5	49.4	70.8	73.8
1980	65.6	61.6	49.6	70.8	74.1
1970	64.2	60.3	48.9	70.6	71.6
1965	63.3	59.7	48.0	72.0	69.1
Percentage point change					
2000 to 2006	1.4	1.9	2.9	2.1	0.7
1965 to 2006	5.5	7.7	6.3	4.1	6.8

Note: The term "central cities" was changed to "principal cities" in 2005. Approximately every ten years, the Office of Management and Budget redefines metropolitan and nonmetropolitan areas. Therefore, metropolitan area data for 1986 to 1994, 1995 to 2004, and 2005 and later are not strictly comparable to one another.
Source: Bureau of the Census, Housing Vacancy Surveys, Internet site http://www.census.gov/hhes/www/housing/hvs/annual06/ann06t12.html; calculations by New Strategist

Table 4.14 Homeownership Rate by Metropolitan Area, 1986 to 2004

(percentage of households that own a home in the 75 largest metropolitan areas, 1986 to 2004; percentage point change for selected years)

	2004	2000	1990	1986	percentage point change 2000–04	percentage point change 1986–04
Total metropolitan households	**67.3%**	**65.5%**	**61.3%**	**61.2%**	**1.8**	**6.1**
Akron, OH	79.1	63.6	–	–	15.5	–
Albany–Schenectady–Troy, NY	67.3	71.1	69.9	62.4	–3.8	4.9
Atlanta, GA	68.4	67.7	61.0	57.5	0.7	10.9
Austin–San Marcos, TX	62.1	54.7	–	–	7.4	–
Baltimore, MD	71.3	68.2	63.0	58.8	3.1	12.5
Bergen–Passaic, NJ	68.8	63.2	61.4	58.6	5.6	10.2
Birmingham, AL	73.6	69.9	65.7	68.6	3.7	5.0
Boston, MA–NH	59.4	58.7	55.0	55.9	0.7	3.5
Buffalo, NY	68.2	72.5	61.4	64.1	–4.3	4.1
Charlotte–Gastonia–Rock Hill, NC–SC	70.4	75.8	64.8	63.0	–5.4	7.4
Chicago, IL	70.1	66.4	56.9	54.7	3.7	15.4
Cincinnati, OH–KY–IN	71.3	72.5	57.9	63.8	–1.2	7.5
Cleveland–Lorain–Elyria, OH	73.9	72.0	64.5	64.7	1.9	9.2
Columbus, OH	69.1	61.6	61.8	59.2	7.5	9.9
Dallas, TX	63.0	62.4	54.0	51.2	0.6	11.8
Dayton–Springfield, OH	62.3	62.8	67.6	62.8	–0.5	–0.5
Denver, CO	71.0	68.2	55.7	60.7	2.8	10.3
Detroit, MI	76.5	75.3	71.4	70.5	1.2	6.0
Fresno, CA	54.7	56.2	–	–	–1.5	–
Ft. Lauderdale, FL	73.8	76.3	68.2	74.3	–2.5	–0.5
Ft. Worth–Arlington, TX	65.7	62.4	61.4	64.8	3.3	0.9
Grand Rapids–Muskegon–Holland, MI	74.4	80.1	–	–	–5.7	–
Greensboro–Winston–Salem– High Point, NC	68.6	68.9	68.2	68.2	–0.3	0.4
Greenville–Spartanburg–Anderson, SC	73.5	76.5	–	–	–3.0	–
Hartford, CT	72.7	69.7	65.5	68.3	3.0	4.4
Honolulu, HI	59.4	56.8	52.9	50.0	2.6	9.4
Houston, TX	58.0	53.6	53.9	56.3	4.4	1.7
Indianapolis, IN	73.1	67.5	55.3	61.4	5.6	11.7
Jacksonville, FL	69.1	70.4	61.0	61.0	–1.3	8.1
Kansas City, MO–KS	74.2	73.6	61.7	63.8	0.6	10.4
Las Vegas, NV–AZ	63.4	61.9	–	–	1.5	–
Los Angeles–Long Beach, CA	51.6	49.0	47.9	48.3	2.6	3.3
Louisville, KY–IN	67.5	70.2	69.3	66.4	–2.7	1.1
Memphis, TN–AR–MS	64.5	61.1	60.8	60.2	3.4	4.3
Miami, FL	62.5	56.2	47.9	47.9	6.3	14.6
Middlesex–Somerset–Hunterdon, NJ	74.7	69.7	72.4	67.5	5.0	7.2
Milwaukee–Waukesha, WI	67.0	67.5	72.2	65.9	–0.5	1.1
Minneapolis–St. Paul, MN–WI	73.9	73.1	62.5	64.2	0.8	9.7

(continued)

	2004	2000	1990	1986	percentage point change	
					2000–04	1986–04
Monmouth–Ocean, NJ	86.9%	83.5%	76.1%	76.6%	3.4	10.3
Nashville, TN	71.1	67.9	57.3	60.6	3.2	10.5
Nassau–Suffolk, NY	85.7	79.7	81.8	81.8	6.0	3.9
New Orleans, LA	68.5	64.6	59.9	59.9	3.9	8.6
New York, NY	36.6	34.1	34.0	32.1	2.5	4.5
Newark, NJ	64.7	60.3	60.7	62.0	4.4	2.7
Norfolk–Virginia Beach–Newport News, VA	73.2	70.1	62.6	57.2	3.1	16.0
Oakland, CA	63.4	60.3	54.2	57.0	3.1	6.4
Oklahoma City, OK	71.0	70.5	65.1	67.8	0.5	3.2
Omaha, NE–IA	70.8	69.6	–	–	1.2	–
Orange County, CA	61.4	62.3	55.1	57.3	–0.9	4.1
Orlando, FL	69.1	60.5	66.8	71.2	8.6	–2.1
Philadelphia, PA–NJ	74.1	74.7	73.6	69.8	–0.6	4.3
Phoenix–Mesa, AZ	70.8	70.7	64.3	61.8	0.1	9.0
Pittsburgh, PA	74.9	71.8	71.9	70.5	3.1	4.4
Portland–Vancouver, OR–WA	66.9	62.1	66.5	65.2	4.8	1.7
Providence–Fall River–Pawtucket, RI	60.2	61.2	59.5	63.0	–1.0	–2.8
Raleigh–Durham–Chapel Hill, NC	67.7	65.6	–	–	2.1	–
Richmond–Petersburg, VA	69.5	74.1	69.4	71.5	–4.6	–2.0
Rochester, NY	70.2	65.2	65.9	61.7	5.0	8.5
Sacramento, CA	63.5	61.6	53.5	54.3	1.9	9.2
Salt Lake City–Ogden, UT	73.7	72.1	73.6	71.2	1.6	2.5
San Antonio, TX	68.3	66.6	57.9	60.1	1.7	8.2
San Bernardino–Riverside, CA	67.2	62.6	60.0	65.9	4.6	1.3
San Diego, CA	65.7	59.1	51.2	53.6	6.6	12.1
San Francisco, CA	50.6	48.9	48.8	48.7	1.7	1.9
San Jose, CA	58.7	60.9	63.2	50.9	–2.2	7.8
Scranton–Wilkes-Barre–Hazelton, PA	73.4	71.8	–	–	1.6	–
Seattle–Bellevue–Everett, WA	64.1	63.4	64.8	63.0	0.7	1.1
St. Louis, MO–IL	73.9	70.6	59.4	64.8	3.3	9.1
Syracuse, NY	58.9	59.2	–	–	–0.3	–
Tampa–St. Petersburg–Clearwater, FL	71.5	70.0	67.0	67.6	1.5	3.9
Tucson, AZ	60.3	60.5	–	–	–0.2	–
Tulsa, OK	66.6	65.2	–	–	1.4	–
Ventura, CA	72.5	66.2	–	–	6.3	–
Washington, DC–MD–VA–WV	69.7	67.1	63.2	60.2	2.6	9.5
West Palm Beach–Boca Raton, FL	78.1	71.3	–	–	6.8	–

Note: Data for 1986 and 1990 are based on 1980 metropolitan definitions. Data for 2000 and 2004 are based on 1990 metropolitan definitions; "–" means data are not available.
Source: Bureau of the Census, Housing Vacancy Surveys, Internet site http://www.census.gov/hhes/www/housing/hvs/annual06/ann06t14a.html; calculations by New Strategist

Table 4.15 Homeownership Rate by Metropolitan Area, 2005 and 2006

(percentage of households that own a home in the 75 largest metropolitan areas, 2005 and 2006; percentage point change for 2005 to 2006)

	2006	2005	percentage point change 2005–06
Total metropolitan households	**67.4%**	**67.4%**	**0.0**
Akron, OH	78.1	77.1	1.0
Albany–Schenectady–Troy, NY	66.3	67.0	–0.7
Alburquerque, NM	69.2	70.0	–0.8
Allentown–Bethlehem–Easton, PA–NJ	73.5	75.1	–1.6
Atlanta–Sandy Springs–Marietta, GA	66.4	67.9	–1.5
Austin–Round Rock, TX	63.9	66.7	–2.8
Bakersfield, CA	60.5	62.3	–1.8
Baltimore–Towson, MD	70.6	72.9	–2.3
Baton Rouge, LA	71.0	65.0	6.0
Birmingham–Hoover, AL	75.1	76.1	–1.0
Boston–Cambridge–Quincy, MA–NH	63.0	64.7	–1.7
Bridgeport–Stamford–Norwalk, CT	68.2	70.4	–2.2
Buffalo–Cheektowaga–Tonawanda, NY	66.3	66.3	0.0
Charlotte–Gastonia–Concord, NC–SC	65.8	66.1	–0.3
Chicago–Naperville–Joliet, IL	70.0	69.6	0.4
Cincinnati–Middletown, OH–KY–IN	68.4	65.5	2.9
Cleveland–Elyria–Mentor, OH	74.4	76.9	–2.5
Columbia, SC	76.3	72.2	4.1
Columbus, OH	68.9	65.8	3.1
Dallas–Ft Worth–Arlington, TX	62.3	60.7	1.6
Dayton, OH	66.1	64.6	1.5
Denver–Aurora, CO	70.7	70.0	0.7
Detroit–Warren–Livonia, MI	75.1	75.8	–0.7
El Paso, TX	72.6	65.0	7.6
Fresno, CA	51.8	53.9	–2.1
Grand Rapids–Wyoming, MI	72.6	76.5	–3.9
Greensboro–High Point, NC	66.3	62.2	4.1
Hartford–West Hartford–East Hartford, CT	72.2	73.8	–1.6
Honolulu, HI	58.0	58.4	–0.4
Houston–Baytown–Sugar Land, TX	61.7	63.5	–1.8
Indianapolis, IN	77.1	79.0	–1.9
Jacksonville, FL	67.9	70.0	–2.1
Kansas City, MO–KS	71.3	69.5	1.8
Las Vegas–Paradise, NV	61.4	63.3	–1.9
Los Angeles–Long Beach–Santa Ana, CA	54.6	54.4	0.2
Louisville, KY–IN	62.9	66.4	–3.5
Memphis, TN–AR–MS	64.8	61.6	3.2
Miami–Fort Lauderdale–Miami Beach, FL	69.2	67.4	1.8
Milwaukee–Waukesha–West Allis, WI	65.7	65.2	0.5

(continued)

	2006	2005	percentage point change 2005–06
Minneapolis–St. Paul–Bloomington, MN–WI	74.9%	73.4%	1.5
Nashville–Davidson–Murfreesboro, TN	73.0	72.4	0.6
New Haven–Milford, CT	66.9	63.9	3.0
New Orleans–Metairie–Kenner, LA	71.2	70.3	0.9
New York–Northern New Jersey–Long Island, NY–NJ–PA	54.6	53.6	1.0
Oklahoma City, OK	72.9	71.8	1.1
Omaha–Council Bluffs, NE–IA	69.7	68.1	1.6
Orlando, FL	70.5	71.1	−0.6
Oxnard–Thousand Oaks–Ventura, CA	73.4	69.8	3.6
Philadelphia–Camden–Wilmington, PA–NJ–DE–MD	73.5	73.1	0.4
Phoenix–Mesa–Scottsdale, AZ	71.2	72.5	−1.3
Pittsburgh, PA	73.1	72.2	0.9
Portland–Vancouver–Beaverton, OR–WA	68.3	66.0	2.3
Poughkeepsie–Newburgh–Middletown, NY	74.2	74.0	0.2
Providence–New Bedford–Fall River RI–MA	63.1	65.5	−2.4
Raleigh–Cary, NC	71.4	71.1	0.3
Richmond, VA	69.7	68.9	0.8
Riverside–San Bernardino–Ontario, CA	68.5	68.3	0.2
Rochester, NY	74.9	73.4	1.5
Sacramento–Arden–Arcade–Roseville, CA	64.1	64.2	−0.1
St. Louis, MO–IL	74.4	72.8	1.6
Salt Lake City, UT	68.8	69.6	−0.8
San Antonio, TX	66.0	62.6	3.4
San Diego–Carlsbad–San Marcos, CA	60.5	61.2	−0.7
San Francisco–Oakland–Freemont, CA	57.8	59.4	−1.6
San Jose–Sunnyvale–Santa Clara, CA	59.2	59.4	−0.2
Seattle–Bellevue–Everett, WA	64.5	63.7	0.8
Springfield, MA	64.5	62.3	2.2
Syracuse, NY	59.8	66.0	−6.2
Tampa–St. Petersburg–Clearwater, FL	71.7	71.6	0.1
Toledo, OH	72.4	70.7	1.7
Tucson, AZ	66.1	67.5	−1.4
Tulsa, OK	71.7	67.9	3.8
Virginia Beach–Norfolk–Newport News, VA	68.0	68.3	−0.3
Washington–Arlington–Alexandria, DC–VA–MD–WV	68.4	68.9	−0.5
Worcester, MA	65.3	71.0	−5.7

Note: Data for 2005 and later are based on 2000 metropolitan definitions.
Source: Bureau of the Census, Housing Vacancy Surveys, Internet site http://www.census.gov/hhes/www/housing/hvs/annual06/ ann06t14.html; calculations by New Strategist

Living Conditions Have Improved

Few households today lack complete plumbing or heat with wood.

During the past half-century, the nation's housing has improved dramatically. In 1950, one-third of housing units did not have complete plumbing facilities, meaning they lacked hot and cold piped water, a bathtub or shower, or a flush toilet. In 2005, a miniscule 0.4 percent of housing units lacked complete plumbing facilities.

The primary fuel used to heat homes has also changed dramatically during the past 55 years. In 1950, fully 45 percent of housing units depended on coal or wood for their primary heating fuel. In 2005, fewer than 2 percent used coal or wood. The majority of households now depend on utility gas, but the figure fell slightly between 2000 and 2005. In contrast, the percentage of households that use electricity as their primary heating fuel is on the rise. In 1950, less than 1 percent of households used electricity as their primary heating fuel. Today, the figure is nearly one-third.

While big changes have occurred in the use of heating fuels and the prevalence of plumbing facilities, there has been surprisingly little change in second homes as a proportion of the nation's total housing units. The share rose from 2.3 percent in 1950 to just 3.1 percent in 2005.

■ The baby-boom generation may be under too much financial stress to boost the vacation home market as much as the real estate industry expects.

Electricity is a much more important heating fuel today

(percent of households that use electricity as the primary heating fuel, 1950 to 2005)

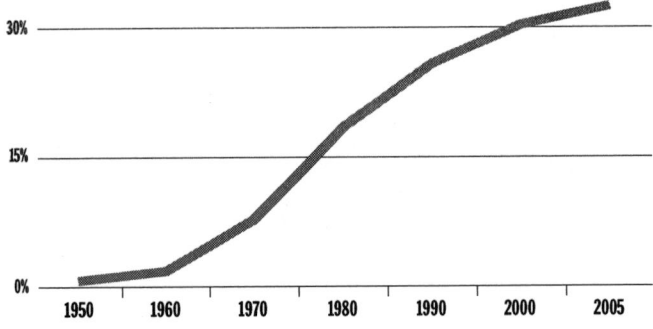

Table 4.16   House Heating Fuel, 1950 to 2005

(total number of occupied housing units that report heating fuel use and percent distribution by primary house heating fuel, 1950 to 2005; numbers in thousands)

	total occupied housing units		utility gas	electricity	fuel oil	bottled, tank or LP gas	coal or coke	wood	other/none
	number	percent							
2005	111,091	100.0%	50.5%	32.5%	8.0%	6.0%	0.1%	1.7%	1.3%
2000	105,480	100.0	51.2	30.3	9.0	6.5	0.1	1.7	1.1
1990	91,947	100.0	51.0	25.8	12.2	5.7	0.4	3.9	1.0
1980	80,390	100.0	53.1	18.4	18.2	5.6	0.6	3.2	0.9
1970	63,447	100.0	55.2	7.7	26.0	6.0	2.9	1.3	1.0
1960	53,022	100.0	43.1	1.8	32.4	5.1	12.2	4.2	1.3
1950	41,829	100.0	26.6	0.7	22.6	2.3	34.6	10.0	3.2

Source: Bureau of the Census, 1950 to 2000 censuses, Internet site http://www.census.gov/hhes/www/housing/census/historic/fuels.html; and 2005 American Community Survey, Internet site http://www.census.gov/acs/www/; calculations by New Strategist

Table 4.17   Plumbing Facilities in Housing Units, 1950 to 2005

(total number of housing units that report plumbing facilities, and number and percent without complete plumbing, 1950 to 2005; numbers in thousands)

		lacking complete plumbing	
	total	number	percent
2005	124,522	490	0.4%
2000	115,905	671	0.6
1990	102,264	1,102	1.1
1980	86,693	2,334	2.7
1970	67,657	4,672	6.9
1960	58,315	9,778	16.8
1950	44,502	15,773	35.4

Note: Complete plumbing facilities are defined as hot and cold piped water, a bathtub or shower, and a flush toilet.
Source: Bureau of the Census, Historical Census of Housing Tables—Plumbing Facilities, Internet site http://www.census.gov/hhes/www/housing/census/historic/plumbing.html; and Table DP-4, Profile of Selected Housing Characteristics: 2000, Internet site http://censtats.census.gov/data/US/01000.pdf; and 2005 American Community Survey, Internet site http://www.census.gov/acs/www/; calculations by New Strategist

Table 4.18 Vacation Homes, 1950 to 2005

(total number of housing units, and number and percent that are seasonal, recreational, or for occasional use, 1950 to 2005; numbers in thousands)

	total	vacation housing units	
		number	percent
2005	124,522	3,916	3.1%
2000	115,905	3,604	3.1
1990	102,264	3,117	3.0
1980	88,411	2,794	3.2
1970	68,679	2,020	2.9
1960	58,326	2,024	3.5
1950	45,983	1,050	2.3

Source: Bureau of the Census, Historical Census of Housing Tables—Vacation Homes, Internet site http://www.census.gov/hhes/ www/housing/census/historic/vacation.html and 2005 American Community Survey, Internet site http://www.census.gov/acs/www/; calculations by New Strategist

5

Income

■ In 2005, a substantial 17.2 percent of households had an income of $100,000 or more, matching the peak reached in 2000. This share is more than four times the 4.1 percent of 1967, after adjusting for inflation.

■ Between 1967 and 2005, median household income grew 31 percent, after adjusting for inflation. But the $46,326 median of 2005 was 3 percent below the level of 2000. Some households have fared better than others over the years, with older householders seeing a bigger increase in median household income.

■ Since 1987, the median income of married couples in which both husband and wife work full-time has grown much faster (up 13 percent) than the income of couples in which only the husband works full-time and the wife does not work (up 2 percent). Consequently, the income gap between these households has grown.

■ Women's earnings have been growing faster than men's for more than four decades. As a result, women are closing the earnings gap with men. Among full-time workers in 1960, women earned only 61 percent as much as men. By 2005, the figure had grown to 77 percent.

■ The number of Americans living in poverty was lower in 2005 than it was in 1959, despite the enormous expansion in our population during those years. Behind the decline in the number of poor is the plummeting poverty rate, which fell from 22.4 percent in 1959 to 12.6 percent in 2005.

Household Affluence Is at a Peak

The proportion of households with incomes of $100,000 or more is matching its all-time high.

In 2005, a substantial 17.2 percent of households had an income of $100,000 or more, matching the peak reached in 2000. This share is more than four times the 4.1 percent of 1967, after adjusting for inflation. The proportion of households with incomes between $75,000 and $99,999 also increased between 1967 and 2005, climbing from 5.7 to 11.1 percent. Behind the rise in household affluence is the aging of dual-income baby-boom couples into their peak earning years.

As the ranks of the affluent have expanded, the ranks of the middle and lower classes have shrunk. The proportion of households with incomes below $35,000 fell from 50.2 to 38.5 percent between 1967 and 2005. The share of households with incomes between $35,000 and $74,999 fell from 40.1 to 33.3 percent during those years.

Not only has household affluence grown, but the economic elite are controlling a growing share of income. Households with incomes in the top fifth of the income distribution control slightly more than half of all household income, up from 44 percent in 1967. Meanwhile, the share controlled by the bottom three income quintiles dropped from 32 to 27 percent.

■ Behind the growing affluence of American households is the rise of working women. Many of the most affluent households are dual-income couples, while the less affluent are single-parent and single-earner households.

Nearly one in six households has an income of $100,000 or more

(percent of households with incomes of $100,000 or more, 1967 and 2005; in 2005 dollars)

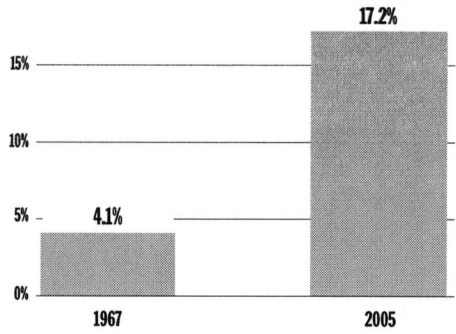

Table 5.1 Distribution of Households by Income, 1967 to 2005

(total number of households and percent distribution by income, 1967 to 2005; percentage point change for selected years; in 2005 dollars; households in thousands as of the following year)

	total households		under $15,000	$15,000– $24,999	$25,000– $34,999	$35,000– $49,999	$50,000– $74,999	$75,000– $99,999	$100,000 or more
	number	percent							
2005	114,384	100.0%	14.7%	12.4%	11.4%	14.9%	18.4%	11.1%	17.2%
2004	113,343	100.0	14.9	12.7	11.6	14.6	18.3	11.2	16.7
2003	112,000	100.0	15.0	12.3	11.5	14.7	18.0	11.4	17.0
2002	111,278	100.0	14.6	12.4	11.8	14.7	17.9	11.9	16.6
2001	109,297	100.0	14.3	12.2	11.7	15.0	18.1	11.9	16.9
2000	108,209	100.0	13.7	12.0	11.6	14.9	18.7	11.9	17.2
1999	106,434	100.0	13.6	12.4	11.2	15.1	18.7	11.9	17.0
1998	103,874	100.0	14.5	12.3	11.4	15.2	19.0	11.7	15.9
1997	102,528	100.0	15.1	12.9	11.4	15.5	18.7	11.5	14.9
1996	101,018	100.0	15.5	13.3	12.0	15.2	19.0	11.4	13.6
1995	99,627	100.0	15.4	13.5	12.0	15.8	18.9	11.2	13.2
1994	98,990	100.0	16.5	13.6	12.2	15.6	18.3	11.0	12.7
1993	97,107	100.0	17.0	13.3	12.6	15.7	18.6	10.5	12.3
1992	96,426	100.0	16.9	13.6	12.2	15.9	19.2	10.8	11.5
1991	95,669	100.0	16.5	13.0	12.6	16.1	19.4	10.7	11.6
1990	94,312	100.0	15.9	12.8	12.2	16.4	19.7	10.9	12.0
1989	93,347	100.0	15.5	13.0	11.8	16.1	19.7	11.4	12.6
1988	92,830	100.0	16.0	13.0	12.1	16.1	19.8	11.2	11.8
1987	91,124	100.0	16.4	13.0	12.2	16.0	19.9	11.1	11.4
1986	89,479	100.0	16.7	12.9	12.5	16.0	20.3	10.8	10.8
1985	88,458	100.0	17.2	13.3	13.0	16.4	19.9	10.5	9.7
1984	86,789	100.0	17.4	13.6	13.1	16.9	19.6	10.2	9.2
1983	85,290	100.0	17.8	14.3	13.1	17.2	19.5	9.6	8.4
1982	83,918	100.0	18.1	14.1	13.2	17.6	19.5	9.6	8.0
1981	83,527	100.0	17.9	14.6	13.1	17.0	20.4	9.4	7.7
1980	82,368	100.0	17.5	14.0	13.0	17.6	20.6	9.7	7.7
1979	80,776	100.0	16.8	13.4	12.9	17.2	21.5	9.9	8.3
1978	77,330	100.0	16.8	13.7	12.7	17.5	21.4	10.1	7.8
1977	76,030	100.0	18.1	14.2	13.4	18.0	20.9	8.9	6.5
1976	74,142	100.0	17.8	14.8	13.3	18.4	21.0	8.9	6.0
1975	72,867	100.0	18.5	14.6	13.6	19.0	20.5	8.5	5.5
1974	71,163	100.0	17.5	14.0	13.8	18.8	21.1	8.5	6.2
1973	69,859	100.0	17.4	13.6	12.8	19.1	21.1	9.4	6.7
1972	68,251	100.0	18.0	13.6	13.2	19.4	21.0	8.5	6.4
1971	66,676	100.0	18.8	13.7	14.1	19.9	20.6	7.7	5.2
1970	64,778	100.0	18.6	13.4	14.0	20.5	20.7	7.6	5.2
1969	63,874	100.0	18.4	13.1	14.1	20.8	21.3	7.4	4.9
1968	62,214	100.0	18.9	13.9	14.8	21.6	20.2	6.4	4.1
1967	60,813	100.0	20.5	14.0	15.7	21.8	18.3	5.7	4.1
Percentage point change									
2000 to 2005	–	–	1.0	0.4	–0.2	0.0	–0.3	–0.8	0.0
1967 to 2005	–	–	–5.8	–1.6	–4.3	–6.9	0.1	5.4	13.1

Note: "–" means not applicable.
Source: Bureau of the Census, Income, Poverty, and Health Insurance Coverage in the United States: 2005, Current Population Report, P60-231, 2006, Internet site http://www.census.gov/hhes/www/income/reports.html; calculations by New Strategist

Table 5.2 Share of Aggregate Income Received by Each Fifth and Top 5 Percent of Households, 1967 to 2005

(total number of households and percent distribution of aggregate income by household income quintile, 1967 to 2005; percentage point change for selected years; households in thousands as of the following year)

	total households number	total households percent	bottom fifth	second fifth	third fifth	fourth fifth	top fifth	top 5 percent
2005	114,384	100.0%	3.4%	8.6%	14.6%	23.0%	50.4%	22.2%
2004	113,343	100.0	3.4	8.7	14.7	23.2	50.1	21.8
2003	112,000	100.0	3.4	8.7	14.8	23.4	49.8	21.4
2002	111,278	100.0	3.5	8.8	14.8	23.3	49.7	21.7
2001	109,297	100.0	3.5	8.7	14.6	23.0	50.1	22.4
2000	108,209	100.0	3.6	8.9	14.8	23.0	49.8	22.1
1999	106,434	100.0	3.6	8.9	14.9	23.2	49.4	21.5
1998	103,874	100.0	3.6	9.0	15.0	23.2	49.2	21.4
1997	102,528	100.0	3.6	8.9	15.0	23.2	49.4	21.7
1996	101,018	100.0	3.7	9.0	15.1	23.3	49.0	21.4
1995	99,627	100.0	3.7	9.1	15.2	23.3	48.7	21.0
1994	98,990	100.0	3.6	8.9	15.0	23.4	49.1	21.2
1993	97,107	100.0	3.6	9.0	15.1	23.5	48.9	21.0
1992	96,426	100.0	3.8	9.4	15.8	24.2	46.9	18.6
1991	95,669	100.0	3.8	9.6	15.9	24.2	46.5	18.1
1990	94,312	100.0	3.9	9.6	15.9	24.0	46.6	18.6
1989	93,347	100.0	3.8	9.5	15.8	24.0	46.8	18.9
1988	92,830	100.0	3.8	9.6	16.0	24.3	46.3	18.3
1987	91,124	100.0	3.8	9.6	16.1	24.3	46.2	18.2
1986	89,479	100.0	3.9	9.7	16.2	24.5	45.7	17.5
1985	88,458	100.0	4.0	9.7	16.3	24.6	45.3	17.0
1984	86,789	100.0	4.1	9.9	16.4	24.7	44.9	16.5
1983	85,290	100.0	4.1	10.0	16.5	24.7	44.7	16.4
1982	83,918	100.0	4.1	10.1	16.6	24.7	44.5	16.2
1981	83,527	100.0	4.2	10.2	16.8	25.0	43.8	15.6
1980	82,368	100.0	4.3	10.3	16.9	24.9	43.7	15.8
1979	80,776	100.0	4.2	10.3	16.9	24.7	44.0	16.4
1978	77,330	100.0	4.3	10.3	16.9	24.8	43.7	16.2
1977	76,030	100.0	4.4	10.3	17.0	24.8	43.6	16.1
1976	74,142	100.0	4.4	10.4	17.1	24.8	43.3	16.0
1975	72,867	100.0	4.4	10.5	17.1	24.8	43.2	15.9
1974	71,163	100.0	4.4	10.6	17.1	24.7	43.1	15.9
1973	69,859	100.0	4.2	10.5	17.1	24.6	43.6	16.6
1972	68,251	100.0	4.1	10.5	17.1	24.5	43.9	17.0
1971	66,676	100.0	4.1	10.6	17.3	24.5	43.5	16.7
1970	64,778	100.0	4.1	10.8	17.4	24.5	43.3	16.6
1969	63,874	100.0	4.1	10.9	17.5	24.5	43.0	16.6
1968	62,214	100.0	4.2	11.1	17.5	24.4	42.8	16.6
1967	60,813	100.0	4.0	10.8	17.3	24.2	43.8	17.5
Percentage point change								
2000 to 2005	–	–	–0.2	–0.3	–0.2	0.0	0.6	0.1
1967 to 2005	–	–	–0.6	–2.2	–2.7	–1.2	6.6	4.7

Note: "–" means not applicable.
Source: Bureau of the Census, Current Population Surveys, Internet site http://www.census.gov/hhes/www/income/histinc/inchhtoc.html; calculations by New Strategist

Household Income Is Up and Down

Median household income is greater than it was in 1967, less than in 2000.

Between 1967 and 2005, median household income grew 31 percent, after adjusting for inflation. But the $46,326 median of 2005 was 3 percent below the level of 2000. Some households have fared better than others over the years. The older the householder, the greater the growth in median household income. Householders aged 65 or older saw their median income rise by more than 90 percent between 1967 and 2005, after adjusting for inflation. Householders aged 55 to 64 were the only ones experiencing income growth between 2000 and 2005, a consequence of their greater labor force participation.

Every household type has lost ground since 2005, as has every racial and ethnic group. Blacks saw their median household income fall the most between 2000 and 2005—down 8 percent, after adjusting for inflation. Since 1967, however, blacks have experienced the biggest gain in median household income—up 44 percent. Most educational attainment groups, including college graduates, experienced income losses between 2000 and 2005. By region, only the Northeast made any gains during those years. In the Midwest, median household income fell by 8 percent between 2000 and 2005.

■ Job losses in the manufacturing sector during the past few years have reduced men's earnings and cut household incomes.

Older householders have seen their incomes grow the most

(percent change in median household income by age of householder, 1967 to 2005; in 2005 dollars)

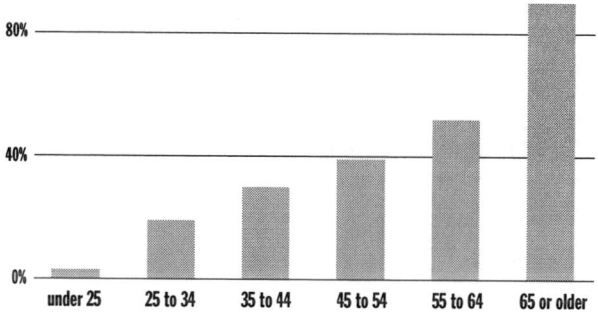

Table 5.3 Median Income of Households by Age of Householder, 1967 to 2005

(median income of households by age of householder, 1967 to 2005; percent change in income for selected years; in 2005 dollars)

	total households	under 25	25 to 34	35 to 44	45 to 54	55 to 64	65 or older
2005	$46,326	$28,770	$47,379	$58,084	$62,424	$52,260	$26,036
2004	45,817	28,497	46,985	58,578	63,068	52,077	25,336
2003	45,970	28,709	47,520	58,414	63,930	52,228	25,243
2002	46,036	30,208	49,207	58,099	64,069	51,240	25,132
2001	46,569	31,094	49,714	58,801	64,012	50,578	25,494
2000	47,599	31,567	50,346	60,943	65,341	50,844	26,166
1999	47,671	29,458	49,304	59,518	66,654	52,320	26,705
1998	46,508	28,184	47,924	57,950	64,763	51,630	25,989
1997	44,883	27,391	46,301	56,228	62,918	50,160	25,181
1996	43,967	26,557	44,457	55,027	62,524	49,322	24,092
1995	43,346	26,686	44,141	55,289	61,131	48,435	24,291
1994	42,038	25,199	43,194	54,289	61,578	45,905	23,577
1993	41,562	25,720	41,615	54,362	61,472	44,533	23,615
1992	41,774	24,084	42,596	54,342	60,591	46,351	23,364
1991	42,108	25,597	43,109	55,000	61,152	46,550	23,727
1990	43,366	26,072	43,969	55,848	60,715	46,874	24,411
1989	43,946	28,374	45,341	57,217	63,128	46,855	23,977
1988	43,168	27,019	45,044	57,960	60,591	45,829	23,662
1987	42,827	27,028	44,315	57,821	61,141	45,291	23,735
1986	42,309	26,017	44,010	55,716	60,599	45,502	23,527
1985	40,868	26,040	43,406	53,756	57,488	44,223	22,934
1984	40,079	25,083	42,439	53,255	56,352	43,081	22,885
1983	38,833	24,919	40,434	51,466	56,436	42,353	21,788
1982	39,064	26,757	41,214	51,069	54,197	42,752	21,383
1981	39,125	27,162	42,077	52,068	55,473	43,160	20,313
1980	39,739	28,522	43,390	53,016	56,369	43,861	19,704
1979	41,015	29,683	45,356	55,056	57,428	44,691	19,632
1978	41,061	30,022	44,981	54,320	57,735	43,689	19,301
1977	38,585	27,210	42,858	51,390	55,089	40,686	18,045
1976	38,368	26,803	42,327	50,572	53,424	40,564	18,032
1975	37,736	26,025	41,980	49,703	52,197	39,927	17,861
1974	38,774	28,091	43,016	51,548	53,234	39,719	18,325
1973	40,008	28,529	45,039	53,142	53,591	41,397	17,442
1972	39,216	28,555	43,988	51,311	53,079	40,578	16,860
1971	37,634	27,434	42,007	48,423	50,090	38,952	15,895
1970	38,026	29,035	42,188	48,462	49,689	38,775	15,229
1969	38,282	29,023	42,558	48,974	49,910	37,726	15,192
1968	36,873	28,706	40,916	46,793	46,536	36,330	15,144
1967	35,379	27,811	39,683	44,557	45,062	34,458	13,670

Percent change

2000 to 2005	–2.7%	–8.9%	–5.9%	–4.7%	–4.5%	2.8%	–0.5%
1967 to 2005	30.9	3.4	19.4	30.4	38.5	51.7	90.5

Source: Bureau of the Census, Current Population Surveys, Annual Social and Economic Supplement, Internet site http://www .census.gov/hhes/www/income/histinc/inchhtoc.html; calculations by New Strategist

Table 5.4 Median Income of Households by Type of Household, 1980 to 2005

(median household income by type of household, 1980 to 2005; percent change for selected years; in 2005 dollars)

	total households	family households			nonfamily households	
		married couples	female hh, no spouse present	male hh, no spouse present	women living alone	men living alone
2005	$46,326	$66,067	$30,650	$46,756	$20,166	$30,020
2004	45,817	65,946	30,823	46,526	20,166	28,330
2003	45,970	66,225	31,101	44,528	19,819	29,118
2002	46,036	66,493	31,481	45,278	19,418	29,101
2001	46,569	66,687	31,035	44,900	19,705	31,190
2000	47,599	67,189	32,039	47,786	20,208	30,779
1999	47,671	66,364	30,684	48,930	20,243	31,363
1998	46,508	64,917	29,175	47,141	19,622	31,122
1997	44,883	62,683	27,945	44,433	18,836	28,953
1996	43,967	61,763	26,713	44,172	18,118	29,793
1995	43,346	59,950	27,155	42,656	18,230	28,730
1994	42,038	58,685	25,892	39,703	17,500	27,643
1993	41,562	57,378	24,672	39,710	17,288	28,433
1992	41,774	57,223	25,043	41,329	17,635	27,242
1991	42,108	57,412	25,110	43,344	17,939	28,317
1990	43,366	57,926	26,169	45,697	18,173	28,914
1989	43,946	58,782	26,428	46,120	18,533	29,824
1988	43,168	57,773	25,451	45,415	18,428	28,991
1987	42,827	57,440	25,439	43,886	17,613	27,927
1986	42,309	55,868	24,363	44,696	16,953	27,985
1985	40,868	53,920	24,772	42,141	16,913	28,226
1984	40,079	53,080	24,090	43,898	17,235	27,182
1983	38,833	50,815	22,757	42,546	16,997	26,255
1982	39,064	50,483	23,013	41,088	15,797	26,759
1981	39,125	51,498	23,468	42,136	15,189	26,332
1980	39,739	52,013	24,301	42,129	15,012	25,865
Percent change						
2000 to 2005	−2.7%	−1.7%	−4.3%	−2.2%	−0.2%	−2.5%
1980 to 2005	16.6	27.0	26.1	11.0	34.3	16.1

*Source: Bureau of the Census, Current Population Surveys, Annual Social and Economic Supplement, Internet site http://www
.census.gov/hhes/www/income/histinc/inchhtoc.html; calculations by New Strategist*

Table 5.5   Median Income of Households by Race and Hispanic Origin of Householder, 1967 to 2005

(median income of households by race and Hispanic origin of householder, 1967 to 2005; percent change for selected years; in 2005 dollars)

	total households	Asian	black	Hispanic	white total	white non-Hispanic
2005	$46,326	$61,048	$30,954	$35,967	$48,554	$50,784
2004	45,817	59,370	31,246	35,417	48,218	50,546
2003	45,970	58,645	31,506	35,017	48,424	50,702
2002	46,036	56,757	31,672	35,934	48,942	50,911
2001	46,569	59,148	32,499	37,015	49,093	51,065
2000	47,599	63,205	33,630	37,598	49,782	51,717
1999	47,671	59,695	32,694	36,016	49,580	51,726
1998	46,508	55,780	30,321	33,884	48,933	50,759
1997	44,883	54,882	30,383	32,297	47,269	49,215
1996	43,967	53,609	29,089	30,853	46,034	48,049
1995	43,346	51,662	28,485	29,079	45,496	47,292
1994	42,038	52,745	27,397	30,516	44,336	45,767
1993	41,562	51,016	25,986	30,447	43,849	45,463
1992	41,774	51,544	25,573	30,812	43,919	45,393
1991	42,108	50,946	26,287	31,716	44,125	45,179
1990	43,366	55,687	27,048	32,340	45,232	46,266
1989	43,946	54,887	27,492	33,327	46,227	47,221
1988	43,168	51,163	26,015	32,281	45,635	46,893
1987	42,827	52,959	25,755	31,776	45,123	46,364
1986	42,309	–	25,626	31,186	44,480	45,491
1985	40,868	–	25,642	30,221	43,100	44,069
1984	40,079	–	24,087	30,383	42,282	43,160
1983	38,833	–	23,110	29,575	40,724	–
1982	39,064	–	23,178	29,394	40,896	41,582
1981	39,125	–	23,197	31,384	41,338	41,935
1980	39,739	–	24,153	30,631	41,925	42,667
1979	41,015	–	25,248	32,496	43,004	43,609
1978	41,061	–	25,652	32,173	42,686	43,490
1977	38,585	–	23,944	30,269	40,575	41,380
1976	38,368	–	23,899	28,941	40,192	41,012
1975	37,736	–	23,691	28,350	39,463	39,760
1974	38,774	–	24,115	30,840	40,550	40,896
1973	40,008	–	24,681	30,995	41,929	42,299
1972	39,216	–	24,014	31,047	41,141	41,727
1971	37,634	–	23,253	–	39,364	–
1970	38,026	–	24,107	–	39,606	–
1969	38,282	–	24,150	–	39,953	–
1968	36,873	–	22,639	–	38,392	–
1967	35,379	–	21,422	–	36,895	–
Percent change						
2000 to 2005	–2.7%	–3.4%	–8.0%	–4.3%	–2.5%	–1.8%
1967 to 2005	30.9	–	44.5	–	31.6	–

Note: Beginning in 2002, data for Asians and blacks are for those who identify themselves as being of the race alone and those who identify themselves as being of the race in combination with one or more other races. Hispanics may be of any race. Beginning in 2002, data for non-Hispanic whites are for those who identify themselves as white alone and not Hispanic. "–" means data are not available.
Source: Bureau of the Census, Current Population Surveys, Annual Social and Economic Supplement, Internet site http://www .census.gov/hhes/www/income/histinc/inchhtoc.html; calculations by New Strategist

Table 5.6 Median Income of Households by Years of Schooling, 1967 to 1990

(median income of households by years of schooling for householders aged 25 or older, 1967 to 1990; percent change, 1967–90; in 2005 dollars)

	total households	fewer than 9 years	high school 1–3 years	4 years	college, 1–3 years	college, 4 years or more total	4 years	5+ years
1990	$44,545	$19,585	$26,346	$41,630	$51,739	$73,210	$68,190	$79,129
1989	45,403	19,302	27,012	42,660	53,337	74,769	69,652	82,050
1988	44,597	19,603	26,320	42,826	51,902	73,388	66,716	81,434
1987	44,113	19,605	27,789	42,607	52,674	72,260	67,333	79,265
1986	43,685	19,791	27,417	42,764	51,069	72,110	67,605	77,957
1985	42,441	19,635	27,390	41,742	49,637	69,978	65,218	77,410
1984	41,576	19,556	27,811	41,717	48,143	67,842	64,043	73,555
1983	40,118	19,334	26,682	40,120	47,823	65,925	61,661	71,445
1982	40,205	19,700	27,169	40,803	47,568	64,901	60,755	70,190
1981	40,622	19,848	27,966	42,157	48,415	63,931	59,502	69,194
1980	41,249	19,914	29,648	44,065	48,782	64,803	61,346	68,851
1979	42,456	20,616	30,623	45,413	50,596	66,047	62,100	71,018
1978	42,296	20,822	31,625	45,172	49,890	65,599	61,788	70,069
1977	40,172	19,989	30,420	43,523	47,805	63,166	59,865	67,064
1976	39,905	20,373	31,588	43,262	48,056	63,178	59,670	67,391
1975	39,322	20,240	30,643	42,392	48,369	63,067	59,511	67,576
1974	40,304	21,342	33,462	43,999	48,892	64,527	61,473	68,609
1973	41,576	–	35,220	45,800	50,919	67,654	–	–
1972	40,671	–	35,212	45,132	50,305	66,954	–	–
1971	38,952	–	34,841	43,387	48,293	63,096	–	–
1970	38,997	–	35,322	43,812	49,110	62,868	–	–
1969	39,309	–	36,138	43,991	49,449	62,774	–	–
1968	37,707	–	35,435	42,221	47,436	60,417	–	–
1967	36,325	–	34,468	40,931	46,082	58,767	–	–
Percent change								
1967 to 1990	22.6%	–	–23.6%	1.7%	12.3%	24.6%	–	–

Note: Because educational attainment categories changed in 1991, these data are not strictly comparable with those in the educational attainment table that follows. "–" means data are not available.
Source: Bureau of the Census, Current Population Surveys, Annual Social and Economic Supplement, Internet site http://www .census.gov/hhes/www/income/histinc/inchhtoc.html; calculations by New Strategist

Table 5.7 Median Income of Households by Educational Attainment of Householder, 1991 to 2005

(median income of households by educational attainment of householders aged 25 or older, 1991 to 2005; percent change for selected years; in 2005 dollars)

	total households	less than 9th grade	9th to 12th grade	high school graduate	some college	associate's degree	bachelor's degree or more total	bachelor's degree	master's degree	professional degree	doctoral degree
2005	$47,716	$20,224	$24,675	$38,191	$48,284	$54,709	$77,179	$72,424	$81,023	>$100k	>$100k
2004	47,490	20,158	23,241	38,578	48,933	55,713	76,788	70,705	82,812	103,344	103,344
2003	47,772	19,937	24,109	39,090	48,661	55,151	77,942	72,935	83,349	106,122	102,758
2002	47,806	19,952	25,257	38,695	49,210	55,425	79,895	75,071	83,010	108,553	107,068
2001	48,073	19,983	25,641	39,761	50,519	56,421	79,714	74,069	87,013	110,279	102,346
2000	49,061	19,843	25,700	41,405	50,583	57,247	81,438	75,514	88,793	113,357	107,778
1999	49,067	20,172	25,445	41,729	51,563	57,605	81,669	75,266	87,123	117,141	113,781
1998	48,196	19,321	24,787	41,112	49,825	58,133	79,506	74,380	85,022	113,994	100,587
1997	46,320	18,849	24,077	40,970	48,534	54,893	76,766	71,618	82,616	111,862	105,802
1996	45,235	19,047	24,345	40,006	47,567	55,137	74,300	68,303	79,142	111,916	100,538
1995	44,820	19,135	23,276	39,911	47,264	53,576	73,844	67,236	82,631	104,320	101,769
1994	43,630	18,599	22,857	39,181	46,748	52,453	74,840	68,235	79,538	101,631	101,833
1993	42,793	18,519	23,901	38,182	46,856	52,660	74,655	68,487	80,276	116,628	99,449
1992	43,087	18,299	23,619	39,435	48,046	52,191	73,524	67,333	78,741	115,514	95,473
1991	43,375	18,480	24,509	39,817	49,131	55,490	73,060	68,077	77,117	108,952	98,283
Percent change											
2000 to 2005	–2.7%	1.9%	–4.0%	–7.8%	–4.5%	–4.4%	–5.2%	–4.1%	–8.8%	–	–
1991 to 2005	10.0	9.4	0.7	–4.1	–1.7	–1.4	5.6	6.4	5.1	–	–

Note: Because educational attainment categories changed in 1991, these data are not strictly comparable with those in the preceding years of schooling table. "–" means data are not available.
Source: Bureau of the Census, Current Population Surveys, Annual Social and Economic Supplement, Internet site http://www.census.gov/hhes/www/income/histinc/inchhtoc.html; calculations by New Strategist

Table 5.8 Median Income of Households by Region, 1975 to 2005

(median income of households by region, 1975 to 2005; percent change in income for selected years; in 2005 dollars)

	total households	Northeast	Midwest	South	West
2005	$46,326	$50,882	$45,950	$42,138	$50,002
2004	45,817	49,462	46,134	42,108	49,245
2003	45,970	49,603	47,470	42,261	49,686
2002	46,036	49,785	47,353	42,902	49,004
2001	46,569	50,415	48,340	42,903	49,722
2000	47,599	49,594	50,173	43,517	50,914
1999	47,671	49,061	49,799	43,746	49,861
1998	46,508	48,600	48,570	42,815	49,018
1997	44,883	47,216	46,473	41,656	47,499
1996	43,967	46,338	45,313	40,164	45,990
1995	43,346	45,934	45,588	39,359	45,767
1994	42,038	45,506	42,352	39,115	44,889
1993	41,562	44,896	41,774	37,837	44,885
1992	41,774	44,996	42,003	37,646	45,439
1991	42,108	46,778	41,830	37,988	45,081
1990	43,366	47,324	43,300	39,020	45,999
1989	43,946	49,628	43,709	39,331	47,261
1988	43,168	48,242	43,668	39,017	45,723
1987	42,827	46,283	42,374	39,388	45,800
1986	42,309	45,022	42,230	38,368	45,884
1985	40,868	44,099	40,752	37,025	44,612
1984	40,079	42,109	40,385	36,875	43,730
1983	38,833	40,568	39,174	36,046	41,310
1982	39,064	40,102	40,321	36,004	41,041
1981	39,125	40,666	40,391	35,570	41,935
1980	39,739	40,821	41,092	36,571	42,654
1979	41,015	42,020	43,123	37,295	43,470
1978	41,061	42,274	42,721	37,221	42,280
1977	38,585	40,462	40,570	35,273	39,745
1976	38,368	39,542	41,384	34,663	39,433
1975	37,736	39,460	40,211	33,703	38,980
Percent change					
2000 to 2005	−2.7%	2.6%	−8.4%	−3.2%	−1.8%
1975 to 2005	22.8	28.9	14.3	25.0	28.3

Source: Bureau of the Census, Current Population Surveys, Annual Social and Economic Supplement, Internet site http://www.census.gov/hhes/www/income/histinc/inchhtoc.html; calculations by New Strategist

Working Wives Have Kept Families Afloat

Incomes have barely grown for married couples with nonworking wives.

Between 2000 and 2005, the median income of the average household fell 2.7 percent, after adjusting for inflation. Among all married couples, median household income fell a smaller 1.6 percent during those years. For married couples in which the wife works full-time, household income continued to climb despite the recession and slow economic recovery. For couples in which both husband and wife work full-time, median household income rose 2.1 percent between 2000 and 2005. This compares with a 1.7 percent decline in the median income of couples in which the husband works full-time and the wife does not work.

Since 1987, the median income of married couples in which both husband and wife work full-time has grown much faster (up 13 percent) than the income of couples in which only the husband works full-time and the wife does not work (up 2 percent). Consequently, the income gap between these households has grown. In 1987, the median income of single-earner couples was 73 percent as high as that of dual-earners. By 2005, it was only 66 percent as high.

■ More than 25 percent of wives earn more than their husbands, up from only 16 percent in 1981.

The income gap between dual- and single-earner couples is growing

(median household income of married couples by earner status, 1987 and 2005; in 2005 dollars)

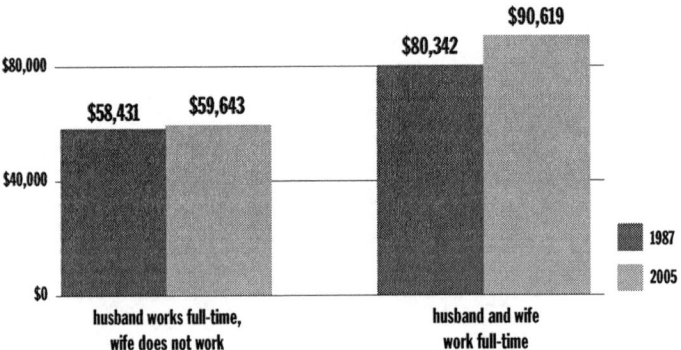

Table 5.9 Median Income of Households by Number of Earners, 1987 to 2005

(median income of households by number of earners, 1987 to 2005; in 2005 dollars)

	total households	no earners	one earner	two earners	three earners	four or more earners
2005	$46,326	$16,893	$37,541	$70,952	$87,905	$100,000+
2004	45,817	16,667	37,371	71,224	86,627	103,344
2003	45,970	16,620	38,179	71,471	87,512	106,122
2002	46,036	16,718	37,775	71,150	87,069	107,299
2001	46,569	17,040	37,610	71,187	85,196	104,312
2000	47,599	17,265	38,110	70,533	85,986	104,647
1999	47,671	18,108	37,437	69,925	86,775	104,828
1998	46,508	17,273	37,271	68,639	83,738	103,668
1997	44,883	17,153	36,120	65,729	81,484	102,872
1996	43,967	16,501	34,556	64,932	77,335	97,249
1995	43,346	16,666	35,066	63,602	80,381	94,440
1994	42,038	15,863	34,150	62,194	78,725	96,777
1993	41,562	15,708	34,004	61,810	76,193	96,109
1992	41,774	15,628	34,435	60,803	76,481	94,363
1991	42,108	16,088	34,711	60,150	77,447	96,677
1990	43,366	16,162	35,592	60,330	77,135	97,036
1989	43,946	16,277	36,197	61,134	78,338	99,128
1988	43,168	15,745	35,736	60,600	77,762	101,579
1987	42,827	15,641	35,470	59,951	77,852	99,170

Percent change

2000 to 2005	−2.7%	−2.2%	−1.5%	0.6%	2.2%	–
1987 to 2005	8.2	8.0	5.8	18.3	12.9	–

Note: "–" means data are not available.
Source: Bureau of the Census, Current Population Surveys, Annual Social and Economic Supplement, Internet site http://www.census.gov/hhes/www/income/histinc/inchhtoc.html; calculations by New Strategist

Table 5.10 Median Income of Married Couples by Work Experience of Husband and Wife, 1987 to 2005

(median household income of married couples with husband working full-time, year-round, by work experience of wife, 1987 to 2005; percent change for selected years; in 2005 dollars)

	total married couples	husband works full-time		wife does not work
		wife works		
		total	full-time	
2005	$65,906	$85,565	$90,619	$59,643
2004	65,758	85,385	90,656	57,923
2003	66,094	86,229	90,752	59,021
2002	66,358	85,547	90,989	60,473
2001	66,537	84,320	89,476	59,508
2000	66,993	84,329	88,725	60,687
1999	66,186	83,491	89,253	59,051
1998	64,802	81,421	87,228	58,025
1997	62,574	78,718	84,304	58,837
1996	61,575	77,094	81,917	55,723
1995	59,864	76,167	81,770	54,860
1994	58,578	75,413	81,253	54,813
1993	57,212	74,523	80,767	55,577
1992	57,119	74,285	80,569	56,134
1991	57,300	73,671	79,799	56,634
1990	57,780	72,835	79,755	56,604
1989	58,603	73,905	80,566	58,532
1988	57,699	73,663	80,692	57,311
1987	57,319	73,183	80,342	58,431
Percent change				
2000 to 2005	−1.6%	1.5%	2.1%	−1.7%
1987 to 2005	15.0	16.9	12.8	2.1

Source: Bureau of the Census, Current Population Surveys, Annual Social and Economic Supplement, Internet site http://www .census.gov/hhes/www/income/histinc/incfamdet.html; calculations by New Strategist

Table 5.11 Wives Who Earn More than Their Husbands, 1981 to 2005

(number of married couples, dual-earner couples, and wives who earn more than their husbands; wives who earn more than their husbands as a percent of all dual-earner couples, 1981 to 2005; married couples in thousands)

	total married couples	dual-earner couples	wives who earn more than their husbands	percent of dual-earner couples with wives earning more
2005	58,189	33,364	8,521	25.5%
2004	57,983	33,110	8,387	25.3
2003	57,725	33,189	8,355	25.2
2002	57,327	33,531	8,394	25.0
2001	56,755	33,666	8,109	24.1
2000	56,598	33,876	7,906	23.3
1999	55,315	33,344	7,420	22.3
1998	54,778	32,783	7,435	22.7
1997	54,321	32,745	7,446	22.7
1996	53,604	32,390	7,327	22.6
1995	53,570	32,030	7,028	21.9
1994	53,865	32,093	7,218	22.5
1993	53,181	31,267	6,960	22.3
1992	53,171	31,224	6,979	22.4
1991	52,457	31,003	6,499	21.0
1987	51,809	29,079	5,266	18.1
1983	50,090	26,120	4,800	18.4
1981	49,630	25,744	4,088	15.9

Note: Earnings include wages and salaries only.
Source: Bureau of the Census, Current Population Survey Annual Demographic Supplements, Internet site http://www.census
.gov/hhes/www/income/histinc/f22.html; calculations by New Strategist

Women's Incomes Are Rising Faster than Men's

Women are narrowing the income gap.

The median income of women nearly tripled between 1950 and 2005, rising from just $6,544 to $18,576, after adjusting for inflation. Men's median income grew only 77 percent during those years. Consequently, women have narrowed the income gap with men. In 1950, women's median income was just 37 percent as high as men's. By 2005, it was 59 percent of men's. Women's incomes are much lower than men's in part because these figures include both full- and part-time workers, and women are more likely than men to work part-time.

Among both men and women, people aged 65 or older have seen their incomes grow the most since 1950. Since 2000, however, only men and women aged 55 to 64 have made any gains, primarily because of increased labor force participation. By race and Hispanic origin, men's median income declined across the board between 2000 and 2005. Among women, only blacks have lost ground since 2000. Gains and losses have been mixed for both men and women by educational level. Men in every region have lost ground since 2000, while women saw their median incomes rise in every region but the West.

■ Women's median income peaks at nearly $60,000 among those with professional degrees. Their male counterparts have a median income of more than $90,000.

Women's median income is still far below men's

(median income of men and women, 2005)

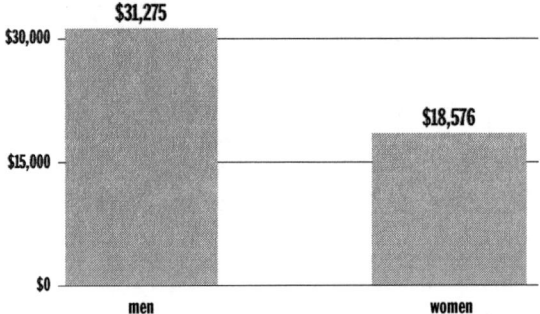

Table 5.12 Median Income by Sex, 1950 to 2005

(median income of people aged 15 or older with income by sex, and women's income as a percent of men's, 1950 to 2005; percent and percentage point change for selected years; in 2005 dollars)

	men	women	women's income as a percent of men's
2005	$31,275	$18,576	59.4%
2004	31,537	18,258	57.9
2003	31,763	18,316	57.7
2002	31,739	18,250	57.5
2001	32,092	18,322	57.1
2000	32,129	18,209	56.7
1999	31,971	17,927	56.1
1998	31,686	17,259	54.5
1997	30,579	16,620	54.4
1996	29,525	15,875	53.8
1995	28,700	15,430	53.8
1994	28,300	14,939	52.8
1993	28,073	14,695	52.3
1992	27,891	14,609	52.4
1991	28,610	14,643	51.2
1990	29,390	14,584	49.6
1989	30,244	14,632	48.4
1988	29,981	14,087	47.0
1987	29,229	13,632	46.6
1986	29,083	12,932	44.5
1985	28,224	12,488	44.2
1984	27,894	12,280	44.0
1983	27,205	11,749	43.2
1982	27,016	11,401	42.2
1981	27,636	11,196	40.5
1980	28,116	11,040	39.3
1979	29,349	10,844	36.9
1978	29,807	11,089	37.2
1977	28,780	11,204	38.9
1976	28,509	10,815	37.9
1975	28,312	10,825	38.2
1974	29,268	10,673	36.5
1973	30,660	10,641	34.7
1972	30,129	10,511	34.9
1971	28,776	10,038	34.9
1970	29,040	9,739	33.5
1969	29,338	9,729	33.2
1968	28,478	9,615	33.8
1967	27,504	8,920	32.4
1966	27,083	8,361	30.9
1965	26,348	7,978	30.3
1960	22,789	7,043	30.9
1955	20,709	6,907	33.4
1950	17,649	6,544	37.1

	percent change		percentage point change
2000 to 2005	−2.7%	2.0%	2.7
1950 to 2005	77.2	183.9	22.3

Source: Bureau of the Census, Current Population Survey Annual Demographic Supplements, Internet site http://www.census .gov/hhes/www/income/histinc/incpertoc.html; calculations by New Strategist

Table 5.13 Median Income of Men by Age, 1950 to 2005

(median income of men with income by age, 1950 to 2005; percent change for selected years; in 2005 dollars)

	total men	under 25	25 to 34	35 to 44	45 to 54	55 to 64	65+
2005	$31,275	$10,469	$31,161	$40,964	$43,627	$40,654	$21,784
2004	31,537	10,419	32,028	41,890	43,265	40,602	21,838
2003	31,763	10,571	32,433	41,594	44,655	41,297	21,610
2002	31,739	10,467	33,301	41,133	44,473	39,380	21,098
2001	32,092	10,257	33,646	42,281	45,329	39,300	21,712
2000	32,129	10,821	34,295	42,987	46,521	38,756	22,004
1999	31,971	9,781	34,412	42,636	47,798	39,224	22,608
1998	31,686	9,796	33,629	42,073	46,552	39,202	21,727
1997	30,579	9,058	31,530	39,844	45,634	37,790	21,551
1996	29,525	8,622	31,191	39,848	44,883	36,576	20,668
1995	28,700	8,794	30,031	39,967	45,267	36,864	20,968
1994	28,300	9,183	29,454	40,009	45,515	35,277	19,870
1993	28,073	8,553	29,171	40,366	44,107	33,444	19,933
1992	27,891	8,586	29,312	40,212	43,880	34,927	19,904
1991	28,610	8,779	30,184	40,955	44,419	35,586	20,067
1990	29,390	9,152	30,983	43,120	44,907	35,923	20,541
1989	30,244	9,598	32,485	44,754	47,072	37,137	19,927
1988	29,981	9,265	32,952	45,261	46,899	35,909	19,774
1987	29,229	8,968	32,747	44,440	46,814	35,961	19,600
1986	29,083	8,978	32,563	44,475	47,167	35,744	19,617
1985	28,224	8,643	32,292	43,879	44,721	35,052	18,861
1984	27,894	8,420	32,351	43,925	43,966	34,915	18,685
1983	27,205	7,966	31,247	41,725	42,980	34,759	18,114
1982	27,016	8,574	31,792	41,927	41,721	34,527	17,794
1981	27,636	6,301	33,008	43,316	43,121	35,620	16,693
1980	28,116	10,315	34,960	44,961	44,819	35,709	16,468
1979	29,349	10,605	36,558	45,707	45,386	37,445	16,029
1978	29,807	9,955	36,553	45,172	45,177	37,136	16,262
1977	28,780	9,203	35,142	44,362	43,586	34,807	15,710
1976	28,509	8,986	35,438	43,329	42,627	34,851	16,009
1975	28,312	9,101	35,296	42,632	42,236	34,026	15,859
1974	29,268	9,395	36,301	43,635	42,534	34,535	16,061
1973	30,660	–	38,394	45,785	44,419	36,354	15,627
1972	30,129	–	37,278	44,627	43,559	36,001	15,149
1971	28,776	–	35,692	41,549	40,240	33,074	14,378
1970	29,040	–	35,945	41,208	39,937	33,428	13,392
1969	29,338	–	36,389	41,276	39,332	33,217	12,905
1968	28,478	–	34,911	39,431	37,159	31,987	12,629
1967	27,504	–	33,675	37,821	36,543	30,322	11,412
1966	27,083	–	33,213	37,286	35,310	29,349	11,035
1965	26,348	–	31,509	35,218	33,376	27,538	11,099
1960	22,789	–	27,391	30,882	28,933	23,956	9,484
1955	20,709	–	23,965	26,241	25,519	21,215	8,245
1950	17,649	–	20,334	22,346	21,226	17,127	6,771

Percent change

2000 to 2005	–2.7%	–3.3%	–9.1%	–4.7%	–6.2%	4.9%	–1.0%
1950 to 2005	77.2	–	53.2	83.3	105.5	137.4	221.7

Note: "–" means data are not available.
Source: Bureau of the Census, Current Population Survey Annual Demographic Supplements, Internet site http://www.census
.gov/hhes/www/income/histinc/incpertoc.html; calculations by New Strategist

Table 5.14 Median Income of Women by Age, 1950 to 2005

(median income of women with income by age, 1950 to 2005; percent change for selected years; in 2005 dollars)

	total women	under 25	25 to 34	35 to 44	45 to 54	55 to 64	65+
2005	$18,576	$8,220	$22,815	$25,435	$26,476	$22,122	$12,495
2004	18,258	7,961	22,805	25,218	27,109	21,498	12,485
2003	18,316	7,890	23,338	24,909	27,449	21,615	12,570
2002	18,250	8,230	23,501	24,231	27,317	20,804	12,382
2001	18,322	8,235	23,680	24,781	26,616	19,655	12,476
2000	18,209	8,343	23,861	25,026	26,902	19,180	12,495
1999	17,927	7,823	22,617	24,201	26,436	18,675	12,836
1998	17,259	7,815	21,836	24,262	25,820	17,552	12,563
1997	16,620	7,692	21,404	22,688	24,905	17,436	12,204
1996	15,875	7,285	20,296	22,852	23,594	16,496	11,924
1995	15,430	6,755	19,789	22,130	22,544	15,749	11,900
1994	14,939	7,177	19,393	21,093	22,216	14,159	11,661
1993	14,695	7,119	18,609	21,078	21,717	14,407	11,307
1992	14,609	7,050	18,587	21,022	21,615	13,817	11,158
1991	14,643	7,264	18,120	21,141	20,580	13,840	11,446
1990	14,584	7,100	18,233	21,006	20,609	13,614	11,650
1989	14,632	7,205	18,595	20,988	19,982	13,931	11,638
1988	14,087	7,111	18,338	19,893	19,059	13,283	11,263
1987	13,632	7,244	18,042	19,712	18,509	12,393	11,333
1986	12,932	6,872	17,520	18,802	17,639	12,536	10,918
1985	12,488	6,560	17,094	17,780	16,644	12,412	10,924
1984	12,280	6,453	16,793	17,096	15,919	12,225	10,764
1983	11,749	6,428	15,810	16,474	15,256	11,396	10,411
1982	11,401	6,492	15,439	15,205	14,529	11,440	10,390
1981	11,196	4,094	15,585	15,109	14,420	11,025	9,653
1980	11,040	7,010	15,647	14,507	14,368	11,053	9,483
1979	10,844	7,034	15,822	14,668	13,943	10,928	9,371
1978	11,089	7,038	15,916	15,820	15,461	12,192	9,213
1977	11,204	6,508	16,779	15,745	16,120	12,887	8,805
1976	10,815	6,073	16,247	15,600	16,123	12,261	8,517
1975	10,825	6,025	16,156	15,046	16,201	12,472	8,631
1974	10,673	6,136	15,631	15,413	16,341	12,546	8,446
1973	10,641	–	15,764	15,642	16,377	13,058	8,065
1972	10,511	–	15,388	15,618	16,447	12,978	7,680
1971	10,038	–	14,778	15,140	16,337	12,844	7,112
1970	9,739	–	14,041	15,020	16,096	12,826	6,626
1969	9,729	–	13,690	14,772	16,237	12,736	6,375
1968	9,615	–	13,720	14,496	15,539	12,267	6,243
1967	8,920	–	12,957	14,047	15,260	11,649	5,562
1966	8,361	–	11,995	13,220	14,077	11,301	5,538
1965	7,978	–	11,839	13,030	13,428	10,590	5,161
1960	7,043	–	9,802	11,361	11,741	7,903	4,586
1955	6,907	–	9,873	9,756	10,638	7,752	4,317
1950	6,544	–	9,305	8,982	8,529	6,304	3,646

Percent change

2000 to 2005	2.0%	–1.5%	–4.4%	1.6%	–1.6%	15.3%	0.0%
1950 to 2005	183.9	–	145.2	183.2	210.4	250.9	242.7

Note: "–" means data are not available.
Source: Bureau of the Census, Current Population Survey Annual Demographic Supplements, Internet site http://www.census
.gov/hhes/www/income/histinc/incpertoc.html; calculations by New Strategist

Table 5.15 Median Income of Men by Race and Hispanic Origin, 1950 to 2005

(median income of men aged 15 or older with income by race and Hispanic origin, 1950 to 2005; percent change for selected years; in 2005 dollars)

	total men	Asian	black	Hispanic	white total	white non-Hispanic
2005	$31,275	$33,036	$22,609	$22,089	$32,179	$35,345
2004	31,537	33,552	23,473	22,277	32,393	34,804
2003	31,763	33,680	23,278	22,342	32,613	34,310
2002	31,739	33,477	23,349	22,473	32,982	34,774
2001	32,092	34,292	23,673	22,264	33,348	35,059
2000	32,129	34,951	24,194	22,102	33,777	35,717
1999	31,971	32,656	23,945	20,929	33,577	36,160
1998	31,686	30,049	23,109	20,640	33,066	35,716
1997	30,579	30,378	21,948	19,668	31,674	33,426
1996	29,525	28,955	20,429	19,123	30,906	32,568
1995	28,700	28,191	20,360	18,877	30,395	32,413
1994	28,300	29,824	19,521	18,893	29,536	31,429
1993	28,073	28,791	19,430	18,211	29,243	30,826
1992	27,891	27,121	17,813	18,282	29,188	30,542
1991	28,610	27,435	18,117	19,314	29,905	30,993
1990	29,390	28,088	18,637	19,509	30,660	31,802
1989	30,244	31,334	19,170	20,372	31,718	32,930
1988	29,981	29,210	19,097	20,661	31,647	32,827
1987	29,229	–	18,430	20,098	31,068	32,364
1986	29,083	–	18,390	19,597	30,690	32,070
1985	28,224	–	18,633	19,785	29,608	30,614
1984	27,894	–	16,893	19,849	29,444	30,320
1983	27,205	–	16,673	20,970	28,636	–
1982	27,016	–	17,116	20,279	28,562	29,292
1981	27,636	–	17,437	20,929	29,324	30,096
1980	28,116	–	17,971	21,674	29,906	30,699
1979	29,349	–	18,979	22,104	30,660	31,305
1978	29,807	–	18,702	22,842	31,218	31,551
1977	28,780	–	17,888	22,167	30,144	30,756
1976	28,509	–	18,095	21,323	30,054	30,605
1975	28,312	–	17,781	21,673	29,741	30,426
1974	29,268	–	18,997	22,311	30,660	31,308
1973	30,660	–	19,460	23,597	32,171	32,632
1972	30,129	–	19,141	23,399	31,601	31,960
1971	28,776	–	17,992	–	30,168	–
1970	29,040	–	18,099	–	30,524	–
1969	29,338	–	17,966	–	30,871	–
1968	28,478	–	17,706	–	29,844	–
1967	27,504	–	16,573	–	28,955	–
1966	27,083	–	15,807	–	28,542	–
1965	26,348	–	14,934	–	27,748	–
1960	22,789	–	12,623	–	23,995	–
1955	20,709	–	11,502	–	21,856	–
1950	17,649	–	10,102	–	18,603	–
Percent change						
2000 to 2005	–2.7%	–5.5%	–6.6%	–0.1%	–4.7%	–1.0%
1950 to 2005	77.2	–	123.8	–	73.0	–

Note: "–" means data are not available.
Source: Bureau of the Census, Current Population Survey Annual Demographic Supplements, Internet site http://www.census
.gov/hhes/www/income/histinc/incpertoc.html; calculations by New Strategist

Table 5.16 Median Income of Women by Race and Hispanic Origin, 1950 to 2005

(median income of women aged 15 or older with income by race and Hispanic origin, 1950 to 2005; percent change for selected years; in 2005 dollars)

	total women	Asian	black	Hispanic	white total	white non-Hispanic
2005	$18,576	$21,623	$17,595	$15,036	$18,669	$19,451
2004	18,258	21,305	17,927	14,935	18,291	19,052
2003	18,316	18,973	17,553	14,477	18,489	19,421
2002	18,250	19,429	18,097	14,507	18,278	18,876
2001	18,322	20,429	17,956	13,876	18,364	19,000
2000	18,209	19,674	18,002	13,884	18,227	18,891
1999	17,927	19,676	17,309	13,326	17,983	18,638
1998	17,259	18,213	15,712	12,991	17,483	18,200
1997	16,620	17,359	15,826	12,444	16,728	17,452
1996	15,875	18,128	14,583	11,749	16,056	16,741
1995	15,430	16,361	13,943	11,357	15,666	16,291
1994	14,939	16,107	13,738	11,222	15,153	15,564
1993	14,695	16,450	12,649	10,776	14,988	15,431
1992	14,609	16,187	12,118	11,328	14,949	15,343
1991	14,643	15,411	12,322	11,200	14,985	15,375
1990	14,584	16,056	12,061	10,909	14,942	15,324
1989	14,632	17,041	11,973	11,626	14,917	15,223
1988	14,087	14,657	11,653	11,083	14,434	14,772
1987	13,632	–	11,420	10,895	13,980	14,294
1986	12,932	–	11,158	10,770	13,187	13,410
1985	12,488	–	10,862	10,417	12,730	12,871
1984	12,280	–	11,022	10,424	12,425	12,624
1983	11,749	–	10,307	10,044	11,939	–
1982	11,401	–	10,193	9,954	11,556	11,901
1981	11,196	–	10,057	10,379	11,321	11,524
1980	11,040	–	10,277	9,884	11,100	11,175
1979	10,844	–	9,962	10,340	10,946	11,230
1978	11,089	–	10,105	10,325	11,222	11,718
1977	11,204	–	9,823	10,431	11,375	11,895
1976	10,815	–	10,277	10,159	10,906	11,653
1975	10,825	–	9,936	10,240	10,937	11,564
1974	10,673	–	9,744	10,416	10,794	11,334
1973	10,641	–	9,697	10,093	10,744	10,972
1972	10,511	–	9,884	10,705	10,579	10,676
1971	10,038	–	8,942	–	10,205	–
1970	9,739	–	8,982	–	9,866	–
1969	9,729	–	8,397	–	9,957	–
1968	9,615	–	7,853	–	9,900	–
1967	8,920	–	7,231	–	9,188	–
1966	8,361	–	6,661	–	8,754	–
1965	7,978	–	6,158	–	8,461	–
1960	7,043	–	4,675	–	7,552	–
1955	6,907	–	4,027	–	7,721	–
1950	6,544	–	3,255	–	7,279	–
Percent change						
2000 to 2005	2.0%	9.9%	–2.3%	8.3%	2.4%	3.0%
1950 to 2005	183.9	–	440.6	–	156.5	–

Note: "–" means data are not available.
Source: Bureau of the Census, Current Population Survey Annual Demographic Supplements, Internet site http://www.census .gov/hhes/www/income/histinc/incpertoc.html; calculations by New Strategist

Table 5.17 Median Income of Men by Years of School Completed, 1963 to 1990

(median income of men aged 25 or older by years of school completed, 1963 to 1990; percent change, 1963 to 1990; in 2005 dollars)

	total men	less than 9 years	high school 1–3 years	4 years	college 1–3 years	college, 4 years or more total	4 years	5+ years
1990	$33,805	$14,917	$21,914	$31,447	$39,373	$54,832	$50,952	$61,670
1989	34,755	15,208	21,952	32,915	40,140	57,093	52,725	63,590
1988	34,944	15,732	22,305	33,593	40,270	56,602	51,260	63,499
1987	34,874	16,010	23,239	33,298	40,569	56,117	51,611	62,212
1986	34,901	15,702	22,773	33,599	40,339	56,595	53,703	61,586
1985	34,061	15,566	22,270	32,872	39,074	55,278	51,389	60,994
1984	33,798	15,384	22,402	33,660	38,225	54,174	50,434	58,811
1983	32,682	15,619	22,530	32,666	37,796	52,262	48,627	56,784
1982	32,782	15,633	23,393	33,030	38,694	51,207	47,700	55,708
1981	33,958	16,400	24,483	34,848	40,007	52,278	48,491	56,078
1980	34,957	16,703	25,885	36,376	40,412	52,018	49,002	56,622
1979	36,276	16,936	27,276	38,536	41,897	53,431	50,145	57,762
1978	36,463	17,772	28,400	39,091	42,138	54,927	51,174	58,408
1977	35,182	17,439	28,495	37,548	40,504	52,681	49,443	57,167
1976	34,969	17,599	28,841	37,482	40,368	52,393	49,801	55,820
1975	34,788	17,503	28,222	37,845	41,766	53,349	50,077	57,289
1974	36,027	18,405	30,885	39,262	42,981	55,409	49,869	55,967
1973	37,298	20,011	32,814	41,225	44,415	55,962	53,050	60,997
1972	36,352	19,788	32,256	40,057	44,368	57,123	54,676	60,484
1971	34,358	19,130	31,556	37,884	42,949	54,717	52,412	57,694
1970	34,355	19,244	31,935	38,191	43,011	55,210	52,872	58,453
1969	34,581	19,554	32,304	38,488	42,869	55,925	54,273	58,060
1968	33,264	19,449	31,283	36,816	41,040	53,607	51,745	55,893
1967	32,026	18,410	30,495	35,879	40,391	52,279	49,975	55,409
1966	31,278	17,803	30,533	35,341	39,348	50,225	49,653	51,251
1965	29,364	16,901	29,028	33,875	37,882	47,460	45,887	50,424
1964	28,857	16,701	28,547	33,423	37,508	46,966	44,965	49,953
1963	28,219	16,485	27,852	32,424	36,764	43,169	42,180	45,585

Percent change

1963 to 1990	19.8%	−9.5%	−21.3%	−3.0%	7.1%	27.0%	20.8%	35.3%

Source: Bureau of the Census, Current Population Survey Annual Demographic Supplements, Internet site http://www.census.gov/hhes/www/income/histinc/incpertoc.html; calculations by New Strategist

Table 5.18 Median Income of Men by Educational Attainment, 1991 to 2005

(median income of men aged 25 or older by educational attainment, 1991 to 2005; percent change for selected years; in 2005 dollars)

	total men	less than 9th grade	9th to 12th grade, no degree	high school graduate	some college	associate's degree	bachelor's degree or more				
							total	bachelor's degree	master's degree	professional degree	doctoral degree
2005	$35,758	$16,321	$20,934	$30,134	$36,930	$41,903	$58,114	$51,700	$64,468	$90,878	$76,937
2004	35,988	16,712	20,248	30,313	37,371	41,095	58,321	52,789	65,376	93,227	82,709
2003	35,569	16,407	20,153	30,524	37,220	41,403	59,164	54,033	65,475	93,950	78,374
2002	35,248	16,424	21,496	29,880	38,018	41,218	59,908	54,928	66,033	95,761	82,660
2001	35,834	16,094	21,432	31,256	37,249	42,866	59,627	55,123	68,329	89,990	80,109
2000	36,450	16,019	21,442	31,151	37,770	43,105	60,633	55,636	67,711	94,881	80,791
1999	36,952	15,848	20,679	31,848	38,159	42,824	61,201	55,395	69,334	95,522	82,538
1998	36,664	15,035	20,885	31,745	37,827	43,012	60,128	54,718	66,720	91,332	78,124
1997	35,075	14,745	20,398	30,872	37,037	39,940	57,158	50,879	63,713	87,660	83,256
1996	33,754	15,081	19,892	30,739	36,123	40,960	54,706	49,085	61,943	89,030	77,120
1995	33,513	14,912	20,087	29,721	35,622	39,467	55,107	49,660	62,426	84,281	72,959
1994	33,179	14,754	19,002	29,169	34,877	39,926	54,758	50,425	60,762	80,442	74,890
1993	32,734	14,494	19,357	28,978	35,019	39,560	55,409	49,854	60,661	92,697	74,169
1992	32,581	14,145	19,387	29,514	35,886	39,258	55,301	50,104	60,396	93,306	70,470
1991	33,107	14,423	20,597	30,116	37,167	41,035	55,634	50,412	60,277	89,093	72,466
Percent change											
2000–2005	−1.9%	1.9%	−2.4%	−3.3%	−2.2%	−2.8%	−4.2%	−7.1%	−4.8%	−4.2%	−4.8%
1991–2005	8.0	13.2	1.6	0.1	-0.6	2.1	4.5	2.6	7.0	2.0	6.2

Source: Bureau of the Census, Current Population Survey Annual Demographic Supplements, Internet site http://www.census.gov/hhes/www/income/histinc/incpertoc.html; calculations by New Strategist

Table 5.19 Median Income of Women by Years of School Completed, 1963 to 1990

(median income of women aged 25 or older by years of school completed, 1963 to 1990; percent change, 1963 to 1990; in 2005 dollars)

	total women	less than 9 years	high school 1–3 years	4 years	college 1–3 years	college, 4 years or more		
						total	4 years	5+ years
1990	$16,325	$8,571	$10,199	$15,429	$21,359	$32,600	$29,492	$39,116
1989	16,441	8,555	10,265	15,871	21,655	32,929	29,576	39,644
1988	15,986	8,253	9,981	15,457	21,195	32,450	29,199	37,225
1987	15,505	8,309	10,340	15,025	20,521	31,013	27,761	36,782
1986	14,584	8,303	9,909	14,217	19,668	30,699	27,404	36,704
1985	14,109	8,463	9,844	14,080	19,065	29,823	26,399	35,781
1984	13,868	8,445	9,940	14,017	18,726	28,378	24,396	35,196
1983	13,274	8,144	9,594	13,694	17,709	27,294	23,227	33,681
1982	12,842	8,122	9,548	13,489	16,622	26,114	22,692	32,449
1981	12,474	7,932	9,548	13,323	16,937	24,789	21,532	31,560
1980	12,323	7,914	9,541	13,246	16,894	24,707	21,557	31,280
1979	12,092	7,679	9,812	13,253	16,193	24,688	20,706	30,264
1978	12,637	7,856	10,088	14,231	16,911	25,276	22,052	30,979
1977	12,953	7,872	10,459	15,000	17,737	25,857	22,963	31,503
1976	12,530	7,848	10,353	14,896	16,641	25,829	23,116	31,754
1975	12,514	7,662	10,579	14,548	17,279	26,630	23,854	33,326
1974	12,186	7,757	10,835	14,554	17,207	26,709	22,429	31,796
1973	12,438	7,676	10,794	15,109	17,370	26,801	23,650	34,009
1972	12,258	7,348	10,887	15,194	16,670	27,892	24,293	34,698
1971	11,856	6,995	10,759	14,982	15,557	27,596	23,911	34,770
1970	11,298	6,814	10,392	14,803	16,205	26,884	23,345	34,347
1969	11,171	6,421	10,669	14,785	16,013	26,545	23,766	32,656
1968	10,962	6,567	10,367	14,634	15,463	25,263	21,130	32,168
1967	10,431	6,033	10,104	14,408	15,270	25,622	21,922	33,220
1966	9,831	6,074	9,764	13,643	14,429	24,336	21,259	31,207
1965	9,589	5,623	9,573	13,344	14,037	24,464	22,518	29,741
1964	9,206	5,291	8,726	12,636	13,314	23,245	20,968	29,433
1963	8,707	5,151	8,551	12,367	12,577	21,804	18,339	28,960
Percent change								
1963 to 1990	87.5%	66.4%	19.3%	24.8%	69.8%	49.5%	60.8%	35.1%

Source: Bureau of the Census, Current Population Survey Annual Demographic Supplements, Internet site http://www.census .gov/hhes/www/income/histinc/incpertoc.html; calculations by New Strategist

Table 5.20 Median Income of Women by Educational Attainment, 1991 to 2005

(median income of women aged 25 or older by educational attainment, 1991 to 2005; percent change for selected years; in 2005 dollars)

	total women	less than 9th grade	9th to 12th grade, no degree	high school graduate	some college	associate's degree	bachelor's degree or more total	bachelor's degree	master's degree	professional degree	doctoral degree
2005	$20,806	$9,496	$11,136	$16,695	$21,545	$26,074	$37,055	$32,668	$44,385	$59,934	$56,820
2004	20,821	9,896	11,111	16,706	21,867	26,042	36,921	32,641	43,656	51,994	57,869
2003	20,884	9,865	11,446	16,939	22,293	26,327	37,275	33,226	43,864	51,507	56,248
2002	20,587	9,732	11,521	17,338	22,364	25,799	37,225	33,421	44,440	48,575	56,812
2001	20,456	9,755	11,392	17,275	22,167	24,965	37,321	34,157	44,932	51,429	57,545
2000	20,441	9,688	11,407	17,177	22,860	26,213	37,576	34,481	46,045	52,240	58,334
1999	19,940	9,677	11,283	17,163	22,958	25,673	37,021	33,408	46,519	53,219	54,483
1998	19,445	9,466	11,461	16,489	22,061	25,464	36,709	32,790	44,120	52,016	55,347
1997	18,888	9,103	10,747	16,261	20,805	25,559	36,121	32,021	43,521	54,821	56,454
1996	18,188	9,013	10,584	15,735	20,136	25,345	34,136	31,207	41,254	52,102	52,563
1995	17,581	9,026	10,249	15,323	19,783	24,741	34,145	30,612	42,625	49,085	50,654
1994	16,633	8,945	9,926	14,840	19,003	23,393	34,185	30,495	41,784	46,653	53,151
1993	16,276	8,621	9,561	14,752	19,276	24,407	33,587	29,869	41,759	43,559	56,856
1992	16,256	8,641	9,944	14,864	19,636	23,632	34,216	30,520	41,137	49,960	53,617
1991	16,186	8,761	9,861	15,121	19,517	24,270	33,024	29,306	41,579	47,613	52,055
Percent change											
2000–2005	1.8%	−2.0%	−2.4%	−2.8%	−5.8%	−0.5%	−1.4%	−5.3%	−3.6%	14.7%	−2.6%
1991–2005	28.5	8.4	12.9	10.4	10.4	7.4	12.2	11.5	6.7	25.9	9.2

Source: Bureau of the Census, Current Population Survey Annual Demographic Supplements, Internet site http://www.census .gov/hhes/www/income/histinc/incpertoc.html; calculations by New Strategist

Table 5.21 Median Income of Men by Region, 1953 to 2005

(median income of men aged 15 or older with income by region, 1953 to 2005; percent change in income for selected years; in 2005 dollars)

	total men	Northeast	Midwest	South	West
2005	$31,275	$32,623	$31,988	$29,984	$31,586
2004	31,537	33,015	32,183	29,744	31,684
2003	31,763	33,335	32,143	29,303	32,289
2002	31,739	33,270	32,824	29,878	31,582
2001	32,092	33,785	33,395	30,156	31,631
2000	32,129	34,390	34,131	30,160	32,023
1999	31,971	33,859	34,566	30,360	31,690
1998	31,686	32,916	33,092	30,256	31,525
1997	30,579	31,993	31,881	28,983	30,118
1996	29,525	31,319	31,472	27,543	28,981
1995	28,700	31,305	30,908	26,919	28,384
1994	28,300	30,891	29,023	26,506	28,702
1993	28,073	29,645	28,864	26,227	28,651
1992	27,891	30,121	28,595	25,348	28,633
1991	28,610	31,238	28,753	25,822	30,152
1990	29,390	31,728	29,941	26,691	30,398
1989	30,244	33,710	30,352	27,141	31,078
1988	29,981	34,160	30,374	26,595	30,810
1987	29,229	32,566	29,441	26,859	30,325
1986	29,083	32,167	29,633	26,282	31,101
1985	28,224	30,422	28,338	25,843	30,091
1984	27,894	29,800	28,053	25,406	30,245
1983	27,205	28,772	27,649	24,875	28,939
1982	27,016	28,167	28,256	24,828	28,312
1981	27,636	28,641	29,111	25,037	29,948
1980	28,116	29,534	29,933	25,625	30,779
1979	29,349	30,294	31,510	26,629	30,777
1978	29,807	30,425	32,053	26,884	31,881
1977	28,780	30,056	30,756	25,439	29,965
1976	28,509	30,003	30,925	25,248	29,718
1975	28,312	30,416	30,394	24,823	29,808
1974	29,268	31,817	31,664	25,358	30,272
1973	30,660	32,696	33,355	25,850	32,696
1972	30,129	32,329	32,361	25,696	32,260
1971	28,776	31,015	30,639	24,261	30,635
1970	29,040	31,330	31,025	24,385	31,016
1969	29,338	31,456	32,094	23,721	32,263
1968	28,478	30,078	30,878	22,934	31,849
1967	27,504	29,743	29,658	21,689	31,075
1966	27,083	29,471	29,185	20,544	30,523
1965	26,348	27,727	27,753	18,700	29,233
1960	22,789	24,989	24,191	16,226	27,536
1955	20,709	22,183	22,824	15,233	22,892
1953	19,951	21,493	21,815	14,351	21,586
Percent change					
2000 to 2005	−2.7%	−5.1%	−6.3%	−0.6%	−1.4%
1953 to 2005	56.8	51.8	46.6	108.9	46.3

Note: Men aged 14 or older in years prior to 1980.
Source: Bureau of the Census, Current Population Survey Annual Demographic Supplements, Internet site http://www.census.gov/hhes/www/income/histinc/incpertoc.html; calculations by New Strategist

Table 5.22 Median Income of Women by Region, 1953 to 2005

(median income of women aged 15 or older with income by region, 1953 to 2005; percent change in income for selected years; in 2005 dollars)

	total women	Northeast	Midwest	South	West
2005	$18,576	$19,467	$18,857	$18,011	$18,569
2004	18,258	18,909	18,491	17,742	18,558
2003	18,316	19,050	18,569	17,683	18,570
2002	18,250	18,718	18,368	17,611	18,761
2001	18,322	18,822	18,622	17,564	18,725
2000	18,209	18,478	18,685	17,602	18,571
1999	17,927	18,463	18,166	17,248	18,213
1998	17,259	17,715	17,370	16,717	17,548
1997	16,620	17,384	16,858	15,811	16,983
1996	15,875	16,663	16,167	15,308	15,895
1995	15,430	15,878	15,748	14,742	15,846
1994	14,939	15,587	15,078	14,253	15,371
1993	14,695	15,133	14,675	14,045	15,390
1992	14,609	15,408	14,368	13,835	15,469
1991	14,643	15,441	14,256	14,051	15,342
1990	14,584	15,543	14,655	13,639	15,159
1989	14,632	16,029	13,900	13,757	15,670
1988	14,087	15,239	13,159	13,357	15,379
1987	13,632	14,368	12,861	13,119	14,692
1986	12,932	13,629	12,346	12,381	13,901
1985	12,488	13,052	11,858	11,758	14,042
1984	12,280	12,522	11,671	11,969	13,534
1983	11,749	11,881	11,089	11,467	12,930
1982	11,401	11,571	10,868	10,996	12,792
1981	11,196	11,284	10,794	10,701	12,254
1980	11,040	11,085	10,744	10,665	12,095
1979	10,844	11,262	10,575	10,012	11,753
1978	11,089	11,999	10,911	10,148	11,726
1977	11,204	11,966	11,096	10,258	11,872
1976	10,815	11,505	10,876	10,096	11,160
1975	10,825	11,679	10,828	9,971	11,183
1974	10,673	11,642	10,586	9,693	11,119
1973	10,641	11,570	10,599	9,595	11,216
1972	10,511	11,615	10,579	9,552	10,713
1971	10,038	11,818	9,971	8,804	10,184
1970	9,739	11,424	9,430	8,629	9,922
1969	9,729	11,276	9,090	8,734	10,126
1968	9,615	10,891	9,158	8,524	10,439
1967	8,920	10,490	8,504	7,712	9,886
1966	8,361	10,198	8,080	7,079	8,968
1965	7,978	10,181	7,942	6,698	9,557
1960	7,043	9,115	6,853	5,368	8,054
1955	6,907	8,714	6,907	5,180	8,541
1953	7,222	9,470	7,334	5,575	6,683

Percent change

	total women	Northeast	Midwest	South	West
2000 to 2005	2.0%	5.4%	0.9%	2.3%	0.0%
1953 to 2005	157.2	105.6	157.1	223.1	177.9

Note: Women aged 14 or older in years prior to 1980.
Source: Bureau of the Census, Current Population Survey Annual Demographic Supplements, Internet site http://www.census
.gov/hhes/www/income/histinc/incpertoc.html; calculations by New Strategist

Women Earn 77 Percent as Much as Men

Among full-time workers, women's earnings have grown nearly twice as fast as men's since 1960.

Women who worked full-time earned a median of $31,858 in 2005, up from just $18,192 in 1960, after adjusting for inflation. Men earned $41,386 in 2005, up from $29,983 in 1960. Women's earnings have been growing faster than men's for more than four decades. Consequently, women are closing the earnings gap with men.

Among full-time workers in 1960, women earned only 61 percent as much as men. By 2005, the figure had grown to 77 percent. Among men working full-time, earnings have grown the fastest for blacks. The median earnings of black men rose from $23,660 in 1967 to $32,976 in 2005—up 39 percent, after adjusting for inflation. White men saw their earnings rise just 15 percent during those years. Among women, the same pattern is true, with the median earnings of black women who work full-time rising 88 percent between 1967 and 2005 versus a 52 percent increase for white women.

By educational level, the earnings of men and women with college degrees grew the most between 1991 and 2005, while incomes grew more slowly or even declined for those with less education. Between 2000 and 2005, earnings growth by educational attainment was more mixed.

■ Without the rapidly rising earnings of women, most American families would be unable to afford a middle class lifestyle of homeownership and a college education for their children.

Women's median earnings are approaching those of men

(median earnings of full-time workers by sex, 1960 and 2005; in 2005 dollars)

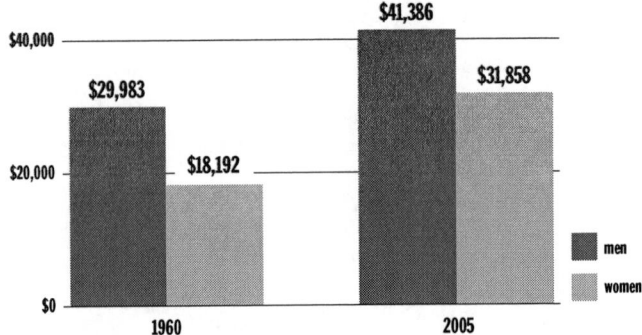

Table 5.23 Median Earnings of Full-Time Workers by Sex, 1960 to 2005

(median earnings of people aged 15 or older who work full-time, year-round by sex, and women's earnings as a percent of men's, 1960 to 2005; percent change for selected years; in 2005 dollars)

	median earnings		women's earnings as a percent of men's
	men	women	
2005	$41,386	$31,858	77.0%
2004	42,160	32,285	76.6
2003	43,158	32,605	75.5
2002	42,801	32,786	76.6
2001	42,209	32,218	76.3
2000	42,228	31,130	73.7
1999	42,629	30,827	72.3
1998	42,274	30,932	73.2
1997	40,843	30,289	74.2
1996	39,819	29,371	73.8
1995	40,064	28,617	71.4
1994	40,201	28,932	72.0
1993	40,453	28,932	71.5
1992	41,175	29,146	70.8
1991	41,123	28,728	69.9
1990	40,086	28,708	71.6
1989	41,552	28,535	68.7
1988	42,266	27,916	66.0
1987	42,638	27,791	65.2
1986	42,919	27,584	64.3
1985	41,866	27,035	64.6
1984	41,515	26,427	63.7
1983	40,685	25,873	63.6
1982	40,819	25,204	61.7
1981	41,558	24,617	59.2
1980	41,763	25,125	60.2
1979	42,393	25,293	59.7
1978	42,877	25,486	59.4
1977	41,582	24,501	58.9
1976	40,694	24,495	60.2
1975	40,800	23,998	58.8
1974	41,080	24,136	58.8
1973	42,573	24,110	56.6
1972	41,258	23,872	57.9
1971	39,181	23,315	59.5
1970	39,036	23,175	59.4
1969	38,584	22,712	58.9
1968	36,497	21,225	58.2
1967	35,572	20,555	57.8
1966	34,994	20,141	57.6
1965	33,508	20,079	59.9
1964	33,087	19,570	59.1
1963	32,322	19,052	58.9
1962	31,520	18,690	59.3
1961	30,947	18,336	59.2
1960	29,983	18,192	60.7

	percent change		percentage point change
2000 to 2005	–2.0%	2.3%	3.3
1960 to 2005	38.0	75.1	16.3

Source: Bureau of the Census, Current Population Survey Annual Demographic Supplements, Internet site http://www.census .gov/hhes/www/income/histinc/incpertoc.html; calculations by New Strategist

Table 5.24 Median Earnings of Men Who Work Full-Time by Race and Hispanic Origin, 1967 to 2005

(median earnings of men who work full-time, year-round by race and Hispanic origin, 1967 to 2005; percent change for selected years; in 2005 dollars)

	total men	Asian	black	Hispanic	white total	white non-Hispanic
2005	$41,386	$47,102	$32,976	$26,769	$41,982	$46,437
2004	42,160	47,267	32,324	27,547	42,941	47,064
2003	43,158	47,857	34,231	27,680	43,734	47,497
2002	42,801	45,311	34,137	28,192	44,007	46,111
2001	42,209	46,155	34,574	27,661	43,929	45,966
2000	42,228	45,973	34,122	26,954	43,798	46,758
1999	42,629	43,215	34,836	26,261	43,565	47,379
1998	42,274	41,656	32,353	26,654	43,263	45,133
1997	40,843	42,065	32,059	26,216	42,685	44,388
1996	39,819	42,678	32,709	26,084	40,838	43,905
1995	40,064	40,163	31,073	25,923	40,924	43,761
1994	40,201	41,773	30,934	26,468	41,170	42,526
1993	40,453	41,112	30,624	26,806	41,360	42,533
1992	41,175	41,618	30,539	26,645	42,074	43,253
1991	41,123	42,154	30,855	27,635	42,304	43,396
1990	40,086	38,764	30,579	27,715	41,828	43,641
1989	41,552	42,799	31,054	27,910	43,391	45,561
1988	42,266	43,003	32,300	28,305	43,173	44,805
1987	42,638	–	31,426	28,650	43,597	44,656
1986	42,919	–	31,164	28,574	44,059	–
1985	41,866	–	30,245	29,505	43,367	–
1984	41,515	–	29,746	30,290	42,845	–
1983	40,685	–	30,035	30,064	41,682	–
1982	40,819	–	30,024	29,790	41,835	–
1981	41,558	–	30,208	30,194	42,473	–
1980	41,763	–	30,398	30,423	42,986	–
1979	42,393	–	31,490	30,847	43,365	–
1978	42,877	–	33,647	31,987	43,599	–
1977	41,582	–	29,695	30,673	42,816	–
1976	40,694	–	30,583	31,052	41,777	–
1975	40,800	–	31,043	30,103	41,746	–
1974	41,080	–	30,189	30,767	41,963	–
1973	42,573	–	29,990	–	43,829	–
1972	41,258	–	29,526	–	42,839	–
1971	39,181	–	27,801	–	40,265	–
1970	39,036	–	27,725	–	40,155	–
1969	38,584	–	26,833	–	39,866	–
1968	36,497	–	25,306	–	37,478	–
1967	35,572	–	23,660	–	36,632	–
Percent change						
2000 to 2005	–2.0%	2.5%	–3.4%	–0.7%	–4.1%	–0.7%
1967 to 2005	16.3	–	39.4	–	14.6	–

Note: "–" means data are not available.
Source: Bureau of the Census, Current Population Survey Annual Demographic Supplements, Internet site http://www.census
.gov/hhes/www/income/histinc/incpertoc.html; calculations by New Strategist

Table 5.25 Median Earnings of Women Who Work Full-Time by Race and Hispanic Origin, 1967 to 2005

(median earnings of women who work full-time, year-round by race and Hispanic origin, 1967 to 2005; percent change for selected years; in 2005 dollars)

	total women	Asian	black	Hispanic	white total	white non-Hispanic
2005	$31,858	$35,980	$29,680	$24,214	$32,173	$34,114
2004	32,285	37,101	28,710	24,260	32,694	33,614
2003	32,605	34,432	28,641	23,732	33,077	34,018
2002	32,786	34,151	29,214	23,784	33,175	34,088
2001	32,218	33,839	29,329	23,702	33,007	33,967
2000	31,130	34,546	28,440	23,418	32,015	33,822
1999	30,827	33,468	28,378	22,708	31,213	32,135
1998	30,932	32,376	27,088	22,989	31,388	32,149
1997	30,289	33,695	26,726	23,012	30,724	31,432
1996	29,371	31,657	26,600	23,122	29,929	30,833
1995	28,617	31,644	26,287	21,851	29,144	30,099
1994	28,932	31,859	25,941	22,891	29,476	30,223
1993	28,932	32,388	26,363	22,294	29,299	29,778
1992	29,146	31,090	26,949	23,298	29,444	29,854
1991	28,728	29,596	26,166	22,705	29,065	29,484
1990	28,708	30,883	26,127	22,698	29,035	29,483
1989	28,535	32,477	26,437	23,811	28,768	29,252
1988	27,916	30,678	26,223	23,538	28,254	28,722
1987	27,791	–	25,884	23,870	28,060	28,364
1986	27,584	–	25,038	23,512	27,907	–
1985	27,035	–	24,758	22,609	27,333	–
1984	26,427	–	24,532	22,431	26,649	–
1983	25,873	–	23,596	21,688	26,154	–
1982	25,204	–	23,495	21,520	25,486	–
1981	24,617	–	22,972	22,008	24,836	–
1980	25,125	–	23,947	21,719	25,304	–
1979	25,293	–	23,482	21,037	25,490	–
1978	25,486	–	24,044	22,011	25,691	–
1977	24,501	–	23,020	21,368	24,654	–
1976	24,495	–	23,137	21,105	24,662	–
1975	23,998	–	23,144	20,566	24,026	–
1974	24,136	–	22,727	20,517	24,309	–
1973	24,110	–	20,883	–	24,487	–
1972	23,872	–	20,815	–	24,256	–
1971	23,315	–	20,901	–	23,557	–
1970	23,175	–	19,361	–	23,563	–
1969	22,712	–	18,295	–	23,173	–
1968	21,225	–	16,606	–	21,811	–
1967	20,555	–	15,820	–	21,194	–
Percent change						
2000 to 2005	2.3%	4.2%	4.4%	3.4%	0.5%	0.9%
1967 to 2005	55.0	–	87.6	–	51.8	–

Note: "–" means data are not available.
Source: Bureau of the Census, Current Population Survey Annual Demographic Supplements, Internet site http://www.census
.gov/hhes/www/income/histinc/incpertoc.html; calculations by New Strategist

Table 5.26 Median Earnings of Men Who Work Full-Time by Education, 1991 to 2005

(median earnings of men aged 25 or older who work full-time, year-round, by educational attainment, 1991 to 2005; in 2005 dollars)

	total men	less than 9th grade	9th to 12th grade, no degree	high school graduate	some college	associate's degree	bachelor's degree or more				
							total	bachelor's degree	master's degree	professional degree	doctoral degree
2005	$43,317	$22,330	$27,189	$36,302	$42,418	$47,180	$66,166	$60,020	$75,025	$100,000+	$85,864
2004	43,491	22,370	27,159	36,921	43,307	45,880	64,778	59,112	73,823	103,344	85,153
2003	44,506	22,516	28,088	37,580	43,879	45,495	65,875	59,961	74,964	106,122	92,465
2002	44,672	22,708	28,118	36,046	44,345	46,521	66,977	60,873	73,035	108,553	90,430
2001	44,890	23,312	28,515	36,433	44,287	45,940	66,777	58,567	73,814	110,279	89,411
2000	45,443	22,955	27,938	36,764	43,274	46,457	68,412	59,513	74,000	105,735	85,433
1999	44,736	22,880	28,050	37,518	43,536	47,351	66,104	59,735	72,412	112,481	89,873
1998	43,870	22,190	28,033	36,920	42,997	46,027	62,569	59,781	71,964	108,425	82,752
1997	43,318	22,500	29,402	37,181	42,556	44,485	62,097	56,102	69,805	94,957	85,758
1996	42,692	21,364	27,508	37,275	41,243	44,685	62,105	54,234	69,466	96,803	81,956
1995	41,797	22,250	27,841	36,306	41,167	42,572	61,138	54,191	65,909	95,763	78,485
1994	41,865	22,347	28,336	35,488	40,839	45,760	61,207	54,787	66,911	93,928	78,528
1993	42,040	21,791	28,473	35,681	41,611	43,391	61,180	55,095	66,287	102,685	81,614
1992	42,705	22,980	28,712	36,405	42,735	44,097	59,654	55,011	64,396	100,360	76,831
1991	43,154	23,594	29,344	36,646	43,377	45,037	59,218	55,761	65,697	98,239	76,353

Percent change

	total men	less than 9th grade	9th to 12th grade, no degree	high school graduate	some college	associate's degree	total	bachelor's degree	master's degree	professional degree	doctoral degree
2000–2005	−4.7%	−2.7%	−2.7%	−1.3%	−2.0%	1.6%	−3.3%	0.9%	1.4%	–	0.5%
1991–2005	0.4	−5.4	−7.3	−0.9	−2.2	4.8	11.7	7.6	14.2	–	12.5

Note: Earnings include wages and salaries only; "–" means data are not available.
Source: Bureau of the Census, Current Population Survey Annual Demographic Supplements, Internet site http://www.census.gov/hhes/www/income/histinc/incpertoc.html; calculations by New Strategist

Table 5.27 Median Earnings of Women Who Work Full-Time by Education, 1991 to 2005

(median earnings of women aged 25 or older who work full-time, year-round, by educational attainment, 1991 to 2005; in 2005 dollars)

	total women	less than 9th grade	9th to 12th grade, no degree	high school graduate	some college	associate's degree	bachelor's degree or more				
							total	bachelor's degree	master's degree	professional degree	doctoral degree
2005	$33,075	$16,142	$20,125	$26,289	$31,399	$33,939	$46,948	$42,172	$51,412	$80,458	$66,852
2004	33,078	17,584	19,808	26,916	31,853	34,609	47,473	43,098	53,035	77,612	70,674
2003	33,497	17,942	20,097	27,670	31,987	34,227	47,878	43,857	53,234	70,561	71,329
2002	33,662	17,922	20,958	27,336	31,915	34,330	46,944	44,347	53,072	61,895	71,336
2001	33,576	17,832	19,781	26,706	31,803	34,401	46,368	43,911	53,238	66,270	66,636
2000	33,067	17,709	19,482	26,719	30,951	34,802	46,919	43,593	53,263	68,560	65,012
1999	31,759	16,892	19,127	25,719	30,947	35,269	46,989	42,551	53,135	66,401	65,976
1998	31,948	16,903	18,954	26,269	31,126	33,940	44,752	42,350	50,236	66,333	62,394
1997	31,320	16,310	19,293	25,824	30,365	32,998	44,083	40,549	50,766	66,136	61,564
1996	30,725	16,813	19,984	25,396	29,523	33,166	43,517	39,529	50,065	69,906	64,403
1995	30,044	16,252	19,212	24,994	28,636	33,430	42,485	39,176	49,092	61,199	53,324
1994	30,182	15,673	18,859	25,445	28,887	32,852	43,395	40,052	48,920	62,911	60,559
1993	29,830	15,799	19,556	25,501	29,264	33,348	42,959	40,369	49,123	64,398	61,756
1992	30,190	16,571	18,687	25,382	29,931	33,839	42,730	39,824	47,726	60,423	59,693
1991	29,733	16,265	18,923	25,218	29,811	33,353	42,481	38,653	46,296	59,549	56,150

Percent change

2000–2005	0.0%	−8.8%	3.3%	−1.6%	1.4%	−2.5%	0.1%	−3.3%	−3.5%	17.4%	2.8%
1991–2005	11.2	−0.8	6.4	4.2	5.3	1.8	10.5	9.1	11.1	35.1	19.1

Note: Earnings include wages and salaries only.
Source: Bureau of the Census, Current Population Survey Annual Demographic Supplements, Internet site http://www.census
.gov/hhes/www/income/histinc/incpertoc.html; calculations by New Strategist

Less Poverty for Most Americans

The poverty rate fell by nearly 10 percentage points between 1959 and 2005.

The number of Americans living in poverty was lower in 2005 than it was in 1959, despite the enormous expansion in our population during those years. Behind the decline in the number of poor is the plummeting poverty rate, which fell from 22.4 percent in 1959 to 12.6 percent in 2005. The poverty rate was higher in 2005, however, than the all-time lows of 11.1 to 11.3 percent achieved in 1973, 1974, and 2000.

The poverty rate of males and females has changed little over the decades. Much bigger changes have occurred in poverty rates by age. Americans aged 65 or older are far less likely to be poor today than in 1959, their poverty rate falling from 35.2 percent to just 10.1 percent. Children are also less likely to be poor, with the poverty rate for people under age 18 falling from 27.3 to 17.6 percent between 1959 and 2005. Blacks continue to have a higher poverty rate than whites, but the black rate has declined sharply. In 1959, the 55.1 percent majority of blacks was poor. By 2005, a considerably smaller 24.7 percent lived in poverty.

■ Among Americans aged 18 to 64, the poverty rate bottomed out during the 1970s at less than 9 percent. By 2005, it had climbed to 11.1 percent.

Poverty has fallen sharply among blacks

(percent of blacks with incomes below poverty level, 1959 and 2005)

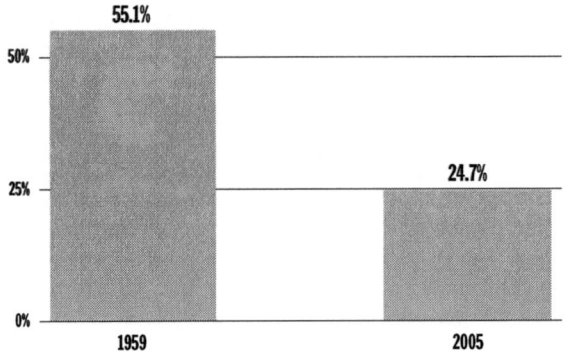

Table 5.28 People in Poverty, 1959 to 2005

(number and percent of people below poverty level, 1959 to 2005; percent and percentage point change for selected years; people in thousands as of the following year)

	number	percent
2005	36,950	12.6%
2004	37,040	12.7
2003	35,861	12.5
2002	34,570	12.1
2001	32,907	11.7
2000	31,581	11.3
1999	32,791	11.9
1998	34,476	12.7
1997	35,574	13.3
1996	36,529	13.7
1995	36,425	13.8
1994	38,059	14.5
1993	39,265	15.1
1992	38,014	14.8
1991	35,708	14.2
1990	33,585	13.5
1989	31,528	12.8
1988	31,745	13.0
1987	32,221	13.4
1986	32,370	13.6
1985	33,064	14.0
1984	33,700	14.4
1983	35,303	15.2
1982	34,398	15.0
1981	31,822	14.0
1980	29,272	13.0
1979	26,072	11.7
1978	24,497	11.4
1977	24,720	11.6
1976	24,975	11.8
1975	25,877	12.3
1974	23,370	11.2
1973	22,973	11.1
1972	24,460	11.9
1971	25,559	12.5
1970	25,420	12.6
1969	24,147	12.1
1968	25,389	12.8
1967	27,769	14.2
1966	28,510	14.7
1965	33,185	17.3
1960	39,851	22.2
1959	39,490	22.4
	percent change	percentage point change
2000 to 2005	17.0%	1.3
1959 to 2005	−6.4	−9.8

Source: Bureau of the Census, Current Population Survey Annual Demographic Supplements, Internet site http://www.census
.gov/hhes/www/poverty/histpov/perindex.html; calculations by New Strategist

Table 5.29 Females in Poverty, 1966 to 2005

(number of total people below poverty, number and percent of females below poverty, and female share of poor, 1966 to 2005; percent and percentage point change for selected years; people in thousands as of the following year)

	total poor	females		
		number of poor	percent in poverty	share of poor
2005	36,950	21,000	14.1%	56.8%
2004	37,040	20,641	13.9	55.7
2003	35,861	20,078	13.7	56.0
2002	34,570	19,408	13.3	56.1
2001	32,907	18,580	12.9	56.5
2000	31,581	18,045	12.6	57.1
1999	32,791	18,712	13.2	57.1
1998	34,476	19,764	14.3	57.3
1997	35,574	20,387	14.9	57.3
1996	36,529	20,918	15.4	57.3
1995	36,425	20,742	15.4	56.9
1994	38,059	21,744	16.3	57.1
1993	39,265	22,365	16.9	57.0
1992	38,014	21,792	16.6	57.3
1991	35,708	20,626	16.0	57.8
1990	33,585	19,373	15.2	57.7
1989	31,528	18,162	14.4	57.6
1988	31,745	18,146	14.5	57.2
1987	32,221	18,518	15.0	57.5
1986	32,370	18,649	15.2	57.6
1985	33,064	18,923	15.6	57.2
1984	33,700	19,163	15.9	56.9
1983	35,303	20,084	16.8	56.9
1982	34,398	19,556	16.5	56.9
1981	31,822	18,462	15.8	58.0
1980	29,272	17,065	14.7	58.3
1979	26,072	14,810	13.2	56.8
1978	24,497	14,480	13.0	59.1
1977	24,720	14,381	13.0	58.2
1976	24,975	14,603	13.4	58.5
1975	25,877	14,970	13.8	57.9
1974	23,370	13,881	12.9	59.4
1973	22,973	13,316	12.5	58.0
1972	24,460	14,258	13.4	58.3
1971	25,559	14,841	14.1	58.1
1970	25,420	14,632	14.0	57.6
1969	24,147	13,978	13.6	57.9
1968	25,389	14,578	14.3	57.4
1967	27,769	15,951	15.8	57.4
1966	28,510	16,265	16.3	57.1

	percent change		percentage point change	
2000 to 2005	17.0%	16.4%	1.5	–0.3
1966 to 2005	29.6	29.1	–2.2	–0.2

Source: Bureau of the Census, Current Population Survey Annual Demographic Supplements, Internet site http://www.census .gov/hhes/www/poverty/histpov/perindex.html; calculations by New Strategist

Table 5.30 Males in Poverty, 1966 to 2005

(number of total people below poverty, number and percent of males below poverty, and male share of poor, 1966 to 2005; percent and percentage point change for selected years; people in thousands as of the following year)

| | | males | | |
	total poor	number of poor	percent in poverty	share of poor
2005	36,950	15,950	11.1%	43.2%
2004	37,040	16,399	11.5	44.3
2003	35,861	15,783	11.2	44.0
2002	34,570	15,162	10.9	43.9
2001	32,907	14,327	10.4	43.5
2000	31,581	13,536	9.9	42.9
1999	32,791	14,079	10.4	42.9
1998	34,476	14,712	11.1	42.7
1997	35,574	15,187	11.6	42.7
1996	36,529	15,611	12.0	42.7
1995	36,425	15,683	12.2	43.1
1994	38,059	16,316	12.8	42.9
1993	39,265	16,900	13.3	43.0
1992	38,014	16,222	12.9	42.7
1991	35,708	15,082	12.3	42.2
1990	33,585	14,211	11.7	42.3
1989	31,528	13,366	11.2	42.4
1988	31,745	13,599	11.5	42.8
1987	32,221	14,029	12.0	43.5
1986	32,370	13,721	11.8	42.4
1985	33,064	14,140	12.3	42.8
1984	33,700	14,537	12.8	43.1
1983	35,303	15,182	13.5	43.0
1982	34,398	14,842	13.4	43.1
1981	31,822	13,360	12.1	42.0
1980	29,272	12,207	11.2	41.7
1979	26,072	10,535	10.0	40.4
1978	24,497	10,017	9.6	40.9
1977	24,720	10,340	10.0	41.8
1976	24,975	10,373	10.1	41.5
1975	25,877	10,908	10.7	42.2
1974	23,370	10,313	10.2	44.1
1973	22,973	9,642	9.6	42.0
1972	24,460	10,190	10.2	41.7
1971	25,559	10,708	10.8	41.9
1970	25,420	10,879	11.1	42.8
1969	24,147	10,292	10.6	42.6
1968	25,389	10,793	11.3	42.5
1967	27,769	11,813	12.5	42.5
1966	28,510	12,225	13.0	42.9

	percent change		percentage point change	
2000 to 2005	17.0%	17.8%	1.2	0.3
1966 to 2005	29.6	30.5	−1.9	0.3

Source: Bureau of the Census, Current Population Survey Annual Demographic Supplements, Internet site http://www.census .gov/hhes/www/poverty/histpov/perindex.html; calculations by New Strategist

Table 5.31 Number of People in Poverty by Age, 1959 to 2005

(number of people below poverty level by age, 1959 to 2005; percent change for selected years; people in thousands as of the following year)

	total poor	under 18	18 to 64	65 or older
2005	36,950	12,896	20,450	3,603
2004	37,040	13,041	20,545	3,453
2003	35,861	12,866	19,443	3,552
2002	34,570	12,133	18,861	3,576
2001	32,907	11,733	17,760	3,414
2000	31,581	11,587	16,671	3,323
1999	32,791	12,280	17,289	3,222
1998	34,476	13,467	17,623	3,386
1997	35,574	14,113	18,085	3,376
1996	36,529	14,463	18,638	3,428
1995	36,425	14,665	18,442	3,318
1994	38,059	15,289	19,107	3,663
1993	39,265	15,727	19,781	3,755
1992	38,014	15,294	18,793	3,928
1991	35,708	14,341	17,586	3,781
1990	33,585	13,431	16,496	3,658
1989	31,528	12,590	15,575	3,363
1988	31,745	12,455	15,809	3,481
1987	32,221	12,843	15,815	3,563
1986	32,370	12,876	16,017	3,477
1985	33,064	13,010	16,598	3,456
1984	33,700	13,420	16,952	3,330
1983	35,303	13,911	17,767	3,625
1982	34,398	13,647	17,000	3,751
1981	31,822	12,505	15,464	3,853
1980	29,272	11,543	13,858	3,871
1979	26,072	10,377	12,014	3,682
1978	24,497	9,931	11,332	3,233
1977	24,720	10,288	11,316	3,177
1976	24,975	10,273	11,389	3,313
1975	25,877	11,104	11,456	3,317
1974	23,370	10,156	10,132	3,085
1973	22,973	9,642	9,977	3,354
1972	24,460	10,284	10,438	3,738
1971	25,559	10,551	10,735	4,273
1970	25,420	10,440	10,187	4,793
1969	24,147	9,691	9,669	4,787
1968	25,389	10,954	9,803	4,632
1967	27,769	11,656	10,725	5,388
1966	28,510	12,389	11,007	5,114
1965	33,185	14,676	–	–
1964	36,055	16,051	–	–
1963	36,436	16,005	–	–
1962	38,625	16,963	–	–
1961	39,628	16,909	–	–
1960	39,851	17,634	–	–
1959	39,490	17,552	16,457	5,481
Percent change				
2000 to 2005	17.0%	11.3%	22.7%	8.4%
1959 to 2005	–6.4	–26.5	24.3	–34.3

Note: "–" means data are not available.
Source: Bureau of the Census, Current Population Survey Annual Demographic Supplements, Internet site http://www.census
.gov/hhes/www/poverty/histpov/perindex.html; calculations by New Strategist

Table 5.32 Percent Distribution of People in Poverty by Age, 1959 to 2005

(percent distribution of people below poverty level by age, 1959 to 2005; percentage point change for selected years)

	total poor	under 18	18 to 64	65 or older
2005	100.0%	34.9%	55.3%	9.8%
2004	100.0	35.2	55.5	9.3
2003	100.0	35.9	54.2	9.9
2002	100.0	35.1	54.6	10.3
2001	100.0	35.7	54.0	10.4
2000	100.0	36.7	52.8	10.5
1999	100.0	37.4	52.7	9.8
1998	100.0	39.1	51.1	9.8
1997	100.0	39.7	50.8	9.5
1996	100.0	39.6	51.0	9.4
1995	100.0	40.3	50.6	9.1
1994	100.0	40.2	50.2	9.6
1993	100.0	40.1	50.4	9.6
1992	100.0	40.2	49.4	10.3
1991	100.0	40.2	49.2	10.6
1990	100.0	40.0	49.1	10.9
1989	100.0	39.9	49.4	10.7
1988	100.0	39.2	49.8	11.0
1987	100.0	39.9	49.1	11.1
1986	100.0	39.8	49.5	10.7
1985	100.0	39.3	50.2	10.5
1984	100.0	39.8	50.3	9.9
1983	100.0	39.4	50.3	10.3
1982	100.0	39.7	49.4	10.9
1981	100.0	39.3	48.6	12.1
1980	100.0	39.4	47.3	13.2
1979	100.0	39.8	46.1	14.1
1978	100.0	40.5	46.3	13.2
1977	100.0	41.6	45.8	12.9
1976	100.0	41.1	45.6	13.3
1975	100.0	42.9	44.3	12.8
1974	100.0	43.5	43.4	13.2
1973	100.0	42.0	43.4	14.6
1972	100.0	42.0	42.7	15.3
1971	100.0	41.3	42.0	16.7
1970	100.0	41.1	40.1	18.9
1969	100.0	40.1	40.0	19.8
1968	100.0	43.1	38.6	18.2
1967	100.0	42.0	38.6	19.4
1966	100.0	43.5	38.6	17.9
1965	100.0	44.2	–	–
1964	100.0	44.5	–	–
1963	100.0	43.9	–	–
1962	100.0	43.9	–	–
1961	100.0	42.7	–	–
1960	100.0	44.2	–	–
1959	100.0	44.4	41.7	13.9
Percentage point change				
2000 to 2005	–	–1.8	2.6	–0.8
1959 to 2005	–	–9.5	13.7	–4.1

Note: "–" means not applicable or data are not available.
Source: Bureau of the Census, Current Population Survey Annual Demographic Supplements, Internet site http://www.census
.gov/hhes/www/poverty/histpov/perindex.html; calculations by New Strategist

Table 5.33 Percent of People in Poverty by Age, 1959 to 2005

(percent of people below poverty level by age, 1959 to 2005; percentage point change for selected years)

	total people	under 18	18 to 64	65 or older
2005	12.6%	17.6%	11.1%	10.1%
2004	12.7	17.8	11.3	9.8
2003	12.5	17.6	10.8	10.2
2002	12.1	16.7	10.6	10.4
2001	11.7	16.3	10.1	10.1
2000	11.3	16.2	9.6	9.9
1999	11.9	17.1	10.1	9.7
1998	12.7	18.9	10.5	10.5
1997	13.3	19.9	10.9	10.5
1996	13.7	20.5	11.4	10.8
1995	13.8	20.8	11.4	10.5
1994	14.5	21.8	11.9	11.7
1993	15.1	22.7	12.4	12.2
1992	14.8	22.3	11.9	12.9
1991	14.2	21.8	11.4	12.4
1990	13.5	20.6	10.7	12.2
1989	12.8	19.6	10.2	11.4
1988	13.0	19.5	10.5	12.0
1987	13.4	20.3	10.6	12.5
1986	13.6	20.5	10.8	12.4
1985	14.0	20.7	11.3	12.6
1984	14.4	21.5	11.7	12.4
1983	15.2	22.3	12.4	13.8
1982	15.0	21.9	12.0	14.6
1981	14.0	20.0	11.1	15.3
1980	13.0	18.3	10.1	15.7
1979	11.7	16.4	8.9	15.2
1978	11.4	15.9	8.7	14.0
1977	11.6	16.2	8.8	14.1
1976	11.8	16.0	9.0	15.0
1975	12.3	17.1	9.2	15.3
1974	11.2	15.4	8.3	14.6
1973	11.1	14.4	8.3	16.3
1972	11.9	15.1	8.8	18.6
1971	12.5	15.3	9.3	21.6
1970	12.6	15.1	9.0	24.6
1969	12.1	14.0	8.7	25.3
1968	12.8	15.6	9.0	25.0
1967	14.2	16.6	10.0	29.5
1966	14.7	17.6	10.5	28.5
1965	17.3	21.0	–	–
1964	19.0	23.0	–	–
1963	19.5	23.1	–	–
1962	21.0	25.0	–	–
1961	21.9	25.6	–	–
1960	22.2	26.9	–	–
1959	22.4	27.3	17.0	35.2
Percentage point change				
2000 to 2005	1.3	1.4	1.5	0.2
1959 to 2005	–9.8	–9.7	–5.9	–25.1

Note: "–" means data are not available.
Source: Bureau of the Census, Current Population Survey Annual Demographic Supplements, Internet site http://www.census
.gov/hhes/www/poverty/histpov/perindex.html; calculations by New Strategist

Table 5.34 Number of People in Poverty by Race and Hispanic Origin, 1959 to 2005

(number of people below poverty level by race and Hispanic origin, 1959 to 2005; percent change for selected years; people in thousands as of the following year)

	total poor	Asian	black	Hispanic	white total	white non-Hispanic
2005	36,950	1,501	9,517	9,368	24,872	16,227
2004	37,040	1,295	9,411	9,122	25,327	16,908
2003	35,861	1,527	9,108	9,051	24,272	15,902
2002	34,570	1,243	8,884	8,555	23,466	15,567
2001	32,907	1,275	8,136	7,997	22,739	15,271
2000	31,581	1,258	7,982	7,747	21,645	14,366
1999	32,791	1,285	8,441	7,876	22,169	14,735
1998	34,476	1,360	9,091	8,070	23,454	15,799
1997	35,574	1,468	9,116	8,308	24,396	16,491
1996	36,529	1,454	9,694	8,697	24,650	16,462
1995	36,425	1,411	9,872	8,574	24,423	16,267
1994	38,059	974	10,196	8,416	25,379	18,110
1993	39,265	1,134	10,877	8,126	26,226	18,882
1992	38,014	985	10,827	7,592	25,259	18,202
1991	35,708	996	10,242	6,339	23,747	17,741
1990	33,585	858	9,837	6,006	22,326	16,622
1989	31,528	939	9,302	5,430	20,785	15,599
1988	31,745	1,117	9,356	5,357	20,715	15,565
1987	32,221	1,021	9,520	5,422	21,195	16,029
1986	32,370	–	8,983	5,117	22,183	17,244
1985	33,064	–	8,926	5,236	22,860	17,839
1984	33,700	–	9,490	4,806	22,955	18,300
1983	35,303	–	9,882	4,633	23,984	19,538
1982	34,398	–	9,697	4,301	23,517	19,362
1981	31,822	–	9,173	3,713	21,553	17,987
1980	29,272	–	8,579	3,491	19,699	16,365
1979	26,072	–	8,050	2,921	17,214	14,419
1978	24,497	–	7,625	2,607	16,259	13,755
1977	24,720	–	7,726	2,700	16,416	13,802
1976	24,975	–	7,595	2,783	16,713	14,025
1975	25,877	–	7,545	2,991	17,770	14,883
1974	23,370	–	7,182	2,575	15,736	13,217
1973	22,973	–	7,388	2,366	15,142	12,864
1972	24,460	–	7,710	2,414	16,203	–
1971	25,559	–	7,396	–	17,780	–
1970	25,420	–	7,548	–	17,484	–
1969	24,147	–	7,095	–	16,659	–
1968	25,389	–	7,616	–	17,395	–
1967	27,769	–	8,486	–	18,983	–
1966	28,510	–	8,867	–	19,290	–
1965	33,185	–	9,927	–	22,496	–
1964	36,055	–	–	–	24,957	–
1963	36,436	–	–	–	25,238	–
1962	38,625	–	–	–	26,672	–
1961	39,628	–	–	–	27,890	–
1960	39,851	–	–	–	28,309	–
1959	39,490	–	9,927	–	28,484	–
Percent change						
2000 to 2005	17.0%	19.3%	19.2%	20.9%	14.9%	13.0%
1959 to 2005	–6.4	–	–4.1	–	–12.7	–

Note: "–" means data are not available.
Source: Bureau of the Census, Current Population Survey Annual Demographic Supplements, Internet site http://www.census
.gov/hhes/www/poverty/histpov/perindex.html; calculations by New Strategist

Table 5.35 Percent Distribution of People in Poverty by Race and Hispanic Origin, 1959 to 2005

(percent distribution of people below poverty level by race and Hispanic origin, 1959 to 2005; percentage point change for selected years)

	total poor	Asian	black	Hispanic	white total	white non-Hispanic
2005	100.0%	4.1%	25.8%	25.4%	67.3%	43.9%
2004	100.0	3.5	25.4	24.6	68.4	45.6
2003	100.0	4.3	25.4	25.2	67.7	44.3
2002	100.0	3.6	25.7	24.7	67.9	45.0
2001	100.0	3.9	24.7	24.3	69.1	46.4
2000	100.0	4.0	25.3	24.5	68.5	45.5
1999	100.0	3.9	25.7	24.0	67.6	44.9
1998	100.0	3.9	26.4	23.4	68.0	45.8
1997	100.0	4.1	25.6	23.4	68.6	46.4
1996	100.0	4.0	26.5	23.8	67.5	45.1
1995	100.0	3.9	27.1	23.5	67.1	44.7
1994	100.0	2.6	26.8	22.1	66.7	47.6
1993	100.0	2.9	27.7	20.7	66.8	48.1
1992	100.0	2.6	28.5	20.0	66.4	47.9
1991	100.0	2.8	28.7	17.8	66.5	49.7
1990	100.0	2.6	29.3	17.9	66.5	49.5
1989	100.0	3.0	29.5	17.2	65.9	49.5
1988	100.0	3.5	29.5	16.9	65.3	49.0
1987	100.0	3.2	29.5	16.8	65.8	49.7
1986	100.0	–	27.8	15.8	68.5	53.3
1985	100.0	–	27.0	15.8	69.1	54.0
1984	100.0	–	28.2	14.3	68.1	54.3
1983	100.0	–	28.0	13.1	67.9	55.3
1982	100.0	–	28.2	12.5	68.4	56.3
1981	100.0	–	28.8	11.7	67.7	56.5
1980	100.0	–	29.3	11.9	67.3	55.9
1979	100.0	–	30.9	11.2	66.0	55.3
1978	100.0	–	31.1	10.6	66.4	56.1
1977	100.0	–	31.3	10.9	66.4	55.8
1976	100.0	–	30.4	11.1	66.9	56.2
1975	100.0	–	29.2	11.6	68.7	57.5
1974	100.0	–	30.7	11.0	67.3	56.6
1973	100.0	–	32.2	10.3	65.9	56.0
1972	100.0	–	31.5	9.9	66.2	–
1971	100.0	–	28.9	–	69.6	–
1970	100.0	–	29.7	–	68.8	–
1969	100.0	–	29.4	–	69.0	–
1968	100.0	–	30.0	–	68.5	–
1967	100.0	–	30.6	–	68.4	–
1966	100.0	–	31.1	–	67.7	–
1965	100.0	–	29.9	–	67.8	–
1964	100.0	–	–	–	69.2	–
1963	100.0	–	–	–	69.3	–
1962	100.0	–	–	–	69.1	–
1961	100.0	–	–	–	70.4	–
1960	100.0	–	–	–	71.0	–
1959	100.0	–	25.1	–	72.1	–
Percentage point change						
2000 to 2005	–	0.1	0.5	0.8	–1.2	–1.6
1959 to 2005	–	–	0.6	–	–4.8	–

Note: "–" means not applicable or data are not available.
Source: Bureau of the Census, Current Population Survey Annual Demographic Supplements, Internet site http://www.census
.gov/hhes/www/poverty/histpov/perindex.html; calculations by New Strategist

Table 5.36 Percent of People in Poverty by Race and Hispanic Origin, 1959 to 2005

(percent of people below poverty level by race and Hispanic origin, 1959 to 2005; percentage point change for selected years)

	total people	Asian	black	Hispanic	white total	white non-Hispanic
2005	12.6%	10.9%	24.7%	21.8%	10.6%	8.3%
2004	12.7	9.7	24.7	21.9	10.8	8.7
2003	12.5	11.8	24.3	22.5	10.5	8.2
2002	12.1	10.0	23.9	21.8	10.2	8.0
2001	11.7	10.2	22.7	21.4	9.9	7.8
2000	11.3	9.9	22.5	21.5	9.5	7.4
1999	11.9	10.7	23.6	22.7	9.8	7.7
1998	12.7	12.5	26.1	25.6	10.5	8.2
1997	13.3	14.0	26.5	27.1	11.0	8.6
1996	13.7	14.5	28.4	29.4	11.2	8.6
1995	13.8	14.6	29.3	30.3	11.2	8.5
1994	14.5	14.6	30.6	30.7	11.7	9.4
1993	15.1	15.3	33.1	30.6	12.2	9.9
1992	14.8	12.7	33.4	29.6	11.9	9.6
1991	14.2	13.8	32.7	28.7	11.3	9.4
1990	13.5	12.2	31.9	28.1	10.7	8.8
1989	12.8	14.1	30.7	26.2	10.0	8.3
1988	13.0	17.3	31.3	26.7	10.1	8.4
1987	13.4	16.1	32.4	28.0	10.4	8.7
1986	13.6	–	31.1	27.3	11.0	9.4
1985	14.0	–	31.3	29.0	11.4	9.7
1984	14.4	–	33.8	28.4	11.5	10.0
1983	15.2	–	35.7	28.0	12.1	10.8
1982	15.0	–	35.6	29.9	12.0	10.6
1981	14.0	–	34.2	26.5	11.1	9.9
1980	13.0	–	32.5	25.7	10.2	9.1
1979	11.7	–	31.0	21.8	9.0	8.1
1978	11.4	–	30.6	21.6	8.7	7.9
1977	11.6	–	31.3	22.4	8.9	8.0
1976	11.8	–	31.1	24.7	9.1	8.1
1975	12.3	–	31.3	26.9	9.7	8.6
1974	11.2	–	30.3	23.0	8.6	7.7
1973	11.1	–	31.4	21.9	8.4	7.5
1972	11.9	–	33.3	22.8	9.0	–
1971	12.5	–	32.5	–	9.9	–
1970	12.6	–	33.5	–	9.9	–
1969	12.1	–	32.2	–	9.5	–
1968	12.8	–	34.7	–	10.0	–
1967	14.2	–	39.3	–	11.0	–
1966	14.7	–	41.8	–	11.3	–
1965	17.3	–	–	–	13.3	–
1964	19.0	–	–	–	14.9	–
1963	19.5	–	–	–	15.3	–
1962	21.0	–	–	–	16.4	–
1961	21.9	–	–	–	17.4	–
1960	22.2	–	–	–	17.8	–
1959	22.4	–	55.1	–	18.1	–
Percentage point change						
2000 to 2005	1.3	1.0	2.2	0.3	1.1	0.9
1959 to 2005	–9.8	–	–30.4	–	–7.5	–

Note: "–" means data are not available.
Source: Bureau of the Census, Current Population Survey Annual Demographic Supplements, Internet site http://www.census .gov/hhes/www/poverty/histpov/perindex.html; calculations by New Strategist

Few Married Couples Are Poor

Poverty among female-headed families has fallen.

Families are less likely to be poor today than in 1959. The poverty rate for all families fell from 18.5 to 9.9 percent between 1959 and 2005. Among families with children under age 18, the rate did not drop as much, falling from 20.3 to 14.5 percent.

Thirty years ago, married couples accounted for the majority of the poor. Today, women head most poor families. The poverty rate among married couples has remained stable over the decades, at about 5 percent. Non-Hispanic white couples have the lowest poverty rate, at 3.3 percent in 2005. The black poverty rate is not much higher, at 8.2 percent. Hispanic couples are more likely to be poor, with 13.8 percent living below the poverty level.

The poverty rate is much higher among female-headed families, at 28.7 percent in 2005. But this rate is somewhat less than the 32.2 percent of 1973. The poverty rate among black female-headed families fell from 52.7 to 42.0 percent between 1973 and 2005. Among Hispanics, the poverty rate fell from 51.4 to 38.9 percent during those years.

■ Poverty rates will remain stubbornly high as long as female-headed families account for such a large share of total families.

Married couples now account for a minority of poor families

(percent distribution of families in poverty, by family type, 1973 and 2005)

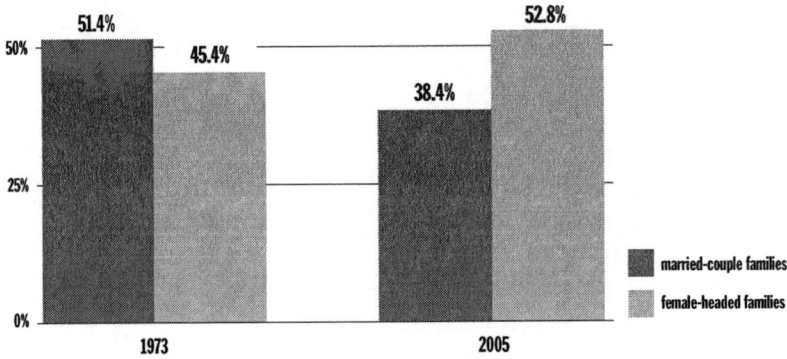

Table 5.37 Families in Poverty, 1959 to 2005

(total number of families, and number and percent below poverty level by presence of children under age 18 at home, 1959 to 2005; percent and percentage point change for selected years; families in thousands as of the following year)

	total families			families with children under age 18		
		in poverty			in poverty	
	total	number	percent	total	number	percent
2005	77,418	7,657	9.9%	39,394	5,729	14.5%
2004	76,866	7,835	10.2	39,375	5,819	14.8
2003	76,232	7,607	10.0	39,029	5,772	14.8
2002	75,616	7,229	9.6	38,846	5,397	13.9
2001	74,340	6,813	9.2	38,427	5,138	13.4
2000	73,778	6,400	8.7	38,190	4,866	12.7
1999	73,206	6,792	9.3	37,688	5,210	13.8
1998	71,551	7,186	10.0	37,268	5,628	15.1
1997	70,884	7,324	10.3	37,427	5,884	15.7
1996	70,241	7,708	11.0	37,204	6,131	16.5
1995	69,597	7,532	10.8	36,719	5,976	16.3
1994	69,313	8,053	11.6	36,782	6,408	17.4
1993	68,506	8,393	12.3	36,456	6,751	18.5
1992	68,216	8,144	11.9	35,851	6,457	18.0
1991	67,175	7,712	11.5	34,862	6,170	17.7
1990	66,322	7,098	10.7	34,503	5,676	16.4
1989	66,090	6,784	10.3	34,279	5,308	15.5
1988	65,837	6,874	10.4	34,251	5,373	15.7
1987	65,204	7,005	10.7	33,996	5,465	16.1
1986	64,491	7,023	10.9	33,801	5,516	16.3
1985	63,558	7,223	11.4	33,536	5,586	16.7
1984	62,706	7,277	11.6	32,942	5,662	17.2
1983	62,015	7,647	12.3	32,787	5,871	17.9
1982	61,393	7,512	12.2	32,565	5,712	17.5
1981	61,019	6,851	11.2	32,587	5,191	15.9
1980	60,309	6,217	10.3	32,773	4,822	14.7
1979	59,550	5,461	9.2	32,397	4,081	12.6
1978	57,804	5,280	9.1	31,735	4,060	12.8
1977	57,215	5,311	9.3	31,637	4,081	12.9
1976	56,710	5,311	9.4	31,434	4,060	12.9
1975	56,245	5,450	9.7	31,377	4,172	13.3
1974	55,698	4,922	8.8	31,319	3,789	12.1
1973	55,053	4,828	8.8	30,977	3,520	11.4
1972	54,373	5,075	9.3	30,807	3,621	11.8
1971	53,296	5,303	10.0	30,725	3,683	12.0
1970	52,227	5,260	10.1	30,070	3,491	11.6
1969	51,586	5,008	9.7	29,827	3,226	10.8
1968	50,511	5,047	10.0	29,325	3,347	11.4
1967	49,835	5,667	11.4	29,032	3,586	12.4
1966	48,921	5,784	11.8	28,592	3,734	13.4
1965	48,278	6,721	13.9	28,100	4,379	15.6
1960	45,435	8,243	18.1	27,102	5,328	19.7
1959	45,054	8,320	18.5	26,992	5,443	20.3

	percent change		percentage point change	percent change		percentage point change
2000 to 2005	4.9%	19.6%	1.2	3.2%	17.7%	1.8
1959 to 2005	71.8	−8.0	−8.6	45.9	5.3	−5.8

Source: Bureau of the Census, Current Population Survey Annual Demographic Supplements, Internet site http://www.census .gov/hhes/www/poverty/histpov/perindex.html; calculations by New Strategist

Table 5.38 Number and Percent Distribution of Families in Poverty by Family Type, 1973 to 2005

(number and percent distribution of families below poverty level by family type, 1973 to 2005; percent and percentage point change for selected years; families in thousands as of the following year)

	total poor	married couples	female-headed families	total poor	married couples	female-headed families
2005	7,657	2,944	4,044	100.0%	38.4%	52.8%
2004	7,835	3,216	3,962	100.0	41.0	50.6
2003	7,607	3,115	3,856	100.0	40.9	50.7
2002	7,229	3,052	3,613	100.0	42.2	50.0
2001	6,813	2,760	3,470	100.0	40.5	50.9
2000	6,400	2,637	3,278	100.0	41.2	51.2
1999	6,792	2,748	3,559	100.0	40.5	52.4
1998	7,186	2,879	3,831	100.0	40.1	53.3
1997	7,324	2,821	3,995	100.0	38.5	54.5
1996	7,708	3,010	4,167	100.0	39.1	54.1
1995	7,532	2,982	4,057	100.0	39.6	53.9
1994	8,053	3,272	4,232	100.0	40.6	52.6
1993	8,393	3,481	4,424	100.0	41.5	52.7
1992	8,144	3,385	4,275	100.0	41.6	52.5
1991	7,712	3,158	4,161	100.0	40.9	54.0
1990	7,098	2,981	3,768	100.0	42.0	53.1
1989	6,784	2,931	3,504	100.0	43.2	51.7
1988	6,874	2,897	3,642	100.0	42.1	53.0
1987	7,005	3,011	3,654	100.0	43.0	52.2
1986	7,023	3,123	3,613	100.0	44.5	51.4
1985	7,223	3,438	3,474	100.0	47.6	48.1
1984	7,277	3,488	3,498	100.0	47.9	48.1
1983	7,647	3,815	3,564	100.0	49.9	46.6
1982	7,512	3,789	3,434	100.0	50.4	45.7
1981	6,851	3,394	3,252	100.0	49.5	47.5
1980	6,217	3,032	2,972	100.0	48.8	47.8
1979	5,461	2,640	2,645	100.0	48.3	48.4
1978	5,280	2,474	2,654	100.0	46.9	50.3
1977	5,311	2,524	2,610	100.0	47.5	49.1
1976	5,311	2,606	2,543	100.0	49.1	47.9
1975	5,450	2,904	2,430	100.0	53.3	44.6
1974	4,922	2,474	2,324	100.0	50.3	47.2
1973	4,828	2,482	2,193	100.0	51.4	45.4

	percent change			percentage point change		
2000 to 2005	19.6%	11.6%	23.4%	–	−2.8	1.6
1973 to 2005	58.6	18.6	84.4	–	−13.0	7.4

Note: Numbers will not add to total because not all family types are shown. "–" means not applicable.
Source: Bureau of the Census, Current Population Survey Annual Demographic Supplements, Internet site http://www.census
.gov/hhes/www/poverty/histpov/perindex.html; calculations by New Strategist

Table 5.39 Number of Married Couples in Poverty by Race and Hispanic Origin, 1973 to 2005

(number of married couples below poverty level by race and Hispanic origin of householder, 1973 to 2005; percent change for selected years; families in thousands as of the following year)

	total married couples in poverty	black	Hispanic	white total	white non-Hispanic
2005	2,944	348	917	2,317	1,450
2004	3,216	386	934	2,585	1,710
2003	3,115	331	976	2,504	1,575
2002	3,052	340	927	2,510	1,628
2001	2,760	328	799	2,242	1,477
2000	2,637	266	772	2,181	1,435
1999	2,748	295	758	2,207	1,474
1998	2,879	290	775	2,400	1,639
1997	2,821	312	836	2,312	1,501
1996	3,010	352	815	2,416	1,628
1995	2,982	314	803	2,443	1,664
1994	3,272	336	827	2,629	1,915
1993	3,481	458	770	2,757	2,042
1992	3,385	490	743	2,677	1,978
1991	3,158	399	674	2,573	1,918
1990	2,981	448	605	2,386	1,799
1989	2,931	443	549	2,329	1,798
1988	2,897	421	547	2,294	1,763
1987	3,011	439	556	2,382	1,847
1986	3,123	403	518	2,591	2,081
1985	3,438	447	505	2,815	2,316
1984	3,488	479	469	2,858	2,400
1983	3,815	535	437	3,125	2,649
1982	3,789	543	465	3,104	2,648
1981	3,394	543	366	2,712	2,353
1980	3,032	474	363	2,437	2,083
1979	2,640	453	298	2,099	1,810
1978	2,474	366	248	2,033	1,790
1977	2,524	429	280	2,028	1,750
1976	2,606	450	312	2,071	1,759
1975	2,904	479	335	2,363	2,036
1974	2,474	435	278	1,977	1,700
1973	2,482	–	239	2,306	–
Percent change					
2000 to 2005	11.6%	30.8%	18.8%	6.2%	1.0%
1973 to 2005	18.6	–	283.7	0.5	–

Note: "–" means data are not available.
Source: Bureau of the Census, Current Population Survey Annual Demographic Supplements, Internet site http://www.census.gov/hhes/www/poverty/histpov/perindex.html; calculations by New Strategist

Table 5.40 Percent Distribution of Married Couples in Poverty by Race and Hispanic Origin, 1973 to 2005

(percent distribution of married couples below poverty level by race and Hispanic origin of householder, 1973 to 2005; percentage point change for selected years)

	total married couples in poverty	black	Hispanic	white total	white non-Hispanic
2005	100.0%	11.8%	31.1%	78.7%	49.3%
2004	100.0	12.0	29.0	80.4	53.2
2003	100.0	10.6	31.3	80.4	50.6
2002	100.0	11.1	30.4	82.2	53.3
2001	100.0	11.9	28.9	81.2	53.5
2000	100.0	10.1	29.3	82.7	54.4
1999	100.0	10.7	27.6	80.3	53.6
1998	100.0	10.1	26.9	83.4	56.9
1997	100.0	11.1	29.6	82.0	53.2
1996	100.0	11.7	27.1	80.3	54.1
1995	100.0	10.5	26.9	81.9	55.8
1994	100.0	10.3	25.3	80.3	58.5
1993	100.0	13.2	22.1	79.2	58.7
1992	100.0	14.5	21.9	79.1	58.4
1991	100.0	12.6	21.3	81.5	60.7
1990	100.0	15.0	20.3	80.0	60.3
1989	100.0	15.1	18.7	79.5	61.3
1988	100.0	14.5	18.9	79.2	60.9
1987	100.0	14.6	18.5	79.1	61.3
1986	100.0	12.9	16.6	83.0	66.6
1985	100.0	13.0	14.7	81.9	67.4
1984	100.0	13.7	13.4	81.9	68.8
1983	100.0	14.0	11.5	81.9	69.4
1982	100.0	14.3	12.3	81.9	69.9
1981	100.0	16.0	10.8	79.9	69.3
1980	100.0	15.6	12.0	80.4	68.7
1979	100.0	17.2	11.3	79.5	68.6
1978	100.0	14.8	10.0	82.2	72.4
1977	100.0	17.0	11.1	80.3	69.3
1976	100.0	17.3	12.0	79.5	67.5
1975	100.0	16.5	11.5	81.4	70.1
1974	100.0	17.6	11.2	79.9	68.7
1973	100.0	–	9.6	92.9	–
Percentage point change					
2000 to 2005	–	1.7	1.9	–4.0	–5.2
1973 to 2005	–	–	21.5	–14.2	–

Note: "–" means not applicable or data are not available.
Source: Bureau of the Census, Current Population Survey Annual Demographic Supplements, Internet site http://www.census .gov/hhes/www/poverty/histpov/perindex.html; calculations by New Strategist

Table 5.41 Percent of Married Couples in Poverty by Race and Hispanic Origin, 1973 to 2005

(percent of married couples below poverty level by race and Hispanic origin of householder, 1973 to 2005; percentage point change for selected years)

	total married couples	black	Hispanic	white total	white non-Hispanic
2005	5.1%	8.2%	13.8%	4.6%	3.3%
2004	5.5	9.1	14.7	5.2	3.9
2003	5.4	7.8	15.7	5.0	3.6
2002	5.3	8.0	15.0	5.0	3.7
2001	4.9	7.8	13.8	4.5	3.3
2000	4.7	6.3	14.2	4.4	3.2
1999	4.9	7.1	14.4	4.5	3.3
1998	5.3	7.3	15.7	5.0	3.8
1997	5.2	8.0	17.4	4.8	3.5
1996	5.6	9.1	18.0	5.1	3.8
1995	5.6	8.5	18.9	5.1	3.8
1994	6.1	8.7	19.5	5.5	4.3
1993	6.5	12.3	19.1	5.8	4.7
1992	6.4	13.0	18.8	5.7	4.5
1991	6.0	11.0	19.1	5.5	4.4
1990	5.7	12.6	17.5	5.1	4.1
1989	5.6	11.8	16.2	5.0	4.1
1988	5.6	11.3	16.1	4.9	4
1987	5.8	11.9	17.4	5.1	4.3
1986	6.1	10.8	16.6	5.6	4.8
1985	6.7	12.2	17.0	6.1	5.4
1984	6.9	13.8	16.6	6.3	5.6
1983	7.6	15.5	17.7	6.9	6.2
1982	7.6	15.6	19.0	6.9	6.2
1981	6.8	15.4	15.1	6.0	5.5
1980	6.2	14.0	15.3	5.4	4.9
1979	5.4	13.2	13.1	4.7	4.3
1978	5.2	11.3	11.9	4.7	4.3
1977	5.3	13.1	13.3	4.7	4.2
1976	5.5	13.2	15.8	4.8	4.2
1975	6.1	14.3	17.7	5.5	4.9
1974	5.3	13.0	14.4	4.6	4.1
1973	5.3	–	12.7	5.3	–
Percentage point change					
2000 to 2005	0.4	1.9	–0.4	0.2	0.1
1973 to 2005	–0.2	–	1.1	–0.7	–

Note: "–" means data are not available.
Source: Bureau of the Census, Current Population Survey Annual Demographic Supplements, Internet site http://www.census
.gov/hhes/www/poverty/histpov/perindex.html; calculations by New Strategist

Table 5.42 Number of Female-Headed Families in Poverty by Race and Hispanic Origin, 1973 to 2005

(number of female-headed families below poverty level by race and Hispanic origin of householder, 1973 to 2005; percent change for selected years; families in thousands as of the following year)

	total female-headed families in poverty	black	Hispanic	white total	white non-Hispanic
2005	4,044	1,335	876	2,312	1,537
2004	3,962	1,339	872	2,273	1,491
2003	3,856	1,341	792	2,171	1,455
2002	3,613	1,288	717	2,004	1,374
2001	3,470	1,351	711	1,939	1,305
2000	3,278	1,300	664	1,820	1,226
1999	3,559	1,487	717	1,901	1,248
1998	3,831	1,557	756	2,123	1,428
1997	3,995	1,563	767	2,305	1,598
1996	4,167	1,724	823	2,276	1,538
1995	4,057	1,701	792	2,200	1,463
1994	4,232	1,715	773	2,329	1,678
1993	4,424	1,908	772	2,376	1,699
1992	4,275	1,878	664	2,245	1,637
1991	4,161	1,834	627	2,192	1,610
1990	3,768	1,648	573	2,010	1,480
1989	3,504	1,524	530	1,858	1,355
1988	3,642	1,579	546	1,945	1,426
1987	3,654	1,577	565	1,961	1,443
1986	3,613	1,488	528	2,041	1,542
1985	3,474	1,452	521	1,950	1,460
1984	3,498	1,533	483	1,878	1,422
1983	3,564	1,541	454	1,926	1,501
1982	3,434	1,535	425	1,813	1,413
1981	3,252	1,377	399	1,814	1,436
1980	2,972	1,301	362	1,609	1,264
1979	2,645	1,234	300	1,350	1,062
1978	2,654	1,208	288	1,391	1,047
1977	2,610	1,162	301	1,400	1,039
1976	2,543	1,122	275	1,379	1,059
1975	2,430	1,004	279	1,394	1,079
1974	2,324	1,010	229	1,289	1,005
1973	2,193	974	211	1,190	–
Percent change					
2000 to 2005	23.4%	2.7%	31.9%	27.0%	25.4%
1973 to 2005	84.4	37.1	315.2	94.3	–

Note: "–" means data are not available.
Source: Bureau of the Census, Current Population Survey Annual Demographic Supplements, Internet site http://www.census .gov/hhes/www/poverty/histpov/perindex.html; calculations by New Strategist

Table 5.43 Percent Distribution of Female-Headed Families in Poverty by Race and Hispanic Origin, 1973 to 2005

(percent distribution of female-headed families below poverty level by race and Hispanic origin of householder, 1973 to 2005; percentage point change for selected years)

	total female-headed families in poverty	black	Hispanic	white total	white non-Hispanic
2005	100.0%	33.0%	21.7%	57.2%	38.0%
2004	100.0	33.8	22.0	57.4	37.6
2003	100.0	34.8	20.5	56.3	37.7
2002	100.0	35.6	19.8	55.5	38.0
2001	100.0	38.9	20.5	55.9	37.6
2000	100.0	39.7	20.3	55.5	37.4
1999	100.0	41.8	20.1	53.4	35.1
1998	100.0	40.6	19.7	55.4	37.3
1997	100.0	39.1	19.2	57.7	40.0
1996	100.0	41.4	19.8	54.6	36.9
1995	100.0	41.9	19.5	54.2	36.1
1994	100.0	40.5	18.3	55.0	39.7
1993	100.0	43.1	17.5	53.7	38.4
1992	100.0	43.9	15.5	52.5	38.3
1991	100.0	44.1	15.1	52.7	38.7
1990	100.0	43.7	15.2	53.3	39.3
1989	100.0	43.5	15.1	53.0	38.7
1988	100.0	43.4	15.0	53.4	39.2
1987	100.0	43.2	15.5	53.7	39.5
1986	100.0	41.2	14.6	56.5	42.7
1985	100.0	41.8	15.0	56.1	42.0
1984	100.0	43.8	13.8	53.7	40.7
1983	100.0	43.2	12.7	54.0	42.1
1982	100.0	44.7	12.4	52.8	41.1
1981	100.0	42.3	12.3	55.8	44.2
1980	100.0	43.8	12.2	54.1	42.5
1979	100.0	46.7	11.3	51.0	40.2
1978	100.0	45.5	10.9	52.4	39.4
1977	100.0	44.5	11.5	53.6	39.8
1976	100.0	44.1	10.8	54.2	41.6
1975	100.0	41.3	11.5	57.4	44.4
1974	100.0	43.5	9.9	55.5	43.2
1973	100.0	44.4	9.6	54.3	–
Percentage point change					
2000 to 2005	–	−6.6	1.4	1.6	0.6
1973 to 2005	–	−11.4	12.0	2.9	–

Note: "–" means not applicable or data are not available.
Source: Bureau of the Census, Current Population Survey Annual Demographic Supplements, Internet site http://www.census .gov/hhes/www/poverty/histpov/perindex.html; calculations by New Strategist

Table 5.44 Percent of Female-Headed Families in Poverty by Race and Hispanic Origin, 1973 to 2005

(percent of female-headed families below poverty level by race and Hispanic origin of householder, 1973 to 2005; percentage point change for selected years)

	total female-headed families	black	Hispanic	white total	white non-Hispanic
2005	28.7%	42.0%	38.9%	25.3%	21.5%
2004	28.3	43.3	38.9	24.7	20.8
2003	28.0	42.7	37.0	24.0	20.4
2002	26.5	41.3	35.3	22.6	19.4
2001	26.4	35.2	37.0	22.4	19.0
2000	25.4	34.3	36.4	21.2	17.8
1999	27.8	39.2	39.3	22.5	18.4
1998	29.9	40.8	43.7	24.9	20.7
1997	31.6	39.8	47.6	27.7	23.4
1996	32.6	43.7	50.9	27.3	22.4
1995	32.4	45.1	49.4	26.6	21.5
1994	34.6	46.2	52.1	29.0	24.8
1993	35.6	49.9	51.6	29.2	25.0
1992	35.4	50.2	49.3	28.5	24.7
1991	35.6	51.2	49.7	28.4	24.6
1990	33.4	48.1	48.3	26.8	23.1
1989	32.2	46.5	47.5	25.4	21.7
1988	33.4	49.0	49.1	26.5	22.7
1987	34.2	51.1	52.2	26.9	23.0
1986	34.6	50.1	51.2	28.2	24.7
1985	34.0	50.5	53.1	27.4	23.6
1984	34.5	51.7	53.4	27.1	23.4
1983	36.0	53.7	52.8	28.3	25.1
1982	36.3	56.2	55.4	27.9	24.5
1981	34.6	52.9	53.2	27.4	24.3
1980	32.7	49.4	51.3	25.7	22.6
1979	30.4	49.4	49.2	22.3	19.4
1978	31.4	50.6	53.1	23.5	20.0
1977	31.7	51.0	53.6	24.0	20.2
1976	33.0	52.2	53.1	25.2	21.8
1975	32.5	50.1	53.6	25.9	22.5
1974	32.1	52.2	49.6	24.8	21.5
1973	32.2	52.7	51.4	24.5	–
Percentage point change					
2000 to 2005	3.3	7.7	2.5	4.1	3.7
1973 to 2005	–3.5	–10.7	–12.5	0.8	–

Note: "–" means data are not available.
Source: Bureau of the Census, Current Population Survey Annual Demographic Supplements, Internet site http://www.census
.gov/hhes/www/poverty/histpov/perindex.html; calculations by New Strategist

6

Labor Force

■ During the past half-century, the American labor force has changed dramatically. In 1950, women accounted for only 30 percent of the nation's workers. Today, they account for nearly half the labor force.

■ Between 1950 and 2006, the labor force participation rate of men fell in every age group, with the largest decline among men aged 65 or older because of early retirement. In more recent years, however, the labor force participation rate of older men has begun to climb.

■ Women are increasingly working at jobs once overwhelmingly dominated by men. Women accounted for more than half of managers and professionals in 2006, up from 41 percent in 1983.

■ The occupations projected to grow the fastest are in the fields of health care and computers. They include home health care aide, physician's assistant, dental hygienist, network systems analyst, and computer software engineer.

■ Dual earners have accounted for the majority of the nation's married couples for nearly two decades. In 2006, 65 percent of couples with children under age 18 were dual earners.

■ Fewer men are holding long-term jobs. In 1983, the majority of men aged 40 to 64 had been with their current employer for 10 or more years. By 2006, only men aged 55 to 59 could make that claim.

■ Sixty percent of the nation's workers in private industry had access to a retirement plan in 2006. The 54 percent majority had access to a defined-contribution plan, such as a 401(k), but only 43 percent participated in the plan.

The Face of the Labor Force Has Changed

Women and minorities have become a much larger share of the total.

During the past half-century, the American labor force has changed dramatically. In 1950, women accounted for only 30 percent of the nation's workers. Today, they account for nearly half the labor force. The age distribution of the labor force has also changed. The median age of workers bottomed out in the 1980s as the large baby-boom generation went to work. Since then, the median age of workers has topped 40 years, and it is projected to rise to nearly 42 by 2014. The share of workers aged 16 to 24 fell between 1950 and 2006 as colleges lured young adults away from jobs. The proportion of workers aged 55 or older also declined as early retirement became more popular. The older worker share of the labor force will grow during the next decade as the large baby-boom generation fills the age group and early retirement becomes less common.

The minority share of the labor force increased substantially between 1980 and 2006. The Hispanic share of workers has climbed from just 6 percent of workers in 1980 to 14 percent in 2006. By 2014, Hispanics will account for 16 percent of workers, according to projections by the Bureau of Labor Statistics. The Asian share of workers is also growing rapidly, but by 2014 Asians will still account for a relatively small 5 percent of workers. The black share of workers is increasing more slowly than the Hispanic or Asian share. By 2014, blacks will account for 12 percent of workers.

■ The non-Hispanic white share of the labor force is declining and is projected to fall from 69 percent today to 66 percent by 2014, according to the Bureau of Labor Statistics.

Non-Hispanic whites are the oldest workers

(median age of the labor force by race and Hispanic origin, 2004)

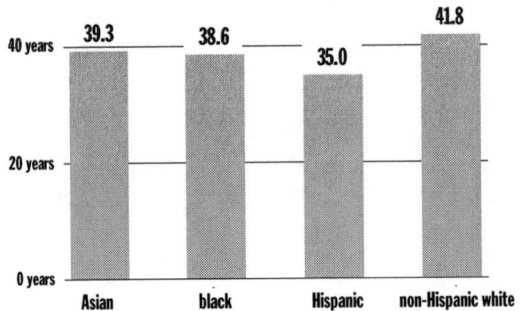

Table 6.1 Labor Force by Sex and Age, 1950 to 2006

(number and percent distribution of people aged 16 or older in the civilian labor force by sex and age, 1950 to 2006; percent change in number and percentage point change in share for selected years; numbers in thousands)

	2006	2000	1990	1980	1970	1960	1950	percent change 2000–06	percent change 1950–06
Total	151,428	142,583	125,840	106,940	82,771	69,628	62,208	6.2%	143.4%
Men	81,255	76,280	69,011	61,453	51,228	46,388	43,819	6.5	85.4
Women	70,173	66,303	56,829	45,487	31,543	23,240	18,389	5.8	281.6
Aged 16 to 24	22,394	22,521	22,492	25,300	17,846	11,545	11,522	–0.6	94.4
Aged 25 to 34	32,573	32,755	35,929	29,227	17,036	14,382	14,619	–0.6	122.8
Aged 35 to 44	35,848	37,567	32,145	20,463	16,437	16,269	13,954	–4.6	156.9
Aged 45 to 54	35,146	31,071	20,248	16,910	16,949	14,852	11,444	13.1	207.1
Aged 55 to 64	19,984	14,356	11,575	11,985	11,283	9,385	7,633	39.2	161.8
Aged 65 or older	5,484	4,312	3,451	3,054	3,222	3,195	3,036	27.2	80.6

	2006	2000	1990	1980	1970	1960	1950	percentage point change 2000–06	percentage point change 1950–2006
Total	100.0%	100.0%	100.0%	100.0%	100.0%	100.0%	100.0%	–	–
Men	53.7	53.5	54.8	57.5	61.9	66.6	70.4	0.2	–16.8
Women	46.3	46.5	45.2	42.5	38.1	33.4	29.6	–0.2	16.8
Aged 16 to 24	14.8	15.8	17.9	23.7	21.6	16.6	18.5	–1.0	–3.7
Aged 25 to 34	21.5	23.0	28.6	27.3	20.6	20.7	23.5	–1.5	–2.0
Aged 35 to 44	23.7	26.3	25.5	19.1	19.9	23.4	22.4	–2.7	1.2
Aged 45 to 54	23.2	21.8	16.1	15.8	20.5	21.3	18.4	1.4	4.8
Aged 55 to 64	13.2	10.1	9.2	11.2	13.6	13.5	12.3	3.1	0.9
Aged 65 or older	3.6	3.0	2.7	2.9	3.9	4.6	4.9	0.6	–1.3

Note: "–" means not applicable.
Source: Bureau of Labor Statistics, Labor Force Statistics from the Current Population Survey, Internet site http://www.bls.gov/cps/home.htm; calculations by New Strategist

Table 6.2 Projections of the Labor Force by Sex and Age, 2006 and 2014

(projected number and percent distribution of people aged 16 or older in the civilian labor force by sex and age, 2006 and 2014; percent change, 2006–14; numbers in thousands)

	2006 number	2006 percent distribution	2014 number	2014 percent distribution	percent change in number, 2006–14
Total labor force	**151,428**	**100.0%**	**162,100**	**100.0%**	**7.0%**
Total men in labor force	**81,255**	**53.7**	**86,194**	**53.2**	**6.1**
Aged 16 to 24	11,809	7.8	11,389	7.0	–3.6
Aged 25 to 34	17,944	11.8	20,565	12.7	14.6
Aged 35 to 44	19,407	12.8	18,067	11.1	–6.9
Aged 45 to 54	18,489	12.2	18,355	11.3	–0.7
Aged 55 to 59	6,763	4.5	7,849	4.8	16.1
Aged 60 to 64	3,746	2.5	5,173	3.2	38.1
Aged 65 or older	3,096	2.0	4,795	3.0	54.9
Total women in labor force	**70,173**	**46.3**	**75,906**	**46.8**	**8.2**
Aged 16 to 24	10,585	7.0	10,769	6.6	1.7
Aged 25 to 34	14,628	9.7	16,189	10.0	10.7
Aged 35 to 44	16,441	10.9	15,277	9.4	–7.1
Aged 45 to 54	16,656	11.0	17,172	10.6	3.1
Aged 55 to 59	6,182	4.1	7,654	4.7	23.8
Aged 60 to 64	3,293	2.2	4,953	3.1	50.4
Aged 65 or older	2,388	1.6	3,892	2.4	63.0

Source: Bureau of Labor Statistics, Labor Force Statistics from the Current Population Survey, Internet site http://www.bls .gov/cps/home.htm#empstat; and Projected Labor Force Data, Internet site http://www.bls.gov/emp/emplab1.htm; calculations by New Strategist

Table 6.3 Labor Force by Race and Hispanic Origin, 1980 to 2006

(number and percent distribution of people aged 16 or older in the civilian labor force by race and Hispanic origin, 1980 to 2006; percent change in number and percentage point change in share for selected years; numbers in thousands)

	2006	2000	1990	1980	percent change 2000–06	percent change 1980–06
RACE						
Total labor force	**151,428**	**142,583**	**125,840**	**106,940**	**6.2%**	**41.6%**
Asian	6,727	6,270	4,653	2,476	7.3	171.7
Black	17,314	16,397	13,740	10,865	5.6	59.4
White	123,834	118,545	107,447	93,600	4.5	32.3
HISPANIC ORIGIN						
Total labor force	**151,428**	**142,583**	**125,840**	**106,940**	**6.2**	**41.6**
Hispanic	20,694	16,689	10,720	6,146	24.0	236.7
Non-Hispanic	130,734	125,894	115,120	100,794	3.8	29.7

	2006	2000	1990	1980	percentage point change 2000–06	percentage point change 1980–2006
RACE						
Total labor force	**100.0%**	**100.0%**	**100.0%**	**100.0%**	–	–
Asian	4.4	4.4	3.7	2.3	0.0	2.1
Black	11.4	11.5	10.9	10.2	–0.1	1.3
White	81.8	83.1	85.4	87.5	–1.4	–5.7
HISPANIC ORIGIN						
Total labor force	**100.0**	**100.0**	**100.0**	**100.0**	–	–
Hispanic	13.7	11.7	8.5	5.7	2.0	7.9
Non-Hispanic	86.3	88.3	91.5	94.3	–2.0	–7.9

Note: Hispanics may be of any race; "–" means not applicable.
Source: Bureau of the Census, Statistical Abstract of the United States: 2007, http://www.census.gov/compendia/statab/2007 edition.html; calculations by New Strategist

Table 6.4 Projections of the Labor Force by Race and Hispanic Origin, 2006 and 2014

(projected number and percent distribution of people aged 16 or older in the civilian labor force by race and Hispanic origin, 2006 and 2014; percent change in number, 2006–14; numbers in thousands)

	2006		2014		percent change in number, 2006–14
	number	percent distribution	number	percent distribution	
Total in labor force	**151,428**	**100.0%**	**162,100**	**100.0%**	**7.0%**
Asian	6,727	4.4	8,304	5.1	23.4
Black	17,314	11.4	19,433	12.0	12.2
Hispanic	20,694	13.7	25,760	15.9	24.5
Non-Hispanic white	104,419	69.0	106,373	65.6	1.9

Source: Bureau of Labor Statistics, Labor Force Statistics from the Current Population Survey, Internet site http://www.bls.gov/cps/home.htm; and Projected Labor Force Data, Internet site http://www.bls.gov/emp/emplab1.htm; calculations by New Strategist

Table 6.5 Median Age of the Labor Force by Sex, Race, and Hispanic Origin, 1962 to 2014

(median age of the civilian labor force by sex, race, and Hispanic origin, 1962 to 2014; change in years for selected years)

	total	men	women	Asian	black	Hispanic	white total	white non-Hispanic
2014	41.6	41.2	42.2	42.0	38.6	37.4	42.3	43.8
2004	40.3	40.1	40.5	39.3	38.6	35.0	40.8	41.8
2000	39.3	39.3	39.3	37.8	37.3	34.9	39.7	40.4
1990	36.6	36.7	36.8	36.5	34.9	33.2	36.8	37.0
1980	34.6	35.1	33.9	34.1	33.3	32.0	34.8	35.0
1970	39.0	39.4	38.3	–	–	–	39.3	–
1962	40.5	40.5	40.4	–	–	–	40.9	–
Change in years								
2000 to 2014	2.3	1.9	2.9	4.2	1.3	2.5	2.6	3.4
1962 to 2014	1.1	0.7	1.8	–	–	–	1.4	–

Note: Prior to 2004, Asians are those who identified themselves as being Asian or of "other" race. In 2004 and 2014, Asians are those who identify themselves as being Asian alone. "–" means data not available.
Source: Bureau of Labor Statistics, Monthly Labor Review, November 2001 and Employment Projections, http://www.bls.gov/emp/home.htm; calculations by New Strategist

Labor Force Participation Is below the Record High

The peak was reached in the late 1990s.

Among Americans aged 16 or older, 66.2 percent were working or looking for work in 2006. This is a relatively high percentage, but it is below the all-time record of 67.1 percent achieved from 1997 to 2000. In 1950, only 59 percent of Americans were at work. Behind the increase in the proportion of Americans in the labor force is the rise of working women.

Seventy-three percent of men aged 16 or older were in the labor force in 2006, down from 86 percent in 1950. The proportion of men not in the labor force grew from 14 to 27 percent during those years as early retirement became increasingly popular and labor force participation among older men fell. Fifty-nine percent of women were in the labor force in 2006, up from just 34 percent in 1950. The proportion of women not in the labor force fell from 66 to 41 percent during those years as more women went to work.

■ During the past half-century, the unemployment rate has ranged from a low of 2.9 percent in 1953 to a high of 9.7 percent in 1982.

Trends in labor force participation differ for men and women

(labor force participation rate of people aged 16 or older, by sex, 1950 and 2006)

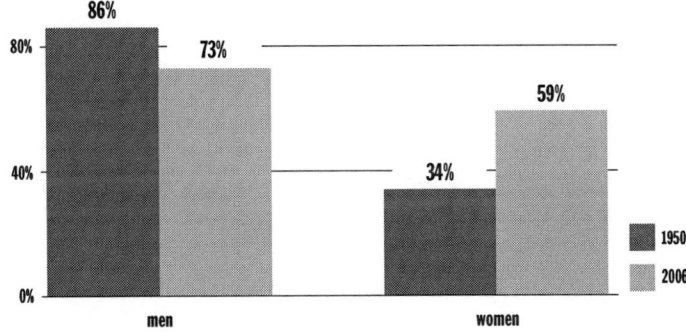

Table 6.6 Employment Status of the Population, 1950 to 2006

(employment status of the civilian noninstitutional population aged 16 or older, 1950 to 2006; numbers in thousands)

	civilian noninstitutional population	total	percent of population	employed total	agricultural	nonagric.	unemployed number	percent	not in labor force
2006	228,815	151,428	66.2%	144,427	2,206	142,221	7,001	4.6%	77,387
2005	226,082	149,320	66.0	141,730	2,197	139,532	7,591	5.1	76,762
2004	223,357	147,401	66.0	139,252	2,232	137,020	8,149	5.5	75,956
2003	221,168	146,510	66.2	137,736	2,275	135,461	8,774	6.0	74,658
2002	217,570	144,863	66.6	136,485	2,311	134,174	8,378	5.8	72,707
2001	215,092	143,734	66.8	136,933	2,299	134,635	6,801	4.7	71,359
2000	212,577	142,583	67.1	136,891	2,464	134,427	5,692	4.0	69,994
1999	207,753	139,368	67.1	133,488	3,281	130,207	5,880	4.2	68,385
1998	205,220	137,673	67.1	131,463	3,378	128,085	6,210	4.5	67,547
1997	203,133	136,297	67.1	129,558	3,399	126,159	6,739	4.9	66,836
1996	200,591	133,943	66.8	126,708	3,443	123,264	7,236	5.4	66,647
1995	198,584	132,304	66.6	124,900	3,440	121,460	7,404	5.6	66,280
1994	196,814	131,056	66.6	123,060	3,409	119,651	7,996	6.1	65,758
1993	194,838	129,200	66.3	120,259	3,115	117,144	8,940	6.9	65,638
1992	192,805	128,105	66.4	118,492	3,247	115,245	9,613	7.5	64,700
1991	190,925	126,346	66.2	117,718	3,269	114,449	8,628	6.8	64,578
1990	189,164	125,840	66.5	118,793	3,223	115,570	7,047	5.6	63,324
1989	186,393	123,869	66.5	117,342	3,199	114,142	6,528	5.3	62,523
1988	184,613	121,669	65.9	114,968	3,169	111,800	6,701	5.5	62,944
1987	182,753	119,865	65.6	112,440	3,208	109,232	7,425	6.2	62,888
1986	180,587	117,834	65.3	109,597	3,163	106,434	8,237	7.0	62,752
1985	178,206	115,461	64.8	107,150	3,179	103,971	8,312	7.2	62,744
1984	176,383	113,544	64.4	105,005	3,321	101,685	8,539	7.5	62,839
1983	174,215	111,550	64.0	100,834	3,383	97,450	10,717	9.6	62,665
1982	172,271	110,204	64.0	99,526	3,401	96,125	10,678	9.7	62,067
1981	170,130	108,670	63.9	100,397	3,368	97,030	8,273	7.6	61,460
1980	167,745	106,940	63.8	99,302	3,364	95,938	7,637	7.1	60,806
1979	164,863	104,962	63.7	98,824	3,347	95,477	6,137	5.8	59,900
1978	161,910	102,250	63.2	96,048	3,387	92,661	6,202	6.1	59,659
1977	159,033	99,008	62.3	92,017	3,283	88,734	6,991	7.1	60,025
1976	156,150	96,158	61.6	88,752	3,331	85,421	7,406	7.7	59,991
1975	153,153	93,774	61.2	85,846	3,408	82,438	7,929	8.5	59,377
1974	150,120	91,949	61.3	86,794	3,515	83,279	5,156	5.6	58,171
1973	147,096	89,429	60.8	85,064	3,470	81,594	4,365	4.9	57,667
1972	144,126	87,034	60.4	82,153	3,484	78,669	4,882	5.6	57,091
1971	140,216	84,382	60.2	79,367	3,394	75,972	5,016	5.9	55,834
1970	137,085	82,771	60.4	78,678	3,463	75,215	4,093	4.9	54,315
1969	134,335	80,734	60.1	77,902	3,606	74,296	2,832	3.5	53,602
1968	132,028	78,737	59.6	75,920	3,817	72,103	2,817	3.6	53,291
1967	129,874	77,347	59.6	74,372	3,844	70,527	2,975	3.8	52,527
1966	128,058	75,770	59.2	72,895	3,979	68,915	2,875	3.8	52,288
1965	126,513	74,455	58.9	71,088	4,361	66,726	3,366	4.5	52,058
1960	117,245	69,628	59.4	65,778	5,458	60,318	3,852	5.5	47,617
1955	109,683	65,023	59.3	62,170	6,450	55,722	2,852	4.4	44,660
1950	104,995	62,208	59.2	58,918	7,160	51,758	3,288	5.3	42,787

Note: The civilian labor force includes both the employed and the unemployed. The civilian population includes both those in the labor force and those not in the labor force.
Source: Bureau of Labor Statistics, Labor Force Characteristics from the Current Population Survey, Internet site http://www .bls.gov/cps/home.htm

Table 6.7 Employment Status of Men, 1950 to 2006

(employment status of men aged 16 or older, 1950 to 2006; numbers in thousands)

| | civilian noninstitutional men | civilian labor force | | | | | | |
| | | total | percent of men | employed | unemployed | | not in labor force | |
					number	percent	number	percent
2006	110,605	81,255	73.5%	77,502	3,753	4.6%	29,350	26.5%
2005	109,151	80,033	73.3	75,973	4,059	5.1	29,119	26.7
2004	107,710	78,980	73.3	74,524	4,456	5.6	28,730	26.7
2003	106,435	78,238	73.5	73,332	4,906	6.3	28,197	26.5
2002	104,585	77,500	74.1	72,903	4,597	5.9	27,085	25.9
2001	103,282	76,886	74.4	73,196	3,690	4.8	26,396	25.6
2000	101,964	76,280	74.8	73,305	2,975	3.9	25,684	25.2
1999	99,722	74,512	74.7	71,446	3,066	4.1	25,210	25.3
1998	98,758	73,959	74.9	70,693	3,266	4.4	24,799	25.1
1997	97,715	73,261	75.0	69,685	3,577	4.9	24,454	25.0
1996	96,206	72,086	74.9	68,207	3,880	5.4	24,119	25.1
1995	95,178	71,360	75.0	67,377	3,983	5.6	23,818	25.0
1994	94,354	70,817	75.1	66,450	4,367	6.2	23,538	24.9
1993	93,332	70,404	75.4	65,349	5,055	7.2	22,927	24.6
1992	92,270	69,964	75.8	64,440	5,523	7.9	22,306	24.2
1991	91,278	69,168	75.8	64,223	4,946	7.2	22,110	24.2
1990	90,377	69,011	76.4	65,104	3,906	5.7	21,367	23.6
1989	88,762	67,840	76.4	64,315	3,525	5.2	20,923	23.6
1988	87,857	66,927	76.2	63,273	3,655	5.5	20,930	23.8
1987	86,899	66,207	76.2	62,107	4,101	6.2	20,692	23.8
1986	85,798	65,422	76.3	60,892	4,530	6.9	20,376	23.7
1985	84,469	64,411	76.3	59,891	4,521	7.0	20,058	23.7
1984	83,605	63,835	76.4	59,091	4,744	7.4	19,771	23.6
1983	82,531	63,047	76.4	56,787	6,260	9.9	19,484	23.6
1982	81,523	62,450	76.6	56,271	6,179	9.9	19,073	23.4
1981	80,511	61,974	77.0	57,397	4,577	7.4	18,537	23.0
1980	79,398	61,453	77.4	57,186	4,267	6.9	17,945	22.6
1979	78,020	60,726	77.8	57,607	3,120	5.1	17,293	22.2
1978	76,576	59,620	77.9	56,479	3,142	5.3	16,956	22.1
1977	75,193	58,396	77.7	54,728	3,667	6.3	16,797	22.3
1976	73,759	57,174	77.5	53,138	4,036	7.1	16,585	22.5
1975	72,291	56,299	77.9	51,857	4,442	7.9	15,993	22.1
1974	70,808	55,739	78.7	53,024	2,714	4.9	15,069	21.3
1973	69,292	54,624	78.8	52,349	2,275	4.2	14,667	21.2
1972	67,835	53,555	78.9	50,896	2,659	5.0	14,280	21.1
1971	65,942	52,180	79.1	49,390	2,789	5.3	13,762	20.9
1970	64,304	51,228	79.7	48,990	2,238	4.4	13,076	20.3
1969	62,898	50,221	79.8	48,818	1,403	2.8	12,677	20.2
1968	61,847	49,533	80.1	48,114	1,419	2.9	12,315	19.9
1967	60,905	48,987	80.4	47,479	1,508	3.1	11,919	19.6
1966	60,262	48,471	80.4	46,919	1,551	3.2	11,792	19.6
1965	59,782	48,255	80.4	46,340	1,914	4.0	11,527	19.3
1960	55,662	46,388	82.9	43,904	2,486	5.4	9,274	16.7
1955	52,109	44,475	85.4	42,621	1,854	4.2	7,634	14.7
1950	50,725	43,819	86.4	41,578	2,239	5.1	6,906	13.6

Note: The civilian labor force includes both the employed and the unemployed. The civilian population includes both those in the labor force and those not in the labor force.
Source: Bureau of Labor Statistics, Handbook of Labor Statistics, Bulletin 2340, 1989; and Labor Force Characteristics from the Current Population Survey, Internet site http://www.bls.gov/cps/home.htm; calculations by New Strategist

Table 6.8 Employment Status of Women, 1950 to 2006

(employment status of women aged 16 or older, 1950 to 2006; numbers in thousands)

| | civilian noninstitutional women | civilian labor force | | | | | | |
| | | total | percent of women | employed | unemployed | | not in labor force | |
					number	percent	number	percent
2006	118,210	70,173	59.4%	66,925	3,247	4.6%	48,037	40.6%
2005	116,931	69,288	59.3	65,757	3,531	5.1	47,643	40.7
2004	115,647	68,421	59.2	64,728	3,694	5.4	47,225	40.8
2003	114,733	68,272	59.5	64,404	3,868	5.7	46,461	40.5
2002	112,985	67,363	59.6	63,582	3,781	5.6	45,621	40.4
2001	111,811	66,848	59.8	63,737	3,111	4.7	44,962	40.2
2000	110,613	66,303	59.9	63,586	2,717	4.1	44,310	40.1
1999	108,031	64,855	60.0	62,042	2,814	4.3	43,175	40.0
1998	106,462	63,714	59.8	60,771	2,944	4.6	42,748	40.2
1997	105,418	63,036	59.8	59,873	3,162	5.0	42,382	40.2
1996	104,385	61,857	59.3	58,501	3,356	5.4	42,528	40.7
1995	103,406	60,944	58.9	57,523	3,421	5.6	42,462	41.1
1994	102,460	60,239	58.8	56,610	3,629	6.0	42,221	41.2
1993	101,506	58,795	57.9	54,910	3,885	6.6	42,711	42.1
1992	100,535	58,141	57.8	54,052	4,090	7.0	42,394	42.2
1991	99,646	57,178	57.4	53,496	3,683	6.4	42,468	42.6
1990	98,787	56,829	57.5	53,689	3,140	5.5	41,957	42.5
1989	97,630	56,030	57.4	53,027	3,003	5.4	41,601	42.6
1988	96,756	54,742	56.6	51,696	3,046	5.6	42,014	43.4
1987	95,853	53,658	56.0	50,334	3,324	6.2	42,195	44.0
1986	94,789	52,413	55.3	48,706	3,707	7.1	42,376	44.7
1985	93,736	51,050	54.5	47,259	3,791	7.4	42,686	45.5
1984	92,778	49,709	53.6	45,915	3,794	7.6	43,068	46.4
1983	91,684	48,503	52.9	44,047	4,457	9.2	43,181	47.1
1982	90,748	47,755	52.6	43,256	4,499	9.4	42,993	47.4
1981	89,618	46,696	52.1	43,000	3,696	7.9	42,922	47.9
1980	88,348	45,487	51.5	42,117	3,370	7.4	42,861	48.5
1979	86,843	44,235	50.9	41,217	3,018	6.8	42,608	49.1
1978	85,334	42,631	50.0	39,569	3,061	7.2	42,703	50.0
1977	83,840	40,613	48.4	37,289	3,324	8.2	43,227	51.6
1976	82,390	38,983	47.3	35,615	3,369	8.6	43,406	52.7
1975	80,860	37,475	46.3	33,989	3,486	9.3	43,386	53.7
1974	79,312	36,211	45.7	33,769	2,441	6.7	43,101	54.3
1973	77,804	34,804	44.7	32,715	2,089	6.0	43,000	55.3
1972	76,290	33,479	43.9	31,257	2,222	6.6	42,811	56.1
1971	74,274	32,202	43.4	29,976	2,227	6.9	42,072	56.6
1970	72,782	31,543	43.3	29,688	1,855	5.9	41,239	56.7
1969	71,436	30,513	42.7	29,084	1,429	4.7	40,924	57.3
1968	70,179	29,204	41.6	27,807	1,397	4.8	40,976	58.4
1967	68,968	28,360	41.1	26,893	1,468	5.2	40,608	58.9
1966	67,795	27,299	40.3	25,976	1,324	4.8	40,496	59.7
1965	66,731	26,200	39.3	24,748	1,452	5.5	40,531	60.7
1960	61,582	23,240	37.7	21,874	1,366	5.9	38,343	62.3
1955	57,574	20,548	35.7	19,551	998	4.9	37,026	64.3
1950	54,270	18,408	33.9	17,359	1,049	5.7	35,881	66.1

Note: The civilian labor force includes both the employed and the unemployed. The civilian population includes both those in the labor force and those not in the labor force.
Source: Bureau of Labor Statistics, Handbook of Labor Statistics, Bulletin 2340, 1989; and Labor Force Characteristics from the Current Population Survey, Internet site http://www.bls.gov/cps/home.htm; calculations by New Strategist

The Labor Force Participation Rate of Older Men Is Rising

Women's labor force participation rate has stabilized after decades of growth.

Between 1950 and 2006, the labor force participation rate of men fell in every age group, with the largest decline among men aged 65 or older because of early retirement. In more recent years, however, the labor force participation rate of older men has begun to climb. Among men aged 55 to 64, labor force participation rose from 67 to 70 percent between 2000 and 2006. Among men aged 65 or older, the rate grew from 18 to 20 percent during those years and is now at the highest level since 1978. Behind the rising labor force participation rate of older men is the disappearance of generous retirement benefits.

The labor force participation rate of women aged 16 or older climbed from just 34 percent in 1950 to 59 percent in 2006. At the same time, the labor force participation rate of men fell from 86 to 73 percent. Consequently, the gap between the labor force participation rate of men and women dropped from an enormous 53 percentage points to just 14 percentage points during the past half-century. The gap is projected to shrink to 12 percentage points by 2014.

During the next few years, the percentage of Americans aged 16 or older in the labor force will continue to fall slightly as the large baby-boom generation begins to retire. By 2014, fewer than 66 percent of Americans will be in the labor force. Big gains are foreseen in the labor force participation of men and women aged 65 or older, however, with their rates climbing by more than 4 percentage points.

■ Hispanic men have the highest labor force participation rate, with 81 percent being at work. Hispanic women have the lowest rate, with only 56 percent working.

Older men are returning to the workforce

(percentage of men aged 65 or older in the labor force, selected years, 1950 to 2014)

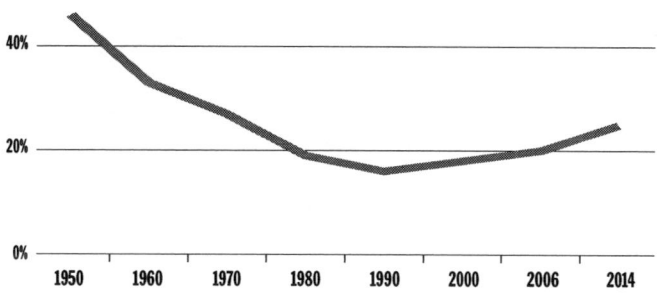

Table 6.9 Labor Force Participation Rate by Sex, 1950 to 2006

(percent of people aged 16 or older in the civilian labor force by sex, and percentage point difference between men and women, 1950 to 2006; percentage point change for selected years)

	total people	men	women	percentage point difference between men and women
2006	66.2%	73.5%	59.4%	14.1
2005	66.0	73.3	59.3	14.0
2004	66.0	73.3	59.2	14.1
2003	66.2	73.5	59.5	14.0
2002	66.6	74.1	59.6	14.5
2001	66.8	74.4	59.8	14.6
2000	67.1	74.8	59.9	14.9
1999	67.1	74.7	60.0	14.7
1998	67.1	74.9	59.8	15.1
1997	67.1	75.0	59.8	15.2
1996	66.8	74.9	59.3	15.6
1995	66.6	75.0	58.9	16.1
1994	66.6	75.1	58.8	16.3
1993	66.3	75.4	57.9	17.5
1992	66.4	75.8	57.8	18.0
1991	66.2	75.8	57.4	18.4
1990	66.5	76.4	57.5	18.9
1989	66.5	76.4	57.4	19.0
1988	65.9	76.2	56.6	19.6
1987	65.6	76.2	56.0	20.2
1986	65.3	76.3	55.3	21.0
1985	64.8	76.3	54.5	21.8
1984	64.4	76.4	53.6	22.8
1983	64.0	76.4	52.9	23.5
1982	64.0	76.6	52.6	24.0
1981	63.9	77.0	52.1	24.9
1980	63.8	77.4	51.5	25.9
1979	63.7	77.8	50.9	26.9
1978	63.2	77.9	50.0	27.9
1977	62.3	77.7	48.4	29.3
1976	61.6	77.5	47.3	30.2
1975	61.2	77.9	46.3	31.6
1974	61.3	78.7	45.7	33.0
1973	60.8	78.8	44.7	34.1
1972	60.4	78.9	43.9	35.0
1971	60.2	79.1	43.4	35.7
1970	60.4	79.7	43.3	36.4
1969	60.1	79.8	42.7	37.1
1968	59.6	80.1	41.6	38.5
1967	59.6	80.4	41.1	39.3
1966	59.2	80.4	40.3	40.1
1965	58.9	80.4	39.3	41.1
1960	59.4	82.9	37.7	45.2
1955	59.3	85.4	35.7	49.7
1950	59.2	86.4	33.9	52.5
Percentage point change				
2000 to 2006	−0.9	−1.3	−0.5	−0.8
1950 to 2006	7.0	−12.9	25.5	−38.4

Source: Bureau of Labor Statistics, Handbook of Labor Statistics, Bulletin 2340, 1989; and Labor Force Statistics from the Current Population Survey, http://www.bls.gov/cps/home.htm; calculations by New Strategist

Table 6.10   Labor Force Participation Rate of Men by Age, 1950 to 2006

(percent of men aged 16 or older in the civilian labor force by age, 1950 to 2006; percentage point change for selected years)

	total men	16–19	20–24	25–34	35–44	45–54	55–64	65+
2006	73.5%	43.7%	79.6%	91.7%	92.1%	88.1%	69.6%	20.3%
2005	73.3	43.2	79.1	91.7	92.1	87.7	69.3	19.8
2004	73.3	43.9	79.6	91.9	91.9	87.5	68.7	19.0
2003	73.5	44.3	80.0	91.8	92.1	87.7	68.7	18.6
2002	74.1	47.5	80.7	92.4	92.1	88.5	69.2	17.9
2001	74.4	50.2	81.6	92.7	92.5	88.5	68.3	17.7
2000	74.8	52.8	82.6	93.4	92.7	88.6	67.3	17.7
1999	74.7	52.9	81.9	93.3	92.8	88.8	67.9	16.9
1998	74.9	53.3	82.0	93.2	92.6	89.2	68.1	16.5
1997	75.0	52.3	82.5	93.0	92.6	89.5	67.6	17.1
1996	74.9	53.2	82.5	93.2	92.4	89.1	67.0	16.9
1995	75.0	54.8	83.1	93.0	92.3	88.8	66.0	16.8
1994	75.1	54.1	83.1	92.6	92.8	89.1	65.5	16.8
1993	75.4	53.2	83.2	93.4	93.4	90.1	66.5	15.6
1992	75.8	53.4	83.3	93.8	93.7	90.7	67.0	16.1
1991	75.8	53.2	83.5	93.6	94.1	90.5	67.0	15.7
1990	76.4	55.7	84.4	94.1	94.3	90.7	67.8	16.3
1989	76.4	57.9	85.3	94.4	94.5	91.1	67.2	16.6
1988	76.2	56.9	85.0	94.3	94.5	90.9	67.0	16.5
1987	76.2	56.1	85.2	94.6	94.6	90.7	67.6	16.3
1986	76.3	56.4	85.8	94.6	94.8	91.0	67.3	16.0
1985	76.3	56.8	85.0	94.7	95.0	91.0	67.9	15.8
1984	76.4	56.0	85.0	94.4	95.4	91.2	68.5	16.3
1983	76.4	56.2	84.8	94.2	95.2	91.2	69.4	17.4
1982	76.6	56.7	84.9	94.7	95.3	91.2	70.2	17.8
1981	77.0	59.0	85.5	94.9	95.4	91.4	70.6	18.4
1980	77.4	60.5	85.9	95.2	95.5	91.2	72.1	19.0
1979	77.8	61.5	86.4	95.3	95.7	91.4	72.8	19.9
1978	77.9	62.0	85.9	95.3	95.7	91.3	73.3	20.4
1977	77.7	60.9	85.6	95.3	95.7	91.1	73.8	20.0
1976	77.5	59.3	85.2	95.2	95.4	91.6	74.3	20.2
1975	77.9	59.1	84.5	95.2	95.6	92.1	75.6	21.6
1974	78.7	60.7	85.9	95.8	96.0	92.2	77.3	22.4
1973	78.8	59.7	85.2	95.7	96.2	93.0	78.2	22.7
1972	78.9	58.1	83.9	95.7	96.4	93.2	80.4	24.3
1971	79.1	56.1	83.0	95.9	96.5	93.9	82.1	25.5
1970	79.7	56.1	83.3	96.4	96.9	94.3	83.0	26.8
1969	79.8	55.9	82.8	96.7	96.9	94.6	83.4	27.2
1968	80.1	55.1	82.8	96.9	97.1	94.9	84.3	27.3
1967	80.4	55.6	84.4	97.2	97.3	95.2	84.4	27.1
1966	80.4	55.3	85.1	97.3	97.2	95.3	84.5	27.1
1965	80.4	53.8	85.8	97.2	97.3	95.6	84.6	27.9
1960	82.9	56.1	88.1	97.5	97.7	95.7	86.8	33.1
1955	85.4	58.9	86.9	97.6	98.1	96.4	87.9	39.6
1950	86.4	63.2	87.9	96.0	97.6	95.8	86.9	45.8
Percentage point change								
2000 to 2006	–1.3	–9.1	–3.0	–1.7	–0.6	–0.5	2.3	2.6
1950 to 2006	–12.9	–19.5	–8.3	–4.3	–5.5	–7.7	–17.3	–25.5

Source: Bureau of Labor Statistics, Labor Force Statistics from the Current Population Survey, Internet site http://www.bls.gov/ cps/home.htm#empstat; calculations by New Strategist

Table 6.11 Labor Force Participation Rate of Women by Age, 1950 to 2006

(percent of women aged 16 or older in the civilian labor force by age, 1950 to 2006; percentage point change for selected years)

	total women	16–19	20–24	25–34	35–44	45–54	55–64	65+
2006	59.4%	43.7%	69.5%	74.4%	75.9%	76.0%	58.2%	11.7%
2005	59.3	44.2	70.1	73.9	75.8	76.0	57.0	11.5
2004	59.2	43.8	70.5	73.6	75.6	76.5	56.3	11.1
2003	59.5	44.8	70.8	74.1	76.0	76.8	56.6	10.6
2002	59.6	47.3	72.1	75.1	76.4	76.0	55.2	9.8
2001	59.8	49.0	72.7	75.5	77.1	76.4	53.2	9.6
2000	59.9	51.2	73.1	76.1	77.2	76.8	51.9	9.4
1999	60.0	51.0	73.2	76.4	77.2	76.7	51.5	8.9
1998	59.8	52.3	73.0	76.3	77.1	76.2	51.2	8.6
1997	59.8	51.0	72.7	76.0	77.7	76.0	50.9	8.6
1996	59.3	51.3	71.3	75.2	77.5	75.4	49.6	8.6
1995	58.9	52.2	70.3	74.9	77.2	74.4	49.2	8.8
1994	58.8	51.3	71.0	74.0	77.1	74.6	48.9	9.2
1993	57.9	49.7	70.9	73.4	76.6	73.5	47.2	8.1
1992	57.8	49.1	70.9	73.9	76.7	72.6	46.5	8.3
1991	57.4	50.0	70.1	73.1	76.5	72.0	45.2	8.5
1990	57.5	51.6	71.3	73.5	76.4	71.2	45.2	8.6
1989	57.4	53.9	72.4	73.5	76.0	70.5	45.0	8.4
1988	56.6	53.6	72.7	72.7	75.2	69.0	43.5	7.9
1987	56.0	53.3	73.0	72.4	74.5	67.1	42.7	7.4
1986	55.3	53.0	72.4	71.6	73.1	65.9	42.3	7.4
1985	54.5	52.1	71.8	70.9	71.8	64.4	42.0	7.3
1984	53.6	51.8	70.4	69.8	70.1	62.9	41.7	7.5
1983	52.9	50.8	69.9	69.0	68.7	61.9	41.5	7.8
1982	52.6	51.4	69.8	68.0	68.0	61.6	41.8	7.9
1981	52.1	51.8	69.6	66.7	66.8	61.1	41.4	8.0
1980	51.5	52.9	68.9	65.5	65.5	59.9	41.3	8.1
1979	50.9	54.2	69.0	63.9	63.6	58.3	41.7	8.3
1978	50.0	53.7	68.3	62.2	61.6	57.1	41.3	8.3
1977	48.4	51.2	66.5	59.7	59.6	55.8	40.9	8.1
1976	47.3	49.8	65.0	57.3	57.8	55.0	41.0	8.2
1975	46.3	49.1	64.1	54.9	55.8	54.6	40.9	8.2
1974	45.7	49.1	63.1	52.6	54.7	54.6	40.7	8.1
1973	44.7	47.8	61.1	50.4	53.3	53.7	41.1	8.9
1972	43.9	45.8	59.1	47.8	52.0	53.9	42.1	9.3
1971	43.4	43.4	57.7	45.6	51.6	54.3	42.9	9.5
1970	43.3	44.0	57.7	45.0	51.1	54.4	43.0	9.7
1969	42.7	43.2	56.7	43.7	49.9	53.8	43.1	9.9
1968	41.6	41.9	54.5	42.6	48.9	52.3	42.4	9.6
1967	41.1	41.6	53.3	41.9	48.1	51.8	42.4	9.6
1966	40.3	41.4	51.5	39.8	46.8	51.7	41.8	9.6
1965	39.3	38.0	49.9	38.5	46.1	50.9	41.1	10.0
1960	37.7	39.3	46.1	36.0	43.4	49.9	37.2	10.8
1955	35.7	39.7	45.9	34.9	41.6	43.8	32.5	10.6
1950	33.9	41.0	46.0	34.0	39.1	37.9	27.0	9.7
Percentage point change								
2000 to 2006	–0.5	–7.5	–3.6	–1.7	–1.3	–0.8	6.3	2.3
1950 to 2006	25.5	2.7	23.5	40.4	36.8	38.1	31.2	2.0

Source: Bureau of Labor Statistics, Labor Force Statistics from the Current Population Survey, Internet site http://www.bls.gov/cps/home.htm#empstat; calculations by New Strategist

Table 6.12 Projections of Labor Force Participation Rate by Sex and Age, 2006 and 2014

(projected percent of people aged 16 or older in the civilian labor force by sex and age, 2006 and 2014; percentage point change in rate, 2006–14)

	2006	2014	percentage point change 2006–14
Percent in labor force	**66.2%**	**65.6%**	**–0.6**
Percent of men in labor force	**73.5**	**71.8**	**–1.7**
Aged 16 to 24	63.3	60.5	–2.8
Aged 25 to 34	91.7	95.3	3.6
Aged 35 to 44	92.1	90.7	–1.4
Aged 45 to 54	88.1	86.6	–1.5
Aged 55 to 59	77.7	76.6	–1.1
Aged 60 to 64	58.6	59.4	0.8
Aged 65 or older	20.3	24.6	4.3
Percent of women in labor force	**59.4**	**59.7**	**0.3**
Aged 16 to 24	57.9	57.8	–0.1
Aged 25 to 34	74.4	75.4	1.0
Aged 35 to 44	75.9	75.4	–0.5
Aged 45 to 54	76.0	78.1	2.1
Aged 55 to 59	66.7	70.7	4.0
Aged 60 to 64	47.0	51.8	4.8
Aged 65 or older	11.7	15.9	4.2

Source: Bureau of Labor Statistics, Labor Force Statistics from the Current Population Survey, Internet site http://www.bls .gov/cps/home.htm#empstat; and Projected Labor Force Data, Internet site http://www.bls.gov/emp/emplab1.htm; calculations by New Strategist

Table 6.13 Labor Force Participation Rate of Men by Race and Hispanic Origin, 1980 to 2006

(percent of men aged 16 or older in the civilian labor force by race and Hispanic origin, 1980 to 2006; percentage point change for selected years)

	total men	Asian	black	Hispanic	white
2006	73.5%	75.0%	67.0%	80.7%	74.3%
2005	73.3	74.8	67.3	80.1	74.1
2004	73.3	75.0	66.7	80.4	74.1
2003	73.5	75.6	67.3	80.1	74.2
2002	74.1	75.9	68.4	80.2	74.8
2001	74.4	76.2	68.4	81.0	75.1
2000	74.8	76.1	69.2	81.5	75.5
1999	74.7	74.1	68.7	79.8	75.6
1998	74.9	75.5	69.0	79.8	75.6
1997	75.0	74.7	68.3	80.1	75.9
1996	74.9	73.4	68.7	79.6	75.8
1995	75.0	75.2	69.0	79.1	75.7
1994	75.1	74.3	69.1	79.2	75.9
1993	75.4	74.9	69.6	80.2	76.2
1992	75.8	75.2	70.7	80.7	76.5
1991	75.8	74.4	70.4	80.3	76.5
1990	76.4	75.0	71.1	81.4	77.1
1989	76.4	75.5	71.0	82.0	77.1
1988	76.2	74.4	71.0	81.9	76.9
1987	76.2	75.7	71.1	81.0	76.8
1986	76.3	75.0	71.2	81.0	76.9
1985	76.3	75.1	70.8	80.4	77.0
1984	76.4	74.0	70.8	80.6	77.1
1983	76.4	75.1	70.6	80.3	77.1
1982	76.6	76.0	70.1	79.5	77.4
1981	77.0	74.0	70.0	80.6	77.9
1980	77.4	74.5	70.6	81.4	78.2
Percentage point change					
2000 to 2006	−1.3	−1.1	−2.2	−0.8	−1.2
1980 to 2006	−3.9	0.5	−3.6	−0.7	−3.9

Source: Bureau of Labor Statistics, Handbook of Labor Statistics, Bulletin 2340, 1989; and Internet site http://www.bls.gov/cps/home.htm; calculations by New Strategist

Table 6.14 Labor Force Participation Rate of Women by Race and Hispanic Origin, 1980 to 2006

(percent of women aged 16 or older in the civilian labor force by race and Hispanic origin, 1980 to 2006; percentage point change for selected years)

	total women	Asian	black	Hispanic	white
2006	59.4%	58.3%	61.7%	56.1%	59.0%
2005	59.3	58.2	61.6	55.3	58.9
2004	59.2	57.6	61.5	56.1	58.9
2003	59.5	58.3	61.9	55.9	59.2
2002	59.6	59.1	61.8	57.6	59.3
2001	59.8	59.0	62.8	57.6	59.4
2000	59.9	59.2	63.1	57.5	59.5
1999	60.0	59.0	63.5	55.9	59.6
1998	59.8	59.2	62.8	55.6	59.4
1997	59.8	59.0	61.7	55.1	59.5
1996	59.3	58.8	60.4	53.4	59.1
1995	58.9	57.2	59.5	52.6	59.0
1994	58.8	56.9	58.7	52.9	59.0
1993	57.9	57.1	57.9	52.1	58.0
1992	57.8	58.2	58.5	52.8	57.7
1991	57.4	56.6	57.5	52.3	57.4
1990	57.5	57.4	58.3	53.1	57.4
1989	57.4	58.8	58.7	53.5	57.2
1988	56.6	56.5	58.0	53.2	56.4
1987	56.0	57.4	58.0	52.0	55.7
1986	55.3	57.0	56.9	50.1	55.0
1985	54.5	56.8	56.5	49.3	54.1
1984	53.6	55.6	55.2	49.7	53.3
1983	52.9	55.2	54.2	47.7	52.7
1982	52.6	54.8	53.7	48.2	52.4
1981	52.1	54.4	53.5	48.3	51.9
1980	51.5	55.4	53.2	47.4	51.2
Percentage point change					
2000 to 2006	−0.5	−0.9	−1.4	−1.4	−0.5
1980 to 2006	7.9	2.9	8.5	8.7	7.8

Source: Bureau of Labor Statistics, Handbook of Labor Statistics, Bulletin 2340, 1989; and Internet site http://www.bls.gov/cps/home.htm; calculations by New Strategist

Table 6.15 Projections of Labor Force Participation Rate by Race and Hispanic Origin, 2006 and 2014

(projected percent of people aged 16 or older in the civilian labor force by sex, race, and Hispanic origin, 2006 and 2014; percentage point change in rate, 2006–14)

	2006	2014	percentage point change 2006–14
Percent in labor force	**66.2%**	**65.6%**	**–0.6**
Percent of men in labor force	**73.5**	**71.8**	**–1.7**
Asian	75.0	74.4	–0.6
Black	67.0	64.7	–2.3
Hispanic	80.7	78.6	–2.1
Non-Hispanic white	72.9	71.5	–1.4
Percent of women in labor force	**59.4**	**59.7**	**0.3**
Asian	58.3	58.1	–0.2
Black	61.7	62.3	0.6
Hispanic	56.1	59.3	3.2
Non-Hispanic white	59.5	59.5	0.0

Source: Bureau of Labor Statistics, Labor Force Statistics from the Current Population Survey, Internet site http://www.bls.gov/cps/home.htm#empstat; and Projected Labor Force Data, Internet site http://www.bls.gov/emp/emplab1.htm; calculations by New Strategist

Women and Blacks Have Made Big Gains

Most occupations are much more diverse than they were several decades ago.

Women are increasingly working at jobs once overwhelmingly dominated by men. Women accounted for half of managers and professionals in 2000, up from 41 percent in 1983. By 2006, women's share of managers and professional had inched up to the 51 percent majority. Since 2000, the Bureau of Labor Statistics has updated the occupational classification system, making occupational comparisons over time more difficult. But some occupations are comparable, such as physicians and lawyers. Women accounted for 32 percent of physicians and 33 percent of lawyers in 2006, more than double their share of those occupations in 1983.

Blacks have also made gains in professional jobs. Blacks accounted for 11 percent of all employed workers in 2006, but they accounted for a larger 14 percent of educational administrators, 21 percent of dieticians, and 23 percent of social workers. Hispanics accounted for 14 percent of all employed workers in 2006, but they were underrepresented in most managerial jobs and overrepresented in blue-collar and service jobs. In 2006, Hispanics accounted for 32 percent of the nation's cooks, 37 percent of dishwashers, 41 percent of grounds maintenance workers, and 47 percent of roofers. Because the government only recently began to distinguish Asians in its data collection efforts, there are no historical data on the occupations held by Asians.

■ Hispanics are overrepresented in blue-collar and service jobs because of their low levels of education.

Women's share of lawyers has more than doubled

(women's share of lawyers, 1983 and 2006)

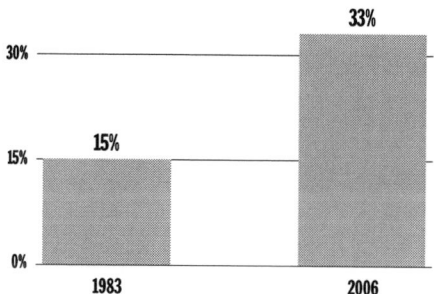

Table 6.16 Women's Share of Workers by Detailed Occupation, 1983 to 2000

(women's share of employed civilians aged 16 or older, by detailed occupation, 1983 to 2000; percentage point change, 1983–2000)

	percent women			percentage point change
	2000	1990	1983	1983–2000
TOTAL EMPLOYED	**46.5%**	**45.4%**	**43.7%**	**2.8**
MANAGERIAL AND PROFESSIONAL SPECIALITY	**49.8**	**45.8**	**40.9**	**8.9**
Executive, administrative, and managerial	**45.3**	**40.0**	**32.4**	**12.9**
Officials and administrators, public administration	52.7	42.4	38.5	14.2
Financial managers	50.1	44.3	38.6	11.5
Personnel and labor relations managers	61.8	55.1	43.9	17.9
Purchasing managers	41.3	31.9	23.6	17.7
Managers, marketing, advertising, and public relations	37.6	31.1	21.8	15.8
Administrators, education and related fields	67.0	54.4	41.4	25.6
Managers, medicine and health	77.9	66.5	57.0	20.9
Managers, properties and real estate	50.9	45.2	42.8	8.1
Management–related occupations	56.5	49.9	40.3	16.2
Accountants and auditors	56.7	50.8	38.7	18.0
Professional specialty	**53.9**	**51.2**	**48.1**	**5.8**
Architects	23.5	18.4	12.7	10.8
Engineers	9.9	8.0	5.8	4.1
Aerospace engineers	9.7	7.3	6.9	2.8
Chemical engineers	10.4	10.9	6.1	4.3
Civil engineers	9.7	5.0	4.0	5.7
Electrical and electronic engineers	9.8	8.7	6.1	3.7
Industrial engineers	15.3	11.9	11.0	4.3
Mechanical engineers	6.3	5.4	2.8	3.5
Mathematical and computer scientists	31.4	36.5	29.6	1.8
Computer systems analysts and scientists	29.2	34.5	27.8	1.4
Operations and systems researchers and analysts	45.5	41.5	31.3	14.2
Natural scientists	33.5	26.0	20.5	13.0
Chemists, except biochemists	30.3	27.0	23.3	7.0
Biological and life scientists	45.4	40.9	40.8	4.6
Health-diagnosing occupations	27.1	17.8	13.3	13.8
Physicians	27.9	19.3	15.8	12.1
Dentists	18.7	9.5	6.7	12.0
Health assessment and treating occupations	85.7	86.2	85.8	–0.1
Registered nurses	92.8	94.5	95.8	–3.0
Pharmacists	46.5	37.2	26.7	19.8
Dietitians	89.9	95.0	90.8	–0.9
Therapists	74.7	76.6	76.3	–1.6
Respiratory therapists	62.4	60.1	69.4	–7.0
Physical therapists	61.1	75.0	77.0	–15.9
Speech therapists	93.5	88.1	90.5	3.0
Physicians' assistants	57.6	39.6	36.3	21.3

(continued)

	percent women			percentage point change
	2000	1990	1983	1983–2000
Teachers, college and university	43.7%	37.7%	36.3%	7.4
Teachers, except college and university	75.4	73.7	70.9	4.5
Prekindergarten and kindergarten	98.5	98.4	98.2	0.3
Elementary school	83.3	85.2	83.3	0.0
Secondary school	57.9	53.1	51.8	6.1
Special education	82.6	84.8	82.2	0.4
Counselors, educational and vocational	70.2	61.9	53.1	17.1
Librarians, archivists, and curators	84.4	81.1	84.4	0.0
Librarians	85.2	83.3	87.3	−2.1
Social scientists and urban planners	58.9	51.5	46.8	12.1
Economists	53.3	43.8	37.9	15.4
Psychologists	64.6	58.4	57.1	7.5
Social, recreation, and religious workers	56.4	50.4	43.1	13.3
Social workers	72.4	68.2	64.3	8.1
Recreation workers	71.0	70.9	71.9	−0.9
Clergy	13.8	9.6	5.6	8.2
Lawyers and judges	29.7	20.8	15.8	13.9
Lawyers	29.6	20.6	15.3	14.3
Writers, artists, entertainers, and athletes	50.0	47.4	42.7	7.3
Authors	54.1	59.9	46.7	7.4
Designers	57.2	53.3	52.7	4.5
Musicians and composers	34.1	31.9	28.0	6.1
Actors and directors	41.5	36.5	30.8	10.7
Painters, sculptors, craft artists, and artist printmakers	46.5	51.2	47.4	−0.9
Photographers	32.6	27.8	20.7	11.9
Editors and reporters	55.8	52.0	48.4	7.4
Public relations specialists	61.1	58.7	50.1	11.0
Athletes	19.8	26.4	17.6	2.2
TECHNICAL, SALES, ADMINISTRATIVE SUPPORT	**63.8**	**64.7**	**64.6**	**−0.8**
Technicians and related support	**51.7**	**49.2**	**48.2**	**3.5**
Health technologists and technicians	80.5	83.5	84.3	−3.8
Clinical laboratory technologists and technicians	75.0	76.3	76.2	−1.2
Dental hygienists	98.5	99.1	98.6	−0.1
Radiologic technicians	69.2	76.4	71.7	−2.5
Licensed practical nurses	93.6	96.3	97.0	−3.4
Engineering and related technologists and technicians	20.4	19.8	18.4	2.0
Electrical and electronic technicians	16.9	15.4	12.5	4.4
Drafting occupations	23.4	18.9	17.5	5.9
Science technicians	41.4	31.9	29.1	12.3
Biological technicians	59.5	40.7	37.7	21.8
Chemical technicians	21.2	28.1	26.9	−5.7
Technicians, except health, engineering, and science	40.5	40.2	35.3	5.2
Airplane pilots and navigators	3.7	5.1	2.1	1.6
Computer programmers	26.5	36.0	32.5	−6.0
Legal assistants	84.4	78.8	74.0	10.4

(continued)

	percent women			percentage point change
	2000	1990	1983	1983–2000
Sales occupations	**49.6%**	**49.2%**	**47.5%**	**2.1**
Supervisors and proprietors	40.3	34.8	28.4	11.9
Sales representatives, finance and business services	44.5	42.9	37.2	7.3
Insurance sales	42.5	32.7	25.1	17.4
Real estate sales	54.3	51.1	48.9	5.4
Securities and financial services sales	31.3	23.4	23.6	7.7
Advertising and related sales	61.9	50.9	47.9	14.0
Sales representatives, commodities, except retail	27.5	22.0	15.1	12.4
Sales workers, retail and personal services	63.5	67.4	69.7	−6.2
Cashiers	77.5	81.4	84.4	−6.9
Sales-related occupations	69.1	63.7	58.7	10.4
Administrative support occupations, including clerical	**79.0**	**79.8**	**79.9**	**−0.9**
Supervisors, administrative support	60.3	31.5	53.4	6.9
Computer equipment operators	48.6	65.7	63.9	−15.3
Computer operators	48.7	65.7	63.7	−15.0
Secretaries, stenographers, and typists	98.0	98.3	98.2	−0.2
Secretaries	98.9	99.0	99.0	−0.1
Typists	94.6	95.5	95.6	−1.0
Information clerks	88.0	88.3	88.9	−0.9
Receptionists	96.7	97.0	96.8	−0.1
Records processing, except financial	81.5	81.3	82.4	−0.9
Order clerks	77.1	77.9	78.1	−1.0
Personnel clerks, except payroll and timekeeping	82.5	88.6	91.1	−8.6
Library clerks	87.0	76.2	81.9	5.1
File clerks	80.2	83.8	83.5	−3.3
Records clerks	85.9	81.4	82.8	3.1
Financial records processing	91.8	91.6	89.4	2.4
Bookkeepers, accounting, and auditing clerks	92.2	92.2	91.0	1.2
Payroll and timekeeping clerks	91.3	91.0	82.2	9.1
Billing clerks	92.2	92.1	88.4	3.8
Cost and rate clerks	77.9	80.6	75.6	2.3
Duplicating, mail and other office machine operators	54.2	62.4	62.6	−8.4
Communications equipment operators	84.3	87.2	89.1	−4.8
Telephone operators	83.9	89.0	90.4	−6.5
Mail and message distributing	41.2	35.9	31.6	9.6
Postal clerks, except mail carriers	54.4	45.2	36.7	17.7
Mail carriers, postal service	30.6	24.9	17.1	13.5
Mail clerks, except postal service	54.0	47.0	50.0	4.0
Messengers	23.9	28.2	26.2	−2.3
Material recording, scheduling, and distributing clerks	46.7	41.9	37.5	9.2
Dispatchers	51.7	54.8	45.7	6.0
Production coordinators	58.5	49.3	44.0	14.5
Traffic, shipping, and receiving clerks	33.8	26.8	22.6	11.2
Stock and inventory clerks	44.9	43.2	38.7	6.2
Expediters	66.5	66.7	57.5	9.0

(continued)

	percent women			percentage point change
	2000	1990	1983	1983–2000
Adjusters and investigators	75.5%	75.1%	69.9%	5.6
Insurance adjusters, examiners, and investigators	73.9	72.2	65.0	8.9
Investigators and adjusters, except insurance	76.0	76.6	70.1	5.9
Eligibility clerks, social welfare	89.2	90.1	88.7	0.5
Bill and account collectors	69.4	67.5	66.4	3.0
Miscellaneous administrative support	83.9	84.6	85.2	−1.3
General office clerks	83.6	81.8	80.6	3.0
Bank tellers	90.0	90.4	91.0	−1.0
Data-entry keyers	83.5	87.2	93.6	−10.1
Statistical clerks	88.5	72.3	75.7	12.8
Teachers' aides	91.0	94.5	93.7	−2.7
SERVICE OCCUPATIONS	**60.4**	**60.1**	**60.1**	**0.3**
Private household	**95.5**	**96.3**	**96.1**	**−0.6**
Child care workers	97.5	97.9	96.9	0.6
Cleaners and servants	94.8	95.5	95.8	−1.0
Protective service	**19.0**	**14.6**	**12.8**	**6.2**
Supervisors	15.1	8.0	4.7	10.4
Police and detectives	14.3	8.6	4.2	10.1
Firefighting and fire prevention	3.8	2.4	1.0	2.8
Firefighting	3.0	1.2	1.0	2.0
Police and detectives	16.5	13.8	9.4	7.1
Police and detectives, public service	12.1	12.1	5.7	6.4
Sheriffs, bailiffs, and other law enforcement officers	19.2	12.8	13.2	6.0
Correctional institution officers	22.5	17.7	17.8	4.7
Guards	27.0	20.5	20.6	6.4
Guards and police, except public services	20.1	14.8	13.0	7.1
Service occupations, excl. private household, protective service	**65.1**	**64.9**	**64.0**	**1.1**
Food preparation and service occupations	57.7	59.5	63.3	−5.6
Bartenders	51.8	55.6	48.4	3.4
Waiters and waitresses	76.7	80.8	87.8	−11.1
Cooks	43.3	47.7	50.0	−6.7
Food counter, fountain, and related occupations	67.9	72.7	76.0	−8.1
Kitchen workers, food preparation	71.1	70.7	77.0	−5.9
Waiters' and waitresses' assistants	51.4	39.1	38.8	12.6
Health service occupations	89.5	90.2	89.2	0.3
Dental assistants	96.4	98.7	98.1	−1.7
Health aides, except nursing	82.6	84.8	86.8	−4.2
Nursing aides, orderlies, and attendants	89.9	90.8	88.7	1.2
Cleaning and building service occupations	45.0	44.0	38.8	6.2
Maids and housemen	81.3	82.0	81.2	0.1
Janitors and cleaners	36.3	32.8	28.6	7.7
Personal service occupations	80.5	81.6	79.2	1.3
Barbers	25.3	18.7	12.9	12.4
Hairdressers and cosmetologists	91.2	89.8	88.7	2.5

(continued)

	percent women			percentage point change
	2000	1990	1983	1983–2000
Attendants, amusement and recreation facilities	39.4%	40.2%	40.2%	–0.8
Public transportation attendants	80.9	83.2	74.3	6.6
Welfare service aides	87.2	92.1	92.5	–5.3
PRECISION PRODUCTION, CRAFT, AND REPAIR	**9.1**	**8.5**	**8.1**	**1.0**
Mechanics and repairers	**5.1**	**3.6**	**3.0**	**2.1**
Mechanics and repairers, except supervisors	5.0	3.3	2.8	2.2
Vehicle and mobile equipment mechanics and repairers	1.6	0.9	0.8	0.8
Automobile mechanics	1.2	0.8	0.5	0.7
Aircraft engine mechanics	6.1	2.8	2.5	3.6
Electrical and electronic equipment repairers	11.5	8.6	7.4	4.1
Data processing equipment repairers	15.4	11.4	9.3	6.1
Telephone installers and repairers	13.1	11.3	9.9	3.2
Construction trades	**2.6**	**1.9**	**1.8**	**0.8**
Construction trades, except supervisors	2.7	1.9	1.9	0.8
Carpenters	1.7	1.3	1.4	0.3
Extractive occupations	**1.9**	**1.9**	**2.3**	**–0.4**
Precision production occupations	**25.0**	**23.1**	**21.5**	**3.5**
OPERATORS, FABRICATORS, AND LABORERS	**23.6**	**25.5**	**26.6**	**–3.0**
Machine operators, assemblers, and inspectors	**36.9**	**40.0**	**42.1**	**–5.2**
Textile, apparel, and furnishings machine operators	69.2	78.3	82.1	–12.9
Textile sewing machine operators	78.4	89.1	94.0	–15.6
Pressing machine operators	66.6	69.0	66.4	0.2
Fabricators, assemblers, and hand working occupations	33.5	32.5	33.7	–0.2
Production inspectors, testers, samplers, and weighers	48.5	51.4	53.8	–5.3
Transportation and material-moving occupations	**10.0**	**9.0**	**7.8**	**2.2**
Motor vehicle operators	11.5	10.8	9.2	2.3
Truck drivers	4.7	2.1	3.1	1.6
Transportation occupations, except motor vehicles	3.5	3.0	2.4	1.1
Material moving equipment operators	5.4	3.9	4.8	0.6
Industrial truck and tractor equipment operators	7.0	5.7	5.6	1.4
Handlers, equipment cleaners, helpers, and laborers	**19.8**	**17.7**	**16.8**	**3.0**
Freight, stock, and material handlers	22.4	19.1	15.4	7.0
Laborers, except construction	20.8	18.8	19.4	1.4
FARMING, FORESTRY, FISHING	**20.6**	**16.0**	**16.0**	**4.6**
Farm operators and managers	**25.4**	**15.7**	**12.1**	**13.3**
Other agricultural and related occupations	**18.9**	**17.1**	**19.9**	**–1.0**
Farm workers	18.7	21.0	24.8	–6.1
Forestry and logging occupations	**8.4**	**5.7**	**1.4**	**7.0**
Fishers, hunters, trappers	**11.9**	**4.7**	**4.5**	**7.4**

Source: Bureau of the Census, Statistical Abstract of the United States, 2001; and Bureau of Labor Statistics, Employment and Earnings, January 1991; calculations by New Strategist

Table 6.17   Black Share of Workers by Detailed Occupation, 1983 to 2000

(black share of employed civilians aged 16 or older, by detailed occupation, 1983 to 2000; percentage point change, 1983 to 2000)

	percent black			percentage point change
	2000	1990	1983	1983–2000
TOTAL EMPLOYED	11.3%	10.1%	9.3%	2.0
MANAGERIAL AND PROFESSIONAL SPECIALTY	8.2	6.2	5.6	2.6
Executive, administrative, and managerial	**7.6**	**5.7**	**4.7**	**2.9**
Officials and administrators, public administration	13.1	9.2	8.3	4.8
Financial managers	6.1	4.1	3.5	2.6
Personnel and labor relations managers	7.9	6.7	4.9	3.0
Purchasing managers	7.0	4.8	5.1	1.9
Managers, marketing, advertising, and public relations	4.2	2.9	2.7	1.5
Administrators, education and related fields	13.5	9.5	11.3	2.2
Managers, medicine and health	9.7	7.5	5.0	4.7
Managers, properties and real estate	8.2	6.5	5.5	2.7
Management-related occupations	9.5	7.6	5.8	3.7
Accountants and auditors	8.9	7.4	5.5	3.4
Professional specialty	**8.7**	**6.7**	**6.4**	**2.3**
Architects	1.6	0.9	1.6	0.0
Engineers	5.7	3.6	2.7	3.0
Aerospace engineers	5.4	4.8	1.5	3.9
Chemical engineers	5.1	1.7	3.0	2.1
Civil engineers	6.1	4.0	1.9	4.2
Electrical and electronic engineers	6.3	3.8	3.4	2.9
Industrial engineers	6.4	4.4	3.3	3.1
Mechanical engineers	4.7	3.5	3.2	1.5
Mathematical and computer scientists	8.1	6.5	5.4	2.7
Computer systems analysts and scientists	8.0	7.0	6.2	1.8
Operations and systems researchers and analysts	10.9	5.2	4.9	6.0
Natural scientists	5.4	2.7	2.6	2.8
Chemists, except biochemists	11.0	4.6	4.3	6.7
Biological and life scientists	4.0	2.7	2.4	1.6
Health-diagnosing occupations	5.2	3.0	2.7	2.5
Physicians	6.3	3.0	3.2	3.1
Dentists	3.4	4.9	2.4	1.0
Health assessment and treating occupations	9.0	7.4	7.1	1.9
Registered nurses	9.5	7.4	6.7	2.8
Pharmacists	3.3	4.1	3.8	−0.5
Dietitians	18.4	20.1	21.0	−2.6
Therapists	8.1	6.0	7.6	0.5
Respiratory therapists	10.8	11.7	6.5	4.3
Physical therapists	6.5	4.1	9.7	−3.2
Speech therapists	4.5	2.8	1.5	3.0
Physicians' assistants	5.6	6.4	7.7	−2.1

(continued)

	percent black			percentage point change
	2000	**1990**	**1983**	**1983–2000**
Teachers, college and university	6.4%	4.5%	4.4%	2.0
Teachers, except college and university	10.4	8.7	9.1	1.3
Prekindergarten and kindergarten	13.3	10.7	11.8	1.5
Elementary school	11.3	9.7	11.1	0.2
Secondary school	8.9	7.1	7.2	1.7
Special education	9.2	11.8	10.2	−1.0
Counselors, educational and vocational	17.1	16.3	13.9	3.2
Librarians, archivists, and curators	6.0	5.3	7.8	−1.8
Librarians	6.7	5.5	7.9	−1.2
Social scientists and urban planners	7.8	5.4	7.1	0.7
Economists	6.3	4.0	6.3	0.0
Psychologists	8.1	6.6	8.6	−0.5
Social, recreation, and religious workers	17.4	15.2	12.1	5.3
Social workers	22.7	21.8	18.2	4.5
Recreation workers	9.5	14.7	15.7	−6.2
Clergy	14.1	6.9	4.9	9.2
Lawyers and judges	5.7	3.4	2.7	3.0
Lawyers	5.4	3.2	2.6	2.8
Writers, artists, entertainers, and athletes	6.9	4.5	4.8	2.1
Authors	7.7	2.3	2.1	5.6
Designers	4.0	2.6	3.1	0.9
Musicians and composers	13.5	9.6	7.9	5.6
Actors and directors	12.8	5.9	6.6	6.2
Painters, sculptors, craft artists, and artist printmakers	6.8	2.8	2.1	4.7
Photographers	5.7	2.9	4.0	1.7
Editors and reporters	5.0	3.8	2.9	2.1
Public relations specialists	10.8	7.7	6.2	4.6
Athletes	10.9	9.7	9.4	1.5
TECHNICAL, SALES, ADMINISTRATIVE SUPPORT	**11.4**	**9.2**	**7.6**	**3.8**
Technicians and related support	**11.2**	**9.1**	**8.2**	**3.0**
Health technologists and technicians	15.0	14.1	12.7	2.3
Clinical laboratory technologists and technicians	18.0	15.1	10.5	7.5
Dental hygienists	2.4	2.5	1.6	0.8
Radiologic technicians	10.8	12.8	8.6	2.2
Licensed practical nurses	20.0	17.6	17.7	2.3
Engineering and related technologists and technicians	10.0	7.2	6.1	3.9
Electrical and electronic technicians	11.0	8.2	8.2	2.8
Drafting occupations	6.2	6.4	5.5	0.7
Science technicians	8.7	7.5	6.6	2.1
Biological technicians	7.1	4.6	2.9	4.2
Chemical technicians	7.2	10.8	9.5	−2.3
Technicians, except health, engineering, and science	7.9	5.7	5.0	2.9
Airplane pilots and navigators	1.9	0.6	–	–
Computer programmers	8.1	5.8	4.4	3.7
Legal assistants	8.4	6.1	4.3	4.1

(continued)

	percent black			percentage point change
	2000	**1990**	**1983**	**1983–2000**
Sales occupations	**8.8%**	**6.4%**	**4.7%**	**4.1**
Supervisors and proprietors	6.6	4.5	3.6	3.0
Sales representatives, finance and business services	7.6	4.4	2.7	4.9
Insurance sales	6.5	5.2	3.8	2.7
Real estate sales	5.3	3.0	1.3	4.0
Securities and financial services sales	8.2	3.6	3.1	5.1
Advertising and related sales	9.2	4.4	4.5	4.7
Sales representatives, commodities, except retail	2.8	2.6	2.1	0.7
Sales workers, retail and personal services	12.3	9.5	6.7	5.6
Cashiers	16.5	13.5	10.1	6.4
Sales-related occupations	9.3	2.5	2.8	6.5
Administrative support occupations, including clerical	**13.7**	**11.4**	**9.6**	**4.1**
Supervisors, administrative support	17.0	14.2	9.3	7.7
Computer equipment operators	16.6	13.1	12.5	4.1
Computer operators	16.6	12.9	12.1	4.5
Secretaries, stenographers, and typists	9.9	8.6	7.3	2.6
Secretaries	8.5	7.6	5.8	2.7
Typists	17.8	15.1	13.8	4.0
Information clerks	11.3	9.5	8.5	2.8
Receptionists	9.7	8.1	7.5	2.2
Records processing, except financial	16.9	14.1	13.9	3.0
Order clerks	24.4	15.1	10.6	13.8
Personnel clerks, except payroll and timekeeping	18.7	21.7	14.9	3.8
Library clerks	10.8	9.1	15.4	−4.6
File clerks	15.3	14.0	16.7	−1.4
Records clerks	13.4	14.7	11.6	1.8
Financial records processing	9.2	6.2	4.6	4.6
Bookkeepers, accounting, and auditing clerks	7.8	5.2	4.3	3.5
Payroll and timekeeping clerks	8.7	11.5	5.9	2.8
Billing clerks	16.3	8.7	6.2	10.1
Cost and rate clerks	9.4	8.4	5.9	3.5
Duplicating, mail and other office machine operators	16.8	19.3	16.0	0.8
Communications equipment operators	21.8	19.9	17.0	4.8
Telephone operators	22.9	19.7	17.0	5.9
Mail and message distributing	21.9	20.0	18.1	3.8
Postal clerks, except mail carriers	32.4	25.1	26.2	6.2
Mail carriers, postal service	14.7	14.4	12.5	2.2
Mail clerks, except postal service	22.6	23.8	15.8	6.8
Messengers	16.7	17.9	16.7	0.0
Material recording, scheduling, and distributing clerks	15.3	12.6	10.9	4.4
Dispatchers	15.1	9.2	11.4	3.7
Production coordinators	12.0	7.4	6.1	5.9
Traffic, shipping, and receiving clerks	16.1	15.3	9.1	7.0
Stock and inventory clerks	15.1	13.3	13.3	1.8
Expediters	13.4	11.1	8.4	5.0

(continued)

| | percent black | | | percentage point change |
	2000	1990	1983	1983–2000
Adjusters and investigators	17.5%	12.9%	11.1%	6.4
Insurance adjusters, examiners, and investigators	14.6	12.1	11.5	3.1
Investigators and adjusters, except insurance	17.0	13.1	11.3	5.7
Eligibility clerks, social welfare	16.1	14.7	12.9	3.2
Bill and account collectors	28.2	13.1	8.5	19.7
Miscellaneous administrative support	14.3	14.0	12.5	1.8
General office clerks	12.9	13.1	12.7	0.2
Bank tellers	13.7	9.9	7.5	6.2
Data-entry keyers	18.8	19.5	18.6	0.2
Statistical clerks	15.8	12.9	7.5	8.3
Teachers' aides	12.8	14.1	17.8	−5.0
SERVICE OCCUPATIONS	**18.1**	**17.3**	**16.6**	**1.5**
Private household	**14.9**	**24.7**	**27.8**	**−12.9**
Child care workers	11.6	9.8	7.9	3.7
Cleaners and servants	16.9	35.6	42.4	−25.5
Protective service	**19.6**	**16.6**	**13.6**	**6.0**
Supervisors	13.9	13.6	7.7	6.2
Police and detectives	10.5	12.9	9.3	1.2
Firefighting and fire prevention	8.7	11.0	6.7	2.0
Firefighting	9.0	11.5	7.3	1.7
Police and detectives	18.3	16.0	13.1	5.2
Police and detectives, public service	13.0	13.5	9.5	3.5
Sheriffs, bailiffs, and other law enforcement officers	0.2	0.1	0.1	0.1
Correctional institution officers	25.9	22.8	24.0	1.9
Guards	25.7	19.4	17.0	8.7
Guards and police, except public services	27.5	21.2	18.9	8.6
Service occupations, excl. private household, protective service	**18.0**	**17.0**	**16.0**	**2.0**
Food preparation and service occupations	11.9	12.4	10.5	1.4
Bartenders	2.0	3.6	2.7	−0.7
Waiters and waitresses	4.4	4.7	4.1	0.3
Cooks	17.6	18.3	15.8	1.8
Food counter, fountain, and related occupations	12.6	11.5	9.1	3.5
Kitchen workers, food preparation	13.0	12.8	13.7	−0.7
Waiters' and waitresses' assistants	10.5	16.0	12.6	−2.1
Health service occupations	31.4	26.3	23.5	7.9
Dental assistants	5.1	5.6	6.1	−1.0
Health aides, except nursing	26.4	21.0	16.5	9.9
Nursing aides, orderlies, and attendants	35.2	30.7	27.3	7.9
Cleaning and building service occupations	22.2	22.4	24.4	−2.2
Maids and housemen	27.7	24.8	32.3	−4.6
Janitors and cleaners	20.9	21.8	22.6	−1.7
Personal service occupations	14.8	12.0	11.1	3.7
Barbers	27.8	17.4	8.4	19.4
Hairdressers and cosmetologists	10.9	9.2	7.0	3.9

(continued)

	percent black			percentage point change
	2000	1990	1983	1983–2000
Attendants, amusement and recreation facilities	9.9%	9.1%	7.1%	2.8
Public transportation attendants	12.3	11.2	11.3	1.0
Welfare service aides	30.3	24.1	24.2	6.1
PRECISION PRODUCTION, CRAFT, AND REPAIR	**8.0**	**7.8**	**6.8**	**1.2**
Mechanics and repairers	**8.2**	**8.1**	**6.8**	**1.4**
Mechanics and repairers, except supervisors	8.3	8.3	7.0	1.3
Vehicle and mobile equipment mechanics and repairers	7.1	7.5	6.9	0.2
Automobile mechanics	7.3	8.7	7.8	–0.5
Aircraft engine mechanics	8.3	9.8	4.0	4.3
Electrical and electronic equipment repairers	10.7	10.6	7.3	3.4
Data processing equipment repairers	9.8	10.6	6.1	3.7
Telephone installers and repairers	11.6	9.7	7.8	3.8
Construction trades	**7.0**	**6.9**	**6.6**	**0.4**
Construction trades, except supervisors	7.2	7.3	7.1	0.1
Carpenters	6.0	4.8	5.0	1.0
Extractive occupations	**3.6**	**6.9**	**3.3**	**0.3**
Precision production occupations	**9.5**	**8.6**	**7.3**	**2.2**
OPERATORS, FABRICATORS, AND LABORERS	**15.4**	**15.0**	**14.0**	**1.4**
Machine operators, assemblers, and inspectors	**14.7**	**14.4**	**14.0**	**0.7**
Textile, apparel, and furnishings machine operators	18.3	20.1	18.7	–0.4
Textile sewing machine operators	16.3	16.4	15.5	0.8
Pressing machine operators	13.9	26.8	27.1	–13.2
Fabricators, assemblers, and hand working occupations	13.9	11.8	11.3	2.6
Production inspectors, testers, samplers, and weighers	16.3	13.5	13.0	3.3
Transportation and material-moving occupations	**16.5**	**15.4**	**13.0**	**3.5**
Motor vehicle operators	16.7	15.4	13.5	3.2
Truck drivers	14.4	–	12.3	2.1
Transportation occupations, except motor vehicles	13.7	10.8	6.7	7.0
Material moving equipment operators	16.0	16.4	12.9	3.1
Industrial truck and tractor equipment operators	22.1	23.5	19.6	2.5
Handlers, equipment cleaners, helpers, and laborers	**15.3**	**15.7**	**15.1**	**0.2**
Freight, stock, and material handlers	17.7	16.4	15.3	2.4
Laborers, except construction	15.5	16.0	16.0	–0.5
FARMING, FORESTRY, FISHING	**4.9**	**6.1**	**7.5**	**–2.6**
Farm operators and managers	**0.9**	**0.9**	**1.3**	**–0.4**
Other agricultural and related occupations	**7.1**	**9.1**	**11.7**	**–4.6**
Farm workers	4.7	8.2	11.6	–6.9
Forestry and logging occupations	**4.4**	**10.1**	**12.8**	**–8.4**
Fishers, hunters, trappers	**3.6**	**7.0**	**1.8**	**1.8**

Note: "–" means data not available or sample is too small to make a reliable estimate.
Source: Bureau of the Census, Statistical Abstract of the United States, 2001; and Bureau of Labor Statistics, Employment and Earnings, January 1991; calculations by New Strategist

Table 6.18 Hispanic Share of Workers by Detailed Occupation, 1983 to 2000

(Hispanic share of employed civilians aged 16 or older, by detailed occupation, 1983 to 2000; percentage point change, 1983 to 2000)

	percent Hispanic			percentage point change
	2000	**1990**	**1983**	**1983–2000**
TOTAL EMPLOYED	**10.7%**	**7.5%**	**5.3%**	**5.4**
MANAGERIAL AND PROFESSIONAL SPECIALTY	**5.0**	**3.6**	**2.6**	**2.4**
Executive, administrative, and managerial	**5.4**	**3.9**	**2.8**	**2.6**
Officials and administrators, public administration	7.0	3.2	3.8	3.2
Financial managers	4.3	2.9	3.1	1.2
Personnel and labor relations managers	4.0	3.2	2.6	1.4
Purchasing managers	3.2	3.5	1.4	1.8
Managers, marketing, advertising, and public relations	4.2	3.1	1.7	2.5
Administrators, education and related fields	5.7	3.8	2.4	3.3
Managers, medicine and health	5.4	2.9	2.0	3.4
Managers, properties and real estate	7.2	5.1	5.2	2.0
Management-related occupations	5.4	4.1	3.5	1.9
Accountants and auditors	5.1	3.8	3.3	1.8
Professional specialty	**4.6**	**3.4**	**2.5**	**2.1**
Architects	5.5	3.5	1.5	4.0
Engineers	3.7	2.8	2.2	1.5
Aerospace engineers	3.6	2.4	2.1	1.5
Chemical engineers	1.0	2.2	1.4	–0.4
Civil engineers	2.7	3.2	3.2	–0.5
Electrical and electronic engineers	3.6	3.3	3.1	0.5
Industrial engineers	4.0	3.2	2.4	1.6
Mechanical engineers	3.7	1.9	1.1	2.6
Mathematical and computer scientists	3.7	3.4	2.6	1.1
Computer systems analysts and scientists	3.6	3.3	2.7	0.9
Operations and systems researchers and analysts	4.4	4.2	2.2	2.2
Natural scientists	3.2	3.8	2.1	1.1
Chemists, except biochemists	2.2	5.9	1.2	1.0
Biological and life scientists	6.0	3.1	1.8	4.2
Health-diagnosing occupations	3.4	3.7	3.3	0.1
Physicians	3.7	4.5	4.5	-0.8
Dentists	2.2	3.5	1.0	1.2
Health assessment and treating occupations	3.4	2.8	2.2	1.2
Registered nurses	2.8	2.5	1.8	1.0
Pharmacists	3.8	4.1	2.6	1.2
Dietitians	4.8	3.5	3.7	1.1
Therapists	5.0	2.9	2.7	2.3
Respiratory therapists	5.3	2.8	3.7	1.6
Physical therapists	6.8	2.7	1.5	5.3
Speech therapists	2.0	3.3	–	–
Physicians' assistants	7.8	5.2	4.4	3.4

(continued)

	percent Hispanic			percentage point change
	2000	**1990**	**1983**	**1983–2000**
Teachers, college and university	4.6%	2.5%	1.8%	2.8
Teachers, except college and university	5.2	3.5	2.7	2.5
Prekindergarten and kindergarten	8.0	5.7	3.4	4.6
Elementary school	5.6	3.2	3.1	2.5
Secondary school	4.2	3.3	2.3	1.9
Special education	3.2	2.2	2.3	0.9
Counselors, educational and vocational	5.3	4.1	3.2	2.1
Librarians, archivists, and curators	5.8	3.3	1.6	4.2
Librarians	6.6	3.3	1.8	4.8
Social scientists and urban planners	4.1	3.3	2.1	2.0
Economists	4.4	3.3	2.7	1.7
Psychologists	4.0	3.6	1.1	2.9
Social, recreation, and religious workers	6.4	4.6	3.8	2.6
Social workers	8.5	6.1	6.3	2.2
Recreation workers	4.9	6.1	2.0	2.9
Clergy	4.5	2.1	1.4	3.1
Lawyers and judges	4.1	2.7	1.0	3.1
Lawyers	3.9	2.8	0.9	3.0
Writers, artists, entertainers, and athletes	5.6	4.0	2.9	2.7
Authors	2.2	0.7	0.9	1.3
Designers	6.3	4.4	2.7	3.6
Musicians and composers	6.0	4.5	4.4	1.6
Actors and directors	6.1	1.9	3.4	2.7
Painters, sculptors, craft artists, and artist printmakers	4.2	4.5	2.3	1.9
Photographers	5.9	5.5	3.4	2.5
Editors and reporters	3.0	2.9	2.1	0.9
Public relations specialists	5.5	2.8	1.9	3.6
Athletes	5.5	4.3	1.7	3.8
TECHNICAL, SALES, ADMINISTRATIVE SUPPORT	**8.9**	**5.8**	**4.3**	**4.6**
Technicians and related support	**6.9**	**4.3**	**3.1**	**3.8**
Health technologists and technicians	8.2	4.5	3.1	5.1
Clinical laboratory technologists and technicians	7.5	4.1	2.9	4.6
Dental hygienists	1.7	3.0	–	–
Radiologic technicians	7.7	4.8	4.5	3.2
Licensed practical nurses	5.0	3.8	3.1	1.9
Engineering and related technologists and technicians	6.1	4.8	3.5	2.6
Electrical and electronic technicians	7.1	5.8	4.6	2.5
Drafting occupations	4.7	5.1	2.3	2.4
Science technicians	8.4	7.2	2.8	5.6
Biological technicians	8.2	9.0	2.0	6.2
Chemical technicians	7.6	7.1	3.5	4.1
Technicians, except health, engineering, and science	5.7	3.1	2.7	3.0
Airplane pilots and navigators	4.3	3.3	1.6	2.7
Computer programmers	3.5	2.5	2.1	1.4
Legal assistants	9.8	3.7	3.6	6.2

(continued)

| | percent Hispanic | | | percentage point change |
	2000	1990	1983	1983–2000
Sales occupations	**8.5%**	**5.3%**	**3.7%**	**4.8**
Supervisors and proprietors	7.3	4.4	3.4	3.9
Sales representatives, finance and business services	4.9	3.6	2.2	2.7
Insurance sales	4.4	3.5	2.5	1.9
Real estate sales	5.0	3.6	1.5	3.5
Securities and financial services sales	3.4	3.2	1.1	2.3
Advertising and related sales	5.7	2.8	3.3	2.4
Sales representatives, commodities, except retail	6.4	3.3	2.2	4.2
Sales workers, retail and personal services	11.4	7.0	4.8	6.6
Cashiers	13.5	8.4	5.4	8.1
Sales-related occupations	2.2	3.4	1.3	0.9
Administrative support occupations, including clerical	**9.7**	**6.5**	**5.0**	**4.7**
Supervisors, administrative support	9.4	7.0	5.0	4.4
Computer equipment operators	7.4	6.9	6.0	1.4
Computer operators	7.4	6.9	6.0	1.4
Secretaries, stenographers, and typists	8.6	5.4	4.5	4.1
Secretaries	8.7	5.2	4.0	4.7
Typists	9.3	7.3	6.4	2.9
Information clerks	10.4	7.3	5.5	4.9
Receptionists	11.6	6.7	6.6	5.0
Records processing, except financial	10.6	7.2	4.8	5.8
Order clerks	12.4	6.5	4.4	8.0
Personnel clerks, except payroll and timekeeping	4.8	7.3	4.6	0.2
Library clerks	6.5	5.0	2.5	4.0
File clerks	12.0	9.0	6.1	5.9
Records clerks	10.7	7.5	5.6	5.1
Financial records processing	7.3	5.1	3.7	3.6
Bookkeepers, accounting, and auditing clerks	6.1	5.0	3.3	2.8
Payroll and timekeeping clerks	8.4	3.6	5.0	3.4
Billing clerks	12.4	6.3	3.9	8.5
Cost and rate clerks	10.9	5.6	5.3	5.6
Duplicating, mail and other office machine operators	9.6	6.1	6.1	3.5
Communications equipment operators	10.7	7.1	4.4	6.3
Telephone operators	10.4	7.2	4.3	6.1
Mail and message distributing	7.7	6.3	4.5	3.2
Postal clerks, except mail carriers	6.2	4.7	5.2	1.0
Mail carriers, postal service	5.9	6.1	2.7	3.2
Mail clerks, except postal service	11.2	7.7	5.9	5.3
Messengers	10.4	7.9	5.2	5.2
Material recording, scheduling, and distributing clerks	12.8	8.0	6.6	6.2
Dispatchers	9.0	4.4	4.3	4.7
Production coordinators	6.6	4.5	2.2	4.4
Traffic, shipping, and receiving clerks	17.5	11.7	11.1	6.4
Stock and inventory clerks	13.1	8.0	5.5	7.6
Expediters	10.5	4.9	4.3	6.2

(continued)

	percent Hispanic			percentage point change
	2000	**1990**	**1983**	**1983–2000**
Adjusters and investigators	10.1%	5.6%	5.1%	5.0
Insurance adjusters, examiners, and investigators	7.0	3.9	3.3	3.7
Investigators and adjusters, except insurance	11.5	6.7	4.8	6.7
Eligibility clerks, social welfare	9.5	4.0	9.4	0.1
Bill and account collectors	9.5	6.7	6.5	3.0
Miscellaneous administrative support	10.4	7.7	5.9	4.5
General office clerks	10.5	7.0	5.2	5.3
Bank tellers	8.2	7.0	4.3	3.9
Data-entry keyers	11.2	8.0	5.6	5.6
Statistical clerks	8.4	6.7	3.4	5.0
Teachers' aides	14.4	11.8	12.6	1.8
SERVICE OCCUPATIONS	**15.7**	**11.2**	**6.8**	**8.9**
Private household	**31.7**	**19.7**	**8.5**	**23.2**
Child care workers	19.9	13.3	3.6	16.3
Cleaners and servants	37.7	23.8	11.8	25.9
Protective service	**8.7**	**5.9**	**4.6**	**4.1**
Supervisors	7.8	4.1	3.1	4.7
Police and detectives	3.0	2.4	1.2	1.8
Firefighting and fire prevention	5.4	4.4	4.1	1.3
Firefighting	5.0	4.5	3.8	1.2
Police and detectives	8.4	5.3	4.0	4.4
Police and detectives, public service	10.1	5.5	4.4	5.7
Sheriffs, bailiffs, and other law enforcement officers	5.8	5.7	4.0	1.8
Correctional institution officers	6.9	4.7	2.8	4.1
Guards	10.0	7.4	5.6	4.4
Guards and police, except public services	10.6	7.8	6.2	4.4
Service occupations, excl. private household, protective service	**16.0**	**11.5**	**6.9**	**9.1**
Food preparation and service occupations	17.2	12.5	6.8	10.4
Bartenders	13.2	6.7	4.4	8.8
Waiters and waitresses	11.0	7.6	3.6	7.4
Cooks	21.6	14.6	6.5	15.1
Food counter, fountain, and related occupations	11.8	7.3	6.7	5.1
Kitchen workers, food preparation	12.3	12.5	8.1	4.2
Waiters' and waitresses' assistants	18.8	21.4	14.2	4.6
Health service occupations	10.1	6.4	4.8	5.3
Dental assistants	10.6	7.4	5.7	4.9
Health aides, except nursing	8.7	5.6	4.8	3.9
Nursing aides, orderlies, and attendants	10.4	6.5	4.7	5.7
Cleaning and building service occupations	23.4	16.7	9.2	14.2
Maids and housemen	28.3	21.7	10.1	18.2
Janitors and cleaners	22.5	15.7	8.9	13.6
Personal service occupations	10.8	7.3	6.0	4.8
Barbers	12.7	9.9	12.1	0.6
Hairdressers and cosmetologists	10.7	7.1	5.7	5.0

(continued)

	percent Hispanic			percentage point change
	2000	**1990**	**1983**	**1983–2000**
Attendants, amusement and recreation facilities	6.0%	5.7%	4.3%	1.7
Public transportation attendants	7.9	6.0	5.9	2.0
Welfare service aides	12.7	13.7	10.5	2.2
PRECISION PRODUCTION, CRAFT, AND REPAIR	**13.9**	**8.5**	**6.2**	**7.7**
Mechanics and repairers	**10.7**	**7.0**	**5.3**	**5.4**
Mechanics and repairers, except supervisors	10.8	7.2	5.5	5.3
Vehicle and mobile equipment mechanics and repairers	13.1	8.4	6.0	7.1
Automobile mechanics	15.6	9.4	6.0	9.6
Aircraft engine mechanics	9.0	8.4	7.6	1.4
Electrical and electronic equipment repairers	7.8	6.0	4.5	3.3
Data processing equipment repairers	4.8	5.6	4.5	0.3
Telephone installers and repairers	9.5	3.8	3.7	5.8
Construction trades	**16.4**	**8.9**	**6.0**	**10.4**
Construction trades, except supervisors	18.1	9.5	6.1	12.0
Carpenters	16.3	8.7	5.0	11.3
Extractive occupations	**7.8**	**6.9**	**6.0**	**1.8**
Precision production occupations	**14.4**	**9.8**	**7.4**	**7.0**
OPERATORS, FABRICATORS, AND LABORERS	**17.5**	**12.2**	**8.3**	**9.2**
Machine operators, assemblers, and inspectors	**19.3**	**13.9**	**9.4**	**9.9**
Textile, apparel, and furnishings machine operators	33.0	19.9	12.5	20.5
Textile sewing machine operators	40.6	23.1	14.5	26.1
Pressing machine operators	49.9	27.9	14.2	35.7
Fabricators, assemblers, and hand working occupations	17.1	12.7	8.7	8.4
Production inspectors, testers, samplers, and weighers	17.3	10.4	7.7	9.6
Transportation and material-moving occupations	**11.9**	**8.5**	**5.9**	**6.0**
Motor vehicle operators	11.8	8.6	6.0	5.8
Truck drivers	12.5	–	5.7	6.8
Transportation occupations, except motor vehicles	3.6	5.1	3.0	0.6
Material-moving equipment operators	13.7	8.9	6.3	7.4
Industrial truck and tractor equipment operators	18.4	10.5	8.2	10.2
Handlers, equipment cleaners, helpers, and laborers	**20.7**	**12.9**	**8.6**	**12.1**
Freight, stock, and material handlers	14.6	10.1	7.1	7.5
Laborers, except construction	18.4	12.0	8.6	9.8
FARMING, FORESTRY, FISHING	**23.7**	**14.2**	**8.2**	**15.5**
Farm operators and managers	**3.0**	**1.7**	**0.7**	**2.3**
Other agricultural and related occupations	**36.1**	**22.8**	**14.0**	**22.1**
Farm workers	47.4	26.9	15.9	31.5
Forestry and logging occupations	**7.8**	**5.4**	**2.1**	**5.7**
Fishers, hunters, trappers	**2.0**	**6.0**	**2.5**	**–0.5**

Note: "–" means data not available or sample is too small to make a reliable estimate.
Source: Bureau of the Census, Statistical Abstract of the United States, 2001; and Bureau of Labor Statistics, Employment and Earnings, January 1991; calculations by New Strategist

Table 6.19 Workers by Detailed Occupation, Sex, Race, and Hispanic Origin, 2006

(total number of employed workers agd 16 or older and percent female, Asian, black, and Hispanic, by detailed occupation, 2006; numbers in thousands)

	total number	percent			
		female	Asian	black	Hispanic
TOTAL EMPLOYED	**144,427**	**46.3%**	**4.5%**	**10.9%**	**13.6%**
MANAGEMENT, PROFESSIONAL, AND RELATED OCCUPATIONS	**50,420**	**50.6**	**6.1**	**8.4**	**6.6**
Management, business, financial operations occupations	**21,233**	**41.9**	**4.8**	**7.3**	**7.0**
Management occupations	15,249	36.7	4.3	6.2	7.1
Chief executives	1,689	23.4	3.9	3.1	4.6
General and operations managers	998	29.1	3.4	5.7	7.7
Advertising and promotions managers	75	52.5	1.7	5.4	5.1
Marketing and sales managers	888	40.2	3.8	4.8	5.3
Administrative services managers	87	24.4	5.2	7.3	8.3
Computer and information systems managers	401	27.2	9.1	6.4	4.7
Financial managers	1,083	55.0	5.5	7.0	7.7
Human resources managers	280	65.8	1.2	11.0	9.9
Industrial production managers	298	16.4	3.2	3.0	8.0
Purchasing managers	165	40.7	1.7	8.7	3.3
Transportation, storage, and distribution managers	249	14.6	2.9	9.8	14.9
Farm, ranch, and other agricultural managers	242	21.8	0.8	2.4	8.5
Farmers and ranchers	784	25.0	1.0	0.8	2.0
Construction managers	1,010	7.8	2.3	3.7	8.3
Education administrators	796	63.9	2.2	14.2	7.2
Engineering managers	103	7.3	10.9	2.9	3.4
Food service managers	900	43.2	12.0	5.8	13.6
Lodging managers	174	51.0	13.3	6.5	8.5
Medical and health services managers	511	68.3	4.8	10.3	5.3
Property, real estate, community association managers	618	51.3	3.2	7.2	11.4
Social and community service managers	315	66.0	2.7	15.0	7.2
Business and financial operations occupations	5,983	55.0	6.2	10.0	6.6
Wholesale and retail buyers, except farm products	222	55.8	3.5	3.2	8.9
Purchasing agents, except wholesale, retail, farm products	290	51.1	3.2	7.9	7.0
Claims adjusters, appraisers, examiners, and investigators	283	58.2	3.4	14.1	6.7
Compliance officers, ex. agriculture, construction, health and safety, and transportation	149	54.0	5.8	17.4	8.3
Cost estimators	114	12.7	4.1	1.0	2.6
Human resources, training, labor relations specialists	765	71.5	4.5	14.5	7.7
Management analysts	572	42.2	7.5	5.9	4.4
Accountants and auditors	1,779	60.2	9.4	10.2	6.0
Appraisers and assessors of real estate	134	35.7	2.2	1.5	4.6
Budget analysts	52	55.7	12.5	18.1	4.5
Financial analysts	103	38.4	12.3	4.0	3.9
Personal financial advisors	389	34.4	5.4	7.0	6.1
Insurance underwriters	92	69.2	2.5	16.2	5.2
Loan counselors and officers	468	52.7	5.6	11.1	10.8
Tax examiners, collectors, and revenue agents	67	56.7	0.9	21.4	6.5
Tax preparers	98	59.6	4.3	10.6	9.0

(continued)

		percent			
	total number	female	Asian	black	Hispanic
Professional and related occupations	**29,187**	**56.9%**	**7.1%**	**9.3%**	**6.4%**
Computer and mathematical occupations	3,209	26.7	16.2	7.3	5.0
Computer scientists and systems analysts	715	31.9	12.7	9.5	5.0
Computer programmers	562	25.3	18.1	3.9	5.3
Computer software engineers	846	21.8	26.9	5.8	3.4
Computer support specialists	314	28.9	7.4	10.5	7.2
Database administrators	90	37.0	14.8	8.9	3.0
Network and computer systems administrators	180	16.6	11.0	4.4	7.0
Network systems and data communications analysts	356	25.5	8.1	7.9	6.0
Operations research analysts	85	40.3	6.6	18.1	4.0
Architecture and engineering occupations	2,830	14.5	9.7	5.6	5.9
Architects, except naval	221	22.2	11.5	3.2	7.7
Aerospace engineers	110	13.1	12.9	5.6	5.1
Chemical engineers	70	17.1	13.0	4.2	3.3
Civil engineers	304	11.9	8.2	5.0	4.0
Computer hardware engineers	80	16.2	26.5	3.8	7.4
Electrical and electronics engineers	382	7.7	15.8	5.9	4.2
Industrial engineers, including health and safety	174	22.6	5.9	7.0	2.9
Mechanical engineers	322	5.8	9.5	4.3	4.0
Drafters	181	21.8	6.8	3.0	10.3
Engineering technicians, except drafters	396	20.6	5.3	9.3	11.2
Surveying and mapping technicians	96	9.9	0.3	3.0	8.5
Life, physical, and social science occupations	1,434	43.3	12.2	5.7	4.1
Biological scientists	116	46.6	11.9	3.5	3.8
Medical scientists	164	45.4	35.6	5.3	2.4
Chemists and materials scientists	116	34.1	13.3	7.4	1.7
Environmental scientists and geoscientists	101	22.0	3.4	2.9	1.8
Market and survey researchers	129	61.3	8.7	9.0	3.4
Psychologists	189	67.7	2.2	2.6	3.5
Chemical technicians	76	35.9	4.4	11.4	8.8
Community and social services occupations	2,156	61.6	3.3	18.6	8.5
Counselors	614	66.8	2.3	17.9	8.2
Social workers	698	82.6	3.3	22.7	10.3
Miscellaneous community and social service specialists	293	70.5	3.2	23.9	11.8
Clergy	416	12.8	4.5	12.4	4.7
Legal occupations	1,637	51.7	2.8	6.5	5.7
Lawyers	965	32.6	2.9	5.0	3.0
Judges, magistrates, and other judicial workers	66	35.5	1.9	11.3	2.0
Paralegals and legal assistants	345	89.1	1.9	8.4	11.3
Miscellaneous legal support workers	261	76.8	3.8	8.7	9.0
Education, training, and library occupations	8,126	74.2	3.5	9.8	7.3
Postsecondary teachers	1,194	46.3	10.3	6.7	4.5
Preschool and kindergarten teachers	690	97.7	2.5	13.9	10.5
Elementary and middle school teachers	2,701	82.2	1.7	9.7	6.5
Secondary school teachers	1,098	56.0	1.9	7.3	6.5
Special education teachers	401	83.5	1.7	9.0	4.7
Other teachers and instructors	705	64.9	4.6	9.4	7.5
Librarians	229	84.2	1.1	8.8	2.9
Teacher assistants	942	92.3	2.3	14.9	14.1
Arts, design, entertainment, sports, and media occupations	2,735	48.8	4.2	6.7	7.8
Artists and related workers	223	52.4	6.2	5.1	4.6
Designers	821	55.5	7.0	3.2	9.4

(continued)

	total number	percent			
		female	Asian	black	Hispanic
Producers and directors	134	40.0%	3.3%	6.4%	6.9%
Athletes, coaches, umpires, and related workers	270	36.9	2.2	9.5	5.8
Musicians, singers, and related workers	203	33.5	3.4	9.0	11.5
Announcers	62	30.8	2.0	21.6	9.4
News analysts, reporters and correspondents	78	53.4	2.5	4.0	4.2
Public relations specialists	141	64.6	1.3	8.8	3.7
Editors	157	53.7	1.3	5.1	5.6
Technical writers	60	49.5	0.8	8.9	4.7
Writers and authors	174	58.5	1.9	5.7	2.8
Miscellaneous media and communication workers	67	69.3	8.7	7.5	29.2
Broadcast and sound engineering technicians, radio operators	89	15.6	2.5	11.7	10.1
Photographers	127	43.3	1.7	7.1	6.7
Healthcare practitioner and technical occupations	7,060	73.4	8.2	10.6	5.6
Chiropractors	69	23.1	1.8	3.3	1.9
Dentists	196	22.6	11.4	3.1	4.3
Dietitians and nutritionists	96	91.0	7.6	21.2	4.6
Pharmacists	245	48.9	19.5	6.0	5.6
Physicians and surgeons	863	32.2	17.0	5.2	5.7
Physician assistants	85	71.7	6.2	10.9	6.7
Registered nurses	2,529	91.3	7.5	10.9	4.2
Occupational therapists	78	90.3	4.7	3.1	2.0
Physical therapists	198	62.7	13.7	5.8	5.0
Respiratory therapists	85	66.0	4.6	15.3	6.2
Speech-language pathologists	114	95.3	1.4	8.1	3.6
Veterinarians	67	50.4	0.4	0.4	2.0
Clinical laboratory technologists and technicians	321	78.1	9.6	14.2	7.8
Dental hygienists	144	98.6	4.2	1.4	4.6
Diagnostic related technologists and technicians	281	72.9	2.9	7.5	6.3
Emergency medical technicians and paramedics	156	31.9	2.2	11.9	7.4
Health diagnosing, treating practitioner support technicians	425	80.1	5.6	11.8	8.2
Licensed practical and licensed vocational nurses	556	94.2	3.1	23.2	7.0
Medical records and health information technicians	98	92.0	1.4	20.5	15.1
SERVICE OCCUPATIONS	**23,811**	**57.3**	**4.3**	**15.9**	**19.5**
Healthcare support occupations	**3,132**	**89.4**	**4.1**	**24.7**	**13.1**
Nursing, psychiatric, and home health aides	1,906	88.9	4.0	34.8	13.1
Physical therapist assistants and aides	61	78.4	0.6	2.7	9.1
Massage therapists	124	84.1	5.0	5.4	8.0
Dental assistants	274	95.4	4.2	5.4	14.9
Protective service occupations	**2,939**	**22.3**	**1.7**	**19.7**	**10.2**
First-line supervisors/managers of police and detectives	103	15.5	0.2	5.5	6.9
Fire fighters	253	3.5	0.4	9.9	7.5
Bailiffs, correctional officers, and jailers	451	28.2	0.4	24.2	7.4
Detectives and criminal investigators	144	26.0	1.8	17.6	13.5
Police and sheriff's patrol officers	655	12.8	2.3	14.9	11.8
Private detectives and investigators	85	38.2	0.6	11.4	5.5
Security guards and gaming surveillance officers	835	23.0	3.1	29.8	12.2
Food preparation and serving related occupations	**7,606**	**56.6**	**5.3**	**11.7**	**21.1**
Chefs and head cooks	313	23.9	15.8	14.1	19.1
First-line supervisors/managers of food preparation and serving workers	652	58.7	3.0	14.7	15.0
Cooks	1,868	43.4	6.2	17.4	31.6

(continued)

	total number	percent			
		female	Asian	black	Hispanic
Food preparation workers	698	59.2%	5.2%	12.3%	25.4%
Bartenders	389	55.0	2.1	2.5	9.4
Combined food preparation, serving workers, incl. fast food	344	67.6	4.3	12.5	13.3
Counter attendants, cafeteria, food concession, coffee shop	308	66.2	3.5	12.1	13.9
Waiters and waitresses	1,960	71.5	5.3	7.0	14.3
Food servers, nonrestaurant	155	65.3	5.1	23.7	13.2
Dining room and cafeteria attendants and bartender helpers	380	48.5	5.4	8.4	30.5
Dishwashers	279	23.9	3.1	10.0	36.7
Hosts and hostesses, restaurant, lounge, and coffee shop	257	86.4	4.3	6.3	14.7
Building and grounds cleaning and maintenance occupations	**5,381**	**40.0**	**2.6**	**15.6**	**31.8**
First-line supervisors/managers of housekeeping and janitorial workers	305	32.6	3.2	16.2	17.1
First-line supervisors/managers of landscaping, lawn service, and groundskeeping workers	235	8.0	1.0	5.8	17.2
Janitors and building cleaners	2,082	32.2	3.0	18.7	26.8
Maids and housekeeping cleaners	1,423	90.3	3.4	19.9	37.2
Pest control workers	78	2.2	2.2	7.7	21.8
Grounds maintenance workers	1,259	6.2	1.2	7.8	40.9
Personal care and service occupations	**4,754**	**78.7**	**6.4**	**15.0**	**13.0**
First-line supervisors/managers of gaming workers	124	43.7	5.7	5.8	3.6
First-line supervisors/managers of personal service workers	176	66.7	10.9	11.2	6.0
Nonfarm animal caretakers	137	72.1	0.9	3.6	9.3
Gaming services workers	106	48.1	18.0	7.6	9.2
Barbers	100	17.7	1.9	36.7	10.0
Hairdressers, hairstylists, and cosmetologists	767	93.4	4.8	11.9	12.4
Miscellaneous personal appearance workers	230	83.0	45.5	6.5	8.0
Baggage porters, bellhops, and concierges	78	20.6	6.1	14.8	24.2
Transportation attendants	134	74.2	4.8	21.8	11.0
Child care workers	1,401	94.2	2.8	17.0	17.3
Personal and home care aides	703	87.3	5.8	22.4	14.9
Recreation and fitness workers	322	68.7	2.3	11.3	8.1
Residential advisors	62	69.0	3.0	25.6	6.6
SALES AND OFFICE OCCUPATIONS	**36,141**	**63.3**	**4.0**	**11.2**	**11.5**
Sales and related occupations	**16,641**	**49.1**	**4.6**	**9.0**	**11.1**
First-line supervisors/managers of retail sales workers	3,435	41.8	4.5	7.4	9.6
First-line supervisors/managers of non-retail sales workers	1,433	27.2	6.0	5.6	9.9
Cashiers	3,063	74.8	5.5	15.3	16.8
Counter and rental clerks	146	51.7	8.9	11.1	14.3
Parts salespersons	149	16.3	1.1	3.0	11.7
Retail salespersons	3,386	51.4	4.2	11.1	11.9
Advertising sales agents	220	53.9	4.2	6.7	7.2
Insurance sales agents	548	45.3	2.6	6.9	6.8
Securities, commodities, and financial services sales agents	398	29.3	7.9	9.3	5.5
Travel agents	82	77.3	8.8	7.1	6.6
Sales representatives, services, all other	563	32.8	2.9	5.9	8.0
Sales representatives, wholesale and manufacturing	1,422	27.2	2.5	2.9	7.3
Models, demonstrators, and product promoters	75	84.2	5.3	3.2	11.5
Real estate brokers and sales agents	1,046	59.9	5.9	5.8	9.1
Telemarketers	142	65.3	1.1	19.5	16.2
Door-to-door sales workers, news and street vendors, and related workers	261	62.4	3.0	6.5	14.6

(continued)

		percent			
	total number	female	Asian	black	Hispanic
Office and administrative support occupations	**19,500**	**75.4%**	**3.6%**	**13.1%**	**11.9%**
First-line supervisors/managers of office and administrative support workers	1,543	72.2	2.7	9.0	9.9
Bill and account collectors	213	62.2	2.1	25.1	17.3
Billing and posting clerks and machine operators	422	88.1	3.5	13.3	10.7
Bookkeeping, accounting, and auditing clerks	1,511	90.3	3.7	7.8	8.4
Payroll and timekeeping clerks	158	92.4	2.3	11.0	11.9
Tellers	432	84.8	4.0	10.6	14.5
Court, municipal, and license clerks	114	80.7	1.4	12.4	13.9
Credit authorizers, checkers, and clerks	56	77.3	5.7	10.8	11.5
Customer service representatives	1,916	70.4	3.6	18.3	13.8
Eligibility interviewers, government programs	61	86.3	5.4	25.4	11.6
File clerks	363	79.2	5.2	13.9	15.1
Hotel, motel, and resort desk clerks	117	63.7	3.7	18.1	18.3
Interviewers, except eligibility and loan	141	82.1	1.6	17.3	9.8
Library assistants, clerical	119	87.9	5.0	8.2	14.8
Loan interviewers and clerks	190	76.7	6.5	12.0	13.2
Order clerks	128	69.4	1.8	8.8	19.0
Human resources assistants, except payroll and timekeeping	56	91.9	3.1	17.9	13.3
Receptionists and information clerks	1,403	92.7	3.8	10.8	12.6
Reservation and transportation ticket agents and travel clerks	156	64.8	5.0	19.3	13.1
Couriers and messengers	273	17.9	3.0	15.3	12.9
Dispatchers	303	53.4	1.0	11.7	13.5
Postal service clerks	153	49.5	12.4	22.7	7.8
Postal service mail carriers	329	35.7	5.0	15.7	8.7
Postal service mail sorters, processors, and processing machine operators	98	47.5	12.3	28.2	7.8
Production, planning, and expediting clerks	296	56.8	2.5	7.5	12.6
Shipping, receiving, and traffic clerks	543	30.1	2.6	14.0	20.1
Stock clerks and order fillers	1,462	39.1	3.4	17.8	16.4
Weighers, measurers, checkers, and samplers, recordkeeping	81	50.4	7.3	15.3	17.8
Secretaries and administrative assistants	3,455	96.9	2.2	9.8	8.6
Computer operators	185	49.6	7.7	15.2	10.3
Data entry keyers	475	81.6	6.1	15.2	11.8
Word processors and typists	256	91.2	1.9	18.1	9.5
Insurance claims and policy processing clerks	274	87.6	0.9	11.4	10.3
Mail clerks and mail machine operators, except postal service	123	54.2	7.5	25.8	8.4
Office clerks, general	1,035	81.9	5.8	12.4	14.5
Office machine operators, except computer	52	57.8	6.3	20.3	20.0
NATURAL RESOURCES, CONSTRUCTION, AND MAINTENANCE OCCUPATIONS	**15,830**	**4.7**	**1.8**	**6.8**	**24.6**
Farming, fishing, and forestry occupations	**961**	**22.0**	**1.6**	**4.9**	**39.7**
Graders and sorters, agricultural products	68	64.9	1.7	11.5	44.5
Logging workers	78	0.2	0.0	7.5	3.0
Construction and extraction occupations	**9,507**	**3.1**	**1.2**	**6.6**	**29.3**
First-line supervisors/managers of construction trades and extraction workers	976	2.6	1.3	4.6	12.0
Brickmasons, blockmasons, and stonemasons	244	1.6	0.1	7.1	40.3
Carpenters	1,843	2.4	1.6	4.5	26.6
Carpet, floor, and tile installers and finishers	279	2.4	1.2	5.3	39.4
Cement masons, concrete finishers, and terrazzo workers	107	0.7	0.0	13.8	51.5
Construction laborers	1,693	3.7	1.4	7.5	44.7

(continued)

	total number	percent			
		female	Asian	black	Hispanic
Operating engineers, other construction equipment operators	451	1.7%	0.3%	8.3%	9.7%
Drywall installers, ceiling tile installers, and tapers	295	2.9	0.1	3.8	51.8
Electricians	882	1.9	1.7	7.5	14.4
Painters, construction and maintenance	713	7.7	1.2	7.0	41.0
Pipelayers, plumbers, pipefitters, and steamfitters	662	1.8	0.4	8.5	20.9
Roofers	242	1.1	1.2	7.0	46.7
Sheet metal workers	125	3.1	2.8	2.2	13.7
Structural iron and steel workers	59	2.2	0.6	2.6	15.5
Helpers, construction trades	132	6.2	0.4	9.9	43.2
Construction and building inspectors	102	8.8	1.3	10.1	12.3
Highway maintenance workers	103	3.8	0.6	10.5	23.1
Installation, maintenance, and repair occupations	**5,362**	**4.6**	**3.0**	**7.6**	**13.4**
First-line supervisors/managers of mechanics, installers, and repairers	357	8.5	2.3	7.8	8.7
Computer, automated teller, and office machine repairers	371	9.7	6.8	8.4	10.2
Radio and telecommunications equipment installers, repairers	205	15.2	5.1	11.2	8.8
Electric motor, power tool, and related repairers	69	2.4	2.5	4.2	5.7
Security and fire alarm systems installers	141	5.3	3.7	6.6	7.6
Aircraft mechanics and service technicians	162	0.6	4.8	4.1	25.6
Automotive body and related repairers	875	1.6	4.4	6.1	16.8
Automotive service technicians and mechanics	367	0.9	1.6	6.3	14.1
Bus and truck mechanics and diesel engine specialists	237	1.4	0.3	2.6	13.5
Heavy vehicle, mobile equip. service technicians, mechanics	61	3.4	2.4	6.0	6.1
Small engine mechanics	405	2.7	1.1	4.8	13.7
Heating, air conditioning, refrigeration mechanics, installers	56	1.5	5.5	5.3	12.0
Industrial and refractory machinery mechanics	436	3.8	2.5	9.1	11.7
Maintenance and repair workers, general	435	4.0	1.2	11.3	16.6
Millwrights	67	2.9	0.0	6.2	7.4
Electrical power-line installers and repairers	109	0.9	0.0	12.0	6.5
Telecommunications line installers and repairers	210	8.6	2.1	11.3	12.8
Precision instrument and equipment repairers	73	13.9	10.0	5.3	10.0
Coin, vending, amusement machine servicers and repairers	62	14.3	3.4	8.2	9.3
PRODUCTION, TRANSPORTATION, AND MATERIAL-MOVING OCCUPATIONS	**18,224**	**22.8**	**3.6**	**14.2**	**19.6**
Production occupations	**9,378**	**30.4**	**4.8**	**12.2**	**20.6**
First-line supervisors/mgrs. of production, operating workers	868	19.4	4.8	9.8	10.8
Electrical, electronics, and electromechanical assemblers	213	51.7	14.0	14.0	19.6
Bakers	186	57.9	4.6	9.4	28.5
Butchers and other meat, poultry, and fish processing workers	292	29.9	3.1	12.8	46.1
Food batchmakers	81	58.6	4.0	10.5	27.7
Computer control programmers and operators	54	8.2	3.9	4.8	8.3
Cutting, punching, and press machine setters, operators, and tenders, metal and plastic	119	17.9	1.5	13.8	15.8
Grinding, lapping, polishing, and buffing machine tool setters, operators, and tenders, metal and plastic	62	5.6	0.1	12.6	19.6
Machinists	415	6.7	4.1	5.2	12.1
Molders and molding machine setters, operators, and tenders, metal and plastic	70	17.1	0.7	9.8	13.7
Tool and die makers	105	0.9	0.0	3.0	5.4
Welding, soldering, and brazing workers	546	5.9	2.7	7.5	19.4
Printing machine operators	208	22.2	3.8	9.5	16.5
Laundry and dry-cleaning workers	190	62.4	5.2	18.3	32.1

(continued)

		percent			
	total number	**female**	**Asian**	**black**	**Hispanic**
Pressers, textile, garment, and related materials	63	70.8%	6.5%	21.7%	49.5%
Sewing machine operators	292	77.9	15.3	10.7	41.4
Tailors, dressmakers, and sewers	111	74.7	11.0	7.6	21.1
Upholsterers	54	14.0	2.4	10.9	23.1
Cabinetmakers and bench carpenters	113	4.4	2.3	1.8	18.5
Sawing machine setters, operators, and tenders, wood	58	10.5	1.9	8.6	26.3
Stationary engineers and boiler operators	94	2.3	3.0	8.5	9.8
Water and liquid waste treatment plant and system operators	95	4.0	0.4	13.4	5.4
Chemical processing machine setters, operators, and tenders	57	13.0	0.0	12.1	12.9
Crushing, grinding, polishing, mixing, and blending workers	105	11.2	5.1	19.3	24.6
Cutting workers	78	24.8	2.7	5.8	27.3
Inspectors, testers, sorters, samplers, and weighers	702	38.8	6.4	11.4	14.4
Medical, dental, and ophthalmic laboratory technicians	95	50.8	11.2	9.7	17.8
Packaging and filling machine operators and tenders	275	55.5	5.0	21.5	38.0
Painting workers	173	16.6	1.4	9.0	25.0
Photographic process workers, processing machine operators	62	51.8	2.2	15.2	6.4
Helpers—production workers	53	25.2	3.8	16.1	26.8
Transportation and material moving occupations	**8,846**	**14.8**	**2.3**	**16.3**	**18.6**
Supervisors, transportation and material moving workers	228	16.7	2.2	13.0	12.1
Aircraft pilots and flight engineers	115	2.2	2.8	0.0	5.3
Bus drivers	565	49.6	1.3	29.4	12.2
Driver/sales workers and truck drivers	3,475	5.2	1.2	13.9	16.0
Taxi drivers and chauffeurs	282	16.0	12.6	23.8	15.0
Railroad conductors and yardmasters	50	6.5	0.0	14.8	9.6
Parking lot attendants	65	19.5	7.2	16.6	30.8
Service station attendants	96	9.8	7.5	5.9	12.0
Crane and tower operators	54	1.5	0.8	13.5	10.2
Dredge, excavating, and loading machine operators	63	1.5	0.4	4.7	16.8
Industrial truck and tractor operators	574	7.2	0.8	20.1	25.8
Cleaners of vehicles and equipment	401	15.0	1.0	16.9	32.7
Laborers and freight, stock, and material movers, hand	1,899	16.9	2.7	16.2	19.4
Packers and packagers, hand	432	57.5	5.4	18.9	39.2
Refuse and recyclable material collectors	91	6.1	4.4	28.0	24.7

Source: Bureau of Labor Statistics, 2006 Current Population Survey, Internet site http://www.bls.gov/cps/home.htm

Computers and Health Care Lead the Pack

Farming should continue to decline.

Every two years, the Bureau of Labor Statistics produces occupational projections that look 10 years ahead, based on demographic and technological change. The most recent set of projections holds few surprises: computing and health care jobs are projected to be the big gainers. Farming will continue to shed workers, and technological change will reduce the demand for secretaries, typists, file clerks, telephone operators, and telemarketers.

Among the 10 fastest growing occupations, home health care aide is on top, with a 56 percent increase in the number of home health care jobs projected for 2014. Other health care occupations that rank among the top 10 fastest growing occupations are medical assistant, physician's assistant, physical therapist assistant, dental hygienist, and dental assistant. Among the computer jobs in the top 10 are network systems analyst and computer software engineer.

The jobs expected to offer the largest number of employment opportunities include retail salesperson, registered nurse, college teacher, janitor, waiter, and home health aide. Quite a few of the occupations that will require many more workers during the next decade are those that do not pay much. For these, it is likely that immigrants—many of them illegal—will fill the positions.

■ Among industries, three are expected to grow more than twice as fast as the average: educational services, health care services, and professional and business services.

Retail sales is on top, farming is on the bottom

(occupations with the largest projected job gain and loss, 2004 to 2014)

+736,000

600,000

300,000

0

−155,000

retail salespeople

farmers and ranchers

Table 6.20 Employment by Major Occupational Group, 2004 and 2014

(number and percent distribution of people aged 16 or older employed by major occupational group, 2004 and 2014; percent change, 2004–14; numbers in thousands)

	2004		2014		
	number	percent distribution	number	percent distribution	percent change 2004–14
Total employed	**145,612**	**100.0%**	**164,540**	**100.0%**	**13.0%**
Management occupations	9,115	6.3	10,147	6.2	11.3
Business and financial operations occupations	5,873	4.0	6,996	4.3	19.1
Professional and related occupations	28,544	19.6	34,590	21.0	21.2
Computer and mathematical	3,153	2.2	4,120	2.5	30.7
Architecture and engineering	2,520	1.7	2,835	1.7	12.5
Life, physical, and social science	1,316	0.9	1,532	0.9	16.4
Community and social services	2,317	1.6	2,800	1.7	20.8
Legal	1,220	0.8	1,414	0.9	15.9
Education, training, and library	8,698	6.0	10,438	6.3	20.0
Art, design, entertainment, sports, and media	2,515	1.7	2,890	1.8	14.9
Health care practitioner, technical occupations	6,805	4.7	8,561	5.2	25.8
Service occupations	27,673	19.0	32,930	20.0	19.0
Health care support	3,492	2.4	4,656	2.8	33.3
Protective service	3,138	2.2	3,578	2.2	14.0
Food preparation and serving related	10,739	7.4	12,453	7.6	16.0
Building and grounds cleaning, maintenance	5,582	3.8	6,530	4.0	17.0
Personal care and service	4,721	3.2	5,713	3.5	21.0
Sales and related occupations	15,330	10.5	16,806	10.2	9.6
Office and administrative support occupations	23,907	16.4	25,287	15.4	5.8
Farming, fishing, and forestry occupations	1,026	0.7	1,013	0.6	−1.3
Construction and extraction occupations	7,738	5.3	8,669	5.3	12.0
Installation, maintenance, and repair occupations	5,747	3.9	6,404	3.9	11.4
Production occupations	10,562	7.3	10,483	6.4	−0.7
Transportation and material-moving occupations	10,098	6.9	11,214	6.8	11.1

Source: Bureau of Labor Statistics, Occupational Employment Projections to 2014, Monthly Labor Review, November 2005, Internet site http://www.bls.gov/opub/mlr/2005/11/art5exc.htm; calculations by New Strategist

Table 6.21 Fastest Growing Occupations, 2004 to 2014

(number of people aged 16 or older employed in the 30 fastest-growing occupations, 2004 to 2014; numerical and percent change, 2004–14; numbers in thousands)

	2004	2014	change, 2004–14 number	change, 2004–14 percent
Home health aides	624	974	350	56.0%
Network systems and data communications analysts	231	357	126	54.6
Medical assistants	387	589	202	52.1
Physician assistants	62	93	31	49.6
Computer software engineers, applications	460	682	222	48.4
Physical therapist assistants	59	85	26	44.2
Dental hygienists	158	226	68	43.3
Computer software engineers, systems software	340	486	146	43.0
Dental assistants	267	382	114	42.7
Personal and home care aides	701	988	287	41.0
Network and computer systems administrators	278	385	107	38.4
Database administrators	104	144	40	38.2
Physical therapists	155	211	57	36.7
Forensic science technicians	10	13	4	36.4
Veterinary technologists and technicians	60	81	21	35.3
Diagnostic medical sonographers	42	57	15	34.8
Physical therapist aides	43	57	15	34.4
Occupational therapist assistants	21	29	7	34.1
Medical scientists, except epidemiologists	72	97	25	34.1
Occupational therapists	92	123	31	33.6
Preschool teachers	431	573	143	33.1
Cardiovascular technologists and technicians	45	60	15	32.6
Postsecondary teachers	1,628	2,153	524	32.2
Hydrologists	8	11	3	31.6
Computer systems analysts	487	640	153	31.4
Hazardous materials removal workers	38	50	12	31.2
Biomedical engineers	10	13	3	30.7
Employment, recruitment, and placement specialists	182	237	55	30.5
Environmental engineers	49	64	15	30.0
Paralegals and legal assistants	224	291	67	29.7

Source: Bureau of Labor Statistics, Occupational Employment Projections to 2014, Monthly Labor Review, November 2005, Internet site http://www.bls.gov/opub/mlr/2005/11/art5exc.htm; calculations by New Strategist

Table 6.22 Occupations with the Largest Job Growth, 2004 to 2014

(number of people aged 16 or older employed in the 30 occupations with the largest projected job growth, 2004 to 2014; numerical and percent change, 2004–14; numbers in thousands)

	2004	2014	change, 2004–14 number	change, 2004–14 percent
Retail salespersons	4,256	4,992	736	17.3%
Registered nurses	2,394	3,096	703	29.4
Postsecondary teachers	1,628	2,153	524	32.2
Customer service representatives	2,063	2,534	471	22.8
Janitors and cleaners (except housekeeping)	2,374	2,813	440	18.5
Waiters and waitresses	2,252	2,627	376	16.7
Food prep and serving workers, incl. fast food	2,150	2,516	367	17.1
Home health aides	624	974	350	56.0
Nursing aides, orderlies, and attendants	1,455	1,781	325	22.3
General and operations managers	1,807	2,115	308	17.0
Personal and home care aides	701	988	287	41.0
Elementary school teachers, except special education	1,457	1,722	265	18.2
Accountants and auditors	1,176	1,440	264	22.4
Office clerks, general	3,138	3,401	263	8.4
Laborers and material movers, hand	2,430	2,678	248	10.2
Receptionists and information clerks	1,133	1,379	246	21.7
Landscaping and groundskeeping workers	1,177	1,407	230	19.5
Truck drivers, heavy and tractor-trailer	1,738	1,962	223	12.9
Computer software engineers, applications	460	682	222	48.4
Maintenance and repair workers, general	1,332	1,533	202	15.2
Medical assistants	387	589	202	52.1
Executive secretaries and administrative assistants	1,547	1,739	192	12.4
Sales reps, wholesale, except technical	1,454	1,641	187	12.9
Carpenters	1,349	1,535	186	13.8
Teacher assistants	1,296	1,478	183	14.1
Child care workers	1,280	1,456	176	13.8
Food preparation workers	869	1,064	175	19.7
Maids and housekeeping cleaners	1,422	1,587	165	11.6
Truck drivers, light or delivery services	1,042	1,206	164	15.7
Computer systems analysts	487	640	153	31.4

Source: Bureau of Labor Statistics, Occupational Employment Projections to 2014, Monthly Labor Review, November 2005, Internet site http://www.bls.gov/opub/mlr/2005/11/art5exc.htm; calculations by New Strategist

Table 6.23 Occupations with the Largest Job Decline, 2004 to 2014

(number of people aged 16 or older employed in the 30 occupations with the largest projected employment decline, 2004 to 2014; numerical and percent change, 2004–14; numbers in thousands)

	2004	2014	change, 2004–14 number	change, 2004–14 percent
Farmers and ranchers	1,065	910	−155	−14.5%
Stock clerks and order fillers	1,566	1,451	−115	−7.3
Sewing machine operators	256	163	−93	−36.5
File clerks	255	163	−93	−36.3
Order clerks	293	230	−63	−21.4
Mail clerks and mail machine operators, except postal	160	101	−59	−37.1
Computer operators	149	101	−49	−32.6
Secretaries, except legal, medical, executive	1,934	1,887	−48	−2.5
Cutting, punching, press machine workers, metal, plastic	251	208	−43	−17.2
Telemarketers	415	373	−42	−10.0
Word processors and typists	194	165	−30	−15.3
Credit authorizers, checkers, and clerks	67	39	−27	−41.2
Machine feeders and offbearers	148	122	−27	−18.0
Textile knitting and weaving machine workers	46	20	−26	−56.2
Textile winding, twisting, drawing out machine workers	53	29	−24	−45.5
Meter readers, utilities	50	27	−22	−44.9
Office machine operators, except computer	100	78	−22	−21.9
Extruding and drawing machine workers, metal and plastic	89	70	−19	−21.3
Switchboard operators, including answering service	213	195	−19	−8.8
Door-to-door sales workers, news and street vendors	239	221	−18	−7.4
Photographic processing machine operators	54	38	−17	−30.7
Farmworkers and laborers, crop, nursery, and greenhouse	611	595	−16	−2.7
Parts salespersons	239	223	−16	−6.6
Molding, coremaking, and casting machine workers, metal and plastic	157	142	−15	−9.5
Electrical and electronic equipment assemblers	221	207	−14	−6.4
Telephone operators	39	25	−14	−35.7
Inspectors, testers, sorters, samplers, and weighers	508	494	−13	−2.6
Couriers and messengers	147	134	−13	−8.6
Chemical plant and system operators	60	49	−11	−17.7
Parking lot attendants	122	111	−11	−8.7

Source: Bureau of Labor Statistics, Occupational Employment Projections to 2014, Monthly Labor Review, November 2005, Internet site http://www.bls.gov/opub/mlr/2005/11/art5exc.htm; calculations by New Strategist

Table 6.24 Employment by Major Industry, 2004 and 2014

(number and percent distribution of people aged 16 or older employed by major industry, 2004 and 2014; percent change in number, 2004–14; numbers in thousands)

| | 2004 | | 2014 | | |
	number	percent distribution	number	percent distribution	percent change 2004–14
Total employed	**145,612**	**100.0%**	**164,540**	**100.0%**	**13.0%**
Nonfarm wage and salary	132,192	90.8	150,877	91.7	14.1
Goods producing	21,817	15.0	21,787	13.2	−0.1
Mining	523	0.4	477	0.3	−8.8
Construction	6,965	4.8	7,757	4.7	11.4
Manufacturing	14,330	9.8	13,553	8.2	−5.4
Service providing	110,374	75.8	129,090	78.5	17.0
Utilities	570	0.4	563	0.3	−1.3
Wholesale trade	5,655	3.9	6,131	3.7	8.4
Retail trade	15,035	10.3	16,683	10.1	11.0
Transportation and warehousing	4,250	2.9	4,756	2.9	11.9
Information	3,138	2.2	3,502	2.1	11.6
Financial activities	8,052	5.5	8,901	5.4	10.5
Professional and business services	16,414	11.3	20,980	12.8	27.8
Education	2,766	1.9	3,665	2.2	32.5
Health care and social assistance	14,187	9.7	18,482	11.2	30.3
Leisure and hospitality	12,479	8.6	14,694	8.9	17.7
Other services	6,210	4.3	6,943	4.2	11.8
Federal government	2,728	1.9	2,771	1.7	1.6
State and local government	18,891	13.0	21,019	12.8	11.3
Agriculture	2,140	1.5	1,910	1.2	−10.7
Nonagricultural self-employed and unpaid family workers	9,556	6.6	10,012	6.1	4.8
Secondary wage, salary jobs in agriculture, forestry, fishing, or private households	138	0.1	127	0.1	−7.8
Secondary jobs as self-employed or unpaid family workers	1,587	1.1	1,614	1.0	1.7

Source: Bureau of Labor Statistics, Industry Output and Employment Projections to 2014, Monthly Labor Review, November 2005, Internet site http://www.bls.gov/opub/mlr/2005/11/art4exc.htm; calculations by New Strategist

Table 6.25 Industries with the Fastest Wage and Salary Employment Growth, 2004 to 2014

(number of people aged 16 or older employed in industries with the fastest wage and salary employment growth, 2004–2014; numerical and percent change in employment, 2004–14; ranked by percent change; numbers in thousands)

	2004	2014	change, 2004–2014 number	change, 2004–2014 percent
Home health care services	773	1,310	537	69.5%
Software publishers	239	400	161	67.6
Management, scientific, technical consulting services	779	1,250	471	60.5
Residential care facilities	1,240	1,840	601	48.5
Facilities support services	116	170	54	47.1
Employment services	3,470	5,050	1,580	45.5
Independent artists, writers, and performers	42	61	19	45.1
Office administrative services	319	450	131	40.9
Computer systems design and related services	1,147	1,600	453	39.5
Outpatient, laboratory, other ambulatory care services	836	1,160	324	38.8

Source: Bureau of Labor Statistics, Industry Output and Employment Projections to 2014, Monthly Labor Review, November 2005, Internet site http://www.bls.gov/opub/mlr/2005/11/art4exc.htm; calculations by New Strategist

Most Married Couples Are Dual Earners

Among couples with children under age 18, nearly two out of three are dual earners.

Dual earners have accounted for the majority of the nation's married couples for nearly two decades. In 2006, 55 percent of couples were dual earners, while only the husband worked in a much smaller 22 percent. Among couples with children under age 18, an even larger 65 percent are dual-earner, and in 30 percent only the husband works.

No matter how young the child, the majority of married women with children under age 18 are in the labor force. Among wives with children under age 3, the 57 percent majority was in the labor force in 2005—up from just 33 percent in 1975. Among wives with children aged 6 to 17, fully 75 percent are in the labor force.

Sixty-one percent of preschoolers are in some type of regular day care. This proportion has been stable for the past decade, but the type of day care is changing. Fewer children are being cared for in a home (the child's or another home) by a nonrelative, with the proportion falling from 18 to 14 percent between 1995 and 2005. A larger percentage of children are being cared for in a day care center, the figure rising from 31 to 36 percent between 1995 and 2005. Twenty-two percent of children are cared for by a relative.

■ Children whose mother works full-time are most likely to be in a center-based child care program. Forty-eight percent were in day care centers in 2005, up from 39 percent 1995.

Nearly two out of three couples with children are dual-earners

(percent distribution of married couples by labor force status of husband and wife, 2005)

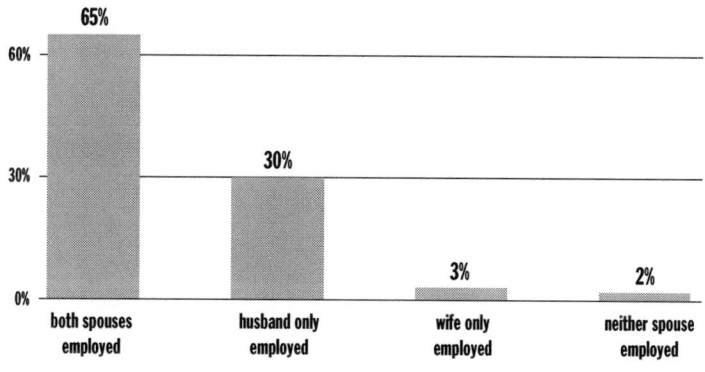

Table 6.26 Married Couples by Labor Force Status of Husband and Wife, 1986 to 2006: Total Couples

(number and percent distribution of married couples by labor force status of husband and wife, 1986 to 2006; percent and percentage point change for selected years; numbers in thousands)

	total couples	husband and wife in labor force	husband only in labor force	wife only in labor force	neither husband nor wife in labor force
2006	58,179	31,783	12,990	3,754	9,652
2005	57,975	31,398	13,385	3,641	9,551
2004	57,719	31,536	12,980	3,684	9,519
2003	57,320	31,951	12,443	3,553	9,373
2002	56,747	31,637	12,327	3,388	9,395
2001	56,592	31,794	12,213	3,274	9,311
2000	55,311	31,095	11,815	3,301	9,098
1999	54,770	30,635	11,704	3,185	9,245
1998	54,317	30,591	11,582	3,087	9,057
1997	53,604	30,466	11,369	2,891	8,878
1996	53,567	29,952	11,684	2,835	9,096
1995	53,858	29,999	11,777	3,043	9,039
1994	53,171	29,279	11,665	3,069	9,158
1993	53,171	28,898	12,268	2,804	9,200
1992	52,457	28,592	12,283	2,620	8,963
1991	52,147	28,167	12,680	2,454	8,845
1990	52,317	28,056	13,013	2,453	8,794
1989	52,100	27,731	13,292	2,348	8,729
1988	51,809	27,016	13,737	2,358	8,698
1987	51,537	26,466	14,144	2,317	8,611
1986	50,933	25,428	14,675	2,362	8,468
Percent change					
2000 to 2006	5.2%	2.2%	9.9%	13.7%	6.1%
1986 to 2006	14.2	25.0	−11.5	58.9	14.0

(continued)

	total couples	husband and wife in labor force	husband only in labor force	wife only in labor force	neither husband nor wife in labor force
Percent distribution					
2006	100.0%	54.6%	22.3%	6.5%	16.6%
2005	100.0	54.2	23.1	6.3	16.5
2004	100.0	54.6	22.5	6.4	16.5
2003	100.0	55.7	21.7	6.2	16.4
2002	100.0	55.8	21.7	6.0	16.6
2001	100.0	56.2	21.6	5.8	16.5
2000	100.0	56.2	21.4	6.0	16.4
1999	100.0	55.9	21.4	5.8	16.9
1998	100.0	56.3	21.3	5.7	16.7
1997	100.0	56.8	21.2	5.4	16.6
1996	100.0	55.9	21.8	5.3	17.0
1995	100.0	55.7	21.9	5.7	16.8
1994	100.0	55.1	21.9	5.8	17.2
1993	100.0	54.3	23.1	5.3	17.3
1992	100.0	54.5	23.4	5.0	17.1
1991	100.0	54.0	24.3	4.7	17.0
1990	100.0	53.6	24.9	4.7	16.8
1989	100.0	53.2	25.5	4.5	16.8
1988	100.0	52.1	26.5	4.6	16.8
1987	100.0	51.4	27.4	4.5	16.7
1986	100.0	49.9	28.8	4.6	16.6
Percentage point change					
2000 to 2006	–	–1.6	1.0	0.5	0.1
1986 to 2006	–	4.7	–6.5	1.8	0.0

Note: "–" means not applicable.
Source: Bureau of the Census, Current Population Surveys, Internet site http://www.census.gov/population/socdemo/hh-fam/ mc1.xls; calculations by New Strategist

Table 6.27 Married Couples by Labor Force Status of Husband and Wife, 1986 to 2006: Couples with Children under Age 18

(number and percent distribution of married couples with children under age 18 at home by labor force status of husband and wife, 1986 to 2006; percent and percentage point change for selected years; numbers in thousands)

	total couples w/ children < age 18	husband and wife in labor force	husband only in labor force	wife only in labor force	neither husband nor wife in labor force
2006	25,982	16,909	7,754	900	420
2005	25,919	16,789	7,806	925	400
2004	25,793	16,691	7,715	952	433
2003	25,914	17,065	7,499	893	457
2002	25,792	17,233	7,301	777	482
2001	25,980	17,563	7,210	784	422
2000	25,248	17,116	6,950	795	387
1999	25,066	16,887	6,998	765	418
1998	25,269	17,168	6,856	753	491
1997	25,083	17,160	6,713	732	478
1996	24,920	16,769	6,883	739	528
1995	25,241	17,024	6,863	756	598
1994	25,058	16,635	7,029	754	641
1993	24,707	16,064	7,431	680	532
1992	24,420	16,054	7,228	580	557
1991	24,397	15,778	7,542	581	495
1990	24,537	15,768	7,667	558	544
1989	24,735	15,757	7,929	488	560
1988	24,600	15,489	8,031	541	539
1987	24,645	15,238	8,345	528	534
1986	24,630	14,606	8,916	518	590
Percent change					
2000 to 2006	2.9%	−1.2%	11.6%	13.2%	8.5%
1986 to 2006	5.5	15.8	−13.0	73.7	−28.8

(continued)

	total couples w/ children < age 18	husband and wife in labor force	husband only in labor force	wife only in labor force	neither husband nor wife in labor force
Percent distribution					
2006	100.0%	65.1%	29.8%	3.5%	1.6%
2005	100.0	64.8	30.1	3.6	1.5
2004	100.0	64.7	29.9	3.7	1.7
2003	100.0	65.9	28.9	3.4	1.8
2002	100.0	66.8	28.3	3.0	1.9
2001	100.0	67.6	27.8	3.0	1.6
2000	100.0	67.8	27.5	3.1	1.5
1999	100.0	67.4	27.9	3.1	1.7
1998	100.0	67.9	27.1	3.0	1.9
1997	100.0	68.4	26.8	2.9	1.9
1996	100.0	67.3	27.6	3.0	2.1
1995	100.0	67.4	27.2	3.0	2.4
1994	100.0	66.4	28.1	3.0	2.6
1993	100.0	65.0	30.1	2.8	2.2
1992	100.0	65.7	29.6	2.4	2.3
1991	100.0	64.7	30.9	2.4	2.0
1990	100.0	64.3	31.2	2.3	2.2
1989	100.0	63.7	32.1	2.0	2.3
1988	100.0	63.0	32.6	2.2	2.2
1987	100.0	61.8	33.9	2.1	2.2
1986	100.0	59.3	36.2	2.1	2.4
Percentage point change					
2000 to 2006	–	–2.7	2.3	0.3	0.1
1986 to 2006	–	5.8	–6.4	1.4	–0.8

Note: "–" means not applicable.
Source: Bureau of the Census, Current Population Surveys, Internet site http://www.census.gov/population/socdemo/hh-fam/ mc1.xls; calculations by New Strategist

Table 6.28 Married Couples by Labor Force Status of Husband and Wife, 1986 to 2006: Couples with Children under Age 6

(number and percent distribution of married couples with children under age 6 at home by labor force status of husband and wife, 1986 to 2006; percent and percentage point change for selected years; numbers in thousands)

	total couples w/ children < age 6	husband and wife in labor force	husband only in labor force	wife only in labor force	neither husband nor wife in labor force
2006	11,984	6,939	4,572	324	149
2005	11,802	6,813	4,553	299	137
2004	11,711	6,657	4,579	317	158
2003	11,743	6,747	4,507	298	191
2002	11,531	6,796	4,311	250	175
2001	11,732	7,054	4,296	247	134
2000	11,393	6,984	4,077	211	121
1999	11,461	6,878	4,182	257	144
1998	11,773	7,310	4,079	223	161
1997	11,584	7,142	4,022	260	162
1996	11,782	7,189	4,159	229	205
1995	11,951	7,406	4,059	233	253
1994	12,118	7,283	4,328	250	255
1993	11,942	6,934	4,535	231	241
1992	11,925	6,972	4,482	217	254
1991	12,100	7,061	4,593	223	222
1990	12,051	6,932	4,692	192	235
1989	12,011	6,772	4,867	148	224
1988	11,915	6,651	4,875	182	206
1987	11,966	6,618	4,947	199	202
1986	11,924	6,271	5,284	155	215
Percent change					
2000 to 2006	5.2%	−0.6%	12.1%	53.6%	23.1%
1986 to 2006	0.5	10.7	−13.5	109.0	−30.7

(continued)

	total couples w/ children < age 6	husband and wife in labor force	husband only in labor force	wife only in labor force	neither husband nor wife in labor force
Percent distribution					
2006	100.0%	57.9%	38.2%	2.7%	1.2%
2005	100.0	57.7	38.6	2.5	1.2
2004	100.0	56.8	39.1	2.7	1.3
2003	100.0	57.5	38.4	2.5	1.6
2002	100.0	58.9	37.4	2.2	1.5
2001	100.0	60.1	36.6	2.1	1.1
2000	100.0	61.3	35.8	1.9	1.1
1999	100.0	60.0	36.5	2.2	1.3
1998	100.0	62.1	34.6	1.9	1.4
1997	100.0	61.7	34.7	2.2	1.4
1996	100.0	61.0	35.3	1.9	1.7
1995	100.0	62.0	34.0	1.9	2.1
1994	100.0	60.1	35.7	2.1	2.1
1993	100.0	58.1	38.0	1.9	2.0
1992	100.0	58.5	37.6	1.8	2.1
1991	100.0	58.4	38.0	1.8	1.8
1990	100.0	57.5	38.9	1.6	2.0
1989	100.0	56.4	40.5	1.2	1.9
1988	100.0	55.8	40.9	1.5	1.7
1987	100.0	55.3	41.3	1.7	1.7
1986	100.0	52.6	44.3	1.3	1.8
Percentage point change					
2000 to 2006	–	–3.4	2.4	0.9	0.2
1986 to 2006	–	5.3	–6.2	1.4	–0.6

Note: "–" means not applicable.
Source: Bureau of the Census, Current Population Surveys, Internet site http://www.census.gov/population/socdemo/hh-fam/mc1.xls; calculations by New Strategist

Table 6.29 Labor Force Participation of Wives by Age of Children at Home, 1960 to 2005

(labor force participation rate of wives aged 16 or older by presence and age of own children under age 18 at home, 1960 to 2005; percentage point change for selected years; numbers in thousands)

	total wives	no children under 18	with children under age 18 total	6 to 17	under age 6	under 3
2005	60.2%	53.8%	68.1%	75.0%	59.8%	57.0%
2004	60.9	55.0	68.2	75.6	59.3	55.1
2003	61.8	55.7	69.2	77.0	59.8	56.5
2002	61.5	54.9	69.6	76.8	60.8	59.0
2001	61.8	54.8	70.4	77.5	61.9	59.4
2000	62.0	54.7	70.6	77.2	62.8	59.0
1999	61.6	54.4	70.1	77.1	61.8	59.2
1998	61.8	54.1	70.6	76.8	63.7	61.4
1997	62.1	54.2	71.1	77.6	63.6	61.3
1996	61.1	53.4	70.0	76.7	62.7	60.5
1995	61.1	53.2	70.2	76.2	63.5	60.9
1994	60.6	53.2	69.0	76.0	61.7	59.7
1993	59.4	52.4	67.5	74.9	59.6	57.3
1992	59.3	51.9	67.8	75.4	59.9	57.5
1991	58.5	51.2	66.8	73.6	59.9	56.8
1990	58.2	51.1	66.3	73.6	58.9	55.5
1989	57.6	50.5	65.6	73.4	57.4	55.2
1988	56.5	48.9	65.0	72.5	57.1	54.5
1987	55.8	48.4	63.8	70.6	56.8	54.2
1986	54.6	48.2	61.3	68.4	53.8	50.9
1985	54.2	48.2	60.8	67.8	53.4	50.5
1984	52.8	47.2	58.8	65.4	51.8	48.2
1983	51.8	46.6	57.2	63.8	49.9	46.0
1982	51.2	46.2	56.3	63.2	48.7	45.3
1981	51.0	46.3	55.7	62.5	47.8	43.7
1980	50.1	46.0	54.1	61.7	45.1	41.3
1979	49.3	46.6	51.9	59.0	43.3	39.6
1978	47.5	44.6	50.2	57.1	41.7	37.9
1977	46.6	44.8	48.2	55.5	39.4	34.7
1976	45.1	43.7	46.1	53.6	37.5	32.7
1975	44.4	43.8	44.9	52.2	36.7	32.7
1974	43.1	43.0	43.1	51.2	34.4	–
1973	42.2	42.8	41.7	50.1	32.7	–
1972	41.5	42.7	40.5	50.2	30.1	–
1971	40.8	42.1	39.7	49.4	29.6	–
1970	40.8	42.2	39.7	49.2	30.3	–
1969	39.6	41.0	38.6	48.6	28.5	–
1968	38.3	40.1	36.9	46.9	27.6	–
1967	36.8	38.9	35.3	45.0	26.5	–
1966	35.4	38.4	33.2	43.7	24.2	–
1965	34.7	38.3	32.2	42.7	23.3	–
1964	34.4	37.8	32.0	43.0	22.7	–
1963	33.7	37.4	31.2	41.5	22.5	–
1962	32.7	36.1	30.3	41.8	21.3	–
1961	32.7	37.3	29.6	41.7	20.0	–
1960	30.5	34.7	27.6	39.0	18.6	–
Percentage point change						
2000 to 2005	–1.8	–0.9	–2.5	–2.2	–3.0	–2.0
1960 to 2005	29.7	19.1	40.5	36.0	41.2	–

Note: "–" means data not available.
Source: Bureau of Labor Statistics, Handbook of Labor Statistics, Bulletin 2340, 1989; and Bureau of the Census, Statistical Abstracts of the United States, 1993 through 2007; calculations by New Strategist

Table 6.30 Child Care Arrangements, 1995 and 2005

(percent distribution of children aged 0 to 6 and not yet in kindergarten by type of care arrangement and family characteristics, 1995 and 2005)

	parental care only		nonparental care							
			total		in a home				center-based program	
					by a relative		by a nonrelative			
	2005	1995	2005	1995	2005	1995	2005	1995	2005	1995
Total children	39.2%	39.9%	60.8%	60.1%	22.3%	21.1%	13.9%	18.0%	36.1%	30.5%
Aged 0 to 2	49.3	50.5	50.7	49.5	22.0	22.5	15.6	18.9	19.6	11.9
Aged 3 to 6	23.6	25.9	73.7	74.1	22.7	19.4	11.7	16.9	57.1	55.0
Race and Hispanic origin										
Asian	43.5	41.8	56.5	58.2	21.3	26.6	9.0	9.1	37.0	29.6
Black, non-Hispanic	30.1	34.2	69.9	65.8	27.7	31.4	10.2	11.6	43.9	33.0
Hispanic	50.5	53.7	49.5	46.3	21.2	23.4	10.4	11.8	25.2	17.0
White, non-Hispanic	37.2	38.3	62.8	61.7	21.0	17.9	17.0	21.3	37.8	32.9
Mother's employment status										
35 hours or more per week	14.7	11.9	85.3	88.1	31.8	33.4	23.3	31.7	47.6	38.9
Less than 35 hours per week	30.3	24.9	69.7	75.1	30.5	30.1	18.0	25.6	37.8	35.0
Not in labor force	66.1	67.7	33.9	32.3	7.8	7.2	3.6	5.5	25.8	22.0
Family type										
Two parents	42.9	42.0	57.1	58.0	18.8	17.2	14.1	19.2	34.4	29.9
One parent	24.9	33.0	75.1	67.0	36.0	33.3	13.4	15.2	42.3	32.4
Educational attainment of mother										
Less than high school	63.7	61.7	36.3	38.3	16.1	19.8	5.5	6.6	18.9	15.7
High school graduate	44.4	43.7	55.6	56.3	24.1	23.4	9.9	15.0	30.7	26.0
Some college or associate's degree	36.5	34.1	63.5	65.9	25.8	23.6	14.5	19.3	35.2	33.5
Bachelor's degree or more	30.5	27.7	69.5	72.3	19.1	15.2	19.2	28.4	45.8	42.7
Region										
Northeast	38.3	43.3	61.7	56.7	21.0	21.1	15.1	15.1	37.9	30.4
Midwest	38.0	34.3	62.0	65.7	22.3	24.3	11.1	16.0	38.8	35.2
South	36.7	37.7	63.3	62.3	23.8	20.4	18.8	23.4	33.5	29.5
West	43.9	47.7	56.1	52.3	21.8	17.2	12.6	17.8	33.1	24.7

Note: Numbers may not sum to total in nonparental care because multiple types of child care arrangements may be used.
Source: National Center for Education Statistics, America's Children: Key National Indicators of Children's Well-Being, 2007, Internet site http://childstats.gov/americaschildren/tables.asp

Self-Employment Is Becoming Less Common

Self-employment might expand if health insurance were more affordable.

Although many Americans claim to want to be their own boss, few manage to do so. Only 7.3 percent of workers aged 16 or older were self-employed in 2006, down from 17.6 percent in 1950. The long-term decline in self-employment occurred in part because of the dwindling number of farmers. In 1950, 7.4 percent of workers were self-employed farmers. The figure fell below 1 percent beginning in 2000 and is now just 0.6 percent.

Nonagricultural self-employment has also been declining during the past half-century. In 1950, more than 1 in 10 workers was self-employed in a nonagricultural industry. By 2006, the figure was just 6.7 percent.

■ The cost of health insurance for the self-employed is so high that few can afford to be an entrepreneur without a spouse who has employer-provided health insurance.

Few Americans work for themselves

(percent of people aged 16 or older self-employed in nonagricultural industries, 1950 and 2006)

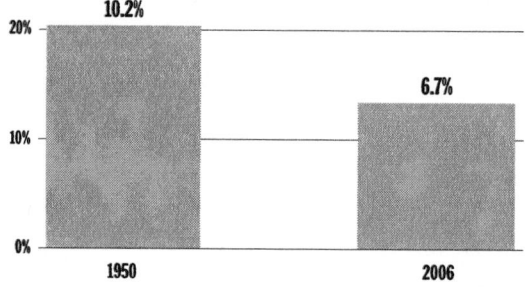

Table 6.31 Self-Employment, 1950 to 2006

(number and percent distribution of employed people aged 16 or older by self-employment status, 1950 to 2006; percent and percentage point change for selected years; numbers in thousands)

	total employed	self-employed total	self-employed nonagricultural	self-employed agricultural	total employed	self-employed total	self-employed nonagricultural	self-employed agricultural
2006	144,427	10,586	9,685	901	100.0%	7.3%	6.7%	0.6%
2005	141,730	10,464	9,509	955	100.0	7.4	6.7	0.7
2004	139,252	10,431	9,467	964	100.0	7.5	6.8	0.7
2003	137,736	10,295	9,344	951	100.0	7.5	6.8	0.7
2002	136,485	9,926	8,923	1,003	100.0	7.3	6.5	0.7
2001	136,933	10,109	9,121	988	100.0	7.4	6.7	0.7
2000	135,208	9,907	8,674	1,233	100.0	7.3	6.4	0.9
1999	133,488	10,087	8,790	1,297	100.0	7.6	6.6	1.0
1998	131,463	10,303	8,962	1,341	100.0	7.8	6.8	1.0
1997	129,558	10,513	9,056	1,457	100.0	8.1	7.0	1.1
1996	126,708	10,490	8,971	1,518	100.0	8.3	7.1	1.2
1995	124,900	10,482	8,902	1,580	100.0	8.4	7.1	1.3
1994	123,060	10,648	9,003	1,645	100.0	8.7	7.3	1.3
1993	119,306	10,335	9,003	1,332	100.0	8.7	7.5	1.1
1992	117,598	10,017	8,619	1,398	100.0	8.5	7.3	1.2
1991	116,877	10,341	8,899	1,442	100.0	8.8	7.6	1.2
1990	117,914	10,160	8,760	1,400	100.0	8.6	7.4	1.2
1989	117,342	10,008	8,605	1,403	100.0	8.5	7.3	1.2
1988	114,968	9,917	8,519	1,398	100.0	8.6	7.4	1.2
1987	112,440	9,624	8,201	1,423	100.0	8.6	7.3	1.3
1986	109,597	9,328	7,881	1,447	100.0	8.5	7.2	1.3
1985	107,150	9,269	7,811	1,458	100.0	8.7	7.3	1.4
1984	105,005	9,338	7,785	1,553	100.0	8.9	7.4	1.5
1983	100,834	9,140	7,575	1,565	100.0	9.1	7.5	1.6
1982	99,526	8,898	7,262	1,636	100.0	8.9	7.3	1.6
1981	100,397	8,735	7,097	1,638	100.0	8.7	7.1	1.6
1980	99,303	8,642	7,000	1,642	100.0	8.7	7.0	1.7
1979	98,824	8,384	6,791	1,593	100.0	8.5	6.9	1.6
1978	96,048	8,047	6,429	1,618	100.0	8.4	6.7	1.7
1977	92,017	7,694	6,114	1,580	100.0	8.4	6.6	1.7
1976	88,752	7,429	5,783	1,646	100.0	8.4	6.5	1.9
1975	85,846	7,427	5,705	1,722	100.0	8.7	6.6	2.0
1974	86,794	7,455	5,697	1,758	100.0	8.6	6.6	2.0
1973	85,064	7,254	5,474	1,780	100.0	8.5	6.4	2.1
1972	82,153	7,157	5,365	1,792	100.0	8.7	6.5	2.2
1971	79,367	7,077	5,327	1,750	100.0	8.9	6.7	2.2
1970	78,678	7,031	5,221	1,810	100.0	8.9	6.6	2.3
1969	77,902	7,148	5,252	1,896	100.0	9.2	6.7	2.4
1968	75,920	7,087	5,102	1,985	100.0	9.3	6.7	2.6
1967	74,372	7,170	5,174	1,996	100.0	9.6	7.0	2.7
1966	72,895	8,127	5,991	2,136	100.0	11.1	8.2	2.9
1965	71,088	8,394	6,097	2,297	100.0	11.8	8.6	3.2
1960	65,778	9,098	6,303	2,795	100.0	13.8	9.6	4.2
1955	62,170	9,577	5,851	3,726	100.0	15.4	9.4	6.0
1950	58,918	10,359	6,019	4,340	100.0	17.6	10.2	7.4

	percent change				percentage point change			
1990 to 2006	6.8%	6.9%	11.7%	26.9%	–	0.0	0.3	–0.3
1950 to 2006	145.1	2.2	60.9	–79.2	–	–10.3	–3.5	–6.7

Source: Bureau of Labor Statistics, Handbook of Labor Statistics, Bulletin 2340, 1989; and Employment and Earnings, various issues; calculations by New Strategist

Job Tenure Has Been Stable

Fewer men have long-term jobs, however.

Job tenure for men and women has been stable over the past few decades. The average male worker in 2006 had been working for his current employer for a median of 4.1 years—the same as in 1983. For the average female worker, job tenure rose during those years from 3.1 to 3.9 years.

Although job tenure has been stable, there is a troubling trend in the percentage of workers who have been with their current employer for 10 or more years. Among all male wage and salary workers aged 25 or older, 31 percent had been with their employer for at least 10 years in 2006, down from 38 percent in 1983. Among men aged 35 to 64, however, there have been double-digit declines in the percentage holding long-term jobs. In 1983, the 51 percent majority of men aged 40 to 44 had been with their current employer for 10 or more years. By 2006, only 35 percent had that kind of tenure. In 1983, the majority of men spanning the ages from 40 to 64 had been with their current employer for 10 or more years. By 2006, only men aged 55 to 59 could make that claim.

■ While some of the decline in long-term jobs may be due to job hopping, the steep decline for middle-aged men suggests that much of it is involuntary.

Middle-aged men have seen steep declines in long-term jobs

(percentage of male wage and salary workers who have been with their current employer for 10 or more years, for selected age groups, 1983 and 2006)

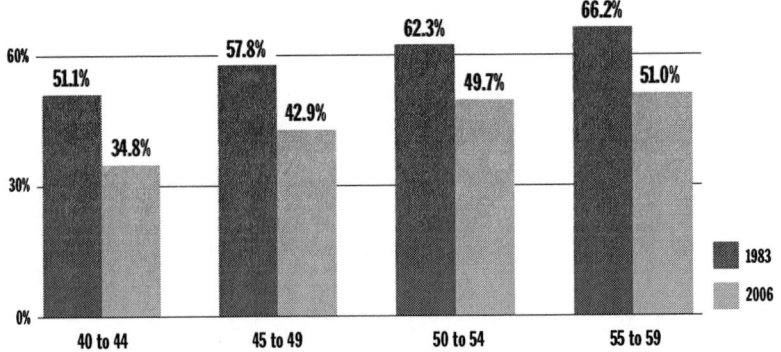

Table 6.32 Job Tenure by Sex and Age, 1983 to 2006

(median number of years workers aged 16 or older have been with their current employer by sex and age, 1983 to 2006; change for selected years)

	2006	2004	2002	2000	1998	1996	1991	1987	1983	change in years 2000–06	change in years 1983–06
Total employed men	**4.1**	**4.1**	**3.9**	**3.8**	**3.8**	**4.0**	**4.1**	**4.0**	**4.1**	**0.3**	**0.0**
Aged 16 to 17	0.7	0.7	0.8	0.6	0.6	0.6	0.7	0.6	0.7	0.1	0.0
Aged 18 to 19	0.7	0.8	0.8	0.7	0.7	0.7	0.8	0.7	0.8	0.0	–0.1
Aged 20 to 24	1.4	1.3	1.4	1.2	1.2	1.2	1.4	1.3	1.5	0.2	–0.1
Aged 25 to 34	2.9	3.0	2.8	2.7	2.8	3.0	3.1	3.1	3.2	0.2	–0.3
Aged 35 to 44	5.1	5.2	5.0	5.3	5.5	6.1	6.5	7.0	7.3	–0.2	–2.2
Aged 45 to 54	8.1	9.6	9.1	9.5	9.4	10.1	11.2	11.8	12.8	–1.4	–4.7
Aged 55 to 64	9.5	9.8	10.2	10.2	11.2	10.5	13.4	14.5	15.3	–0.7	–5.8
Aged 65 or older	8.3	8.2	8.1	9.0	7.1	8.3	7.0	8.3	8.3	–0.7	0.0
Total employed women	**3.9**	**3.8**	**3.4**	**3.3**	**3.4**	**3.5**	**3.2**	**3.0**	**3.1**	**0.6**	**0.8**
Aged 16 to 17	0.6	0.6	0.7	0.6	0.6	0.7	0.7	0.6	0.7	0.0	–0.1
Aged 18 to 19	0.7	0.8	0.8	0.7	0.7	0.7	0.8	0.7	0.8	0.0	–0.1
Aged 20 to 24	1.2	1.3	1.1	1.0	1.1	1.2	1.3	1.3	1.5	0.2	–0.3
Aged 25 to 34	2.8	2.8	2.5	2.5	2.5	2.7	2.7	2.6	2.8	0.3	0.0
Aged 35 to 44	4.6	4.5	4.2	4.3	4.5	4.8	4.5	4.4	4.1	0.3	0.5
Aged 45 to 54	6.7	6.4	6.5	7.3	7.2	7.0	6.7	6.8	6.3	–0.6	0.4
Aged 55 to 64	9.2	9.2	9.6	9.9	9.6	10.0	9.9	9.7	9.8	–0.7	–0.6
Aged 65 or older	9.5	9.6	9.4	9.7	8.7	8.4	9.5	9.9	10.1	–0.2	–0.6

Source: Bureau of Labor Statistics, Current Population Surveys, Employee Tenure, Internet site http://www.bls.gov/news.release/ tenure.toc.htm; calculations by New Strategist

Table 6.33 Long-Term Jobs by Sex and Age, 1983 to 2006

(percent of employed wage and salary workers aged 25 or older who have been with their current employer for 10 years or more, by sex and age, 1983 to 2006; percentage point change for selected years)

	2006	2004	2002	2000	1998	1996	1991	1987	1983	percentage point change 2000–06	percentage point change 1983–06
Total employed men	**31.1%**	**32.4%**	**32.6%**	**33.4%**	**32.7%**	**33.1%**	**35.9%**	**35.0%**	**37.7%**	**−2.3**	**−6.6**
Aged 25 to 29	2.6	2.7	2.6	3.0	3.1	3.3	5.7	4.5	4.0	−0.4	−1.4
Aged 30 to 34	11.6	11.9	13.0	15.1	15.3	15.6	21.1	18.7	18.7	−3.5	−7.1
Aged 35 to 39	24.7	24.9	27.2	29.4	29.7	30.5	35.6	34.8	36.9	−4.7	−12.2
Aged 40 to 44	34.8	36.2	37.4	40.2	39.1	41.7	46.3	48.5	51.1	−5.4	−16.3
Aged 45 to 49	42.9	48.1	45.4	49.0	47.4	50.8	53.5	53.0	57.8	−6.1	−14.9
Aged 50 to 54	49.7	53.0	54.0	51.6	52.8	54.9	58.5	59.4	62.3	−1.9	−12.6
Aged 55 to 59	51.0	53.4	56.5	53.7	56.5	55.7	61.0	63.2	66.2	−2.7	−15.2
Aged 60 to 64	48.1	48.5	48.4	52.4	55.7	50.4	57.5	58.7	65.6	−4.3	−17.5
Aged 65 or older	47.2	46.8	46.4	48.6	42.3	47.6	42.6	47.4	47.6	−1.4	−0.4
Total employed women	**28.8**	**28.6**	**28.8**	**29.5**	**28.4**	**27.6**	**28.2**	**25.7**	**24.9**	**−0.7**	**3.9**
Aged 25 to 29	2.1	1.9	1.8	1.9	2.2	2.2	4.4	3.6	2.5	0.2	−0.4
Aged 30 to 34	9.4	9.8	10.2	12.5	14.0	13.6	17.3	14.7	14.8	−3.1	−5.4
Aged 35 to 39	20.5	21.3	22.9	22.3	24.0	22.9	26.1	23.8	21.6	−1.8	−1.1
Aged 40 to 44	28.4	28.5	30.2	31.2	31.8	30.4	32.0	27.9	23.4	−2.8	5.0
Aged 45 to 49	36.9	36.2	37.0	41.4	38.4	38.1	39.3	36.4	33.0	−4.5	3.9
Aged 50 to 54	43.6	44.1	44.8	45.8	44.6	45.8	43.4	43.0	42.5	−2.2	1.1
Aged 55 to 59	49.1	48.4	49.9	52.5	49.2	52.1	51.4	50.8	51.0	−3.4	−1.9
Aged 60 to 64	48.7	51.0	52.6	53.6	53.0	52.7	53.1	52.4	52.6	−4.9	−3.9
Aged 65 or older	49.9	50.7	49.7	51.0	47.7	47.2	49.9	53.1	54.5	−1.1	−4.6

Source: Bureau of Labor Statistics, Current Population Surveys, Employee Tenure, Internet site http://www.bls.gov/news.release/tenure.toc.htm; calculations by New Strategist

More Cars, Less Carpooling

Few people walk to work.

Despite the efforts of many to encourage carpooling and the use of public transportation for the commute to work, Americans are increasingly likely to drive alone to their jobs. In 2005, 77 percent of workers drove to work alone versus the 64 percent who did so in 1980. The percentage of workers who carpool fell from 20 percent in 1980 to 11 percent in 2005.

Most other means of transportation to work have also experienced declines over the decades. The percentage of people who use public transportation stood at 5 percent in 2005, down from 12 percent in 1960. The percentage of Americans who walk to work fell from 10 to 2 percent during those years as suburban sprawl increased the distance between home and work.

■ Since 1980, the percentage of people who work at home has increased, rising from 2 to 4 percent. Nearly 5 million people worked at home in 2005.

More people are driving alone to work

(percentage of workers aged 16 or older who drive to work alone, 1980 to 2005)

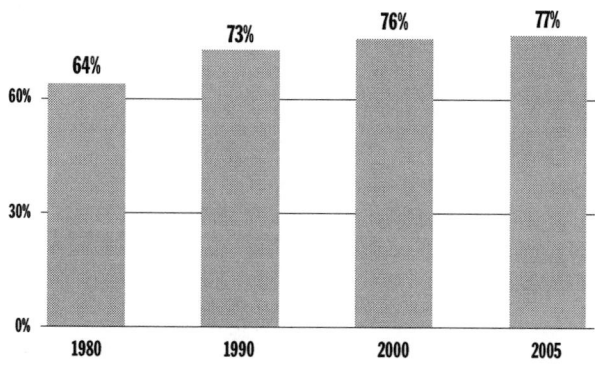

Table 6.34 Transportation to Work, 1960 to 2005

(number and percent distribution of workers aged 16 or older by primary means of transportation to work, 1960 to 2005; percent change in number and percentage point change in distribution, for selected years; numbers in thousands)

	2005	2000	1990	1980	1970	1960	percent change 2000–05	percent change 1960–05
Total workers	**133,091**	**128,279**	**115,070**	**96,617**	**76,852**	**64,656**	**3.8%**	**105.8%**
Car, truck, or van	116,658	112,736	99,593	81,258	59,723	41,368	3.5	182.0
Drove alone	102,458	97,102	84,215	62,193	–	–	5.5	–
Carpooled	14,200	15,634	15,378	19,065	–	–	–9.2	–
Public transportation	6,202	6,068	6,070	6,175	6,810	7,807	2.2	–20.6
Walked only	3,291	3,759	4,489	5,413	5,690	6,416	–12.5	–48.7
Other means	2,143	1,532	1,513	1,590	1,944	1,620	39.9	32.3
Worked at home	4,796	4,184	3,406	2,180	2,685	4,663	14.6	2.9

	2005	2000	1990	1980	1970	1960	percentage point change 2000–05	percentage point change 1960–05
Total workers	**100.0%**	**100.0%**	**100.0%**	**100.0%**	**100.0%**	**100.0%**	–	–
Car, truck, or van	87.7	87.9	86.5	84.1	77.7	64.0	–0.2	23.7
Drove alone	77.0	75.7	73.2	64.4	–	–	1.3	–
Carpooled	10.7	12.2	13.4	19.7	–	–	–1.5	–
Public transportation	4.7	4.7	5.3	6.4	8.9	12.1	–0.1	–7.4
Walked only	2.5	2.9	3.9	5.6	7.4	9.9	–0.5	–7.5
Other means	1.6	1.2	1.3	1.6	2.5	2.5	0.4	–0.9
Worked at home	3.6	3.3	3.0	2.3	3.5	7.2	0.3	–3.6

Note: Workers aged 14 or older in 1960 and 1970. Numbers in 1960 will not add to total because not reported is not shown. "–" means data are not available or not applicable.
Source: Bureau of the Census, Censuses of Population and Housing, Internet site http://www.census.gov/population/socdemo/ journey/mode6790.txt; and Census 2000 Demographic Profiles, Internet site http://www.census.gov/Press-Release/www/2002/ demoprofiles.html; and 2005 American Community Survey, Internet site http://www.census.gov/acs/www/; calculations by New Strategist

Most Workers Have Access to a Defined-Contribution Retirement Plan

Fewer than half participate in such a plan, however.

Sixty percent of the nation's workers in private industry had access to a retirement plan in 2006. The 54 percent majority had access to a defined-contribution plan, such as a 401(k), but only 43 percent participated in the plan. Only 21 percent of workers in private industry had access to a defined-benefit retirement plan, a figure that has not changed much since 1999. Comparable benefit data are not available for years earlier than 1999 because the Bureau of Labor Statistics replaced the Employee Benefit Survey, which collected data separately from small and large employers, with the National Compensation Survey, which collects data on employers of all sizes.

Seventy-one percent of workers in private industry had access to medical care benefits in 2006. Most were required to contribute to the cost of medical coverage. For family benefits, the average monthly employee contribution was $297. Only 46 percent of workers in private industry receive dental benefits, while a larger 67 percent receive prescription drug benefits.

■ The percentage of workers represented by unions fell between 1983 and 2006, from 23 to 13 percent. With the strength of unions on the decline, employee benefits are not likely to improve much in the years ahead.

Most workers have access to retirement and medical benefits

(percent of workers in private industry with access to selected benefits, 2006)

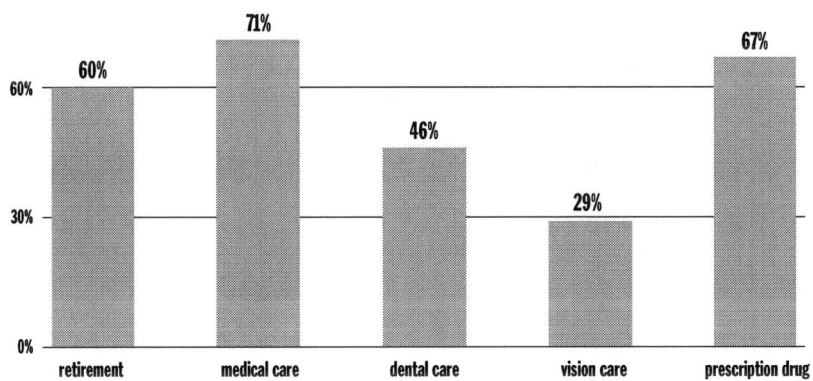

Table 6.35 Workers in Private Industry with Access to Employee Benefits, 2006

(percentage of workers in private industry with access to employee benefits, 2006)

Retirement benefits	**60%**
Defined-benefit penion plan	21
Defined-contribution plan	54
Health care benefits	
Medical care	71
Single coverage	
Employee contributions required	75
Average flat monthly contribution	$76.05
Family coverage	
Employee contributions required	87%
Average flat monthly contribution	$296.88
Dental care	46%
Vision care	29
Prescription drugs coverage	67
Paid leave	
Paid vacations	77
Paid holidays	76
Paid jury duty leave	70
Paid funeral leave	68
Paid sick leave	57
Paid military leave	48
Paid personal leave	37
Paid family leave	8
Other benefits	
Life insurance	52
Education assistance, work-related	49
Nonproduction bonus	46
Employee assistance programs	40
Short-term disability benefits	39
Health care reimbursement account	32
Long-term disability benefits	30
Dependent care reimbursement account	30
Wellness programs	23
Travel accident insurance	22
Flexible benefit plans	17
Employer assistance for child care	15
Education assistance, nonwork-related	14
Fitness centers	13
Long-term care insurance	12
Adoption assistance	10
Health savings accounts	6
Flexible work place	4

Source: Bureau of Labor Statistics, Employee Benefits in Private Industry, March 2006 Summary, National Compensation Survey, Internet site http://www.bls.gov/ncs/ebs/home.htm

Table 6.36   Workers in Private Industry Participating in Employee Benefits, 1999 to 2006

(percentage of all workers in private industry who participate in selected employee benefits, 1999 to 2006; percentage point change, 1999–2006)

	participating in defined-benefit pension plan	participating in defined-contribution retirement plan	participating in medical benefits	percent of employees required to contribute to single medical coverage
2006	20%	43%	52%	75%
2005	21	42	53	76
2004	21	42	53	76
2003	20	40	53	78
2000	19	36	52	68
1999	21	36	53	67
Percentage point change				
1999 to 2006	−1	7	−1	8

Source: Bureau of Labor Statistics, Employee Benefits Survey, Internet site http://www.bls.gov/ncs/ebs/home.htm; calculations by New Strategist

Table 6.37 **Workers in Private Industry with 100 or More Employees Who Participate in Employee Benefits, 1980 to 1997**

(percentage of workers in private industry with 100 or more employees who participate in selected employee benefits, 1980 to 1997; percentage point change, 1980–97)

	participating in defined-benefit pension plan	participating in defined-contribution retirement plan	participating in medical benefits	percent of employees required to contribute to single medical coverage
1997	50%	57%	76%	69%
1995	52	55	77	67
1993	56	49	82	61
1991	59	48	83	51
1989	63	48	92	47
1988	63	45	90	44
1986	76	60	95	43
1985	80	53	96	36
1984	82	–	97	36
1983	82	–	96	33
1982	84	–	97	27
1981	84	–	97	27
1980	84	–	97	26
Percentage point change				
1980 to 1997	–34	–	–21	43

Note: "–" means data are not available.
Source: Bureau of Labor Statistics, Employee Benefits Survey, Internet site http://www.bls.gov/ncs/ebs/home.htm; calculations by New Strategist

Table 6.38 Workers Represented by Unions, 1983 to 2006

(number and percent of employed wage and salary workers aged 16 or older represented by unions, 1983 to 2006; percent and percentage point change for selected years; numbers in thousands)

	number	percent
2006	16,860	13.1%
2005	17,223	13.7
2004	17,087	13.8
2003	17,448	14.3
2002	17,695	14.5
2001	18,026	14.7
2000	18,153	14.9
1999	18,182	15.3
1998	17,918	15.4
1997	17,923	15.6
1996	18,158	16.2
1995	18,346	16.7
1994	18,843	17.5
1993	18,646	17.7
1992	18,540	17.9
1991	18,734	18.2
1990	19,058	18.3
1989	19,198	18.6
1988	19,241	19.0
1985	19,358	20.5
1983	20,532	23.3

	percent change	percentage point change
2000 to 2006	−7.1%	−1.8
1983 to 2006	−17.9	−10.2

Source: Bureau of Labor Statistics, Labor Force Statistics from the Current Population Survey, Internet site http://www.bls.gov/ webapps/legacy/cpslutab1.htm; and Employment and Earnings for selected years; calculations by New Strategist

Living Arrangements

■ In 1950, married couples headed fully 78 percent of the nation's households. By 2006, the share was just 51 percent as lifestyles grew more diverse.

■ One of the biggest lifestyle changes of the past half-century is the disappearance of children from the nation's households. In 1950, nearly half—47 percent—of households included children under age 18. By 2006 the figure had fallen to just 32 percent.

■ Single-parent households have become much more numerous as divorce and out-of-wedlock births have become common. In 2006, only 67 percent of children lived with both parents, down from 88 percent in 1960.

■ Americans of all ages were more likely to live alone in 2006 than in 1970. The increase in lone living has been especially pronounced among women aged 75 or older, 48 percent of whom now live alone.

■ As young adults postponed marriage, the percentage of not-yet-married Americans grew enormously. Fully 75 percent of women aged 20 to 24 had not yet married in 2006, up from 32 percent in 1950.

Lifestyles Have Changed Dramatically

Married couples head barely half of households today.

Americans live differently than they once did. In 1950, married couples headed fully 78 percent of the nation's households. By 2006, the share was just 51 percent as lifestyles grew more diverse. In 1950, people who lived alone or with nonrelatives headed only 11 percent of households. Today, nonfamily households account for nearly one-third of the total. The share of households consisting of female- or male-headed families also grew during those years, rising from 11 to 17 percent.

The age distribution of householders has shifted less than household types over the years. Householders had a median age of 48 in 2006, just one year older than in 1960. The distribution of householders by age is similar to what it was in 1950, with one notable exception. The percentage of households headed by people aged 75 or older has nearly doubled in the past half-century, rising from 6 to 10 percent as Americans live longer.

To examine households historically by race of householder, it is necessary to revert to the simple categories used in the past—black and white. The black share of households grew from 10 percent in 1970 to 13 percent in 2006. The white share of households fell slightly over those years, from 89 to 82 percent. These figures include Hispanics, however, since most Hispanics are white. The Hispanic share of households has grown from just 4 percent in the mid-1970s to 11 percent today.

■ As baby boomers age into their sixties and seventies, the share of households headed by the elderly will greatly expand.

Married couples are a much smaller share of households

(percentage of households headed by married couples, 1950 and 2006)

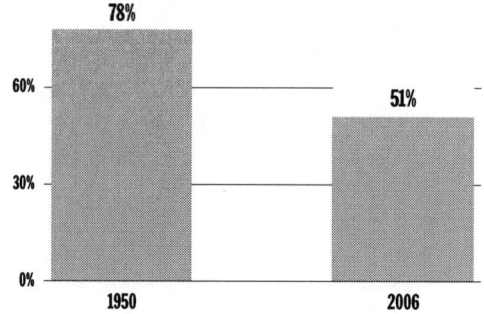

Table 7.1 Households by Type, 1950 to 2006

(number of households by type, 1950 to 2006; percent change for selected years; numbers in thousands)

	total households	family households				nonfamily households		
		total	married couples	female hh, no spouse present	male hh, no spouse present	total	female householder	male householder
2006	114,384	77,402	58,179	14,093	5,130	36,982	20,230	16,753
2005	113,343	76,858	57,975	13,981	4,901	36,485	19,942	16,543
2004	112,000	76,217	57,719	13,781	4,716	35,783	19,647	16,136
2003	111,278	75,596	57,320	13,620	4,656	35,682	19,662	16,020
2002	109,297	74,329	56,747	13,143	4,438	34,969	19,390	15,579
2001	108,209	73,767	56,592	12,900	4,275	34,442	19,097	15,345
2000	104,705	72,025	55,311	12,687	4,028	32,680	18,039	14,641
1999	103,874	71,535	54,770	12,789	3,976	32,339	17,971	14,368
1998	102,528	70,880	54,317	12,652	3,911	31,648	17,516	14,133
1997	101,018	70,241	53,604	12,790	3,847	30,777	17,070	13,707
1996	99,627	69,594	53,567	12,514	3,513	30,033	16,685	13,348
1995	98,990	69,305	53,858	12,220	3,226	29,686	16,496	13,190
1994	97,107	68,490	53,171	12,406	2,913	28,617	16,155	12,462
1993	96,426	68,216	53,090	12,061	3,065	28,210	15,914	12,297
1992	95,669	67,173	52,457	11,692	3,025	28,496	16,068	12,428
1991	94,312	66,322	52,147	11,268	2,907	27,990	15,840	12,150
1990	93,347	66,090	52,317	10,890	2,884	27,257	15,651	11,606
1989	92,830	65,837	52,100	10,890	2,847	26,994	15,120	11,874
1988	91,124	65,204	51,675	10,696	2,834	25,919	14,637	11,282
1987	89,479	64,491	51,537	10,445	2,510	24,988	14,336	10,652
1986	88,458	63,558	50,933	10,211	2,414	24,900	14,252	10,648
1985	86,789	62,706	50,350	10,129	2,228	24,082	13,968	10,114
1984	85,290	62,015	50,081	9,896	2,038	23,276	13,587	9,689
1983	83,918	61,393	49,908	9,469	2,016	22,525	13,011	9,514
1982	83,527	61,019	49,630	9,403	1,986	22,508	13,051	9,457
1981	82,368	60,309	49,294	9,082	1,933	22,059	12,780	9,279
1980	80,776	59,550	49,112	8,705	1,733	21,226	12,419	8,807
1979	77,330	57,498	47,662	8,220	1,616	19,831	11,767	8,064
1978	76,030	56,958	47,357	8,037	1,564	19,071	11,261	7,811
1977	74,142	56,472	47,471	7,540	1,461	17,669	10,698	6,971
1976	72,867	56,056	47,297	7,335	1,424	16,811	10,263	6,548
1975	71,120	55,563	46,951	7,127	1,485	15,557	9,645	5,912
1974	69,859	54,917	46,787	6,709	1,421	14,942	9,288	5,654
1973	68,251	54,264	46,297	6,535	1,432	13,986	8,858	5,129
1972	66,676	53,163	45,724	6,108	1,331	13,513	8,674	4,839
1971	64,778	52,102	44,928	5,920	1,254	12,676	8,273	4,403
1970	63,401	51,456	44,728	5,500	1,228	11,945	7,882	4,063
1965	57,436	47,838	41,689	4,982	1,167	9,598	6,321	3,277
1960	52,799	44,905	39,254	4,422	1,228	7,895	5,179	2,716
1955	47,874	41,732	36,251	4,153	1,328	6,142	4,083	2,059
1950	43,554	38,838	34,075	3,594	1,169	4,716	3,048	1,668
Percent change								
2000 to 2006	9.2%	7.5%	5.2%	11.1%	27.4%	13.2%	12.1%	14.4%
1950 to 2006	162.6	99.3	70.7	292.1	338.8	684.2	563.7	904.4

Source: Bureau of the Census, Families and Living Arrangements, Historical Tables—Households, Internet site http://www .census.gov/population/www/socdemo/hh-fam.html; calculations by New Strategist

Table 7.2 Distribution of Households by Type, 1950 to 2006

(percent distribution of households by type, 1950 to 2006; percentage point change for selected years)

	total households	family households				nonfamily households		
		total	married couples	female hh, no spouse present	male hh, no spouse present	total	female householder	male householder
2006	100.0%	67.7%	50.9%	12.3%	4.5%	32.3%	17.7%	14.6%
2005	100.0	67.8	51.2	12.3	4.3	32.2	17.6	14.6
2004	100.0	68.1	51.5	12.3	4.2	31.9	17.5	14.4
2003	100.0	67.9	51.5	12.2	4.2	32.1	17.7	14.4
2002	100.0	68.0	51.9	12.0	4.1	32.0	17.7	14.3
2001	100.0	68.2	52.3	11.9	4.0	31.8	17.6	14.2
2000	100.0	68.8	52.8	12.1	3.8	31.2	17.2	14.0
1999	100.0	68.9	52.7	12.3	3.8	31.1	17.3	13.8
1998	100.0	69.1	53.0	12.3	3.8	30.9	17.1	13.8
1997	100.0	69.5	53.1	12.7	3.8	30.5	16.9	13.6
1996	100.0	69.9	53.8	12.6	3.5	30.1	16.7	13.4
1995	100.0	70.0	54.4	12.3	3.3	30.0	16.7	13.3
1994	100.0	70.5	54.8	12.8	3.0	29.5	16.6	12.8
1993	100.0	70.7	55.1	12.5	3.2	29.3	16.5	12.8
1992	100.0	70.2	54.8	12.2	3.2	29.8	16.8	13.0
1991	100.0	70.3	55.3	11.9	3.1	29.7	16.8	12.9
1990	100.0	70.8	56.0	11.7	3.1	29.2	16.8	12.4
1989	100.0	70.9	56.1	11.7	3.1	29.1	16.3	12.8
1988	100.0	71.6	56.7	11.7	3.1	28.4	16.1	12.4
1987	100.0	72.1	57.6	11.7	2.8	27.9	16.0	11.9
1986	100.0	71.9	57.6	11.5	2.7	28.1	16.1	12.0
1985	100.0	72.3	58.0	11.7	2.6	27.7	16.1	11.7
1984	100.0	72.7	58.7	11.6	2.4	27.3	15.9	11.4
1983	100.0	73.2	59.5	11.3	2.4	26.8	15.5	11.3
1982	100.0	73.1	59.4	11.3	2.4	26.9	15.6	11.3
1981	100.0	73.2	59.8	11.0	2.3	26.8	15.5	11.3
1980	100.0	73.7	60.8	10.8	2.1	26.3	15.4	10.9
1979	100.0	74.4	61.6	10.6	2.1	25.6	15.2	10.4
1978	100.0	74.9	62.3	10.6	2.1	25.1	14.8	10.3
1977	100.0	76.2	64.0	10.2	2.0	23.8	14.4	9.4
1976	100.0	76.9	64.9	10.1	2.0	23.1	14.1	9.0
1975	100.0	78.1	66.0	10.0	2.1	21.9	13.6	8.3
1974	100.0	78.6	67.0	9.6	2.0	21.4	13.3	8.1
1973	100.0	79.5	67.8	9.6	2.1	20.5	13.0	7.5
1972	100.0	79.7	68.6	9.2	2.0	20.3	13.0	7.3
1971	100.0	80.4	69.4	9.1	1.9	19.6	12.8	6.8
1970	100.0	81.2	70.5	8.7	1.9	18.8	12.4	6.4
1965	100.0	83.3	72.6	8.7	2.0	16.7	11.0	5.7
1960	100.0	85.0	74.3	8.4	2.3	15.0	9.8	5.1
1955	100.0	87.2	75.7	8.7	2.8	12.8	8.5	4.3
1950	100.0	89.2	78.2	8.3	2.7	10.8	7.0	3.8

Percentage point change

2000 to 2006	–	–1.1	–2.0	0.2	0.6	1.1	0.5	0.7
1950 to 2006	–	–21.5	–27.4	4.1	1.8	21.5	10.7	10.8

Note: "–" means not applicable.
Source: Bureau of the Census, Families and Living Arrangements, Historical Tables—Households, Internet site http://www
.census.gov/population/www/socdemo/hh-fam.html; calculations by New Strategist

Table 7.3 Households by Age of Householder, 1960 to 2006

(number of households by age of householder, and median age of householders, 1960 to 2006; percent change for selected years; numbers in thousands)

	total households	< 25	25–29	30–34	35–44	45–54	55–64	65–74	75+	median age
2006	114,384	6,795	9,223	9,896	23,016	23,732	18,264	11,687	11,772	48.3 yrs.
2005	113,343	6,734	9,173	10,141	23,248	23,392	17,503	11,528	11,623	48.0
2004	112,000	6,609	8,738	10,421	23,221	23,138	16,824	11,499	11,550	47.8
2003	111,278	6,611	8,535	10,521	24,069	22,623	16,261	11,361	11,299	47.5
2002	109,297	6,391	8,412	10,576	24,031	22,208	15,203	11,472	11,004	47.2
2001	108,209	6,409	8,521	10,510	24,054	21,969	14,277	11,490	10,979	47.0
2000	104,705	5,860	8,520	10,107	23,955	20,927	13,592	11,325	10,419	46.8
1999	103,874	5,770	8,519	10,300	23,969	20,158	13,571	11,373	10,216	46.6
1998	102,528	5,435	8,463	10,570	23,943	19,547	13,072	11,272	10,225	46.3
1997	101,018	5,160	8,647	10,667	23,823	18,843	12,469	11,679	9,729	46.1
1996	99,627	5,282	8,354	10,871	23,227	18,007	12,401	11,908	9,578	46.0
1995	98,990	5,444	8,400	11,052	22,914	17,590	12,224	11,803	9,562	45.9
1994	97,107	5,265	8,472	11,245	22,293	16,837	12,188	11,639	9,168	45.7
1993	96,426	5,257	8,859	11,198	21,862	16,413	12,154	11,668	9,014	45.6
1992	95,669	4,859	8,810	11,197	21,774	15,547	12,559	12,043	8,878	45.7
1991	94,312	4,882	9,246	11,077	21,304	14,751	12,524	12,001	8,526	45.4
1990	93,347	5,121	9,423	11,049	20,555	14,514	12,529	11,733	8,423	45.3
1989	92,830	5,415	9,624	11,300	19,952	14,018	12,805	11,590	8,127	45.1
1988	91,124	5,228	9,614	10,969	19,323	13,630	12,846	11,410	8,045	45.3
1987	89,479	5,197	9,652	10,850	18,703	13,211	12,868	11,250	7,748	45.3
1986	88,458	5,503	9,781	10,629	17,997	13,099	12,852	11,157	7,439	45.2
1985	86,789	5,438	9,637	10,377	17,481	12,628	13,073	10,851	7,305	45.4
1984	85,290	5,510	9,848	9,960	16,596	12,471	13,121	10,700	7,201	45.6
1983	83,918	5,695	9,465	9,639	16,020	12,354	13,074	10,603	7,067	45.9
1982	83,527	6,109	9,525	9,802	15,326	12,505	12,947	10,379	6,933	45.8
1981	82,368	6,443	9,514	9,639	14,463	12,694	12,704	10,226	6,685	45.9
1980	80,776	6,569	9,252	9,252	13,980	12,654	12,525	10,112	6,432	46.1
1979	77,330	6,342	8,679	8,317	13,328	12,585	12,284	9,753	6,042	46.6
1978	76,030	6,220	8,598	8,233	12,969	12,602	12,183	9,383	5,842	46.6
1977	74,142	5,991	8,385	7,782	12,482	12,905	11,780	9,210	5,606	46.9
1976	72,867	5,877	8,298	7,212	12,227	12,820	11,631	9,258	5,544	47.2
1975	71,120	5,834	7,810	7,137	11,861	12,916	11,301	8,910	5,350	47.3
1974	69,859	5,857	7,527	6,804	11,703	12,939	11,149	8,716	5,162	47.3
1973	68,251	5,476	7,116	6,447	11,721	12,805	11,212	8,369	5,104	47.6
1972	66,676	5,194	6,794	6,009	11,529	12,758	11,138	8,165	5,090	48.0
1971	64,778	4,737	6,239	5,682	11,813	12,588	11,021	7,793	4,909	48.1
1970	63,401	4,359	6,101	5,593	11,810	12,216	10,824	7,744	4,756	48.1
1969	62,214	4,094	5,910	5,447	11,817	12,230	10,622	7,540	4,554	48.1
1968	60,813	3,852	5,336	5,325	12,003	12,038	10,394	7,536	4,327	48.2
1967	59,236	3,587	5,288	5,099	11,998	11,892	9,909	7,321	4,143	48.1
1966	58,406	3,571	4,991	5,086	11,944	11,806	9,745	7,224	4,038	48.1
1965	57,436	3,413	4,808	5,119	12,009	11,523	9,600	7,173	3,790	47.9
1960	52,799	2,559	4,317	5,407	11,614	10,878	8,599	6,380	3,045	47.3

Percent change

	total households	< 25	25–29	30–34	35–44	45–54	55–64	65–74	75+	median age
2000 to 2006	9.2%	16.0%	8.3%	–2.1%	–3.9%	13.4%	34.4%	3.2%	13.0%	–
1960 to 2006	116.6	165.5	113.6	83.0	98.2	118.2	112.4	83.2	286.6	–

Note: "–" means not applicable.
*Source: Bureau of the Census, Families and Living Arrangements, Historical Tables—Households, Internet site http://www
.census.gov/population/www/socdemo/hh-fam.html; calculations by New Strategist*

Table 7.4 Distribution of Households by Age of Householder, 1960 to 2006

(percent distribution of households by age of householder, 1960 to 2006; percentage point change for selected years)

	total households	< 25	25–29	30–34	35–44	45–54	55–64	65–74	75+
2006	100.0%	5.9%	8.1%	8.7%	20.1%	20.7%	16.0%	10.2%	10.3%
2005	100.0	5.9	8.1	8.9	20.5	20.6	15.4	10.2	10.3
2004	100.0	5.9	7.8	9.3	20.7	20.7	15.0	10.3	10.3
2003	100.0	5.9	7.7	9.5	21.6	20.3	14.6	10.2	10.2
2002	100.0	5.8	7.7	9.7	22.0	20.3	13.9	10.5	10.1
2001	100.0	5.9	7.9	9.7	22.2	20.3	13.2	10.6	10.1
2000	100.0	5.6	8.1	9.7	22.9	20.0	13.0	10.8	10.0
1999	100.0	5.6	8.2	9.9	23.1	19.4	13.1	10.9	9.8
1998	100.0	5.3	8.3	10.3	23.4	19.1	12.7	11.0	10.0
1997	100.0	5.1	8.6	10.6	23.6	18.7	12.3	11.6	9.6
1996	100.0	5.3	8.4	10.9	23.3	18.1	12.4	12.0	9.6
1995	100.0	5.5	8.5	11.2	23.1	17.8	12.3	11.9	9.7
1994	100.0	5.4	8.7	11.6	23.0	17.3	12.6	12.0	9.4
1993	100.0	5.5	9.2	11.6	22.7	17.0	12.6	12.1	9.3
1992	100.0	5.1	9.2	11.7	22.8	16.3	13.1	12.6	9.3
1991	100.0	5.2	9.8	11.7	22.6	15.6	13.3	12.7	9.0
1990	100.0	5.5	10.1	11.8	22.0	15.5	13.4	12.6	9.0
1989	100.0	5.8	10.4	12.2	21.5	15.1	13.8	12.5	8.8
1988	100.0	5.7	10.6	12.0	21.2	15.0	14.1	12.5	8.8
1987	100.0	5.8	10.8	12.1	20.9	14.8	14.4	12.6	8.7
1986	100.0	6.2	11.1	12.0	20.3	14.8	14.5	12.6	8.4
1985	100.0	6.3	11.1	12.0	20.1	14.6	15.1	12.5	8.4
1984	100.0	6.5	11.5	11.7	19.5	14.6	15.4	12.5	8.4
1983	100.0	6.8	11.3	11.5	19.1	14.7	15.6	12.6	8.4
1982	100.0	7.3	11.4	11.7	18.3	15.0	15.5	12.4	8.3
1981	100.0	7.8	11.6	11.7	17.6	15.4	15.4	12.4	8.1
1980	100.0	8.1	11.5	11.5	17.3	15.7	15.5	12.5	8.0
1979	100.0	8.2	11.2	10.8	17.2	16.3	15.9	12.6	7.8
1978	100.0	8.2	11.3	10.8	17.1	16.6	16.0	12.3	7.7
1977	100.0	8.1	11.3	10.5	16.8	17.4	15.9	12.4	7.6
1976	100.0	8.1	11.4	9.9	16.8	17.6	16.0	12.7	7.6
1975	100.0	8.2	11.0	10.0	16.7	18.2	15.9	12.5	7.5
1974	100.0	8.4	10.8	9.7	16.8	18.5	16.0	12.5	7.4
1973	100.0	8.0	10.4	9.4	17.2	18.8	16.4	12.3	7.5
1972	100.0	7.8	10.2	9.0	17.3	19.1	16.7	12.2	7.6
1971	100.0	7.3	9.6	8.8	18.2	19.4	17.0	12.0	7.6
1970	100.0	6.9	9.6	8.8	18.6	19.3	17.1	12.2	7.5
1969	100.0	6.6	9.5	8.8	19.0	19.7	17.1	12.1	7.3
1968	100.0	6.3	8.8	8.8	19.7	19.8	17.1	12.4	7.1
1967	100.0	6.1	8.9	8.6	20.3	20.1	16.7	12.4	7.0
1966	100.0	6.1	8.5	8.7	20.4	20.2	16.7	12.4	6.9
1965	100.0	5.9	8.4	8.9	20.9	20.1	16.7	12.5	6.6
1960	100.0	4.8	8.2	10.2	22.0	20.6	16.3	12.1	5.8

Percentage point change

2000 to 2006	–	0.3	–0.1	–1.0	–2.8	0.8	3.0	–0.6	0.3
1960 to 2006	–	1.1	–0.1	–1.6	–1.9	0.1	–0.3	–1.9	4.5

Note: "–" means not applicable.
Source: Bureau of the Census, Families and Living Arrangements, Historical Tables—Households, Internet site http://www
.census.gov/population/www/socdemo/hh-fam.html; calculations by New Strategist

Table 7.5 Households by Race and Hispanic Origin of Householder, 1970 to 2006

(number and percent distribution of households by race and Hispanic origin of householder, 1970 to 2006; percent and percentage point change for selected years; numbers in thousands)

| | number of households | | | | percent distribution | | | |
	total	black	Hispanic	white	total	black	Hispanic	white
2006	114,384	14,399	12,519	93,588	100.0%	12.6%	10.9%	81.8%
2005	113,343	14,151	12,178	92,880	100.0	12.5	10.7	81.9
2004	112,000	13,969	11,692	91,962	100.0	12.5	10.4	82.1
2003	111,278	13,778	11,339	91,645	100.0	12.4	10.2	82.4
2002	109,297	13,315	10,499	90,682	100.0	12.2	9.6	83.0
2001	108,209	13,174	10,034	90,030	100.0	12.2	9.3	83.2
2000	104,705	12,849	9,319	87,671	100.0	12.3	8.9	83.7
1999	103,874	12,579	9,060	87,212	100.0	12.1	8.7	84.0
1998	102,528	12,474	8,590	86,106	100.0	12.2	8.4	84.0
1997	101,018	12,109	8,225	85,059	100.0	12.0	8.1	84.2
1996	99,627	11,577	7,939	84,511	100.0	11.6	8.0	84.8
1995	98,990	11,655	7,735	83,737	100.0	11.8	7.8	84.6
1994	97,107	11,281	7,362	82,387	100.0	11.6	7.6	84.8
1993	96,391	11,190	6,626	82,083	100.0	11.6	6.9	85.2
1992	95,669	11,083	6,379	81,675	100.0	11.6	6.7	85.4
1991	94,312	10,671	6,220	80,968	100.0	11.3	6.6	85.9
1990	93,347	10,486	5,933	80,163	100.0	11.2	6.4	85.9
1989	92,830	10,561	5,910	79,734	100.0	11.4	6.4	85.9
1988	91,066	10,186	5,698	78,469	100.0	11.2	6.3	86.2
1987	89,479	9,922	5,418	77,284	100.0	11.1	6.1	86.4
1986	88,458	9,797	5,213	76,576	100.0	11.1	5.9	86.6
1985	86,789	9,480	4,883	75,328	100.0	10.9	5.6	86.8
1984	85,407	9,236	4,326	74,376	100.0	10.8	5.1	87.1
1983	83,918	8,916	4,085	73,182	100.0	10.6	4.9	87.2
1982	83,527	8,961	3,980	72,845	100.0	10.7	4.8	87.2
1981	82,368	8,847	3,906	71,872	100.0	10.7	4.7	87.3
1980	80,776	8,586	3,684	70,766	100.0	10.6	4.6	87.6
1979	77,330	8,066	3,291	68,028	100.0	10.4	4.3	88.0
1978	76,030	7,977	3,304	66,934	100.0	10.5	4.3	88.0
1977	74,142	7,776	3,081	65,353	100.0	10.5	4.2	88.1
1976	72,867	7,486	2,948	64,392	100.0	10.3	4.0	88.4
1975	71,120	7,262	–	62,945	100.0	10.2	–	88.5
1974	69,859	7,040	–	61,965	100.0	10.1	–	88.7
1973	68,251	6,809	–	60,618	100.0	10.0	–	88.8
1972	66,676	6,578	–	59,463	100.0	9.9	–	89.2
1971	64,374	6,180	–	57,575	100.0	9.6	–	89.4
1970	63,401	6,223	–	56,602	100.0	9.8	–	89.3

	percent change				percentage point change			
2000 to 2006	9.2%	12.1%	34.3%	6.7%	–	0.3	2.0	–1.9
1970 to 2006	80.4	131.4	–	65.3	–	2.8	–	–7.5

Note: Numbers will not add to total because Hispanics may be of any race and not all races are shown. Beginning in 2003, figures for blacks are for those who identify themselves as being of the race alone and those who identify themselves as being of the race in combination with one or more other races. Beginning in 2003, white figures are for those who identify themselves as being of the race alone. "–" means data are not available or not applicable.
Source: Bureau of the Census, Families and Living Arrangements, Historical Tables—Households, Internet site http://www .census.gov/population/www/socdemo/hh-fam.html; calculations by New Strategist

Fewer Households include Children

Less than one-third of households are home to children under age 18.

One of the biggest lifestyle changes of the past half-century is the disappearance of children from the nation's households. In 1950, nearly half—47 percent—of households included children under age 18. By 2006 the figure had fallen to just 32 percent. Even more dramatic, the nuclear family (married couples with children under age 18 at home) share of households fell from 43 to just 23 percent during those years. Only 6 percent of households include three or more children today, down from 17 percent in 1960.

With fewer households including children, and fewer children per household, household size has fallen. In 1950, the average household contained 3.37 people. By 2006, average household size was just 2.57 people. The share of households containing only one or two people climbed from 40 to 60 percent. Today, single-person households outnumber nuclear families.

■ The number of single-person households will grow rapidly as boomers age into their sixties and seventies.

Nuclear families are a small share of households today

(percentage of households containing married couples with children under age 18, 1950 and 2006)

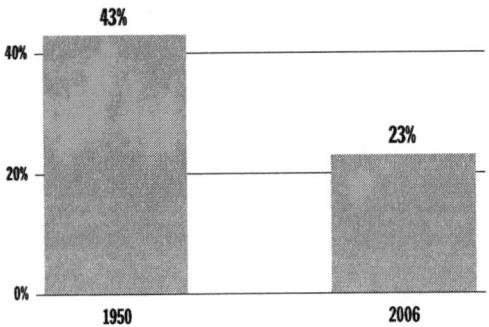

Table 7.6 Households with Children under Age 18 by Household Type, 1950 to 2006

(number of households by presence of own children under age 18 at home, 1950 to 2006; percent change for selected years; numbers in thousands)

| | total households | families with children under age 18 | | | | |
		total	married couples	total	mother only	father only
				single parent		
2006	114,384	36,466	25,982	10,484	8,389	2,095
2005	113,343	36,211	25,919	10,291	8,270	2,021
2004	112,000	35,944	25,793	10,152	8,221	1,931
2003	111,278	35,968	25,914	10,054	8,139	1,915
2002	109,297	35,705	25,792	9,913	8,010	1,903
2001	108,209	35,355	25,980	9,374	7,538	1,836
2000	104,705	34,605	25,248	9,357	7,571	1,786
1999	103,874	34,613	25,066	9,547	7,841	1,706
1998	102,528	34,760	25,269	9,491	7,693	1,798
1997	101,018	34,665	25,083	9,583	7,874	1,709
1996	99,627	34,203	24,920	9,284	7,656	1,628
1995	98,990	34,296	25,241	9,055	7,615	1,440
1994	97,107	34,018	25,058	8,961	7,647	1,314
1993	96,426	33,257	24,707	8,550	7,226	1,324
1992	95,669	32,746	24,420	8,326	7,043	1,283
1991	94,312	32,401	24,397	8,004	6,823	1,181
1990	93,347	32,289	24,537	7,752	6,599	1,153
1989	92,830	32,322	24,735	7,587	6,519	1,068
1988	91,124	31,920	24,600	7,320	6,273	1,047
1987	89,479	31,898	24,646	7,252	6,297	955
1986	88,458	31,670	24,630	7,040	6,105	935
1985	86,789	31,112	24,210	6,902	6,006	896
1984	85,290	31,046	24,340	6,706	5,907	799
1983	83,918	30,818	24,363	6,455	5,718	737
1982	83,527	31,012	24,465	6,547	5,868	679
1981	82,368	31,227	24,927	6,300	5,634	666
1980	80,776	31,022	24,961	6,061	5,445	616
1979	77,330	30,371	24,514	5,857	5,288	569
1978	76,030	30,369	24,625	5,744	5,206	539
1977	74,142	30,145	24,875	5,270	4,784	486
1976	72,867	30,177	25,110	5,067	4,621	446
1975	71,120	30,057	25,169	4,888	4,404	484
1974	69,859	29,750	25,278	4,472	4,081	391
1973	68,251	29,571	25,387	4,184	3,798	386
1972	66,676	29,445	25,482	3,963	3,598	365
1971	64,778	28,786	25,091	3,695	3,365	331
1970	63,401	28,812	25,541	3,271	2,971	345
1965	57,436	27,140	24,406	2,734	2,485	249
1960	52,799	25,690	23,358	2,332	2,099	232
1955	47,874	23,190	21,064	2,126	1,870	256
1950	43,554	20,324	18,824	1,500	1,272	229
Percent change						
2000 to 2006	9.2%	5.4%	2.9%	12.0%	10.8%	17.3%
1950 to 2006	162.6	79.4	38.0	598.9	559.5	814.8

Source: Bureau of the Census, Families and Living Arrangements, Historical Tables—Households, Internet site http://www .census.gov/population/www/socdemo/hh-fam.html; calculations by New Strategist

Table 7.7 Distribution of Households with Children under Age 18 by Household Type, 1950 to 2006

(percent distribution of households by presence of own children under age 18 at home, 1950 to 2006; percentage point change for selected years)

| | | families with children under age 18 | | | | |
| | | | | single parent | | |
	total households	total	married couples	total	mother only	father only
2006	100.0%	31.9%	22.7%	9.2%	7.3%	1.8%
2005	100.0	31.9	22.9	9.1	7.3	1.8
2004	100.0	32.1	23.0	9.1	7.3	1.7
2003	100.0	32.3	23.3	9.0	7.3	1.7
2002	100.0	32.7	23.6	9.1	7.3	1.7
2001	100.0	32.7	24.0	8.7	7.0	1.7
2000	100.0	33.0	24.1	8.9	7.2	1.7
1999	100.0	33.3	24.1	9.2	7.5	1.6
1998	100.0	33.9	24.6	9.3	7.5	1.8
1997	100.0	34.3	24.8	9.5	7.8	1.7
1996	100.0	34.3	25.0	9.3	7.7	1.6
1995	100.0	34.6	25.5	9.1	7.7	1.5
1994	100.0	35.0	25.8	9.2	7.9	1.4
1993	100.0	34.5	25.6	8.9	7.5	1.4
1992	100.0	34.2	25.5	8.7	7.4	1.3
1991	100.0	34.4	25.9	8.5	7.2	1.3
1990	100.0	34.6	26.3	8.3	7.1	1.2
1989	100.0	34.8	26.6	8.2	7.0	1.2
1988	100.0	35.0	27.0	8.0	6.9	1.1
1987	100.0	35.6	27.5	8.1	7.0	1.1
1986	100.0	35.8	27.8	8.0	6.9	1.1
1985	100.0	35.8	27.9	8.0	6.9	1.0
1984	100.0	36.4	28.5	7.9	6.9	0.9
1983	100.0	36.7	29.0	7.7	6.8	0.9
1982	100.0	37.1	29.3	7.8	7.0	0.8
1981	100.0	37.9	30.3	7.6	6.8	0.8
1980	100.0	38.4	30.9	7.5	6.7	0.8
1979	100.0	39.3	31.7	7.6	6.8	0.7
1978	100.0	39.9	32.4	7.6	6.8	0.7
1977	100.0	40.7	33.6	7.1	6.5	0.7
1976	100.0	41.4	34.5	7.0	6.3	0.6
1975	100.0	42.3	35.4	6.9	6.2	0.7
1974	100.0	42.6	36.2	6.4	5.8	0.6
1973	100.0	43.3	37.2	6.1	5.6	0.6
1972	100.0	44.2	38.2	5.9	5.4	0.5
1971	100.0	44.4	38.7	5.7	5.2	0.5
1970	100.0	45.4	40.3	5.2	4.7	0.5
1965	100.0	47.3	42.5	4.8	4.3	0.4
1960	100.0	48.7	44.2	4.4	4.0	0.4
1955	100.0	48.4	44.0	4.4	3.9	0.5
1950	100.0	46.7	43.2	3.4	2.9	0.5
Percentage point change						
2000 to 2006	–	–1.2	–1.4	0.2	0.1	0.1
1950 to 2006	–	–14.8	–20.5	5.7	4.4	1.3

Note: "–" means not applicable.
Source: Bureau of the Census, Families and Living Arrangements, Historical Tables—Households, Internet site http://www
.census.gov/population/www/socdemo/hh-fam.html; calculations by New Strategist

Table 7.8 Households by Presence and Number of Children under Age 18, 1950 to 2006

(number and percent distribution of households by presence and number of own children under age 18 at home 1950 to 2006; percent and percentage point change for selected years; numbers in thousands)

	total households	no children	households with children				
			total	one child	two children	three children	four or more children
2006	114,384	77,918	36,466	15,528	13,664	5,278	1,997
2000	104,705	70,100	34,605	14,311	13,215	5,063	2,017
1990	93,347	61,058	32,289	13,530	12,263	4,650	1,846
1980	80,776	49,754	31,022	12,443	11,470	4,674	2,435
1970	63,401	34,589	28,812	9,364	8,961	5,445	5,042
1960	52,799	27,109	25,690	8,349	8,118	5,010	4,213
1950	43,554	23,230	20,324	8,292	6,483	3,069	2,480
Percent change							
2000 to 2006	9.2%	11.2%	5.4%	8.5%	3.4%	4.2%	−1.0%
1950 to 2006	162.6	235.4	79.4	87.3	110.8	72.0	−19.5
Percent distribution							
2006	100.0%	68.1%	31.9%	13.6%	11.9%	4.6%	1.7%
2000	100.0	67.0	33.0	13.7	12.6	4.8	1.9
1990	100.0	65.4	34.6	14.5	13.1	5.0	2.0
1980	100.0	61.6	38.4	15.4	14.2	5.8	3.0
1970	100.0	54.6	45.4	14.8	14.1	8.6	8.0
1960	100.0	51.3	48.7	15.8	15.4	9.5	8.0
1950	100.0	53.3	46.7	19.0	14.9	7.0	5.7
Percentage point change							
2000 to 2006	−	1.1	−1.1	−0.1	−0.7	−0.2	−0.2
1950 to 2006	−	14.8	−14.8	−5.4	−3.0	−2.4	−4.0

Note: "–" means not applicable.
Source: Bureau of the Census, America's Families and Living Arrangements, Internet site http://www.census.gov/population/ www/socdemo/hh-fam.html; and Historical Statistics of the United States: Colonial Times to 1970, Part 1, 1975; calculations by New Strategist

Table 7.9 Households by Size, 1950 to 2006

(number of households by size, and average number of persons per household, 1950 to 2006; percent change for selected years; numbers in thousands)

	total households	one person	two people	three people	four people	five people	six people	seven+ people	avg. per household
2006	114,384	30,453	37,775	18,924	15,998	7,306	2,562	1,366	2.57
2005	113,343	30,137	37,446	18,285	16,382	7,166	2,497	1,430	2.57
2004	112,000	29,586	37,366	17,968	16,066	7,150	2,476	1,388	2.57
2003	111,278	29,431	37,078	17,889	15,967	7,029	2,521	1,364	2.57
2002	109,297	28,775	36,240	17,742	15,794	6,948	2,438	1,360	2.58
2001	108,209	28,207	35,917	17,444	15,692	6,978	2,555	1,415	2.58
2000	104,705	26,724	34,666	17,172	15,309	6,981	2,445	1,428	2.62
1999	103,874	26,606	34,262	17,386	15,030	6,962	2,367	1,261	2.61
1998	102,528	26,327	32,965	17,331	15,358	7,048	2,232	1,267	2.62
1997	101,018	25,402	32,736	17,065	15,396	6,774	2,311	1,334	2.64
1996	99,627	24,900	32,526	16,724	15,118	6,631	2,357	1,372	2.65
1995	98,990	24,732	31,834	16,827	15,321	6,616	2,279	1,382	2.65
1994	97,107	23,611	31,211	16,898	15,073	6,749	2,186	1,379	2.67
1993	96,426	23,558	31,041	16,964	14,997	6,404	2,217	1,244	2.66
1992	95,669	23,974	30,734	16,398	14,710	6,389	2,126	1,338	2.62
1991	94,312	23,590	30,181	16,082	14,556	6,206	2,237	1,459	2.63
1990	93,347	22,999	30,114	16,128	14,456	6,213	2,143	1,295	2.63
1989	92,830	22,708	29,976	16,276	14,550	6,232	2,003	1,084	2.62
1988	91,124	21,889	29,295	16,163	14,143	6,081	2,176	1,320	2.64
1987	89,479	21,128	28,602	16,159	13,984	6,162	2,176	1,268	2.66
1986	88,458	21,178	27,732	16,088	13,774	6,276	2,138	1,272	2.67
1985	86,789	20,602	27,389	15,465	13,631	6,108	2,299	1,296	2.69
1984	85,290	19,954	26,890	15,134	13,593	6,070	2,372	1,394	2.71
1983	83,918	19,250	26,439	14,793	13,303	6,105	2,460	1,568	2.73
1982	83,527	19,354	26,486	14,617	12,868	6,103	2,480	1,619	2.72
1981	82,368	18,936	25,787	14,569	12,768	6,117	2,549	1,643	2.73
1980	80,776	18,296	25,327	14,130	12,666	6,059	2,519	1,778	2.76
1979	77,330	17,201	23,928	13,392	12,274	6,187	2,573	1,774	2.78
1978	76,030	16,715	23,334	13,040	11,955	6,356	2,723	1,906	2.81
1977	74,142	15,532	22,775	12,794	11,630	6,285	2,864	2,263	2.86
1976	72,867	14,983	22,321	12,520	11,407	6,268	3,001	2,367	2.89
1975	71,120	13,939	21,753	12,384	11,103	6,399	3,059	2,484	2.94
1974	69,859	13,368	21,495	11,913	10,900	6,469	3,063	2,651	2.97
1973	68,251	12,635	20,632	11,804	10,739	6,426	3,245	2,769	3.01
1972	66,676	12,189	19,482	11,542	10,679	6,431	3,374	2,979	3.06
1971	64,778	11,446	18,892	11,071	10,059	6,640	3,435	3,234	3.11
1970	63,401	10,851	18,333	10,949	9,991	6,548	3,534	3,195	3.14
1965	57,436	8,631	16,119	10,263	9,269	6,313	3,327	3,514	3.29
1960	52,799	6,917	14,678	9,979	9,293	6,072	3,010	2,851	3.33
1950	43,468	4,737	12,529	9,808	7,729	4,357	2,196	2,113	3.37

Percent change

	total households	one person	two people	three people	four people	five people	six people	seven+ people	avg. per household
2000 to 2006	9.2%	14.0%	9.0%	10.2%	4.5%	4.7%	4.8%	−4.3%	−1.8%
1950 to 2006	163.1	542.9	201.5	92.9	107.0	67.7	16.7	−35.4	−23.7

Source: Bureau of the Census, America's Families and Living Arrangements, Internet site http://www.census.gov/population/ www/socdemo/hh-fam.html; and Historical Statistics of the United States: Colonial Times to 1970, Part 1, 1975; calculations by New Strategist

Table 7.10 Distribution of Households by Size, 1950 to 2006

(percent distribution of households by size, 1950 to 2006; percentage point change for selected years)

	total households	one person	two people	three people	four people	five people	six people	seven+ people
2006	100.0%	26.6%	33.0%	16.5%	14.0%	6.4%	2.2%	1.2%
2005	100.0	26.6	33.0	16.1	14.5	6.3	2.2	1.3
2004	100.0	26.4	33.4	16.0	14.3	6.4	2.2	1.2
2003	100.0	26.4	33.3	16.1	14.3	6.3	2.3	1.2
2002	100.0	26.3	33.2	16.2	14.5	6.4	2.2	1.2
2001	100.0	26.1	33.2	16.1	14.5	6.4	2.4	1.3
2000	100.0	25.5	33.1	16.4	14.6	6.7	2.3	1.4
1999	100.0	25.6	33.0	16.7	14.5	6.7	2.3	1.2
1998	100.0	25.7	32.2	16.9	15.0	6.9	2.2	1.2
1997	100.0	25.1	32.4	16.9	15.2	6.7	2.3	1.3
1996	100.0	25.0	32.6	16.8	15.2	6.7	2.4	1.4
1995	100.0	25.0	32.2	17.0	15.5	6.7	2.3	1.4
1994	100.0	24.3	32.1	17.4	15.5	7.0	2.3	1.4
1993	100.0	24.4	32.2	17.6	15.6	6.6	2.3	1.3
1992	100.0	25.1	32.1	17.1	15.4	6.7	2.2	1.4
1991	100.0	25.0	32.0	17.1	15.4	6.6	2.4	1.5
1990	100.0	24.6	32.3	17.3	15.5	6.7	2.3	1.4
1989	100.0	24.5	32.3	17.5	15.7	6.7	2.2	1.2
1988	100.0	24.0	32.1	17.7	15.5	6.7	2.4	1.4
1987	100.0	23.6	32.0	18.1	15.6	6.9	2.4	1.4
1986	100.0	23.9	31.4	18.2	15.6	7.1	2.4	1.4
1985	100.0	23.7	31.6	17.8	15.7	7.0	2.6	1.5
1984	100.0	23.4	31.5	17.7	15.9	7.1	2.8	1.6
1983	100.0	22.9	31.5	17.6	15.9	7.3	2.9	1.9
1982	100.0	23.2	31.7	17.5	15.4	7.3	3.0	1.9
1981	100.0	23.0	31.3	17.7	15.5	7.4	3.1	2.0
1980	100.0	22.7	31.4	17.5	15.7	7.5	3.1	2.2
1979	100.0	22.2	30.9	17.3	15.9	8.0	3.3	2.3
1978	100.0	22.0	30.7	17.2	15.7	8.4	3.6	2.5
1977	100.0	20.9	30.7	17.3	15.7	8.5	3.9	3.1
1976	100.0	20.6	30.6	17.2	15.7	8.6	4.1	3.2
1975	100.0	19.6	30.6	17.4	15.6	9.0	4.3	3.5
1974	100.0	19.1	30.8	17.1	15.6	9.3	4.4	3.8
1973	100.0	18.5	30.2	17.3	15.7	9.4	4.8	4.1
1972	100.0	18.3	29.2	17.3	16.0	9.6	5.1	4.5
1971	100.0	17.7	29.2	17.1	15.5	10.3	5.3	5.0
1970	100.0	17.1	28.9	17.3	15.8	10.3	5.6	5.0
1965	100.0	15.0	28.1	17.9	16.1	11.0	5.8	6.1
1960	100.0	13.1	27.8	18.9	17.6	11.5	5.7	5.4
1950	100.0	10.9	28.8	22.6	17.8	10.0	5.1	4.9
Percentage point change								
2000 to 2006	–	1.1	–0.1	–0.3	–0.2	–0.3	–0.1	–0.1
1950 to 2006	–	15.7	4.2	–6.4	–3.3	–3.7	–2.8	–3.6

Note: "–" means not applicable.
Source: Bureau of the Census, America's Families and Living Arrangements, Internet site http://www.census.gov/population/www/ socdemo/hh-fam.html; and Historical Statistics of the United States: Colonial Times to 1970, Part 1, 1975; calculations by New Strategist

More Children Live with Mother Only

Few live only with their father.

Single-parent households have become much more numerous as divorce and out-of-wedlock births have become common. In 2006, only 67 percent of children lived with both parents, down from 88 percent in 1960. The percentage of children who live with their mother only climbed from 8 percent in 1960 to 23 percent in 2006.

Most black children live with their mother only. In 2006, the 51 percent majority of black children lived with their mother. Just 35 percent lived with both parents, down from 67 percent in 1960. Among Hispanic children, 66 percent live with both parents, down from 78 percent in 1970. Among white children 74 percent lived with both parents in 2006, down from 91 percent in 1960. Children are about as likely to live with their father only as they are to live with neither mother nor father.

As out-of-wedlock births have soared, many more children live with mothers who have never married. Among children who lived with only their mother in 2006, fully 43 percent lived with a never-married mother. The share was only 4 percent in 1960. Five percent of children live with grandparents, up from 4 percent in 1970. Most who live in the home of a grandparent also live with one or both parents.

■ Children who live in single-parent families have a much higher poverty rate than those who live with both parents.

Only two-thirds of the nation's children live with both parents

(percentage of children under age 18 who live with both parents, 1960 and 2006)

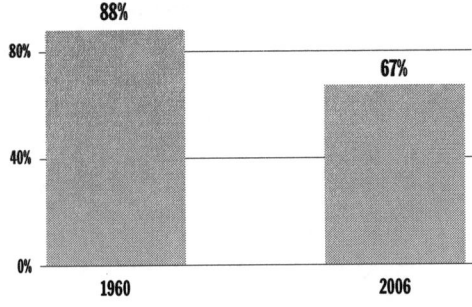

Table 7.11 Living Arrangements of Children under Age 18, 1960 to 2006: Total Children

(number and percent of children under age 18 by living arrangement, 1960 to 2006; numbers in thousands)

	total children	living with both parents		living with mother only		living with father only		living with others	
		number	percent	number	percent	number	percent	number	percent
2006	73,664	49,661	67.4%	17,161	23.3%	3,458	4.7%	3,383	4.6%
2005	73,494	49,481	67.3	17,225	23.4	3,497	4.8	3,291	4.5
2004	73,205	49,603	67.8	17,072	23.3	3,402	4.6	3,129	4.3
2003	73,001	49,903	68.4	16,770	23.0	3,323	4.6	3,005	4.1
2002	72,321	49,666	68.7	16,473	22.8	3,297	4.6	2,885	4.0
2001	72,006	49,792	69.1	16,117	22.4	3,133	4.4	2,962	4.1
2000	72,012	49,795	69.1	16,162	22.4	3,058	4.2	2,997	4.2
1999	71,703	48,775	68.0	16,805	23.4	3,094	4.3	3,029	4.2
1998	71,377	48,642	68.1	16,634	23.3	3,143	4.4	2,959	4.1
1997	70,983	48,386	68.2	16,740	23.6	3,059	4.3	2,798	3.9
1996	70,908	48,224	68.0	16,993	24.0	2,759	3.9	2,932	4.1
1995	70,254	48,276	68.7	16,477	23.5	2,461	3.5	3,040	4.3
1994	69,508	48,084	69.2	16,334	23.5	2,257	3.2	2,834	4.1
1993	66,893	47,181	70.5	15,586	23.3	2,286	3.4	1,840	2.8
1992	65,965	46,638	70.7	15,396	23.3	2,182	3.3	1,749	2.7
1991	65,093	46,658	71.7	14,608	22.4	2,016	3.1	1,811	2.8
1990	64,137	46,503	72.5	13,874	21.6	1,993	3.1	1,767	2.8
1989	63,637	46,549	73.1	13,700	21.5	1,793	2.8	1,595	2.5
1988	63,179	45,942	72.7	13,521	21.4	1,808	2.9	1,908	3.0
1987	62,932	46,009	73.1	13,420	21.3	1,651	2.6	1,852	2.9
1986	62,763	46,384	73.9	13,180	21.0	1,579	2.5	1,620	2.6
1985	62,475	46,149	73.9	13,081	20.9	1,554	2.5	1,691	2.7
1984	62,139	46,555	74.9	12,646	20.4	1,378	2.2	1,560	2.5
1983	62,281	46,632	74.9	12,739	20.5	1,267	2.0	1,643	2.6
1982	62,407	46,797	75.0	12,512	20.0	1,189	1.9	1,909	3.1
1981	62,918	48,040	76.4	11,416	18.1	1,203	1.9	2,259	3.6
1980	63,427	48,624	76.7	11,406	18.0	1,060	1.7	2,337	3.7
1979	62,389	48,295	77.4	10,531	16.9	997	1.6	2,566	4.1
1978	63,206	49,132	77.7	10,725	17.0	985	1.6	2,364	3.7
1977	64,062	50,735	79.2	10,419	16.3	892	1.4	2,016	3.1
1976	65,129	52,101	80.0	10,310	15.8	811	1.2	1,907	2.9
1975	66,087	53,072	80.3	10,231	15.5	1,014	1.5	1,770	2.7
1974	67,047	54,561	81.4	9,647	14.4	842	1.3	1,997	3.0
1973	67,950	55,807	82.1	9,272	13.6	821	1.2	2,050	3.0
1972	68,811	57,201	83.1	8,838	12.8	796	1.2	1,976	2.9
1971	70,255	58,606	83.4	8,714	12.4	764	1.1	2,171	3.1
1970	69,162	58,939	85.2	7,452	10.8	748	1.1	2,023	2.9
1969	70,317	59,857	85.1	7,744	11.0	765	1.1	1,951	2.8
1968	70,326	60,030	85.4	7,556	10.7	776	1.1	1,964	2.8
1960	63,727	55,877	87.7	5,105	8.0	724	1.1	2,021	3.2

Source: Bureau of the Census, Families and Living Arrangements—Historical Tables, Internet site http://www.census.gov/population/www/socdemo/hh-fam.html; calculations by New Strategist

Table 7.12 Living Arrangements of Children under Age 18, 1960 to 2006: Black Children

(number and percent of black children under age 18 by living arrangement, 1960 to 2006; numbers in thousands)

	total black children	living with both parents		living with mother only		living with father only		living with others	
		number	percent	number	percent	number	percent	number	percent
2006	12,261	4,338	35.4%	6,199	50.6%	608	5.0%	1,115	9.1%
2005	12,256	4,377	35.7	6,074	49.6	607	5.0	1,197	9.8
2004	12,277	4,340	35.4	6,153	50.1	688	5.6	1,095	8.9
2003	12,187	4,468	36.7	6,130	50.3	565	4.6	1,024	8.4
2002	11,646	4,481	38.5	5,605	48.1	605	5.2	955	8.2
2001	11,578	4,356	37.6	5,573	48.1	542	4.7	1,108	9.6
2000	11,412	4,286	37.6	5,596	49.0	484	4.2	1,046	9.2
1999	11,425	3,967	34.7	5,891	51.6	461	4.0	1,093	9.6
1998	11,414	4,137	36.2	5,830	51.1	424	3.7	1,015	8.9
1997	11,369	3,940	34.7	5,888	51.8	581	5.1	960	8.4
1996	11,434	3,816	33.4	6,056	53.0	504	4.4	1,058	9.3
1995	11,301	3,746	33.1	5,881	52.0	458	4.1	1,216	10.8
1994	11,177	3,722	33.3	5,967	53.4	417	3.7	1,071	9.6
1993	10,660	3,796	35.6	5,757	54.0	322	3.0	784	7.4
1992	10,427	3,714	35.6	5,607	53.8	327	3.1	779	7.5
1991	10,209	3,669	35.9	5,516	54.0	358	3.5	666	6.5
1990	10,018	3,781	37.7	5,132	51.2	353	3.5	753	7.5
1989	9,835	3,738	38.0	5,023	51.1	339	3.4	735	7.5
1988	9,699	3,739	38.6	4,959	51.1	288	3.0	713	7.4
1987	9,612	3,852	40.1	4,844	50.4	243	2.5	673	7.0
1986	9,532	3,869	40.6	4,827	50.6	231	2.4	605	6.3
1985	9,479	3,741	39.5	4,837	51.0	276	2.9	624	6.6
1984	9,375	3,845	41.0	4,705	50.2	273	2.9	552	5.9
1983	9,377	3,818	40.7	4,789	51.1	234	2.5	535	5.7
1982	9,377	3,978	42.4	4,422	47.2	192	2.0	785	8.4
1981	9,400	4,016	42.7	4,074	43.3	236	2.5	1,075	11.4
1980	9,375	3,956	42.2	4,117	43.9	180	1.9	1,122	12.0
1979	9,285	4,030	43.4	3,891	41.9	198	2.1	1,166	12.6
1978	9,394	4,094	43.6	3,978	42.3	195	2.1	1,127	12.0
1977	9,374	4,384	46.8	3,911	41.7	135	1.4	944	10.1
1976	9,461	4,688	49.6	3,791	40.1	145	1.5	837	8.8
1975	9,472	4,682	49.4	3,870	40.9	172	1.8	747	7.9
1974	9,526	4,831	50.7	3,602	37.8	171	1.8	921	9.7
1973	9,523	4,904	51.5	3,583	37.6	199	2.1	837	8.8
1972	9,583	5,201	54.3	3,207	33.5	178	1.9	997	10.4
1971	10,004	5,446	54.4	3,264	32.6	173	1.7	1,121	11.2
1970	9,422	5,508	58.5	2,783	29.5	213	2.3	919	9.8
1969	9,832	5,784	58.8	2,907	29.6	179	1.8	962	9.8
1968	9,714	5,702	58.7	2,842	29.3	210	2.2	960	9.9
1960	8,650	5,795	67.0	1,723	19.9	173	2.0	958	11.1

Note: Beginning in 2002, data are for those who identify themselves as being of the race alone and those who identify themselves as being of the race in combination with other races.
Source: Bureau of the Census, Families and Living Arrangements—Historical Tables, Internet site http://www.census.gov/population/www/socdemo/hh-fam.html; calculations by New Strategist

Table 7.13 Living Arrangements of Children under Age 18, 1970 to 2006: Hispanic Children

(number and percent of Hispanic children under age 18 by living arrangement, 1970 to 2006; numbers in thousands)

	total Hispanic children	living with both parents		living with mother only		living with father only		living with others	
		number	percent	number	percent	number	percent	number	percent
2006	14,697	9,686	65.9%	3,674	25.0%	603	4.1%	734	5.0%
2005	14,241	9,209	64.7	3,619	25.4	679	4.8	733	5.1
2004	13,752	8,886	64.6	3,489	25.4	731	5.3	647	4.7
2003	13,284	8,584	64.6	3,261	24.5	737	5.5	702	5.3
2002	12,817	8,338	65.1	3,212	25.1	641	5.0	626	4.9
2001	12,446	8,111	65.2	3,055	24.5	570	4.6	710	5.7
2000	11,613	7,561	65.1	2,919	25.1	506	4.4	627	5.4
1999	11,236	7,127	63.4	3,023	26.9	506	4.5	580	5.2
1998	10,863	6,909	63.6	2,915	26.8	482	4.4	551	5.1
1997	10,526	6,748	64.1	2,819	26.8	441	4.2	517	4.9
1996	10,251	6,381	62.2	2,937	28.7	384	3.7	549	5.4
1995	9,843	6,191	62.9	2,798	28.4	417	4.2	438	4.4
1994	9,496	6,022	63.4	2,646	27.9	373	3.9	455	4.8
1993	7,776	5,017	64.5	2,176	28.0	296	3.8	287	3.7
1992	7,619	4,935	64.8	2,168	28.5	279	3.7	237	3.1
1991	7,462	4,944	66.3	1,983	26.6	239	3.2	296	4.0
1990	7,174	4,789	66.8	1,943	27.1	211	2.9	231	3.2
1989	6,973	4,673	67.0	1,940	27.8	189	2.7	171	2.5
1988	6,786	4,497	66.3	1,845	27.2	202	3.0	241	3.6
1987	6,647	4,355	65.5	1,843	27.7	184	2.8	265	4.0
1986	6,430	4,275	66.5	1,784	27.7	171	2.7	200	3.1
1985	6,057	4,110	67.9	1,612	26.6	134	2.2	201	3.3
1984	5,625	3,946	70.2	1,399	24.9	110	2.0	170	3.0
1983	5,513	3,774	68.5	1,475	26.8	99	1.8	165	3.0
1982	5,358	3,700	69.1	1,353	25.3	83	1.5	222	4.1
1981	5,267	3,703	70.3	1,212	23.0	129	2.4	223	4.2
1980	5,459	4,116	75.4	1,069	19.6	83	1.5	191	3.5
1970	4,006	3,111	77.7	–	–	–	–	–	–

Note: "–" means data are not available.
Source: Bureau of the Census, Families and Living Arrangements—Historical Tables, Internet site http://www.census.gov/population/www/socdemo/hh-fam.html; calculations by New Strategist

Table 7.14 Living Arrangements of Children under Age 18, 1960 to 2006: White Children

(number and percent of white children under age 18 by living arrangement, 1960 to 2006; numbers in thousands)

	total white children	living with both parents		living with mother only		living with father only		living with others	
		number	percent	number	percent	number	percent	number	percent
2006	56,332	41,599	73.8%	10,090	17.9%	2,603	4.6%	2,040	3.6%
2005	56,234	41,334	73.5	10,367	18.4	2,635	4.7	1,898	3.4
2004	55,902	41,550	74.3	10,050	18.0	2,468	4.4	1,835	3.3
2003	55,920	41,805	74.8	9,799	17.5	2,535	4.5	1,781	3.2
2002	56,276	41,944	74.5	10,052	17.9	2,548	4.5	1,732	3.1
2001	56,135	42,188	75.2	9,826	17.5	2,437	4.3	1,685	3.0
2000	56,455	42,497	75.3	9,765	17.3	2,427	4.3	1,766	3.1
1999	56,265	41,845	74.4	10,200	18.1	2,454	4.4	1,766	3.1
1998	56,124	41,547	74.0	10,210	18.2	2,562	4.6	1,799	3.2
1997	55,869	41,654	74.6	10,204	18.3	2,339	4.2	1,672	3.0
1996	55,714	41,609	74.7	10,239	18.4	2,096	3.8	1,770	3.2
1995	55,327	41,946	75.8	9,827	17.8	1,892	3.4	1,662	3.0
1994	54,795	41,766	76.2	9,724	17.7	1,710	3.1	1,594	2.9
1993	53,075	40,996	77.2	9,256	17.4	1,854	3.5	969	1.8
1992	52,493	40,635	77.4	9,250	17.6	1,721	3.3	887	1.7
1991	51,918	40,733	78.5	8,585	16.5	1,557	3.0	1,043	2.0
1990	51,390	40,593	79.0	8,321	16.2	1,549	3.0	928	1.8
1989	51,134	40,706	79.6	8,220	16.1	1,406	2.7	802	1.6
1988	51,030	40,287	78.9	8,160	16.0	1,464	2.9	1,119	2.2
1987	51,112	40,407	79.1	8,231	16.1	1,338	2.6	1,136	2.2
1986	50,931	40,681	79.9	8,021	15.7	1,282	2.5	947	1.9
1985	50,836	40,690	80.0	7,929	15.6	1,210	2.4	1,007	2.0
1984	50,620	41,009	81.0	7,641	15.1	1,061	2.1	909	1.8
1983	50,873	41,231	81.0	7,616	15.0	998	2.0	1,028	2.0
1982	51,086	41,285	80.8	7,831	15.3	949	1.9	1,020	2.0
1981	51,620	42,493	82.3	7,097	13.7	927	1.8	1,103	2.1
1980	52,242	43,200	82.7	7,059	13.5	842	1.6	1,141	2.2
1979	51,688	43,145	83.5	6,445	12.5	767	1.5	1,332	2.6
1978	52,523	44,001	83.8	6,592	12.6	770	1.5	1,160	2.2
1977	53,394	45,289	84.8	6,359	11.9	747	1.4	1,000	1.9
1976	54,411	46,342	85.2	6,421	11.8	634	1.2	1,014	1.9
1975	55,500	47,415	85.4	6,266	11.3	830	1.5	990	1.8
1974	56,437	48,910	86.7	5,889	10.4	661	1.2	977	1.7
1973	57,398	50,150	87.4	5,514	9.6	614	1.1	1,120	2.0
1972	58,221	51,159	87.9	5,510	9.5	610	1.0	942	1.6
1971	59,264	52,328	88.3	5,336	9.0	587	1.0	1,013	1.7
1970	58,791	52,624	89.5	4,581	7.8	528	0.9	1,057	1.8
1969	59,589	53,360	89.5	4,721	7.9	552	0.9	956	1.6
1968	59,724	53,599	89.7	4,613	7.7	563	0.9	949	1.6
1960	55,077	50,082	90.9	3,381	6.1	551	1.0	1,063	1.9

Note: Beginning in 2002, data are for those who identify themselves as being of the race alone.
Source: Bureau of the Census, Families and Living Arrangements—Historical Tables, Internet site http://www.census.gov/population/www/socdemo/hh-fam.html; calculations by New Strategist

Table 7.15 Children under Age 18 Living with Mother Only, 1960 to 2006

(total number of children under age 18 who live with only their mother and percent distribution by marital status of mother, 1960 to 2006; numbers in thousands)

	living with mother only		mother's marital status			
	number	percent	never married	married, spouse absent	divorced	widowed
2006	17,161	100.0%	43.4%	19.4%	33.6%	3.6%
2005	17,225	100.0	43.1	19.7	33.7	3.5
2004	17,072	100.0	42.3	19.2	34.4	4.1
2003	16,770	100.0	41.8	20.0	34.3	4.0
2002	16,472	100.0	41.7	20.0	34.0	4.4
2001	16,117	100.0	41.8	19.3	34.6	4.3
2000	16,162	100.0	40.8	19.9	35.0	4.3
1999	16,805	100.0	40.1	21.2	34.7	4.0
1998	16,634	100.0	40.3	21.4	34.3	4.0
1997	16,740	100.0	39.4	22.4	34.8	3.4
1996	16,993	100.0	37.5	23.1	35.5	3.9
1995	16,477	100.0	35.6	23.7	36.5	4.2
1994	16,334	100.0	36.7	23.5	35.5	4.3
1993	15,586	100.0	35.4	24.0	36.5	4.2
1992	15,396	100.0	35.1	24.6	35.8	4.5
1991	14,608	100.0	34.5	24.5	35.6	5.3
1990	13,874	100.0	31.5	24.6	36.9	7.0
1989	13,700	100.0	31.3	24.7	38.2	5.9
1988	13,521	100.0	31.8	24.9	37.1	6.2
1987	13,420	100.0	29.7	24.5	39.7	6.1
1986	13,180	100.0	27.4	25.2	40.6	6.8
1985	13,081	100.0	26.7	25.7	40.4	7.2
1984	12,646	100.0	24.8	27.1	40.9	7.3
1983	12,739	100.0	25.2	26.2	40.7	7.9
1982	12,512	100.0	22.1	28.1	40.8	9.0
1981	11,416	100.0	15.8	31.0	43.0	10.1
1980	11,406	100.0	15.3	31.7	41.8	11.3
1979	10,531	100.0	14.7	33.1	40.4	11.8
1978	10,725	100.0	15.2	32.7	40.4	11.7
1977	10,419	100.0	12.8	34.7	40.4	12.0
1976	10,310	100.0	11.0	36.8	39.0	13.2
1975	10,231	100.0	11.4	37.7	35.6	15.3
1974	9,647	100.0	10.0	39.3	34.0	16.7
1973	9,272	100.0	9.6	40.4	33.5	16.5
1972	8,838	100.0	7.2	44.1	31.7	17.0
1971	8,714	100.0	8.9	44.4	30.1	16.6
1970	7,452	100.0	7.1	43.4	30.8	18.7
1969	7,744	100.0	5.7	47.8	26.5	19.9
1968	7,556	100.0	6.2	45.3	27.2	21.4
1960	5,105	100.0	4.3	46.3	23.7	25.7

Source: Bureau of the Census, Families and Living Arrangements—Historical Tables, Internet site http://www.census.gov/ population/www/socdemo/hh-fam.html; calculations by New Strategist

Table 7.16   Grandchildren Living in the Home of Their Grandparents, 1970 to 2006

(number and percent distribution of children under age 18 who live with their grandparents by presence of parent in the home, 1970 to 2006; numbers in thousands)

	total children	living with grandparents total	with parents present both	with parents present mother only	with parents present father only	neither parent present
2006	73,664	3,731	412	1,650	184	1,484
2005	73,494	4,141	486	1,821	240	1,595
2004	73,205	4,050	526	1,765	259	1,501
2003	73,001	3,767	547	1,576	227	1,416
2002	72,321	3,681	477	1,658	275	1,274
2001	72,006	3,844	510	1,755	231	1,348
2000	72,012	3,842	531	1,732	220	1,359
1999	71,703	3,919	535	1,803	250	1,331
1998	71,377	3,989	503	1,827	241	1,417
1997	70,983	3,894	554	1,785	247	1,309
1996	70,908	4,060	467	1,943	220	1,431
1995	70,254	3,965	427	1,876	195	1,466
1994	69,508	3,735	436	1,764	175	1,359
1993	66,893	3,368	475	1,647	229	1,017
1992	65,965	3,253	502	1,740	144	867
1991	65,093	3,320	559	1,674	151	937
1990	64,137	3,155	467	1,563	191	935
1980	63,369	2,306	310	922	86	988
1970	69,276	2,214	363	817	78	957

Percent distribution by living arrangement

2006	100.0%	5.1%	0.6%	2.2%	0.2%	2.0%
2005	100.0	5.6	0.7	2.5	0.3	2.2
2004	100.0	5.5	0.7	2.4	0.4	2.1
2003	100.0	5.2	0.7	2.2	0.3	1.9
2002	100.0	5.1	0.7	2.3	0.4	1.8
2001	100.0	5.3	0.7	2.4	0.3	1.9
2000	100.0	5.3	0.7	2.4	0.3	1.9
1998	100.0	5.5	0.7	2.5	0.3	1.9
1997	100.0	5.6	0.7	2.6	0.3	2.0
1996	100.0	5.5	0.8	2.5	0.3	1.8
1995	100.0	5.7	0.7	2.7	0.3	2.0
1994	100.0	5.6	0.6	2.7	0.3	2.1
1993	100.0	5.4	0.6	2.5	0.3	2.0
1992	100.0	5.0	0.7	2.5	0.3	1.5
1991	100.0	4.9	0.8	2.6	0.2	1.3
1990	100.0	5.1	0.9	2.6	0.2	1.4
1980	100.0	4.9	0.7	2.4	0.3	1.5
1970	100.0	3.6	0.5	1.5	0.1	1.6

Source: Bureau of the Census, Families and Living Arrangements—Historical Tables, Internet site http://www.census.gov/ population/www/socdemo/hh-fam.html; calculations by New Strategist

The Young Are More Dependent

The old are more independent.

The living arrangements of both the young and the old have changed over the past few decades. Young adults are more likely to live with mom and dad and less likely to head their own households. Older Americans are more likely to live alone and less likely to live with adult children. The unmarried-couple share of households has increased as men and women opt for living together outside of marriage.

Among men aged 18 to 24, the 54 percent majority lived with their parents in 2006, up from 52 percent in 1960. Among women in the age group, the proportion of those who live with their parents climbed from 35 to 47 percent. Men and women aged 25 to 34 are also more likely to live with their parents than they once were. The rate rose from 11 to 14 percent among men and from 7 to 9 percent among women between 1960 and 2006. Behind this increase is more schooling, as young adults who live in college dormitories are counted as still living with their parents.

Among Americans of all ages, a larger share lived alone in 2006 than in 1970. The increase in lone living has been especially pronounced among women aged 75 or older—most of them widows living alone following the death of their husband. In 1970, 37 percent of women in the age group lived alone. By 2006, 48 percent lived by themselves, although this was down from 54 percent in 1990.

■ The percentage of elderly women who live alone has fallen in recent years because the life expectancy of older men has grown.

Older women are much more likely than older men to live alone

(percentage of people aged 75 or older who live alone, by sex, 2006)

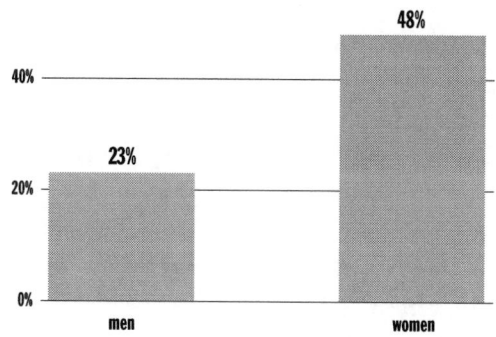

Table 7.17 Living Arrangements of Young Men, 1960 to 2006

(total number of men aged 18 to 34, and number and percent of men who live with their parents, by age, 1960 to 2006; numbers in thousands)

	men aged 18 to 24			men aged 25 to 34		
		living with parents			living with parents	
	total	number	share of total	total	number	share of total
2006	14,100	7,573	53.7%	19,824	2,840	14.3%
2005	14,060	7,448	53.0	19,656	2,660	13.5
2004	14,165	8,010	56.5	19,553	2,720	13.9
2003	13,811	7,569	54.8	19,543	2,631	13.5
2002	13,696	7,575	55.3	19,220	2,610	13.6
2001	13,412	7,385	55.1	19,308	2,520	13.1
2000	13,291	7,593	57.1	18,563	2,387	12.9
1999	12,936	7,440	57.5	18,924	2,636	13.9
1998	12,633	7,399	58.6	19,526	2,845	14.6
1997	12,534	7,501	59.8	20,039	2,909	14.5
1996	12,402	7,327	59.0	20,390	3,213	16.0
1995	12,545	7,328	58.4	20,589	3,166	15.4
1994	12,683	7,547	59.5	20,873	3,261	15.6
1993	12,049	7,145	59.3	20,856	3,300	15.8
1992	12,083	7,296	60.4	21,125	3,225	15.3
1991	12,275	7,385	60.2	21,319	3,172	14.9
1990	12,450	7,232	58.1	21,462	3,213	15.0
1989	12,574	7,308	58.1	21,461	3,130	14.6
1988	12,835	7,792	60.7	21,320	3,207	15.0
1987	13,029	7,981	61.3	21,142	3,071	14.5
1986	13,324	7,831	58.8	20,956	2,981	14.2
1985	13,695	8,172	59.7	20,184	2,685	13.3
1984	14,196	8,764	61.7	19,876	2,626	13.2
1983	14,344	8,803	61.4	19,438	2,664	13.7
1980	14,278	7,755	54.3	18,107	1,894	10.5
1970	10,398	5,641	54.3	11,929	1,129	9.5
1960	6,842	3,583	52.4	10,896	1,185	10.9

Note: Unmarried college students living in dormitories are counted as living in their parents' home.
Source: Bureau of the Census, Families and Living Arrangements—Historical Tables, Internet site http://www.census.gov/population/www/socdemo/hh-fam.html; calculations by New Strategist

Table 7.18 Living Arrangements of Young Women, 1960 to 2006

(total number of women aged 18 to 34, and number and percent of women who live with their parents, by age, 1960 to 2006; numbers in thousands)

| | women aged 18 to 24 | | | women aged 25 to 34 | | |
| | | living with parents | | | living with parents | |
	total	number	share of total	total	number	share of total
2006	13,841	6,466	46.7%	19,653	1,731	8.8%
2005	13,933	6,413	46.0	19,632	1,597	8.1
2004	13,611	6,327	46.5	19,587	1,559	8.0
2003	13,592	6,215	45.7	19,659	1,375	7.0
2002	13,602	6,252	46.0	19,428	1,618	8.3
2001	13,361	6,068	45.4	19,527	1,583	8.1
2000	13,242	6,232	47.1	19,222	1,602	8.3
1999	13,031	6,389	49.0	19,551	1,690	8.6
1998	12,568	5,974	47.5	19,828	1,680	8.5
1997	12,452	6,006	48.2	20,217	1,745	8.6
1996	12,441	5,955	48.0	20,528	1,810	9.0
1995	12,613	5,896	46.7	20,800	1,759	8.5
1994	12,792	5,924	46.3	21,073	1,859	8.8
1993	12,260	5,746	46.9	21,007	1,844	8.8
1992	12,351	5,929	48.0	21,368	1,874	8.8
1991	12,627	6,163	48.8	21,586	1,887	8.7
1990	12,860	6,135	47.7	21,779	1,774	8.1
1989	13,055	6,141	47.0	21,777	1,728	7.9
1988	13,226	6,398	48.4	21,649	1,791	8.3
1987	13,433	6,375	47.5	21,494	1,655	7.7
1986	13,787	6,433	46.7	21,097	1,686	8.0
1985	14,149	6,758	47.8	20,673	1,661	8.0
1984	14,482	6,779	46.8	20,297	1,548	7.6
1983	14,702	7,001	47.6	19,903	1,520	7.6
1980	14,844	6,336	42.7	18,689	1,300	7.0
1970	11,959	4,941	41.3	12,637	829	6.6
1960	7,876	2,750	34.9	11,587	853	7.4

Note: Unmarried college students living in dormitories are counted as living in their parents' home.
Source: Bureau of the Census, Families and Living Arrangements—Historical Tables, Internet site http://www.census.gov/population/www/socdemo/hh-fam.html; calculations by New Strategist

Table 7.19 Men Living Alone by Age, 1970 to 2006

(number and percent of men who live alone by age, 1970 to 2006, percent change in number and percentage point change in share for selected years; numbers in thousands)

	2006	2000	1990	1980	1970	percent change 2000–06	percent change 1970–2006
NUMBER LIVING ALONE							
Total men living alone	**13,061**	**11,181**	**9,049**	**6,966**	**3,532**	**16.8%**	**269.8%**
Aged 15 to 24	826	556	674	947	274	48.6	201.5
Aged 25 to 34	2,219	2,279	2,395	1,975	535	–2.6	314.8
Aged 35 to 44	2,353	2,569	1,836	945	398	8.4	491.2
Aged 45 to 54	2,640	2,146	1,167	804	513	23.0	414.6
Aged 55 to 64	2,077	1,276	1,036	809	639	62.8	225.0
Aged 65 to 74	1,436	1,108	1,042	775	611	29.6	135.0
Aged 75 or older	1,511	1,247	901	711	563	21.2	168.4

	2006	2000	1990	1980	1970	percentage point change 2000–06	percentage point change 1970–2006
PERCENT LIVING ALONE							
Total men	**11.6%**	**10.8%**	**9.8%**	**8.5%**	**5.0%**	**0.8**	**6.6**
Aged 15 to 24	3.9	2.9	3.8	4.6	1.5	1.0	2.4
Aged 25 to 34	11.2	12.3	11.2	10.9	4.4	–1.1	6.8
Aged 35 to 44	11.0	11.6	10.0	7.6	3.5	–0.6	7.5
Aged 45 to 54	12.6	12.0	9.5	7.4	4.6	0.6	8.0
Aged 55 to 64	14.0	11.5	10.4	8.1	7.2	2.5	6.8
Aged 65 to 74	16.9	13.8	13.0	11.6	11.3	3.1	5.6
Aged 75 or older	22.7	21.4	20.9	21.6	19.1	1.3	3.6

Source: Bureau of the Census, Marital Status and Living Arrangements: March 1994, Current Population Reports, P20-484, 1996; and America's Families and Living Arrangements: March 2000 and 2006, Internet site http://www.census.gov/population/www/socdemo/hh-fam.html; calculations by New Strategist

Table 7.20 Women Living Alone by Age, 1970 to 2006

(number and percent of women who live alone by age, 1970 to 2006, percent change in number and percentage point change in share for selected years; numbers in thousands)

	2006	2000	1990	1980	1970	percent change 2000–06	percent change 1970–2006
NUMBER LIVING ALONE							
Total women living alone	**17,392**	**15,543**	**13,950**	**11,330**	**7,319**	**11.9%**	**137.6%**
Aged 15 to 24	765	588	536	779	282	30.1	171.3
Aged 25 to 34	1,532	1,568	1,578	1,284	358	–2.3	327.9
Aged 35 to 44	1,534	1,540	1,303	525	313	–0.4	390.1
Aged 45 to 54	2,606	2,158	1,256	901	790	20.8	229.9
Aged 55 to 64	3,168	2,262	2,044	2,000	1,680	40.1	88.6
Aged 65 to 74	2,859	2,983	3,309	3,076	2,204	–4.2	29.7
Aged 75 or older	4,930	4,444	3,924	2,766	1,693	10.9	191.2

	2006	2000	1990	1980	1970	percentage point change 2000–06	percentage point change 1970–2006
PERCENT LIVING ALONE							
Total women	**14.5%**	**14.0%**	**14.0%**	**12.6%**	**9.4%**	**0.5**	**5.1**
Aged 15 to 24	3.8	3.1	3.0	3.7	1.4	0.7	2.4
Aged 25 to 34	7.8	8.2	7.2	6.9	2.8	–0.4	5.0
Aged 35 to 44	7.1	6.8	6.9	4.0	2.6	0.3	4.5
Aged 45 to 54	11.9	11.5	9.7	7.7	6.6	0.4	5.3
Aged 55 to 64	19.7	18.5	18.2	17.4	17.1	1.2	2.6
Aged 65 to 74	28.5	30.6	33.2	35.6	31.6	–2.1	–3.1
Aged 75 or older	48.0	49.4	54.0	49.3	37.0	–1.4	11.0

Source: Bureau of the Census, Marital Status and Living Arrangements: March 1994, Current Population Reports, P20-484, 1996; and America's Families and Living Arrangements: March 2000 and 2006, Internet site http://www.census.gov/population/www/socdemo/hh-fam.html; calculations by New Strategist

Table 7.21 Unmarried-Couple Households, 1960 to 2006

(total number of households, number and percent of households headed by people of the opposite sex who share living quarters, and number and percent headed by unmarried partners, 1960 to 2006; numbers in thousands)

	total households	persons of opposite sex sharing living quarters		unmarried partners	
		number	percent	number	percent
2006	114,384	5,368	4.7%	5,012	4.4%
2005	113,343	5,214	4.6	4,875	4.3
2004	112,000	5,080	4.5	4,677	4.2
2003	111,278	5,054	4.5	4,622	4.2
2002	109,297	4,898	4.5	4,193	3.8
2001	108,209	4,893	4.5	4,101	3.8
2000	104,705	4,736	4.5	3,822	3.7
1999	103,874	4,486	4.3	3,380	3.3
1998	102,528	4,236	4.1	3,139	3.1
1997	101,018	4,130	4.1	3,087	3.1
1996	99,627	3,958	4.0	2,858	2.9
1995	98,990	3,668	3.7	–	–
1994	97,107	3,661	3.8	–	–
1993	96,426	3,510	3.6	–	–
1992	95,669	3,308	3.5	–	–
1991	94,312	3,039	3.2	–	–
1990	93,347	2,856	3.1	–	–
1989	92,830	2,764	3.0	–	–
1988	91,124	2,588	2.8	–	–
1987	89,479	2,334	2.6	–	–
1986	88,458	2,220	2.5	–	–
1985	86,789	1,983	2.3	–	–
1984	85,290	1,988	2.3	–	–
1983	83,918	1,891	2.3	–	–
1982	83,527	1,863	2.2	–	–
1981	82,368	1,808	2.2	–	–
1980	80,776	1,589	2.0	–	–
1979	77,330	1,346	1.7	–	–
1978	76,030	1,137	1.5	–	–
1977	74,142	957	1.3	–	–
1970	63,401	523	0.8	–	–
1960	52,799	439	0.8	–	–

Note: People of the opposite sex who share living quarters may or may not be unmarried partners; "–" means data are not available.
Source: Bureau of the Census, Families and Living Arrangements—Historical Tables, Internet site http://www.census.gov/ population/www/socdemo/hh-fam.html; calculations by New Strategist

Most People Marry, but Later than in the Past

In the 1950s, nearly half of women married in their teens.

The median age at first marriage hit a record high in 2006. For women the age by which half have married stood at 25.5 years. Among men, the median age at first marriage stood at 27.5 years in 2006. In 1950, half of women had married by age 20, and most men had married before their 23rd birthday.

As young adults postponed marriage, the percentage of those not yet married grew enormously. Fully 75 percent of women aged 20 to 24 had not yet married in 2006, up from 32 percent in 1950—an impressive 43 percentage point increase. Among men aged 20 to 24, the proportion of the not-yet-married climbed from 59 to 87 percent.

As people postpone marriage, the married share of the adult population is declining. In 1950, two-thirds of men and women aged 15 or older were currently married. By 2006, only 56 percent of men and 53 percent of women were currently married.

■ Although young adults are postponing marriage, most women marry before age 30 and most men before age 35.

The percentage of young women who have never married has soared

(percentage of women aged 20 to 24 who have never married, 1950 and 2006)

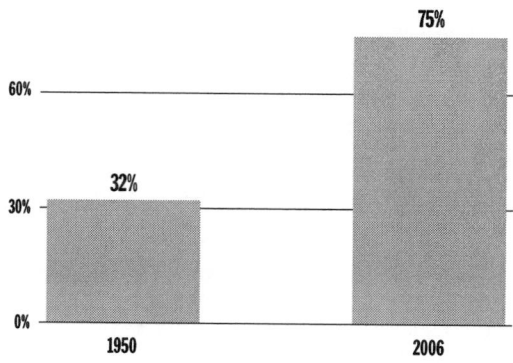

Table 7.22 Never-Married by Sex and Age, 1950 to 2006

(percent of people aged 18 or older who have never married, by sex and age, 1950 to 2006; percentage point change for selected years)

	2006	2000	1990	1980	1970	1960	1950	percentage point change 2000–06	1950–06
Total men	**28.6%**	**27.0%**	**25.8%**	**23.8%**	**18.9%**	**17.3%**	**20.2%**	**1.6**	**8.4**
Aged 18 to 19	97.8	98.3	96.8	94.3	92.8	91.1	93.4	–0.5	4.4
Aged 20 to 24	86.7	83.7	79.3	68.8	54.7	53.1	59.0	3.0	27.7
Aged 25 to 29	57.4	51.7	45.2	33.1	19.1	20.8	23.8	5.7	33.6
Aged 30 to 34	33.4	30.0	27.0	15.9	9.4	11.9	13.2	3.4	20.2
Aged 35 to 39	23.3	20.3	14.7	7.8	7.2	8.8	–	3.0	–
Aged 40 to 44	18.5	15.7	10.5	7.1	6.3	7.3	–	2.8	–
Aged 45 to 54	12.4	9.5	6.3	6.1	7.5	7.4	8.5	2.9	3.9
Aged 55 to 64	6.9	5.5	5.8	5.3	7.8	8.0	8.4	1.4	–1.5
Aged 65 or older	3.8	4.2	4.2	4.9	7.5	7.7	8.4	–0.4	–4.6
Total women	**22.0**	**21.1**	**18.9**	**17.1**	**13.7**	**11.9**	**14.1**	**0.9**	**7.9**
Aged 18 to 19	94.7	93.0	90.3	82.8	75.6	67.9	68.9	1.7	25.8
Aged 20 to 24	75.3	72.8	62.8	50.2	35.8	28.4	32.3	2.5	43.0
Aged 25 to 29	43.1	38.9	31.1	20.9	10.5	10.5	13.3	4.2	29.8
Aged 30 to 34	24.0	21.9	16.4	9.5	6.2	6.9	9.3	2.1	14.7
Aged 35 to 39	16.7	14.3	10.4	6.2	5.4	6.1	–	2.4	–
Aged 40 to 44	13.1	11.8	8.0	4.8	4.9	6.1	–	1.3	–
Aged 45 to 54	10.3	8.6	5.0	4.7	4.9	7.0	7.8	1.7	2.5
Aged 55 to 64	6.5	4.9	3.9	4.5	6.8	8.0	7.9	1.6	–1.4
Aged 65 or older	3.6	3.6	4.9	5.9	7.7	8.5	8.9	0.0	–5.3

Note: "–" means data are not available for five-year age groups. Among 35-to-44-year-olds in 1950, 9.6 percent of men and 8.3 percent of women had not married.
Source: Bureau of the Census, America's Families and Living Arrangements, Internet site http://www.census.gov/population/www/socdemo/hh-fam.html; and Historical Statistics of the United States: Colonial Times to 1970, Part 1, 1975; and Statistical Abstract of the United States for 1980, 1993, and 2001; calculations by New Strategist

Table 7.23 Median Age at First Marriage by Sex, 1950 to 2006

(median age at first marriage by sex, 1950 to 2006)

	men	women
2006	27.5 yrs.	25.5 yrs.
2005	27.1	25.3
2004	27.4	25.3
2003	27.1	25.3
2002	26.9	25.3
2001	26.9	25.1
2000	26.8	25.1
1999	26.9	25.1
1998	26.7	25.0
1997	26.8	25.0
1996	27.1	24.8
1995	26.9	24.5
1994	26.7	24.5
1993	26.5	24.5
1992	26.5	24.4
1991	26.3	24.1
1990	26.1	23.9
1989	26.2	23.8
1988	25.9	23.6
1987	25.8	23.6
1986	25.7	23.1
1985	25.5	23.3
1984	25.4	23.0
1983	25.4	22.8
1982	25.2	22.5
1981	24.8	22.3
1980	24.7	22.0
1979	24.4	22.1
1978	24.2	21.8
1977	24.0	21.6
1976	23.8	21.3
1975	23.5	21.1
1974	23.1	21.1
1973	23.2	21.0
1972	23.3	20.9
1971	23.1	20.9
1970	23.2	20.8
1969	23.2	20.8
1968	23.1	20.8
1967	23.1	20.6
1966	22.8	20.5
1965	22.8	20.6
1964	23.1	20.5
1963	22.8	20.5
1962	22.7	20.3
1961	22.8	20.3
1960	22.8	20.3
1955	22.6	20.2
1950	22.8	20.3

Source: Bureau of the Census, Families and Living Arrangements, Historical Tables—Households, Internet site http://www.census.gov/population/www/socdemo/hh-fam.html; calculations by New Strategist

Table 7.24 Marital Status of Men, 1950 to 2006

(total number of men aged 15 or older and percent distribution by marital status, 1950 to 2006; numbers in thousands)

	total men		never married	married	divorced	widowed
	number	percent				
2006	113,073	100.0%	32.8%	56.3%	8.6%	2.3%
2005	111,591	100.0	32.6	56.7	8.3	2.4
2004	110,048	100.0	32.6	56.8	8.2	2.4
2003	108,696	100.0	32.1	57.2	8.3	2.5
2002	106,819	100.0	32.0	57.4	8.1	2.5
2001	105,584	100.0	31.3	58.0	8.3	2.4
2000	103,114	100.0	31.3	57.9	8.3	2.5
1999	102,048	100.0	31.3	57.9	8.4	2.5
1998	101,123	100.0	31.2	58.0	8.2	2.5
1997	100,159	100.0	31.3	57.8	8.2	2.7
1996	98,593	100.0	31.1	58.5	7.9	2.5
1995	97,704	100.0	31.0	58.9	7.6	2.3
1994	96,768	100.0	31.2	59.0	7.5	2.3
1993	94,854	100.0	30.3	59.9	7.1	2.6
1992	93,760	100.0	30.2	59.9	7.2	2.7
1991	92,840	100.0	30.1	60.2	7.1	2.6
1990	91,955	100.0	29.9	60.7	6.8	2.5
1980	81,947	100.0	29.6	63.2	4.8	2.4
1970	70,559	100.0	28.1	66.8	2.2	2.9
1960	60,273	100.0	25.3	69.3	1.8	3.5
1950	54,601	100.0	26.4	67.5	2.0	4.1

Note: Figures for 1950 and 1960 are for men aged 14 or older.
Source: Bureau of the Census, Families and Living Arrangements—Historical Tables, Internet site http://www.census.gov/population/www/socdemo/hh-fam.html; and Statistical Abstract of the United States for 1992 and 1993; calculations by New Strategist

Table 7.25 Marital Status of Women, 1950 to 2006

(total number of women aged 15 or older and percent distribution by marital status, 1950 to 2006; numbers in thousands)

	total women		never			
	number	percent	married	married	divorced	widowed
2006	119,966	100.0%	26.2%	53.4%	10.9%	9.4%
2005	118,681	100.0	25.8	53.8	11.0	9.4
2004	117,295	100.0	25.6	54.0	10.9	9.5
2003	116,361	100.0	25.4	54.0	10.9	9.7
2002	114,639	100.0	25.2	54.2	10.7	10.0
2001	113,451	100.0	24.7	54.6	10.6	10.2
2000	110,660	100.0	25.1	54.7	10.2	10.0
1999	109,628	100.0	25.1	54.7	10.2	10.0
1998	108,168	100.0	24.7	54.9	10.3	10.2
1997	107,076	100.0	24.3	54.9	10.4	10.3
1996	106,031	100.0	24.1	55.6	9.9	10.4
1995	105,028	100.0	23.5	56.2	9.8	10.6
1994	104,032	100.0	23.7	55.9	9.7	10.6
1993	102,400	100.0	23.0	56.4	9.7	11.0
1992	101,483	100.0	23.0	56.4	9.4	11.2
1991	100,680	100.0	23.2	56.5	9.1	11.2
1990	99,838	100.0	22.8	56.9	8.9	11.5
1980	89,914	100.0	22.5	58.9	6.6	12.0
1970	77,766	100.0	22.1	61.9	3.5	12.5
1960	64,607	100.0	19.0	65.9	2.6	12.5
1950	57,102	100.0	20.0	65.8	2.4	11.8

Note: Figures for 1950 and 1960 are for women aged 14 or older.
Source: Bureau of the Census, Families and Living Arrangements—Historical Tables, Internet site http://www.census.gov/ population/www/socdemo/hh-fam.html; and Statistical Abstract of the United States for 1992 and 1993; calculations by New Strategist

Interracial Marriage Has Become More Common

Changes in racial and ethnic categories make comparisons difficult.

In 2006, more than 4 million married couples had mixed marriages—meaning the husband and wife were of different races or Hispanic origins. The number of mixed marriages is growing. In 1960, just 0.4 percent of couples were interracial. By 2002, the most recent year with comparable statistics, the figure had grown to 2.9 percent. Since 2003, statistics on mixed marriages include both race and Hispanic origin, boosting the number of mixed marriages to 7 percent of the total.

The most common type of mixed marriage is a non-Hispanic white husband and a Hispanic wife (989,000). Second is a non-Hispanic white husband and a wife of other race, mostly Asian (956,000). Third are marriages between a non-Hispanic white wife and a Hispanic husband (946,000). Together, these three types of mixed marriages account for more than two-thirds of the total.

■ Marriages between blacks and non-Hispanic whites are still uncommon, numbering only 336,000 in 2006.

Most marriages are between spouses of the same race and Hispanic origin

(percent distribution of marriages by race and Hispanic origin of spouses, 2006)

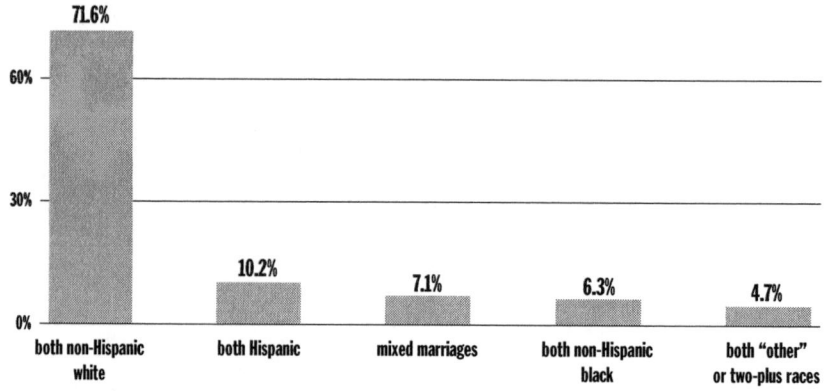

Table 7.26 Interracial and Interethnic Married Couples, 1960 to 2006

(total number of married couples, number of interracial couples through 2002, number of interracial and inter-ethnic couples from 2003 through 2006, and interracial/interethnic couple share of total, 1960 to 2006; numbers in thousands)

	total couples	interracial and interethnic couples	
		number	share of total
2006	59,528	4,256	7.1%
2005	59,373	4,176	7.0
2004	59,064	3,972	6.7
2003	58,586	3,719	6.3

	total couples	interracial couples	
		number	share of total
2002	57,919	1,674	2.9%
2001	57,838	1,596	2.8
2000	56,497	1,464	2.6
1999	55,849	1,481	2.7
1998	55,305	1,348	2.4
1997	54,666	1,264	2.3
1996	54,664	1,260	2.3
1995	54,937	1,392	2.5
1994	54,251	1,283	2.4
1993	54,199	1,195	2.2
1992	53,512	1,161	2.2
1991	53,227	994	1.9
1990	53,256	964	1.8
1989	52,924	953	1.8
1988	52,613	956	1.8
1987	52,286	799	1.5
1986	51,704	827	1.6
1985	51,114	792	1.5
1984	50,864	762	1.5
1983	50,665	719	1.4
1982	50,294	697	1.4
1981	49,896	639	1.3
1980	49,714	651	1.3
1970	44,598	310	0.7
1960	40,491	149	0.4

Note: Before 2003, interracial marriages include only marriages between blacks, whites, and Asians. From 2003 on, interracial and interethnic marriages include those between husbands and wives of differing races and Hispanic origins.
Source: Bureau of the Census, America's Families and Living Arrangements, Internet site http://www.census.gov/population/www/socdemo/hh-fam.html; and 1960 and 1970 censuses; calculations by New Strategist

Table 7.27 Race/Hispanic Origin Difference between Husbands and Wives, 2006

(number and percent distribution of married-couple family groups by race/Hispanic origin difference between husband and wife, 2006; numbers in thousands)

	number	percent distribution
Total married couples	**59,528**	**100.0%**
SAME RACE/HISPANIC ORIGIN MARRIAGES	**55,271**	**92.8**
Both white, non-Hispanic	42,610	71.6
Both black, non-Hispanic	3,778	6.3
Both Hispanic	6,065	10.2
Both other race or two-plus races, non-Hispanic	2,818	4.7
MIXED RACE/HISPANIC ORIGIN MARRIAGES	**4,256**	**7.1**
Husband white, non-Hispanic; wife black, non-Hispanic	100	0.2
Husband white, non-Hispanic; wife Hispanic	989	1.7
Husband white, non-Hispanic; wife other race or two-plus races, non-Hispanic	956	1.6
Husband black, non-Hispanic; wife white, non-Hispanic	236	0.4
Husband black, non-Hispanic; wife Hispanic	91	0.2
Husband black, non-Hispanic; wife other race or two-plus races, non-Hispanic	76	0.1
Husband Hispanic; wife white, non-Hispanic	946	1.6
Husband Hispanic; wife black, non-Hispanic	49	0.1
Husband Hispanic; wife other race or two-plus races, non-Hispanic	72	0.1
Husband other race or two-plus races, non-Hispanic; wife white, non-Hispanic	634	1.1
Husband other race or two-plus races, non-Hispanic; wife black, non-Hispanic	28	0.0
Husband other race or two-plus races, non-Hispanic; wife Hispanic	79	0.1

Source: Bureau of the Census, America's Families and Living Arrangements: 2006, Internet site http://www.census.gov/population/www/socdemo/hh-fam/cps2006.html; calculations by New Strategist

CHAPTER

8

Population

■ Since the 2000 census counted 282 million Americans, the U.S. population has grown by 17 million people. Our 1 percent annual growth rate is relatively rapid for a developed country.

■ The biggest ongoing change in the U.S. population is growing diversity. In 1950, 90 percent of Americans were white. By 2006, non-Hispanic whites accounted for only 66 percent of the population.

■ The proportion of Americans who were born in another country is growing rapidly as immigrants arrive in the United States. In 2006, 12 percent of the population was foreign-born, up from 7 percent in 1950.

■ The West is by far the most diverse region, and non-Hispanic whites accounted for only 55 percent of its population in 2006. The Midwest is the least diverse region; non-Hispanic whites accounted for 80 percent of its population.

■ In Maine, fully 96 percent of the population was non-Hispanic white in 2006. In California, the nation's most populous state, non-Hispanic whites accounted for just 43 percent of the population.

■ Among the nation's 361 metropolitan areas, New York is by far the most populous, with 19 million people in 2006.

The U.S. Population Is Growing

The population is increasing by about 3 million people each year.

Since the 2000 census counted 282 million Americans, the U.S. population has grown by 17 million people, to just under 300 million as of July 1, 2006. Our 1 percent annual growth rate is relatively rapid for a developed country. Fueling the growth is the steady stream of immigrants arriving at our shores looking for a better life.

Females slightly outnumber males in the population. Females accounted for 51 percent of the total in 2006—a figure that has barely changed over the past half-century. The age distribution of the population has changed, however, as age groups expand and contract with the aging of the large baby-boom generation (born between 1946 and 1964). Between 2000 and 2006, the 55-to-59 age group grew faster than any other, up 34 percent as it filled with the oldest boomers.

■ The population will continue to age as boomers become the nation's elders.

The U.S. population has doubled since 1950

(population of the United States as of July 1, 1950, and July 1, 2006)

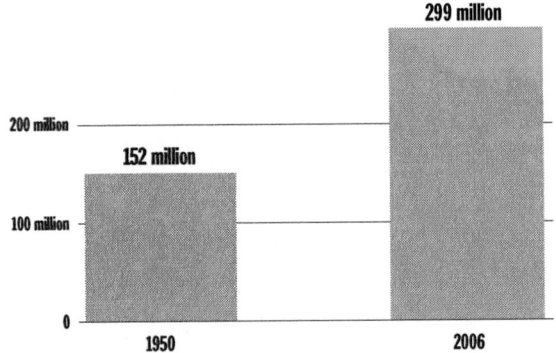

Table 8.1 Population of the United States, 1950 to 2006

(population of the United States, 1950 to 2006; numerical and percent change from preceding year and decade; numbers in thousands)

		increase from preceding year/decade	
	population	numerical	percent
2006	299,398	2,891	1.0%
2005	296,507	2,869	1.0
2004	293,638	2,842	1.0
2003	290,796	2,670	0.9
2002	288,126	2,900	1.0
2001	285,226	3,009	1.1
2000	282,217	3,177	1.1
1990 to 2000	–	32,594	13.1
1999	279,040	3,186	1.2
1998	275,854	3,207	1.2
1997	272,647	3,253	1.2
1996	269,394	3,116	1.2
1995	266,278	3,152	1.2
1994	263,126	3,207	1.2
1993	259,919	3,405	1.3
1992	256,514	3,533	1.4
1991	252,981	3,358	1.3
1990	249,623	2,645	1.1
1980 to 1990	–	22,398	9.9
1989	246,819	2,320	0.9
1988	244,499	2,210	0.9
1987	242,289	2,156	0.9
1986	240,133	2,209	0.9
1985	237,924	2,099	0.9
1984	235,825	2,033	0.9
1983	233,792	2,128	0.9
1982	231,664	2,199	1.0
1981	229,466	2,241	1.0
1980	227,225	2,169	1.0
1970 to 1980	–	22,173	10.8
1979	225,055	2,471	1.1
1978	222,585	2,345	1.1
1977	220,239	2,204	1.0
1976	218,035	2,062	1.0
1975	215,973	2,119	1.0
1974	213,854	1,945	0.9
1973	211,909	2,013	1.0
1972	209,896	2,235	1.1
1971	207,661	2,609	1.3
1970	205,052	2,375	1.2

(continued)

| | population | increase from preceding year/decade | |
		numerical	percent
1960 to 1970	–	24,381	13.5%
1969	202,677	1,971	1.0
1968	200,706	1,994	1.0
1967	198,712	2,152	1.1
1966	196,560	2,257	1.2
1965	194,303	2,414	1.3
1964	191,889	2,647	1.4
1963	189,242	2,704	1.4
1962	186,538	2,846	1.5
1961	183,691	3,020	1.7
1960	180,671	2,842	1.6
1950 to 1960	–	28,400	18.7
1959	177,830	2,948	1.7
1958	174,882	2,898	1.7
1957	171,984	3,081	1.8
1956	168,903	2,972	1.8
1955	165,931	2,905	1.8
1954	163,026	2,842	1.8
1953	160,184	2,631	1.7
1952	157,553	2,675	1.7
1951	154,878	2,606	1.7
1950	152,271	–	–

Note: Figures are for July 1 of the year shown. "–" means not applicable.
Source: Bureau of the Census, National Population Estimates, Internet site http://www.census.gov/popest/national/index.html; calculations by New Strategist

Table 8.2 Population by Sex, 1950 to 2006

(number of people by sex and female share of total, 1950 to 2006; numbers in thousands)

	total	males	females	
			number	share of total
2006	299,398	147,512	151,886	50.7%
2000	281,422	138,054	143,368	50.9
1990	248,791	121,284	127,507	51.3
1980	226,546	110,053	116,493	51.4
1970	203,235	98,926	104,309	51.3
1960	179,323	88,331	90,992	50.7
1950	151,326	75,187	76,139	50.3

Source: Bureau of the Census, National Population Estimates, Internet site http://www.census.gov/popest/national/index.html; calculations by New Strategist

Table 8.3 Population by Age, 1950 to 2006

(number and percent distribution of people by age, 1950 to 2006; numbers in thousands)

	total	under 15	15 to 24	25 to 34	35 to 44	45 to 54	55 to 64	65 or older	median age (years)
Number									
2006	299,398	60,755	42,435	40,416	43,667	43,278	31,587	37,260	36.4
2000	281,422	60,253	39,184	39,892	45,149	37,678	24,275	34,992	35.3
1990	248,791	53,874	37,036	43,174	37,444	25,062	21,116	31,084	32.8
1980	226,546	51,290	42,487	37,082	25,634	22,800	21,703	25,550	30.0
1970	203,212	57,900	35,441	24,907	23,088	23,220	18,590	20,066	27.9
1960	179,323	55,786	24,020	22,818	24,081	20,485	15,572	16,560	29.4
1950	150,697	40,483	22,098	23,759	21,450	17,343	13,295	12,270	30.2
Percent distribution									
2006	100.0%	20.3%	14.2%	13.5%	14.6%	14.5%	10.6%	12.4%	–
2000	100.0	21.4	13.9	14.2	16.0	13.4	8.6	12.4	–
1990	100.0	21.7	14.9	17.4	15.1	10.1	8.5	12.5	–
1980	100.0	22.6	18.8	16.4	11.3	10.1	9.6	11.3	–
1970	100.0	28.5	17.4	12.3	11.4	11.4	9.1	9.9	–
1960	100.0	31.1	13.4	12.7	13.4	11.4	8.7	9.2	–
1950	100.0	26.9	14.7	15.8	14.2	11.5	8.8	8.1	–

Note: "–" means not applicable.
Source: Bureau of the Census, Historical Statistics of the United States: Colonial Times to 1970, Part 1, 1975; and Statistical Abstract of the United States: 2001; and National Population Estimates, Internet site http://www.census.gov/popest/national/index .html; calculations by New Strategist

Table 8.4 Population by Age and Sex, 2006

(number of people by age and sex, and sex ratio by age, 2006; numbers in thousands)

	total	female	male	sex ratio
Total people	**299,398**	**151,886**	**147,512**	**97**
Under age 5	20,418	9,976	10,442	105
Aged 5 to 9	19,710	9,633	10,077	105
Aged 10 to 14	20,627	10,065	10,563	105
Aged 15 to 19	21,324	10,389	10,935	105
Aged 20 to 24	21,111	10,201	10,910	107
Aged 25 to 29	20,709	10,125	10,584	105
Aged 30 to 34	19,706	9,726	9,980	103
Aged 35 to 39	21,186	10,536	10,650	101
Aged 40 to 44	22,481	11,281	11,200	99
Aged 45 to 49	22,798	11,536	11,262	98
Aged 50 to 54	20,481	10,453	10,028	96
Aged 55 to 59	18,224	9,379	8,845	94
Aged 60 to 64	13,362	6,984	6,379	91
Aged 65 or older	37,260	21,603	15,657	72

Note: The sex ratio is the number of men per 100 women; "–" means not applicable.
Source: Bureau of the Census, National Population Estimates, Internet site http://www.census.gov/popest/national/asrh/NC-EST2006-sa.html; calculations by New Strategist

Table 8.5 Population by Age, 2000 and 2006

(number of people by age, 2000 and 2006; percent change, 2000–06; numbers in thousands)

	2006	2000	percent change
Total people	**299,398**	**282,217**	**6.1%**
Under age 5	20,418	19,188	6.4
Aged 5 to 9	19,710	20,478	–3.8
Aged 10 to 14	20,627	20,622	0.0
Aged 15 to 19	21,324	20,264	5.2
Aged 20 to 24	21,111	19,132	10.3
Aged 25 to 29	20,709	19,309	7.3
Aged 30 to 34	19,706	20,543	–4.1
Aged 35 to 39	21,186	22,662	–6.5
Aged 40 to 44	22,481	22,525	–0.2
Aged 45 to 49	22,798	20,223	12.7
Aged 50 to 54	20,481	17,775	15.2
Aged 55 to 59	18,224	13,559	34.4
Aged 60 to 64	13,362	10,857	23.1
Aged 65 or older	37,260	35,078	6.2

Source: Bureau of the Census, National Population Estimates, Internet site http://www.census.gov/popest/national/asrh/NC-EST2006-sa.html; calculations by New Strategist

The United States Is Increasingly Diverse

In 2006, only two-thirds of Americans were non-Hispanic white.

The United States is becoming increasingly diverse, and our ways of measuring diversity are becoming more complex. Racial identification was once limited to three categories—white, black, and other. In 1980, the number of racial categories expanded and Hispanic identification was added to the mix. In 2006, the complexity grew by leaps and bounds as the government added yet another racial identification (Native Hawaiians) and allowed Americans to identify themselves as being of more than one race.

In 2006, non-Hispanic whites accounted for only 66 percent of the U.S. population. The Hispanic population has surged past blacks as the largest minority group. By 2006, they accounted for 15 percent of the total population versus the black share of 13 percent. Between 2000 and 2006, the Asian and Hispanic populations expanded by 24 and 26 percent, respectively, compared with a small 2 percent increase in the number of non-Hispanic whites. These differences in growth rates guarantee the increasingly diversity of the American population.

■ Although the number of Asians is growing rapidly, the Asian share of the total population was a small 4 percent in 2006.

The non-Hispanic white share of the population is declining

(non-Hispanic white share of the total U.S. population, 1980 to 2006)

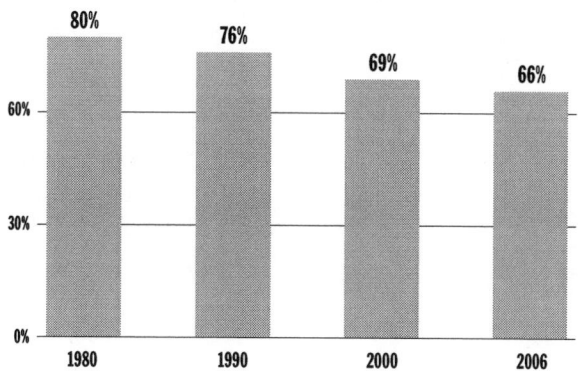

Table 8.6 Population by Race, 1950 to 1970

(number and percent distribution of people by race, 1950 to 1970; numbers in thousands)

	1970		1960		1950	
	number	percent distribution	number	percent distribution	number	percent distribution
Total population	**205,052**	**100.0%**	**180,671**	**100.0%**	**150,697**	**100.0%**
Black	22,801	11.1	19,006	10.5	15,042	10.0
White	179,644	87.6	160,023	88.6	134,942	89.5
Other	2,607	1.3	1,642	0.9	713	0.5

Source: Bureau of the Census, Historical Statistics of the United States: Colonial Times to 1970, Part 1, 1975; calculations by New Strategist

Table 8.7 Population by Race and Hispanic Origin, 1980 and 1990

(number and percent distribution of people by race and Hispanic origin, 1980 and 1990; numbers in thousands)

	1990		1980	
	number	percent distribution	number	percent distribution
RACE				
Total population	**248,791**	**100.0%**	**226,546**	**100.0%**
American Indian	2,067	0.8	1,420	0.6
Asian	7,467	3.0	3,729	1.6
Black	30,517	12.3	26,683	11.8
White	208,741	83.9	194,713	85.9
HISPANIC ORIGIN				
Total population	**248,791**	**100.0**	**226,546**	**100.0**
Hispanic	22,379	9.0	14,609	6.4
Non-Hispanic	226,412	91.0	211,937	93.6
Non-Hispanic white	188,315	75.7	180,906	79.9

Note: Hispanics may be of any race.
Source: Bureau of the Census, National Population Estimates, Internet site http://www.census.gov/popest/national/index.html; calculations by New Strategist

Table 8.8 Population by Race and Hispanic Origin, 2000 and 2006

(number and percent distribution of people by race and Hispanic origin, 2000 and 2006, and percent change in number, 2000–06; numbers in thousands)

	2006		2000		percent change in number 2000–06
	number	percent distribution	number	percent distribution	
RACE					
Total population	**299,398**	**100.0%**	**281,422**	**100.0%**	**6.4%**
One race	294,680	98.4	277,524	98.6	6.2
American Indian	2,903	1.0	2,664	0.9	9.0
Asian	13,159	4.4	10,589	3.8	24.3
Black	38,343	12.8	35,704	12.7	7.4
Native Hawaiian	529	0.2	463	0.2	14.3
White	239,746	80.1	228,104	81.1	5.1
Two or more races	4,719	1.6	3,898	1.4	21.1
HISPANIC ORIGIN					
Total population	**299,398**	**100.0**	**281,422**	**100.0**	**6.4**
Hispanic	44,321	14.8	35,306	12.5	25.5
Non-Hispanic	255,077	85.2	246,116	87.5	3.6
Non-Hispanic white	198,744	66.4	195,575	69.5	1.6

Note: Native Hawaiians include other Pacific Islanders. Hispanics may be of any race.
Source: Bureau of the Census, National Population Estimates, Internet site http://www.census.gov/popest/national/index.html; calculations by New Strategist

Table 8.9 Population by Age and Race, 2006

(number of people by age and race, 2006; numbers in thousands)

	total population	American Indian	Asian	black	white	Native Hawaiian	two or more races
				one race			
Total people	**299,398**	**2,903**	**13,159**	**38,343**	**239,746**	**529**	**4,719**
Under age 5	20,418	203	890	3,073	15,549	38	665
Aged 5 to 9	19,710	226	807	2,967	15,044	40	627
Aged 10 to 14	20,627	253	814	3,246	15,721	45	548
Aged 15 to 19	21,324	272	818	3,359	16,357	45	472
Aged 20 to 24	21,111	264	906	3,096	16,395	47	403
Aged 25 to 29	20,709	236	1,098	2,899	16,092	51	333
Aged 30 to 34	19,706	208	1,283	2,624	15,279	45	267
Aged 35 to 39	21,186	206	1,217	2,738	16,736	42	247
Aged 40 to 44	22,481	215	1,088	2,875	18,027	40	236
Aged 45 to 49	22,798	206	978	2,781	18,570	35	226
Aged 50 to 54	20,481	174	863	2,338	16,887	29	191
Aged 55 to 59	18,224	142	725	1,903	15,275	23	157
Aged 60 to 64	13,362	96	497	1,275	11,371	16	109
Aged 65 or older	37,260	202	1,177	3,168	32,444	33	238
Median age (years)	36.4	29.9	34.9	31.0	37.8	29.7	20.6

PERCENT DISTRIBUTION BY RACE

Total people	**100.0%**	**1.0%**	**4.4%**	**12.8%**	**80.1%**	**0.2%**	**1.6%**
Under age 5	100.0	1.0	4.4	15.1	76.2	0.2	3.3
Aged 5 to 9	100.0	1.1	4.1	15.1	76.3	0.2	3.2
Aged 10 to 14	100.0	1.2	3.9	15.7	76.2	0.2	2.7
Aged 15 to 19	100.0	1.3	3.8	15.8	76.7	0.2	2.2
Aged 20 to 24	100.0	1.2	4.3	14.7	77.7	0.2	1.9
Aged 25 to 29	100.0	1.1	5.3	14.0	77.7	0.2	1.6
Aged 30 to 34	100.0	1.1	6.5	13.3	77.5	0.2	1.4
Aged 35 to 39	100.0	1.0	5.7	12.9	79.0	0.2	1.2
Aged 40 to 44	100.0	1.0	4.8	12.8	80.2	0.2	1.1
Aged 45 to 49	100.0	0.9	4.3	12.2	81.5	0.2	1.0
Aged 50 to 54	100.0	0.8	4.2	11.4	82.5	0.1	0.9
Aged 55 to 59	100.0	0.8	4.0	10.4	83.8	0.1	0.9
Aged 60 to 64	100.0	0.7	3.7	9.5	85.1	0.1	0.8
Aged 65 or older	100.0	0.5	3.2	8.5	87.1	0.1	0.6

Source: Bureau of the Census, National Population Estimates, Internet site http://www.census.gov/popest/national/asrh/ NC-EST2006-asrh.html; calculations by New Strategist

Table 8.10 Population by Age and Hispanic Origin, 2006

(number of people by age and Hispanic origin, 2006; numbers in thousands)

| | | | Hispanic origin | |
| | | | non-Hispanic | |
	total population	Hispanic	total	white
Total people	**299,398**	**44,321**	**255,077**	**198,744**
Under age 5	20,418	4,705	15,713	11,162
Aged 5 to 9	19,710	4,091	15,619	11,291
Aged 10 to 14	20,627	3,942	16,685	12,125
Aged 15 to 19	21,324	3,623	17,701	13,049
Aged 20 to 24	21,111	3,752	17,359	12,938
Aged 25 to 29	20,709	4,163	16,547	12,236
Aged 30 to 34	19,706	3,929	15,778	11,622
Aged 35 to 39	21,186	3,532	17,653	13,455
Aged 40 to 44	22,481	3,127	19,354	15,125
Aged 45 to 49	22,798	2,557	20,240	16,200
Aged 50 to 54	20,481	1,960	18,521	15,072
Aged 55 to 59	18,224	1,500	16,724	13,883
Aged 60 to 64	13,362	1,040	12,322	10,400
Aged 65 or older	37,260	2,399	34,861	30,188
Median age (years)	36.4	27.4	38.6	40.5

PERCENT DISTRIBUTION BY HISPANIC ORIGIN

Total people	**100.0%**	**14.8%**	**85.2%**	**66.4%**
Under age 5	100.0	23.0	77.0	54.7
Aged 5 to 9	100.0	20.8	79.2	57.3
Aged 10 to 14	100.0	19.1	80.9	58.8
Aged 15 to 19	100.0	17.0	83.0	61.2
Aged 20 to 24	100.0	17.8	82.2	61.3
Aged 25 to 29	100.0	20.1	79.9	59.1
Aged 30 to 34	100.0	19.9	80.1	59.0
Aged 35 to 39	100.0	16.7	83.3	63.5
Aged 40 to 44	100.0	13.9	86.1	67.3
Aged 45 to 49	100.0	11.2	88.8	71.1
Aged 50 to 54	100.0	9.6	90.4	73.6
Aged 55 to 59	100.0	8.2	91.8	76.2
Aged 60 to 64	100.0	7.8	92.2	77.8
Aged 65 or older	100.0	6.4	93.6	81.0

Source: Bureau of the Census, National Population Estimates, Internet site http://www.census.gov/popest/national/asrh/ NC-EST2006-asrh.html; calculations by New Strategist

The Mobility Rate Has Fallen Since 1950

Most movers stay within the same county.

Between 2004 and 2005, only 14 percent of people aged 1 or older moved from one residence to another. This mobility rate is much lower than the 21 percent who moved between 1950 and 1951. No one knows why the mobility rate has fallen so much, but there are a number of likely reasons. Homeownership has increased, and homeowners are less likely than renters to move. Another reason may be the rise in two-earner couples, as it is more difficult to relocate when both husband and wife must find a new job. The aging of the population is also important, since older people move less frequently than young adults.

Most moves are local, and 57 percent of movers remain in the same county. Local moves dominate the total because most movers move for housing-related reasons, according to Census Bureau research. Only 19 percent of movers crossed state lines in 2004–05, slightly more than the 16 percent of 1950–51.

■ The mobility rate should continue to decline with the aging of the population.

Americans are moving less often than they once did

(percentage of people aged 1 or older who moved in the past 12 months, for selected years, 1950–51 to 2004–05)

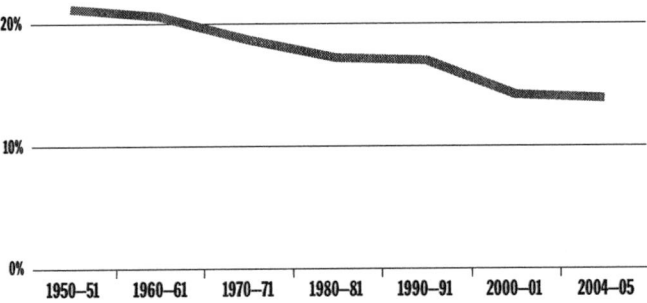

20%						
10%						
0%						
1950–51	1960–61	1970–71	1980–81	1990–91	2000–01	2004–05

Table 8.11 Geographical Mobility, 1950 to 2005

(total number of people aged 1 or older, and number and percent of movers by type of move, 1950–51 to 2004–05; numbers in thousands)

	total people aged 1+	same house (nonmovers)	total movers	different house in United States					movers from abroad
				total	same county	different county	same state	different state	
2004–05	287,148	247,261	39,888	38,023	22,736	15,287	7,847	7,441	1,865
2003–04	284,367	245,372	38,995	37,723	22,551	15,172	7,842	7,330	1,272
2002–03	282,556	242,463	40,093	38,824	23,468	15,356	7,728	7,628	1,269
2001–02	278,160	237,049	41,111	39,548	23,712	15,836	8,066	7,770	1,563
2000–01	275,611	236,605	39,007	37,251	21,918	15,333	7,550	7,783	1,756
1999–00	270,219	226,831	43,388	41,642	24,399	17,242	8,814	8,428	1,746
1998–99	267,933	225,297	42,636	41,207	25,268	15,939	8,423	7,516	1,429
1997–98	265,209	222,702	42,507	41,304	27,082	14,222	7,867	6,355	1,203
1996–97	262,976	219,585	43,391	42,088	27,740	14,348	7,960	6,389	1,303
1995–96	260,406	217,868	42,537	41,176	26,696	14,480	8,009	6,471	1,361
1994–95	258,248	215,931	42,317	41,539	27,908	13,631	7,888	5,743	778
1993–94	255,774	212,939	42,835	41,590	26,638	14,952	8,226	6,726	1,245
1992–93	252,799	209,700	43,099	41,704	26,932	14,772	7,855	6,916	1,395
1991–92	247,380	204,580	42,800	41,545	26,587	14,957	7,853	7,105	1,255
1990–91	244,884	203,345	41,539	40,154	25,151	15,003	7,881	7,122	1,385
1980–81	221,641	183,442	38,200	36,887	23,097	13,789	7,614	6,175	1,313
1970–71	201,506	163,800	37,705	36,161	23,018	13,143	6,197	6,946	1,544
1960–61	177,354	140,821	36,533	35,535	24,289	11,246	5,493	5,753	998
1950–51	148,400	116,936	31,464	31,158	20,694	10,464	5,276	5,188	306

Percent distribution of population by mobility status

	total people aged 1+	same house (nonmovers)	total movers	total	same county	different county	same state	different state	movers from abroad
2004–05	100.0%	86.1%	13.9%	13.2%	7.9%	5.3%	2.7%	2.6%	0.6%
2003–04	100.0	86.3	13.7	13.3	7.9	5.3	2.8	2.6	0.4
2002–03	100.0	85.8	14.2	13.7	8.3	5.4	2.7	2.7	0.4
2001–02	100.0	85.2	14.8	14.2	8.5	5.7	2.9	2.8	0.6
2000–01	100.0	85.8	14.2	13.5	8.0	5.6	2.7	2.8	0.6
1999–00	100.0	83.9	16.1	15.4	9.0	6.4	3.3	3.1	0.6
1998–99	100.0	84.1	15.9	15.4	9.4	5.9	3.1	2.8	0.5
1997–98	100.0	84.0	16.0	15.6	10.2	5.4	3.0	2.4	0.5
1996–97	100.0	83.5	16.5	16.0	10.5	5.5	3.0	2.4	0.5
1995–96	100.0	83.7	16.3	15.8	10.3	5.6	3.1	2.5	0.5
1994–95	100.0	83.6	16.4	16.1	10.8	5.3	3.1	2.2	0.3
1993–94	100.0	83.3	16.7	16.3	10.4	5.8	3.2	2.6	0.5
1992–93	100.0	83.0	17.0	16.5	10.7	5.8	3.1	2.7	0.6
1991–92	100.0	82.7	17.3	16.8	10.7	6.0	3.2	2.9	0.5
1990–91	100.0	83.0	17.0	16.4	10.3	6.1	3.2	2.9	0.6
1980–81	100.0	82.8	17.2	16.6	10.4	6.2	3.4	2.8	0.6
1970–71	100.0	81.3	18.7	17.9	11.4	6.5	3.1	3.4	0.8
1960–61	100.0	79.4	20.6	20.0	13.7	6.3	3.1	3.2	0.6
1950–51	100.0	78.8	21.2	21.0	13.9	7.1	3.6	3.5	0.2

(continued)

	total people aged 1+	same house (nonmovers)	total movers	different house in United States					movers from abroad
				total	same county	different county	same state	different state	
Percent distribution of movers by type of move									
2004–05	–	–	100.0%	95.3%	57.0%	38.3%	19.7%	18.7%	4.7%
2003–04	–	–	100.0	96.7	57.8	38.9	20.1	18.8	3.3
2002–03	–	–	100.0	96.8	58.5	38.3	19.3	19.0	3.2
2001–02	–	–	100.0	96.2	57.7	38.5	19.6	18.9	3.8
2000–01	–	–	100.0	95.5	56.2	39.3	19.4	20.0	4.5
1999–00	–	–	100.0	96.0	56.2	39.7	20.3	19.4	4.0
1998–99	–	–	100.0	96.6	59.3	37.4	19.8	17.6	3.4
1997–98	–	–	100.0	97.2	63.7	33.5	18.5	15.0	2.8
1996–97	–	–	100.0	97.0	63.9	33.1	18.3	14.7	3.0
1995–96	–	–	100.0	96.8	62.8	34.0	18.8	15.2	3.2
1994–95	–	–	100.0	98.2	65.9	32.2	18.6	13.6	1.8
1993–94	–	–	100.0	97.1	62.2	34.9	19.2	15.7	2.9
1992–93	–	–	100.0	96.8	62.5	34.3	18.2	16.0	3.2
1991–92	–	–	100.0	97.1	62.1	34.9	18.3	16.6	2.9
1990–91	–	–	100.0	96.7	60.5	36.1	19.0	17.1	3.3
1980–81	–	–	100.0	96.6	60.5	36.1	19.9	16.2	3.4
1970–71	–	–	100.0	95.9	61.0	34.9	16.4	18.4	4.1
1960–61	–	–	100.0	97.3	66.5	30.8	15.0	15.7	2.7
1950–51	–	–	100.0	99.0	65.8	33.3	16.8	16.5	1.0

Note: "–" means not applicable.
Source: Bureau of the Census, Geographical Mobility, Internet site http://www.census.gov/population/socdemo/migration/tab-a-1.txt; calculations by New Strategist

Many Americans Were Born Abroad

One in eight U.S. residents is foreign-born.

The proportion of Americans who were born in another country is growing rapidly as immigrants arrive in the United States. In 2006, 12 percent of the population was foreign-born, up from 7 percent in 1950.

The 53 percent majority of the foreign-born are from Latin America, according to the Census Bureau's 2005 American Community Survey. Another 27 percent are from Asia, and only 14 percent are from Europe. Mexico is the number one country of birth among the nation's foreign-born, according to the 2000 census. Italy was once the leading country of birth for the nation's foreign-born.

Nearly 10 million legal immigrants came to the United States during the 1990s, and that figure will probably be surpassed during this decade. Already, more than 7 million legal immigrants have come to the U.S. between 2000 and 2006, the largest number from Mexico. The Department of Homeland Security estimates that the U.S. is also home to 10.5 million undocumented immigrants.

■ Americans are of two minds about immigration, a division that prevents politicians from crafting a workable immigration policy.

About 1 million immigrants a year come to the United States

(number of legal immigrants coming to the United States, 2000 to 2006)

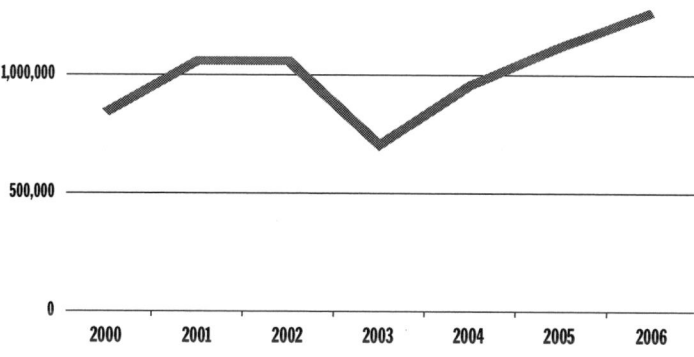

Table 8.12 Foreign-Born Population, 1950 to 2005

(number and percent of people by foreign-born status, 1950 to 2005; numbers in thousands)

| | total population | native-born | | | foreign-born | |
| | | total | born in state of residence | | | |
			number	percent of total population	number	percent of total population
2005	288,378	252,688	170,473	59.1%	35,690	12.4%
2000	281,422	250,314	168,729	60.0	31,108	11.1
1990	248,710	228,943	153,685	61.8	19,767	7.9
1980	226,546	212,466	144,871	63.9	14,080	6.2
1970	203,194	193,454	131,296	64.6	9,740	4.8
1960	178,467	168,806	118,802	66.6	9,661	5.4
1950	150,216	139,869	102,788	68.4	10,347	6.9

Source: Bureau of the Census, Statistical Abstract of the United States: 2001; and Census 2000, Table DP-2: Profile of Selected Social Characteristics: 2000; and 2005 American Community Survey, 2005 Data Profiles, Selected Social Characteristics in the United States: 2005; calculations by New Strategist

Table 8.13 Foreign-Born Population by Country of Birth, 1960 to 2005

(number and percent distribution of foreign-born by country of birth for the 10 largest foreign-born populations, 1960 to 2000; and number and percent distribution of foreign-born by world region of birth, 2005; numbers in thousands)

	number	percent distribution
2005		
Total foreign-born	**35,689**	**100.0%**
Latin America	19,019	53.3
Asia	9,534	26.7
Europe	4,870	13.6
Africa	1,252	3.5
North America	829	2.3
Oceania	185	0.5
2000		
Total foreign-born	**31,108**	**100.0**
Total from top 10 countries	18,158	58.4
Mexico	9,177	29.5
China	1,519	4.9
Philippines	1,369	4.4
India	1,023	3.3
Vietnam	988	3.2
Cuba	873	2.8
Korea	864	2.8
Canada	821	2.6
El Salvador	817	2.6
Germany	707	2.3
1990		
Total foreign-born	**19,767**	**100.0**
Total from top 10 countries	10,267	51.9
Mexico	4,298	21.7
Philippines	913	4.6
Canada	745	3.8
Cuba	737	3.7
Germany	712	3.6
United Kingdom	640	3.2
Italy	581	2.9
Korea	568	2.9
Vietnam	543	2.7
China	530	2.7

(continued)

	number	percent distribution
1980		
Total foreign-born	**14,080**	**100.0%**
Total from top 10 countries	7,615	54.1
Mexico	2,199	15.6
Germany	849	6.0
Canada	843	6.0
Italy	832	5.9
United Kingdom	669	4.8
Cuba	608	4.3
Philippines	501	3.6
Poland	418	3.0
Soviet Union	406	2.9
Korea	290	2.1
1970		
Total foreign-born	**9,740**	**100.0**
Total from top 10 countries	6,015	61.8
Italy	1,009	10.4
Germany	833	8.6
Canada	812	8.3
Mexico	760	7.8
United Kingdom	686	7.0
Poland	548	5.6
Soviet Union	463	4.8
Cuba	439	4.5
Ireland	251	2.6
Austria	214	2.2
1960		
Total foreign-born	**9,661**	**100.0**
Total from top 10 countries	6,937	71.8
Italy	1,257	13.0
Germany	990	10.2
Canada	953	9.9
United Kingdom	833	8.6
Poland	748	7.7
Soviet Union	691	7.2
Mexico	576	6.0
Ireland	339	3.5
Austria	305	3.2
Hungary	245	2.5

Source: Bureau of the Census, Profile of the Foreign-Born Population in the United States: 1997, Current Population Reports, P23-195, 1999; and The Foreign-Born Population: 2000, Census 2000 Brief C2KBR-34, 2003; and 2005 American Community Survey, 2005 Data Profiles, Selected Social Characteristics in the United States: 2005; calculations by New Strategist

Table 8.14   Legal Immigration to the United States, 1950 to 2006

(number of immigrants granted permanent residence in the United States by decade and by single year, 1951 to 2006; percent change from previous year)

	number of immigrants	percent change from preceding year
2000 to 2006	**7,009,322**	–
2006	1,266,264	12.8%
2005	1,122,373	17.2
2004	957,883	36.2
2003	703,542	–33.6
2002	1,059,356	0.0
2001	1,058,902	25.9
2000	841,002	30.4
1990 to 1999	**9,775,398**	–
1999	644,787	–1.3
1998	653,206	–18.1
1997	797,847	–12.9
1996	915,560	27.1
1995	720,177	–10.4
1994	803,993	–11.1
1993	903,916	–7.1
1992	973,445	–46.7
1991	1,826,595	18.9
1990	1,535,872	40.9
1980 to 1989	**6,244,379**	–
1989	1,090,172	70.0
1988	641,346	6.9
1987	599,889	0.0
1986	600,027	5.6
1985	568,149	4.9
1984	541,811	–1.5
1983	550,052	3.1
1982	533,624	–10.3
1981	595,014	13.5
1980	524,295	33.0
1970 to 1979	**4,248,203**	–
1979	394,244	–33.2
1978	589,810	28.6
1977	458,755	–8.1
1976	499,093	29.5
1975	385,378	–2.2
1974	393,919	–1.2
1973	398,515	3.6
1972	384,685	3.8
1971	370,478	–0.8
1970	373,326	4.1

(continued)

	number of immigrants	percent change from preceding year
1960 to 1969	**3,213,749**	–
1969	358,579	–21.1%
1968	454,448	25.5
1967	361,972	12.1
1966	323,040	8.9
1965	296,697	1.5
1964	292,248	–4.6
1963	306,260	7.9
1962	283,763	4.6
1961	271,344	2.2
1960	265,398	1.8
1950 to 1959	**2,499,268**	–
1959	260,686	2.9
1958	253,265	–22.5
1957	326,867	1.6
1956	321,625	35.3
1955	237,790	14.2
1954	208,177	22.1
1953	170,434	–35.8
1952	265,520	29.1
1951	205,717	–17.4
1950	249,187	–

Note: Immigrants are people granted legal permanent residence in the United States. They either arrive in the U.S. with immigrant visas issued abroad or adjust their status in the United States from temporary to permanent residence. "–" means not applicable.
Source: Department of Homeland Security, 2006 Yearbook of Immigration Statistics, Internet site http://www.dhs.gov/ximgtn/statistics/publications/LPR06.shtm; calculations by New Strategist

Table 8.15 Legal Immigrants by Country of Last Residence, 1950 to 2006

(country of last residence for legal immigrants from the 10 countries sending the largest number of immigrants to the U.S., 1950 to 2006)

2000–06		1970–79	
TOTAL IMMIGRANTS	**7,009,322**	**TOTAL IMMIGRANTS**	**4,248,203**
Total from top 10	**3,640,210**	**Total from top ten**	**2,336,621**
Percent from top 10	**51.9%**	**Percent from top ten**	**55.0%**
Mexico	1,208,908	Mexico	621,218
India	421,006	Philippines	337,726
China	384,553	Cuba	256,497
Philippines	366,176	Korea	241,192
Russia	348,991	Canada	179,267
Vietnam	203,906	Italy	150,031
El Salvador	192,950	India	147,997
Dominican Republic	182,436	Dominican Republic	139,249
Canada	171,151	United Kingdom	133,218
Cuba	160,133	Jamaica	130,226
1990–99		**1960–69**	
TOTAL IMMIGRANTS	**9,775,398**	**TOTAL IMMIGRANTS**	**3,213,749**
Total from top ten	**5,702,541**	**Total from top ten**	**2,005,875**
Percent from top ten	**58.3%**	**Percent from top ten**	**62.4%**
Mexico	2,757,418	Mexico	441,824
Philippines	534,338	Canada	433,128
Russia	433,427	United Kingdom	220,213
Dominican Republic	359,818	Germany	209,616
India	352,528	Cuba	202,030
China	342,058	Italy	200,111
Vietnam	275,379	Dominican Republic	83,552
El Salvador	273,017	Greece	74,173
Canada	194,788	Philippines	70,660
Korea	179,770	Portugal	70,568
1980–89		**1950–59**	
TOTAL IMMIGRANTS	**6,244,379**	**TOTAL IMMIGRANTS**	**2,499,268**
Total from top ten	**3,162,911**	**Total from top ten**	**1,882,786**
Percent from top ten	**50.7%**	**Percent from top ten**	**75.3%**
Mexico	1,009,586	Germany	576,905
Philippines	502,056	Canada	353,169
Korea	322,708	Mexico	273,847
India	231,649	United Kingdom	195,709
Dominican Republic	221,552	Italy	184,576
Vietnam	200,632	Austria	81,354
Jamaica	193,874	Cuba	73,221
China	170,897	France	50,113
Canada	156,313	Ireland	47,189
United Kingdom	153,644	Netherlands	46,703

Note: Immigrants are persons granted legal permanent residence in the United States. They either arrive in the U.S. with immigrant visas issued abroad or adjust their status in the United States from temporary to permanent residence.
Source: Department of Homeland Security, 2006 Yearbook of Immigration Statistics, Internet site http://www.dhs.gov/ximgtn/ statistics/publications/LPR06.shtm; calculations by New Strategist

Table 8.16 Unauthorized Immigrant Population, 2000 and 2005

(estimated number and percent distribution of unauthorized immigrants in the U.S. by country of birth and state of residence, 2000 and 2005; percent change in number, 2000–05; numbers in thousands)

	2005		2000		
	number	percent distribution	number	percent distribution	percent change in number, 2000–05
COUNTRY OF BIRTH					
Total unauthorized immigrants	**10,500**	**100.0%**	**8,460**	**100.0%**	**24.1%**
Mexico	5,970	56.9	4,680	55.3	27.6
El Salvador	470	4.5	430	5.1	9.3
Guatemala	370	3.5	290	3.4	27.6
India	280	2.7	120	1.4	133.3
China	230	2.2	190	2.2	21.1
Korea	210	2.0	180	2.1	16.7
Philippines	210	2.0	200	2.4	5.0
Honduras	180	1.7	160	1.9	12.5
Brazil	170	1.6	100	1.2	70.0
Vietnam	160	1.5	160	1.9	0.0
Other countries	2,250	21.4	1,950	23.0	15.4
STATE OF RESIDENCE					
Total unauthorized immigrants	**10,500**	**100.0**	**8,460**	**100.0**	**24.1**
California	2,770	26.4	2,510	29.7	10.4
Texas	1,360	13.0	1,090	12.9	24.8
Florida	850	8.1	800	9.5	6.3
New York	560	5.3	540	6.4	3.7
Illinois	520	5.0	440	5.2	18.2
Arizona	480	4.6	330	3.9	45.5
Georgia	470	4.5	220	2.6	113.6
New Jersey	380	3.6	350	4.1	8.6
North Carolina	360	3.4	260	3.1	38.5
Nevada	240	2.3	170	2.0	41.2
Other states	2,510	23.9	1,750	20.7	43.4

Source: Department of Homeland Security, Estimates of the Unauthorized Immigrant Population Residing in the United States: January 2005, Internet site http://www.uscis.gov/graphics/shared/statistics/publications/index.htm

Some Regions Are More Diverse than Others

The more diverse regions are growing faster.

The populations of the South and West have more than doubled since 1950. Much of their growth is from immigration, making the South and West much more diverse than the Northeast or Midwest.

The West is by far the most diverse region, and non-Hispanic whites accounted for only 55 percent of its population in 2006. In the Pacific states, which include California, fully 29 percent of the population is Hispanic and 12 percent is Asian. The Midwest is the least diverse region, as non-Hispanic whites account for 80 percent of its population. The South is home to the 55 percent majority of the nation's black population.

■ Some regions struggle with the problems of integrating their diverse populations, while other regions are bystanders to the diversity trend.

The West is the most diverse region

(non-Hispanic white share of the population, by region, 2006)

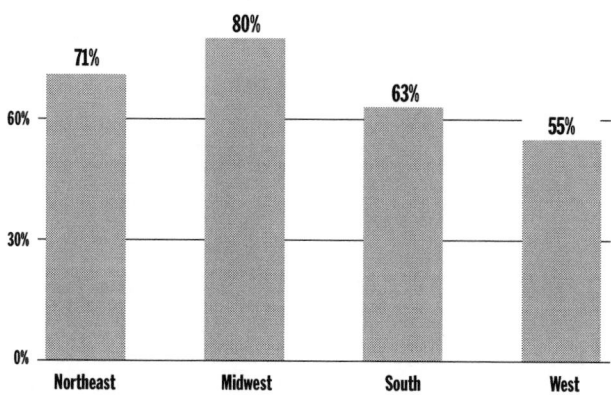

Table 8.17 Regional Populations, 1950 to 2006

(population by region and division, 1950 to 2006; percent change for selected years; numbers in thousands)

	2006	2000	1990	1980	1970	1960	1950	percent change 2000–06	percent change 1950–2006
UNITED STATES	299,398	281,422	248,791	226,546	203,302	179,323	151,326	6.4%	97.8%
Northeast	54,741	53,594	50,828	49,135	49,061	44,678	39,478	2.1	38.7
New England	14,270	13,923	13,207	12,348	11,847	10,509	9,315	2.5	53.2
Middle Atlantic	40,471	39,672	37,621	36,787	37,213	34,168	30,163	2.0	34.2
Midwest	66,218	64,393	59,669	58,866	56,590	51,619	44,461	2.8	48.9
East North Central	46,276	45,155	42,009	41,682	40,263	36,224	30,400	2.5	52.2
West North Central	19,942	19,238	17,660	17,183	16,328	15,395	14,062	3.7	41.8
South	109,084	100,237	85,456	75,372	62,813	54,973	47,197	8.8	131.1
South Atlantic	57,144	51,769	43,571	36,959	30,679	25,972	21,183	10.4	169.8
East South Central	17,754	17,023	15,180	14,666	12,808	12,050	11,478	4.3	54.7
West South Central	34,186	31,445	26,704	23,747	19,326	16,951	14,538	8.7	135.1
West	69,356	63,198	52,837	43,172	34,838	28,053	20,190	9.7	243.5
Mountain	20,846	18,172	13,659	11,373	8,290	6,855	5,076	14.7	310.7
Pacific	48,510	45,026	39,179	31,800	26,548	21,198	15,115	7.7	220.9

Note: The population totals for 1950 through 2000 are slightly different from those shown in some of the other tables in this chapter because these are from censuses and the others are estimates.
Source: Bureau of the Census, Selected Historical Decennial Census Population and Housing Counts, Internet site http://www .census.gov/population/www/censusdata/hiscendata.html; and 2000 Census, Table DP-1. Profiles of General Demographic Characteristics, 2001; and State Population Estimates, Internet site http://www.census.gov/popest/states/NST-ann-est.html; calculations by New Strategist

Table 8.18 Regional Populations by Race and Hispanic Origin, 1990

(number and percent distribution of people by region and division, race, and Hispanic origin, 1990; numbers in thousands)

	total people	race Amer. Indian	Asian	black	white	Hispanic origin Hispanic	non-Hispanic total	white
UNITED STATES	248,765	2,065	7,462	30,511	208,727	22,372	226,394	188,307
Northeast	50,828	132	1,362	5,915	43,420	3,762	47,066	40,422
New England	13,207	34	236	667	12,269	568	12,639	11,792
Middle Atlantic	37,621	98	1,126	5,247	31,150	3,194	34,427	28,630
Midwest	59,669	348	781	5,750	52,790	1,727	57,943	51,202
East North Central	42,009	156	583	4,847	36,423	1,438	40,571	35,094
West North Central	17,660	192	198	904	16,367	289	17,371	16,108
South	85,456	578	1,145	15,907	67,825	6,767	78,689	61,403
South Atlantic	43,571	175	640	8,964	33,793	2,133	41,439	31,840
East South Central	15,180	41	85	2,982	12,071	95	15,085	11,994
West South Central	26,704	362	420	3,962	21,961	4,539	22,165	17,569
West	52,837	1,007	4,174	2,939	44,692	10,116	42,721	35,281
Mountain	13,659	502	225	384	12,547	1,992	11,667	10,655
Pacific	39,153	505	3,949	2,554	32,145	8,124	31,029	24,626

Percent distribution by race and Hispanic origin

	total people	Amer. Indian	Asian	black	white	Hispanic	total	white
UNITED STATES	100.0%	0.8%	3.0%	12.3%	83.9%	9.0%	91.0%	75.7%
Northeast	100.0	0.3	2.7	11.6	85.4	7.4	92.6	79.5
New England	100.0	0.3	1.8	5.1	92.9	4.3	95.7	89.3
Middle Atlantic	100.0	0.3	3.0	13.9	82.8	8.5	91.5	76.1
Midwest	100.0	0.6	1.3	9.6	88.5	2.9	97.1	85.8
East North Central	100.0	0.4	1.4	11.5	86.7	3.4	96.6	83.5
West North Central	100.0	1.1	1.1	5.1	92.7	1.6	98.4	91.2
South	100.0	0.7	1.3	18.6	79.4	7.9	92.1	71.9
South Atlantic	100.0	0.4	1.5	20.6	77.6	4.9	95.1	73.1
East South Central	100.0	0.3	0.6	19.6	79.5	0.6	99.4	79.0
West South Central	100.0	1.4	1.6	14.8	82.2	17.0	83.0	65.8
West	100.0	1.9	7.9	5.6	84.6	19.1	80.9	66.8
Mountain	100.0	3.7	1.6	2.8	91.9	14.6	85.4	78.0
Pacific	100.0	1.3	10.1	6.5	82.1	20.7	79.3	62.9

Percent distribution by region/division

	total people	Amer. Indian	Asian	black	white	Hispanic	total	white
UNITED STATES	100.0%	100.0%	100.0%	100.0%	100.0%	100.0%	100.0%	100.0%
Northeast	20.4	6.4	18.3	19.4	20.8	16.8	20.8	21.5
New England	5.3	1.6	3.2	2.2	5.9	2.5	5.6	6.3
Middle Atlantic	15.1	4.7	15.1	17.2	14.9	14.3	15.2	15.2
Midwest	24.0	16.9	10.5	18.8	25.3	7.7	25.6	27.2
East North Central	16.9	7.6	7.8	15.9	17.5	6.4	17.9	18.6
West North Central	7.1	9.3	2.7	3.0	7.8	1.3	7.7	8.6
South	34.4	28.0	15.3	52.1	32.5	30.2	34.8	32.6
South Atlantic	17.5	8.5	8.6	29.4	16.2	9.5	18.3	16.9
East South Central	6.1	2.0	1.1	9.8	5.8	0.4	6.7	6.4
West South Central	10.7	17.5	5.6	13.0	10.5	20.3	9.8	9.3
West	21.2	48.8	55.9	9.6	21.4	45.2	18.9	18.7
Mountain	5.5	24.3	3.0	1.3	6.0	8.9	5.2	5.7
Pacific	15.7	24.5	52.9	8.4	15.4	36.3	13.7	13.1

Note: Numbers will not add to total because Hispanics may be of any race.
Source: Bureau of the Census, Internet site http://eire.census.gov/popest/archives/state/srh/srhmars.txt; calculations by New Strategist

Table 8.19 Regional Populations by Race, 2000

(number and percent distribution of people by region, division, and race, 2000; numbers in thousands)

	total	race alone						two or more races
		American Indian	Asian	black	Native Hawaiian	white	some other race	
UNITED STATES	281,422	2,476	10,243	34,658	399	211,461	15,359	6,826
Northeast	53,594	163	2,119	6,100	21	41,534	2,430	1,228
New England	13,923	42	374	719	5	12,051	448	282
Middle Atlantic	39,672	120	1,745	5,381	16	29,483	1,981	946
Midwest	64,393	399	1,198	6,500	22	53,834	1,417	1,022
East North Central	45,155	177	881	5,405	14	36,827	1,124	728
West North Central	19,238	222	317	1,094	9	17,007	294	295
South	100,237	726	1,922	18,982	51	72,819	3,889	1,847
South Atlantic	51,769	233	1,102	11,027	26	37,284	1,175	923
East South Central	17,023	58	136	3,419	6	13,113	121	170
West South Central	31,445	435	684	4,536	20	22,423	2,592	755
West	63,198	1,188	5,004	3,077	304	43,274	7,623	2,728
Mountain	18,172	615	353	523	39	14,592	1,542	509
Pacific	45,026	573	4,650	2,554	266	28,682	6,081	2,219

Percent distribution by race

	total	American Indian	Asian	black	Native Hawaiian	white	some other race	two or more races
UNITED STATES	100.0%	0.9%	3.6%	12.3%	0.1%	75.1%	5.5%	2.4%
Northeast	100.0	0.3	4.0	11.4	0.0	77.5	4.5	2.3
New England	100.0	0.3	2.7	5.2	0.0	86.6	3.2	2.0
Middle Atlantic	100.0	0.3	4.4	13.6	0.0	74.3	5.0	2.4
Midwest	100.0	0.6	1.9	10.1	0.0	83.6	2.2	1.6
East North Central	100.0	0.4	2.0	12.0	0.0	81.6	2.5	1.6
West North Central	100.0	1.2	1.6	5.7	0.0	88.4	1.5	1.5
South	100.0	0.7	1.9	18.9	0.1	72.6	3.9	1.8
South Atlantic	100.0	0.5	2.1	21.3	0.0	72.0	2.3	1.8
East South Central	100.0	0.3	0.8	20.1	0.0	77.0	0.7	1.0
West South Central	100.0	1.4	2.2	14.4	0.1	71.3	8.2	2.4
West	100.0	1.9	7.9	4.9	0.5	68.5	12.1	4.3
Mountain	100.0	3.4	1.9	2.9	0.2	80.3	8.5	2.8
Pacific	100.0	1.3	10.3	5.7	0.6	63.7	13.5	4.9

Percent distribution by region/division

	total	American Indian	Asian	black	Native Hawaiian	white	some other race	two or more races
UNITED STATES	100.0%	100.0%	100.0%	100.0%	100.0%	100.0%	100.0%	100.0%
Northeast	19.0	6.6	20.7	17.6	5.2	19.6	15.8	18.0
New England	4.9	1.7	3.7	2.1	1.3	5.7	2.9	4.1
Middle Atlantic	14.1	4.8	17.0	15.5	3.9	13.9	12.9	13.9
Midwest	22.9	16.1	11.7	18.8	5.6	25.5	9.2	15.0
East North Central	16.0	7.1	8.6	15.6	3.4	17.4	7.3	10.7
West North Central	6.8	9.0	3.1	3.2	2.2	8.0	1.9	4.3
South	35.6	29.3	18.8	54.8	12.8	34.4	25.3	27.1
South Atlantic	18.4	9.4	10.8	31.8	6.5	17.6	7.7	13.5
East South Central	6.0	2.3	1.3	9.9	1.4	6.2	0.8	2.5
West South Central	11.2	17.6	6.7	13.1	4.9	10.6	16.9	11.1
West	22.5	48.0	48.8	8.9	76.3	20.5	49.6	40.0
Mountain	6.5	24.8	3.5	1.5	9.7	6.9	10.0	7.5
Pacific	16.0	23.1	45.4	7.4	66.6	13.6	39.6	32.5

Source: Bureau of the Census, 2000 Census, Population by Race and Hispanic or Latino Origin for the United States, Regions, Divisions, States, Puerto Rico, and Places of 100,000 or More Population (PHC-T-6), Internet site http://www.census.gov/ population/www/cen2000/phc-t6.html; calculations by New Strategist

Table 8.20 Regional Populations by Hispanic Origin, 2000

(number and percent distribution of people by region, division, and Hispanic origin, 2000; numbers in thousands)

| | | | Hispanic origin | |
| | | | non-Hispanic | |
	total	Hispanic	total	white
UNITED STATES	**281,422**	**35,306**	**246,116**	**194,553**
Northeast	**53,594**	**5,254**	**48,340**	**39,327**
New England	13,923	875	13,047	11,687
Middle Atlantic	39,672	4,379	35,293	27,641
Midwest	**64,393**	**3,125**	**61,268**	**52,386**
East North Central	45,155	2,479	42,676	35,670
West North Central	19,238	646	18,592	16,716
South	**100,237**	**11,587**	**88,650**	**65,928**
South Atlantic	51,769	4,244	47,525	34,576
East South Central	17,023	299	16,724	12,968
West South Central	31,445	7,044	24,401	18,384
West	**63,198**	**15,341**	**47,857**	**36,912**
Mountain	18,172	3,544	14,629	12,884
Pacific	45,026	11,797	33,229	24,028

Percent distribution by Hispanic origin

UNITED STATES	**100.0%**	**12.5%**	**87.5%**	**69.1%**
Northeast	**100.0**	**9.8**	**90.2**	**73.4**
New England	100.0	6.3	93.7	83.9
Middle Atlantic	100.0	11.0	89.0	69.7
Midwest	**100.0**	**4.9**	**95.1**	**81.4**
East North Central	100.0	5.5	94.5	79.0
West North Central	100.0	3.4	96.6	86.9
South	**100.0**	**11.6**	**88.4**	**65.8**
South Atlantic	100.0	8.2	91.8	66.8
East South Central	100.0	1.8	98.2	76.2
West South Central	100.0	22.4	77.6	58.5
West	**100.0**	**24.3**	**75.7**	**58.4**
Mountain	100.0	19.5	80.5	70.9
Pacific	100.0	26.2	73.8	53.4

Percent distribution by region/division

UNITED STATES	**100.0%**	**100.0%**	**100.0%**	**100.0%**
Northeast	**19.0**	**14.9**	**19.6**	**20.2**
New England	4.9	2.5	5.3	6.0
Middle Atlantic	14.1	12.4	14.3	14.2
Midwest	**22.9**	**8.9**	**24.9**	**26.9**
East North Central	16.0	7.0	17.3	18.3
West North Central	6.8	1.8	7.6	8.6
South	**35.6**	**32.8**	**36.0**	**33.9**
South Atlantic	18.4	12.0	19.3	17.8
East South Central	6.0	0.8	6.8	6.7
West South Central	11.2	20.0	9.9	9.4
West	**22.5**	**43.5**	**19.4**	**19.0**
Mountain	6.5	10.0	5.9	6.6
Pacific	16.0	33.4	13.5	12.4

Source: Bureau of the Census, 2000 Census, Population by Race and Hispanic or Latino Origin for the United States, Regions, Divisions, States, Puerto Rico, and Places of 100,000 or More Population (PHC-T-6), Internet site http://www.census.gov/ population/www/cen2000/phc-t6.html; calculations by New Strategist

Table 8.21 Regional Populations by Race, 2006

(number and percent distribution of people by region, division, and race, 2006; numbers in thousands)

	total	American Indian	Asian	black	Native Hawaiian	white	two or more races
UNITED STATES	299,398	2,903	13,159	38,343	529	239,746	4,719
Northeast	54,741	209	2,770	6,855	42	44,169	697
New England	14,270	52	504	901	10	12,623	180
Middle Atlantic	40,471	157	2,267	5,954	31	31,546	517
Midwest	66,218	445	1,562	6,877	33	56,463	837
East North Central	46,276	200	1,150	5,645	21	38,692	567
West North Central	19,942	245	412	1,232	12	17,771	270
South	109,084	860	2,691	21,094	84	82,980	1,375
South Atlantic	57,144	294	1,567	12,582	42	41,944	716
East South Central	17,754	66	186	3,629	8	13,698	169
West South Central	34,186	500	938	4,884	35	27,339	491
West	69,356	1,389	6,135	3,516	370	56,135	1,810
Mountain	20,846	702	524	717	56	18,481	366
Pacific	48,510	687	5,612	2,799	314	37,654	1,444

Percent distribution by race

	total	American Indian	Asian	black	Native Hawaiian	white	two or more races
UNITED STATES	100.0%	1.0%	4.4%	12.8%	0.2%	80.1%	1.6%
Northeast	100.0	0.4	5.1	12.5	0.1	80.7	1.3
New England	100.0	0.4	3.5	6.3	0.1	88.5	1.3
Middle Atlantic	100.0	0.4	5.6	14.7	0.1	77.9	1.3
Midwest	100.0	0.7	2.4	10.4	0.1	85.3	1.3
East North Central	100.0	0.4	2.5	12.2	0.0	83.6	1.2
West North Central	100.0	1.2	2.1	6.2	0.1	89.1	1.4
South	100.0	0.8	2.5	19.3	0.1	76.1	1.3
South Atlantic	100.0	0.5	2.7	22.0	0.1	73.4	1.3
East South Central	100.0	0.4	1.0	20.4	0.0	77.1	0.9
West South Central	100.0	1.5	2.7	14.3	0.1	80.0	1.4
West	100.0	2.0	8.8	5.1	0.5	80.9	2.6
Mountain	100.0	3.4	2.5	3.4	0.3	88.7	1.8
Pacific	100.0	1.4	11.6	5.8	0.6	77.6	3.0

Percent distribution by region/division

	total	American Indian	Asian	black	Native Hawaiian	white	two or more races
UNITED STATES	100.0%	100.0%	100.0%	100.0%	100.0%	100.0%	100.0%
Northeast	18.3	7.2	21.1	17.9	7.9	18.4	14.8
New England	4.8	1.8	3.8	2.4	1.9	5.3	3.8
Middle Atlantic	13.5	5.4	17.2	15.5	6.0	13.2	11.0
Midwest	22.1	15.3	11.9	17.9	6.3	23.6	17.7
East North Central	15.5	6.9	8.7	14.7	4.0	16.1	12.0
West North Central	6.7	8.5	3.1	3.2	2.3	7.4	5.7
South	36.4	29.6	20.5	55.0	15.8	34.6	29.1
South Atlantic	19.1	10.1	11.9	32.8	7.9	17.5	15.2
East South Central	5.9	2.3	1.4	9.5	1.4	5.7	3.6
West South Center	11.4	17.2	7.1	12.7	6.5	11.4	10.4
West	23.2	47.9	46.6	9.2	70.0	23.4	38.4
Mountain	7.0	24.2	4.0	1.9	10.6	7.7	7.8
Pacific	16.2	23.7	42.6	7.3	59.4	15.7	30.6

Source: Bureau of the Census, State Population Estimates, Internet site http://www.census.gov/popest/states/asrh/ SC-EST2006-04.html; calculations by New Strategist

Table 8.22 Regional Populations by Hispanic Origin, 2006

(number and percent distribution of people by region, division, and Hispanic origin, 2006; numbers in thousands)

	total	Hispanic	non-Hispanic total	non-Hispanic white
UNITED STATES	299,398	44,321	255,077	198,744
Northeast	54,741	6,102	48,639	39,070
New England	14,270	1,071	13,199	11,719
Middle Atlantic	40,471	5,031	35,440	27,351
Midwest	66,218	3,978	62,240	52,765
East North Central	46,276	3,108	43,168	35,792
West North Central	19,942	870	19,072	16,973
South	109,084	15,376	93,708	68,467
South Atlantic	57,144	6,030	51,113	36,394
East South Central	17,754	448	17,307	13,298
West South Central	34,186	8,898	25,288	18,775
West	69,356	18,865	50,491	38,442
Mountain	20,846	4,693	16,153	14,066
Pacific	48,510	14,172	34,338	24,376

Percent distribution by Hispanic origin

	total	Hispanic	non-Hispanic total	non-Hispanic white
UNITED STATES	100.0%	14.8%	85.2%	66.4%
Northeast	100.0	11.1	88.9	71.4
New England	100.0	7.5	92.5	82.1
Middle Atlantic	100.0	12.4	87.6	67.6
Midwest	100.0	6.0	94.0	79.7
East North Central	100.0	6.7	93.3	77.3
West North Central	100.0	4.4	95.6	85.1
South	100.0	14.1	85.9	62.8
South Atlantic	100.0	10.6	89.4	63.7
East South Central	100.0	2.5	97.5	74.9
West South Central	100.0	26.0	74.0	54.9
West	100.0	27.2	72.8	55.4
Mountain	100.0	22.5	77.5	67.5
Pacific	100.0	29.2	70.8	50.2

Percent distribution by region/division

	total	Hispanic	non-Hispanic total	non-Hispanic white
Northeast	100.0%	100.0%	100.0%	100.0%
New England	18.3	13.8	19.1	19.7
Middle Atlantic	4.8	2.4	5.2	5.9
Midwest	13.5	11.4	13.9	13.8
East North Central	22.1	9.0	24.4	26.5
West North Central	15.5	7.0	16.9	18.0
South	6.7	2.0	7.5	8.5
South Atlantic	36.4	34.7	36.7	34.4
East South Central	19.1	13.6	20.0	18.3
West South Central	5.9	1.0	6.8	6.7
West	11.4	20.1	9.9	9.4
Mountain	23.2	42.6	19.8	19.3
Pacific	7.0	10.6	6.3	7.1
Pacific	16.2	32.0	13.5	12.3

Source: Bureau of the Census, State Population Estimates, Internet site http://www.census.gov/popest/states/asrh/ SC-EST2006-04.html; calculations by New Strategist

Nevada Is Growing the Fastest

North Dakota is losing population.

Since 1950, the population of Nevada has increased more than tenfold while West Virginia's population has declined. Nevada had a population of just 160,000 in 1950. By 2006, it was home to 2.5 million people. West Virginia is the only state to have fewer residents in 2006 than in 1950, its population declining by 9 percent during those years.

In 1950, New York was the nation's most populous state with 15 million people. In 2006, California was number one with 36 million, followed by Texas with 24 million. New York is now in third place with 19 million people.

Between 2000 and 2006, Nevada has been the fastest growing state with a population increase of 25 percent. In contrast, North Dakota's population fell by 1 percent between 2000 and 2006. Louisiana's population shrank an even larger 4 percent during those years because of the devastation of Hurricane Katrina.

■ California will remain the most populous state for years to come.

Wyoming is the least populous state

(most and least populous states, 2006)

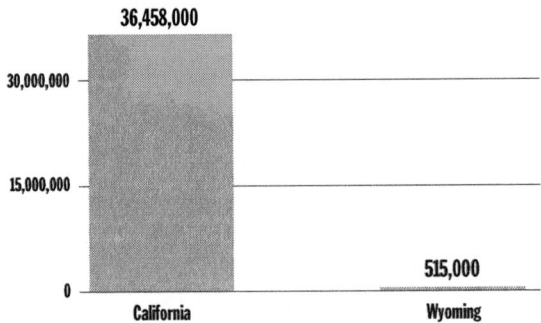

Table 8.23 State Populations, 1950 to 2006

(population by state, 1950 to 2006; percent change for selected years; numbers in thousands)

	2006	2000	1990	1980	1970	1960	1950	percent change 1990–00	percent change 1950–00
United States	299,398	281,422	248,791	226,546	203,302	179,323	151,326	6.4%	97.8%
Alabama	4,599	4,447	4,040	3,894	3,444	3,267	3,062	3.4	50.2
Alaska	670	627	550	402	303	226	129	6.9	419.4
Arizona	6,166	5,131	3,665	2,718	1,775	1,302	750	20.2	722.2
Arkansas	2,811	2,673	2,351	2,286	1,923	1,786	1,910	5.2	47.2
California	36,458	33,872	29,811	23,668	19,971	15,717	10,586	7.6	244.4
Colorado	4,753	4,301	3,294	2,890	2,210	1,754	1,325	10.5	258.7
Connecticut	3,505	3,406	3,287	3,108	3,032	2,535	2,007	2.9	74.6
Delaware	853	784	666	594	548	446	318	8.9	168.4
District of Columbia	582	572	607	638	757	764	802	1.7	−27.5
Florida	18,090	15,982	12,938	9,746	6,791	4,952	2,771	13.2	552.8
Georgia	9,364	8,186	6,478	5,463	4,588	3,943	3,445	14.4	171.8
Hawaii	1,285	1,212	1,108	965	770	633	500	6.1	157.1
Idaho	1,466	1,294	1,007	944	713	667	589	13.3	149.0
Illinois	12,832	12,419	11,431	11,427	11,110	10,081	8,712	3.3	47.3
Indiana	6,314	6,080	5,544	5,490	5,195	4,662	3,934	3.8	60.5
Iowa	2,982	2,926	2,777	2,914	2,825	2,758	2,621	1.9	13.8
Kansas	2,764	2,688	2,478	2,364	2,249	2,179	1,905	2.8	45.1
Kentucky	4,206	4,042	3,687	3,661	3,221	3,038	2,945	4.1	42.8
Louisiana	4,288	4,469	4,222	4,206	3,645	3,257	2,684	−4.1	59.8
Maine	1,322	1,275	1,228	1,125	994	969	914	3.7	44.6
Maryland	5,616	5,296	4,781	4,217	3,924	3,101	2,343	6.0	139.7
Massachusetts	6,437	6,349	6,016	5,737	5,689	5,149	4,691	1.4	37.2
Michigan	10,096	9,938	9,295	9,262	8,882	7,823	6,372	1.6	58.4
Minnesota	5,167	4,919	4,376	4,076	3,806	3,414	2,982	5.0	73.3
Mississippi	2,911	2,845	2,575	2,521	2,217	2,178	2,179	2.3	33.6
Missouri	5,843	5,595	5,117	4,917	4,678	4,320	3,955	4.4	47.7
Montana	945	902	799	787	694	675	591	4.7	59.8
Nebraska	1,768	1,711	1,578	1,570	1,485	1,411	1,326	3.4	33.4
Nevada	2,496	1,998	1,202	800	489	285	160	24.9	1,459.7
New Hampshire	1,315	1,236	1,109	921	738	607	533	6.4	146.7
New Jersey	8,725	8,414	7,748	7,365	7,171	6,067	4,835	3.7	80.4
New Mexico	1,955	1,819	1,515	1,303	1,017	951	681	7.5	187.0
New York	19,306	18,976	17,991	17,558	18,241	16,782	14,830	1.7	30.2
North Carolina	8,857	8,049	6,632	5,882	5,084	4,556	4,062	10.0	118.0
North Dakota	636	642	639	653	618	632	620	−1.0	2.6
Ohio	11,478	11,353	10,847	10,798	10,657	9,706	7,947	1.1	44.4
Oklahoma	3,579	3,451	3,146	3,025	2,559	2,328	2,233	3.7	60.3
Oregon	3,701	3,421	2,842	2,633	2,092	1,769	1,521	8.2	143.3
Pennsylvania	12,441	12,281	11,883	11,864	11,801	11,319	10,498	1.3	18.5
Rhode Island	1,068	1,048	1,003	947	950	859	792	1.9	34.8
South Carolina	4,321	4,012	3,486	3,122	2,591	2,383	2,117	7.7	104.1
South Dakota	782	755	696	691	666	681	653	3.6	19.7
Tennessee	6,039	5,689	4,877	4,591	3,926	3,567	3,292	6.1	83.4
Texas	23,508	20,852	16,986	14,229	11,199	9,580	7,711	12.7	204.9
Utah	2,550	2,233	1,723	1,461	1,059	891	689	14.2	270.1
Vermont	624	609	563	511	445	390	378	2.4	65.1
Virginia	7,643	7,079	6,189	5,347	4,651	3,967	3,319	8.0	130.3
Washington	6,396	5,894	4,867	4,132	3,413	2,853	2,379	8.5	168.8
West Virginia	1,818	1,808	1,793	1,950	1,744	1,860	2,006	0.6	−9.3
Wisconsin	5,557	5,364	4,892	4,706	4,418	3,952	3,435	3.6	61.8
Wyoming	515	494	454	470	332	330	291	4.3	77.0

*Source: Bureau of the Census, Selected Historical Decennial Census Population and Housing Counts, Internet site http://www
.census.gov/population/www/censusdata/hiscendata.html; and State Population Estimates, Internet site http://www.census.gov/
popest/states/NST-ann-est.html; calculations by New Strategist*

Table 8.24 States Ranked by Population, 1950, 2000, and 2006

(states ranked by population in 1950, 2000, and 2006; numbers in thousands)

2006		2000		1950	
California	36,458	California	33,872	New York	14,830
Texas	23,508	Texas	20,852	California	10,586
New York	19,306	New York	18,976	Pennsylvania	10,498
Florida	18,090	Florida	15,982	Illinois	8,712
Illinois	12,832	Illinois	12,419	Ohio	7,947
Pennsylvania	12,441	Pennsylvania	12,281	Texas	7,711
Ohio	11,478	Ohio	11,353	Michigan	6,372
Michigan	10,096	Michigan	9,938	New Jersey	4,835
Georgia	9,364	New Jersey	8,414	Massachusetts	4,691
North Carolina	8,857	Georgia	8,186	North Carolina	4,062
New Jersey	8,725	North Carolina	8,049	Missouri	3,955
Virginia	7,643	Virginia	7,079	Indiana	3,934
Massachusetts	6,437	Massachusetts	6,349	Georgia	3,445
Washington	6,396	Indiana	6,080	Wisconsin	3,435
Indiana	6,314	Washington	5,894	Virginia	3,319
Arizona	6,166	Tennessee	5,689	Tennessee	3,292
Tennessee	6,039	Missouri	5,595	Alabama	3,062
Missouri	5,843	Wisconsin	5,364	Minnesota	2,982
Maryland	5,616	Maryland	5,296	Kentucky	2,945
Wisconsin	5,557	Arizona	5,131	Florida	2,771
Minnesota	5,167	Minnesota	4,919	Louisiana	2,684
Colorado	4,753	Louisiana	4,469	Iowa	2,621
Alabama	4,599	Alabama	4,447	Washington	2,379
South Carolina	4,321	Colorado	4,301	Maryland	2,343
Louisiana	4,288	Kentucky	4,042	Oklahoma	2,233
Kentucky	4,206	South Carolina	4,012	Mississippi	2,179
Oregon	3,701	Oklahoma	3,451	South Carolina	2,117
Oklahoma	3,579	Oregon	3,421	Connecticut	2,007
Connecticut	3,505	Connecticut	3,406	West Virginia	2,006
Iowa	2,982	Iowa	2,926	Arkansas	1,910
Mississippi	2,911	Mississippi	2,845	Kansas	1,905
Arkansas	2,811	Kansas	2,688	Oregon	1,521
Kansas	2,764	Arkansas	2,673	Nebraska	1,326
Utah	2,550	Utah	2,233	Colorado	1,325
Nevada	2,496	Nevada	1,998	Maine	914
New Mexico	1,955	New Mexico	1,819	District of Columbia	802
West Virginia	1,818	West Virginia	1,808	Rhode Island	792
Nebraska	1,768	Nebraska	1,711	Arizona	750
Idaho	1,466	Idaho	1,294	Utah	689
Maine	1,322	Maine	1,275	New Mexico	681
New Hampshire	1,315	New Hampshire	1,236	South Dakota	653
Hawaii	1,285	Hawaii	1,212	North Dakota	620
Rhode Island	1,068	Rhode Island	1,048	Montana	591
Montana	945	Montana	902	Idaho	589
Delaware	853	Delaware	784	New Hampshire	533
South Dakota	782	South Dakota	755	Hawaii	500
Alaska	670	North Dakota	642	Vermont	378
North Dakota	636	Alaska	627	Delaware	318
Vermont	624	Vermont	609	Wyoming	291
District of Columbia	582	District of Columbia	572	Nevada	160
Wyoming	515	Wyoming	494	Alaska	129

Source: Bureau of the Census, Selected Historical Decennial Census Population and Housing Counts, Internet site http://www .census.gov/population/www/censusdata/hiscendata.html; and 2000 Census, http://www.census.gov/population/cen2000/ phc-t2/tab01.xls; and State Population Estimates, Internet site http://www.census.gov/popest/states/NST-ann-est.html; calculations by New Strategist

Table 8.25 States Ranked by Population Change, 1950 to 2000

(states ranked by numerical and percent change in population, 1950 to 2000; numbers in thousands)

numerical change, 1950–2000		percent change, 1950–2000	
California	23,286	Nevada	1,149.0%
Florida	13,211	Arizona	584.1
Texas	13,141	Florida	476.8
Georgia	4,741	Alaska	386.0
Arizona	4,381	Colorado	224.6
New York	4,146	Utah	224.1
North Carolina	3,987	California	220.0
Virginia	3,760	Texas	170.4
Illinois	3,707	New Mexico	167.1
New Jersey	3,579	Washington	147.8
Michigan	3,566	Delaware	146.4
Washington	3,515	Hawaii	142.3
Ohio	3,406	Georgia	137.6
Colorado	2,976	New Hampshire	131.9
Maryland	2,953	Maryland	126.1
Tennessee	2,397	Oregon	124.9
Indiana	2,146	Idaho	119.7
Minnesota	1,937	Virginia	113.3
Wisconsin	1,929	North Carolina	98.2
Oregon	1,900	South Carolina	89.5
South Carolina	1,895	New Jersey	74.0
Nevada	1,838	Tennessee	72.8
Louisiana	1,785	Wyoming	69.7
Pennsylvania	1,783	Connecticut	69.7
Massachusetts	1,658	Louisiana	66.5
Missouri	1,640	Minnesota	65.0
Utah	1,544	Vermont	61.1
Connecticut	1,399	Wisconsin	56.1
Alabama	1,385	Michigan	56.0
Oklahoma	1,218	Indiana	54.6
New Mexico	1,138	Oklahoma	54.5
Kentucky	1,097	Montana	52.7
Kansas	783	Alabama	45.2
Arkansas	763	Ohio	42.9
Hawaii	712	Illinois	42.6
Idaho	705	Missouri	41.5
New Hampshire	703	Kansas	41.1
Mississippi	666	Arkansas	40.0
Alaska	498	Maine	39.5
Delaware	466	Kentucky	37.2
Nebraska	385	Massachusetts	35.3
Maine	361	Rhode Island	32.4
Montana	311	Mississippi	30.5
Iowa	305	Nebraska	29.1
Rhode Island	256	New York	28.0
Vermont	231	Pennsylvania	17.0
Wyoming	203	South Dakota	15.6
South Dakota	102	Iowa	11.6
North Dakota	22	North Dakota	3.6
West Virginia	−198	West Virginia	−9.9
District of Columbia	−230	District of Columbia	−28.7

Source: Calculations by New Strategist based on Bureau of the Census, Internet sites http://www.census.gov/population/www/censusdata/hiscendata.html and http://www.census.gov/population/cen2000/phc-t2/tab01.xls

Table 8.26 States Ranked by Population Change, 2000 to 2006

(states ranked by numerical and percent change in population, 2000 to 2006; numbers in thousands)

numerical change, 2000–06		percent change, 2000–06	
Texas	2,656	Nevada	24.9%
California	2,586	Arizona	20.2
Florida	2,108	Georgia	14.4
Georgia	1,178	Utah	14.2
Arizona	1,035	Idaho	13.3
North Carolina	808	Florida	13.2
Virginia	564	Texas	12.7
Washington	502	Colorado	10.5
Nevada	498	North Carolina	10.0
Colorado	452	Delaware	8.9
Illinois	413	Washington	8.5
Tennessee	350	Oregon	8.2
New York	330	Virginia	8.0
Maryland	320	South Carolina	7.7
Utah	317	California	7.6
New Jersey	311	New Mexico	7.5
South Carolina	309	Alaska	6.9
Oregon	280	New Hampshire	6.4
Minnesota	248	Tennessee	6.1
Missouri	248	Hawaii	6.1
Indiana	234	Maryland	6.0
Wisconsin	193	Arkansas	5.2
Idaho	172	Minnesota	5.0
Kentucky	164	Montana	4.7
Pennsylvania	160	Missouri	4.4
Michigan	158	Wyoming	4.3
Alabama	152	Kentucky	4.1
Arkansas	138	Indiana	3.8
New Mexico	136	Oklahoma	3.7
Oklahoma	128	New Jersey	3.7
Ohio	125	Maine	3.7
Connecticut	99	Wisconsin	3.6
Massachusetts	88	South Dakota	3.6
New Hampshire	79	Alabama	3.4
Kansas	76	Nebraska	3.4
Hawaii	73	Illinois	3.3
Delaware	69	Connecticut	2.9
Mississippi	66	Kansas	2.8
Nebraska	57	Vermont	2.4
Iowa	56	Mississippi	2.3
Maine	47	Iowa	1.9
Alaska	43	Rhode Island	1.9
Montana	43	New York	1.7
South Dakota	27	District of Columbia	1.7
Wyoming	21	Michigan	1.6
Rhode Island	20	Massachusetts	1.4
Vermont	15	Pennsylvania	1.3
West Virginia	10	Ohio	1.1
District of Columbia	10	West Virginia	0.6
North Dakota	–6	North Dakota	–1.0
Louisiana	–181	Louisiana	–4.1

Source: Calculations by New Strategist based on Bureau of the Census, 200 Census, Internet site http://www.census.gov/ population/cen2000/phc-t2/tab01.xls; and State Population Estimates, Internet site http://www.census.gov/popest/states/ NST-ann-est.html

Texas and California Have Minority Majorities

The two most populous states are highly diverse.

In Maine, fully 96 percent of the population was non-Hispanic white in 2006. In California, the nation's most populous state, non-Hispanic whites accounted for just 43 percent of the population. The enormous differences among states in racial and ethnic diversity create social, economic, and political divisions that are difficult to reconcile.

The Hispanic share of state populations ranges from a high of 44 percent in New Mexico and 36 percent in California and Texas to a low of just 1 percent in Maine, Vermont, and West Virginia. The black share of state populations also varies greatly, from a high of 37 percent in Mississippi to less than 1 percent in seven states including Maine and Vermont. The Asian population accounted for fully 40 percent of Hawaii's population in 2006 and 12 percent of California's population. But in eight states, again including Maine and Vermont, the Asian share was less than 1 percent in 2006.

■ Because the nation's most populous state, California, is also one of the most diverse, it is a leader in social and economic change.

California is one of the most diverse states

(percent distribution of California's population by race and Hispanic origin, 2006)

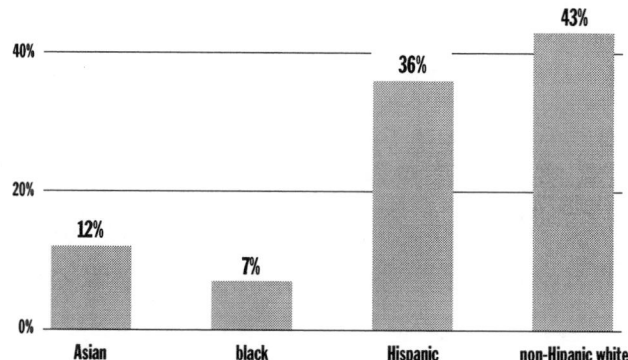

Table 8.27 State Populations by Race and Hispanic Origin, 1990

(number of people by state, race, and Hispanic origin, 1990; numbers in thousands)

		race				Hispanic origin	non-Hispanic	
	total	Amer. Indian	Asian	black	white	Hispanic	total	white
United States	**248,765**	**2,065**	**7,462**	**30,511**	**208,727**	**22,372**	**226,394**	**188,307**
Alabama	4,040	17	22	1,021	2,980	25	4,016	2,960
Alaska	550	86	20	23	421	18	532	407
Arizona	3,665	214	58	115	3,278	688	2,977	2,630
Arkansas	2,351	13	13	374	1,951	20	2,331	1,933
California	29,786	285	2,947	2,304	24,249	7,697	22,088	17,064
Colorado	3,294	31	62	136	3,066	424	2,870	2,663
Connecticut	3,287	7	52	282	2,946	213	3,074	2,757
Delaware	666	2	9	113	541	16	650	528
District of Columbia	607	2	12	402	191	33	574	166
Florida	12,938	37	156	1,772	10,972	1,574	11,364	9,482
Georgia	6,478	14	77	1,751	4,636	109	6,369	4,545
Hawaii	1,108	5	696	28	379	81	1,027	349
Idaho	1,007	15	10	4	979	53	954	929
Illinois	11,431	24	292	1,707	9,407	904	10,526	8,556
Indiana	5,544	13	38	434	5,059	99	5,445	4,967
Iowa	2,777	8	26	48	2,695	33	2,744	2,665
Kansas	2,478	23	32	145	2,277	94	2,384	2,192
Kentucky	3,687	6	18	264	3,399	22	3,665	3,380
Louisiana	4,222	19	42	1,303	2,858	93	4,129	2,778
Maine	1,228	6	7	5	1,210	7	1,221	1,204
Maryland	4,781	13	141	1,196	3,430	125	4,656	3,328
Massachusetts	6,016	13	146	327	5,530	288	5,729	5,298
Michigan	9,295	58	106	1,298	7,833	202	9,094	7,654
Minnesota	4,376	51	79	96	4,150	54	4,322	4,104
Mississippi	2,575	9	13	917	1,636	16	2,559	1,625
Missouri	5,117	20	42	550	4,505	62	5,055	4,450
Montana	799	48	4	2	744	12	787	734
Nebraska	1,578	13	13	58	1,495	37	1,541	1,461
Nevada	1,202	21	39	80	1,061	124	1,077	947
New Hampshire	1,109	2	9	7	1,090	11	1,098	1,080
New Jersey	7,748	16	277	1,077	6,378	748	7,000	5,726
New Mexico	1,515	138	15	32	1,331	579	936	767
New York	17,991	66	709	3,065	14,150	2,214	15,777	12,475
North Carolina	6,632	81	53	1,462	5,037	77	6,556	4,975
North Dakota	639	26	4	4	606	5	634	602
Ohio	10,847	21	92	1,160	9,575	140	10,707	9,450
Oklahoma	3,146	258	35	236	2,617	86	3,059	2,549
Oregon	2,842	41	70	47	2,685	113	2,730	2,581
Pennsylvania	11,883	15	140	1,105	10,622	232	11,651	10,428
Rhode Island	1,003	4	19	43	937	46	958	901
South Carolina	3,486	8	23	1,042	2,414	31	3,456	2,390
South Dakota	696	51	3	3	639	5	691	635
Tennessee	4,877	10	32	779	4,056	33	4,844	4,029
Texas	16,986	72	331	2,048	14,534	4,340	12,646	10,308
Utah	1,723	25	34	12	1,651	85	1,638	1,572
Vermont	563	2	3	2	556	4	559	552
Virginia	6,189	16	161	1,168	4,844	160	6,029	4,706
Washington	4,867	87	215	153	4,411	215	4,652	4,225
West Virginia	1,793	2	7	56	1,727	8	1,785	1,719
Wisconsin	4,892	40	54	247	4,550	93	4,799	4,466
Wyoming	454	10	3	4	437	26	428	413

Note: Asians include Pacific Islanders; numbers will not add to total because Hispanics may be of any race.
Source: Bureau of the Census, Population Estimates, Archives, 1990s, Internet site http://www.census.gov/popest/archives/1990s/strh/srhmars.txt

Table 8.28 Distribution of State Populations by Race and Hispanic Origin, 1990

(percent distribution of people by race and Hispanic origin, by state, 1990)

| | total | | race | | | | Hispanic origin | | |
		Amer. Indian	Asian	black	white	Hispanic	non-Hispanic total	non-Hispanic white
United States	**100.0%**	**0.8%**	**3.0%**	**12.3%**	**83.9%**	**9.0%**	**91.0%**	**75.7%**
Alabama	100.0	0.4	0.5	25.3	73.8	0.6	99.4	73.3
Alaska	100.0	15.7	3.7	4.2	76.5	3.2	96.8	74.0
Arizona	100.0	5.9	1.6	3.1	89.4	18.8	81.2	71.7
Arkansas	100.0	0.6	0.5	15.9	83.0	0.8	99.2	82.2
California	100.0	1.0	9.9	7.7	81.4	25.8	74.2	57.3
Colorado	100.0	0.9	1.9	4.1	93.1	12.9	87.1	80.8
Connecticut	100.0	0.2	1.6	8.6	89.6	6.5	93.5	83.9
Delaware	100.0	0.3	1.4	17.0	81.3	2.4	97.6	79.3
District of Columbia	100.0	0.3	1.9	66.3	31.5	5.4	94.6	27.4
Florida	100.0	0.3	1.2	13.7	84.8	12.2	87.8	73.3
Georgia	100.0	0.2	1.2	27.0	71.6	1.7	98.3	70.2
Hawaii	100.0	0.5	62.8	2.5	34.2	7.3	92.7	31.5
Idaho	100.0	1.5	1.0	0.3	97.2	5.3	94.7	92.3
Illinois	100.0	0.2	2.6	14.9	82.3	7.9	92.1	74.9
Indiana	100.0	0.2	0.7	7.8	91.2	1.8	98.2	89.6
Iowa	100.0	0.3	0.9	1.7	97.1	1.2	98.8	96.0
Kansas	100.0	0.9	1.3	5.8	91.9	3.8	96.2	88.5
Kentucky	100.0	0.2	0.5	7.2	92.2	0.6	99.4	91.7
Louisiana	100.0	0.4	1.0	30.9	67.7	2.2	97.8	65.8
Maine	100.0	0.5	0.5	0.4	98.5	0.6	99.4	98.0
Maryland	100.0	0.3	3.0	25.0	71.7	2.6	97.4	69.6
Massachusetts	100.0	0.2	2.4	5.4	91.9	4.8	95.2	88.1
Michigan	100.0	0.6	1.1	14.0	84.3	2.2	97.8	82.3
Minnesota	100.0	1.2	1.8	2.2	94.8	1.2	98.8	93.8
Mississippi	100.0	0.3	0.5	35.6	63.5	0.6	99.4	63.1
Missouri	100.0	0.4	0.8	10.7	88.0	1.2	98.8	87.0
Montana	100.0	6.0	0.5	0.3	93.1	1.5	98.5	91.9
Nebraska	100.0	0.8	0.8	3.7	94.7	2.3	97.7	92.6
Nevada	100.0	1.8	3.3	6.6	88.3	10.4	89.6	78.8
New Hampshire	100.0	0.2	0.8	0.7	98.3	1.0	99.0	97.4
New Jersey	100.0	0.2	3.6	13.9	82.3	9.7	90.3	73.9
New Mexico	100.0	9.1	1.0	2.1	87.8	38.2	61.8	50.6
New York	100.0	0.4	3.9	17.0	78.7	12.3	87.7	69.3
North Carolina	100.0	1.2	0.8	22.0	75.9	1.2	98.8	75.0
North Dakota	100.0	4.1	0.5	0.6	94.8	0.7	99.3	94.2
Ohio	100.0	0.2	0.8	10.7	88.3	1.3	98.7	87.1
Oklahoma	100.0	8.2	1.1	7.5	83.2	2.7	97.3	81.0
Oregon	100.0	1.4	2.5	1.7	94.4	4.0	96.0	90.8
Pennsylvania	100.0	0.1	1.2	9.3	89.4	2.0	98.0	87.8
Rhode Island	100.0	0.4	1.9	4.3	93.4	4.6	95.4	89.8
South Carolina	100.0	0.2	0.7	29.9	69.2	0.9	99.1	68.6
South Dakota	100.0	7.3	0.5	0.5	91.8	0.8	99.2	91.2
Tennessee	100.0	0.2	0.7	16.0	83.2	0.7	99.3	82.6
Texas	100.0	0.4	2.0	12.1	85.6	25.5	74.5	60.7
Utah	100.0	1.5	2.0	0.7	95.9	4.9	95.1	91.2
Vermont	100.0	0.3	0.6	0.4	98.8	0.7	99.3	98.2
Virginia	100.0	0.3	2.6	18.9	78.3	2.6	97.4	76.0
Washington	100.0	1.8	4.4	3.1	90.6	4.4	95.6	86.8
West Virginia	100.0	0.1	0.4	3.1	96.3	0.5	99.5	95.9
Wisconsin	100.0	0.8	1.1	5.0	93.0	1.9	98.1	91.3
Wyoming	100.0	2.2	0.6	0.8	96.4	5.7	94.3	91.0

Note: Asians include Pacific Islanders; numbers will not add to total because Hispanics may be of any race.
Source: Bureau of the Census, Population Estimates, Archives, 1990s, Internet site http://www.census.gov/popest/archives/1990s/strh/srhmars.txt; calculations by New Strategist

Table 8.29　State Populations by Race, 2000

(number of people by state and race, 2000; numbers in thousands)

	total	American Indian	Asian	black	Native Hawaiian	white	some other race	two or more races
					race alone			
United States	281,422	2,476	10,243	34,658	399	211,461	15,359	6,826
Alabama	4,447	22	31	1,156	1	3,163	29	44
Alaska	627	98	25	22	3	435	10	34
Arizona	5,131	256	92	159	7	3,874	597	147
Arkansas	2,673	18	20	419	2	2,139	40	36
California	33,872	333	3,698	2,264	117	20,170	5,682	1,608
Colorado	4,301	44	95	165	5	3,560	310	122
Connecticut	3,406	10	82	310	1	2,780	147	75
Delaware	784	3	16	151	0	585	16	13
District of Columbia	572	2	15	343	0	176	22	13
Florida	15,982	54	266	2,336	9	12,465	477	376
Georgia	8,186	22	173	2,350	4	5,327	196	114
Hawaii	1,212	4	504	22	114	294	15	259
Idaho	1,294	18	12	5	1	1,177	55	26
Illinois	12,419	31	424	1,877	5	9,125	723	235
Indiana	6,080	16	59	510	2	5,320	98	76
Iowa	2,926	9	37	62	1	2,749	37	32
Kansas	2,688	25	47	154	1	2,314	91	56
Kentucky	4,042	9	30	296	1	3,641	23	42
Louisiana	4,469	25	55	1,452	1	2,856	31	48
Maine	1,275	7	9	7	0	1,236	3	13
Maryland	5,296	15	211	1,477	2	3,391	96	104
Massachusetts	6,349	15	238	343	2	5,367	237	146
Michigan	9,938	58	177	1,413	3	7,966	130	192
Minnesota	4,919	55	142	172	2	4,400	66	83
Mississippi	2,845	12	19	1,034	1	1,746	14	20
Missouri	5,595	25	62	629	3	4,748	46	82
Montana	902	56	5	3	0	817	5	16
Nebraska	1,711	15	22	69	1	1,533	48	24
Nevada	1,998	26	90	135	8	1,502	159	76
New Hampshire	1,236	3	16	9	0	1,187	7	13
New Jersey	8,414	19	480	1,142	3	6,105	451	214
New Mexico	1,819	173	19	34	2	1,214	310	66
New York	18,976	82	1,045	3,014	9	12,894	1,342	590
North Carolina	8,049	100	114	1,738	4	5,805	187	103
North Dakota	642	31	4	4	0	593	3	7
Ohio	11,353	24	133	1,301	3	9,645	89	158
Oklahoma	3,451	273	47	261	2	2,628	83	156
Oregon	3,421	45	101	56	8	2,962	145	105
Pennsylvania	12,281	18	220	1,225	3	10,484	188	142
Rhode Island	1,048	5	24	47	1	891	53	28
South Carolina	4,012	14	36	1,185	2	2,696	40	40
South Dakota	755	62	4	5	0	669	4	10
Tennessee	5,689	15	57	933	2	4,563	56	63
Texas	20,852	118	562	2,405	14	14,800	2,438	515
Utah	2,233	30	37	18	15	1,993	93	47
Vermont	609	2	5	3	0	589	1	7
Virginia	7,079	21	261	1,390	4	5,120	139	143
Washington	5,894	93	322	190	24	4,822	229	214
West Virginia	1,808	4	9	57	0	1,719	3	16
Wisconsin	5,364	47	89	304	2	4,770	85	67
Wyoming	494	11	3	4	0	455	12	9

Note: Most who identified themselves as "some other race" on the 2000 census were Hispanic.
Source: Bureau of the Census, 2000 Census, Population by Race and Hispanic or Latino Origin for the United States, Regions, Divisions, States, Puerto Rico, and Places of 100,000 or More Population (PHC-T-6), Internet site http://www.census.gov/population/www/cen2000/phc-t6.html; calculations by New Strategist

Table 8.30 Distribution of State Populations by Race, 2000

(percent distribution of people by race, by state, 2000)

	total	American Indian	Asian	black	Native Hawaiian	white	some other race	two or more races
					race alone			
United States	**100.0%**	**0.9%**	**3.6%**	**12.3%**	**0.1%**	**75.1%**	**5.5%**	**2.4%**
Alabama	100.0	0.5	0.7	26.0	0.0	71.1	0.7	1.0
Alaska	100.0	15.6	4.0	3.5	0.5	69.4	1.6	5.4
Arizona	100.0	5.0	1.8	3.1	0.1	75.5	11.6	2.9
Arkansas	100.0	0.7	0.8	15.7	0.1	80.0	1.5	1.3
California	100.0	1.0	10.9	6.7	0.3	59.5	16.8	4.7
Colorado	100.0	1.0	2.2	3.8	0.1	82.8	7.2	2.8
Connecticut	100.0	0.3	2.4	9.1	0.0	81.6	4.3	2.2
Delaware	100.0	0.4	2.1	19.3	0.0	74.6	2.0	1.7
District of Columbia	100.0	0.3	2.7	60.0	0.1	30.8	3.8	2.4
Florida	100.0	0.3	1.7	14.6	0.1	78.0	3.0	2.4
Georgia	100.0	0.3	2.1	28.7	0.1	65.1	2.4	1.4
Hawaii	100.0	0.3	41.6	1.8	9.4	24.3	1.2	21.4
Idaho	100.0	1.4	0.9	0.4	0.1	91.0	4.2	2.0
Illinois	100.0	0.2	3.4	15.1	0.0	73.5	5.8	1.9
Indiana	100.0	0.3	1.0	8.4	0.0	87.5	1.6	1.2
Iowa	100.0	0.3	1.3	2.1	0.0	94.0	1.3	1.1
Kansas	100.0	0.9	1.7	5.7	0.0	86.1	3.4	2.1
Kentucky	100.0	0.2	0.7	7.3	0.0	90.1	0.6	1.1
Louisiana	100.0	0.6	1.2	32.5	0.0	63.9	0.7	1.1
Maine	100.0	0.5	0.7	0.5	0.0	96.9	0.2	1.0
Maryland	100.0	0.3	4.0	27.9	0.0	64.0	1.8	2.0
Massachusetts	100.0	0.2	3.8	5.4	0.0	84.5	3.7	2.3
Michigan	100.0	0.6	1.8	14.2	0.0	80.2	1.3	1.9
Minnesota	100.0	1.1	2.9	3.5	0.0	89.4	1.3	1.7
Mississippi	100.0	0.4	0.7	36.3	0.0	61.4	0.5	0.7
Missouri	100.0	0.4	1.1	11.2	0.1	84.9	0.8	1.5
Montana	100.0	6.2	0.5	0.3	0.1	90.6	0.6	1.7
Nebraska	100.0	0.9	1.3	4.0	0.0	89.6	2.8	1.4
Nevada	100.0	1.3	4.5	6.8	0.4	75.2	8.0	3.8
New Hampshire	100.0	0.2	1.3	0.7	0.0	96.0	0.6	1.1
New Jersey	100.0	0.2	5.7	13.6	0.0	72.6	5.4	2.5
New Mexico	100.0	9.5	1.1	1.9	0.1	66.7	17.0	3.6
New York	100.0	0.4	5.5	15.9	0.0	67.9	7.1	3.1
North Carolina	100.0	1.2	1.4	21.6	0.0	72.1	2.3	1.3
North Dakota	100.0	4.8	0.6	0.6	0.0	92.4	0.4	1.2
Ohio	100.0	0.2	1.2	11.5	0.0	85.0	0.8	1.4
Oklahoma	100.0	7.9	1.4	7.6	0.1	76.2	2.4	4.5
Oregon	100.0	1.3	3.0	1.6	0.2	86.6	4.2	3.1
Pennsylvania	100.0	0.1	1.8	10.0	0.0	85.4	1.5	1.2
Rhode Island	100.0	0.5	2.3	4.5	0.1	85.0	5.0	2.7
South Carolina	100.0	0.3	0.9	29.5	0.0	67.2	1.0	1.0
South Dakota	100.0	8.2	0.6	0.7	0.0	88.6	0.5	1.3
Tennessee	100.0	0.3	1.0	16.4	0.0	80.2	1.0	1.1
Texas	100.0	0.6	2.7	11.5	0.1	71.0	11.7	2.5
Utah	100.0	1.3	1.7	0.8	0.7	89.3	4.2	2.1
Vermont	100.0	0.3	0.9	0.5	0.0	96.7	0.2	1.2
Virginia	100.0	0.3	3.7	19.6	0.1	72.3	2.0	2.0
Washington	100.0	1.6	5.5	3.2	0.4	81.8	3.9	3.6
West Virginia	100.0	0.2	0.5	3.2	0.0	95.1	0.2	0.9
Wisconsin	100.0	0.9	1.7	5.7	0.0	88.9	1.6	1.2
Wyoming	100.0	2.2	0.6	0.8	0.1	92.1	2.5	1.8

Note: Most who identified themselves as "some other race" on the 2000 census were Hispanic.
Source: Bureau of the Census, 2000 Census, Population by Race and Hispanic or Latino Origin for the United States, Regions, Divisions, States, Puerto Rico, and Places of 100,000 or More Population (PHC-T-6), Internet site http://www.census.gov/ population/www/cen2000/phc-t6.html; calculations by New Strategist

Table 8.31 State Populations by Hispanic Origin, 2000

(number of people by state and Hispanic origin, 2000; numbers in thousands)

			Hispanic origin	
			non-Hispanic	
	total	Hispanic	total	white
United States	**281,422**	**35,306**	**246,116**	**194,553**
Alabama	4,447	76	4,371	3,126
Alaska	627	26	601	424
Arizona	5,131	1,296	3,835	3,274
Arkansas	2,673	87	2,587	2,100
California	33,872	10,967	22,905	15,817
Colorado	4,301	736	3,566	3,203
Connecticut	3,406	320	3,085	2,639
Delaware	784	37	746	568
Distrist of Columbia	572	45	527	159
Florida	15,982	2,683	13,300	10,459
Georgia	8,186	435	7,751	5,129
Hawaii	1,212	88	1,124	277
Idaho	1,294	102	1,192	1,139
Illinois	12,419	1,530	10,889	8,424
Indiana	6,080	215	5,866	5,219
Iowa	2,926	82	2,844	2,710
Kansas	2,688	188	2,500	2,234
Kentucky	4,042	60	3,982	3,608
Louisiana	4,469	108	4,361	2,794
Maine	1,275	9	1,266	1,230
Maryland	5,296	228	5,069	3,287
Massachusetts	6,349	429	5,920	5,198
Michigan	9,938	324	9,615	7,807
Minnesota	4,919	143	4,776	4,337
Mississippi	2,845	40	2,805	1,728
Missouri	5,595	119	5,477	4,686
Montana	902	18	884	808
Nebraska	1,711	94	1,617	1,494
Nevada	1,998	394	1,604	1,303
New Hampshire	1,236	20	1,215	1,175
New Jersey	8,414	1,117	7,297	5,557
New Mexico	1,819	765	1,054	813
New York	18,976	2,868	16,109	11,761
North Carolina	8,049	379	7,670	5,647
North Dakota	642	8	634	589
Ohio	11,353	217	11,136	9,538
Oklahoma	3,451	179	3,271	2,556
Oregon	3,421	275	3,146	2,858
Pennsylvania	12,281	394	11,887	10,322
Rhode Island	1,048	91	957	858
South Carolina	4,012	95	3,917	2,652
South Dakota	755	11	744	665
Tennessee	5,689	124	5,565	4,506
Texas	20,852	6,670	14,182	10,933
Utah	2,233	202	2,032	1,904
Vermont	609	6	603	585
Virginia	7,079	330	6,749	4,966
Washington	5,894	442	5,453	4,652
West Virginia	1,808	12	1,796	1,710
Wisconsin	5,364	193	5,171	4,682
Wyoming	494	32	462	439

Source: Bureau of the Census, 2000 Census, Population by Race and Hispanic or Latino Origin for the United States, Regions, Divisions, States, Puerto Rico, and Places of 100,000 or More Population (PHC-T-6), Internet site http://www.census.gov/population/www/cen2000/phc-t6.html; calculations by New Strategist

Table 8.32 Distribution of State Populations by Hispanic Origin, 2000

(percent distribution of people by Hispanic origin, by state, 2000)

	total	Hispanic	non-Hispanic total	white
United States	**100.0%**	**12.5%**	**87.5%**	**69.1%**
Alabama	100.0	1.7	98.3	70.3
Alaska	100.0	4.1	95.9	67.6
Arizona	100.0	25.3	74.7	63.8
Arkansas	100.0	3.3	96.8	78.6
California	100.0	32.4	67.6	46.7
Colorado	100.0	17.1	82.9	74.5
Connecticut	100.0	9.4	90.6	77.5
Delaware	100.0	4.7	95.2	72.4
Distrist of Columbia	100.0	7.9	92.1	27.8
Florida	100.0	16.8	83.2	65.4
Georgia	100.0	5.3	94.7	62.7
Hawaii	100.0	7.3	92.7	22.9
Idaho	100.0	7.9	92.1	88.0
Illinois	100.0	12.3	87.7	67.8
Indiana	100.0	3.5	96.5	85.8
Iowa	100.0	2.8	97.2	92.6
Kansas	100.0	7.0	93.0	83.1
Kentucky	100.0	1.5	98.5	89.3
Louisiana	100.0	2.4	97.6	62.5
Maine	100.0	0.7	99.3	96.5
Maryland	100.0	4.3	95.7	62.1
Massachusetts	100.0	6.8	93.2	81.9
Michigan	100.0	3.3	96.7	78.6
Minnesota	100.0	2.9	97.1	88.2
Mississippi	100.0	1.4	98.6	60.7
Missouri	100.0	2.1	97.9	83.8
Montana	100.0	2.0	98.0	89.6
Nebraska	100.0	5.5	94.5	87.3
Nevada	100.0	19.7	80.3	65.2
New Hampshire	100.0	1.6	98.3	95.1
New Jersey	100.0	13.3	86.7	66.0
New Mexico	100.0	42.1	57.9	44.7
New York	100.0	15.1	84.9	62.0
North Carolina	100.0	4.7	95.3	70.2
North Dakota	100.0	1.2	98.8	91.7
Ohio	100.0	1.9	98.1	84.0
Oklahoma	100.0	5.2	94.8	74.1
Oregon	100.0	8.0	92.0	83.5
Pennsylvania	100.0	3.2	96.8	84.0
Rhode Island	100.0	8.7	91.3	81.9
South Carolina	100.0	2.4	97.6	66.1
South Dakota	100.0	1.5	98.5	88.1
Tennessee	100.0	2.2	97.8	79.2
Texas	100.0	32.0	68.0	52.4
Utah	100.0	9.0	91.0	85.3
Vermont	100.0	1.0	99.0	96.1
Virginia	100.0	4.7	95.3	70.2
Washington	100.0	7.5	92.5	78.9
West Virginia	100.0	0.7	99.3	94.6
Wisconsin	100.0	3.6	96.4	87.3
Wyoming	100.0	6.5	93.5	88.9

Source: Bureau of the Census, 2000 Census, Population by Race and Hispanic or Latino Origin for the United States, Regions, Divisions, States, Puerto Rico, and Places of 100,000 or More Population (PHC-T-6), Internet site http://www.census.gov/population/www/cen2000/phc-t6.html; calculations by New Strategist

Table 8.33 State Populations by Race, 2006

(number of people by state and race, 2006; numbers in thousands)

	total	American Indian	Asian	black	Native Hawaiian	white	two or more races
				race alone			
United States	**299,398**	**2,903**	**13,159**	**38,343**	**529**	**239,746**	**4,719**
Alabama	4,599	24	42	1,212	2	3,277	43
Alaska	670	103	31	25	4	474	33
Arizona	6,166	294	147	232	12	5,381	101
Arkansas	2,811	22	29	442	3	2,280	35
California	36,458	421	4,511	2,445	153	28,044	884
Colorado	4,753	55	126	196	7	4,283	87
Connecticut	3,505	12	118	358	3	2,966	47
Delaware	853	3	24	178	0	636	12
District of Columbia	582	2	19	329	1	223	8
Florida	18,090	80	397	2,864	15	14,504	229
Georgia	9,364	31	261	2,800	7	6,159	106
Hawaii	1,285	6	514	32	117	367	249
Idaho	1,466	21	16	10	2	1,397	22
Illinois	12,832	41	541	1,928	8	10,170	143
Indiana	6,314	19	84	563	3	5,575	70
Iowa	2,982	11	47	73	1	2,820	29
Kansas	2,764	27	61	165	2	2,462	47
Kentucky	4,206	10	42	317	2	3,793	42
Louisiana	4,288	27	60	1,358	2	2,802	39
Maine	1,322	8	11	11	0	1,278	13
Maryland	5,616	19	278	1,657	4	3,574	85
Massachusetts	6,437	19	314	447	5	5,569	84
Michigan	10,096	61	237	1,444	4	8,199	150
Minnesota	5,167	60	181	231	3	4,616	76
Mississippi	2,911	14	22	1,081	1	1,772	21
Missouri	5,843	28	83	673	4	4,975	79
Montana	945	61	6	4	1	858	15
Nebraska	1,768	17	29	78	1	1,623	20
Nevada	2,496	35	150	196	12	2,038	64
New Hampshire	1,315	3	24	14	1	1,260	13
New Jersey	8,725	28	648	1,265	7	6,665	112
New Mexico	1,955	191	26	49	3	1,654	32
New York	19,306	105	1,326	3,353	19	14,220	283
North Carolina	8,857	111	164	1,921	6	6,558	96
North Dakota	636	34	5	5	0	584	7
Ohio	11,478	28	177	1,377	4	9,748	145
Oklahoma	3,579	288	60	279	3	2,804	145
Oregon	3,701	51	134	69	10	3,348	88
Pennsylvania	12,441	24	293	1,336	5	10,660	122
Rhode Island	1,068	7	29	67	1	947	16
South Carolina	4,321	17	50	1,253	2	2,959	40
South Dakota	782	67	6	7	0	691	11
Tennessee	6,039	19	80	1,020	3	4,856	62
Texas	23,508	163	788	2,805	27	19,453	272
Utah	2,550	34	50	26	19	2,384	38
Vermont	624	2	7	4	0	603	7
Virginia	7,643	26	363	1,520	6	5,605	123
Washington	6,396	104	422	228	30	5,421	191
West Virginia	1,818	4	12	60	1	1,726	16
Wisconsin	5,557	52	111	332	2	5,000	59
Wyoming	515	13	4	5	0	486	7

Source: Bureau of the Census, State Population Estimates, Internet site http://www.census.gov/popest/states/asrh/SC-EST2006-04.html; calculations by New Strategist

Table 8.34 Distribution of State Populations by Race, 2006

(percent distribution of people by race, by state, 2006)

	total	American Indian	Asian	black	Native Hawaiian	white	two or more races
							race alone
United States	100.0%	1.0%	4.4%	12.8%	0.2%	80.1%	1.6%
Alabama	100.0	0.5	0.9	26.3	0.0	71.2	0.9
Alaska	100.0	15.4	4.6	3.7	0.6	70.7	4.9
Arizona	100.0	4.8	2.4	3.8	0.2	87.3	1.6
Arkansas	100.0	0.8	1.0	15.7	0.1	81.1	1.3
California	100.0	1.2	12.4	6.7	0.4	76.9	2.4
Colorado	100.0	1.1	2.6	4.1	0.1	90.1	1.8
Connecticut	100.0	0.4	3.4	10.2	0.1	84.6	1.4
Delaware	100.0	0.4	2.8	20.9	0.1	74.5	1.4
District of Columbia	100.0	0.4	3.2	56.5	0.1	38.4	1.4
Florida	100.0	0.4	2.2	15.8	0.1	80.2	1.3
Georgia	100.0	0.3	2.8	29.9	0.1	65.8	1.1
Hawaii	100.0	0.5	40.0	2.5	9.1	28.6	19.4
Idaho	100.0	1.4	1.1	0.7	0.1	95.2	1.5
Illinois	100.0	0.3	4.2	15.0	0.1	79.3	1.1
Indiana	100.0	0.3	1.3	8.9	0.0	88.3	1.1
Iowa	100.0	0.4	1.6	2.5	0.0	94.6	1.0
Kansas	100.0	1.0	2.2	6.0	0.1	89.1	1.7
Kentucky	100.0	0.2	1.0	7.5	0.0	90.2	1.0
Louisiana	100.0	0.6	1.4	31.7	0.0	65.4	0.9
Maine	100.0	0.6	0.9	0.8	0.0	96.7	1.0
Maryland	100.0	0.3	4.9	29.5	0.1	63.6	1.5
Massachusetts	100.0	0.3	4.9	6.9	0.1	86.5	1.3
Michigan	100.0	0.6	2.4	14.3	0.0	81.2	1.5
Minnesota	100.0	1.2	3.5	4.5	0.1	89.3	1.5
Mississippi	100.0	0.5	0.8	37.1	0.0	60.9	0.7
Missouri	100.0	0.5	1.4	11.5	0.1	85.1	1.3
Montana	100.0	6.4	0.6	0.4	0.1	90.8	1.6
Nebraska	100.0	1.0	1.7	4.4	0.1	91.8	1.2
Nevada	100.0	1.4	6.0	7.9	0.5	81.7	2.6
New Hampshire	100.0	0.3	1.9	1.1	0.0	95.8	1.0
New Jersey	100.0	0.3	7.4	14.5	0.1	76.4	1.3
New Mexico	100.0	9.8	1.3	2.5	0.1	84.6	1.6
New York	100.0	0.5	6.9	17.4	0.1	73.7	1.5
North Carolina	100.0	1.3	1.9	21.7	0.1	74.0	1.1
North Dakota	100.0	5.4	0.7	0.8	0.0	91.9	1.1
Ohio	100.0	0.2	1.5	12.0	0.0	84.9	1.3
Oklahoma	100.0	8.0	1.7	7.8	0.1	78.3	4.1
Oregon	100.0	1.4	3.6	1.9	0.3	90.5	2.4
Pennsylvania	100.0	0.2	2.4	10.7	0.0	85.7	1.0
Rhode Island	100.0	0.6	2.7	6.3	0.1	88.7	1.5
South Carolina	100.0	0.4	1.1	29.0	0.1	68.5	0.9
South Dakota	100.0	8.5	0.7	0.9	0.0	88.4	1.4
Tennessee	100.0	0.3	1.3	16.9	0.1	80.4	1.0
Texas	100.0	0.7	3.4	11.9	0.1	82.7	1.2
Utah	100.0	1.3	2.0	1.0	0.8	93.5	1.5
Vermont	100.0	0.4	1.1	0.7	0.0	96.7	1.1
Virginia	100.0	0.3	4.8	19.9	0.1	73.3	1.6
Washington	100.0	1.6	6.6	3.6	0.5	84.8	3.0
West Virginia	100.0	0.2	0.6	3.3	0.0	94.9	0.9
Wisconsin	100.0	0.9	2.0	6.0	0.0	90.0	1.1
Wyoming	100.0	2.5	0.7	0.9	0.1	94.5	1.4

Source: Bureau of the Census, State Population Estimates, Internet site http://www.census.gov/popest/states/asrh/ SC-EST2006-04.html; calculations by New Strategist

Table 8.35 State Populations by Hispanic Origin, 2006

(number of people by state and Hispanic origin, 2006; numbers in thousands)

| | | | Hispanic origin | |
| | | | non-Hispanic | |
	total	Hispanic	total	white
United States	**299,398**	**44,321**	**255,077**	**198,744**
Alabama	4,599	114	4,485	3,175
Alaska	670	38	633	445
Arizona	6,166	1,803	4,363	3,680
Arkansas	2,811	141	2,670	2,149
California	36,458	13,074	23,383	15,723
Colorado	4,753	934	3,819	3,410
Connecticut	3,505	392	3,113	2,622
Delaware	853	54	800	589
District of Columbia	582	48	534	184
Florida	18,090	3,646	14,443	11,093
Georgia	9,364	703	8,661	5,518
Hawaii	1,285	100	1,186	317
Idaho	1,466	139	1,328	1,266
Illinois	12,832	1,887	10,945	8,373
Indiana	6,314	301	6,013	5,296
Iowa	2,982	115	2,867	2,714
Kansas	2,764	237	2,527	2,241
Kentucky	4,206	86	4,120	3,716
Louisiana	4,288	124	4,163	2,694
Maine	1,322	14	1,308	1,266
Maryland	5,616	337	5,278	3,282
Massachusetts	6,437	511	5,926	5,150
Michigan	10,096	393	9,702	7,846
Minnesota	5,167	196	4,971	4,440
Mississippi	2,911	53	2,857	1,726
Missouri	5,843	164	5,679	4,826
Montana	945	24	921	838
Nebraska	1,768	130	1,638	1,501
Nevada	2,496	610	1,885	1,469
New Hampshire	1,315	30	1,285	1,233
New Jersey	8,725	1,365	7,360	5,458
New Mexico	1,955	861	1,094	836
New York	19,306	3,139	16,167	11,677
North Carolina	8,857	594	8,263	6,015
North Dakota	636	11	625	575
Ohio	11,478	268	11,210	9,514
Oklahoma	3,579	247	3,332	2,581
Oregon	3,701	379	3,322	2,996
Pennsylvania	12,441	527	11,914	10,216
Rhode Island	1,068	118	950	850
South Carolina	4,321	151	4,170	2,827
South Dakota	782	17	765	677
Tennessee	6,039	195	5,844	4,681
Texas	23,508	8,385	15,123	11,351
Utah	2,550	286	2,264	2,114
Vermont	624	7	617	597
Virginia	7,643	480	7,163	5,175
Washington	6,396	581	5,814	4,895
West Virginia	1,818	17	1,802	1,710
Wisconsin	5,557	259	5,298	4,761
Wyoming	515	36	479	454

*Source: Bureau of the Census, State Population Estimates, Internet site http://www.census.gov/popest/states/asrh/
SC-EST2006-04.html; calculations by New Strategist*

Table 8.36 Distribution of State Populations by Hispanic Origin, 2006

(percent distribution of people by Hispanic origin, by state, 2006)

| | | | Hispanic origin | |
| | | | | non-Hispanic |
	total	Hispanic	total	white
United States	**100.0%**	**14.8%**	**85.2%**	**66.4%**
Alabama	100.0	2.5	97.5	69.0
Alaska	100.0	5.6	94.4	66.4
Arizona	100.0	29.2	70.8	59.7
Arkansas	100.0	5.0	95.0	76.4
California	100.0	35.9	64.1	43.1
Colorado	100.0	19.7	80.3	71.7
Connecticut	100.0	11.2	88.8	74.8
Delaware	100.0	6.3	93.7	69.0
District of Columbia	100.0	8.2	91.8	31.7
Florida	100.0	20.2	79.8	61.3
Georgia	100.0	7.5	92.5	58.9
Hawaii	100.0	7.8	92.2	24.7
Idaho	100.0	9.5	90.5	86.3
Illinois	100.0	14.7	85.3	65.3
Indiana	100.0	4.8	95.2	83.9
Iowa	100.0	3.8	96.2	91.0
Kansas	100.0	8.6	91.4	81.1
Kentucky	100.0	2.0	98.0	88.4
Louisiana	100.0	2.9	97.1	62.8
Maine	100.0	1.0	99.0	95.8
Maryland	100.0	6.0	94.0	58.4
Massachusetts	100.0	7.9	92.1	80.0
Michigan	100.0	3.9	96.1	77.7
Minnesota	100.0	3.8	96.2	85.9
Mississippi	100.0	1.8	98.2	59.3
Missouri	100.0	2.8	97.2	82.6
Montana	100.0	2.5	97.5	88.7
Nebraska	100.0	7.4	92.6	84.9
Nevada	100.0	24.4	75.6	58.9
New Hampshire	100.0	2.3	97.7	93.8
New Jersey	100.0	15.6	84.4	62.6
New Mexico	100.0	44.0	56.0	42.8
New York	100.0	16.3	83.7	60.5
North Carolina	100.0	6.7	93.3	67.9
North Dakota	100.0	1.7	98.3	90.4
Ohio	100.0	2.3	97.7	82.9
Oklahoma	100.0	6.9	93.1	72.1
Oregon	100.0	10.2	89.8	81.0
Pennsylvania	100.0	4.2	95.8	82.1
Rhode Island	100.0	11.0	89.0	79.6
South Carolina	100.0	3.5	96.5	65.4
South Dakota	100.0	2.1	97.9	86.6
Tennessee	100.0	3.2	96.8	77.5
Texas	100.0	35.7	64.3	48.3
Utah	100.0	11.2	88.8	82.9
Vermont	100.0	1.1	98.9	95.7
Virginia	100.0	6.3	93.7	67.7
Washington	100.0	9.1	90.9	76.5
West Virginia	100.0	0.9	99.1	94.1
Wisconsin	100.0	4.7	95.3	85.7
Wyoming	100.0	6.9	93.1	88.1

Source: Bureau of the Census, State Population Estimates, Internet site http://www.census.gov/popest/states/asrh/ SC-EST2006-04.html; calculations by New Strategist

The Suburbs Are Home to Half of Americans

Eighty percent of the population lives in a metropolitan area.

The suburbs have grown faster than the central cities and nonmetropolitan areas for decades. The 2000 census found half of Americans living in the suburbs of a metropolitan area, up from 23 percent in 1950. Only 20 percent live in a nonmetropolitan area, down from 44 percent in 1950.

Among the nation's 361 metropolitan areas, New York is by far the most populous, with 19 million people in 2006. Los Angeles is well behind in second place, with 13 million. Between 2000 and 2006, St. George, Utah, was the fastest growing metropolitan area, with a 40 percent increase in population. New Orleans lost an enormous 22 percent of its population between 2000 and 2006 because of the devastation caused by Hurricane Katrina. Also because of Katrina, the population of Gulfport-Biloxi, Mississippi, fell 7 percent during those years.

■ Because metropolitan boundaries change every few years, it is difficult to compare metropolitan population figures over more than one decade.

New Orleans lost 22 percent of its population between 2000 and 2006

(metropolitan areas with the largest percent increase and decrease in population, 2000 to 2006)

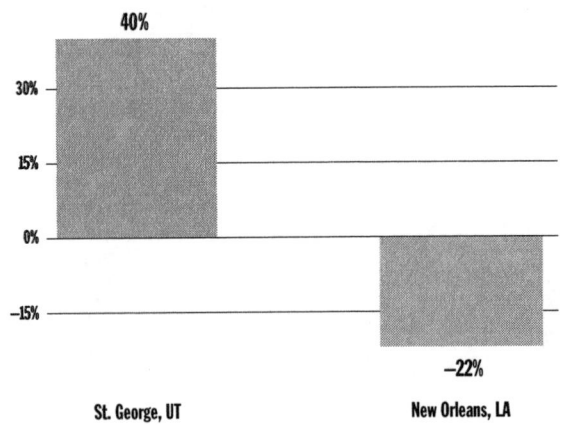

Table 8.37 Population by Metropolitan Status, 1950 to 2000

(number and percent distribution of people by metropolitan status, 1950 to 2000; numbers in thousands; metropolitan areas as defined at each time period)

| | number | | percent distribution by metropolitan status | | | | |
	total	metropolitan	total	metropolitan total	central cities	suburbs	nonmetro areas
2000	281,422	225,968	100.0%	80.3%	30.3%	50.0%	19.7%
1990	249,464	198,249	100.0	77.5	31.3	46.2	22.5
1980	227,225	177,361	100.0	74.8	30.0	44.8	25.2
1970	203,212	139,480	100.0	69.0	31.4	37.6	31.0
1960	179,323	112,885	100.0	63.3	32.3	30.9	36.7
1950	150,697	84,501	100.0	56.1	32.8	23.3	43.9

Note: The suburbs are the portion of a metropolitan area outside the central city.
Source: Bureau of the Census, Metropolitan Areas and Cities, 1990 Census Profile, No. 3, 1991; and 2000 Census, Table DP-1: Profile of General Demographic Characteristics: 2000; and Historical Statistics of the United States, Colonial Times to 1970, Part 1, 1975; calculations by New Strategist

Table 8.38 Metropolitan Populations, 2000 and 2006: Alphabetical Ranking

(number of people by metropolitan area, 2000 and 2006; change and percent change in number, 2000–06; metropolitan area definitions as of December 2005; metropolitan areas ranked alphabetically)

		2006	2000	change 2000–06	
				number	percent
1.	Abilene, TX	158,063	160,241	–2,178	–1.4%
2.	Akron, OH	700,943	694,960	5,983	0.9
3.	Albany, GA	163,961	157,866	6,095	3.9
4.	Albany–Schenectady–Troy, NY	850,957	825,875	25,082	3.0
5.	Albuquerque, NM	816,811	729,653	87,158	11.9
6.	Alexandria, LA	150,080	145,035	5,045	3.5
7.	Allentown–Bethlehem–Easton, PA–NJ	800,336	740,394	59,942	8.1
8.	Altoona, PA	126,494	129,144	–2,650	–2.1
9.	Amarillo, TX	241,515	226,522	14,993	6.6
10.	Ames, IA	80,145	79,981	164	0.2
11.	Anchorage, AK	359,180	319,605	39,575	12.4
12.	Anderson, IN	130,575	133,358	–2,783	–2.1
13.	Anderson, SC	177,963	165,740	12,223	7.4
14.	Ann Arbor, MI	344,047	322,770	21,277	6.6
15.	Anniston–Oxford, AL	112,903	112,243	660	0.6
16.	Appleton, WI	217,313	201,722	15,591	7.7
17.	Asheville, NC	398,009	369,172	28,837	7.8
18.	Athens–Clarke County, GA	185,479	166,079	19,400	11.7
19.	Atlanta–Sandy Springs–Marietta, GA	5,138,223	4,248,012	890,211	21.0
20.	Atlantic City, NJ	271,620	252,552	19,068	7.6
21.	Auburn–Opelika, AL	125,781	115,092	10,689	9.3
22.	Augusta–Richmond County, GA–SC	523,249	499,653	23,596	4.7
23.	Austin–Round Rock, TX	1,513,565	1,249,763	263,802	21.1
24.	Bakersfield, CA	780,117	661,655	118,462	17.9
25.	Baltimore–Towson, MD	2,658,405	2,552,994	105,411	4.1
26.	Bangor, ME	147,180	144,919	2,261	1.6
27.	Barnstable Town, MA	224,816	222,230	2,586	1.2
28.	Baton Rouge, LA	766,514	705,967	60,547	8.6
29.	Battle Creek, MI	137,991	137,985	6	0.0
30.	Bay City, MI	108,390	110,157	–1,767	–1.6
31.	Beaumont–Port Arthur, TX	379,640	385,090	–5,450	–1.4
32.	Bellingham, WA	185,953	166,823	19,130	11.5
33.	Bend, OR	149,140	115,367	33,773	29.3
34.	Billings, MT	148,116	138,904	9,212	6.6
35.	Binghamton, NY	247,554	252,320	–4,766	–1.9
36.	Birmingham–Hoover, AL	1,100,019	1,051,305	48,714	4.6
37.	Bismarck, ND	101,138	94,719	6,419	6.8
38.	Blacksburg–Christiansburg–Radford, VA	151,524	151,324	200	0.1
39.	Bloomington, IN	178,714	175,506	3,208	1.8
40.	Bloomington–Normal, IL	161,202	150,435	10,767	7.2
41.	Boise City–Nampa, ID	567,640	464,840	102,800	22.1
42.	Boston–Cambridge–Quincy, MA–NH	4,455,217	4,392,340	62,877	1.4

(continued)

		2006	2000	change 2000–06	
				number	percent
43.	Boulder, CO	282,304	269,787	12,517	4.6%
44.	Bowling Green, KY	113,320	104,166	9,154	8.8
45.	Bremerton–Silverdale, WA	240,604	231,969	8,635	3.7
46.	Bridgeport–Stamford–Norwalk, CT	900,440	882,567	17,873	2.0
47.	Brownsville–Harlingen, TX	387,717	335,227	52,490	15.7
48.	Brunswick, GA	100,613	93,044	7,569	8.1
49.	Buffalo–Niagara Falls, NY	1,137,520	1,170,109	−32,589	−2.8
50.	Burlington, NC	142,661	130,794	11,867	9.1
51.	Burlington–South Burlington, VT	206,007	198,889	7,118	3.6
52.	Canton–Massillon, OH	409,764	406,968	2,796	0.7
53.	Cape Coral–Fort Myers, FL	571,344	440,888	130,456	29.6
54.	Carson City, NV	55,289	52,457	2,832	5.4
55.	Casper, WY	70,401	66,533	3,868	5.8
56.	Cedar Rapids, IA	249,320	237,230	12,090	5.1
57.	Champaign–Urbana, IL	216,581	210,279	6,302	3.0
58.	Charleston, WV	305,526	309,632	−4,106	−1.3
59.	Charleston–North Charleston, SC	603,178	548,972	54,206	9.9
60.	Charlotte–Gastonia–Concord, NC–SC	1,583,016	1,330,403	252,613	19.0
61.	Charlottesville, VA	190,278	174,021	16,257	9.3
62.	Chattanooga, TN–GA	496,704	476,513	20,191	4.2
63.	Cheyenne, WY	85,384	81,607	3,777	4.6
64.	Chicago–Naperville–Joliet, IL–IN–WI	9,505,748	9,098,615	407,133	4.5
65.	Chico, CA	215,881	203,171	12,710	6.3
66.	Cincinnati–Middletown, OH–KY–IN	2,104,218	2,009,673	94,545	4.7
67.	Clarksville, TN–KY	240,500	232,043	8,457	3.6
68.	Cleveland, TN	109,477	104,003	5,474	5.3
69.	Cleveland–Elyria–Mentor, OH	2,114,155	2,148,010	−33,855	−1.6
70.	Coeur d'Alene, ID	131,507	108,685	22,822	21.0
71.	College Station–Bryan, TX	192,152	184,885	7,267	3.9
72.	Colorado Springs, CO	599,127	537,484	61,643	11.5
73.	Columbia, MO	155,997	145,666	10,331	7.1
74.	Columbia, SC	703,771	647,253	56,518	8.7
75.	Columbus, GA–AL	288,847	281,768	7,079	2.5
76.	Columbus, IN	74,444	71,435	3,009	4.2
77.	Columbus, OH	1,725,570	1,612,841	112,729	7.0
78.	Corpus Christi, TX	415,810	403,280	12,530	3.1
79.	Corvallis, OR	79,061	78,139	922	1.2
80.	Cumberland, MD–WV	99,759	102,008	−2,249	−2.2
81.	Dallas–Fort Worth–Arlington, TX	6,003,967	5,161,518	842,449	16.3
82.	Dalton, GA	134,397	120,061	14,336	11.9
83.	Danville, IL	81,941	83,924	−1,983	−2.4
84.	Danville, VA	107,087	110,156	−3,069	−2.8
85.	Davenport–Moline–Rock Island, IA–IL	377,291	376,052	1,239	0.3
86.	Dayton, OH	838,940	848,157	−9,217	−1.1
87.	Decatur, AL	149,549	145,867	3,682	2.5
88.	Decatur, IL	109,309	114,706	−5,397	−4.7
89.	Deltona–Daytona Beach–Ormond Beach, FL	496,575	443,340	53,235	12.0

(continued)

		2006	2000	change 2000–06	
				number	percent
90.	Denver–Aurora, CO	2,408,750	2,179,320	229,430	10.5%
91.	Des Moines–West Des Moines, IA	534,230	481,398	52,832	11.0
92.	Detroit–Warren–Livonia, MI	4,468,966	4,452,557	16,409	0.4
93.	Dothan, AL	138,234	130,861	7,373	5.6
94.	Dover, DE	147,601	126,700	20,901	16.5
95.	Dubuque, IA	92,384	89,156	3,228	3.6
96.	Duluth, MN–WI	274,244	275,486	−1,242	−0.5
97.	Durham, NC	464,389	423,800	40,589	9.6
98.	Eau Claire, WI	155,041	148,337	6,704	4.5
99.	El Centro, CA	160,301	142,361	17,940	12.6
100.	Elizabethtown, KY	110,878	107,543	3,335	3.1
101.	Elkhart–Goshen, IN	198,105	182,791	15,314	8.4
102.	Elmira, NY	88,641	91,070	−2,429	−2.7
103.	El Paso, TX	736,310	679,622	56,688	8.3
104.	Erie, PA	279,811	280,843	−1,032	−0.4
105.	Eugene–Springfield, OR	337,870	322,977	14,893	4.6
106.	Evansville, IN–KY	350,356	342,816	7,540	2.2
107.	Fairbanks, AK	86,754	82,840	3,914	4.7
108.	Fargo, ND–MN	187,001	174,367	12,634	7.2
109.	Farmington, NM	126,473	113,801	12,672	11.1
110.	Fayetteville, NC	341,363	336,608	4,755	1.4
111.	Fayetteville–Springdale–Rogers, AR–MO	420,876	347,045	73,831	21.3
112.	Flagstaff, AZ	124,953	116,320	8,633	7.4
113.	Flint, MI	441,966	436,148	5,818	1.3
114.	Florence, SC	198,848	193,155	5,693	2.9
115.	Florence–Muscle Shoals, AL	142,657	142,950	−293	−0.2
116.	Fond du Lac, WI	99,243	97,296	1,947	2.0
117.	Fort Collins–Loveland, CO	276,253	251,494	24,759	9.8
118.	Fort Smith, AR–OK	288,818	273,171	15,647	5.7
119.	Fort Walton Beach–Crestview–Destin, FL	180,291	170,497	9,794	5.7
120.	Fort Wayne, IN	408,071	390,154	17,917	4.6
121.	Fresno, CA	891,756	799,407	92,349	11.6
122.	Gadsden, AL	103,362	103,460	−98	−0.1
123.	Gainesville, FL	243,985	232,392	11,593	5.0
124.	Gainesville, GA	173,256	139,315	33,941	24.4
125.	Glens Falls, NY	129,455	124,345	5,110	4.1
126.	Goldsboro, NC	113,847	113,329	518	0.5
127.	Grand Forks, ND–MN	96,523	97,478	−955	−1.0
128.	Grand Junction, CO	134,189	116,935	17,254	14.8
129.	Grand Rapids–Wyoming, MI	774,084	740,482	33,602	4.5
130.	Great Falls, MT	79,385	80,357	−972	−1.2
131.	Greeley, CO	236,857	180,861	55,996	31.0
132.	Green Bay, WI	299,003	282,497	16,506	5.8
133.	Greensboro–High Point, NC	685,378	643,446	41,932	6.5
134.	Greenville, NC	165,776	152,693	13,083	8.6
135.	Greenville, SC	601,986	559,922	42,064	7.5
136.	Gulfport–Biloxi, MS	227,904	246,190	−18,286	−7.4
137.	Hagerstown–Martinsburg, MD–WV	257,619	222,771	34,848	15.6

(continued)

	2006	2000	change 2000–06 number	percent
138. Hanford–Corcoran, CA	146,153	129,461	16,692	12.9%
139. Harrisburg–Carlisle, PA	525,380	509,074	16,306	3.2
140. Harrisonburg, VA	113,449	108,169	5,280	4.9
141. Hartford–West Hartford–East Hartford, CT	1,188,841	1,148,618	40,223	3.5
142. Hattiesburg, MS	134,744	123,812	10,932	8.8
143. Hickory–Lenoir–Morganton, NC	359,856	341,819	18,037	5.3
144. Hinesville–Fort Stewart, GA	74,023	71,914	2,109	2.9
145. Holland–Grand Haven, MI	257,671	238,314	19,357	8.1
146. Honolulu, HI	909,863	876,156	33,707	3.8
147. Hot Springs, AR	95,164	88,066	7,098	8.1
148. Houma–Bayou Cane–Thibodaux, LA	202,902	194,477	8,425	4.3
149. Houston–Sugar Land–Baytown, TX	5,539,949	4,715,402	824,547	17.5
150. Huntington–Ashland, WV–KY–OH	285,475	288,650	–3,175	–1.1
151. Huntsville, AL	376,753	342,627	34,126	10.0
152. Idaho Falls, ID	116,980	101,677	15,303	15.1
153. Indianapolis–Carmel, IN	1,666,032	1,525,104	140,928	9.2
154. Iowa City, IA	139,567	131,676	7,891	6.0
155. Ithaca, NY	100,407	96,502	3,905	4.0
156. Jackson, MI	163,851	158,422	5,429	3.4
157. Jackson, MS	529,456	497,197	32,259	6.5
158. Jackson, TN	111,937	107,365	4,572	4.3
159. Jacksonville, FL	1,277,997	1,122,750	155,247	13.8
160. Jacksonville, NC	150,673	150,355	318	0.2
161. Janesville, WI	159,153	152,307	6,846	4.5
162. Jefferson City, MO	144,958	140,052	4,906	3.5
163. Johnson City, TN	191,136	181,607	9,529	5.2
164. Johnstown, PA	146,967	152,598	–5,631	–3.7
165. Jonesboro, AR	113,330	107,762	5,568	5.2
166. Joplin, MO	168,552	157,322	11,230	7.1
167. Kalamazoo–Portage, MI	319,738	314,866	4,872	1.5
168. Kankakee–Bradley, IL	109,090	103,833	5,257	5.1
169. Kansas City, MO–KS	1,967,405	1,836,420	130,985	7.1
170. Kennewick–Richland–Pasco, WA	226,033	191,825	34,208	17.8
171. Killeen–Temple–Fort Hood, TX	351,322	330,712	20,610	6.2
172. Kingsport–Bristol–Bristol, TN–VA	302,451	298,484	3,967	1.3
173. Kingston, NY	182,742	177,749	4,993	2.8
174. Knoxville, TN	667,384	616,080	51,304	8.3
175. Kokomo, IN	100,877	101,541	–664	–0.7
176. La Crosse, WI–MN	129,236	126,838	2,398	1.9
177. Lafayette, IN	185,745	178,541	7,204	4.0
178. Lafayette, LA	254,432	238,906	15,526	6.5
179. Lake Charles, LA	192,316	193,565	–1,249	–0.6
180. Lakeland, FL	561,606	483,924	77,682	16.1
181. Lancaster, PA	494,486	470,635	23,851	5.1
182. Lansing–East Lansing, MI	454,044	447,822	6,222	1.4
183. Laredo, TX	231,470	193,117	38,353	19.9
184. Las Cruces, NM	193,888	174,682	19,206	11.0

(continued)

	2006	2000	change 2000–06	
			number	percent
185. Las Vegas–Paradise, NV	1,777,539	1,375,738	401,801	29.2%
186. Lawrence, KS	112,123	99,965	12,158	12.2
187. Lawton, OK	109,181	114,996	−5,815	−5.1
188. Lebanon, PA	126,883	120,327	6,556	5.4
189. Lewiston, ID–WA	59,571	57,961	1,610	2.8
190. Lewiston–Auburn, ME	107,552	103,793	3,759	3.6
191. Lexington–Fayette, KY	436,684	408,326	28,358	6.9
192. Lima, OH	105,788	108,473	−2,685	−2.5
193. Lincoln, NE	283,970	266,787	17,183	6.4
194. Little Rock–North Little Rock, AR	652,834	610,520	42,314	6.9
195. Logan, UT–ID	111,156	102,720	8,436	8.2
196. Longview, TX	203,367	194,042	9,325	4.8
197. Longview, WA	99,905	92,948	6,957	7.5
198. Los Angeles–Long Beach–Santa Ana, CA	12,950,129	12,365,619	584,510	4.7
199. Louisville–Jefferson County, KY–IN	1,222,216	1,162,409	59,807	5.1
200. Lubbock, TX	261,411	249,700	11,711	4.7
201. Lynchburg, VA	239,510	228,616	10,894	4.8
202. Macon, GA	229,326	222,385	6,941	3.1
203. Madera, CA	146,345	123,109	23,236	18.9
204. Madison, WI	543,022	501,773	41,249	8.2
205. Manchester–Nashua, NH	402,789	380,843	21,946	5.8
206. Mansfield, OH	127,010	128,852	−1,842	−1.4
207. McAllen–Edinburg–Mission, TX	700,634	569,463	131,171	23.0
208. Medford, OR	197,071	181,323	15,748	8.7
209. Memphis, TN–MS–AR	1,274,704	1,205,194	69,510	5.8
210. Merced, CA	245,658	210,554	35,104	16.7
211. Miami–Fort Lauderdale–Miami Beach, FL	5,463,857	5,007,988	455,869	9.1
212. Michigan City–La Porte, IN	110,479	110,106	373	0.3
213. Midland, TX	124,380	116,009	8,371	7.2
214. Milwaukee–Waukesha–West Allis, WI	1,509,981	1,500,744	9,237	0.6
215. Minneapolis–St. Paul–Bloomington, MN–WI	3,175,041	2,968,817	206,224	6.9
216. Missoula, MT	101,417	95,802	5,615	5.9
217. Mobile, AL	404,157	399,843	4,314	1.1
218. Modesto, CA	512,138	446,997	65,141	14.6
219. Monroe, LA	172,223	170,053	2,170	1.3
220. Monroe, MI	155,035	145,945	9,090	6.2
221. Montgomery, AL	361,748	346,530	15,218	4.4
222. Morgantown, WV	115,136	111,200	3,936	3.5
223. Morristown, TN	132,851	123,081	9,770	7.9
224. Mount Vernon–Anacortes, WA	115,700	102,982	12,718	12.3
225. Muncie, IN	114,879	118,769	−3,890	−3.3
226. Muskegon–Norton Shores, MI	175,231	170,200	5,031	3.0
227. Myrtle Beach–Conway–North Myrtle Beach, SC	238,493	196,629	41,864	21.3
228. Napa, CA	133,522	124,308	9,214	7.4
229. Naples–Marco Island, FL	314,649	251,377	63,272	25.2
230. Nashville–Davidson–Murfreesboro, TN	1,455,097	1,311,789	143,308	10.9
231. New Haven–Milford, CT	845,244	824,008	21,236	2.6

(continued)

	2006	2000	change 2000–06	
			number	percent
232. New Orleans–Metairie–Kenner, LA	1,024,678	1,316,512	–291,834	–22.2%
233. New York–Northern New Jersey– Long Island, NY–NJ–PA	18,818,536	18,323,382	495,154	2.7
234. Niles–Benton Harbor, MI	161,705	162,455	–750	–0.5
235. Norwich–New London, CT	263,293	259,106	4,187	1.6
236. Ocala, FL	316,183	258,916	57,267	22.1
237. Ocean City, NJ	97,724	102,326	–4,602	–4.5
238. Odessa, TX	127,462	121,123	6,339	5.2
239. Ogden–Clearfield, UT	497,640	442,656	54,984	12.4
240. Oklahoma City, OK	1,172,339	1,095,421	76,918	7.0
241. Olympia, WA	234,670	207,355	27,315	13.2
242. Omaha–Council Bluffs, NE–IA	822,549	767,140	55,409	7.2
243. Orlando–Kissimmee, FL	1,984,855	1,644,563	340,292	20.7
244. Oshkosh–Neenah, WI	160,593	156,763	3,830	2.4
245. Owensboro, KY	112,093	109,875	2,218	2.0
246. Oxnard–Thousand Oaks–Ventura, CA	799,720	753,195	46,525	6.2
247. Palm Bay–Melbourne–Titusville, FL	534,359	476,230	58,129	12.2
248. Panama City–Lynn Haven, FL	163,505	148,218	15,287	10.3
249. Parkersburg–Marietta–Vienna, WV–OH	161,724	164,624	–2,900	–1.8
250. Pascagoula, MS	152,405	150,564	1,841	1.2
251. Pensacola–Ferry Pass–Brent, FL	439,987	412,153	27,834	6.8
252. Peoria, IL	370,194	366,875	3,319	0.9
253. Philadelphia–Camden–Wilmington, PA–NJ–DE–MD	5,826,742	5,687,141	139,601	2.5
254. Phoenix–Mesa–Scottsdale, AZ	4,039,182	3,251,876	787,306	24.2
255. Pine Bluff, AR	103,638	107,345	–3,707	–3.5
256. Pittsburgh, PA	2,370,776	2,431,085	–60,309	–2.5
257. Pittsfield, MA	131,117	134,953	–3,836	–2.8
258. Pocatello, ID	86,357	83,103	3,254	3.9
259. Portland–South Portland–Biddeford, ME	513,667	487,568	26,099	5.4
260. Portland–Vancouver–Beaverton, OR–WA	2,137,565	1,927,881	209,684	10.9
261. Port St. Lucie–Fort Pierce, FL	392,117	319,426	72,691	22.8
262. Poughkeepsie–Newburgh–Middletown, NY	671,538	621,517	50,021	8.0
263. Prescott, AZ	208,014	167,517	40,497	24.2
264. Providence–New Bedford–Fall River, RI–MA	1,612,989	1,582,997	29,992	1.9
265. Provo–Orem, UT	474,180	376,778	97,402	25.9
266. Pueblo, CO	152,912	141,472	11,440	8.1
267. Punta Gorda, FL	154,438	141,627	12,811	9.0
268. Racine, WI	196,096	188,831	7,265	3.8
269. Raleigh–Cary, NC	994,551	797,025	197,526	24.8
270. Rapid City, SD	118,763	112,818	5,945	5.3
271. Reading, PA	401,149	373,661	27,488	7.4
272. Redding, CA	179,951	163,256	16,695	10.2
273. Reno–Sparks, NV	400,560	342,885	57,675	16.8
274. Richmond, VA	1,194,008	1,096,957	97,051	8.8
275. Riverside–San Bernardino–Ontario, CA	4,026,135	3,254,821	771,314	23.7
276. Roanoke, VA	295,050	288,254	6,796	2.4

(continued)

	2006	2000	change 2000–06	
			number	percent
277. Rochester, MN	179,573	163,618	15,955	9.8%
278. Rochester, NY	1,035,435	1,037,833	−2,398	−0.2
279. Rockford, IL	348,252	320,204	28,048	8.8
280. Rocky Mount, NC	146,276	142,991	3,285	2.3
281. Rome, GA	95,322	90,565	4,757	5.3
282. Sacramento–Arden–Arcade–Roseville, CA	2,067,117	1,796,857	270,260	15.0
283. Saginaw–Saginaw Township North, MI	206,300	210,042	−3,742	−1.8
284. St. Cloud, MN	182,784	167,396	15,388	9.2
285. St. George, UT	126,312	90,354	35,958	39.8
286. St. Joseph, MO–KS	122,306	123,820	−1,514	−1.2
287. St. Louis, MO–IL	2,796,368	2,698,672	97,696	3.6
288. Salem, OR	384,600	347,218	37,382	10.8
289. Salinas, CA	410,206	401,764	8,442	2.1
290. Salisbury, MD	117,761	109,392	8,369	7.7
291. Salt Lake City, UT	1,067,722	968,883	98,839	10.2
292. San Angelo, TX	105,752	105,781	−29	0.0
293. San Antonio, TX	1,942,217	1,711,716	230,501	13.5
294. San Diego–Carlsbad–San Marcos, CA	2,941,454	2,813,833	127,621	4.5
295. Sandusky, OH	78,116	79,551	−1,435	−1.8
296. San Francisco–Oakland–Fremont, CA	4,180,027	4,123,742	56,285	1.4
297. San Jose–Sunnyvale–Santa Clara, CA	1,787,123	1,735,819	51,304	3.0
298. San Luis Obispo–Paso Robles, CA	257,005	246,681	10,324	4.2
299. Santa Barbara–Santa Maria, CA	400,335	399,347	988	0.2
300. Santa Cruz–Watsonville, CA	249,705	255,600	−5,895	−2.3
301. Santa Fe, NM	142,407	129,287	13,120	10.1
302. Santa Rosa–Petaluma, CA	466,891	458,614	8,277	1.8
303. Sarasota–Bradenton–Venice, FL	682,833	589,963	92,870	15.7
304. Savannah, GA	320,013	293,299	26,714	9.1
305. Scranton—Wilkes–Barre, PA	550,841	560,627	−9,786	−1.7
306. Seattle–Tacoma–Bellevue, WA	3,263,497	3,043,885	219,612	7.2
307. Sebastian–Vero Beach, FL	130,100	112,947	17,153	15.2
308. Sheboygan, WI	114,756	112,656	2,100	1.9
309. Sherman–Denison, TX	118,478	110,595	7,883	7.1
310. Shreveport–Bossier City, LA	386,778	375,968	10,810	2.9
311. Sioux City, IA–NE–SD	143,474	143,053	421	0.3
312. Sioux Falls, SD	212,911	187,093	25,818	13.8
313. South Bend–Mishawaka, IN–MI	318,007	316,661	1,346	0.4
314. Spartanburg, SC	271,087	253,782	17,305	6.8
315. Spokane, WA	446,706	417,938	28,768	6.9
316. Springfield, IL	206,112	201,440	4,672	2.3
317. Springfield, MA	686,174	680,014	6,160	0.9
318. Springfield, MO	407,092	368,374	38,718	10.5
319. Springfield, OH	141,872	144,741	−2,869	−2.0
320. State College, PA	140,953	135,758	5,195	3.8
321. Stockton, CA	673,170	563,598	109,572	19.4
322. Sumter, SC	104,430	104,636	−206	−0.2
323. Syracuse, NY	650,051	650,154	−103	0.0

(continued)

	2006	2000	change 2000–06	
			number	percent
324. Tallahassee, FL	336,502	320,304	16,198	5.1%
325. Tampa–St. Petersburg–Clearwater, FL	2,697,731	2,396,013	301,718	12.6
326. Terre Haute, IN	168,217	170,954	–2,737	–1.6
327. Texarkana, TX–AR	134,510	129,749	4,761	3.7
328. Toledo, OH	653,695	659,184	–5,489	–0.8
329. Topeka, KS	228,894	224,551	4,343	1.9
330. Trenton–Ewing, NJ	367,605	350,761	16,844	4.8
331. Tucson, AZ	946,362	843,746	102,616	12.2
332. Tulsa, OK	897,752	859,530	38,222	4.4
333. Tuscaloosa, AL	198,769	193,106	5,663	2.9
334. Tyler, TX	194,635	174,706	19,929	11.4
335. Utica–Rome, NY	297,286	299,896	–2,610	–0.9
336. Valdosta, GA	126,305	119,566	6,739	5.6
337. Vallejo–Fairfield, CA	411,680	394,513	17,167	4.4
338. Victoria, TX	114,088	111,666	2,422	2.2
339. Vineland–Millville–Bridgeton, NJ	154,823	146,438	8,385	5.7
340. Virginia Beach–Norfolk–Newport News, VA–NC	1,649,457	1,576,917	72,540	4.6
341. Visalia–Porterville, CA	419,909	368,021	51,888	14.1
342. Waco, TX	226,189	213,513	12,676	5.9
343. Warner Robins, GA	127,530	110,765	16,765	15.1
344. Washington–Arlington–Alexandria, DC–VA–MD–WV	5,290,400	4,796,180	494,220	10.3
345. Waterloo–Cedar Falls, IA	162,263	163,707	–1,444	–0.9
346. Wausau, WI	130,223	125,834	4,389	3.5
347. Weirton–Steubenville, WV–OH	125,168	132,008	–6,840	–5.2
348. Wenatchee, WA	106,806	99,219	7,587	7.6
349. Wheeling, WV–OH	147,329	153,178	–5,849	–3.8
350. Wichita, KS	592,126	571,168	20,958	3.7
351. Wichita Falls, TX	145,528	151,524	–5,996	–4.0
352. Williamsport, PA	117,668	120,048	–2,380	–2.0
353. Wilmington, NC	326,166	274,550	51,616	18.8
354. Winchester, VA–WV	118,932	102,997	15,935	15.5
355. Winston–Salem, NC	456,614	421,934	34,680	8.2
356. Worcester, MA	784,992	749,973	35,019	4.7
357. Yakima, WA	233,105	222,578	10,527	4.7
358. York–Hanover, PA	416,322	381,751	34,571	9.1
359. Youngstown–Warren–Boardman, OH–PA	586,939	602,964	–16,025	–2.7
360. Yuba City, CA	161,806	139,149	22,657	16.3
361. Yuma, AZ	187,555	160,026	27,529	17.2

Source: Bureau of the Census, Metropolitan and Micropolitan Statistical Area Estimates, Internet site http://www.census.gov/population/www/estimates/CBSA-est2006-pop-chg.html; calculations by New Strategist

Table 8.39 Metropolitan Populations, 2000 and 2006: Population Ranking

(number of people by metropolitan area, 2000 and 2006; change and percent change in number, 2000–06; metropolitan area definitions as of December 2005; metropolitan areas ranked by population)

		2006	2000	change 2000–06 number	change 2000–06 percent
1.	New York–Northern New Jersey–Long Island, NY–NJ–PA	18,818,536	18,323,382	495,154	2.7%
2.	Los Angeles–Long Beach–Santa Ana, CA	12,950,129	12,365,619	584,510	4.7
3.	Chicago–Naperville–Joliet, IL–IN–WI	9,505,748	9,098,615	407,133	4.5
4.	Dallas–Fort Worth–Arlington, TX	6,003,967	5,161,518	842,449	16.3
5.	Philadelphia–Camden–Wilmington, PA–NJ–DE–MD	5,826,742	5,687,141	139,601	2.5
6.	Houston–Sugar Land–Baytown, TX	5,539,949	4,715,402	824,547	17.5
7.	Miami–Fort Lauderdale–Miami Beach, FL	5,463,857	5,007,988	455,869	9.1
8.	Washington–Arlington–Alexandria, DC–VA–MD–WV	5,290,400	4,796,180	494,220	10.3
9.	Atlanta–Sandy Springs–Marietta, GA	5,138,223	4,248,012	890,211	21.0
10.	Detroit–Warren–Livonia, MI	4,468,966	4,452,557	16,409	0.4
11.	Boston–Cambridge–Quincy, MA–NH	4,455,217	4,392,340	62,877	1.4
12.	San Francisco–Oakland–Fremont, CA	4,180,027	4,123,742	56,285	1.4
13.	Phoenix–Mesa–Scottsdale, AZ	4,039,182	3,251,876	787,306	24.2
14.	Riverside–San Bernardino–Ontario, CA	4,026,135	3,254,821	771,314	23.7
15.	Seattle–Tacoma–Bellevue, WA	3,263,497	3,043,885	219,612	7.2
16.	Minneapolis–St. Paul–Bloomington, MN–WI	3,175,041	2,968,817	206,224	6.9
17.	San Diego–Carlsbad–San Marcos, CA	2,941,454	2,813,833	127,621	4.5
18.	St. Louis, MO–IL	2,796,368	2,698,672	97,696	3.6
19.	Tampa–St. Petersburg–Clearwater, FL	2,697,731	2,396,013	301,718	12.6
20.	Baltimore–Towson, MD	2,658,405	2,552,994	105,411	4.1
21.	Denver–Aurora, CO	2,408,750	2,179,320	229,430	10.5
22.	Pittsburgh, PA	2,370,776	2,431,085	–60,309	–2.5
23.	Portland–Vancouver–Beaverton, OR–WA	2,137,565	1,927,881	209,684	10.9
24.	Cleveland–Elyria–Mentor, OH	2,114,155	2,148,010	–33,855	–1.6
25.	Cincinnati–Middletown, OH–KY–IN	2,104,218	2,009,673	94,545	4.7
26.	Sacramento–Arden–Arcade–Roseville, CA	2,067,117	1,796,857	270,260	15.0
27.	Orlando–Kissimmee, FL	1,984,855	1,644,563	340,292	20.7
28.	Kansas City, MO–KS	1,967,405	1,836,420	130,985	7.1
29.	San Antonio, TX	1,942,217	1,711,716	230,501	13.5
30.	San Jose–Sunnyvale–Santa Clara, CA	1,787,123	1,735,819	51,304	3.0
31.	Las Vegas–Paradise, NV	1,777,539	1,375,738	401,801	29.2
32.	Columbus, OH	1,725,570	1,612,841	112,729	7.0
33.	Indianapolis–Carmel, IN	1,666,032	1,525,104	140,928	9.2
34.	Virginia Beach–Norfolk–Newport News, VA–NC	1,649,457	1,576,917	72,540	4.6
35.	Providence–New Bedford–Fall River, RI–MA	1,612,989	1,582,997	29,992	1.9
36.	Charlotte–Gastonia–Concord, NC–SC	1,583,016	1,330,403	252,613	19.0
37.	Austin–Round Rock, TX	1,513,565	1,249,763	263,802	21.1
38.	Milwaukee–Waukesha–West Allis, WI	1,509,981	1,500,744	9,237	0.6

(continued)

		2006	2000	change 2000–06	
				number	percent
39.	Nashville–Davidson–Murfreesboro, TN	1,455,097	1,311,789	143,308	10.9%
40.	Jacksonville, FL	1,277,997	1,122,750	155,247	13.8
41.	Memphis, TN–MS–AR	1,274,704	1,205,194	69,510	5.8
42.	Louisville–Jefferson County, KY–IN	1,222,216	1,162,409	59,807	5.1
43.	Richmond, VA	1,194,008	1,096,957	97,051	8.8
44.	Hartford–West Hartford–East Hartford, CT	1,188,841	1,148,618	40,223	3.5
45.	Oklahoma City, OK	1,172,339	1,095,421	76,918	7.0
46.	Buffalo–Niagara Falls, NY	1,137,520	1,170,109	−32,589	−2.8
47.	Birmingham–Hoover, AL	1,100,019	1,051,305	48,714	4.6
48.	Salt Lake City, UT	1,067,722	968,883	98,839	10.2
49.	Rochester, NY	1,035,435	1,037,833	−2,398	−0.2
50.	New Orleans–Metairie–Kenner, LA	1,024,678	1,316,512	−291,834	−22.2
51.	Raleigh–Cary, NC	994,551	797,025	197,526	24.8
52.	Tucson, AZ	946,362	843,746	102,616	12.2
53.	Honolulu, HI	909,863	876,156	33,707	3.8
54.	Bridgeport–Stamford–Norwalk, CT	900,440	882,567	17,873	2.0
55.	Tulsa, OK	897,752	859,530	38,222	4.4
56.	Fresno, CA	891,756	799,407	92,349	11.6
57.	Albany–Schenectady–Troy, NY	850,957	825,875	25,082	3.0
58.	New Haven–Milford, CT	845,244	824,008	21,236	2.6
59.	Dayton, OH	838,940	848,157	−9,217	−1.1
60.	Omaha–Council Bluffs, NE–IA	822,549	767,140	55,409	7.2
61.	Albuquerque, NM	816,811	729,653	87,158	11.9
62.	Allentown–Bethlehem–Easton, PA–NJ	800,336	740,394	59,942	8.1
63.	Oxnard–Thousand Oaks–Ventura, CA	799,720	753,195	46,525	6.2
64.	Worcester, MA	784,992	749,973	35,019	4.7
65.	Bakersfield, CA	780,117	661,655	118,462	17.9
66.	Grand Rapids–Wyoming, MI	774,084	740,482	33,602	4.5
67.	Baton Rouge, LA	766,514	705,967	60,547	8.6
68.	El Paso, TX	736,310	679,622	56,688	8.3
69.	Columbia, SC	703,771	647,253	56,518	8.7
70.	Akron, OH	700,943	694,960	5,983	0.9
71.	McAllen–Edinburg–Mission, TX	700,634	569,463	131,171	23.0
72.	Springfield, MA	686,174	680,014	6,160	0.9
73.	Greensboro–High Point, NC	685,378	643,446	41,932	6.5
74.	Sarasota–Bradenton–Venice, FL	682,833	589,963	92,870	15.7
75.	Stockton, CA	673,170	563,598	109,572	19.4
76.	Poughkeepsie–Newburgh–Middletown, NY	671,538	621,517	50,021	8.0
77.	Knoxville, TN	667,384	616,080	51,304	8.3
78.	Toledo, OH	653,695	659,184	−5,489	−0.8
79.	Little Rock–North Little Rock, AR	652,834	610,520	42,314	6.9
80.	Syracuse, NY	650,051	650,154	−103	0.0
81.	Charleston–North Charleston, SC	603,178	548,972	54,206	9.9
82.	Greenville, SC	601,986	559,922	42,064	7.5
83.	Colorado Springs, CO	599,127	537,484	61,643	11.5
84.	Wichita, KS	592,126	571,168	20,958	3.7

(continued)

	2006	2000	change 2000–06 number	change 2000–06 percent
85. Youngstown–Warren–Boardman, OH–PA	586,939	602,964	−16,025	−2.7%
86. Cape Coral–Fort Myers, FL	571,344	440,888	130,456	29.6
87. Boise City–Nampa, ID	567,640	464,840	102,800	22.1
88. Lakeland, FL	561,606	483,924	77,682	16.1
89. Scranton–Wilkes-Barre, PA	550,841	560,627	−9,786	−1.7
90. Madison, WI	543,022	501,773	41,249	8.2
91. Palm Bay–Melbourne–Titusville, FL	534,359	476,230	58,129	12.2
92. Des Moines–West Des Moines, IA	534,230	481,398	52,832	11.0
93. Jackson, MS	529,456	497,197	32,259	6.5
94. Harrisburg–Carlisle, PA	525,380	509,074	16,306	3.2
95. Augusta–Richmond County, GA–SC	523,249	499,653	23,596	4.7
96. Portland–South Portland–Biddeford, ME	513,667	487,568	26,099	5.4
97. Modesto, CA	512,138	446,997	65,141	14.6
98. Ogden–Clearfield, UT	497,640	442,656	54,984	12.4
99. Chattanooga, TN–GA	496,704	476,513	20,191	4.2
100. Deltona–Daytona Beach–Ormond Beach, FL	496,575	443,340	53,235	12.0
101. Lancaster, PA	494,486	470,635	23,851	5.1
102. Provo–Orem, UT	474,180	376,778	97,402	25.9
103. Santa Rosa–Petaluma, CA	466,891	458,614	8,277	1.8
104. Durham, NC	464,389	423,800	40,589	9.6
105. Winston-Salem, NC	456,614	421,934	34,680	8.2
106. Lansing–East Lansing, MI	454,044	447,822	6,222	1.4
107. Spokane, WA	446,706	417,938	28,768	6.9
108. Flint, MI	441,966	436,148	5,818	1.3
109. Pensacola–Ferry Pass–Brent, FL	439,987	412,153	27,834	6.8
110. Lexington–Fayette, KY	436,684	408,326	28,358	6.9
111. Fayetteville–Springdale–Rogers, AR–MO	420,876	347,045	73,831	21.3
112. Visalia–Porterville, CA	419,909	368,021	51,888	14.1
113. York–Hanover, PA	416,322	381,751	34,571	9.1
114. Corpus Christi, TX	415,810	403,280	12,530	3.1
115. Vallejo–Fairfield, CA	411,680	394,513	17,167	4.4
116. Salinas, CA	410,206	401,764	8,442	2.1
117. Canton–Massillon, OH	409,764	406,968	2,796	0.7
118. Fort Wayne, IN	408,071	390,154	17,917	4.6
119. Springfield, MO	407,092	368,374	38,718	10.5
120. Mobile, AL	404,157	399,843	4,314	1.1
121. Manchester–Nashua, NH	402,789	380,843	21,946	5.8
122. Reading, PA	401,149	373,661	27,488	7.4
123. Reno–Sparks, NV	400,560	342,885	57,675	16.8
124. Santa Barbara–Santa Maria, CA	400,335	399,347	988	0.2
125. Asheville, NC	398,009	369,172	28,837	7.8
126. Port St. Lucie–Fort Pierce, FL	392,117	319,426	72,691	22.8
127. Brownsville–Harlingen, TX	387,717	335,227	52,490	15.7
128. Shreveport–Bossier City, LA	386,778	375,968	10,810	2.9
129. Salem, OR	384,600	347,218	37,382	10.8
130. Beaumont–Port Arthur, TX	379,640	385,090	−5,450	−1.4
131. Davenport–Moline–Rock Island, IA–IL	377,291	376,052	1,239	0.3

(continued)

	2006	2000	change 2000–06 number	percent
132. Huntsville, AL	376,753	342,627	34,126	10.0%
133. Peoria, IL	370,194	366,875	3,319	0.9
134. Trenton–Ewing, NJ	367,605	350,761	16,844	4.8
135. Montgomery, AL	361,748	346,530	15,218	4.4
136. Hickory–Lenoir–Morganton, NC	359,856	341,819	18,037	5.3
137. Anchorage, AK	359,180	319,605	39,575	12.4
138. Killeen–Temple–Fort Hood, TX	351,322	330,712	20,610	6.2
139. Evansville, IN–KY	350,356	342,816	7,540	2.2
140. Rockford, IL	348,252	320,204	28,048	8.8
141. Ann Arbor, MI	344,047	322,770	21,277	6.6
142. Fayetteville, NC	341,363	336,608	4,755	1.4
143. Eugene–Springfield, OR	337,870	322,977	14,893	4.6
144. Tallahassee, FL	336,502	320,304	16,198	5.1
145. Wilmington, NC	326,166	274,550	51,616	18.8
146. Savannah, GA	320,013	293,299	26,714	9.1
147. Kalamazoo–Portage, MI	319,738	314,866	4,872	1.5
148. South Bend–Mishawaka, IN–MI	318,007	316,661	1,346	0.4
149. Ocala, FL	316,183	258,916	57,267	22.1
150. Naples–Marco Island, FL	314,649	251,377	63,272	25.2
151. Charleston, WV	305,526	309,632	−4,106	−1.3
152. Kingsport–Bristol–Bristol, TN–VA	302,451	298,484	3,967	1.3
153. Green Bay, WI	299,003	282,497	16,506	5.8
154. Utica–Rome, NY	297,286	299,896	−2,610	−0.9
155. Roanoke, VA	295,050	288,254	6,796	2.4
156. Columbus, GA–AL	288,847	281,768	7,079	2.5
157. Fort Smith, AR–OK	288,818	273,171	15,647	5.7
158. Huntington–Ashland, WV–KY–OH	285,475	288,650	−3,175	−1.1
159. Lincoln, NE	283,970	266,787	17,183	6.4
160. Boulder, CO	282,304	269,787	12,517	4.6
161. Erie, PA	279,811	280,843	−1,032	−0.4
162. Fort Collins–Loveland, CO	276,253	251,494	24,759	9.8
163. Duluth, MN–WI	274,244	275,486	−1,242	−0.5
164. Atlantic City, NJ	271,620	252,552	19,068	7.6
165. Spartanburg, SC	271,087	253,782	17,305	6.8
166. Norwich–New London, CT	263,293	259,106	4,187	1.6
167. Lubbock, TX	261,411	249,700	11,711	4.7
168. Holland–Grand Haven, MI	257,671	238,314	19,357	8.1
169. Hagerstown–Martinsburg, MD–WV	257,619	222,771	34,848	15.6
170. San Luis Obispo–Paso Robles, CA	257,005	246,681	10,324	4.2
171. Lafayette, LA	254,432	238,906	15,526	6.5
172. Santa Cruz–Watsonville, CA	249,705	255,600	−5,895	−2.3
173. Cedar Rapids, IA	249,320	237,230	12,090	5.1
174. Binghamton, NY	247,554	252,320	−4,766	−1.9
175. Merced, CA	245,658	210,554	35,104	16.7
176. Gainesville, FL	243,985	232,392	11,593	5.0
177. Amarillo, TX	241,515	226,522	14,993	6.6
178. Bremerton–Silverdale, WA	240,604	231,969	8,635	3.7

(continued)

	2006	2000	change 2000–06	
			number	percent
179. Clarksville, TN–KY	240,500	232,043	8,457	3.6%
180. Lynchburg, VA	239,510	228,616	10,894	4.8
181. Myrtle Beach–Conway–North Myrtle Beach, SC	238,493	196,629	41,864	21.3
182. Greeley, CO	236,857	180,861	55,996	31.0
183. Olympia, WA	234,670	207,355	27,315	13.2
184. Yakima, WA	233,105	222,578	10,527	4.7
185. Laredo, TX	231,470	193,117	38,353	19.9
186. Macon, GA	229,326	222,385	6,941	3.1
187. Topeka, KS	228,894	224,551	4,343	1.9
188. Gulfport–Biloxi, MS	227,904	246,190	–18,286	–7.4
189. Waco, TX	226,189	213,513	12,676	5.9
190. Kennewick–Richland–Pasco, WA	226,033	191,825	34,208	17.8
191. Barnstable Town, MA	224,816	222,230	2,586	1.2
192. Appleton, WI	217,313	201,722	15,591	7.7
193. Champaign–Urbana, IL	216,581	210,279	6,302	3.0
194. Chico, CA	215,881	203,171	12,710	6.3
195. Sioux Falls, SD	212,911	187,093	25,818	13.8
196. Prescott, AZ	208,014	167,517	40,497	24.2
197. Saginaw–Saginaw Township North, MI	206,300	210,042	–3,742	–1.8
198. Springfield, IL	206,112	201,440	4,672	2.3
199. Burlington–South Burlington, VT	206,007	198,889	7,118	3.6
200. Longview, TX	203,367	194,042	9,325	4.8
201. Houma–Bayou Cane–Thibodaux, LA	202,902	194,477	8,425	4.3
202. Florence, SC	198,848	193,155	5,693	2.9
203. Tuscaloosa, AL	198,769	193,106	5,663	2.9
204. Elkhart–Goshen, IN	198,105	182,791	15,314	8.4
205. Medford, OR	197,071	181,323	15,748	8.7
206. Racine, WI	196,096	188,831	7,265	3.8
207. Tyler, TX	194,635	174,706	19,929	11.4
208. Las Cruces, NM	193,888	174,682	19,206	11.0
209. Lake Charles, LA	192,316	193,565	–1,249	–0.6
210. College Station–Bryan, TX	192,152	184,885	7,267	3.9
211. Johnson City, TN	191,136	181,607	9,529	5.2
212. Charlottesville, VA	190,278	174,021	16,257	9.3
213. Yuma, AZ	187,555	160,026	27,529	17.2
214. Fargo, ND–MN	187,001	174,367	12,634	7.2
215. Bellingham, WA	185,953	166,823	19,130	11.5
216. Lafayette, IN	185,745	178,541	7,204	4.0
217. Athens–Clarke County, GA	185,479	166,079	19,400	11.7
218. St. Cloud, MN	182,784	167,396	15,388	9.2
219. Kingston, NY	182,742	177,749	4,993	2.8
220. Fort Walton Beach–Crestview–Destin, FL	180,291	170,497	9,794	5.7
221. Redding, CA	179,951	163,256	16,695	10.2
222. Rochester, MN	179,573	163,618	15,955	9.8
223. Bloomington, IN	178,714	175,506	3,208	1.8
224. Anderson, SC	177,963	165,740	12,223	7.4
225. Muskegon–Norton Shores, MI	175,231	170,200	5,031	3.0

(continued)

	2006	2000	change 2000–06	
			number	percent
226. Gainesville, GA	173,256	139,315	33,941	24.4%
227. Monroe, LA	172,223	170,053	2,170	1.3
228. Joplin, MO	168,552	157,322	11,230	7.1
229. Terre Haute, IN	168,217	170,954	−2,737	−1.6
230. Greenville, NC	165,776	152,693	13,083	8.6
231. Albany, GA	163,961	157,866	6,095	3.9
232. Jackson, MI	163,851	158,422	5,429	3.4
233. Panama City–Lynn Haven, FL	163,505	148,218	15,287	10.3
234. Waterloo–Cedar Falls, IA	162,263	163,707	−1,444	−0.9
235. Yuba City, CA	161,806	139,149	22,657	16.3
236. Parkersburg–Marietta–Vienna, WV–OH	161,724	164,624	−2,900	−1.8
237. Niles–Benton Harbor, MI	161,705	162,455	−750	−0.5
238. Bloomington–Normal, IL	161,202	150,435	10,767	7.2
239. Oshkosh–Neenah, WI	160,593	156,763	3,830	2.4
240. El Centro, CA	160,301	142,361	17,940	12.6
241. Janesville, WI	159,153	152,307	6,846	4.5
242. Abilene, TX	158,063	160,241	−2,178	−1.4
243. Columbia, MO	155,997	145,666	10,331	7.1
244. Eau Claire, WI	155,041	148,337	6,704	4.5
245. Monroe, MI	155,035	145,945	9,090	6.2
246. Vineland–Millville–Bridgeton, NJ	154,823	146,438	8,385	5.7
247. Punta Gorda, FL	154,438	141,627	12,811	9.0
248. Pueblo, CO	152,912	141,472	11,440	8.1
249. Pascagoula, MS	152,405	150,564	1,841	1.2
250. Blacksburg–Christiansburg–Radford, VA	151,524	151,324	200	0.1
251. Jacksonville, NC	150,673	150,355	318	0.2
252. Alexandria, LA	150,080	145,035	5,045	3.5
253. Decatur, AL	149,549	145,867	3,682	2.5
254. Bend, OR	149,140	115,367	33,773	29.3
255. Billings, MT	148,116	138,904	9,212	6.6
256. Dover, DE	147,601	126,700	20,901	16.5
257. Wheeling, WV–OH	147,329	153,178	−5,849	−3.8
258. Bangor, ME	147,180	144,919	2,261	1.6
259. Johnstown, PA	146,967	152,598	−5,631	−3.7
260. Madera, CA	146,345	123,109	23,236	18.9
261. Rocky Mount, NC	146,276	142,991	3,285	2.3
262. Hanford–Corcoran, CA	146,153	129,461	16,692	12.9
263. Wichita Falls, TX	145,528	151,524	−5,996	−4.0
264. Jefferson City, MO	144,958	140,052	4,906	3.5
265. Sioux City, IA–NE–SD	143,474	143,053	421	0.3
266. Burlington, NC	142,661	130,794	11,867	9.1
267. Florence–Muscle Shoals, AL	142,657	142,950	−293	−0.2
268. Santa Fe, NM	142,407	129,287	13,120	10.1
269. Springfield, OH	141,872	144,741	−2,869	−2.0
270. State College, PA	140,953	135,758	5,195	3.8
271. Iowa City, IA	139,567	131,676	7,891	6.0
272. Dothan, AL	138,234	130,861	7,373	5.6

(continued)

	2006	2000	change 2000–06	
			number	percent
273. Battle Creek, MI	137,991	137,985	6	0.0%
274. Hattiesburg, MS	134,744	123,812	10,932	8.8
275. Texarkana, TX–AR	134,510	129,749	4,761	3.7
276. Dalton, GA	134,397	120,061	14,336	11.9
277. Grand Junction, CO	134,189	116,935	17,254	14.8
278. Napa, CA	133,522	124,308	9,214	7.4
279. Morristown, TN	132,851	123,081	9,770	7.9
280. Coeur d'Alene, ID	131,507	108,685	22,822	21.0
281. Pittsfield, MA	131,117	134,953	–3,836	–2.8
282. Anderson, IN	130,575	133,358	–2,783	–2.1
283. Wausau, WI	130,223	125,834	4,389	3.5
284. Sebastian–Vero Beach, FL	130,100	112,947	17,153	15.2
285. Glens Falls, NY	129,455	124,345	5,110	4.1
286. La Crosse, WI–MN	129,236	126,838	2,398	1.9
287. Warner Robins, GA	127,530	110,765	16,765	15.1
288. Odessa, TX	127,462	121,123	6,339	5.2
289. Mansfield, OH	127,010	128,852	–1,842	–1.4
290. Lebanon, PA	126,883	120,327	6,556	5.4
291. Altoona, PA	126,494	129,144	–2,650	–2.1
292. Farmington, NM	126,473	113,801	12,672	11.1
293. St. George, UT	126,312	90,354	35,958	39.8
294. Valdosta, GA	126,305	119,566	6,739	5.6
295. Auburn–Opelika, AL	125,781	115,092	10,689	9.3
296. Weirton–Steubenville, WV–OH	125,168	132,008	–6,840	–5.2
297. Flagstaff, AZ	124,953	116,320	8,633	7.4
298. Midland, TX	124,380	116,009	8,371	7.2
299. St. Joseph, MO–KS	122,306	123,820	–1,514	–1.2
300. Winchester, VA–WV	118,932	102,997	15,935	15.5
301. Rapid City, SD	118,763	112,818	5,945	5.3
302. Sherman–Denison, TX	118,478	110,595	7,883	7.1
303. Salisbury, MD	117,761	109,392	8,369	7.7
304. Williamsport, PA	117,668	120,048	–2,380	–2.0
305. Idaho Falls, ID	116,980	101,677	15,303	15.1
306. Mount Vernon–Anacortes, WA	115,700	102,982	12,718	12.3
307. Morgantown, WV	115,136	111,200	3,936	3.5
308. Muncie, IN	114,879	118,769	–3,890	–3.3
309. Sheboygan, WI	114,756	112,656	2,100	1.9
310. Victoria, TX	114,088	111,666	2,422	2.2
311. Goldsboro, NC	113,847	113,329	518	0.5
312. Harrisonburg, VA	113,449	108,169	5,280	4.9
313. Jonesboro, AR	113,330	107,762	5,568	5.2
314. Bowling Green, KY	113,320	104,166	9,154	8.8
315. Anniston–Oxford, AL	112,903	112,243	660	0.6
316. Lawrence, KS	112,123	99,965	12,158	12.2
317. Owensboro, KY	112,093	109,875	2,218	2.0
318. Jackson, TN	111,937	107,365	4,572	4.3
319. Logan, UT–ID	111,156	102,720	8,436	8.2

(continued)

	2006	2000	change 2000–06	
			number	percent
320. Elizabethtown, KY	110,878	107,543	3,335	3.1%
321. Michigan City–La Porte, IN	110,479	110,106	373	0.3
322. Cleveland, TN	109,477	104,003	5,474	5.3
323. Decatur, IL	109,309	114,706	–5,397	–4.7
324. Lawton, OK	109,181	114,996	–5,815	–5.1
325. Kankakee–Bradley, IL	109,090	103,833	5,257	5.1
326. Bay City, MI	108,390	110,157	–1,767	–1.6
327. Lewiston–Auburn, ME	107,552	103,793	3,759	3.6
328. Danville, VA	107,087	110,156	–3,069	–2.8
329. Wenatchee, WA	106,806	99,219	7,587	7.6
330. Lima, OH	105,788	108,473	–2,685	–2.5
331. San Angelo, TX	105,752	105,781	–29	0.0
332. Sumter, SC	104,430	104,636	–206	–0.2
333. Pine Bluff, AR	103,638	107,345	–3,707	–3.5
334. Gadsden, AL	103,362	103,460	–98	–0.1
335. Missoula, MT	101,417	95,802	5,615	5.9
336. Bismarck, ND	101,138	94,719	6,419	6.8
337. Kokomo, IN	100,877	101,541	–664	–0.7
338. Brunswick, GA	100,613	93,044	7,569	8.1
339. Ithaca, NY	100,407	96,502	3,905	4.0
340. Longview, WA	99,905	92,948	6,957	7.5
341. Cumberland, MD–WV	99,759	102,008	–2,249	–2.2
342. Fond du Lac, WI	99,243	97,296	1,947	2.0
343. Ocean City, NJ	97,724	102,326	–4,602	–4.5
344. Grand Forks, ND–MN	96,523	97,478	–955	–1.0
345. Rome, GA	95,322	90,565	4,757	5.3
346. Hot Springs, AR	95,164	88,066	7,098	8.1
347. Dubuque, IA	92,384	89,156	3,228	3.6
348. Elmira, NY	88,641	91,070	–2,429	–2.7
349. Fairbanks, AK	86,754	82,840	3,914	4.7
350. Pocatello, ID	86,357	83,103	3,254	3.9
351. Cheyenne, WY	85,384	81,607	3,777	4.6
352. Danville, IL	81,941	83,924	–1,983	–2.4
353. Ames, IA	80,145	79,981	164	0.2
354. Great Falls, MT	79,385	80,357	–972	–1.2
355. Corvallis, OR	79,061	78,139	922	1.2
356. Sandusky, OH	78,116	79,551	–1,435	–1.8
357. Columbus, IN	74,444	71,435	3,009	4.2
358. Hinesville–Fort Stewart, GA	74,023	71,914	2,109	2.9
359. Casper, WY	70,401	66,533	3,868	5.8
360. Lewiston, ID–WA	59,571	57,961	1,610	2.8
361. Carson City, NV	55,289	52,457	2,832	5.4

Source: Bureau of the Census, Metropolitan and Micropolitan Statistical Area Estimates, Internet site http://www.census.gov/ population/www/estimates/CBSA–est2006–pop–chg.html; calculations by New Strategist

Table 8.40 Metropolitan Populations, 2000 and 2006: Percent Change Ranking

(number of people by metropolitan area, 2000 and 2006; change and percent change in number, 2000–06; metropolitan area definitions as of December 2005; metropolitan areas ranked by percent change, 2000–06)

		2006	2000	change 2000–06 number	change 2000–06 percent
1.	St. George, UT	126,312	90,354	35,958	39.8%
2.	Greeley, CO	236,857	180,861	55,996	31.0
3.	Cape Coral–Fort Myers, FL	571,344	440,888	130,456	29.6
4.	Bend, OR	149,140	115,367	33,773	29.3
5.	Las Vegas–Paradise, NV	1,777,539	1,375,738	401,801	29.2
6.	Provo–Orem, UT	474,180	376,778	97,402	25.9
7.	Naples–Marco Island, FL	314,649	251,377	63,272	25.2
8.	Raleigh–Cary, NC	994,551	797,025	197,526	24.8
9.	Gainesville, GA	173,256	139,315	33,941	24.4
10.	Phoenix–Mesa–Scottsdale, AZ	4,039,182	3,251,876	787,306	24.2
11.	Prescott, AZ	208,014	167,517	40,497	24.2
12.	Riverside–San Bernardino–Ontario, CA	4,026,135	3,254,821	771,314	23.7
13.	McAllen–Edinburg–Mission, TX	700,634	569,463	131,171	23.0
14.	Port St. Lucie–Fort Pierce, FL	392,117	319,426	72,691	22.8
15.	Ocala, FL	316,183	258,916	57,267	22.1
16.	Boise City–Nampa, ID	567,640	464,840	102,800	22.1
17.	Myrtle Beach–Conway–North Myrtle Beach, SC	238,493	196,629	41,864	21.3
18.	Fayetteville–Springdale–Rogers, AR–MO	420,876	347,045	73,831	21.3
19.	Austin–Round Rock, TX	1,513,565	1,249,763	263,802	21.1
20.	Coeur d'Alene, ID	131,507	108,685	22,822	21.0
21.	Atlanta–Sandy Springs–Marietta, GA	5,138,223	4,248,012	890,211	21.0
22.	Orlando–Kissimmee, FL	1,984,855	1,644,563	340,292	20.7
23.	Laredo, TX	231,470	193,117	38,353	19.9
24.	Stockton, CA	673,170	563,598	109,572	19.4
25.	Charlotte–Gastonia–Concord, NC–SC	1,583,016	1,330,403	252,613	19.0
26.	Madera, CA	146,345	123,109	23,236	18.9
27.	Wilmington, NC	326,166	274,550	51,616	18.8
28.	Bakersfield, CA	780,117	661,655	118,462	17.9
29.	Kennewick–Richland–Pasco, WA	226,033	191,825	34,208	17.8
30.	Houston–Sugar Land–Baytown, TX	5,539,949	4,715,402	824,547	17.5
31.	Yuma, AZ	187,555	160,026	27,529	17.2
32.	Reno–Sparks, NV	400,560	342,885	57,675	16.8
33.	Merced, CA	245,658	210,554	35,104	16.7
34.	Dover, DE	147,601	126,700	20,901	16.5
35.	Dallas–Fort Worth–Arlington, TX	6,003,967	5,161,518	842,449	16.3
36.	Yuba City, CA	161,806	139,149	22,657	16.3
37.	Lakeland, FL	561,606	483,924	77,682	16.1
38.	Sarasota–Bradenton–Venice, FL	682,833	589,963	92,870	15.7
39.	Brownsville–Harlingen, TX	387,717	335,227	52,490	15.7
40.	Hagerstown–Martinsburg, MD–WV	257,619	222,771	34,848	15.6
41.	Winchester, VA–WV	118,932	102,997	15,935	15.5
42.	Sebastian–Vero Beach, FL	130,100	112,947	17,153	15.2

(continued)

		2006	2000	change 2000–06	
				number	percent
43.	Warner Robins, GA	127,530	110,765	16,765	15.1%
44.	Idaho Falls, ID	116,980	101,677	15,303	15.1
45.	Sacramento–Arden–Arcade–Roseville, CA	2,067,117	1,796,857	270,260	15.0
46.	Grand Junction, CO	134,189	116,935	17,254	14.8
47.	Modesto, CA	512,138	446,997	65,141	14.6
48.	Visalia–Porterville, CA	419,909	368,021	51,888	14.1
49.	Jacksonville, FL	1,277,997	1,122,750	155,247	13.8
50.	Sioux Falls, SD	212,911	187,093	25,818	13.8
51.	San Antonio, TX	1,942,217	1,711,716	230,501	13.5
52.	Olympia, WA	234,670	207,355	27,315	13.2
53.	Hanford–Corcoran, CA	146,153	129,461	16,692	12.9
54.	El Centro, CA	160,301	142,361	17,940	12.6
55.	Tampa–St. Petersburg–Clearwater, FL	2,697,731	2,396,013	301,718	12.6
56.	Ogden–Clearfield, UT	497,640	442,656	54,984	12.4
57.	Anchorage, AK	359,180	319,605	39,575	12.4
58.	Mount Vernon–Anacortes, WA	115,700	102,982	12,718	12.3
59.	Palm Bay–Melbourne–Titusville, FL	534,359	476,230	58,129	12.2
60.	Lawrence, KS	112,123	99,965	12,158	12.2
61.	Tucson, AZ	946,362	843,746	102,616	12.2
62.	Deltona–Daytona Beach–Ormond Beach, FL	496,575	443,340	53,235	12.0
63.	Albuquerque, NM	816,811	729,653	87,158	11.9
64.	Dalton, GA	134,397	120,061	14,336	11.9
65.	Athens–Clarke County, GA	185,479	166,079	19,400	11.7
66.	Fresno, CA	891,756	799,407	92,349	11.6
67.	Colorado Springs, CO	599,127	537,484	61,643	11.5
68.	Bellingham, WA	185,953	166,823	19,130	11.5
69.	Tyler, TX	194,635	174,706	19,929	11.4
70.	Farmington, NM	126,473	113,801	12,672	11.1
71.	Las Cruces, NM	193,888	174,682	19,206	11.0
72.	Des Moines–West Des Moines, IA	534,230	481,398	52,832	11.0
73.	Nashville–Davidson–Murfreesboro, TN	1,455,097	1,311,789	143,308	10.9
74.	Portland–Vancouver–Beaverton, OR–WA	2,137,565	1,927,881	209,684	10.9
75.	Salem, OR	384,600	347,218	37,382	10.8
76.	Denver–Aurora, CO	2,408,750	2,179,320	229,430	10.5
77.	Springfield, MO	407,092	368,374	38,718	10.5
78.	Panama City–Lynn Haven, FL	163,505	148,218	15,287	10.3
79.	Washington–Arlington–Alexandria, DC–VA–MD–WV	5,290,400	4,796,180	494,220	10.3
80.	Redding, CA	179,951	163,256	16,695	10.2
81.	Salt Lake City, UT	1,067,722	968,883	98,839	10.2
82.	Santa Fe, NM	142,407	129,287	13,120	10.1
83.	Huntsville, AL	376,753	342,627	34,126	10.0
84.	Charleston–North Charleston, SC	603,178	548,972	54,206	9.9
85.	Fort Collins–Loveland, CO	276,253	251,494	24,759	9.8
86.	Rochester, MN	179,573	163,618	15,955	9.8
87.	Durham, NC	464,389	423,800	40,589	9.6
88.	Charlottesville, VA	190,278	174,021	16,257	9.3

(continued)

		2006	2000	change 2000–06	
				number	percent
89.	Auburn–Opelika, AL	125,781	115,092	10,689	9.3%
90.	Indianapolis–Carmel, IN	1,666,032	1,525,104	140,928	9.2
91.	St. Cloud, MN	182,784	167,396	15,388	9.2
92.	Savannah, GA	320,013	293,299	26,714	9.1
93.	Miami–Fort Lauderdale–Miami Beach, FL	5,463,857	5,007,988	455,869	9.1
94.	Burlington, NC	142,661	130,794	11,867	9.1
95.	York–Hanover, PA	416,322	381,751	34,571	9.1
96.	Punta Gorda, FL	154,438	141,627	12,811	9.0
97.	Richmond, VA	1,194,008	1,096,957	97,051	8.8
98.	Hattiesburg, MS	134,744	123,812	10,932	8.8
99.	Bowling Green, KY	113,320	104,166	9,154	8.8
100.	Rockford, IL	348,252	320,204	28,048	8.8
101.	Columbia, SC	703,771	647,253	56,518	8.7
102.	Medford, OR	197,071	181,323	15,748	8.7
103.	Baton Rouge, LA	766,514	705,967	60,547	8.6
104.	Greenville, NC	165,776	152,693	13,083	8.6
105.	Elkhart–Goshen, IN	198,105	182,791	15,314	8.4
106.	El Paso, TX	736,310	679,622	56,688	8.3
107.	Knoxville, TN	667,384	616,080	51,304	8.3
108.	Madison, WI	543,022	501,773	41,249	8.2
109.	Winston-Salem, NC	456,614	421,934	34,680	8.2
110.	Logan, UT–ID	111,156	102,720	8,436	8.2
111.	Brunswick, GA	100,613	93,044	7,569	8.1
112.	Holland–Grand Haven, MI	257,671	238,314	19,357	8.1
113.	Allentown–Bethlehem–Easton, PA–NJ	800,336	740,394	59,942	8.1
114.	Pueblo, CO	152,912	141,472	11,440	8.1
115.	Hot Springs, AR	95,164	88,066	7,098	8.1
116.	Poughkeepsie–Newburgh–Middletown, NY	671,538	621,517	50,021	8.0
117.	Morristown, TN	132,851	123,081	9,770	7.9
118.	Asheville, NC	398,009	369,172	28,837	7.8
119.	Appleton, WI	217,313	201,722	15,591	7.7
120.	Salisbury, MD	117,761	109,392	8,369	7.7
121.	Wenatchee, WA	106,806	99,219	7,587	7.6
122.	Atlantic City, NJ	271,620	252,552	19,068	7.6
123.	Greenville, SC	601,986	559,922	42,064	7.5
124.	Longview, WA	99,905	92,948	6,957	7.5
125.	Flagstaff, AZ	124,953	116,320	8,633	7.4
126.	Napa, CA	133,522	124,308	9,214	7.4
127.	Anderson, SC	177,963	165,740	12,223	7.4
128.	Reading, PA	401,149	373,661	27,488	7.4
129.	Fargo, ND–MN	187,001	174,367	12,634	7.2
130.	Omaha–Council Bluffs, NE–IA	822,549	767,140	55,409	7.2
131.	Midland, TX	124,380	116,009	8,371	7.2
132.	Seattle–Tacoma–Bellevue, WA	3,263,497	3,043,885	219,612	7.2
133.	Bloomington–Normal, IL	161,202	150,435	10,767	7.2
134.	Joplin, MO	168,552	157,322	11,230	7.1
135.	Kansas City, MO–KS	1,967,405	1,836,420	130,985	7.1

(continued)

	2006	2000	change 2000–06	
			number	percent
136. Sherman–Denison, TX	118,478	110,595	7,883	7.1%
137. Columbia, MO	155,997	145,666	10,331	7.1
138. Oklahoma City, OK	1,172,339	1,095,421	76,918	7.0
139. Columbus, OH	1,725,570	1,612,841	112,729	7.0
140. Minneapolis–St. Paul–Bloomington, MN–WI	3,175,041	2,968,817	206,224	6.9
141. Lexington–Fayette, KY	436,684	408,326	28,358	6.9
142. Little Rock–North Little Rock, AR	652,834	610,520	42,314	6.9
143. Spokane, WA	446,706	417,938	28,768	6.9
144. Spartanburg, SC	271,087	253,782	17,305	6.8
145. Bismarck, ND	101,138	94,719	6,419	6.8
146. Pensacola–Ferry Pass–Brent, FL	439,987	412,153	27,834	6.8
147. Billings, MT	148,116	138,904	9,212	6.6
148. Amarillo, TX	241,515	226,522	14,993	6.6
149. Ann Arbor, MI	344,047	322,770	21,277	6.6
150. Greensboro–High Point, NC	685,378	643,446	41,932	6.5
151. Lafayette, LA	254,432	238,906	15,526	6.5
152. Jackson, MS	529,456	497,197	32,259	6.5
153. Lincoln, NE	283,970	266,787	17,183	6.4
154. Chico, CA	215,881	203,171	12,710	6.3
155. Killeen–Temple–Fort Hood, TX	351,322	330,712	20,610	6.2
156. Monroe, MI	155,035	145,945	9,090	6.2
157. Oxnard–Thousand Oaks–Ventura, CA	799,720	753,195	46,525	6.2
158. Iowa City, IA	139,567	131,676	7,891	6.0
159. Waco, TX	226,189	213,513	12,676	5.9
160. Missoula, MT	101,417	95,802	5,615	5.9
161. Green Bay, WI	299,003	282,497	16,506	5.8
162. Casper, WY	70,401	66,533	3,868	5.8
163. Memphis, TN–MS–AR	1,274,704	1,205,194	69,510	5.8
164. Manchester–Nashua, NH	402,789	380,843	21,946	5.8
165. Fort Walton Beach–Crestview–Destin, FL	180,291	170,497	9,794	5.7
166. Fort Smith, AR–OK	288,818	273,171	15,647	5.7
167. Vineland–Millville–Bridgeton, NJ	154,823	146,438	8,385	5.7
168. Valdosta, GA	126,305	119,566	6,739	5.6
169. Dothan, AL	138,234	130,861	7,373	5.6
170. Lebanon, PA	126,883	120,327	6,556	5.4
171. Carson City, NV	55,289	52,457	2,832	5.4
172. Portland–South Portland–Biddeford, ME	513,667	487,568	26,099	5.4
173. Hickory–Lenoir–Morganton, NC	359,856	341,819	18,037	5.3
174. Rapid City, SD	118,763	112,818	5,945	5.3
175. Cleveland, TN	109,477	104,003	5,474	5.3
176. Rome, GA	95,322	90,565	4,757	5.3
177. Johnson City, TN	191,136	181,607	9,529	5.2
178. Odessa, TX	127,462	121,123	6,339	5.2
179. Jonesboro, AR	113,330	107,762	5,568	5.2
180. Louisville–Jefferson County, KY–IN	1,222,216	1,162,409	59,807	5.1
181. Cedar Rapids, IA	249,320	237,230	12,090	5.1
182. Lancaster, PA	494,486	470,635	23,851	5.1

(continued)

	2006	2000	change 2000–06 number	change 2000–06 percent
183. Kankakee–Bradley, IL	109,090	103,833	5,257	5.1%
184. Tallahassee, FL	336,502	320,304	16,198	5.1
185. Gainesville, FL	243,985	232,392	11,593	5.0
186. Harrisonburg, VA	113,449	108,169	5,280	4.9
187. Longview, TX	203,367	194,042	9,325	4.8
188. Trenton–Ewing, NJ	367,605	350,761	16,844	4.8
189. Lynchburg, VA	239,510	228,616	10,894	4.8
190. Yakima, WA	233,105	222,578	10,527	4.7
191. Los Angeles–Long Beach–Santa Ana, CA	12,950,129	12,365,619	584,510	4.7
192. Fairbanks, AK	86,754	82,840	3,914	4.7
193. Augusta–Richmond County, GA–SC	523,249	499,653	23,596	4.7
194. Cincinnati–Middletown, OH–KY–IN	2,104,218	2,009,673	94,545	4.7
195. Lubbock, TX	261,411	249,700	11,711	4.7
196. Worcester, MA	784,992	749,973	35,019	4.7
197. Boulder, CO	282,304	269,787	12,517	4.6
198. Birmingham–Hoover, AL	1,100,019	1,051,305	48,714	4.6
199. Cheyenne, WY	85,384	81,607	3,777	4.6
200. Eugene–Springfield, OR	337,870	322,977	14,893	4.6
201. Virginia Beach–Norfolk–Newport News, VA–NC	1,649,457	1,576,917	72,540	4.6
202. Fort Wayne, IN	408,071	390,154	17,917	4.6
203. Grand Rapids–Wyoming, MI	774,084	740,482	33,602	4.5
204. San Diego–Carlsbad–San Marcos, CA	2,941,454	2,813,833	127,621	4.5
205. Eau Claire, WI	155,041	148,337	6,704	4.5
206. Janesville, WI	159,153	152,307	6,846	4.5
207. Chicago–Naperville–Joliet, IL–IN–WI	9,505,748	9,098,615	407,133	4.5
208. Tulsa, OK	897,752	859,530	38,222	4.4
209. Montgomery, AL	361,748	346,530	15,218	4.4
210. Vallejo–Fairfield, CA	411,680	394,513	17,167	4.4
211. Houma–Bayou Cane–Thibodaux, LA	202,902	194,477	8,425	4.3
212. Jackson, TN	111,937	107,365	4,572	4.3
213. Chattanooga, TN–GA	496,704	476,513	20,191	4.2
214. Columbus, IN	74,444	71,435	3,009	4.2
215. San Luis Obispo–Paso Robles, CA	257,005	246,681	10,324	4.2
216. Baltimore–Towson, MD	2,658,405	2,552,994	105,411	4.1
217. Glens Falls, NY	129,455	124,345	5,110	4.1
218. Ithaca, NY	100,407	96,502	3,905	4.0
219. Lafayette, IN	185,745	178,541	7,204	4.0
220. College Station–Bryan, TX	192,152	184,885	7,267	3.9
221. Pocatello, ID	86,357	83,103	3,254	3.9
222. Albany, GA	163,961	157,866	6,095	3.9
223. Racine, WI	196,096	188,831	7,265	3.8
224. Honolulu, HI	909,863	876,156	33,707	3.8
225. State College, PA	140,953	135,758	5,195	3.8
226. Bremerton–Silverdale, WA	240,604	231,969	8,635	3.7
227. Texarkana, TX–AR	134,510	129,749	4,761	3.7
228. Wichita, KS	592,126	571,168	20,958	3.7

(continued)

	2006	2000	change 2000–06	
			number	percent
229. Clarksville, TN–KY	240,500	232,043	8,457	3.6%
230. Lewiston–Auburn, ME	107,552	103,793	3,759	3.6
231. Dubuque, IA	92,384	89,156	3,228	3.6
232. St. Louis, MO–IL	2,796,368	2,698,672	97,696	3.6
233. Burlington–South Burlington, VT	206,007	198,889	7,118	3.6
234. Morgantown, WV	115,136	111,200	3,936	3.5
235. Jefferson City, MO	144,958	140,052	4,906	3.5
236. Hartford–West Hartford–East Hartford, CT	1,188,841	1,148,618	40,223	3.5
237. Wausau, WI	130,223	125,834	4,389	3.5
238. Alexandria, LA	150,080	145,035	5,045	3.5
239. Jackson, MI	163,851	158,422	5,429	3.4
240. Harrisburg–Carlisle, PA	525,380	509,074	16,306	3.2
241. Macon, GA	229,326	222,385	6,941	3.1
242. Corpus Christi, TX	415,810	403,280	12,530	3.1
243. Elizabethtown, KY	110,878	107,543	3,335	3.1
244. Albany–Schenectady–Troy, NY	850,957	825,875	25,082	3.0
245. Champaign–Urbana, IL	216,581	210,279	6,302	3.0
246. Muskegon–Norton Shores, MI	175,231	170,200	5,031	3.0
247. San Jose–Sunnyvale–Santa Clara, CA	1,787,123	1,735,819	51,304	3.0
248. Florence, SC	198,848	193,155	5,693	2.9
249. Hinesville–Fort Stewart, GA	74,023	71,914	2,109	2.9
250. Tuscaloosa, AL	198,769	193,106	5,663	2.9
251. Shreveport–Bossier City, LA	386,778	375,968	10,810	2.9
252. Kingston, NY	182,742	177,749	4,993	2.8
253. Lewiston, ID–WA	59,571	57,961	1,610	2.8
254. New York–Northern New Jersey–Long Island, NY–NJ–PA	18,818,536	18,323,382	495,154	2.7
255. New Haven–Milford, CT	845,244	824,008	21,236	2.6
256. Decatur, AL	149,549	145,867	3,682	2.5
257. Columbus, GA–AL	288,847	281,768	7,079	2.5
258. Philadelphia–Camden–Wilmington, PA–NJ–DE–MD	5,826,742	5,687,141	139,601	2.5
259. Oshkosh–Neenah, WI	160,593	156,763	3,830	2.4
260. Roanoke, VA	295,050	288,254	6,796	2.4
261. Springfield, IL	206,112	201,440	4,672	2.3
262. Rocky Mount, NC	146,276	142,991	3,285	2.3
263. Evansville, IN–KY	350,356	342,816	7,540	2.2
264. Victoria, TX	114,088	111,666	2,422	2.2
265. Salinas, CA	410,206	401,764	8,442	2.1
266. Bridgeport–Stamford–Norwalk, CT	900,440	882,567	17,873	2.0
267. Owensboro, KY	112,093	109,875	2,218	2.0
268. Fond du Lac, WI	99,243	97,296	1,947	2.0
269. Topeka, KS	228,894	224,551	4,343	1.9
270. Providence–New Bedford–Fall River, RI–MA	1,612,989	1,582,997	29,992	1.9
271. La Crosse, WI–MN	129,236	126,838	2,398	1.9
272. Sheboygan, WI	114,756	112,656	2,100	1.9
273. Bloomington, IN	178,714	175,506	3,208	1.8

(continued)

	2006	2000	change 2000–06	
			number	percent
274. Santa Rosa–Petaluma, CA	466,891	458,614	8,277	1.8%
275. Norwich–New London, CT	263,293	259,106	4,187	1.6
276. Bangor, ME	147,180	144,919	2,261	1.6
277. Kalamazoo–Portage, MI	319,738	314,866	4,872	1.5
278. Boston–Cambridge–Quincy, MA–NH	4,455,217	4,392,340	62,877	1.4
279. Fayetteville, NC	341,363	336,608	4,755	1.4
280. Lansing–East Lansing, MI	454,044	447,822	6,222	1.4
281. San Francisco–Oakland–Fremont, CA	4,180,027	4,123,742	56,285	1.4
282. Flint, MI	441,966	436,148	5,818	1.3
283. Kingsport–Bristol–Bristol, TN–VA	302,451	298,484	3,967	1.3
284. Monroe, LA	172,223	170,053	2,170	1.3
285. Pascagoula, MS	152,405	150,564	1,841	1.2
286. Corvallis, OR	79,061	78,139	922	1.2
287. Barnstable Town, MA	224,816	222,230	2,586	1.2
288. Mobile, AL	404,157	399,843	4,314	1.1
289. Springfield, MA	686,174	680,014	6,160	0.9
290. Peoria, IL	370,194	366,875	3,319	0.9
291. Akron, OH	700,943	694,960	5,983	0.9
292. Canton–Massillon, OH	409,764	406,968	2,796	0.7
293. Milwaukee–Waukesha–West Allis, WI	1,509,981	1,500,744	9,237	0.6
294. Anniston–Oxford, AL	112,903	112,243	660	0.6
295. Goldsboro, NC	113,847	113,329	518	0.5
296. South Bend–Mishawaka, IN–MI	318,007	316,661	1,346	0.4
297. Detroit–Warren–Livonia, MI	4,468,966	4,452,557	16,409	0.4
298. Michigan City–La Porte, IN	110,479	110,106	373	0.3
299. Davenport–Moline–Rock Island, IA–IL	377,291	376,052	1,239	0.3
300. Sioux City, IA–NE–SD	143,474	143,053	421	0.3
301. Santa Barbara–Santa Maria, CA	400,335	399,347	988	0.2
302. Jacksonville, NC	150,673	150,355	318	0.2
303. Ames, IA	80,145	79,981	164	0.2
304. Blacksburg–Christiansburg–Radford, VA	151,524	151,324	200	0.1
305. Battle Creek, MI	137,991	137,985	6	0.0
306. Syracuse, NY	650,051	650,154	−103	0.0
307. San Angelo, TX	105,752	105,781	−29	0.0
308. Gadsden, AL	103,362	103,460	−98	−0.1
309. Sumter, SC	104,430	104,636	−206	−0.2
310. Florence–Muscle Shoals, AL	142,657	142,950	−293	−0.2
311. Rochester, NY	1,035,435	1,037,833	−2,398	−0.2
312. Erie, PA	279,811	280,843	−1,032	−0.4
313. Duluth, MN–WI	274,244	275,486	−1,242	−0.5
314. Niles–Benton Harbor, MI	161,705	162,455	−750	−0.5
315. Lake Charles, LA	192,316	193,565	−1,249	−0.6
316. Kokomo, IN	100,877	101,541	−664	−0.7
317. Toledo, OH	653,695	659,184	−5,489	−0.8
318. Utica–Rome, NY	297,286	299,896	−2,610	−0.9
319. Waterloo–Cedar Falls, IA	162,263	163,707	−1,444	−0.9

(continued)

	2006	2000	change, 2000–06	
			number	percent
320. Grand Forks, ND–MN	96,523	97,478	–955	–1.0%
321. Dayton, OH	838,940	848,157	–9,217	–1.1
322. Huntington–Ashland, WV–KY–OH	285,475	288,650	–3,175	–1.1
323. Great Falls, MT	79,385	80,357	–972	–1.2
324. St. Joseph, MO–KS	122,306	123,820	–1,514	–1.2
325. Charleston, WV	305,526	309,632	–4,106	–1.3
326. Abilene, TX	158,063	160,241	–2,178	–1.4
327. Beaumont–Port Arthur, TX	379,640	385,090	–5,450	–1.4
328. Mansfield, OH	127,010	128,852	–1,842	–1.4
329. Cleveland–Elyria–Mentor, OH	2,114,155	2,148,010	–33,855	–1.6
330. Terre Haute, IN	168,217	170,954	–2,737	–1.6
331. Bay City, MI	108,390	110,157	–1,767	–1.6
332. Scranton–Wilkes-Barre, PA	550,841	560,627	–9,786	–1.7
333. Parkersburg–Marietta–Vienna, WV–OH	161,724	164,624	–2,900	–1.8
334. Saginaw–Saginaw Township North, MI	206,300	210,042	–3,742	–1.8
335. Sandusky, OH	78,116	79,551	–1,435	–1.8
336. Binghamton, NY	247,554	252,320	–4,766	–1.9
337. Springfield, OH	141,872	144,741	–2,869	–2.0
338. Williamsport, PA	117,668	120,048	–2,380	–2.0
339. Altoona, PA	126,494	129,144	–2,650	–2.1
340. Anderson, IN	130,575	133,358	–2,783	–2.1
341. Cumberland, MD–WV	99,759	102,008	–2,249	–2.2
342. Santa Cruz–Watsonville, CA	249,705	255,600	–5,895	–2.3
343. Danville, IL	81,941	83,924	–1,983	–2.4
344. Lima, OH	105,788	108,473	–2,685	–2.5
345. Pittsburgh, PA	2,370,776	2,431,085	–60,309	–2.5
346. Youngstown–Warren–Boardman, OH–PA	586,939	602,964	–16,025	–2.7
347. Elmira, NY	88,641	91,070	–2,429	–2.7
348. Buffalo–Niagara Falls, NY	1,137,520	1,170,109	–32,589	–2.8
349. Danville, VA	107,087	110,156	–3,069	–2.8
350. Pittsfield, MA	131,117	134,953	–3,836	–2.8
351. Muncie, IN	114,879	118,769	–3,890	–3.3
352. Pine Bluff, AR	103,638	107,345	–3,707	–3.5
353. Johnstown, PA	146,967	152,598	–5,631	–3.7
354. Wheeling, WV–OH	147,329	153,178	–5,849	–3.8
355. Wichita Falls, TX	145,528	151,524	–5,996	–4.0
356. Ocean City, NJ	97,724	102,326	–4,602	–4.5
357. Decatur, IL	109,309	114,706	–5,397	–4.7
358. Lawton, OK	109,181	114,996	–5,815	–5.1
359. Weirton–Steubenville, WV–OH	125,168	132,008	–6,840	–5.2
360. Gulfport–Biloxi, MS	227,904	246,190	–18,286	–7.4
361. New Orleans–Metairie–Kenner, LA	1,024,678	1,316,512	–291,834	–22.2

Source: Bureau of the Census, Metropolitan and Micropolitan Statistical Area Estimates, Internet site http://www.census.gov/ population/www/estimates/CBSA–est2006–pop–chg.html; calculations by New Strategist

9

Spending

■ Between 1950 and 2005, spending by the average household rose 39 percent, after adjusting for inflation. In 1950, 30 percent of the household budget was devoted to food. Today, the figure is just 13 percent.

■ Baby boomers and younger adults are often accused of spending freely. In fact, the spending of householders aged 65 or older has been climbing much faster—up 29 to 30 percent between 1984 and 2005, after adjusting for inflation.

■ The spending of black and Hispanic households is well below average, but their spending is growing faster than average. Between 1984 and 2005, black households boosted their spending by 19 percent and Hispanic households by 15 percent, after adjusting for inflation.

■ Nobody spends more than married couples with children. In 2005, this household type spent $66,441, fully 43 percent more than the average household. But the spending of married couples without children at home—most of them empty-nesters—is growing faster.

■ The spending of college graduates is not only 41 percent above average, but it is rising faster than average. College graduates increased their spending by 12 percent between 1995 and 2005, after adjusting for inflation.

Spending Patterns Have Changed as Our Standard of Living Has Grown

Food spending has plummeted, while housing has more than doubled.

Between 1950 and 2005, spending by the average household rose 39 percent, after adjusting for inflation. Behind the increase was a substantial rise in our standard of living. Houses grew larger and housing quality improved. Most households now own more than one vehicle. Food and clothing prices dropped, and households could afford to devote more of their dollars to having fun.

In 1950, 30 percent of the household budget was devoted to food. Today, the figure is just 13 percent. At the same time, the share of the budget allotted to shelter rose substantially, from 11 to 19 percent. Vehicle expenses also command more of the household budget, rising from a 12 percent share in 1950 to 17 percent in 2005. The average household spends more on entertainment, health care, and education today than in 1950, but less on alcoholic beverages, apparel, household furnishings, reading material, personal care products and services, and tobacco.

■ Although spending on health care grew by more than 50 percent between 2000 and 2005, the share of total household spending devoted to health care increased only marginally—rising from 5.2 to 5.7 percent.

Household spending has grown strongly since 1950

(average annual spending of households, 1950 and 2005; in 2005 dollars)

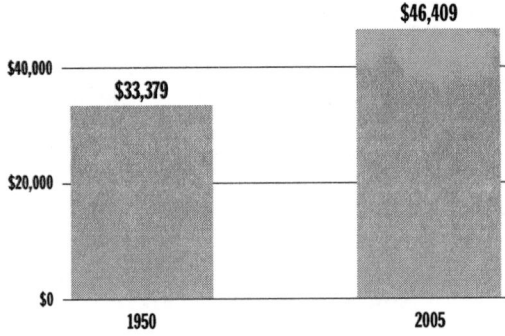

Table 9.1 Household Spending on Major Categories of Goods and Services, 1950, 2000, and 2005

(average annual spending of consumer units on major categories of goods and services, and percent distribution of spending, 1950, 2000, and 2005; percent change and percentage point change, 1950–2000 and 2000–05; in 2005 dollars)

				percent change	
	2005	2000	1950	2000–05	1950–05
Total spending by the average consumer unit	**$46,409**	**$43,127**	**$33,379**	**7.6%**	**39.0%**
Food	5,931	5,847	9,895	1.4	−40.1
Alcoholic beverages	426	422	543	0.9	−21.5
Shelter	8,805	8,064	3,687	9.2	138.8
Utilities, fuels, and public services	3,183	2,821	1,394	12.8	128.4
Household operations	1,412	1,321	1,548	6.9	−8.8
Household furnishings and equipment	1,767	1,756	2,350	0.6	−24.8
Apparel and services	1,886	2,104	3,857	−10.4	−51.1
Vehicle expenses	7,896	7,924	3,971	−0.4	98.9
Public transportation	448	484	559	−7.4	−19.9
Health care	2,664	2,342	1,742	13.7	52.9
Entertainment	2,388	2,112	1,499	13.1	59.3
Reading	126	166	300	−24.1	−58.0
Personal care	541	639	746	−15.3	−27.4
Education	940	716	211	31.3	346.1
Tobacco	319	362	600	−11.9	−46.8
Miscellaneous	7,675	6,045	486	27.0	1,478.5

				percentage point change	
	2005	2000	1950	2000–05	1950–05
PERCENT DISTRIBUTION OF SPENDING					
Total spending by the average consumer unit	**100.0%**	**100.0%**	**100.0%**	–	–
Food	12.8	13.6	29.6	−0.8	−16.9
Alcoholic beverages	0.9	1.0	1.6	−0.1	−0.7
Shelter	19.0	18.7	11.0	0.3	7.9
Utilities, fuels, and public services	6.9	6.5	4.2	0.3	2.7
Household operations	3.0	3.1	4.6	0.0	−1.6
Household furnishings and equipment	3.8	4.1	7.0	−0.3	−3.2
Apparel and services	4.1	4.9	11.6	−0.8	−7.5
Vehicle expenses	17.0	18.4	11.9	−1.4	5.1
Public transportation	1.0	1.1	1.7	−0.2	−0.7
Health care	5.7	5.4	5.2	0.3	0.5
Entertainment	5.1	4.9	4.5	0.2	0.7
Reading	0.3	0.4	0.9	−0.1	−0.6
Personal care	1.2	1.5	2.2	−0.3	−1.1
Education	2.0	1.7	0.6	0.4	1.4
Tobacco	0.7	0.8	1.8	−0.2	−1.1
Miscellaneous	16.5	14.0	1.5	2.5	15.1

Note: Miscellaneous includes cash contributions, personal insurance, and pensions. "–" means not applicable.
Source: Bureau of Labor Statistics, 2000 and 2005 Consumer Expenditure Surveys, Internet site http://www.bls.gov/cex/; and Historical Statistics of the United States, Colonial Times to 1970, Par 1, 1975; calculations by New Strategist

Average Household Spending Is Growing

The average household spent less in 2005 than in 1984 on many items, however.

Between 1984 and 2005, spending by the average household rose by a substantial 12 percent, after adjusting for inflation. In 2005, the average household spent $46,409, according to the Bureau of Labor Statistics' Consumer Expenditure Survey.

Despite the overall increase, average household spending on many individual items declined between 1984 and 2005. Spending on food at home (groceries) fell 11 percent, after adjusting for inflation. Spending on alcoholic beverage was down an even larger 18 percent, apparel fell 24 percent, and reading material was down 49 percent. Many categories gained, however. Average household spending on food away from home (mostly restaurant meals) climbed 6 percent, mortgage interest payments were up 41 percent, and property taxes nearly doubled—rising 95 percent. Despite rising gasoline prices, average household spending on this item has grown by only 1 percent between 1984 and 2005 (although it was up 38 percent between 2000 and 2005). Spending on health insurance climbed 96 percent. Entertainment spending grew 20 percent, after adjusting for inflation, driven largely by the rise in spending on cable television service.

Households are spending less on some items, more on others

(percent change in spending by the average household on selected products and services, 1984 to 2005; in 2005 dollars)

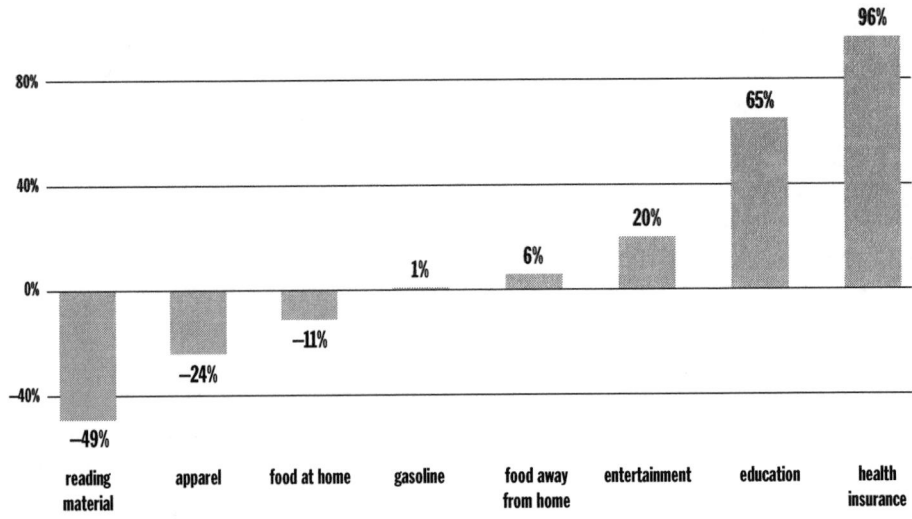

Average household spending patterns will change substantially in the years ahead as the large baby-boom generation enters the empty-nest life stage. Some changes are already apparent: Between 2000 and 2005, spending on alcoholic beverages grew slightly as boomers aged out of the parenting years, when alcohol consumption is limited. Also because of the aging of boomers, spending on household personal services (mostly daycare) is now falling after years of growth.

■ Household spending has recovered from the recession of 2001 and the sluggish economy that followed, but nondiscretionary items—such as education, health insurance, and property taxes—are experiencing some of the biggest spending gains.

Table 9.2 Average Household Spending, 1984 to 2005

(average annual spending of consumer units on products and services, 1984 to 2005; percent change for selected years; in 2005 dollars)

	average spending				percent change	
	2005	2000	1990	1984	2000–05	1984–05
Number of consumer units (in 000s)	117,356	109,367	96,968	90,223	7.3%	30.1%
Average annual spending of consumer units	$46,409	$43,127	$42,409	$41,306	7.6	12.4
FOOD	$5,931	$5,847	$6,419	$6,184	1.4%	–4.1%
Food at home	3,297	3,425	3,713	3,703	–3.7	–11.0
Cereals and bakery products	445	514	550	492	–13.4	–9.6
Cereals and cereal products	143	177	193	158	–19.2	–9.4
Bakery products	302	337	359	335	–10.4	–9.7
Meats, poultry, fish, and eggs	764	901	998	1,101	–15.2	–30.6
Beef	228	270	326	374	–15.6	–39.0
Pork	153	189	197	224	–19.0	–31.6
Other meats	103	114	148	152	–9.6	–32.4
Poultry	134	164	161	160	–18.3	–16.1
Fish and seafood	113	125	123	126	–9.6	–10.3
Eggs	33	39	45	66	–15.4	–49.8
Dairy products	378	368	441	476	2.7	–20.5
Fresh milk and cream	146	148	209	241	–1.4	–39.3
Other dairy products	232	219	232	235	5.9	–1.3
Fruits and vegetables	552	591	610	588	–6.6	–6.2
Fresh fruits	182	185	190	175	–1.6	4.1
Fresh vegetables	175	180	176	173	–2.8	1.2
Processed fruits	106	130	139	135	–18.5	–21.7
Processed vegetables	89	95	105	105	–6.3	–15.4
Other food at home	1,158	1,051	1,115	989	10.2	17.1
Sugar and other sweets	119	133	140	139	–10.5	–14.4
Fats and oils	85	94	102	105	–9.6	–19.2
Miscellaneous foods	609	495	502	410	23.0	48.6
Nonalcoholic beverages	303	283	318	335	7.1	–9.4
Food prepared by consumer unit on trips	41	45	52	56	–8.9	–27.3
Food away from home	2,634	2,422	2,706	2,481	8.8	6.2
ALCOHOLIC BEVERAGES	426	422	438	517	0.9	–17.6
HOUSING	15,167	13,964	13,005	12,545	8.6	20.9
Shelter	8,805	8,064	7,226	6,558	9.2	34.3
Owned dwellings	5,958	5,217	4,413	3,876	14.2	53.7
Mortgage interest and charges	3,317	2,991	2,715	2,351	10.9	41.1
Property taxes	1,541	1,291	892	791	19.4	94.7
Maintenance, repair, insurance, other expenses	1,101	935	807	733	17.8	50.2
Rented dwellings	2,345	2,306	2,291	2,011	1.7	16.6
Other lodging	502	542	521	671	–7.4	–25.2
Utilities, fuels, and public services	3,183	2,821	2,824	3,079	12.8	3.4
Natural gas	473	348	368	558	35.9	–15.3
Electricity	1,155	1,033	1,133	1,182	11.8	–2.3

(continued)

	average spending				percent change	
	2005	2000	1990	1984	2000–05	1984–05
Fuel oil and other fuels	$142	$110	$149	$263	29.1%	–46.0%
Telephone	1,048	994	885	818	5.4	28.2
Water and other public services	366	336	288	259	8.9	41.1
Household services	**801**	**775**	**666**	**592**	**3.4**	**35.3**
Personal services	322	370	327	241	–13.0	33.8
Other household services	479	406	339	352	18.0	36.3
Housekeeping supplies	**611**	**546**	**607**	**577**	**11.9**	**5.9**
Laundry and cleaning supplies	134	148	169	164	–9.5	–18.1
Other household products	320	256	256	252	25.0	27.0
Postage and stationery	157	143	182	162	9.8	–2.9
Household furnishings and equipment	**1,767**	**1,756**	**1,681**	**1,741**	**0.6**	**1.5**
Household textiles	132	120	148	162	10.0	–18.3
Furniture	467	443	463	508	5.4	–8.0
Floor coverings	56	50	137	147	12.0	–61.8
Major appliances	223	214	220	269	4.2	–17.0
Small appliances and miscellaneous housewares	105	99	112	126	6.1	–16.6
Miscellaneous household equipment	782	829	601	530	–5.7	47.5
APPAREL AND RELATED SERVICES	**1,886**	**2,104**	**2,418**	**2,479**	**–10.4**	**–23.9**
Men and boys	**440**	**499**	**587**	**658**	**–11.8**	**–33.1**
Men, aged 16 or older	349	390	484	526	–10.5	–33.7
Boys, aged 2 to 15	91	109	105	132	–16.5	–30.8
Women and girls	**754**	**822**	**1,006**	**985**	**–8.3**	**–23.4**
Women, aged 16 or older	633	688	876	835	–8.0	–24.2
Girls, aged 2 to 15	121	134	130	148	–9.7	–18.5
Children under age 2	**82**	**93**	**105**	**94**	**–11.8**	**–12.8**
Footwear	**320**	**389**	**336**	**348**	**–17.7**	**–8.0**
Other apparel products and services	**290**	**302**	**386**	**397**	**–4.0**	**–26.9**
TRANSPORTATION	**8,344**	**8,408**	**7,651**	**8,090**	**–0.8**	**3.1**
Vehicle purchases	**3,544**	**3,875**	**3,181**	**3,408**	**–8.5**	**4.0**
Cars and trucks, new	1,931	1,819	1,732	1,936	6.2	–0.3
Cars and trucks, used	1,531	2,006	1,417	1,421	–23.7	7.7
Gasoline and motor oil	**2,013**	**1,463**	**1,564**	**1,989**	**37.6**	**1.2**
Other vehicle expenses	**2,339**	**2,586**	**2,454**	**2,214**	**–9.6**	**5.6**
Vehicle finance charges	297	372	448	400	–20.2	–25.8
Maintenance and repairs	671	707	880	904	–5.1	–25.8
Vehicle insurance	913	882	841	656	3.5	39.2
Vehicle rentals, leases, licenses, other charges	458	625	284	252	–26.7	81.8
Public transportation	**448**	**484**	**451**	**479**	**–7.4**	**–6.5**
HEALTH CARE	**2,664**	**2,342**	**2,212**	**1,972**	**13.7**	**35.1**
Health insurance	1,361	1,114	868	695	22.2	95.7
Medical services	677	644	840	853	5.1	–20.7
Drugs	521	472	377	314	10.4	66.0
Medical supplies	105	112	127	109	–6.3	–3.7
ENTERTAINMENT	**2,388**	**2,112**	**2,125**	**1,983**	**13.1**	**20.4**
Fees and admissions	588	584	554	588	0.7	–0.1
Audio and visual equipment and services	888	705	678	605	26.0	46.7

(continued)

	average spending				percent change	
	2005	2000	1990	1984	2000–05	1984–05
Pets, toys, hobbies, playground equipment	$420	$379	$412	$357	10.8%	17.6%
Other entertainment products and services	492	445	480	432	10.6	13.8
PERSONAL CARE PRODUCTS AND SERVICES	**541**	**639**	**544**	**543**	**–15.3**	**–0.4**
READING	**126**	**166**	**229**	**248**	**–24.1**	**–49.2**
EDUCATION	**940**	**716**	**607**	**570**	**31.3**	**65.0**
TOBACCO PRODUCTS AND SMOKING SUPPLIES	**319**	**362**	**409**	**429**	**–11.9**	**–25.6**
MISCELLANEOUS	**808**	**880**	**1,258**	**848**	**–8.2**	**–4.7**
CASH CONTRIBUTIONS	**1,663**	**1,351**	**1,219**	**1,327**	**23.1**	**25.3**
PERSONAL INSURANCE AND PENSIONS	**5,204**	**3,814**	**3,873**	**3,566**	**36.4**	**45.9**
Life and other personal insurance	381	452	516	564	–15.7	–32.4
Pensions and Social Security*	4,823	3,362	3,359	3,004	43.5	60.6
PERSONAL TAXES	**2,408**	**3,533**	**4,411**	**4,186**	**–31.8**	**–42.5**
Federal income taxes	1,696	2,731	3,465	3,258	–37.9	–47.9
State and local income taxes	534	637	834	810	–16.2	–34.1
Other taxes	177	166	112	118	6.6	49.5
GIFTS FOR PEOPLE IN OTHER HOUSEHOLDS	**1,091**	**1,228**	**1,361**	**1,308**	**–11.2**	**–16.6**

* Because of changes in methodology, the 2005 data on pensions and Social Security are not comparable with earlier years.
Note: Spending by category will not add to total spending because gift spending is also included in the preceding product and service categories and personal taxes are not included in the total.
Source: Bureau of Labor Statistics, 1984, 1990, 2000, and 2005 Consumer Expenditure Surveys, Internet site http://www.bls.gov/cex/; calculations by New Strategist

Older Householders Are Spending More

Middle-aged householders have experienced the smallest increases in spending.

While many blame boomers and younger adults for spending freely, in fact the spending of households headed by young and middle-aged adults has been restrained over the past two decades compared with the spending of older Americans. Among householders aged 65 or older, average spending climbed by 29 to 30 percent between 1984 and 2005, after adjusting for inflation. In contrast, householders aged 35 to 54 boosted their spending by just 4 percent during those years. Householders aged 35 to 54 remain the biggest spenders, however, with average annual spending exceeding $55,000 in 2005.

Behind the increase in the spending of older Americans is the entry into the age group of a more affluent and educated generation. Entertainment spending tells the story. Average household spending on entertainment by householders aged 65 to 74 grew by an enormous 92 percent between 1984 and 2005, after adjusting for inflation. In contrast, householders aged 35 to 44 cut their spending on entertainment by 2 percent during those years.

■ Most of the increased spending among the middle aged has been devoted to necessities such as mortgage interest, property taxes, vehicles, health insurance, and education.

Who are the free spenders?

(percent change in average household spending by age of householder, 1984 to 2005; in 2005 dollars)

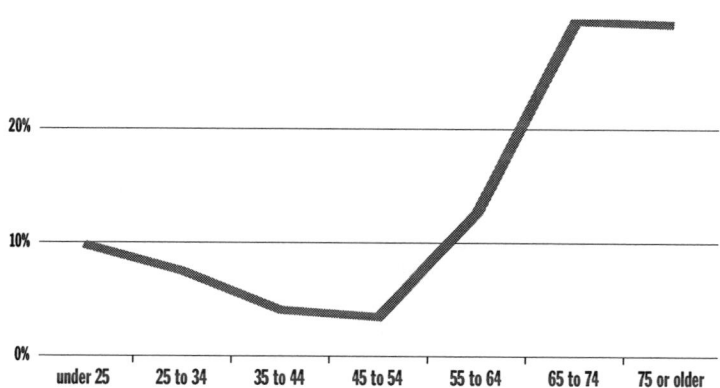

Table 9.3 Average Spending by Householders under Age 25, 1984 to 2005

(average annual spending of consumer units headed by people under age 25 on products and services, 1984 to 2005; percent change for selected years; in 2005 dollars)

	average spending				percent change	
	2005	2000	1990	1984	2000–05	1984–05
Number of consumer units under age 25 (in 000s)	8,543	8,306	7581	8811	2.9%	–3.0%
Average annual spending of consumer units	$27,776	$25,567	$24,693	$25,303	8.6	9.8
FOOD	$3,933	$3,644	$4,126	$3,921	7.9%	0.3%
Food at home	1,917	1,863	1,920	1,981	2.9	–3.2
Cereals and bakery products	273	270	273	258	1.1	6.0
Cereals and cereal products	106	102	108	92	3.8	15.1
Bakery products	167	168	166	165	–0.5	1.0
Meats, poultry, fish, and eggs	449	496	442	536	–9.4	–16.2
Beef	149	153	145	188	–2.7	–20.7
Pork	79	101	88	118	–21.7	–33.3
Other meats	59	62	72	77	–5.4	–23.4
Poultry	83	98	58	79	–14.9	5.1
Fish and seafood	59	59	52	41	0.0	42.7
Eggs	21	24	25	32	–11.8	–34.3
Dairy products	214	198	233	274	7.8	–22.0
Fresh milk and cream	90	83	121	152	8.7	–40.9
Other dairy products	124	115	112	122	8.3	1.5
Fruits and vegetables	298	287	281	284	3.9	5.0
Fresh fruits	87	87	69	77	–0.4	12.9
Fresh vegetables	90	84	85	83	7.2	8.8
Processed fruits	69	70	72	60	–1.9	14.7
Processed vegetables	51	47	55	64	9.7	–20.2
Other food at home	684	614	690	607	11.5	12.7
Sugar and other sweets	60	68	72	66	–11.8	–8.8
Fats and oils	43	48	46	58	–9.7	–26.2
Miscellaneous foods	381	307	360	276	24.0	37.9
Nonalcoholic beverages	186	167	190	209	11.6	–10.9
Food prepared by consumer unit on trips	13	22	22	21	–39.7	–37.1
Food away from home	2,015	1,779	2,206	1,942	13.2	3.8
ALCOHOLIC BEVERAGES	401	445	475	494	–9.8	–18.9
HOUSING	8,940	8,063	7,240	7,053	10.9	26.8
Shelter	5,538	5,188	4,504	4,288	6.8	29.2
Owned dwellings	1,263	719	465	870	75.6	45.1
Mortgage interest and charges	835	438	348	677	90.7	23.4
Property taxes	287	200	40	73	43.8	291.5
Maintenance, repair, insurance, other expenses	140	82	76	120	71.4	16.4
Rented dwellings	4,085	4,103	3,742	3,054	–0.4	33.7
Other lodging	190	365	299	363	–48.0	–47.6
Utilities, fuels, and public services	1,755	1,415	1,354	1,344	24.0	30.6
Natural gas	191	116	140	154	65.1	23.9
Electricity	645	504	474	521	28.1	23.9

(continued)

	average spending				percent change	
	2005	**2000**	**1990**	**1984**	**2000–05**	**1984–05**
Fuel oil and other fuels	$36	$24	$25	$58	51.2%	–38.2%
Telephone	744	668	643	549	11.4	35.6
Water and other public services	140	103	72	62	35.6	125.7
Household services	**387**	**256**	**218**	**218**	**51.0**	**77.5**
Personal services	237	175	149	152	35.7	55.7
Other household services	151	82	69	66	84.9	129.5
Housekeeping supplies	**242**	**220**	**266**	**265**	**10.0**	**–8.7**
Laundry and cleaning supplies	63	62	70	88	1.0	–28.7
Other household products	110	101	88	81	9.0	36.1
Postage and stationery	69	57	108	98	21.7	–29.4
Household furnishings and equipment	**1,018**	**983**	**898**	**938**	**3.5**	**8.5**
Household textiles	58	40	58	75	46.1	–22.9
Furniture	297	306	380	395	–3.0	–24.8
Floor coverings	17	7	13	24	149.8	–30.4
Major appliances	95	87	97	122	8.8	–22.2
Small appliances and miscellaneous housewares	68	57	60	85	19.9	–19.6
Miscellaneous household equipment	483	487	290	237	–0.7	103.9
APPAREL AND RELATED SERVICES	**1,577**	**1,610**	**1,545**	**1761**	**–2.1**	**–10.5**
Men and boys	**316**	**363**	**471**	**464**	**–12.9**	**–31.9**
Men, aged 16 or older	279	333	453	432	–16.3	–35.5
Boys, aged 2 to 15	37	29	19	32	25.5	15.8
Women and girls	**678**	**493**	**471**	**624**	**37.4**	**8.6**
Women, aged 16 or older	636	459	433	600	38.5	6.1
Girls, aged 2 to 15	42	35	39	24	19.5	71.9
Children under age 2	**97**	**115**	**126**	**105**	**–15.3**	**–7.8**
Footwear	**297**	**412**	**140**	**224**	**–27.9**	**32.8**
Other apparel products and services	**189**	**228**	**338**	**344**	**–17.1**	**–45.1**
TRANSPORTATION	**5,987**	**5,885**	**5,221**	**6237**	**1.7**	**–4.0**
Vehicle purchases	**2,721**	**2,981**	**2,377**	**3075**	**–8.7**	**–11.5**
Cars and trucks, new	720	1,203	1,097	998	–40.2	–27.9
Cars and trucks, used	1,907	1,755	1,248	1942	8.7	–1.8
Gasoline and motor oil	**1,538**	**1,074**	**1,079**	**1453**	**43.2**	**5.8**
Other vehicle expenses	**1,536**	**1,584**	**1,497**	**1479**	**–3.1**	**3.8**
Vehicle finance charges	199	259	290	305	–23.0	–34.6
Maintenance and repairs	444	501	581	641	–11.4	–30.7
Vehicle insurance	626	509	483	387	22.9	61.7
Vehicle rentals, leases, licenses, other charges	267	315	145	147	–15.3	82.1
Public transportation	**191**	**245**	**267**	**229**	**–22.0**	**–16.7**
HEALTH CARE	**704**	**572**	**602**	**697**	**23.2**	**1.0**
Health insurance	377	239	158	203	57.5	85.7
Medical services	197	202	284	350	–2.4	–43.7
Drugs	99	92	97	105	7.8	–5.9
Medical supplies	31	39	61	41	–19.6	–25.0
ENTERTAINMENT	**1,393**	**1,237**	**1,245**	**1227**	**12.6**	**13.5**
Fees and admissions	249	307	326	359	–19.0	–30.6
Audio and visual equipment and services	631	536	514	432	17.6	46.0

(continued)

	average spending				percent change	
	2005	**2000**	**1990**	**1984**	**2000–05**	**1984–05**
Pets, toys, hobbies, playground equipment	$184	$196	$175	$165	–6.2%	11.2%
Other entertainment products and services	328	198	232	271	65.3	21.2
PERSONAL CARE PRODUCTS AND SERVICES	337	391	317	301	–13.9	12.1
READING	49	65	112	117	–24.2	–58.0
EDUCATION	1,359	1,426	1,221	1071	–4.7	26.8
TOBACCO PRODUCTS AND SMOKING SUPPLIES	308	269	323	299	14.6	3.1
MISCELLANEOUS	263	365	596	451	–28.0	–41.7
CASH CONTRIBUTIONS	393	214	218	194	83.3	103.0
PERSONAL INSURANCE AND PENSIONS	2,133	1,379	1,452	1479	54.7	44.2
Life and other personal insurance	45	61	73	120	–26.5	–62.6
Pensions and Social Security*	2,088	1,318	1,378	1359	58.4	53.6
PERSONAL TAXES	373	1,056	1,260	1962	–64.7	–81.0
Federal income taxes	200	789	959	1551	–74.7	–87.1
State and local income taxes	161	256	287	397	–37.2	–59.4
Other taxes	13	10	15	13	27.4	–1.2
GIFTS FOR PEOPLE IN OTHER HOUSEHOLDS	367	677	628	718	–45.8	–48.9

Because of changes in methodology, the 2005 data on pensions and Social Security are not comparable with earlier years.
Note: Spending by category will not add to total spending because gift spending is also included in the preceding product and service categories and personal taxes are not included in the total.
Source: Bureau of Labor Statistics, 1984, 1990, 2000, and 2005 Consumer Expenditure Surveys, Internet site http://www.bls .gov/cex/; calculations by New Strategist

Table 9.4 Average Spending by Householders Aged 25 to 34, 1984 to 2005

(average annual spending of consumer units headed by people aged 25 to 34, 1984 to 2005; percent change for selected years; in 2005 dollars)

	average spending				percent change	
	2005	2000	1990	1984	2000–05	1984–05
Number of consumer units 25 to 34 (in 000s)	19,635	18,887	21,287	20058	4.0%	–2.1%
Average annual spending of consumer units	$45,068	$44,169	$42,014	$41,906	2.0	7.5
FOOD	**$5,639**	**$5,966**	**$6,126**	**$5,887**	**–5.5%**	**–4.2%**
Food at home	**2,945**	**3,347**	**3,497**	**3,440**	**–12.0**	**–14.4**
Cereals and bakery products	387	487	496	464	–20.5	–16.6
Cereals and cereal products	138	189	187	162	–27.1	–14.6
Bakery products	249	298	308	303	–16.5	–17.7
Meats, poultry, fish, and eggs	654	873	938	1,000	–25.1	–34.6
Beef	189	271	324	353	–30.3	–46.5
Pork	121	176	170	199	–31.2	–39.3
Other meats	95	111	139	143	–14.5	–33.5
Poultry	137	164	154	152	–16.7	–10.0
Fish and seafood	82	116	109	90	–29.1	–9.1
Eggs	30	34	43	60	–11.8	–50.1
Dairy products	348	360	436	453	–3.2	–23.2
Fresh milk and cream	139	152	212	235	–8.5	–40.8
Other dairy products	209	208	224	218	0.7	–4.1
Fruits and vegetables	461	553	547	500	–16.7	–7.8
Fresh fruits	145	166	169	135	–12.4	7.1
Fresh vegetables	144	168	154	141	–14.2	2.1
Processed fruits	91	128	127	118	–29.0	–23.2
Processed vegetables	82	93	97	105	–11.8	–22.1
Other food at home	1,094	1,073	1,079	976	2.0	12.1
Sugar and other sweets	91	119	121	124	–23.6	–26.6
Fats and oils	76	87	85	96	–13.0	–20.7
Miscellaneous foods	613	550	511	451	11.4	35.9
Nonalcoholic beverages	281	280	309	305	0.3	–7.7
Food prepared by consumer unit on trips	32	35	52	51	–9.0	–36.9
Food away from home	**2,694**	**2,619**	**2,630**	**2,447**	**2.9**	**10.1**
ALCOHOLIC BEVERAGES	**478**	**489**	**545**	**630**	**–2.2**	**–24.1**
HOUSING	**15,516**	**14,801**	**13,761**	**13,472**	**4.8**	**15.2**
Shelter	**9,491**	**8,965**	**8,241**	**7,694**	**5.9**	**23.4**
Owned dwellings	5,206	4,698	4,339	4,227	10.8	23.1
Mortgage interest and charges	3,535	3,275	3,379	3,265	7.9	8.3
Property taxes	1,027	856	454	459	19.9	123.9
Maintenance, repair, insurance, other expenses	645	566	507	502	14.0	28.5
Rented dwellings	4,043	3,985	3,647	3,036	1.4	33.2
Other lodging	241	281	254	430	–14.3	–44.0
Utilities, fuels, and public services	**2,909**	**2,655**	**2,516**	**2,778**	**9.6**	**4.7**
Natural gas	396	310	297	459	27.9	–13.7
Electricity	1,047	937	998	1,083	11.8	–3.3

(continued)

	average spending				percent change	
	2005	2000	1990	1984	2000–05	1984–05
Fuel oil and other fuels	$65	$66	$94	$175	–1.2%	–62.8%
Telephone	1,099	1,077	903	846	2.0	29.9
Water and other public services	302	265	224	216	13.8	39.7
Household services	**1,004**	**988**	**849**	**774**	**1.6**	**29.6**
Personal services	651	727	671	564	–10.5	15.4
Other household services	354	261	178	211	35.7	68.2
Housekeeping supplies	**504**	**496**	**550**	**538**	**1.7**	**–6.2**
Laundry and cleaning supplies	127	142	169	160	–10.4	–20.5
Other household products	253	228	224	241	11.0	5.2
Postage and stationery	123	127	157	137	–3.2	–10.4
Household furnishings and equipment	**1,608**	**1,696**	**1,606**	**1,690**	**–5.2**	**–4.8**
Household textiles	136	136	118	143	–0.1	–4.8
Furniture	537	518	499	607	3.6	–11.6
Floor coverings	41	48	81	47	–13.9	–12.8
Major appliances	184	205	224	293	–10.4	–37.3
Small appliances and miscellaneous housewares	89	88	103	102	0.6	–12.3
Miscellaneous household equipment	621	700	583	498	–11.3	24.7
APPAREL AND RELATED SERVICES	**2,082**	**2,335**	**2,347**	**2,575**	**–10.8**	**–19.2**
Men and boys	**468**	**580**	**586**	**712**	**–19.2**	**–34.3**
Men, aged 16 or older	353	417	448	549	–15.4	–35.7
Boys, aged 2 to 15	115	162	137	162	–29.1	–28.9
Women and girls	**728**	**798**	**849**	**874**	**–8.8**	**–16.7**
Women, aged 16 or older	587	636	705	718	–7.7	–18.2
Girls, aged 2 to 15	141	163	143	156	–13.7	–9.6
Children under age 2	**172**	**187**	**200**	**184**	**–8.1**	**–6.6**
Footwear	**384**	**447**	**312**	**353**	**–14.1**	**8.7**
Other apparel products and services	**330**	**323**	**400**	**451**	**2.1**	**–26.8**
TRANSPORTATION	**8,798**	**9,478**	**8,087**	**8,622**	**–7.2**	**2.0**
Vehicle purchases	**3,949**	**4,694**	**3,618**	**4,019**	**–15.9**	**–1.7**
Cars and trucks, new	1,877	2,093	1,878	2,363	–10.3	–20.6
Cars and trucks, used	2,001	2,514	1,678	1,609	–20.4	24.4
Gasoline and motor oil	**2,123**	**1,521**	**1,614**	**1,938**	**39.6**	**9.5**
Other vehicle expenses	**2,361**	**2,815**	**2,522**	**2,224**	**–16.1**	**6.2**
Vehicle finance charges	402	494	554	496	–18.7	–19.0
Maintenance and repairs	618	646	865	868	–4.4	–28.8
Vehicle insurance	888	878	779	579	1.2	53.4
Vehicle rentals, leases, licenses, other charges	452	795	324	280	–43.1	61.4
Public transportation	**366**	**448**	**333**	**440**	**–18.3**	**–16.8**
HEALTH CARE	**1,522**	**1,424**	**1,466**	**1,402**	**6.8**	**8.5**
Health insurance	822	726	584	466	13.2	76.3
Medical services	399	416	584	679	–4.1	–41.2
Drugs	237	205	202	184	15.5	28.7
Medical supplies	63	78	96	71	–19.5	–11.8
ENTERTAINMENT	**2,455**	**2,128**	**2,200**	**2,265**	**15.4**	**8.4**
Fees and admissions	489	522	511	558	–6.3	–12.4
Audio and visual equipment and services	943	771	752	769	22.3	22.7

(continued)

	average spending				percent change	
	2005	2000	1990	1984	2000–05	1984–05
Pets, toys, hobbies, playground equipment	$443	$398	$459	$462	11.3%	–4.2%
Other entertainment products and services	580	437	480	476	32.8	22.0
PERSONAL CARE PRODUCTS AND SERVICES	**504**	**653**	**471**	**513**	**–22.8**	**–1.8**
READING	**89**	**134**	**200**	**250**	**–33.5**	**–64.4**
EDUCATION	**779**	**663**	**486**	**408**	**17.4**	**91.0**
TOBACCO PRODUCTS AND SMOKING SUPPLIES	**307**	**352**	**411**	**417**	**–12.7**	**–26.4**
MISCELLANEOUS	**697**	**912**	**1,174**	**996**	**–23.6**	**–30.0**
CASH CONTRIBUTIONS	**1,080**	**735**	**614**	**665**	**47.0**	**62.3**
PERSONAL INSURANCE AND PENSIONS	**5,123**	**4,099**	**4,126**	**3,801**	**25.0**	**34.8**
Life and other personal insurance	219	274	336	444	–20.2	–50.6
Pensions and Social Security*	4,903	3,825	3,789	3,357	28.2	46.0
PERSONAL TAXES	**1,809**	**3,213**	**4,414**	**4,835**	**–43.7**	**–62.6**
Federal income taxes	1,189	2,501	3,429	3,769	–52.5	–68.5
State and local income taxes	509	646	935	1,004	–21.3	–49.3
Other taxes	111	66	49	62	68.7	78.9
GIFTS FOR PEOPLE IN OTHER HOUSEHOLDS	**482**	**812**	**900**	**914**	**–40.6**	**–47.2**

* Because of changes in methodology, the 2005 data on pensions and Social Security are not comparable with earlier years.
Note: Spending by category will not add to total spending because gift spending is also included in the preceding product and service categories and personal taxes are not included in the total.
Source: Bureau of Labor Statistics, 1984, 1990, 2000, and 2005 Consumer Expenditure Surveys, Internet site http://www.bls.gov/cex/; calculations by New Strategist

Table 9.5 Average Spending by Householders Aged 35 to 44, 1984 to 2005

(average annual spending of consumer units headed by people aged 35 to 44, 1984 to 2005; percent change for selected years; in 2005 dollars)

	average spending				percent change	
	2005	2000	1990	1984	2000–05	1984–05
Number of consumer units 35 to 44 (in 000s)	23,835	23,983	21,003	17,118	–0.6%	39.2%
Average annual spending of consumer units	$55,190	$51,206	$53,187	$53,034	7.8	4.1
FOOD	$7,359	$6,909	$8,039	$8,086	6.5%	–9.0%
Food at home	4,121	3,951	4,683	4,729	4.3	–12.9
Cereals and bakery products	564	602	710	624	–6.3	–9.6
Cereals and cereal products	183	215	254	212	–15.1	–13.8
Bakery products	381	387	456	412	–1.5	–7.4
Meats, poultry, fish, and eggs	963	1,041	1,197	1,378	–7.5	–30.1
Beef	293	306	391	479	–4.3	–38.9
Pork	199	211	233	274	–5.7	–27.5
Other meats	133	136	173	197	–2.3	–32.6
Poultry	170	202	188	211	–15.8	–19.2
Fish and seafood	131	143	160	137	–8.3	–4.5
Eggs	38	42	51	79	–9.4	–51.9
Dairy products	479	434	563	617	10.3	–22.3
Fresh milk and cream	191	178	261	306	7.3	–37.7
Other dairy products	288	256	302	308	12.4	–6.6
Fruits and vegetables	663	626	732	729	5.9	–9.1
Fresh fruits	218	192	211	207	13.7	5.4
Fresh vegetables	202	186	217	212	8.6	–4.9
Processed fruits	132	142	170	180	–6.9	–26.8
Processed vegetables	111	104	133	130	6.4	–14.4
Other food at home	1,452	1,249	1,481	1,318	16.3	10.2
Sugar and other sweets	144	167	185	182	–13.6	–21.0
Fats and oils	99	102	131	135	–3.0	–26.8
Miscellaneous foods	777	587	690	558	32.3	39.2
Nonalcoholic beverages	389	340	409	442	14.3	–11.9
Food prepared by consumer unit on trips	42	52	64	66	–19.5	–36.2
Food away from home	3,238	2,957	3,356	3,355	9.5	–3.5
ALCOHOLIC BEVERAGES	511	476	553	543	7.3	–5.9
HOUSING	18,482	17,138	16,512	16,485	7.8	12.1
Shelter	10,835	10,128	9,275	9,049	7.0	19.7
Owned dwellings	7,936	7,296	6,461	5,962	8.8	33.1
Mortgage interest and charges	5,169	4,879	4,604	4,385	5.9	17.9
Property taxes	1,760	1,413	1,073	827	24.5	112.8
Maintenance, repair, insurance, other expenses	1,006	1,003	784	748	0.3	34.5
Rented dwellings	2,473	2,344	2,288	2,212	5.5	11.8
Other lodging	427	488	526	874	–12.4	–51.1
Utilities, fuels, and public services	3,569	3,187	3,217	3,645	12.0	–2.1
Natural gas	524	397	409	622	32.0	–15.8
Electricity	1,290	1,144	1,285	1,468	12.7	–12.1

(continued)

	average spending				percent change	
	2005	2000	1990	1984	2000–05	1984–05
Fuel oil and other fuels	$137	$110	$163	$252	24.5%	–45.6%
Telephone	1,208	1,155	1,019	966	4.6	25.0
Water and other public services	410	381	342	336	7.6	21.9
Household services	**1,145**	**1,016**	**911**	**733**	**12.7**	**56.2**
Personal services	666	615	529	348	8.3	91.5
Other household services	479	401	383	385	19.3	24.3
Housekeeping supplies	**716**	**646**	**738**	**726**	**10.8**	**–1.3**
Laundry and cleaning supplies	161	178	212	203	–9.6	–20.7
Other household products	385	318	326	333	21.2	15.7
Postage and stationery	170	151	199	190	12.7	–10.5
Household furnishings and equipment	**2,216**	**2,162**	**2,370**	**2,331**	**2.5**	**–4.9**
Household textiles	155	141	185	209	10.2	–25.7
Furniture	626	566	610	697	10.6	–10.2
Floor coverings	55	60	229	158	–8.5	–65.2
Major appliances	247	240	259	323	2.7	–23.6
Small appliances and miscellaneous housewares	100	105	131	171	–5.2	–41.5
Miscellaneous household equipment	1,033	1,050	956	771	–1.6	34.0
APPAREL AND RELATED SERVICES	**2,365**	**2,635**	**3,455**	**3,551**	**–10.2**	**–33.4**
Men and boys	**598**	**625**	**840**	**1,024**	**–4.3**	**–41.6**
Men, aged 16 or older	405	416	628	684	–2.7	–40.8
Boys, aged 2 to 15	193	209	211	340	–7.5	–43.3
Women and girls	**927**	**1,060**	**1,466**	**1,414**	**–12.6**	**–34.4**
Women, aged 16 or older	671	785	1,161	1,017	–14.5	–34.0
Girls, aged 2 to 15	256	274	305	395	–6.7	–35.1
Children under age 2	**106**	**119**	**103**	**90**	**–11.0**	**17.5**
Footwear	**397**	**455**	**519**	**526**	**–12.7**	**–24.6**
Other apparel products and services	**336**	**375**	**527**	**498**	**–10.5**	**–32.5**
TRANSPORTATION	**9,945**	**9,869**	**9,084**	**9,622**	**0.8**	**3.4**
Vehicle purchases	**4,407**	**4,532**	**3,770**	**3,773**	**–2.8**	**16.8**
Cars and trucks, new	2,381	1,955	2,019	2,229	21.8	6.8
Cars and trucks, used	1,852	2,493	1,715	1,487	–25.7	24.6
Gasoline and motor oil	**2,379**	**1,789**	**1,860**	**2,449**	**33.0**	**–2.9**
Other vehicle expenses	**2,669**	**3,036**	**2,966**	**2,867**	**–12.1**	**–6.9**
Vehicle finance charges	395	460	590	541	–14.2	–27.0
Maintenance and repairs	727	803	1,034	1,171	–9.5	–37.9
Vehicle insurance	1,008	1,003	973	797	0.5	26.5
Vehicle rentals, leases, licenses, other charges	539	771	369	357	–30.1	50.9
Public transportation	**490**	**512**	**487**	**536**	**–4.2**	**–8.5**
HEALTH CARE	**2,272**	**2,012**	**2,114**	**1,835**	**12.9**	**23.8**
Health insurance	1,160	964	725	570	20.3	103.7
Medical services	665	629	965	927	5.6	–28.2
Drugs	354	322	273	252	9.9	40.5
Medical supplies	93	96	149	88	–3.5	5.3
ENTERTAINMENT	**2,765**	**2,795**	**2,745**	**2,808**	**–1.1**	**–1.5**
Fees and admissions	753	811	787	855	–7.1	–12.0
Audio and visual equipment and services	1,029	895	871	784	15.0	31.3

(continued)

	average spending				percent change	
	2005	**2000**	**1990**	**1984**	**2000–05**	**1984–05**
Pets, toys, hobbies, playground equipment	$468	$512	$536	$517	–8.5%	–9.5%
Other entertainment products and services	516	577	548	652	–10.6	–20.9
PERSONAL CARE PRODUCTS AND SERVICES	627	730	668	652	–14.2	–3.9
READING	121	171	281	306	–29.3	–60.5
EDUCATION	931	698	695	742	33.5	25.4
TOBACCO PRODUCTS AND SMOKING SUPPLIES	357	484	472	515	–26.3	–30.7
MISCELLANEOUS	791	966	1,730	1,162	–18.1	–31.9
CASH CONTRIBUTIONS	1,735	1,138	1,309	1,857	52.5	–6.6
PERSONAL INSURANCE AND PENSIONS	6,929	5,183	5,529	4,870	33.7	42.3
Life and other personal insurance	397	467	663	673	–15.0	–41.0
Pensions and Social Security*	6,532	4,716	4,865	4,197	38.5	55.6
PERSONAL TAXES	3,080	4,394	6,681	5,690	–29.9	–45.9
Federal income taxes	2,190	3,418	5,288	4,472	–35.9	–51.0
State and local income taxes	739	832	1,234	1,083	–11.2	–31.7
Other taxes	151	143	158	137	5.7	10.0
GIFTS FOR PEOPLE IN OTHER HOUSEHOLDS	903	1,135	1,340	1,498	–20.5	–39.7

* Because of changes in methodology, the 2005 data on pensions and Social Security are not comparable with earlier years.
Note: Spending by category will not add to total spending because gift spending is also included in the preceding product and service categories and personal taxes are not included in the total.
Source: Bureau of Labor Statistics, 1984, 1990, 2000, and 2005 Consumer Expenditure Surveys, Internet site http://www.bls.gov/cex/; calculations by New Strategist

Table 9.6 Average Spending by Householders Aged 45 to 54, 1984 to 2005

(average annual spending of consumer units headed by people aged 45 to 54 , 1984 to 2005; percent change for selected years; in 2005 dollars)

	average spending				percent change	
	2005	2000	1990	1984	2000–05	1984–05
Number of consumer units 45 to 54 (in 000s)	24,393	21,874	14,855	13,027	11.5%	87.2%
Average annual spending of consumer units	$55,854	$52,352	$55,306	$53,940	6.7	3.5
FOOD	**$6,980**	**$7,139**	**$8,203**	**$8,160**	**–2.2%**	**–14.5%**
Food at home	**3,807**	**4,148**	**4,495**	**4,851**	**–8.2**	**–21.5**
Cereals and bakery products	499	635	657	630	–21.4	–20.8
Cereals and cereal products	159	204	214	195	–22.1	–18.7
Bakery products	340	431	444	434	–21.1	–21.7
Meats, poultry, fish, and eggs	918	1,100	1,270	1,577	–16.6	–41.8
Beef	283	336	400	528	–15.7	–46.4
Pork	179	225	269	303	–20.3	–40.9
Other meats	117	137	194	207	–14.7	–43.4
Poultry	162	192	203	197	–15.5	–17.9
Fish and seafood	140	166	152	252	–15.5	–44.4
Eggs	37	45	52	88	–18.4	–58.1
Dairy products	433	428	516	615	1.3	–29.6
Fresh milk and cream	159	166	242	312	–4.0	–49.0
Other dairy products	274	263	275	301	4.1	–8.9
Fruits and vegetables	614	710	699	754	–13.5	–18.5
Fresh fruits	201	212	215	231	–5.2	–13.1
Fresh vegetables	202	228	209	227	–11.4	–11.2
Processed fruits	114	151	155	165	–24.4	–31.1
Processed vegetables	98	119	120	130	–17.7	–24.4
Other food at home	1,342	1,275	1,351	1,199	5.3	11.9
Sugar and other sweets	142	162	178	173	–12.4	–17.9
Fats and oils	99	116	124	126	–14.4	–21.4
Miscellaneous foods	688	599	589	464	14.9	48.2
Nonalcoholic beverages	366	340	399	436	7.6	–16.1
Food prepared by consumer unit on trips	47	59	61	79	–20.3	–40.5
Food away from home	**3,173**	**2,992**	**3,709**	**3,306**	**6.1**	**–4.0**
ALCOHOLIC BEVERAGES	**458**	**473**	**484**	**690**	**–3.2**	**–33.6**
HOUSING	**17,258**	**16,081**	**15,578**	**15,075**	**7.3**	**14.5**
Shelter	**10,281**	**9,410**	**8,692**	**7,457**	**9.3**	**37.9**
Owned dwellings	7,686	6,764	5,908	5,062	13.6	51.8
Mortgage interest and charges	4,493	4,035	3,922	3,058	11.3	46.9
Property taxes	1,940	1,668	1,062	1,056	16.3	83.6
Maintenance, repair, insurance, other expenses	1,253	1,060	923	947	18.2	32.3
Rented dwellings	1,826	1,831	1,824	1,400	–0.2	30.4
Other lodging	770	815	959	994	–5.6	–22.6
Utilities, fuels, and public services	**3,693**	**3,240**	**3,522**	**3,940**	**14.0**	**–6.3**
Natural gas	536	390	457	731	37.4	–26.7
Electricity	1,332	1,185	1,415	1,523	12.4	–12.5

(continued)

	average spending				percent change	
	2005	2000	1990	1984	2000–05	1984–05
Fuel oil and other fuels	$172	$124	$166	$293	39.1%	–41.3%
Telephone	1,229	1,142	1,121	1,049	7.6	17.2
Water and other public services	425	399	365	344	6.5	23.6
Household services	**668**	**661**	**471**	**562**	**1.0**	**18.9**
Personal services	132	167	81	79	–20.8	67.2
Other household services	536	493	390	483	8.6	11.0
Housekeeping supplies	**717**	**603**	**722**	**744**	**18.8**	**–3.7**
Laundry and cleaning supplies	154	155	205	224	–0.9	–31.2
Other household products	389	280	296	333	38.9	16.9
Postage and stationery	174	167	221	188	4.4	–7.4
Household furnishings and equipment	**1,899**	**2,167**	**2,171**	**2,372**	**–12.4**	**–19.9**
Household textiles	159	142	217	201	12.2	–20.9
Furniture	423	534	559	594	–20.8	–28.8
Floor coverings	91	58	224	286	57.3	–68.1
Major appliances	239	253	261	344	–5.5	–30.5
Small appliances and miscellaneous housewares	124	143	148	179	–13.2	–30.6
Miscellaneous household equipment	863	1,038	759	769	–16.8	12.3
APPAREL AND RELATED SERVICES	**2,318**	**2,689**	**3,237**	**3,047**	**–13.8**	**–23.9**
Men and boys	**573**	**654**	**853**	**821**	**–12.4**	**–30.2**
Men, aged 16 or older	478	547	752	705	–12.6	–32.2
Boys, aged 2 to 15	95	108	102	118	–11.8	–19.8
Women and girls	**955**	**1,108**	**1,352**	**1,218**	**–13.8**	**–21.6**
Women, aged 16 or older	821	964	1,237	1,062	–14.8	–22.7
Girls, aged 2 to 15	135	143	115	158	–5.5	–14.5
Children under age 2	**52**	**61**	**87**	**86**	**–15.1**	**–39.9**
Footwear	**369**	**497**	**430**	**404**	**–25.7**	**–8.7**
Other apparel products and services	**368**	**369**	**516**	**515**	**–0.2**	**–28.5**
TRANSPORTATION	**9,795**	**10,011**	**10,529**	**11,162**	**–2.2**	**–12.2**
Vehicle purchases	**3,945**	**4,381**	**4,433**	**4,765**	**–10.0**	**–17.2**
Cars and trucks, new	2,160	1,917	2,500	2,492	12.7	–13.3
Cars and trucks, used	1,723	2,413	1,893	2,190	–28.6	–21.3
Gasoline and motor oil	**2,424**	**1,806**	**2,079**	**2,793**	**34.3**	**–13.2**
Other vehicle expenses	**2,850**	**3,253**	**3,343**	**3,011**	**–12.4**	**–5.4**
Vehicle finance charges	331	443	641	581	–25.4	–43.0
Maintenance and repairs	810	908	1,155	1,194	–10.8	–32.1
Vehicle insurance	1,159	1,136	1,172	906	2.0	27.9
Vehicle rentals, leases, licenses, other charges	550	764	375	331	–28.0	66.3
Public transportation	**576**	**573**	**672**	**592**	**0.6**	**–2.7**
HEALTH CARE	**2,672**	**2,495**	**2,386**	**2,340**	**7.1**	**14.2**
Health insurance	1,283	1,107	871	741	15.9	73.2
Medical services	771	793	992	1,147	–2.7	–32.8
Drugs	494	462	353	338	7.0	46.0
Medical supplies	124	134	169	115	–7.3	8.1
ENTERTAINMENT	**3,034**	**2,530**	**2,938**	**2,363**	**19.9**	**28.4**
Fees and admissions	753	722	654	782	4.2	–3.7
Audio and visual equipment and services	1,046	789	885	680	32.5	53.7

(continued)

	average spending				percent change	
	2005	2000	1990	1984	2000–05	1984–05
Pets, toys, hobbies, playground equipment	$539	$436	$613	$425	23.8%	26.9%
Other entertainment products and services	697	583	787	476	19.6	46.6
PERSONAL CARE PRODUCTS AND SERVICES	**627**	**773**	**714**	**729**	**–18.9**	**–14.0**
READING	**143**	**202**	**275**	**303**	**–29.2**	**–52.7**
EDUCATION	**1,769**	**1,300**	**1,094**	**932**	**36.1**	**89.7**
TOBACCO PRODUCTS AND SMOKING SUPPLIES	**427**	**426**	**539**	**613**	**0.1**	**–30.3**
MISCELLANEOUS	**949**	**1,051**	**1,639**	**1,090**	**–9.7**	**–13.0**
CASH CONTRIBUTIONS	**2,076**	**1,743**	**1,941**	**2,030**	**19.1**	**2.3**
PERSONAL INSURANCE AND PENSIONS	**7,348**	**5,438**	**5,748**	**5,406**	**35.1**	**35.9**
Life and other personal insurance	474	623	829	912	–23.9	–48.0
Pensions and Social Security*	6,874	4,816	4,919	4,494	42.7	52.9
PERSONAL TAXES	**3,824**	**5,376**	**6,082**	**5,776**	**–28.9**	**–33.8**
Federal income taxes	2,794	4,204	4,783	4,523	–33.5	–38.2
State and local income taxes	823	962	1,157	1,101	–14.4	–25.3
Other taxes	208	210	142	154	–0.9	34.9
GIFTS FOR PEOPLE IN OTHER HOUSEHOLDS	**1,855**	**1,955**	**2,651**	**2,038**	**–5.1**	**–9.0**

* Because of changes in methodology, the 2005 data on pensions and Social Security are not comparable with earlier years.
Note: Spending by category will not add to total spending because gift spending is also included in the preceding product and service categories and personal taxes are not included in the total.
Source: Bureau of Labor Statistics, 1984, 1990, 2000, and 2005 Consumer Expenditure Surveys, Internet site http://www.bls .gov/cex/; calculations by New Strategist

Table 9.7 Average Spending by Householders Aged 55 to 64, 1984 to 2005

(average annual spending of consumer units headed by people aged 55 to 64, 1984 to 2005; percent change for selected years; in 2005 dollars)

	average spending				percent change	
	2005	2000	1990	1984	2000–05	1984–05
Number of consumer units 55 to 64 (in 000s)	18,104	14,161	12,162	13,343	27.8%	35.7%
Average annual spending of consumer units	$49,592	$44,617	$43,727	$43,987	11.1	12.7
FOOD	$6,202	$5,861	$6,620	$6,513	5.8%	–4.8%
Food at home	3,487	3,483	3,887	3,979	0.1	–12.4
Cereals and bakery products	465	500	565	524	–7.0	–11.3
Cereals and cereal products	139	159	193	143	–12.5	–2.7
Bakery products	326	341	372	382	–4.5	–14.6
Meats, poultry, fish, and eggs	827	944	1,116	1,177	–12.4	–29.7
Beef	250	276	345	389	–9.3	–35.7
Pork	167	211	229	246	–20.8	–32.2
Other meats	107	112	172	171	–4.7	–37.4
Poultry	134	166	187	177	–19.1	–24.2
Fish and seafood	132	130	134	113	1.2	17.0
Eggs	36	49	49	79	–26.2	–54.4
Dairy products	377	364	435	494	3.6	–23.7
Fresh milk and cream	139	143	191	237	–2.7	–41.3
Other dairy products	238	221	244	258	7.6	–7.6
Fruits and vegetables	626	633	668	680	–1.1	–8.0
Fresh fruits	211	210	232	214	0.6	–1.5
Fresh vegetables	214	196	196	207	9.1	3.5
Processed fruits	104	130	131	143	–20.3	–27.2
Processed vegetables	97	99	108	117	–1.7	–16.8
Other food at home	1,192	1,041	1,101	1,023	14.5	16.6
Sugar and other sweets	129	130	142	154	–1.1	–16.3
Fats and oils	94	102	108	118	–7.9	–20.6
Miscellaneous foods	594	451	453	404	31.6	47.0
Nonalcoholic beverages	317	298	323	346	6.3	–8.3
Food prepared by consumer unit on trips	58	59	76	79	–1.7	–26.5
Food away from home	2,715	2,378	2,734	2,534	14.2	7.2
ALCOHOLIC BEVERAGES	454	421	380	558	7.9	–18.7
HOUSING	15,769	14,020	12,640	12,643	12.5	24.7
Shelter	8,686	7,471	6,306	5,865	16.3	48.1
Owned dwellings	6,650	5,421	4,292	3,844	22.7	73.0
Mortgage interest and charges	3,076	2,584	1,866	1,440	19.1	113.6
Property taxes	1,883	1,658	1,270	1,348	13.6	39.7
Maintenance, repair, insurance, other expenses	1,692	1,180	1,154	1,056	43.4	60.2
Rented dwellings	1,290	1,274	1,304	1,188	1.3	8.6
Other lodging	747	777	711	833	–3.8	–10.3
Utilities, fuels, and public services	3,427	3,126	3,228	3,530	9.6	–2.9
Natural gas	521	387	435	733	34.7	–28.9
Electricity	1,255	1,189	1,372	1,338	5.6	–6.2

(continued)

	average spending				percent change	
	2005	2000	1990	1984	2000–05	1984–05
Fuel oil and other fuels	$172	$128	$193	$316	34.2%	−45.5%
Telephone	1,077	1,031	882	848	4.5	27.0
Water and other public services	402	391	347	293	2.7	37.1
Household services	**689**	**615**	**577**	**496**	**12.1**	**38.8**
Personal services	71	105	85	73	−32.7	−3.1
Other household services	618	509	490	423	21.4	46.1
Housekeeping supplies	**736**	**663**	**729**	**645**	**10.9**	**14.2**
Laundry and cleaning supplies	150	209	187	179	−28.1	−16.0
Other household products	383	297	336	286	28.9	34.1
Postage and stationery	203	158	206	179	28.8	13.7
Household furnishings and equipment	**2,231**	**2,145**	**1,801**	**2,109**	**4.0**	**5.8**
Household textiles	153	142	182	165	7.9	−7.5
Furniture	527	409	553	532	28.7	−0.9
Floor coverings	83	64	136	318	30.7	−73.9
Major appliances	298	251	281	318	18.9	−6.2
Small appliances and miscellaneous housewares	140	120	134	148	16.5	−5.7
Miscellaneous household equipment	1,031	1,159	516	628	−11.1	64.2
APPAREL AND RELATED SERVICES	**1,784**	**1,921**	**2,331**	**2,513**	**−7.1**	**−29.0**
Men and boys	**397**	**448**	**535**	**598**	**−11.4**	**−33.6**
Men, aged 16 or older	359	399	486	532	−10.1	−32.5
Boys, aged 2 to 15	38	48	51	66	−20.2	−42.2
Women and girls	**709**	**779**	**1,031**	**1,070**	**−9.0**	**−33.7**
Women, aged 16 or older	650	715	986	1,006	−9.0	−35.4
Girls, aged 2 to 15	59	65	45	64	−8.7	−7.7
Children under age 2	**58**	**60**	**76**	**56**	**−3.5**	**2.9**
Footwear	**298**	**340**	**324**	**393**	**−12.4**	**−24.1**
Other apparel products and services	**323**	**294**	**363**	**398**	**10.0**	**−18.9**
TRANSPORTATION	**8,908**	**8,894**	**7,915**	**8,444**	**0.2**	**5.5**
Vehicle purchases	**3,756**	**4,109**	**3,009**	**3,410**	**−8.6**	**10.2**
Cars and trucks, new	2,370	2,378	1,709	2,199	−0.3	7.8
Cars and trucks, used	1,296	1,710	1,275	1,199	−24.2	8.1
Gasoline and motor oil	**2,101**	**1,530**	**1,694**	**2,133**	**37.3**	**−1.5**
Other vehicle expenses	**2,513**	**2,694**	**2,594**	**2,321**	**−6.7**	**8.3**
Vehicle finance charges	289	396	391	353	−27.0	−18.2
Maintenance and repairs	738	762	982	955	−3.2	−22.7
Vehicle insurance	944	903	965	765	4.6	23.4
Vehicle rentals, leases, licenses, other charges	542	634	254	246	−14.5	120.1
Public transportation	**537**	**561**	**619**	**579**	**−4.3**	**−7.2**
HEALTH CARE	**3,410**	**2,844**	**2,676**	**2,359**	**19.9**	**44.6**
Health insurance	1,585	1,284	1,046	852	23.5	86.1
Medical services	979	818	977	987	19.7	−0.8
Drugs	713	610	508	415	16.9	71.6
Medical supplies	134	133	143	105	1.0	27.3
ENTERTAINMENT	**2,429**	**2,217**	**2,252**	**2,004**	**9.5**	**21.2**
Fees and admissions	633	577	545	586	9.7	7.9
Audio and visual equipment and services	862	659	583	523	30.8	65.0

(continued)

	average spending				percent change	
	2005	**2000**	**1990**	**1984**	**2000–05**	**1984–05**
Pets, toys, hobbies, playground equipment	$526	$406	$381	$323	29.5%	62.7%
Other entertainment products and services	408	575	743	571	−29.0	−28.6
PERSONAL CARE PRODUCTS AND SERVICES	**550**	**645**	**616**	**613**	**−14.8**	**−10.2**
READING	**167**	**203**	**244**	**265**	**−17.7**	**−37.0**
EDUCATION	**733**	**431**	**562**	**466**	**70.1**	**57.2**
TOBACCO PRODUCTS AND SMOKING SUPPLIES	**336**	**396**	**487**	**496**	**−15.1**	**−32.3**
MISCELLANEOUS	**981**	**935**	**1,237**	**872**	**5.0**	**12.5**
CASH CONTRIBUTIONS	**1,960**	**1,476**	**1,349**	**1,643**	**32.8**	**19.3**
PERSONAL INSURANCE AND PENSIONS	**5,909**	**4,353**	**4,420**	**4,598**	**35.7**	**28.5**
Life and other personal insurance	541	666	698	868	−18.7	−37.7
Pensions and Social Security*	5,368	3,688	3,722	3,729	45.5	43.9
PERSONAL TAXES	**3,088**	**4,535**	**5,240**	**4,594**	**−31.9**	**−32.8**
Federal income taxes	2,192	3,473	4,157	3,491	−36.9	−37.2
State and local income taxes	631	796	941	906	−20.7	−30.4
Other taxes	264	267	142	197	−0.9	33.8
GIFTS FOR PEOPLE IN OTHER HOUSEHOLDS	**1,855**	**1,525**	**1,706**	**1,821**	**21.6**	**1.8**

* Because of changes in methodology, the 2005 data on pensions and Social Security are not comparable with earlier years.
Note: Spending by category will not add to total spending because gift spending is also included in the preceding product and service categories and personal taxes are not included in the total.
Source: Bureau of Labor Statistics, 1984, 1990, 2000, and 2005 Consumer Expenditure Surveys, Internet site http://www.bls.gov/cex/; calculations by New Strategist

Table 9.8 Average Spending by Householders Aged 65 to 74, 1984 to 2005

(average annual spending of consumer units headed by people aged 65 to 74, 1984 to 2005; percent change for selected years; in 2005 dollars)

	average spending				percent change	
	2005	2000	1990	1984	2000–05	1984–05
Number of consumer units 65 to 74 (in 000s)	11,505	11,538	11,318	10,761	−0.3%	6.9%
Average annual spending of consumer units	$38,573	$34,911	$31,232	$29,778	10.5	29.5
FOOD	**$4,899**	**$4,738**	**$4,939**	**$4,846**	**3.4%**	**1.1%**
Food at home	**2,967**	**3,130**	**3,147**	**3,179**	**−5.2**	**−6.7**
Cereals and bakery products	405	470	484	430	−13.7	−5.9
Cereals and cereal products	114	151	154	133	−24.4	−14.6
Bakery products	291	319	330	297	−8.7	−2.0
Meats, poultry, fish, and eggs	691	825	894	949	−16.2	−27.2
Beef	189	246	309	320	−23.2	−40.9
Pork	152	191	175	212	−20.2	−28.4
Other meats	92	98	123	118	−5.7	−22.3
Poultry	104	147	146	130	−29.5	−19.8
Fish and seafood	124	108	99	109	15.1	13.7
Eggs	30	36	40	60	−17.3	−50.1
Dairy products	344	352	369	383	−2.2	−10.3
Fresh milk and cream	128	134	182	188	−4.4	−31.9
Other dairy products	216	218	188	195	−0.8	10.5
Fruits and vegetables	553	600	586	571	−7.8	−3.2
Fresh fruits	192	186	191	184	3.2	4.2
Fresh vegetables	172	184	172	164	−6.4	5.2
Processed fruits	106	135	133	133	−21.5	−20.6
Processed vegetables	83	95	91	90	−12.9	−8.0
Other food at home	974	884	814	791	10.2	23.1
Sugar and other sweets	118	119	118	124	−0.9	−4.9
Fats and oils	79	99	96	88	−19.9	−10.6
Miscellaneous foods	488	395	330	297	23.6	64.3
Nonalcoholic beverages	238	226	230	284	5.5	−16.1
Food prepared by consumer unit on trips	51	45	40	51	12.4	0.5
Food away from home	**1,933**	**1,608**	**1,792**	**1,665**	**20.2**	**16.1**
ALCOHOLIC BEVERAGES	**325**	**296**	**248**	**295**	**9.8**	**10.1**
HOUSING	**12,474**	**10,968**	**9,636**	**9,212**	**13.7**	**35.4**
Shelter	**6,423**	**5,800**	**4,764**	**4,128**	**10.7**	**55.6**
Owned dwellings	4,664	4,104	3,110	2,365	13.6	97.2
Mortgage interest and charges	1,570	1,337	849	464	17.4	238.2
Property taxes	1,659	1,443	1,231	972	15.0	70.7
Maintenance, repair, insurance, other expenses	1,435	1,325	1,030	930	8.3	54.2
Rented dwellings	1,140	1,080	1,097	1,047	5.6	8.9
Other lodging	619	616	557	716	0.5	−13.6
Utilities, fuels, and public services	**3,091**	**2,765**	**2,746**	**2,985**	**11.8**	**3.6**
Natural gas	504	361	427	596	39.7	−15.4
Electricity	1,151	1,045	1,095	1,100	10.2	4.7

(continued)

	average spending				percent change	
	2005	**2000**	**1990**	**1984**	**2000–05**	**1984–05**
Fuel oil and other fuels	$199	$171	$193	$387	16.2%	–48.6%
Telephone	845	817	711	641	3.5	31.8
Water and other public services	392	372	321	261	5.4	50.0
Household services	**677**	**565**	**511**	**474**	**19.9**	**42.9**
Personal services	95	112	43	41	–15.4	129.7
Other household services	582	453	468	432	28.6	34.6
Housekeeping supplies	**644**	**580**	**541**	**555**	**11.1**	**16.1**
Laundry and cleaning supplies	122	125	129	130	–2.2	–5.9
Other household products	326	273	220	227	19.3	43.3
Postage and stationery	195	181	194	197	7.5	–1.2
Household furnishings and equipment	**1,640**	**1,259**	**1,073**	**1,070**	**30.3**	**53.3**
Household textiles	114	115	134	145	–0.5	–21.2
Furniture	442	290	218	224	52.2	97.6
Floor coverings	34	45	84	86	–25.1	–60.7
Major appliances	217	222	172	216	–2.4	0.4
Small appliances and miscellaneous housewares	120	77	91	100	55.6	20.5
Miscellaneous household equipment	713	510	374	299	39.7	138.6
APPAREL AND RELATED SERVICES	**1,313**	**1,282**	**1,452**	**1,658**	**2.5**	**–20.8**
Men and boys	**276**	**305**	**260**	**376**	**–9.5**	**–26.6**
Men, aged 16 or older	241	272	227	357	–11.5	–32.5
Boys, aged 2 to 15	35	33	33	21	6.4	69.3
Women and girls	**629**	**512**	**776**	**852**	**23.0**	**–26.1**
Women, aged 16 or older	593	477	732	816	24.2	–27.3
Girls, aged 2 to 15	36	35	43	36	2.4	0.8
Children under age 2	**31**	**35**	**28**	**30**	**–11.8**	**3.1**
Footwear	**189**	**211**	**200**	**180**	**–10.4**	**4.7**
Other apparel products and services	**188**	**218**	**190**	**218**	**–13.7**	**–13.8**
TRANSPORTATION	**6,568**	**6,575**	**5,175**	**5,633**	**–0.1**	**16.6**
Vehicle purchases	**2,608**	**2,984**	**1,738**	**2,117**	**–12.6**	**23.2**
Cars and trucks, new	1,761	1,641	1,049	1,440	7.3	22.3
Cars and trucks, used	833	1,330	689	677	–37.4	23.1
Gasoline and motor oil	**1,567**	**1,087**	**1,183**	**1,470**	**44.2**	**6.6**
Other vehicle expenses	**1,926**	**2,003**	**1,850**	**1,564**	**–3.8**	**23.2**
Vehicle finance charges	167	206	212	150	–19.1	11.1
Maintenance and repairs	657	633	732	720	3.8	–8.7
Vehicle insurance	737	763	702	541	–3.4	36.1
Vehicle rentals, leases, licenses, other charges	366	400	202	152	–8.6	140.4
Public transportation	**467**	**501**	**405**	**483**	**–6.8**	**–3.3**
HEALTH CARE	**4,176**	**3,587**	**3,283**	**2,791**	**16.4**	**49.6**
Health insurance	2,352	1,824	1,515	1,229	29.0	91.3
Medical services	733	778	980	868	–5.8	–15.6
Drugs	956	844	680	515	13.3	85.6
Medical supplies	134	143	109	179	–6.2	–25.0
ENTERTAINMENT	**2,143**	**1,591**	**1,366**	**1,118**	**34.7**	**91.6**
Fees and admissions	548	472	492	425	16.1	29.0
Audio and visual equipment and services	797	531	459	312	50.2	155.4

(continued)

	average spending				percent change	
	2005	**2000**	**1990**	**1984**	**2000–05**	**1984–05**
Pets, toys, hobbies, playground equipment	$327	$297	$241	$203	10.0%	61.1%
Other entertainment products and services	471	291	173	179	61.6	163.8
PERSONAL CARE PRODUCTS AND SERVICES	**495**	**543**	**456**	**468**	**–8.9**	**5.8**
READING	**154**	**188**	**233**	**231**	**–18.2**	**–33.4**
EDUCATION	**256**	**169**	**72**	**143**	**51.5**	**79.2**
TOBACCO PRODUCTS AND SMOKING SUPPLIES	**228**	**253**	**312**	**314**	**–9.9**	**–27.4**
MISCELLANEOUS	**1,037**	**863**	**1,058**	**449**	**20.2**	**130.8**
CASH CONTRIBUTIONS	**1,925**	**2,293**	**1,400**	**1,280**	**–16.1**	**50.4**
PERSONAL INSURANCE AND PENSIONS	**2,580**	**1,564**	**1,600**	**1,336**	**65.0**	**93.0**
Life and other personal insurance	449	583	510	430	–23.0	4.3
Pensions and Social Security*	2,132	981	1,091	906	117.3	135.3
PERSONAL TAXES	**1,226**	**2,037**	**2,059**	**1,806**	**–39.8**	**–32.1**
Federal income taxes	862	1,517	1,615	1,331	–43.2	–35.2
State and local income taxes	113	227	317	288	–50.2	–60.7
Other taxes	250	291	127	188	–14.2	33.0
GIFTS FOR PEOPLE IN OTHER HOUSEHOLDS	**1,071**	**1,098**	**1,097**	**972**	**–2.4**	**10.2**

Because of changes in methodology, the 2005 data on pensions and Social Security are not comparable with earlier years.
Note: Spending by category will not add to total spending because gift spending is also included in the preceding product and service categories and personal taxes are not included in the total.
Source: Bureau of Labor Statistics, 1984, 1990, 2000, and 2005 Consumer Expenditure Surveys, Internet site http://www.bls.gov/cex/; calculations by New Strategist

Table 9.9 Average Spending by Householders Aged 75 or Older, 1984 to 2005

(average annual spending of consumer units headed by people aged 75 or older, 1984 to 2005; percent change for selected years; in 2005 dollars)

	average spending				percent change	
	2005	2000	1990	1984	2000–05	1984–05
Number of consumer units 75 or older (in 000s)	11,342	10,617	8,761	7,105	6.8%	59.6%
Average annual spending of consumer units	$27,018	$24,847	$23,086	$20,906	8.7	29.2
FOOD	**$3,388**	**$3,490**	**$3,595**	**$3,273**	**−2.9%**	**3.5%**
Food at home	**2,222**	**2,389**	**2,472**	**2,380**	**−7.0**	**−6.6**
Cereals and bakery products	326	379	400	350	−13.9	−6.8
Cereals and cereal products	97	127	131	103	−23.6	−6.2
Bakery products	229	252	267	246	−9.0	−7.0
Meats, poultry, fish, and eggs	440	584	605	671	−24.7	−34.4
Beef	108	163	173	205	−33.9	−47.3
Pork	98	132	127	124	−25.5	−21.0
Other meats	65	79	82	83	−18.1	−21.4
Poultry	65	95	105	103	−31.8	−37.1
Fish and seafood	79	83	85	111	−4.6	−28.8
Eggs	25	32	33	45	−21.3	−44.6
Dairy products	269	268	300	318	0.5	−15.3
Fresh milk and cream	109	118	151	162	−7.6	−32.6
Other dairy products	160	150	151	156	6.9	2.6
Fruits and vegetables	424	518	519	445	−18.2	−4.8
Fresh fruits	146	198	179	147	−26.4	−0.4
Fresh vegetables	122	145	127	122	−16.0	−0.1
Processed fruits	96	110	134	107	−12.7	−10.4
Processed vegetables	61	65	78	70	−5.6	−12.3
Other food at home	762	639	647	588	19.3	29.5
Sugar and other sweets	95	91	103	102	4.7	−6.4
Fats and oils	64	68	72	75	−5.9	−14.9
Miscellaneous foods	408	290	272	203	40.5	101.0
Nonalcoholic beverages	167	171	185	207	−2.5	−19.2
Food prepared by consumer unit on trips	29	19	15	8	50.4	285.7
Food away from home	**1,166**	**1,101**	**1,124**	**893**	**5.9**	**30.6**
ALCOHOLIC BEVERAGES	**167**	**176**	**106**	**126**	**−5.0**	**32.6**
HOUSING	**9,612**	**8,808**	**8,172**	**7,530**	**9.1**	**27.6**
Shelter	**5,240**	**4,575**	**4,176**	**3,500**	**14.5**	**49.7**
Owned dwellings	3,132	2,742	2,419	1,763	14.2	77.6
Mortgage interest and charges	542	425	160	212	27.4	155.2
Property taxes	1,387	1,214	1,012	737	14.3	88.2
Maintenance, repair, insurance, other expenses	1,204	1,104	1,248	812	9.1	48.3
Rented dwellings	1,850	1,524	1,455	1,466	21.4	26.2
Other lodging	258	308	302	271	−16.4	−4.7
Utilities, fuels, and public services	**2,531**	**2,197**	**2,264**	**2,429**	**15.2**	**4.2**
Natural gas	474	341	321	472	38.8	0.5
Electricity	905	839	906	808	7.8	12.0

(continued)

	average spending				percent change	
	2005	**2000**	**1990**	**1984**	**2000–05**	**1984–05**
Fuel oil and other fuels	$192	$137	$221	$440	39.9%	–56.3%
Telephone	619	580	562	500	6.8	23.8
Water and other public services	341	299	253	209	13.9	63.4
Household services	**623**	**952**	**687**	**626**	**–34.5**	**–0.5**
Personal services	130	386	282	107	–66.3	21.3
Other household services	493	565	405	519	–12.7	–5.0
Housekeeping supplies	**418**	**365**	**408**	**325**	**14.5**	**28.5**
Laundry and cleaning supplies	89	90	105	85	–0.7	5.2
Other household products	212	166	157	124	28.0	70.9
Postage and stationery	116	110	146	115	5.4	1.2
Household furnishings and equipment	**800**	**719**	**635**	**650**	**11.3**	**23.0**
Household textiles	66	49	51	147	35.3	–55.0
Furniture	168	160	136	130	5.1	29.5
Floor coverings	21	41	79	68	–48.6	–69.0
Major appliances	192	138	133	105	38.8	82.4
Small appliances and miscellaneous housewares	68	44	60	41	53.7	64.4
Miscellaneous household equipment	285	288	175	162	–1.1	76.3
APPAREL AND RELATED SERVICES	**584**	**795**	**731**	**810**	**–26.5**	**–27.9**
Men and boys	**101**	**133**	**112**	**150**	**–23.9**	**–32.8**
Men, aged 16 or older	94	122	106	141	–23.3	–33.3
Boys, aged 2 to 15	7	10	6	9	–31.4	–25.5
Women and girls	**257**	**389**	**360**	**383**	**–33.9**	**–33.0**
Women, aged 16 or older	244	375	345	367	–35.0	–33.4
Girls, aged 2 to 15	14	14	15	17	2.9	–17.2
Children under age 2	**13**	**9**	**19**	**15**	**43.3**	**–13.5**
Footwear	**128**	**147**	**130**	**145**	**–13.2**	**–11.6**
Other apparel products and services	**85**	**117**	**109**	**115**	**–27.2**	**–25.9**
TRANSPORTATION	**3,754**	**3,261**	**3,184**	**2,656**	**15.1**	**41.3**
Vehicle purchases	**1,398**	**1,263**	**1,376**	**684**	**10.7**	**104.3**
Cars and trucks, new	973	763	840	430	27.5	126.0
Cars and trucks, used	424	500	536	224	–15.2	89.6
Gasoline and motor oil	**843**	**557**	**592**	**726**	**51.4**	**16.2**
Other vehicle expenses	**1,257**	**1,074**	**944**	**874**	**17.0**	**43.8**
Vehicle finance charges	52	49	42	47	6.6	10.7
Maintenance and repairs	427	356	371	376	19.9	13.6
Vehicle insurance	577	489	442	372	18.0	55.0
Vehicle rentals, leases, licenses, other charges	201	180	90	77	11.5	160.8
Public transportation	**256**	**365**	**272**	**372**	**–29.9**	**–31.2**
HEALTH CARE	**4,210**	**3,786**	**3,322**	**2,827**	**11.2**	**48.9**
Health insurance	2,260	1,850	1,434	1,071	22.2	110.9
Medical services	805	746	1,007	994	7.9	–19.0
Drugs	998	1,030	749	538	–3.1	85.6
Medical supplies	146	160	131	224	–8.7	–34.7
ENTERTAINMENT	**1,032**	**802**	**632**	**699**	**28.7**	**47.6**
Fees and admissions	282	243	229	222	16.2	27.1
Audio and visual equipment and services	484	369	241	353	31.3	37.0

(continued)

	average spending				percent change	
	2005	2000	1990	1984	2000–05	1984–05
Pets, toys, hobbies, playground equipment	$137	$118	$124	$90	16.1%	51.8%
Other entertainment products and services	129	71	39	34	80.5	281.3
PERSONAL CARE PRODUCTS AND SERVICES	**427**	**417**	**326**	**316**	**2.3**	**35.2**
READING	**132**	**145**	**167**	**158**	**–9.1**	**–16.4**
EDUCATION	**165**	**71**	**91**	**171**	**130.9**	**–3.5**
TOBACCO PRODUCTS AND SMOKING SUPPLIES	**102**	**112**	**136**	**126**	**–9.2**	**–19.0**
MISCELLANEOUS	**635**	**627**	**527**	**293**	**1.2**	**116.6**
CASH CONTRIBUTIONS	**1,852**	**1,835**	**1,705**	**1,504**	**0.9**	**23.2**
PERSONAL INSURANCE AND PENSIONS	**959**	**522**	**390**	**417**	**83.8**	**129.8**
Life and other personal insurance	357	261	196	169	36.9	111.0
Pensions and Social Security*	601	262	194	246	129.4	144.1
PERSONAL TAXES	**628**	**912**	**1,239**	**1,425**	**–31.1**	**–55.9**
Federal income taxes	357	651	932	1,171	–45.2	–69.5
State and local income taxes	81	94	167	182	–14.0	–55.6
Other taxes	190	167	139	73	14.0	159.2
GIFTS FOR PEOPLE IN OTHER HOUSEHOLDS	**676**	**856**	**808**	**925**	**–21.1**	**–26.9**

Because of changes in methodology, the 2005 data on pensions and Social Security are not comparable with earlier years.
Note: Spending by category will not add to total spending because gift spending is also included in the preceding product and service categories and personal taxes are not included in the total.
Source: Bureau of Labor Statistics, 1984, 1990, 2000, and 2005 Consumer Expenditure Surveys, Internet site http://www.bls.gov/cex/; calculations by New Strategist

Blacks and Hispanics Spend Less than Average

But their spending has grown faster than average over the past two decades.

Black households spent $32,849 in 2005, just 71 percent as much as the average household. Hispanic households spent $40,123, or 86 percent as much as the average. Between 1984 and 2005, however, the spending of black and Hispanic households grew faster than average. While the average household boosted spending by 12 percent during those years, after adjusting for inflation, black households saw their spending grow by 19 percent. Hispanic spending was up 15 percent.

Black spending grew strongly between 1984 and 2005 on items such as mortgage interest (up 48 percent) and new cars and trucks (up 33 percent). Their spending on entertainment increased 33 percent. Behind these gains was the growing black middle class. The average Hispanic household boosted its spending on food-away-from-home by 43 percent as fast-food substituted for home-cooked meals. They spent only 19 percent more on health insurance, however, since many Hispanics do not have coverage.

■ The spending of black households will remain below average because few are headed by married couples—the most affluent household type. The spending of Hispanics will remain below average because many are recent immigrants with low incomes.

Hispanics spend more than blacks

(average annual spending of consumer units by race and Hispanic origin of householder, 2005)

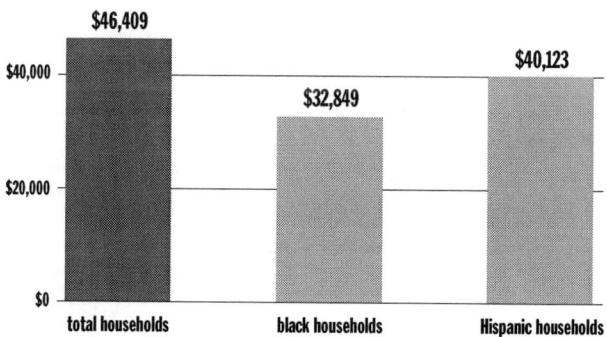

Table 9.10 Average Spending by Black Householders, 1984 to 2005

(average annual spending of consumer units headed by blacks, 1984 to 2005; percent change for selected years; in 2005 dollars)

	average spending				percent change	
	2005	2000	1990	1984	2000–05	1984–05
Number of consumer units headed by blacks (in 000s)	14,042	13,230	11,128	9,389	6.1%	49.6%
Average annual spending of consumer units	$32,849	$31,929	$28,593	$27,502	2.9	19.4
FOOD	$4,319	$4,644	$4,677	$4,318	–7.0%	0.0%
Food at home	2,663	3,052	3,178	2,962	–12.7	–10.1
Cereals and bakery products	363	446	432	387	–18.6	–6.3
Cereals and cereal products	132	180	176	150	–26.8	–12.2
Bakery products	231	265	256	239	–13.0	–3.2
Meats, poultry, fish, and eggs	787	1,031	1,089	1,139	–23.7	–30.9
Beef	193	268	314	325	–27.9	–40.6
Pork	170	226	261	258	–24.7	–34.0
Other meats	90	120	139	133	–25.1	–32.6
Poultry	177	210	199	201	–15.6	–12.0
Fish and seafood	121	158	126	150	–23.2	–19.5
Eggs	35	49	51	71	–28.2	–51.0
Dairy products	245	278	293	316	–11.8	–22.4
Fresh milk and cream	98	116	142	184	–15.3	–46.8
Other dairy products	147	162	151	132	–9.4	11.7
Fruits and vegetables	428	515	544	481	–16.9	–11.1
Fresh fruits	122	149	157	137	–17.9	–11.1
Fresh vegetables	122	146	151	145	–16.6	–15.7
Processed fruits	99	134	137	111	–26.0	–10.7
Processed vegetables	85	86	97	88	–1.4	–3.8
Other food at home	840	784	820	630	7.2	33.4
Sugar and other sweets	82	101	112	98	–18.8	–16.1
Fats and oils	79	94	96	88	–16.1	–10.6
Miscellaneous foods	432	358	369	227	20.5	89.9
Nonalcoholic beverages	230	211	235	216	9.0	6.4
Food prepared by consumer unit on trips	17	19	9	11	–11.8	50.7
Food away from home	1,657	1,592	1,499	1,353	4.1	22.4
ALCOHOLIC BEVERAGES	173	239	242	329	–27.7	–47.4
HOUSING	11,650	11,235	9,394	8,962	3.7	30.0
Shelter	6,524	6,440	5,079	4,530	1.3	44.0
Owned dwellings	3,188	2,957	2,146	1,998	7.8	59.6
Mortgage interest and charges	1,998	1,785	1,473	1,350	11.9	48.0
Property taxes	734	726	256	312	1.1	135.2
Maintenance, repair, insurance, other expenses	456	446	418	335	2.3	36.3
Rented dwellings	3,148	3,224	2,797	2,303	–2.4	36.7
Other lodging	189	257	134	231	–26.6	–18.3
Utilities, fuels, and public services	3,253	2,916	2,646	2,917	11.6	11.5
Natural gas	549	388	417	598	41.5	–8.2
Electricity	1,205	1,064	994	1,060	13.3	13.7

(continued)

	average spending				percent change	
	2005	**2000**	**1990**	**1984**	**2000–05**	**1984–05**
Fuel oil and other fuels	$45	$49	$72	$169	−7.7%	−73.4%
Telephone	1,124	1,118	932	868	0.5	29.4
Water and other public services	330	296	232	224	11.5	47.5
Household services	**530**	**531**	**308**	**299**	**−0.1**	**77.3**
Personal services	289	331	185	179	−12.7	61.8
Other household services	241	200	121	118	20.7	103.5
Housekeeping supplies	**352**	**344**	**444**	**363**	**2.4**	**−3.0**
Laundry and cleaning supplies	119	143	173	152	−16.7	−21.8
Other household products	160	143	163	128	12.0	25.2
Postage and stationery	74	58	108	83	27.9	−10.5
Household furnishings and equipment	**991**	**1,006**	**917**	**852**	**−1.5**	**16.4**
Household textiles	93	65	70	79	43.9	17.8
Furniture	298	321	299	286	−7.2	4.3
Floor coverings	16	28	40	28	−43.6	−43.3
Major appliances	143	122	164	182	16.7	−21.6
Small appliances and miscellaneous housewares	46	41	52	79	12.7	−41.7
Miscellaneous household equipment	393	428	291	197	−8.1	99.1
APPAREL AND RELATED SERVICES	**1,981**	**1,922**	**2,104**	**2,109**	**3.0**	**−6.1**
Men and boys	**420**	**442**	**524**	**457**	**−5.0**	**−8.0**
Men, aged 16 or older	297	278	356	353	6.9	−16.0
Boys, aged 2 to 15	123	164	169	102	−25.2	21.2
Women and girls	**765**	**685**	**784**	**838**	**11.7**	**−8.7**
Women, aged 16 or older	635	536	656	709	18.4	−10.4
Girls, aged 2 to 15	130	149	129	130	−12.5	0.2
Children under age 2	**77**	**101**	**106**	**73**	**−23.7**	**5.0**
Footwear	**493**	**399**	**347**	**378**	**23.5**	**30.5**
Other apparel products and services	**226**	**295**	**341**	**365**	**−23.4**	**−38.0**
TRANSPORTATION	**5,850**	**5,913**	**4,795**	**5,090**	**−1.1**	**14.9**
Vehicle purchases	**2,350**	**2,592**	**1,714**	**1,637**	**−9.3**	**43.5**
Cars and trucks, new	988	986	741	742	0.2	33.1
Cars and trucks, used	1,307	1,604	973	878	−18.5	48.9
Gasoline and motor oil	**1,546**	**1,084**	**1,076**	**1,590**	**42.6**	**−2.8**
Other vehicle expenses	**1,710**	**1,934**	**1,660**	**1,509**	**−11.6**	**13.3**
Vehicle finance charges	229	329	327	271	−30.4	−15.4
Maintenance and repairs	433	513	592	669	−15.5	−35.3
Vehicle insurance	747	719	553	427	3.9	75.1
Vehicle rentals, leases, licenses, other charges	301	374	187	141	−19.6	113.5
Public transportation	**245**	**304**	**345**	**355**	**−19.4**	**−31.0**
HEALTH CARE	**1,448**	**1,256**	**1,166**	**1,158**	**15.3**	**25.1**
Health insurance	841	725	513	483	16.0	74.1
Medical services	321	217	389	408	48.2	−21.3
Drugs	244	267	203	218	−8.5	11.9
Medical supplies	43	47	61	49	−7.5	−12.0
ENTERTAINMENT	**1,242**	**1,150**	**947**	**934**	**8.0**	**32.9**
Fees and admissions	201	205	206	203	−2.1	−1.0
Audio and visual equipment and services	797	643	499	410	23.9	94.5

(continued)

	average spending				percent change	
	2005	2000	1990	1984	2000–05	1984–05
Pets, toys, hobbies, playground equipment	$128	$180	$175	$156	−29.0%	−18.0%
Other entertainment products and services	117	121	69	167	−3.6	−30.1
PERSONAL CARE PRODUCTS AND SERVICES	472	711	450	434	−33.6	8.7
READING	52	82	108	126	−36.3	−58.7
EDUCATION	500	434	311	382	15.1	31.0
TOBACCO PRODUCTS AND SMOKING SUPPLIES	216	276	321	344	−21.6	−37.2
MISCELLANEOUS	416	649	704	590	−35.9	−29.5
CASH CONTRIBUTIONS	1,204	794	804	588	51.7	104.6
PERSONAL INSURANCE AND PENSIONS	3,325	2,623	2,572	2,139	26.7	55.4
Life and other personal insurance	292	406	436	476	−28.1	−38.6
Pensions and Social Security*	3,033	2,217	2,135	1,664	36.8	82.3
PERSONAL TAXES	603	1,844	2,781	2,438	−67.3	−75.3
Federal income taxes	287	1,406	2,105	1,846	−79.6	−84.5
State and local income taxes	257	383	637	541	−33.0	−52.5
Other taxes	59	54	39	49	8.4	20.7
GIFTS FOR PEOPLE IN OTHER HOUSEHOLDS	587	648	589	671	−9.4	−12.5

* Because of changes in methodology, the 2005 data on pensions and Social Security are not comparable with earlier years.
Note: Spending by category will not add to total spending because gift spending is also included in the preceding product and service categories and personal taxes are not included in the total.
Source: Bureau of Labor Statistics, 1984, 1990, 2000, and 2005 Consumer Expenditure Surveys, Internet site http://www.bls.gov/cex/; calculations by New Strategist

Table 9.11 Average Spending by Hispanic Householders, 1994 to 2005

(average annual spending of consumer units headed by Hispanics, 1994 to 2005; percent change for selected years; in 2005 dollars)

	average spending			percent change	
	2005	2000	1994	2000–05	1994–05
Number of consumer units headed by Hispanics (in 000s)	12,462	9,473	7,730	31.6%	61.2%
Average annual spending of consumer units	$40,123	$37,126	$34,834	8.1	15.2
FOOD	$5,551	$6,081	$5,925	–8.7%	–6.3%
Food at home	3,344	3,965	4,378	–15.7	–23.6
Cereals and bakery products	400	557	633	–28.2	–36.8
Cereals and cereal products	147	228	300	–35.5	–51.1
Bakery products	253	329	332	–23.1	–23.8
Meats, poultry, fish, and eggs	876	1,175	1,355	–25.4	–35.3
Beef	285	370	480	–22.9	–40.6
Pork	160	242	264	–33.8	–39.3
Other meats	99	132	150	–24.7	–34.1
Poultry	177	215	237	–17.9	–25.4
Fish and seafood	109	154	140	–29.3	–22.0
Eggs	46	62	84	–26.3	–45.5
Dairy products	364	407	449	–10.6	–19.0
Fresh milk and cream	162	193	241	–16.0	–32.8
Other dairy products	202	214	208	–5.8	–3.0
Fruits and vegetables	640	760	749	–15.8	–14.5
Fresh fruits	219	259	242	–15.3	–9.7
Fresh vegetables	210	259	250	–18.8	–16.1
Processed fruits	119	142	146	–16.1	–18.6
Processed vegetables	92	101	109	–8.9	–15.9
Other food at home	1,064	1,066	1,193	–0.2	–10.8
Sugar and other sweets	90	125	153	–27.9	–41.1
Fats and oils	84	113	141	–25.9	–40.4
Miscellaneous foods	535	459	513	16.5	4.4
Nonalcoholic beverages	321	331	352	–3.1	–8.8
Food prepared by consumer unit on trips	33	39	34	–14.4	–3.7
Food away from home	2,207	2,115	1,547	4.3	42.7
ALCOHOLIC BEVERAGES	286	323	278	–11.5	2.9
HOUSING	14,338	12,305	11,779	16.5	21.7
Shelter	8,937	7,301	7,003	22.4	27.6
Owned dwellings	4,886	3,345	3,047	46.1	60.4
Mortgage interest and charges	3,166	1,986	2,052	59.4	54.3
Property taxes	1,058	754	593	40.3	78.4
Maintenance, repair, insurance, other expenses	662	605	402	9.5	64.7
Rented dwellings	3,876	3,751	3,786	3.3	2.4
Other lodging	175	205	170	–14.8	2.9
Utilities, fuels, and public services	2,986	2,461	2,586	21.3	15.5
Natural gas	378	274	290	37.7	30.4
Electricity	1,071	849	941	26.1	13.8

(continued)

	average spending			percent change	
	2005	2000	1994	2000–05	1994–05
Fuel oil and other fuels	$43	$34	$25	26.4%	71.7%
Telephone	1,130	1,008	1,045	12.1	8.1
Water and other public services	365	294	286	24.3	27.6
Household services	**605**	**527**	**467**	**14.7**	**29.7**
Personal services	336	289	268	16.2	25.6
Other household services	268	239	198	12.0	35.6
Housekeeping supplies	**508**	**538**	**472**	**–5.5**	**7.7**
Laundry and cleaning supplies	156	195	184	–20.0	–15.4
Other household products	252	257	225	–2.1	11.8
Postage and stationery	100	86	61	16.0	65.0
Household furnishings and equipment	**1,303**	**1,478**	**1,253**	**–11.8**	**4.0**
Household textiles	95	101	124	–5.9	–23.3
Furniture	487	507	378	–3.9	28.8
Floor coverings	20	31	22	–34.7	–10.7
Major appliances	171	188	167	–9.2	2.2
Small appliances and miscellaneous housewares	85	75	83	13.6	2.4
Miscellaneous household equipment	445	576	478	–22.8	–7.0
APPAREL AND RELATED SERVICES	**2,195**	**2,354**	**2,488**	**–6.8**	**–11.8**
Men and boys	**529**	**548**	**735**	**–3.4**	**–28.1**
Men, aged 16 or older	416	407	495	2.2	–16.0
Boys, aged 2 to 15	112	141	240	–20.4	–53.3
Women and girls	**787**	**784**	**698**	**0.4**	**12.7**
Women, aged 16 or older	597	612	530	–2.5	12.7
Girls, aged 2 to 15	191	170	169	12.3	13.2
Children under age 2	**149**	**155**	**191**	**–4.1**	**–22.0**
Footwear	**442**	**585**	**535**	**–24.5**	**–17.4**
Other apparel products and services	**288**	**282**	**328**	**2.0**	**–12.2**
TRANSPORTATION	**7,900**	**7,620**	**6,387**	**3.7**	**23.7**
Vehicle purchases	**3,280**	**3,568**	**2,849**	**–8.1**	**15.1**
Cars and trucks, new	1,710	1,224	1,144	39.7	49.5
Cars and trucks, used	1,551	2,334	1,704	–33.5	–9.0
Gasoline and motor oil	**2,171**	**1,411**	**1,194**	**53.9**	**81.8**
Other vehicle expenses	**2,068**	**2,206**	**1,952**	**–6.3**	**6.0**
Vehicle finance charges	269	311	236	–13.4	14.0
Maintenance and repairs	586	619	706	–5.4	–17.0
Vehicle insurance	837	789	687	6.0	21.9
Vehicle rentals, leases, licenses, other charges	376	485	322	–22.5	16.9
Public transportation	**380**	**437**	**394**	**–13.0**	**–3.6**
HEALTH CARE	**1,520**	**1,410**	**1,398**	**7.8**	**8.7**
Health insurance	750	680	629	10.2	19.3
Medical services	444	413	523	7.6	–15.1
Drugs	273	239	195	14.1	40.0
Medical supplies	54	78	51	–31.0	5.1
ENTERTAINMENT	**1,494**	**1,345**	**1,235**	**11.1**	**21.0**
Fees and admissions	337	297	256	13.4	31.8
Audio and visual equipment and services	716	618	608	15.8	17.9

(continued)

	average spending			percent change	
	2005	2000	1994	2000–05	1994–05
Pets, toys, hobbies, playground equipment	$244	$247	$225	−1.3%	8.3%
Other entertainment products and services	197	184	146	7.2	34.7
PERSONAL CARE PRODUCTS AND SERVICES	**501**	**640**	**598**	**−21.7**	**−16.3**
READING	**55**	**67**	**100**	**−17.8**	**−45.1**
EDUCATION	**558**	**412**	**441**	**35.5**	**26.4**
TOBACCO PRODUCTS AND SMOKING SUPPLIES	**158**	**196**	**181**	**−19.5**	**−12.5**
MISCELLANEOUS	**665**	**683**	**763**	**−2.6**	**−12.8**
CASH CONTRIBUTIONS	**927**	**732**	**597**	**26.7**	**55.3**
PERSONAL INSURANCE AND PENSIONS	**3,974**	**2,958**	**2,665**	**34.4**	**49.1**
Life and other personal insurance	140	214	253	−34.7	−44.7
Pensions and Social Security*	3,834	2,745	2,412	39.7	59.0
PERSONAL TAXES	**982**	**1,793**	**2,311**	**−45.2**	**−57.5**
Federal income taxes	655	1,427	1,771	−54.1	−63.0
State and local income taxes	258	307	484	−16.1	−46.7
Other taxes	69	59	57	17.0	21.8
GIFTS FOR PEOPLE IN OTHER HOUSEHOLDS	**636**	**936**	**784**	**−32.0**	**−18.9**

* Because of changes in methodology, the 2005 data on pensions and Social Security are not comparable with earlier years.
Note: Spending by category will not add to total spending because gift spending is also included in the preceding product and service categories and personal taxes are not included in the total.
Source: Bureau of Labor Statistics, 1984, 1990, 2000, and 2005 Consumer Expenditure Surveys, Internet site http://www.bls .gov/cex/; calculations by New Strategist

Married Couples with Children Are the Biggest Spenders

But spending grew the most for married couples without children at home.

Nobody spends more than married couples with children. In 2005, they spent $66,441, fully 43 percent more than the average household. This household type spends much more than others because their households are larger, with children to feed, house, clothe, educate, and entertain. Between 1984 and 2005, the average spending of married couples with children on the category of education more than doubled, after adjusting for inflation.

Married couples without children at home, many of them empty-nesters, saw their spending rise 23 percent between 1984 and 2005, after adjusting for inflation—more than any other household type. Behind the rise in spending for this group is the entry of more affluent and educated generations into the older age groups. Married couples without children at home boosted their spending on entertainment by 49 percent between 1984 and 2000. They spent 16 percent more on food-away-from-home and 27 percent more on new cars and trucks.

Single parents and people who live alone spend much less than the average household because there are fewer earners in the home. Both household types boosted their spending between 1984 and 2005. Single parents spent 28 percent more on food-away-from-home, after adjusting for inflation. They spent 14 percent more on footwear and 39 percent more on entertainment. Although the spending of single-person households rose 10 percent between 1984 and 2005, after adjusting for inflation, they spent less on many items including food, alcoholic beverages, and clothing. They spent more on mortgage interest, however, and doubled their spending on property taxes and health insurance.

■ As the large baby-boom generation fills the empty-nest age groups, average household spending patterns will change.

People living alone spend less than other household types

(average annual household spending by household type, 2005)

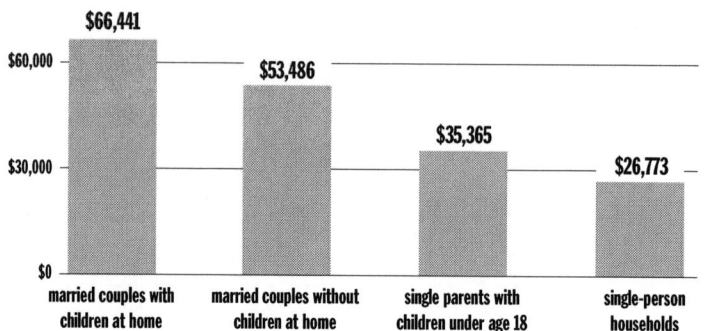

Table 9.12 Average Spending by Married Couples with Children at Home, 1984 to 2005

(average annual spending of consumer units headed by married couples with children at home, 1984 to 2005; percent change for selected years; in 2005 dollars)

	average spending				percent change	
	2005	2000	1990	1984	2000–05	1984–05
Number of consumer units headed by married couples with children at home (in 000s)	29,528	28,777	27,991	28,064	2.6%	5.2%
Average annual spending of consumer units	$66,441	$60,774	$58,306	$55,909	9.3	18.8
FOOD	$8,764	$8,224	$8,975	$8,780	6.6%	−0.2%
Food at home	4,878	4,941	5,363	5,453	−1.3	−10.5
Cereals and bakery products	673	771	819	733	−12.7	−8.2
Cereals and cereal products	221	272	293	244	−18.8	−9.3
Bakery products	452	499	526	490	−9.4	−7.7
Meats, poultry, fish, and eggs	1,108	1,262	1,406	1,639	−12.2	−32.4
Beef	342	380	462	562	−10.0	−39.1
Pork	213	256	276	333	−16.9	−36.0
Other meats	150	168	212	234	−10.6	−36.0
Poultry	196	235	224	222	−16.5	−11.6
Fish and seafood	165	174	170	196	−4.9	−15.8
Eggs	43	50	61	93	−13.8	−53.7
Dairy products	582	546	663	720	6.7	−19.2
Fresh milk and cream	229	228	321	369	0.5	−38.0
Other dairy products	352	318	342	351	10.8	0.2
Fruits and vegetables	794	805	813	811	−1.4	−2.1
Fresh fruits	264	245	245	232	7.8	13.9
Fresh vegetables	248	239	233	231	3.6	7.2
Processed fruits	151	186	191	194	−18.8	−22.1
Processed vegetables	131	135	142	154	−2.9	−14.9
Other food at home	1,721	1,557	1,663	1,465	10.5	17.5
Sugar and other sweets	172	195	209	206	−11.8	−16.6
Fats and oils	120	128	145	151	−6.4	−20.6
Miscellaneous foods	929	768	773	633	21.0	46.8
Nonalcoholic beverages	442	404	465	475	9.5	−7.0
Food prepared by consumer unit on trips	57	61	70	83	−6.9	−31.7
Food away from home	3,886	3,282	3,612	3,327	18.4	16.8
ALCOHOLIC BEVERAGES	476	449	444	551	6.0	−13.5
HOUSING	21,057	19,430	17,257	16,432	8.4	28.1
Shelter	12,043	10,993	9,212	8,302	9.5	45.1
Owned dwellings	9,691	8,605	6,736	5,932	12.6	63.4
Mortgage interest and charges	6,026	5,603	4,685	4,101	7.6	46.9
Property taxes	2,238	1,835	1,180	982	22.0	127.8
Maintenance, repair, insurance, other expenses	1,427	1,167	871	847	22.3	68.4
Rented dwellings	1,643	1,703	1,804	1,511	−3.6	8.7
Other lodging	709	685	672	860	3.5	−17.6
Utilities, fuels, and public services	4,114	3,607	3,595	3,946	14.1	4.3
Natural gas	603	449	475	683	34.3	−11.8
Electricity	1,482	1,317	1,476	1,613	12.6	−8.1

(continued)

	average spending				percent change	
	2005	**2000**	**1990**	**1984**	**2000–05**	**1984–05**
Fuel oil and other fuels	$189	$136	$205	$304	38.9%	–37.9%
Telephone	1,359	1,244	1,039	981	9.2	38.5
Water and other public services	482	459	399	364	4.9	32.6
Household services	**1,422**	**1,385**	**1,145**	**911**	**2.7**	**56.1**
Personal services	830	851	779	534	–2.4	55.4
Other household services	593	534	365	376	11.0	57.7
Housekeeping supplies	**871**	**797**	**853**	**808**	**9.2**	**7.8**
Laundry and cleaning supplies	195	230	253	244	–15.3	–20.2
Other household products	472	383	375	371	23.1	27.2
Postage and stationery	204	184	226	193	11.0	5.5
Household furnishings and equipment	**2,607**	**2,649**	**2,454**	**2,466**	**–1.6**	**5.7**
Household textiles	190	184	236	202	3.4	–6.1
Furniture	707	690	631	651	2.5	8.6
Floor coverings	98	81	276	262	21.7	–62.5
Major appliances	333	329	293	367	1.2	–9.2
Small appliances and miscellaneous housewares	136	138	148	171	–1.7	–20.5
Miscellaneous household equipment	1,142	1,227	871	813	–6.9	40.5
APPAREL AND RELATED SERVICES	**2,953**	**3,118**	**3,401**	**3,450**	**–5.3**	**–14.4**
Men and boys	**701**	**775**	**897**	**1,023**	**–9.5**	**–31.5**
Men, aged 16 or older	497	530	671	739	–6.2	–32.8
Boys, aged 2 to 15	203	245	226	283	–17.1	–28.3
Women and girls	**1,194**	**1,193**	**1,358**	**1,305**	**0.1**	**–8.5**
Women, aged 16 or older	901	882	1,061	989	2.1	–8.9
Girls, aged 2 to 15	294	311	297	315	–5.4	–6.8
Children under age 2	**176**	**196**	**215**	**192**	**–10.3**	**–8.4**
Footwear	**496**	**544**	**438**	**467**	**–8.9**	**6.3**
Other apparel products and services	**386**	**409**	**495**	**462**	**–5.7**	**–16.5**
TRANSPORTATION	**12,319**	**12,575**	**11,147**	**11,119**	**–2.0**	**10.8**
Vehicle purchases	**5,415**	**6,085**	**5,086**	**4,831**	**–11.0**	**12.1**
Cars and trucks, new	3,013	2,810	2,748	2,688	7.2	12.1
Cars and trucks, used	2,289	3,195	2,292	2,076	–28.4	10.2
Gasoline and motor oil	**2,973**	**2,131**	**2,226**	**2,804**	**39.5**	**6.0**
Other vehicle expenses	**3,357**	**3,802**	**3,382**	**3,018**	**–11.7**	**11.2**
Vehicle finance charges	489	606	717	624	–19.3	–21.6
Maintenance and repairs	926	965	1,137	1,148	–4.1	–19.3
Vehicle insurance	1,292	1,244	1,139	898	3.8	43.9
Vehicle rentals, leases, licenses, other charges	649	988	387	348	–34.3	86.4
Public transportation	**574**	**557**	**454**	**466**	**3.1**	**23.1**
HEALTH CARE	**3,081**	**2,615**	**2,527**	**2,275**	**17.8**	**35.4**
Health insurance	1,559	1,283	956	737	21.5	111.4
Medical services	905	792	1,062	1,129	14.3	–19.9
Drugs	486	409	368	304	18.7	59.8
Medical supplies	131	132	140	104	–0.4	25.8
ENTERTAINMENT	**3,486**	**3,248**	**3,012**	**2,934**	**7.3**	**18.8**
Fees and admissions	975	964	787	790	1.1	23.3
Audio and visual equipment and services	1,211	969	931	860	25.0	40.8

(continued)

	average spending				percent change	
	2005	**2000**	**1990**	**1984**	**2000–05**	**1984–05**
Pets, toys, hobbies, playground equipment	$575	$565	$610	$539	1.8%	6.7%
Other entertainment products and services	725	751	684	745	–3.4	–2.6
PERSONAL CARE PRODUCTS AND SERVICES	**735**	**872**	**747**	**731**	**–15.7**	**0.6**
READING	**152**	**200**	**288**	**302**	**–23.9**	**–49.7**
EDUCATION	**1,760**	**1,277**	**1,019**	**856**	**37.8**	**105.6**
TOBACCO PRODUCTS AND SMOKING SUPPLIES	**328**	**406**	**508**	**538**	**–19.2**	**–39.0**
MISCELLANEOUS	**922**	**1,013**	**1,575**	**991**	**–9.0**	**–7.0**
CASH CONTRIBUTIONS	**2,094**	**1,384**	**1,397**	**1,607**	**51.3**	**30.3**
PERSONAL INSURANCE AND PENSIONS	**8,313**	**5,962**	**6,010**	**5,347**	**39.4**	**55.5**
Life and other personal insurance	575	682	814	832	–15.6	–30.9
Pensions and Social Security*	7,738	5,281	5,196	4,514	46.5	71.4
PERSONAL TAXES	**3,780**	**5,055**	**6,019**	**5,597**	**–25.2**	**–32.5**
Federal income taxes	2,639	3,932	4,749	4,321	–32.9	–38.9
State and local income taxes	916	925	1,149	1,115	–1.0	–17.9
Other taxes	225	198	121	161	13.4	40.0
GIFTS FOR PEOPLE IN OTHER HOUSEHOLDS	**1,102**	**1,436**	**1,651**	**1,476**	**–23.2**	**–25.3**

* Because of changes in methodology, the 2005 data on pensions and Social Security are not comparable with earlier years.
Note: Spending by category will not add to total spending because gift spending is also included in the preceding product and service categories and personal taxes are not included in the total.
Source: Bureau of Labor Statistics, 1984, 1990, 2000, and 2005 Consumer Expenditure Surveys, Internet site http://www.bls.gov/cex/; calculations by New Strategist

Table 9.13 Average Spending by Married Couples without Children at Home, 1984 to 2005

(average annual spending of consumer units headed by married couples without children at home, 1984 to 2005; percent change for selected years; in 2005 dollars)

	average spending				percent change	
	2005	2000	1990	1984	2000–05	1984–05
Number of consumer units headed by married couples without children at home (in 000s)	25,293	22,805	20,653	19,337	10.9%	30.8%
Average annual spending of consumer units	$53,486	$47,856	$47,108	$43,509	11.8	22.9
FOOD	$6,351	$6,323	$6,824	$5,902	0.4%	7.6%
Food at home	3,413	3,578	3,746	3,367	–4.6	1.4
Cereals and bakery products	452	517	532	432	–12.6	4.5
Cereals and cereal products	134	169	175	126	–20.7	6.4
Bakery products	319	348	357	306	–8.4	4.1
Meats, poultry, fish, and eggs	806	959	1,042	992	–16.0	–18.8
Beef	233	285	359	353	–18.2	–34.1
Pork	171	214	197	205	–20.2	–16.5
Other meats	110	113	149	130	–3.0	–15.2
Poultry	125	162	169	141	–22.9	–11.3
Fish and seafood	135	143	127	103	–5.5	30.6
Eggs	33	42	42	58	–21.4	–43.4
Dairy products	376	380	412	412	–1.0	–8.7
Fresh milk and cream	131	137	178	184	–4.5	–28.9
Other dairy products	245	243	235	227	0.9	7.7
Fruits and vegetables	604	656	665	596	–7.9	1.4
Fresh fruits	202	204	223	195	–1.1	3.3
Fresh vegetables	197	208	193	175	–5.1	12.7
Processed fruits	109	140	142	130	–21.9	–16.0
Processed vegetables	95	103	108	96	–8.0	–0.9
Other food at home	1,175	1,066	1,094	859	10.2	36.8
Sugar and other sweets	132	140	145	122	–5.4	8.0
Fats and oils	91	107	106	96	–14.6	–5.1
Miscellaneous foods	600	468	465	331	28.1	81.4
Nonalcoholic beverages	291	286	308	310	1.8	–6.2
Food prepared by consumer unit on trips	61	66	70	73	–7.3	–16.8
Food away from home	2,938	2,745	3,080	2,536	7.0	15.9
ALCOHOLIC BEVERAGES	505	523	504	549	–3.4	–8.0
HOUSING	16,359	14,553	13,985	13,329	12.4	22.7
Shelter	9,239	8,113	7,370	6,739	13.9	37.1
Owned dwellings	7,094	5,936	5,015	4,447	19.5	59.5
Mortgage interest and charges	3,391	3,053	2,606	2,342	11.1	44.8
Property taxes	2,114	1,656	1,204	1,047	27.7	101.9
Maintenance, repair, insurance, other expenses	1,589	1,227	1,206	1,060	29.5	49.9
Rented dwellings	1,264	1,271	1,535	1,370	–0.6	–7.8
Other lodging	881	905	820	921	–2.7	–4.3
Utilities, fuels, and public services	3,481	3,050	3,048	3,216	14.1	8.2
Natural gas	532	361	372	570	47.5	–6.6
Electricity	1,265	1,159	1,270	1,273	9.1	–0.6

(continued)

	average spending				percent change	
	2005	**2000**	**1990**	**1984**	**2000–05**	**1984–05**
Fuel oil and other fuels	$190	$146	$193	$321	29.9%	–40.9%
Telephone	1,073	988	879	780	8.6	37.6
Water and other public services	421	395	335	273	6.7	54.5
Household services	**713**	**605**	**572**	**581**	**17.9**	**22.8**
Personal services	40	61	70	66	–34.7	–39.2
Other household services	673	542	502	515	24.1	30.7
Housekeeping supplies	**754**	**650**	**731**	**632**	**16.0**	**19.4**
Laundry and cleaning supplies	140	152	181	152	–7.9	–8.0
Other household products	400	324	309	269	23.3	48.8
Postage and stationery	214	175	241	209	22.5	2.6
Household furnishings and equipment	**2,172**	**2,137**	**2,262**	**2,160**	**1.7**	**0.6**
Household textiles	160	146	193	190	9.4	–15.7
Furniture	603	496	607	701	21.7	–14.0
Floor coverings	76	69	130	167	9.9	–54.6
Major appliances	306	247	293	350	23.8	–12.5
Small appliances and miscellaneous housewares	145	125	157	160	16.2	–9.2
Miscellaneous household equipment	882	1,054	883	592	–16.3	49.0
APPAREL AND RELATED SERVICES	**1,694**	**1,956**	**2,477**	**2,361**	**–13.4**	**–28.2**
Men and boys	**413**	**481**	**593**	**581**	**–14.1**	**–28.9**
Men, aged 16 or older	388	454	562	553	–14.5	–29.8
Boys, aged 2 to 15	25	28	31	30	–11.8	–16.9
Women and girls	**669**	**784**	**1,119**	**1,038**	**–14.6**	**–35.5**
Women, aged 16 or older	630	745	1,083	1,011	–15.5	–37.7
Girls, aged 2 to 15	39	39	34	26	1.1	48.2
Children under age 2	**47**	**43**	**48**	**51**	**9.1**	**–7.4**
Footwear	**221**	**338**	**351**	**308**	**–34.6**	**–28.3**
Other apparel products and services	**343**	**311**	**368**	**382**	**10.4**	**–10.1**
TRANSPORTATION	**10,192**	**9,424**	**8,585**	**8,650**	**8.2**	**17.8**
Vehicle purchases	**4,642**	**4,337**	**3,558**	**3,686**	**7.0**	**25.9**
Cars and trucks, new	3,019	2,396	2,344	2,385	26.0	26.6
Cars and trucks, used	1,532	1,911	1,188	1,278	–19.8	19.9
Gasoline and motor oil	**2,215**	**1,600**	**1,699**	**2,008**	**38.4**	**10.3**
Other vehicle expenses	**2,683**	**2,827**	**2,739**	**2,368**	**–5.1**	**13.3**
Vehicle finance charges	321	397	444	391	–19.1	–17.9
Maintenance and repairs	790	763	974	966	3.5	–18.2
Vehicle insurance	995	949	968	724	4.8	37.5
Vehicle rentals, leases, licenses, other charges	577	718	354	288	–19.6	100.6
Public transportation	**652**	**659**	**587**	**588**	**–1.1**	**10.8**
HEALTH CARE	**4,043**	**3,452**	**3,125**	**2,735**	**17.1**	**47.8**
Health insurance	2,091	1,677	1,284	1,088	24.7	92.1
Medical services	935	837	1,067	1,008	11.7	–7.2
Drugs	864	761	601	470	13.5	83.9
Medical supplies	154	178	173	169	–13.5	–9.0
ENTERTAINMENT	**2,946**	**2,232**	**2,492**	**1,974**	**32.0**	**49.3**
Fees and admissions	706	675	660	635	4.6	11.1
Audio and visual equipment and services	933	646	662	549	44.3	70.0

(continued)

	average spending				percent change	
	2005	2000	1990	1984	2000–05	1984–05
Pets, toys, hobbies, playground equipment	$534	$440	$421	$348	21.4%	53.6%
Other entertainment products and services	773	470	749	442	64.6	75.0
PERSONAL CARE PRODUCTS AND SERVICES	**632**	**693**	**625**	**598**	**–8.8**	**5.7**
READING	**174**	**223**	**278**	**282**	**–22.1**	**–38.3**
EDUCATION	**810**	**507**	**378**	**391**	**59.8**	**107.2**
TOBACCO PRODUCTS AND SMOKING SUPPLIES	**294**	**324**	**402**	**442**	**–9.4**	**–33.4**
MISCELLANEOUS	**1,069**	**996**	**1,349**	**705**	**7.4**	**51.7**
CASH CONTRIBUTIONS	**2,315**	**2,172**	**1,789**	**1,660**	**6.6**	**39.5**
PERSONAL INSURANCE AND PENSIONS	**6,102**	**4,479**	**4,296**	**3,934**	**36.2**	**55.1**
Life and other personal insurance	516	695	669	673	–25.8	–23.3
Pensions and Social Security*	5,586	3,782	3,627	3,261	47.7	71.3
PERSONAL TAXES	**3,338**	**4,943**	**5,454**	**4,534**	**–32.5**	**–26.4**
Federal income taxes	2,448	3,852	4,292	3,511	–36.4	–30.3
State and local income taxes	610	823	979	859	–25.9	–29.0
Other taxes	281	268	184	165	5.0	69.9
GIFTS FOR PEOPLE IN OTHER HOUSEHOLDS	**1,874**	**1,675**	**1,754**	**1,598**	**11.9**	**17.3**

Because of changes in methodology, the 2005 data on pensions and Social Security are not comparable with earlier years.
Note: Spending by category will not add to total spending because gift spending is also included in the preceding product and service categories and personal taxes are not included in the total.
Source: Bureau of Labor Statistics, 1984, 1990, 2000, and 2005 Consumer Expenditure Surveys, Internet site http://www.bls .gov/cex/; calculations by New Strategist

Table 9.14 Average Spending by Single Parents with Children under Age 18 at Home, 1984 to 2005

(average annual spending of consumer units headed by single parents with children under age 18 at home, 1984 to 2005; percent change for selected years; in 2005 dollars)

	average spending				percent change	
	2005	2000	1990	1984	2000–05	1984–05
Number of consumer units headed by single parents with children under age 18 at home (in 000s)	6,902	6,132	6,074	5,086	12.6%	35.7%
Average annual spending of consumer units	$35,365	$32,803	$28,748	$31,646	7.8	11.8
FOOD	**$5,283**	**$4,826**	**$5,288**	**$4,951**	**9.5%**	**6.7%**
Food at home	**3,099**	**3,002**	**3,582**	**3,239**	**3.2**	**–4.3**
Cereals and bakery products	423	440	536	455	–3.9	–7.0
Cereals and cereal products	149	174	211	182	–14.1	–18.3
Bakery products	274	265	327	273	3.2	0.5
Meats, poultry, fish, and eggs	769	855	1,036	1,034	–10.1	–25.6
Beef	235	253	368	359	–7.1	–34.5
Pork	156	180	206	211	–13.5	–25.9
Other meats	105	103	149	135	1.7	–22.4
Poultry	148	174	158	171	–14.7	–13.5
Fish and seafood	91	105	105	88	–13.7	3.0
Eggs	33	37	48	70	–11.8	–52.6
Dairy products	347	316	432	421	9.7	–17.6
Fresh milk and cream	146	133	223	242	10.0	–39.8
Other dairy products	201	184	209	179	9.4	12.6
Fruits and vegetables	461	463	541	474	–0.4	–2.7
Fresh fruits	139	129	148	120	7.5	15.5
Fresh vegetables	132	133	151	143	–0.5	–7.6
Processed fruits	105	119	137	115	–11.8	–8.4
Processed vegetables	86	82	105	98	5.3	–12.0
Other food at home	1,099	928	1,036	838	18.5	31.1
Sugar and other sweets	111	121	134	113	–8.5	–1.6
Fats and oils	81	88	96	86	–8.4	–6.3
Miscellaneous foods	607	407	493	336	49.1	80.4
Nonalcoholic beverages	283	273	288	303	3.5	–6.5
Food prepared by consumer unit on trips	16	36	24	17	–55.9	–5.4
Food away from home	**2,185**	**1,824**	**1,706**	**1,711**	**19.8**	**27.7**
ALCOHOLIC BEVERAGES	**221**	**212**	**245**	**252**	**4.2**	**–12.3**
HOUSING	**12,905**	**12,172**	**10,346**	**10,885**	**6.0**	**18.6**
Shelter	**7,521**	**7,180**	**5,813**	**5,883**	**4.7**	**27.8**
Owned dwellings	3,548	3,172	2,324	2,564	11.8	38.4
Mortgage interest and charges	2,265	1,921	1,490	1,793	17.9	26.3
Property taxes	729	733	383	385	–0.5	89.2
Maintenance, repair, insurance, other expenses	554	518	450	383	6.9	44.5
Rented dwellings	3,802	3,760	3,322	2,887	1.1	31.7
Other lodging	170	248	169	432	–31.6	–60.7
Utilities, fuels, and public services	**2,994**	**2,648**	**2,388**	**2,831**	**13.1**	**5.8**
Natural gas	453	347	327	577	30.5	–21.5
Electricity	1,145	979	944	1,058	17.0	8.2

(continued)

	average spending				percent change	
	2005	**2000**	**1990**	**1984**	**2000–05**	**1984–05**
Fuel oil and other fuels	$54	$49	$72	$154	10.7%	–65.0%
Telephone	1,042	1,013	822	808	2.9	28.9
Water and other public services	**299**	**261**	**224**	**235**	**14.6**	**27.3**
Household services	857	891	865	754	–3.9	13.7
Personal services	598	665	646	560	–10.0	6.8
Other household services	260	227	220	194	14.6	34.3
Housekeeping supplies	**445**	**417**	**405**	**365**	**6.6**	**22.0**
Laundry and cleaning supplies	137	171	146	128	–20.0	7.2
Other household products	218	159	155	148	37.3	46.8
Postage and stationery	89	87	105	88	1.9	0.7
Household furnishings and equipment	**1,089**	**1,034**	**874**	**1,053**	**5.3**	**3.5**
Household textiles	131	68	51	177	92.5	–25.9
Furniture	354	308	311	368	14.8	–3.9
Floor coverings	25	25	43	32	0.2	–21.8
Major appliances	72	118	167	201	–39.0	–64.2
Small appliances and miscellaneous housewares	71	41	48	79	73.9	–10.1
Miscellaneous household equipment	436	473	254	194	–7.8	125.2
APPAREL AND RELATED SERVICES	**2,167**	**2,179**	**2,246**	**2,481**	**–0.5**	**–12.7**
Men and boys	**490**	**460**	**435**	**566**	**6.4**	**–13.4**
Men, aged 16 or older	239	168	124	293	42.4	–18.5
Boys, aged 2 to 15	251	294	311	273	–14.6	–7.9
Women and girls	**903**	**921**	**979**	**1,058**	**–1.9**	**–14.7**
Women, aged 16 or older	628	603	722	673	4.1	–6.7
Girls, aged 2 to 15	275	316	257	385	–13.1	–28.6
Children under age 2	**81**	**126**	**100**	**75**	**–35.7**	**7.7**
Footwear	**528**	**466**	**396**	**464**	**13.3**	**13.7**
Other apparel products and services	**164**	**204**	**335**	**318**	**–19.7**	**–48.4**
TRANSPORTATION	**5,910**	**5,690**	**4,046**	**5,286**	**3.9**	**11.8**
Vehicle purchases	**2,622**	**2,652**	**1,536**	**2,092**	**–1.1**	**25.3**
Cars and trucks, new	894	594	260	1,062	50.4	–15.8
Cars and trucks, used	1,661	2,053	1,230	1,008	–19.1	64.9
Gasoline and motor oil	**1,444**	**1,014**	**919**	**1,318**	**42.4**	**9.6**
Other vehicle expenses	**1,634**	**1,722**	**1,379**	**1,500**	**–5.1**	**8.9**
Vehicle finance charges	203	246	205	269	–17.5	–24.5
Maintenance and repairs	455	533	520	624	–14.6	–27.1
Vehicle insurance	687	628	459	432	9.3	58.9
Vehicle rentals, leases, licenses, other charges	288	313	196	177	–8.0	63.0
Public transportation	**211**	**303**	**212**	**376**	**–30.3**	**–43.9**
HEALTH CARE	**1,376**	**1,150**	**940**	**1,103**	**19.6**	**24.7**
Health insurance	675	514	342	336	31.4	100.6
Medical services	433	412	406	575	5.2	–24.7
Drugs	211	164	126	139	28.3	51.7
Medical supplies	56	61	66	53	–8.6	6.4
ENTERTAINMENT	**1,823**	**1,625**	**1,315**	**1,314**	**12.2**	**38.7**
Fees and admissions	361	458	327	470	–21.2	–23.2
Audio and visual equipment and services	795	670	593	395	18.6	101.4

(continued)

	average spending				percent change	
	2005	**2000**	**1990**	**1984**	**2000–05**	**1984–05**
Pets, toys, hobbies, playground equipment	$333	$289	$248	$299	15.1%	11.4%
Other entertainment products and services	334	206	145	150	61.8	122.1
PERSONAL CARE PRODUCTS AND SERVICES	**463**	**645**	**403**	**429**	**–28.3**	**8.0**
READING	**57**	**86**	**118**	**162**	**–33.9**	**–64.7**
EDUCATION	**713**	**448**	**390**	**555**	**59.2**	**28.6**
TOBACCO PRODUCTS AND SMOKING SUPPLIES	**274**	**339**	**311**	**359**	**–19.2**	**–23.7**
MISCELLANEOUS	**541**	**889**	**844**	**714**	**–39.2**	**–24.3**
CASH CONTRIBUTIONS	**677**	**462**	**524**	**1,303**	**46.7**	**–48.0**
PERSONAL INSURANCE AND PENSIONS	**2,955**	**2,080**	**1,729**	**1,857**	**42.1**	**59.1**
Life and other personal insurance	158	170	205	289	–7.1	–45.4
Pensions and Social Security*	2,796	1,909	1,524	1,570	46.5	78.1
PERSONAL TAXES	**519**	**677**	**1,542**	**1,855**	**–23.3**	**–72.0**
Federal income taxes	187	400	1,121	1,491	–53.3	–87.5
State and local income taxes	269	230	363	338	16.8	–20.5
Other taxes	64	47	58	26	37.6	143.2
GIFTS FOR PEOPLE IN OTHER HOUSEHOLDS	**697**	**775**	**750**	**1,058**	**–10.0**	**–34.1**

* Because of changes in methodology, the 2005 data on pensions and Social Security are not comparable with earlier years.
Note: Spending by category will not add to total spending because gift spending is also included in the preceding product and service categories and personal taxes are not included in the total.
Source: Bureau of Labor Statistics, 1984, 1990, 2000, and 2005 Consumer Expenditure Surveys, Internet site http://www.bls .gov/cex/; calculations by New Strategist

Table 9.15 Average Spending by People Living Alone, 1984 to 2005

(average annual spending of consumer units headed by people living alone, 1984 to 2005; percent change for selected years; in 2005 dollars)

	average spending				percent change	
	2005	2000	1990	1984	2000–05	1984–05
Number of consumer units headed by people living alone (in 000s)	34,339	32,323	27,263	24,563	6.2%	39.8%
Average annual spending of consumer units	$26,773	$26,152	$25,594	$24,425	2.4	9.6
FOOD	$3,073	$3,204	$3,440	$3,335	–4.1%	–7.8%
Food at home	1,638	1,675	1,689	1,609	–2.2	1.8
Cereals and bakery products	227	251	253	220	–9.4	3.2
Cereals and cereal products	69	78	82	62	–11.8	11.2
Bakery products	158	171	170	160	–7.7	–1.1
Meats, poultry, fish, and eggs	332	399	406	425	–16.8	–21.8
Beef	90	113	118	139	–20.6	–35.3
Pork	67	81	76	73	–16.8	–8.6
Other meats	45	53	64	56	–15.6	–20.2
Poultry	61	77	73	70	–20.9	–12.3
Fish and seafood	52	57	55	60	–8.3	–13.5
Eggs	18	20	21	28	–11.8	–36.2
Dairy products	193	184	200	211	5.0	–8.3
Fresh milk and cream	74	74	96	103	0.4	–28.4
Other dairy products	118	111	106	109	6.2	8.2
Fruits and vegetables	290	316	308	288	–8.4	0.8
Fresh fruits	100	105	99	88	–5.2	13.2
Fresh vegetables	91	98	90	85	–6.7	7.6
Processed fruits	58	68	72	68	–14.8	–14.3
Processed vegetables	42	45	48	47	–7.4	–10.6
Other food at home	597	524	520	442	13.9	35.2
Sugar and other sweets	61	64	64	64	–4.0	–4.6
Fats and oils	44	44	46	43	–0.5	1.8
Miscellaneous foods	312	251	227	175	24.5	78.5
Nonalcoholic beverages	161	142	160	158	13.6	2.0
Food prepared by consumer unit on trips	19	25	22	24	–23.9	–22.2
Food away from home	1,435	1,529	1,751	1,726	–6.1	–16.8
ALCOHOLIC BEVERAGES	327	369	390	451	–11.3	–27.5
HOUSING	9,835	9,288	8,785	7,940	5.9	23.9
Shelter	6,179	5,732	5,572	4,741	7.8	30.3
Owned dwellings	3,055	2,645	2,389	1,605	15.5	90.3
Mortgage interest and charges	1,429	1,140	1,252	722	25.4	98.0
Property taxes	907	820	553	444	10.6	104.5
Maintenance, repair, insurance, other expenses	720	685	584	440	5.1	63.7
Rented dwellings	2,889	2,762	2,872	2,716	4.6	6.4
Other lodging	235	326	312	419	–27.8	–43.9
Utilities, fuels, and public services	2,024	1,846	1,790	1,818	9.6	11.4
Natural gas	312	236	233	336	32.3	–7.3
Electricity	719	645	666	607	11.4	18.4

(continued)

	average spending				percent change	
	2005	**2000**	**1990**	**1984**	**2000–05**	**1984–05**
Fuel oil and other fuels	$99	$77	$85	$169	28.4%	–41.5%
Telephone	664	688	657	585	–3.5	13.6
Water and other public services	230	198	149	122	15.9	88.2
Household services	**383**	**439**	**332**	**258**	**–12.7**	**48.7**
Personal services	42	141	66	11	–70.1	272.4
Other household services	341	299	266	248	13.9	37.4
Housekeeping supplies	**321**	**254**	**299**	**274**	**26.4**	**17.0**
Laundry and cleaning supplies	66	60	69	66	9.8	0.3
Other household products	159	116	115	100	37.4	59.6
Postage and stationery	96	78	115	109	22.7	–11.9
Household furnishings and equipment	**928**	**1,015**	**792**	**848**	**–8.6**	**9.5**
Household textiles	65	71	60	102	–9.0	–36.0
Furniture	218	256	261	265	–14.9	–17.7
Floor coverings	25	23	54	32	10.2	–21.8
Major appliances	104	118	102	124	–11.8	–16.2
Small appliances and miscellaneous housewares	62	56	58	64	11.6	–3.0
Miscellaneous household equipment	454	491	257	261	–7.6	73.8
APPAREL AND RELATED SERVICES	**980**	**1,166**	**1,325**	**1,374**	**–15.9**	**–28.7**
Men and boys	**223**	**253**	**321**	**329**	**–11.8**	**–32.2**
Men, aged 16 or older	212	239	309	310	–11.4	–31.6
Boys, aged 2 to 15	11	14	12	21	–19.2	–46.8
Women and girls	**386**	**470**	**526**	**553**	**–17.8**	**–30.2**
Women, aged 16 or older	370	450	510	536	–17.8	–30.9
Girls, aged 2 to 15	16	18	18	17	–11.8	–5.4
Children under age 2	**16**	**19**	**16**	**13**	**–17.0**	**21.6**
Footwear	**172**	**217**	**184**	**169**	**–20.6**	**1.7**
Other apparel products and services	**183**	**208**	**276**	**310**	**–11.8**	**–41.0**
TRANSPORTATION	**4,030**	**4,233**	**3,973**	**4,327**	**–4.8**	**–6.9**
Vehicle purchases	**1,395**	**1,651**	**1,327**	**1,647**	**–15.5**	**–15.3**
Cars and trucks, new	673	904	656	1,017	–25.5	–33.8
Cars and trucks, used	669	712	657	592	–6.1	13.0
Gasoline and motor oil	**1,032**	**773**	**831**	**1,047**	**33.4**	**–1.4**
Other vehicle expenses	**1,336**	**1,443**	**1,414**	**1,186**	**–7.4**	**12.6**
Vehicle finance charges	121	146	206	156	–17.3	–22.4
Maintenance and repairs	437	449	581	528	–2.7	–17.3
Vehicle insurance	521	496	471	346	5.1	50.6
Vehicle rentals, leases, licenses, other charges	258	352	157	154	–26.6	67.4
Public transportation	**267**	**365**	**400**	**447**	**–26.9**	**–40.3**
HEALTH CARE	**1,750**	**1,688**	**1,460**	**1,173**	**3.7**	**49.2**
Health insurance	893	745	581	402	19.8	122.0
Medical services	424	474	532	466	–10.6	–9.0
Drugs	368	398	259	216	–7.6	70.2
Medical supplies	65	70	87	88	–7.6	–26.4
ENTERTAINMENT	**1,335**	**1,164**	**1,257**	**1,220**	**14.7**	**9.4**
Fees and admissions	336	319	351	427	5.4	–21.3
Audio and visual equipment and services	591	487	433	423	21.5	39.7

(continued)

	average spending				percent change	
	2005	**2000**	**1990**	**1984**	**2000–05**	**1984–05**
Pets, toys, hobbies, playground equipment	$233	$201	$251	$173	16.1%	34.7%
Other entertainment products and services	175	158	221	194	11.0	–9.6
PERSONAL CARE PRODUCTS AND SERVICES	328	383	312	321	–14.4	2.0
READING	103	128	163	190	–19.6	–45.7
EDUCATION	500	462	466	487	8.3	2.7
TOBACCO PRODUCTS AND SMOKING SUPPLIES	227	230	233	233	–1.4	–2.6
MISCELLANEOUS	563	636	950	695	–11.5	–19.0
CASH CONTRIBUTIONS	1,313	1,187	910	891	10.6	47.4
PERSONAL INSURANCE AND PENSIONS	2,409	2,017	1,932	1,786	19.5	34.9
Life and other personal insurance	162	176	167	248	–7.8	–34.7
Pensions and Social Security*	2,247	1,841	1,763	1,536	22.1	46.3
PERSONAL TAXES	1,425	2,370	2,944	3,019	–39.9	–52.8
Federal income taxes	1,016	1,838	2,361	2,387	–44.7	–57.4
State and local income taxes	286	408	526	549	–30.0	–47.9
Other taxes	124	124	58	81	0.3	53.4
GIFTS FOR PEOPLE IN OTHER HOUSEHOLDS	769	915	1,055	1,019	–16.0	–24.5

Because of changes in methodology, the 2005 data on pensions and Social Security are not comparable with earlier years.
Note: Spending by category will not add to total spending because gift spending is also included in the preceding product and service categories and personal taxes are not included in the total.
Source: Bureau of Labor Statistics, 1984, 1990, 2000, and 2005 Consumer Expenditure Surveys, Internet site http://www.bls .gov/cex/; calculations by New Strategist

Spending Is Highest in the West

But it is growing the fastest in the Northeast.

In the West, the average household spent $52,891 in 2005, 14 percent more than the average household. This is no surprise, since housing prices are much higher there than in the other regions. Spending is lowest in the South, at just $42,504—8 percent below average. Between 1984 and 2005, spending grew just 5 percent in the South, after adjusting for inflation. In contrast, average household spending increased 18 percent in the Northeast. One factor behind the slow spending growth in the South is the influx of retirees with lower incomes and spending levels.

Households in all four regions increased their spending on food-away-from-home, mortgage interest, property tax, health insurance, and education. They cut their spending on food-at-home (groceries), apparel, and other lodging (mostly hotels and motels). Although spending increases in some regions were much larger than in others, this does not mean households are better off. It means they have bigger bills. In the Northeast, for example, average household spending increased 18 percent overall between 1984 and 2005, but spending on property tax and health insurance more than doubled during those years.

■ Since 2000, spending gains in the Midwest have slowed to a crawl, reflecting job losses in its manufacturing base.

Spending is lowest in the South

(average annual household spending by region, 2005)

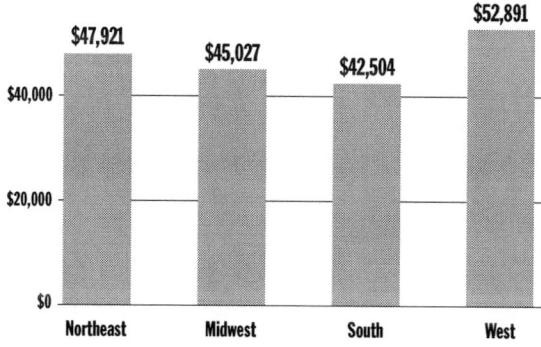

Table 9.16 Average Spending by Households in the Northeast, 1984 to 2005

(average annual spending of consumer units in the Northeast, 1984 to 2005; percent change for selected years; in 2005 dollars)

	average spending				percent change	
	2005	2000	1990	1984	2000–05	1984–05
Number of consumer units in the Northeast (in 000s)	22,356	20,994	20,259	19,686	6.5%	13.6%
Average annual spending of consumer units	$47,921	$44,121	$44,075	$40,588	8.6	18.1
FOOD	$6,495	$6,098	$6,908	$6,554	6.5%	−0.9%
Food at home	3,645	3,632	3,884	3,927	0.4	−7.2
Cereals and bakery products	508	557	608	536	−8.8	−5.2
Cereals and cereal products	162	186	197	147	−12.9	10.5
Bakery products	346	370	411	389	−6.4	−11.1
Meats, poultry, fish, and eggs	885	1,001	1,122	1,229	−11.6	−28.0
Beef	243	281	338	400	−13.6	−39.3
Pork	163	184	194	222	−11.3	−26.5
Other meats	125	132	166	184	−5.0	−32.1
Poultry	159	197	208	190	−19.4	−16.2
Fish and seafood	158	169	167	162	−6.5	−2.3
Eggs	37	40	49	71	−6.8	−48.2
Dairy products	424	401	468	521	5.6	−18.6
Fresh milk and cream	151	150	227	246	0.9	−38.7
Other dairy products	273	252	241	274	8.4	−0.5
Fruits and vegetables	652	657	663	679	−0.7	−3.9
Fresh fruits	214	205	203	207	4.2	3.5
Fresh vegetables	217	209	191	197	4.0	9.9
Processed fruits	127	149	163	164	−14.5	−22.3
Processed vegetables	95	94	108	111	0.9	−14.3
Other food at home	1,176	1,015	1,022	908	15.9	29.5
Sugar and other sweets	126	143	133	128	−11.8	−1.4
Fats and oils	93	101	91	94	−7.9	−1.0
Miscellaneous foods	614	451	433	359	36.0	71.0
Nonalcoholic beverages	306	272	318	329	12.4	−7.0
Food prepared by consumer unit on trips	37	47	48	55	−20.4	−32.1
Food away from home	2,850	2,467	3,024	2,628	15.5	8.5
ALCOHOLIC BEVERAGES	441	442	496	523	−0.3	−15.6
HOUSING	16,421	15,317	14,349	12,284	7.2	33.7
Shelter	10,071	9,325	8,456	6,481	8.0	55.4
Owned dwellings	6,681	5,930	4,939	3,603	12.7	85.4
Mortgage interest and charges	3,049	2,919	2,767	1,741	4.4	75.2
Property taxes	2,344	2,019	1,321	1,092	16.1	114.6
Maintenance, repair, insurance, other expenses	1,288	991	850	771	29.9	67.1
Rented dwellings	2,765	2,761	2,737	2,201	0.2	25.6
Other lodging	624	634	780	675	−1.6	−7.5
Utilities, fuels, and public services	3,409	2,915	2,960	3,303	17.0	3.2
Natural gas	621	468	426	622	32.6	−0.2
Electricity	1,102	925	1,039	1,105	19.1	−0.3

(continued)

	average spending				percent change	
	2005	**2000**	**1990**	**1984**	**2000–05**	**1984–05**
Fuel oil and other fuels	$391	$307	$384	$575	27.2%	−32.0%
Telephone	1,035	971	880	814	6.6	27.2
Water and other public services	261	243	230	188	7.5	38.9
Household services	**765**	**729**	**565**	**513**	**4.9**	**49.1**
Personal services	307	354	275	192	−13.2	60.1
Other household services	458	375	290	323	22.0	41.7
Housekeeping supplies	**654**	**601**	**637**	**558**	**8.8**	**17.1**
Laundry and cleaning supplies	118	166	182	156	−28.7	−24.4
Other household products	342	278	254	237	23.1	44.4
Postage and stationery	194	158	200	164	23.1	18.6
Household furnishings and equipment	**1,522**	**1,747**	**1,730**	**1,429**	**−12.9**	**6.5**
Household textiles	132	152	131	118	−13.1	11.5
Furniture	385	440	510	368	−12.5	4.5
Floor coverings	58	53	236	71	8.8	−18.8
Major appliances	210	203	217	261	3.4	−19.6
Small appliances and miscellaneous housewares	99	103	93	107	−4.1	−7.6
Miscellaneous household equipment	638	796	542	502	−19.9	27.1
APPAREL AND RELATED SERVICES	**2,036**	**2,399**	**2,703**	**2,714**	**−15.1**	**−25.0**
Men and boys	**467**	**549**	**622**	**722**	**−14.9**	**−35.3**
Men, aged 16 or older	379	424	505	549	−10.6	−30.9
Boys, aged 2 to 15	88	125	117	173	−29.5	−49.1
Women and girls	**848**	**963**	**1,112**	**1,070**	**−11.9**	**−20.7**
Women, aged 16 or older	722	800	976	898	−9.7	−19.6
Girls, aged 2 to 15	126	163	136	171	−22.8	−26.3
Children under age 2	**87**	**93**	**106**	**92**	**−6.5**	**−5.5**
Footwear	**354**	**433**	**456**	**412**	**−18.3**	**−14.0**
Other apparel products and services	**281**	**361**	**408**	**421**	**−22.1**	**−33.3**
TRANSPORTATION	**7,732**	**7,558**	**7,187**	**7,491**	**2.3**	**3.2**
Vehicle purchases	**2,911**	**3,084**	**2,869**	**3,094**	**−5.6**	**−5.9**
Cars and trucks, new	1,760	1,651	1,748	2,086	6.6	−15.6
Cars and trucks, used	1,114	1,413	1,104	996	−21.2	11.8
Gasoline and motor oil	**1,761**	**1,241**	**1,296**	**1,662**	**41.9**	**6.0**
Other vehicle expenses	**2,424**	**2,553**	**2,380**	**2,088**	**−5.1**	**16.1**
Vehicle finance charges	241	259	356	306	−6.8	−21.3
Maintenance and repairs	641	646	795	829	−0.8	−22.7
Vehicle insurance	967	916	941	716	5.5	35.0
Vehicle rentals, leases, licenses, other charges	574	733	288	237	−21.7	142.4
Public transportation	**637**	**680**	**643**	**645**	**−6.4**	**−1.2**
HEALTH CARE	**2,581**	**2,112**	**2,086**	**1,850**	**22.2**	**39.5**
Health insurance	1,429	1,030	826	571	38.8	150.1
Medical services	563	572	835	904	−1.5	−37.7
Drugs	482	396	306	286	21.8	68.7
Medical supplies	107	115	120	88	−6.6	21.1
ENTERTAINMENT	**2,263**	**2,172**	**1,989**	**1,833**	**4.2**	**23.5**
Fees and admissions	615	654	595	622	−6.0	−1.2
Audio and visual equipment and services	903	711	641	545	27.0	65.7

(continued)

	average spending				percent change	
	2005	**2000**	**1990**	**1984**	**2000–05**	**1984–05**
Pets, toys, hobbies, playground equipment	$394	$358	$403	$320	9.9%	23.3%
Other entertainment products and services	352	448	351	344	−21.4	2.3
PERSONAL CARE PRODUCTS AND SERVICES	540	656	526	509	−17.6	6.0
READING	148	195	256	288	−24.1	−48.5
EDUCATION	1,387	933	886	724	48.6	91.7
TOBACCO PRODUCTS AND SMOKING SUPPLIES	330	370	417	459	−10.7	−28.0
MISCELLANEOUS	822	837	1,195	679	−1.8	21.1
CASH CONTRIBUTIONS	1,370	1,207	1,058	1,310	13.5	4.6
PERSONAL INSURANCE AND PENSIONS	5,353	3,823	4,020	3,374	40.0	58.7
Life and other personal insurance	374	480	510	455	−22.0	−17.8
Pensions and Social Security*	4,980	3,343	3,510	2,919	48.9	70.6
PERSONAL TAXES	2,160	3,383	4,623	4,058	−36.2	−46.8
Federal income taxes	1,412	2,491	3,600	2,996	−43.3	−52.9
State and local income taxes	509	718	926	921	−29.1	−44.7
Other taxes	239	175	99	141	36.8	69.5
GIFTS FOR PEOPLE IN OTHER HOUSEHOLDS	1,353	1,243	1,648	1,308	8.9	3.4

* Because of changes in methodology, the 2005 data on pensions and Social Security are not comparable with earlier years.
Note: Spending by category will not add to total spending because gift spending is also included in the preceding product and service categories and personal taxes are not included in the total.
Source: Bureau of Labor Statistics, 1984, 1990, 2000, and 2005 Consumer Expenditure Surveys, Internet site http://www.bls.gov/cex/; calculations by New Strategist

Table 9.17 Average Spending by Households in the Midwest, 1984 to 2005

(average annual spending of consumer units in the Midwest, 1984 to 2005; percent change for selected years; in 2005 dollars)

	average spending				percent change	
	2005	2000	1990	1984	2000–05	1984–05
Number of consumer units in the Midwest (in 000s)	27,005	25,717	24,205	23,737	5.0%	13.8%
Average annual spending of consumer units	$45,027	$44,473	$38,754	$39,787	1.2	13.2
FOOD	**$5,754**	**$5,960**	**$6,010**	**$6,079**	**–3.5%**	**–5.3%**
Food at home	**3,232**	**3,326**	**3,456**	**3,688**	**–2.8**	**–12.4**
Cereals and bakery products	454	504	519	515	–9.8	–11.9
Cereals and cereal products	143	172	178	167	–17.0	–14.5
Bakery products	311	331	341	346	–6.1	–10.1
Meats, poultry, fish, and eggs	712	818	883	1,064	–12.9	–33.1
Beef	220	256	294	370	–14.2	–40.6
Pork	150	181	194	242	–17.3	–38.1
Other meats	109	117	146	179	–6.7	–39.0
Poultry	121	142	123	130	–14.6	–6.7
Fish and seafood	85	88	91	83	–3.9	2.8
Eggs	26	32	36	60	–18.1	–56.8
Dairy products	391	374	418	459	4.5	–14.7
Fresh milk and cream	150	150	197	231	0.2	–35.1
Other dairy products	240	223	221	227	7.4	5.5
Fruits and vegetables	517	547	556	556	–5.4	–7.1
Fresh fruits	175	171	181	171	2.2	2.3
Fresh vegetables	150	155	151	158	–3.5	–5.0
Processed fruits	106	128	131	124	–17.3	–14.6
Processed vegetables	87	92	93	103	–5.3	–15.8
Other food at home	1,158	1,085	1,080	1,038	6.7	11.6
Sugar and other sweets	119	141	136	147	–15.4	–18.8
Fats and oils	83	85	97	105	–2.4	–21.1
Miscellaneous foods	615	531	504	445	15.9	38.1
Nonalcoholic beverages	300	282	303	338	6.2	–11.3
Food prepared by consumer unit on trips	40	47	42	55	–14.0	–26.6
Food away from home	**2,522**	**2,633**	**2,554**	**2,393**	**–4.2**	**5.4**
ALCOHOLIC BEVERAGES	**460**	**440**	**438**	**457**	**4.5**	**0.7**
HOUSING	**14,151**	**13,566**	**11,492**	**11,812**	**4.3**	**19.8**
Shelter	**7,886**	**7,523**	**6,062**	**5,804**	**4.8**	**35.9**
Owned dwellings	5,688	5,216	3,834	3,699	9.1	53.8
Mortgage interest and charges	3,001	2,802	2,156	2,002	7.1	49.9
Property taxes	1,671	1,388	955	981	20.4	70.3
Maintenance, repair, insurance, other expenses	1,016	1,024	723	716	–0.8	41.9
Rented dwellings	1,664	1,736	1,793	1,536	–4.2	8.4
Other lodging	534	570	435	570	–6.4	–6.2
Utilities, fuels, and public services	**3,158**	**2,850**	**2,746**	**3,258**	**10.8**	**–3.1**
Natural gas	725	488	557	868	48.7	–16.5
Electricity	994	946	998	1,158	5.1	–14.2

(continued)

	average spending				percent change	
	2005	2000	1990	1984	2000–05	1984–05
Fuel oil and other fuels	$106	$83	$124	$218	28.0%	−51.4%
Telephone	1,000	1,003	817	765	−0.3	30.7
Water and other public services	333	330	250	246	0.9	35.2
Household services	**759**	**760**	**545**	**528**	**−0.1**	**43.7**
Personal services	346	419	303	216	−17.3	60.1
Other household services	413	341	242	312	21.0	32.4
Housekeeping supplies	**618**	**583**	**583**	**602**	**6.0**	**2.7**
Laundry and cleaning supplies	140	151	164	171	−7.2	−18.2
Other household products	317	270	245	261	17.4	21.3
Postage and stationery	162	162	172	169	−0.1	−4.2
Household furnishings and equipment	**1,730**	**1,850**	**1,557**	**1,620**	**−6.5**	**6.8**
Household textiles	144	133	151	150	8.5	−4.2
Furniture	395	429	435	459	−7.9	−13.9
Floor coverings	56	61	157	148	−8.6	−62.3
Major appliances	210	225	196	256	−6.5	−17.9
Small appliances and miscellaneous housewares	108	117	109	124	−7.5	−12.9
Miscellaneous household equipment	817	887	510	483	−7.9	69.1
APPAREL AND RELATED SERVICES	**1,750**	**2,174**	**2,031**	**2,382**	**−19.5**	**−26.5**
Men and boys	**388**	**555**	**496**	**665**	**−30.0**	**−41.7**
Men, aged 16 or older	310	438	400	530	−29.2	−41.5
Boys, aged 2 to 15	78	117	96	135	−33.2	−42.4
Women and girls	**728**	**874**	**864**	**968**	**−16.7**	**−24.8**
Women, aged 16 or older	621	733	738	801	−15.2	−22.4
Girls, aged 2 to 15	107	142	126	165	−24.5	−35.3
Children under age 2	**77**	**100**	**94**	**102**	**−22.8**	**−24.1**
Footwear	**280**	**367**	**245**	**321**	**−23.8**	**−12.9**
Other apparel products and services	**278**	**278**	**332**	**327**	**0.0**	**−15.0**
TRANSPORTATION	**7,753**	**8,893**	**7,161**	**7,851**	**−12.8**	**−1.3**
Vehicle purchases	**3,085**	**4,263**	**3,090**	**3,417**	**−27.6**	**−9.7**
Cars and trucks, new	1,700	1,747	1,331	1,767	−2.7	−3.8
Cars and trucks, used	1,298	2,418	1,726	1,588	−46.3	−18.3
Gasoline and motor oil	**1,975**	**1,533**	**1,494**	**1,996**	**28.8**	**−1.1**
Other vehicle expenses	**2,313**	**2,639**	**2,264**	**2,086**	**−12.4**	**10.9**
Vehicle finance charges	274	400	448	372	−31.6	−26.4
Maintenance and repairs	648	692	798	838	−6.3	−22.7
Vehicle insurance	845	851	725	586	−0.7	44.1
Vehicle rentals, leases, licenses, other charges	546	698	294	289	−21.7	88.6
Public transportation	**380**	**457**	**312**	**353**	**−16.9**	**7.5**
HEALTH CARE	**2,841**	**2,463**	**1,996**	**1,872**	**15.3**	**51.7**
Health insurance	1,409	1,187	822	711	18.7	98.3
Medical services	755	652	683	778	15.8	−3.0
Drugs	558	498	371	299	12.1	86.7
Medical supplies	119	126	123	85	−5.5	40.7
ENTERTAINMENT	**2,384**	**2,314**	**2,026**	**1,863**	**3.0**	**28.0**
Fees and admissions	614	642	519	577	−4.4	6.4
Audio and visual equipment and services	839	754	647	541	11.2	55.0

(continued)

	average spending				percent change	
	2005	**2000**	**1990**	**1984**	**2000–05**	**1984–05**
Pets, toys, hobbies, playground equipment	$411	$408	$403	$338	0.7%	21.5%
Other entertainment products and services	520	509	457	406	2.1	28.1
PERSONAL CARE PRODUCTS AND SERVICES	**514**	**617**	**490**	**562**	**–16.7**	**–8.5**
READING	**132**	**186**	**239**	**259**	**–29.0**	**–49.1**
EDUCATION	**998**	**756**	**589**	**586**	**31.9**	**70.2**
TOBACCO PRODUCTS AND SMOKING SUPPLIES	**374**	**408**	**445**	**442**	**–8.4**	**–15.3**
MISCELLANEOUS	**837**	**905**	**1,125**	**711**	**–7.5**	**17.8**
CASH CONTRIBUTIONS	**1,868**	**1,832**	**1,113**	**1,367**	**2.0**	**36.7**
PERSONAL INSURANCE AND PENSIONS	**5,212**	**3,958**	**3,598**	**3,547**	**31.7**	**46.9**
Life and other personal insurance	380	487	530	562	–21.9	–32.4
Pensions and Social Security*	4,832	3,472	3,068	2,985	39.2	61.9
PERSONAL TAXES	**2,326**	**4,159**	**3,625**	**4,028**	**–44.1**	**–42.3**
Federal income taxes	1,533	3,061	2,624	2,908	–49.9	–47.3
State and local income taxes	572	924	849	921	–38.1	–37.9
Other taxes	221	174	154	199	27.4	10.9
GIFTS FOR PEOPLE IN OTHER HOUSEHOLDS	**1,055**	**1,464**	**1,236**	**1,242**	**–27.9**	**–15.1**

* Because of changes in methodology, the 2005 data on pensions and Social Security are not comparable with earlier years.
Note: Spending by category will not add to total spending because gift spending is also included in the preceding product and service categories and personal taxes are not included in the total.
Source: Bureau of Labor Statistics, 1984, 1990, 2000, and 2005 Consumer Expenditure Surveys, Internet site http://www.bls .gov/cex/; calculations by New Strategist

Table 9.18 Average Spending by Households in the South, 1984 to 2005

(average annual spending of consumer units in the South, 1984 to 2005; percent change for selected years; in 2005 dollars)

	average spending				percent change	
	2005	2000	1990	1984	2000–05	1984–05
Number of consumer units in the South (in 000s)	42,120	38,245	32,651	29,852	10.1%	41.1%
Average annual spending of consumer units	$42,504	$39,363	$40,375	$40,577	8.0	4.7
FOOD	**$5,491**	**$5,358**	**$6,092**	**$5,731**	**2.5%**	**–4.2%**
Food at home	**3,011**	**3,202**	**3,558**	**3,442**	**–6.0**	**–12.5**
Cereals and bakery products	400	479	516	451	–16.4	–11.3
Cereals and cereal products	129	168	190	154	–23.1	–16.3
Bakery products	270	311	326	297	–13.1	–9.1
Meats, poultry, fish, and eggs	732	884	979	1,081	–17.1	–32.3
Beef	227	261	318	368	–13.0	–38.4
Pork	157	200	212	216	–21.3	–27.4
Other meats	89	107	140	122	–16.5	–27.2
Poultry	129	161	157	164	–19.9	–21.1
Fish and seafood	100	113	108	143	–11.8	–30.0
Eggs	30	41	43	68	–26.5	–55.7
Dairy products	332	324	405	425	2.4	–21.8
Fresh milk and cream	137	138	194	231	–1.0	–40.7
Other dairy products	195	186	211	194	4.8	0.7
Fruits and vegetables	475	533	568	511	–10.9	–7.1
Fresh fruits	148	160	170	139	–7.5	6.4
Fresh vegetables	149	158	164	152	–5.5	–2.1
Processed fruits	89	117	121	115	–23.8	–22.4
Processed vegetables	89	98	112	107	–8.8	–16.9
Other food at home	1,072	983	1,091	929	9.0	15.4
Sugar and other sweets	109	121	139	128	–10.2	–14.7
Fats and oils	79	93	108	103	–15.1	–23.6
Miscellaneous foods	563	465	490	380	21.1	48.3
Nonalcoholic beverages	291	270	309	318	7.8	–8.4
Food prepared by consumer unit on trips	30	33	43	43	–8.8	–30.6
Food away from home	**2,480**	**2,156**	**2,534**	**2,289**	**15.0**	**8.3**
ALCOHOLIC BEVERAGES	**350**	**345**	**372**	**479**	**1.5**	**–27.0**
HOUSING	**13,402**	**12,311**	**11,661**	**12,459**	**8.9**	**7.6**
Shelter	**7,167**	**6,622**	**5,929**	**6,184**	**8.2**	**15.9**
Owned dwellings	4,900	4,313	3,628	3,806	13.6	28.7
Mortgage interest and charges	2,815	2,538	2,250	2,603	10.9	8.1
Property taxes	1,085	936	584	476	16.0	128.2
Maintenance, repair, insurance, other expenses	1,000	838	793	727	19.3	37.5
Rented dwellings	1,911	1,863	1,889	1,712	2.6	11.6
Other lodging	355	446	412	665	–20.4	–46.6
Utilities, fuels, and public services	**3,240**	**2,944**	**2,989**	**3,105**	**10.0**	**4.3**
Natural gas	294	215	224	305	36.4	–3.5
Electricity	1,401	1,302	1,420	1,470	7.6	–4.7

(continued)

	average spending				percent change	
	2005	**2000**	**1990**	**1984**	**2000–05**	**1984–05**
Fuel oil and other fuels	$75	$65	$84	$192	16.0%	−60.9%
Telephone	1,085	1,011	920	836	7.4	29.7
Water and other public services	385	353	339	303	9.2	27.2
Household services	**777**	**732**	**699**	**620**	**6.2**	**25.3**
Personal services	313	322	317	273	−2.8	14.8
Other household services	464	409	383	348	13.3	33.4
Housekeeping supplies	**573**	**499**	**568**	**566**	**14.8**	**1.3**
Laundry and cleaning supplies	141	143	163	162	−1.3	−12.8
Other household products	298	242	248	273	23.4	9.3
Postage and stationery	133	115	157	130	16.1	2.5
Household furnishings and equipment	**1,646**	**1,513**	**1,476**	**1,981**	**8.8**	**−16.9**
Household textiles	128	96	142	171	32.8	−25.2
Furniture	463	383	418	622	20.8	−25.6
Floor coverings	56	47	72	218	20.4	−74.3
Major appliances	214	191	229	280	12.3	−23.6
Small appliances and miscellaneous housewares	88	82	103	137	7.8	−35.9
Miscellaneous household equipment	697	715	511	556	−2.5	25.3
APPAREL AND RELATED SERVICES	**1,836**	**1,834**	**2,315**	**2,423**	**0.1**	**−24.2**
Men and boys	**421**	**433**	**568**	**605**	**−2.8**	**−30.4**
Men, aged 16 or older	315	335	468	496	−5.9	−36.5
Boys, aged 2 to 15	106	99	100	107	7.4	−1.1
Women and girls	**738**	**694**	**986**	**972**	**6.3**	**−24.1**
Women, aged 16 or older	617	566	865	844	9.0	−26.9
Girls, aged 2 to 15	121	128	121	128	−5.6	−5.3
Children under age 2	**76**	**93**	**99**	**90**	**−18.3**	**−15.8**
Footwear	**322**	**344**	**288**	**350**	**−6.3**	**−7.9**
Other apparel products and services	**279**	**270**	**375**	**406**	**3.4**	**−31.3**
TRANSPORTATION	**7,990**	**8,178**	**7,930**	**8,132**	**−2.3**	**−1.7**
Vehicle purchases	**3,543**	**4,044**	**3,399**	**3,449**	**−12.4**	**2.7**
Cars and trucks, new	1,777	1,851	1,952	1,968	−4.0	−9.7
Cars and trucks, used	1,689	2,165	1,408	1,440	−22.0	17.3
Gasoline and motor oil	**2,069**	**1,463**	**1,721**	**2,145**	**41.4**	**−3.5**
Other vehicle expenses	**2,085**	**2,351**	**2,437**	**2,184**	**−11.3**	**−4.5**
Vehicle finance charges	336	415	517	485	−19.1	−30.7
Maintenance and repairs	587	662	897	891	−11.4	−34.1
Vehicle insurance	879	847	813	630	3.8	39.6
Vehicle rentals, leases, licenses, other charges	282	426	211	179	−33.9	57.9
Public transportation	**293**	**321**	**372**	**353**	**−8.7**	**−17.1**
HEALTH CARE	**2,606**	**2,435**	**2,391**	**2,179**	**7.0**	**19.6**
Health insurance	1,353	1,206	952	836	12.2	61.8
Medical services	600	605	856	861	−0.7	−30.3
Drugs	557	533	444	363	4.5	53.5
Medical supplies	96	93	139	118	3.2	−18.9
ENTERTAINMENT	**2,112**	**1,834**	**1,892**	**1,861**	**15.2**	**13.5**
Fees and admissions	451	448	457	477	0.7	−5.5
Audio and visual equipment and services	868	651	656	586	33.3	48.0

(continued)

	average spending				percent change	
	2005	2000	1990	1984	2000–05	1984–05
Pets, toys, hobbies, playground equipment	$396	$355	$405	$357	11.6%	10.9%
Other entertainment products and services	397	380	374	438	4.5	–9.4
PERSONAL CARE PRODUCTS AND SERVICES	**508**	**624**	**536**	**528**	**–18.6**	**–3.8**
READING	**94**	**129**	**196**	**209**	**–27.3**	**–54.9**
EDUCATION	**674**	**541**	**477**	**449**	**24.6**	**50.0**
TOBACCO PRODUCTS AND SMOKING SUPPLIES	**318**	**379**	**427**	**449**	**–16.1**	**–29.2**
MISCELLANEOUS	**654**	**827**	**1,255**	**885**	**–20.9**	**–26.1**
CASH CONTRIBUTIONS	**1,710**	**1,081**	**1,254**	**1,274**	**58.2**	**34.2**
PERSONAL INSURANCE AND PENSIONS	**4,760**	**3,490**	**3,579**	**3,521**	**36.4**	**35.2**
Life and other personal insurance	419	462	550	630	–9.2	–33.5
Pensions and Social Security*	4,341	3,028	3,029	2,891	43.4	50.2
PERSONAL TAXES	**2,265**	**2,854**	**4,057**	**4,192**	**–20.6**	**–46.0**
Federal income taxes	1,694	2,328	3,399	3,498	–27.2	–51.6
State and local income taxes	435	364	545	603	19.5	–27.9
Other taxes	136	161	112	90	–15.6	50.7
GIFTS FOR PEOPLE IN OTHER HOUSEHOLDS	**916**	**1,030**	**1,261**	**1,199**	**–11.1**	**–23.6**

* Because of changes in methodology, the 2005 data on pensions and Social Security are not comparable with earlier years.
Note: Spending by category will not add to total spending because gift spending is also included in the preceding product and service categories and personal taxes are not included in the total.
Source: Bureau of Labor Statistics, 1984, 1990, 2000, and 2005 Consumer Expenditure Surveys, Internet site http://www.bls .gov/cex/; calculations by New Strategist

Table 9.19 Average Spending by Households in the West, 1984 to 2005

(average annual spending of consumer units in the West, 1984 to 2005; percent change for selected years; in 2005 dollars)

	average spending				percent change	
	2005	2000	1990	1984	2000–05	1984–05
Number of consumer units in the West (in 000s)	25,875	24,410	19,853	16,948	6.0%	52.7%
Average annual spending of consumer units	$52,891	$46,872	$48,505	$45,560	12.8	16.1
FOOD	**$6,339**	**$6,299**	**$6,960**	**$6,709**	**0.6%**	**−5.5%**
Food at home	**3,527**	**3,708**	**4,108**	**3,929**	**−4.9**	**−10.2**
Cereals and bakery products	456	544	586	489	−16.2	−6.7
Cereals and cereal products	148	189	208	165	−21.9	−10.5
Bakery products	307	355	377	323	−13.5	−5.0
Meats, poultry, fish, and eggs	767	931	1,046	1,038	−17.6	−26.1
Beef	222	289	360	363	−23.2	−38.8
Pork	143	186	182	205	−23.1	−30.2
Other meats	101	107	143	132	−5.3	−23.2
Poultry	135	166	166	160	−18.5	−15.5
Fish and seafood	125	141	140	109	−11.1	14.7
Eggs	40	43	52	70	−7.2	−42.5
Dairy products	401	404	504	539	−0.7	−25.7
Fresh milk and cream	152	164	232	261	−7.6	−41.8
Other dairy products	249	239	272	276	4.1	−9.9
Fruits and vegetables	624	671	686	671	−7.1	−7.0
Fresh fruits	214	222	217	211	−3.7	1.7
Fresh vegetables	206	215	215	201	−4.4	2.4
Processed fruits	117	140	151	156	−16.1	−25.0
Processed vegetables	87	95	103	102	−8.7	−14.3
Other food at home	1,279	1,158	1,287	1,117	10.5	14.6
Sugar and other sweets	128	133	157	160	−3.5	−19.9
Fats and oils	90	99	109	115	−8.8	−21.5
Miscellaneous foods	673	549	586	474	22.6	42.1
Nonalcoholic beverages	324	314	350	368	3.1	−12.1
Food prepared by consumer unit on trips	64	62	85	79	2.6	−18.9
Food away from home	**2,813**	**2,592**	**2,853**	**2,778**	**8.5**	**1.3**
ALCOHOLIC BEVERAGES	**503**	**509**	**490**	**664**	**−1.2**	**−24.2**
HOUSING	**18,016**	**15,846**	**15,687**	**14,034**	**13.7**	**28.4**
Shelter	**11,337**	**9,830**	**9,523**	**8,361**	**15.3**	**35.6**
Owned dwellings	7,337	6,034	5,875	4,566	21.6	60.7
Mortgage interest and charges	4,693	3,967	4,105	3,105	18.3	51.1
Property taxes	1,452	1,119	888	735	29.7	97.6
Maintenance, repair, insurance, other expenses	1,192	946	883	726	26.0	64.3
Rented dwellings	3,398	3,212	3,104	2,983	5.8	13.9
Other lodging	601	584	544	812	2.9	−26.0
Utilities, fuels, and public services	**2,923**	**2,525**	**2,512**	**2,519**	**15.8**	**16.0**
Natural gas	375	308	317	492	21.6	−23.9
Electricity	969	798	920	799	21.4	21.3

(continued)

	average spending				percent change	
	2005	2000	1990	1984	2000–05	1984–05
Fuel oil and other fuels	$73	$40	$49	$85	83.9%	−13.7%
Telephone	1,047	980	913	861	6.8	21.6
Water and other public services	459	398	312	282	15.3	62.8
Household services	**913**	**903**	**867**	**727**	**1.1**	**25.5**
Personal services	323	408	427	280	−20.9	15.3
Other household services	590	494	439	445	19.3	32.4
Housekeeping supplies	**629**	**535**	**668**	**583**	**17.5**	**7.9**
Laundry and cleaning supplies	130	138	170	162	−6.0	−19.6
Other household products	338	245	282	214	38.0	57.7
Postage and stationery	161	153	217	207	5.2	−22.1
Household furnishings and equipment	**2,214**	**2,054**	**2,116**	**1,844**	**7.8**	**20.1**
Household textiles	128	120	169	211	6.5	−39.2
Furniture	621	555	526	534	12.0	16.3
Floor coverings	55	42	118	102	31.1	−45.8
Major appliances	264	251	239	280	5.3	−5.7
Small appliances and miscellaneous housewares	136	105	146	132	28.9	3.4
Miscellaneous household equipment	1,009	981	917	586	2.9	72.0
APPAREL AND RELATED SERVICES	**1,975**	**2,206**	**2,769**	**2,444**	**−10.5**	**−19.2**
Men and boys	**499**	**505**	**698**	**664**	**−1.1**	**−24.8**
Men, aged 16 or older	416	401	590	543	3.6	−23.4
Boys, aged 2 to 15	83	103	108	120	−19.6	−31.0
Women and girls	**724**	**846**	**1,101**	**929**	**−14.4**	**−22.0**
Women, aged 16 or older	594	739	955	793	−19.7	−25.1
Girls, aged 2 to 15	130	108	146	135	20.7	−3.9
Children under age 2	**93**	**85**	**124**	**96**	**9.3**	**−3.0**
Footwear	**330**	**443**	**403**	**306**	**−25.6**	**7.7**
Other apparel products and services	**329**	**327**	**442**	**449**	**0.7**	**−26.8**
TRANSPORTATION	**10,068**	**9,009**	**8,259**	**9,053**	**11.8**	**11.2**
Vehicle purchases	**4,572**	**3,890**	**3,249**	**3,686**	**17.5**	**24.0**
Cars and trucks, new	2,571	1,995	1,839	1,947	28.9	32.0
Cars and trucks, used	1,874	1,837	1,367	1,650	2.0	13.6
Gasoline and motor oil	**2,180**	**1,588**	**1,666**	**2,083**	**37.3**	**4.7**
Other vehicle expenses	**2,708**	**2,933**	**2,784**	**2,592**	**−7.7**	**4.5**
Vehicle finance charges	304	373	429	400	−18.5	−24.1
Maintenance and repairs	860	849	1,039	1,111	1.2	−22.6
Vehicle insurance	993	942	932	729	5.4	36.2
Vehicle rentals, leases, licenses, other charges	550	768	384	353	−28.4	55.6
Public transportation	**608**	**598**	**560**	**692**	**1.7**	**−12.1**
HEALTH CARE	**2,647**	**2,269**	**2,307**	**1,885**	**16.6**	**40.4**
Health insurance	1,264	967	834	570	30.7	121.9
Medical services	820	759	1,010	891	8.1	−8.0
Drugs	459	417	344	278	10.0	65.0
Medical supplies	105	126	120	148	−16.6	−29.3
ENTERTAINMENT	**2,950**	**2,292**	**2,769**	**2,547**	**28.7**	**15.8**
Fees and admissions	760	675	720	765	12.6	−0.7
Audio and visual equipment and services	959	735	789	793	30.5	20.9

(continued)

	average spending				percent change	
	2005	**2000**	**1990**	**1984**	**2000–05**	**1984–05**
Pets, toys, hobbies, playground equipment	$491	$403	$447	$427	22.0%	15.1%
Other entertainment products and services	741	480	811	564	54.5	31.4
PERSONAL CARE PRODUCTS AND SERVICES	**623**	**674**	**640**	**586**	**–7.5**	**6.2**
READING	**155**	**179**	**245**	**258**	**–13.5**	**–39.8**
EDUCATION	**926**	**764**	**560**	**585**	**21.1**	**58.4**
TOBACCO PRODUCTS AND SMOKING SUPPLIES	**254**	**278**	**330**	**342**	**–8.6**	**–25.8**
MISCELLANEOUS	**1,016**	**974**	**1,487**	**1,173**	**4.3**	**–13.4**
CASH CONTRIBUTIONS	**1,627**	**1,398**	**1,457**	**1,382**	**16.3**	**17.8**
PERSONAL INSURANCE AND PENSIONS	**5,789**	**4,173**	**4,546**	**3,900**	**38.7**	**48.4**
Life and other personal insurance	326	378	445	573	–13.7	–43.1
Pensions and Social Security*	5,462	3,795	4,100	3,325	43.9	64.3
PERSONAL TAXES	**2,938**	**4,063**	**5,665**	**4,524**	**–27.7**	**–35.1**
Federal income taxes	2,117	3,206	4,402	3,579	–34.0	–40.8
State and local income taxes	677	696	1,182	904	–2.8	–25.1
Other taxes	144	159	79	41	–9.3	248.2
GIFTS FOR PEOPLE IN OTHER HOUSEHOLDS	**1,188**	**1,283**	**1,387**	**1,393**	**–7.4**	**–14.7**

Because of changes in methodology, the 2005 data on pensions and Social Security are not comparable with earlier years.
Note: Spending by category will not add to total spending because gift spending is also included in the preceding product and service categories and personal taxes are not included in the total.
Source: Bureau of Labor Statistics, 1984, 1990, 2000, and 2005 Consumer Expenditure Surveys, Internet site http://www.bls.gov/cex/; calculations by New Strategist

College Graduates Are the Biggest Spenders

Their spending increased more than that of their less-educated counterparts over the past decade.

Households headed by college graduates spent $65,542 in 2005, fully 41 percent more than the average household. Incomes and spending are directly linked to education. Households headed by people with some college education or an associate's degree spent $45,699—or about an average amount. In contrast, households headed by people who went no further than high school spent $38,162, or 18 percent less than average. Households headed by people who did not graduate from high school spent just $27,435—more than 40 percent below average.

The spending of college graduates is not only above average, but it is rising faster than that of less-educated householders. College graduates boosted their spending by 12 percent between 1995 and 2005, after adjusting for inflation. This compares with increases ranging from 3 to 8 percent for the less-educated groups. Much of the increased spending of college graduates is being devoted to necessities, however. Their spending on property taxes increased 39 percent between 1995 and 2005, after adjusting for inflation. Their spending on health insurance climbed 36 percent during those years, while their spending on education increased 47 percent. College graduates spent just 8 percent more on entertainment in 2005 than in 1995, after adjusting for inflation.

■ The spending patterns of householders with a high school diploma or less education is heavily influenced by the fact that many are older retirees.

College graduates are the only ones who spend more than the average household

(average annual spending of households by educational attainment of householder, 2005)

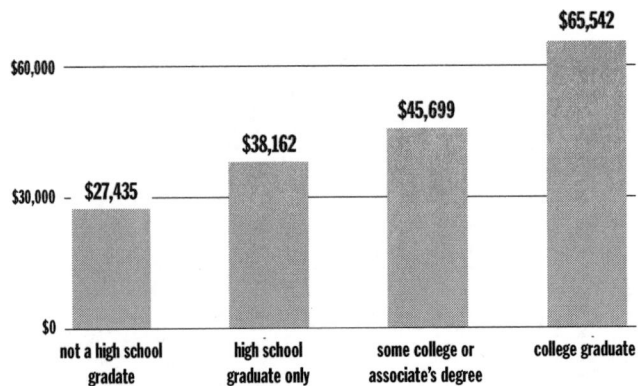

Table 9.20 Average Spending by Households Headed by People without a High School Diploma, 1995 to 2005

(average annual spending of consumer units headed by people without a high school diploma, 1995 to 2005; percent change for selected years; in 2005 dollars)

	average spending			percent change	
	2005	2000	1995	2000–05	1995–05
Number of consumer units headed by people without a high school diploma (in 000s)	18,028	17,991	21,534	0.2%	−16.3%
Average annual spending of consumer units	$27,435	$26,523	$25,354	3.4	8.2
FOOD	**$4,374**	**$4,591**	**$4,343**	**−4.7%**	**0.7%**
Food at home	**2,912**	**3,290**	**3,363**	**−11.5**	**−13.4**
Cereals and bakery products	391	494	509	−20.9	−23.1
Cereals and cereal products	135	188	206	−28.3	−34.6
Bakery products	256	306	304	−16.4	−15.7
Meats, poultry, fish, and eggs	750	988	1,059	−24.1	−29.1
Beef	221	293	320	−24.5	−31.0
Pork	166	230	237	−27.9	−30.0
Other meats	94	118	144	−20.3	−34.5
Poultry	134	174	181	−22.8	−25.8
Fish and seafood	96	118	131	−18.6	−26.6
Eggs	38	57	47	−33.0	−19.9
Dairy products	330	332	337	−0.7	−2.1
Fresh milk and cream	148	158	172	−6.1	−13.8
Other dairy products	182	175	165	4.2	10.1
Fruits and vegetables	488	566	538	−13.8	−9.3
Fresh fruits	155	185	164	−16.2	−5.5
Fresh vegetables	156	181	167	−14.0	−6.4
Processed fruits	91	110	110	−17.3	−17.4
Processed vegetables	86	90	97	−4.0	−11.7
Other food at home	953	910	920	4.8	3.6
Sugar and other sweets	103	125	123	−17.4	−16.3
Fats and oils	79	98	111	−19.0	−29.1
Miscellaneous foods	474	388	378	22.2	25.4
Nonalcoholic beverages	277	276	279	0.5	−0.8
Food prepared by consumer unit on trips	20	25	29	−19.8	−32.1
Food away from home	**1,462**	**1,300**	**979**	**12.5**	**49.3**
ALCOHOLIC BEVERAGES	**192**	**164**	**140**	**16.8**	**37.5**
HOUSING	**9,437**	**8,699**	**8,255**	**8.5**	**14.3**
Shelter	**5,361**	**4,804**	**4,524**	**11.6**	**18.5**
Owned dwellings	2,547	2,370	2,250	7.5	13.2
Mortgage interest and charges	1,308	1,091	1,011	19.9	29.4
Property taxes	732	713	674	2.6	8.6
Maintenance, repair, insurance, other expenses	507	566	565	−10.4	−10.3
Rented dwellings	2,728	2,300	2,148	18.6	27.0
Other lodging	86	134	126	−35.7	−31.5
Utilities, fuels, and public services	**2,613**	**2,367**	**2,378**	**10.4**	**9.9**
Natural gas	374	276	283	35.7	32.1
Electricity	1,013	942	985	7.5	2.8

(continued)

	average spending			percent change	
	2005	**2000**	**1995**	**2000–05**	**1995–05**
Fuel oil and other fuels	$114	$120	$117	−5.2%	−2.2%
Telephone	826	775	727	6.6	13.7
Water and other public services	287	254	265	13.0	8.2
Household services	**287**	**297**	**269**	**−3.4**	**6.6**
Personal services	134	153	140	−12.5	−4.1
Other household services	153	143	129	7.1	18.2
Housekeeping supplies	**386**	**408**	**334**	**−5.5**	**15.4**
Laundry and cleaning supplies	126	151	123	−16.5	2.4
Other household products	193	171	135	12.7	43.4
Postage and stationery	68	86	76	−21.1	−10.1
Household furnishings and equipment	**790**	**823**	**750**	**−4.1**	**5.4**
Household textiles	63	51	41	23.4	53.6
Furniture	247	243	210	1.8	17.5
Floor coverings	15	18	35	−17.3	−56.6
Major appliances	114	138	160	−17.6	−28.8
Small appliances and miscellaneous housewares	54	36	55	48.8	−2.0
Miscellaneous household equipment	297	337	249	−11.8	19.5
APPAREL AND RELATED SERVICES	**1,237**	**1,335**	**1,293**	**−7.3**	**−4.3**
Men and boys	**268**	**304**	**317**	**−11.8**	**−15.3**
Men, aged 16 or older	200	217	199	−7.7	0.7
Boys, aged 2 to 15	68	88	118	−23.1	−42.3
Women and girls	**459**	**459**	**425**	**−0.1**	**7.9**
Women, aged 16 or older	365	362	345	0.9	5.9
Girls, aged 2 to 15	94	98	81	−3.6	16.4
Children under age 2	**82**	**75**	**86**	**9.5**	**−4.5**
Footwear	**282**	**341**	**314**	**−17.4**	**−10.2**
Other apparel products and services	**145**	**155**	**151**	**−6.7**	**−4.1**
TRANSPORTATION	**5,106**	**5,117**	**4,771**	**−0.2**	**7.0**
Vehicle purchases	**2,131**	**2,457**	**2,203**	**−13.3**	**−3.3**
Cars and trucks, new	916	730	633	25.4	44.7
Cars and trucks, used	1,192	1,708	1,551	−30.2	−23.1
Gasoline and motor oil	**1,471**	**1,018**	**956**	**44.4**	**53.9**
Other vehicle expenses	**1,316**	**1,456**	**1,433**	**−9.6**	**−8.1**
Vehicle finance charges	168	204	179	−17.7	−6.4
Maintenance and repairs	387	430	525	−10.0	−26.3
Vehicle insurance	599	574	566	4.4	5.8
Vehicle rentals, leases, licenses, other charges	162	248	163	−34.8	−0.5
Public transportation	**188**	**186**	**179**	**1.1**	**4.8**
HEALTH CARE	**1,835**	**1,896**	**1,989**	**−3.2**	**−7.7**
Health insurance	980	938	1,085	4.5	−9.7
Medical services	353	367	424	−3.9	−16.8
Drugs	447	525	411	−14.9	8.7
Medical supplies	56	67	67	−16.3	−16.0
ENTERTAINMENT	**1,152**	**1,016**	**984**	**13.4**	**17.1**
Fees and admissions	123	150	147	−17.8	−16.5
Audio and visual equipment and services	553	474	491	16.6	12.7

(continued)

	average spending			percent change	
	2005	**2000**	**1995**	**2000–05**	**1995–05**
Pets, toys, hobbies, playground equipment	$261	$218	$213	19.9%	22.7%
Other entertainment products and services	215	175	133	23.1	61.3
PERSONAL CARE PRODUCTS AND SERVICES	**301**	**414**	**297**	**–27.3**	**1.2**
READING	**42**	**67**	**95**	**–37.2**	**–55.7**
EDUCATION	**131**	**145**	**127**	**–9.8**	**3.3**
TOBACCO PRODUCTS, SMOKING SUPPLIES	**379**	**423**	**392**	**–10.4**	**–3.4**
MISCELLANEOUS	**459**	**584**	**645**	**–21.4**	**–28.8**
CASH CONTRIBUTIONS	**659**	**575**	**559**	**14.6**	**17.9**
PERSONAL INSURANCE AND PENSIONS	**2,133**	**1,495**	**1,463**	**42.7**	**45.7**
Life and other personal insurance	164	255	263	–35.7	–37.6
Pensions and Social Security*	1,969	1,240	1,201	58.8	64.0
PERSONAL TAXES	**396**	**737**	**1,252**	**–46.3**	**–68.4**
Federal income taxes	166	540	855	–69.3	–80.6
State and local income taxes	142	134	272	6.1	–47.7
Other taxes	87	65	126	34.6	–30.7
GIFTS FOR PEOPLE IN OTHER HOUSEHOLDS	**383**	**539**	**527**	**–28.9**	**–27.3**

* Because of changes in methodology, the 2005 data on pensions and Social Security are not comparable with earlier years.
Note: Spending by category will not add to total spending because gift spending is also included in the preceding product and service categories and personal taxes are not included in the total.
Source: Bureau of Labor Statistics, 1984, 1990, 2000, and 2005 Consumer Expenditure Surveys, Internet site http://www.bls.gov/cex/; calculations by New Strategist

Table 9.21 Average Spending by Households Headed by High School Graduates, 1995 to 2005

(average annual spending of consumer units headed by high school graduates, 1995 to 2005; percent change for selected years; in 2005 dollars)

	average spending			percent change	
	2005	2000	1995	2000–05	1995–05
Number of consumer units headed by high school graduates (in 000s)	30,389	31,900	33,027	–4.7%	–8.0%
Average annual spending of consumer units	$38,162	$36,800	$37,142	3.7	2.7
FOOD	**$5,150**	**$5,345**	**$5,386**	**–3.7%**	**–4.4%**
Food at home	**3,040**	**3,291**	**3,556**	**–7.6**	**–14.5**
Cereals and bakery products	418	494	557	–15.5	–25.0
Cereals and cereal products	129	168	202	–23.1	–36.3
Bakery products	289	326	355	–11.2	–18.6
Meats, poultry, fish, and eggs	735	922	991	–20.3	–25.8
Beef	219	289	323	–24.3	–32.2
Pork	158	206	217	–23.5	–27.0
Other meats	104	117	133	–11.0	–22.0
Poultry	129	162	167	–20.5	–22.6
Fish and seafood	94	110	114	–14.6	–17.6
Eggs	30	37	37	–19.8	–19.3
Dairy products	343	361	365	–4.9	–6.1
Fresh milk and cream	139	150	154	–7.2	–9.6
Other dairy products	204	211	211	–3.3	–3.5
Fruits and vegetables	472	539	542	–12.4	–12.9
Fresh fruits	142	162	170	–12.4	–16.7
Fresh vegetables	146	162	158	–10.0	–7.4
Processed fruits	97	118	113	–17.8	–14.0
Processed vegetables	86	95	101	–9.7	–15.1
Other food at home	1,072	977	1,101	9.8	–2.6
Sugar and other sweets	111	124	144	–10.2	–22.7
Fats and oils	83	94	105	–11.8	–21.0
Miscellaneous foods	556	455	472	22.3	17.9
Nonalcoholic beverages	292	273	337	6.8	–13.4
Food prepared by consumer unit on trips	31	31	44	1.2	–28.9
Food away from home	**2,110**	**2,054**	**1,829**	**2.7**	**15.4**
ALCOHOLIC BEVERAGES	**326**	**321**	**301**	**1.6**	**8.3**
HOUSING	**12,380**	**11,701**	**11,788**	**5.8**	**5.0**
Shelter	**6,958**	**6,570**	**6,563**	**5.9**	**6.0**
Owned dwellings	4,416	4,188	3,983	5.4	10.9
Mortgage interest and charges	2,362	2,226	2,017	6.1	17.1
Property taxes	1,256	1,125	1,139	11.6	10.2
Maintenance, repair, insurance, other expenses	798	837	828	–4.7	–3.6
Rented dwellings	2,304	2,038	2,245	13.0	2.6
Other lodging	238	344	334	–30.7	–28.8
Utilities, fuels, and public services	**3,066**	**2,738**	**2,803**	**12.0**	**9.4**
Natural gas	444	336	355	32.3	25.1
Electricity	1,154	1,050	1,142	9.9	1.1

(continued)

	average spending			percent change	
	2005	**2000**	**1995**	**2000–05**	**1995–05**
Fuel oil and other fuels	$169	$128	$118	31.9%	43.3%
Telephone	977	910	865	7.4	12.9
Water and other public services	321	314	323	2.2	−0.6
Household services	**520**	**493**	**500**	**5.4**	**4.0**
Personal services	200	259	276	−22.7	−27.4
Other household services	320	235	224	36.3	42.7
Housekeeping supplies	**533**	**473**	**524**	**12.7**	**1.7**
Laundry and cleaning supplies	131	136	150	−3.7	−12.6
Other household products	273	227	245	20.4	11.5
Postage and stationery	129	110	129	17.3	−0.3
Household furnishings and equipment	**1,303**	**1,427**	**1,399**	**−8.7**	**−6.9**
Household textiles	114	101	135	12.9	−15.3
Furniture	312	273	349	14.1	−10.5
Floor coverings	30	56	95	−46.0	−68.4
Major appliances	180	196	199	−8.3	−9.4
Small appliances and miscellaneous housewares	86	77	96	11.5	−10.5
Miscellaneous household equipment	581	724	527	−19.7	10.3
APPAREL AND RELATED SERVICES	**1,464**	**1,702**	**1,902**	**−14.0**	**−23.0**
Men and boys	**362**	**432**	**466**	**−16.2**	**−22.4**
Men, aged 16 or older	283	322	356	−12.1	−20.6
Boys, aged 2 to 15	79	110	110	−28.2	−28.3
Women and girls	**580**	**639**	**739**	**−9.2**	**−21.6**
Women, aged 16 or older	480	524	610	−8.4	−21.3
Girls, aged 2 to 15	100	115	129	−12.7	−22.7
Children under age 2	**74**	**86**	**101**	**−14.1**	**−26.9**
Footwear	**268**	**336**	**297**	**−20.2**	**−9.9**
Other apparel products and services	**179**	**210**	**297**	**−14.7**	**−39.8**
TRANSPORTATION	**7,364**	**7,939**	**7,451**	**−7.2**	**−1.2**
Vehicle purchases	**3,112**	**3,878**	**3,482**	**−19.7**	**−10.6**
Cars and trucks, new	1,585	1,536	1,358	3.2	16.7
Cars and trucks, used	1,456	2,276	2,058	−36.0	−29.3
Gasoline and motor oil	**1,941**	**1,449**	**1,305**	**33.9**	**48.8**
Other vehicle expenses	**2,078**	**2,332**	**2,357**	**−10.9**	**−11.8**
Vehicle finance charges	281	397	373	−29.2	−24.6
Maintenance and repairs	564	622	736	−9.3	−23.3
Vehicle insurance	875	882	903	−0.8	−3.1
Vehicle rentals, leases, licenses, other charges	358	431	343	−16.9	4.2
Public transportation	**232**	**280**	**308**	**−17.2**	**−24.6**
HEALTH CARE	**2,457**	**2,150**	**2,158**	**14.3**	**13.9**
Health insurance	1,346	1,107	1,071	21.6	25.6
Medical services	505	480	641	5.3	−21.2
Drugs	519	468	351	10.8	47.8
Medical supplies	88	95	94	−7.6	−5.9
ENTERTAINMENT	**1,877**	**1,723**	**1,758**	**9.0**	**6.8**
Fees and admissions	331	338	372	−2.1	−10.9
Audio and visual equipment and services	777	642	648	21.0	19.8

(continued)

	average spending			percent change	
	2005	**2000**	**1995**	**2000–05**	**1995–05**
Pets, toys, hobbies, playground equipment	$314	$344	$367	–8.6%	–14.3%
Other entertainment products and services	455	398	370	14.3	22.9
PERSONAL CARE PRODUCTS AND SERVICES	**432**	**563**	**501**	**–23.2**	**–13.8**
READING	**87**	**119**	**164**	**–26.9**	**–47.0**
EDUCATION	**457**	**352**	**320**	**30.0**	**42.6**
TOBACCO PRODUCTS, SMOKING SUPPLIES	**425**	**463**	**422**	**–8.2**	**0.8**
MISCELLANEOUS	**741**	**739**	**987**	**0.2**	**–24.9**
CASH CONTRIBUTIONS	**1,148**	**791**	**879**	**45.2**	**30.6**
PERSONAL INSURANCE AND PENSIONS	**3,854**	**2,893**	**3,126**	**33.2**	**23.3**
Life and other personal insurance	251	403	431	–37.7	–41.7
Pensions and Social Security*	3,604	2,491	2,695	44.7	33.7
PERSONAL TAXES	**1,194**	**2,137**	**2,887**	**–44.1**	**–58.6**
Federal income taxes	772	1,562	2,038	–50.6	–62.1
State and local income taxes	288	417	639	–31.0	–55.0
Other taxes	134	159	209	–15.6	–35.8
GIFTS FOR PEOPLE IN OTHER HOUSEHOLDS	**771**	**849**	**1,030**	**–9.2**	**–25.2**

Because of changes in methodology, the 2005 data on pensions and Social Security are not comparable with earlier years.
Note: Spending by category will not add to total spending because gift spending is also included in the preceding product and service categories and personal taxes are not included in the total.
Source: Bureau of Labor Statistics, 1984, 1990, 2000, and 2005 Consumer Expenditure Surveys, Internet site http://www.bls .gov/cex/; calculations by New Strategist

Table 9.22 Average Spending by Households Headed by People with Some College or an Associate's Degree, 1995 to 2005

(average annual spending of consumer units headed by people with some college or an associate's degree, 1995 to 2005; percent change for selected years; in 2005 dollars)

	average spending			percent change	
	2005	2000	1995	2000–05	1995–05
Number of consumer units headed by people with some college or an associate's degree (in 000s)	36,877	31,416	23,568	17.4%	56.5%
Average annual spending of consumer units	$45,699	$42,625	$42,721	7.2	7.0
FOOD	**$5,818**	**$5,730**	**$5,973**	**1.5%**	**−2.6%**
Food at home	**3,161**	**3,276**	**3,497**	**−3.5**	**−9.6**
Cereals and bakery products	424	496	555	−14.4	−23.5
Cereals and cereal products	136	169	208	−19.1	−34.3
Bakery products	288	328	347	−12.0	−17.0
Meats, poultry, fish, and eggs	748	840	920	−10.9	−18.7
Beef	237	253	276	−6.6	−14.2
Pork	151	170	190	−11.0	−20.2
Other meats	97	109	131	−11.0	−25.9
Poultry	131	159	182	−17.7	−28.0
Fish and seafood	101	114	109	−11.3	−6.9
Eggs	31	34	35	−6.8	−9.7
Dairy products	359	348	383	2.9	−6.4
Fresh milk and cream	140	137	154	2.4	−8.9
Other dairy products	219	212	229	3.4	−4.4
Fruits and vegetables	505	538	559	−6.1	−9.5
Fresh fruits	165	163	174	0.9	−5.5
Fresh vegetables	157	162	167	−2.9	−5.7
Processed fruits	98	121	114	−19.4	−14.4
Processed vegetables	86	92	104	−6.3	−16.8
Other food at home	1,124	1,054	1,079	6.7	4.2
Sugar and other sweets	113	133	132	−15.3	−14.8
Fats and oils	79	90	104	−11.9	−23.8
Miscellaneous foods	590	499	483	18.2	22.1
Nonalcoholic beverages	304	287	301	6.1	1.0
Food prepared by consumer unit on trips	38	45	59	−14.8	−34.9
Food away from home	**2,658**	**2,454**	**2,475**	**8.3**	**7.4**
ALCOHOLIC BEVERAGES	**415**	**437**	**392**	**−5.1**	**5.8**
HOUSING	**14,566**	**13,482**	**13,584**	**8.0**	**7.2**
Shelter	**8,309**	**7,811**	**7,718**	**6.4**	**7.7**
Owned dwellings	5,579	4,942	4,753	12.9	17.4
Mortgage interest and charges	3,231	2,948	2,826	9.6	14.3
Property taxes	1,342	1,169	1,105	14.8	21.5
Maintenance, repair, insurance, other expenses	1,007	824	824	22.2	22.2
Rented dwellings	2,303	2,393	2,448	−3.8	−5.9
Other lodging	427	475	516	−10.2	−17.4
Utilities, fuels, and public services	**3,169**	**2,760**	**2,718**	**14.8**	**16.6**
Natural gas	447	344	323	30.0	38.4
Electricity	1,149	1,012	1,074	13.6	7.0

(continued)

	average spending			percent change	
	2005	2000	1995	2000–05	1995–05
Fuel oil and other fuels	$134	$81	$82	65.0%	63.5%
Telephone	1,069	993	909	7.6	17.6
Water and other public services	370	330	329	12.3	12.5
Household services	**769**	**750**	**683**	**2.5**	**12.6**
Personal services	324	369	361	−12.3	−10.3
Other household services	445	381	322	16.8	38.3
Housekeeping supplies	**588**	**507**	**561**	**16.0**	**4.8**
Laundry and cleaning supplies	132	140	137	−6.0	−3.9
Other household products	316	235	272	34.4	16.5
Postage and stationery	140	132	154	6.5	−8.8
Household furnishings and equipment	**1,731**	**1,654**	**1,903**	**4.6**	**−9.1**
Household textiles	119	114	140	4.5	−14.6
Furniture	503	432	451	16.5	11.6
Floor coverings	48	35	204	39.2	−76.4
Major appliances	236	218	209	8.4	13.2
Small appliances and miscellaneous housewares	99	93	118	7.0	−15.9
Miscellaneous household equipment	724	763	782	−5.1	−7.4
APPAREL AND RELATED SERVICES	**1,847**	**2,091**	**2,211**	**−11.7**	**−16.4**
Men and boys	**435**	**509**	**523**	**−14.5**	**−16.7**
Men, aged 16 or older	332	404	425	−17.9	−22.1
Boys, aged 2 to 15	104	104	97	0.1	7.3
Women and girls	**732**	**823**	**889**	**−11.0**	**−17.7**
Women, aged 16 or older	608	682	745	−10.8	−18.3
Girls, aged 2 to 15	125	141	144	−11.1	−12.9
Children under age 2	**79**	**83**	**104**	**−4.8**	**−23.9**
Footwear	**320**	**398**	**354**	**−19.6**	**−9.6**
Other apparel products and services	**280**	**279**	**342**	**0.3**	**−18.2**
TRANSPORTATION	**8,717**	**8,945**	**8,194**	**−2.6**	**6.4**
Vehicle purchases	**3,845**	**4,266**	**3,661**	**−9.9**	**5.0**
Cars and trucks, new	1,944	2,127	1,715	−8.6	13.4
Cars and trucks, used	1,772	2,092	1,890	−15.3	−6.3
Gasoline and motor oil	**2,119**	**1,558**	**1,351**	**36.0**	**56.9**
Other vehicle expenses	**2,384**	**2,688**	**2,733**	**−11.3**	**−12.8**
Vehicle finance charges	333	412	378	−19.0	−11.9
Maintenance and repairs	647	735	906	−12.0	−28.6
Vehicle insurance	947	900	938	5.3	1.0
Vehicle rentals, leases, licenses, other charges	457	642	511	−28.8	−10.6
Public transportation	**369**	**433**	**447**	**−14.9**	**−17.5**
HEALTH CARE	**2,528**	**2,188**	**2,062**	**15.6**	**22.6**
Health insurance	1,259	1,041	996	21.0	26.5
Medical services	672	606	641	10.8	4.8
Drugs	495	430	318	15.2	55.8
Medical supplies	102	111	108	−8.1	−5.0
ENTERTAINMENT	**2,531**	**2,123**	**2,318**	**19.2**	**9.2**
Fees and admissions	513	526	584	−2.6	−12.3
Audio and visual equipment and services	935	725	777	29.0	20.5

(continued)

	average spending			percent change	
	2005	2000	1995	2000–05	1995–05
Pets, toys, hobbies, playground equipment	$448	$371	$484	20.8%	–7.4%
Other entertainment products and services	635	501	473	26.8	34.4
PERSONAL CARE PRODUCTS AND SERVICES	**512**	**648**	**551**	**–21.0**	**–7.1**
READING	**115**	**154**	**211**	**–25.5**	**–45.7**
EDUCATION	**958**	**811**	**747**	**18.1**	**28.2**
TOBACCO PRODUCTS, SMOKING SUPPLIES	**351**	**375**	**328**	**–6.3**	**7.1**
MISCELLANEOUS	**808**	**900**	**971**	**–10.3**	**–16.8**
CASH CONTRIBUTIONS	**1,601**	**1,107**	**1,229**	**44.7**	**30.3**
PERSONAL INSURANCE AND PENSIONS	**4,932**	**3,632**	**3,952**	**35.8**	**24.8**
Life and other personal insurance	370	385	483	–3.9	–23.4
Pensions and Social Security*	4,562	3,247	3,469	40.5	31.5
PERSONAL TAXES	**2,272**	**3,242**	**3,766**	**–29.9**	**–39.7**
Federal income taxes	1,583	2,486	2,744	–36.3	–42.3
State and local income taxes	531	598	782	–11.2	–32.0
Other taxes	158	158	241	0.2	–34.4
GIFTS FOR PEOPLE IN OTHER HOUSEHOLDS	**988**	**1,092**	**1,280**	**–9.5**	**–22.9**

* Because of changes in methodology, the 2005 data on pensions and Social Security are not comparable with earlier years.
Note: Spending by category will not add to total spending because gift spending is also included in the preceding product and service categories and personal taxes are not included in the total.
Source: Bureau of Labor Statistics, 1984, 1990, 2000, and 2005 Consumer Expenditure Surveys, Internet site http://www.bls.gov/cex/; calculations by New Strategist

Table 9.23 Average Spending by Households Headed by College Graduates, 1995 to 2005

(average annual spending of consumer units headed by college graduates, 1995 to 2005; percent change for selected years; in 2005 dollars)

	average spending			percent change	
	2005	2000	1995	2000–05	1995–05
Number of consumer units headed by college graduates (in 000s)	32,062	28,059	24,994	14.3%	28.3%
Average annual spending of consumer units	$65,542	$61,444	$58,637	6.7	11.8
FOOD	**$7,610**	**$7,290**	**$7,075**	**4.4%**	**7.6%**
Food at home	**3,891**	**3,810**	**3,870**	**2.1**	**0.5**
Cereals and bakery products	522	567	619	–7.9	–15.7
Cereals and cereal products	168	189	228	–11.3	–26.4
Bakery products	354	377	391	–6.0	–9.4
Meats, poultry, fish, and eggs	819	895	910	–8.5	–10.0
Beef	231	253	254	–8.7	–9.0
Pork	145	167	165	–13.0	–12.3
Other meats	113	115	127	–1.4	–10.9
Poultry	143	168	179	–14.8	–20.3
Fish and seafood	153	158	146	–2.9	4.7
Eggs	34	35	38	–3.3	–11.6
Dairy products	459	419	422	9.7	8.9
Fresh milk and cream	159	155	156	2.3	1.7
Other dairy products	300	263	265	14.0	13.1
Fruits and vegetables	710	719	686	–1.3	3.6
Fresh fruits	251	234	223	7.4	12.6
Fresh vegetables	231	218	209	6.1	10.6
Processed fruits	131	166	150	–20.9	–12.6
Processed vegetables	97	101	104	–3.9	–6.6
Other food at home	1,382	1,210	1,235	14.2	11.9
Sugar and other sweets	141	147	167	–4.4	–15.4
Fats and oils	96	98	104	–1.6	–7.5
Miscellaneous foods	750	598	564	25.5	33.0
Nonalcoholic beverages	327	293	302	11.8	8.1
Food prepared by consumer unit on trips	67	76	99	–11.8	–32.1
Food away from home	**3,719**	**3,481**	**3,204**	**6.8**	**16.1**
ALCOHOLIC BEVERAGES	**653**	**675**	**534**	**–3.2**	**22.2**
HOUSING	**21,676**	**20,448**	**19,592**	**6.0**	**10.6**
Shelter	**13,062**	**12,154**	**11,496**	**7.5**	**13.6**
Owned dwellings	9,774	8,530	8,136	14.6	20.1
Mortgage interest and charges	5,450	5,133	4,924	6.2	10.7
Property taxes	2,494	1,987	1,792	25.5	39.2
Maintenance, repair, insurance, other expenses	1,830	1,410	1,422	29.8	28.7
Rented dwellings	2,216	2,519	2,328	–12.0	–4.8
Other lodging	1,071	1,105	1,030	–3.0	3.9
Utilities, fuels, and public services	**3,633**	**3,282**	**3,268**	**10.7**	**11.2**
Natural gas	587	414	400	41.8	46.8
Electricity	1,243	1,098	1,225	13.2	1.5

(continued)

	average spending			percent change	
	2005	**2000**	**1995**	**2000–05**	**1995–05**
Fuel oil and other fuels	$139	$116	$122	20.2%	14.2%
Telephone	1,215	1,233	1,116	–1.4	8.9
Water and other public services	448	422	405	6.2	10.6
Household services	**1,391**	**1,436**	**1,152**	**–3.1**	**20.7**
Personal services	540	636	541	–15.1	–0.1
Other household services	851	801	611	6.3	39.2
Housekeeping supplies	**822**	**754**	**714**	**9.0**	**15.2**
Laundry and cleaning supplies	144	169	147	–14.8	–2.3
Other household products	431	362	309	19.1	39.6
Postage and stationery	247	223	258	10.6	–4.1
Household furnishings and equipment	**2,768**	**2,821**	**2,962**	**–1.9**	**–6.5**
Household textiles	199	191	176	4.4	13.3
Furniture	697	776	661	–10.2	5.4
Floor coverings	114	84	522	35.8	–78.1
Major appliances	310	278	222	11.6	39.8
Small appliances and miscellaneous housewares	157	169	158	–7.1	–0.4
Miscellaneous household equipment	1,291	1,324	1,225	–2.5	5.4
APPAREL AND RELATED SERVICES	**2,670**	**3,043**	**3,138**	**–12.3**	**–14.9**
Men and boys	**608**	**682**	**820**	**–10.8**	**–25.9**
Men, aged 16 or older	508	557	659	–8.8	–22.9
Boys, aged 2 to 15	100	125	161	–19.8	–38.1
Women and girls	**1,088**	**1,246**	**1,221**	**–12.7**	**–10.9**
Women, aged 16 or older	937	1,077	1,067	–13.0	–12.2
Girls, aged 2 to 15	151	169	154	–10.6	–1.8
Children under age 2	**95**	**124**	**120**	**–23.2**	**–21.1**
Footwear	**391**	**467**	**451**	**–16.3**	**–13.3**
Other apparel products and services	**489**	**525**	**525**	**–6.9**	**–6.9**
TRANSPORTATION	**10,664**	**10,465**	**10,102**	**1.9**	**5.6**
Vehicle purchases	**4,402**	**4,351**	**4,001**	**1.2**	**10.0**
Cars and trucks, new	2,815	2,500	2,376	12.6	18.5
Cars and trucks, used	1,514	1,799	1,598	–15.8	–5.3
Gasoline and motor oil	**2,265**	**1,663**	**1,494**	**36.2**	**51.6**
Other vehicle expenses	**3,109**	**3,489**	**3,712**	**–10.9**	**–16.3**
Vehicle finance charges	342	409	372	–16.5	–8.0
Maintenance and repairs	961	950	1,161	1.1	–17.2
Vehicle insurance	1,087	1,062	1,199	2.4	–9.4
Vehicle rentals, leases, licenses, other charges	719	1,067	980	–32.6	–26.7
Public transportation	**889**	**964**	**894**	**–7.8**	**–0.6**
HEALTH CARE	**3,480**	**3,017**	**2,646**	**15.4**	**31.5**
Health insurance	1,706	1,318	1,258	29.5	35.6
Medical services	1,029	1,050	889	–2.0	15.7
Drugs	593	488	359	21.6	65.3
Medical supplies	152	161	140	–5.6	8.8
ENTERTAINMENT	**3,402**	**3,244**	**3,145**	**4.9**	**8.2**
Fees and admissions	1,179	1,207	1,119	–2.3	5.4
Audio and visual equipment and services	1,127	904	852	24.7	32.2

(continued)

	average spending			percent change	
	2005	2000	1995	2000–05	1995–05
Pets, toys, hobbies, playground equipment	$577	$526	$564	9.6%	2.3%
Other entertainment products and services	518	608	610	–14.8	–15.1
PERSONAL CARE PRODUCTS AND SERVICES	**805**	**856**	**661**	**–6.0**	**21.7**
READING	**225**	**296**	**360**	**–24.0**	**–37.5**
EDUCATION	**1,831**	**1,390**	**1,247**	**31.7**	**46.8**
TOBACCO PRODUCTS, SMOKING SUPPLIES	**148**	**191**	**218**	**–22.3**	**–32.1**
MISCELLANEOUS	**1,068**	**1,206**	**1,278**	**–11.4**	**–16.4**
CASH CONTRIBUTIONS	**2,787**	**2,765**	**2,088**	**0.8**	**33.5**
PERSONAL INSURANCE AND PENSIONS	**8,523**	**6,561**	**6,556**	**29.9**	**30.0**
Life and other personal insurance	639	709	721	–9.9	–11.4
Pensions and Social Security*	7,884	5,851	5,835	34.7	35.1
PERSONAL TAXES	**4,845**	**7,260**	**7,740**	**–33.3**	**–37.4**
Federal income taxes	3,562	5,752	5,830	–38.1	–38.9
State and local income taxes	993	1,258	1,578	–21.1	–37.1
Other taxes	290	251	333	15.7	–13.0
GIFTS FOR PEOPLE IN OTHER HOUSEHOLDS	**1,896**	**2,240**	**2,116**	**–15.4**	**–10.4**

Because of changes in methodology, the 2005 data on pensions and Social Security are not comparable with earlier years.
Note: Spending by category will not add to total spending because gift spending is also included in the preceding product and service categories and personal taxes are not included in the total.
Source: Bureau of Labor Statistics, 1984, 1990, 2000, and 2005 Consumer Expenditure Surveys, Internet site http://www.bls .gov/cex/; calculations by New Strategist

10

Wealth

■ The median net worth of the average American household stood at $93,100 in 2004, 35 percent higher than in 1989 after adjusting for inflation. Most of the gains occurred during the 1990s. Between 2001 and 2004, the net worth of the average household climbed just 1 percent.

■ The median value of the financial assets owned by the average household stood at $23,000 in 2004, down 23 percent since 2001 after adjusting for inflation. The recession of 2001 and the stock market decline were behind the falling value of financial assets.

■ For the average household, the value of its nonfinancial assets is more than six times greater than the value of its financial assets. Between 2001 and 2004, the median value of nonfinancial assets grew 22 percent, after adjusting for inflation, thanks to rising housing prices.

■ Seventy-six percent of households have debt, owing a median of $55,300 in 2004. The median amount of debt owed by the average debtor household increased by a substantial 34 percent between 2001 and 2004, after adjusting for inflation.

Net Worth Barely Increased between 2001 and 2004

Since 1989, however, net worth has grown substantially.

The median net worth, or assets minus debts, of the average American household stood at $93,100 in 2004. While modest, the figure is 35 percent higher than in 1989, after adjusting for inflation. Most of the gains occurred during the 1990s. Between 2001 and 2004, the net worth of the average household climbed just 1 percent.

Most, but not all, age groups have seen their net worth increase over the years. Householders aged 55 to 64 experienced an enormous 73 percent increase in net worth between 1989 and 2004, after adjusting for inflation. The net worth of this age group grew substantially even between 2001 and 2004, up 26 percent and more than any other age group. In contrast, householders aged 35 to 44 have seen their net worth decline over the years. In 2004, it was 16 percent below the level of 1989, after adjusting for inflation. Behind the rising net worth of householders aged 55 to 64 is their increased labor force participation. As fewer opt for early retirement, their assets are growing. Householders aged 35 to 44 have lost ground because many have taken on mortgage debt, which lowers net worth.

The net worth of non-Hispanic whites far surpasses that of blacks and Hispanics, $140,700 to $24,800 in 2004. But the net worth of blacks and Hispanics has grown faster over the years thanks to their rising homeownership rate.

Home equity accounts for the largest share of net worth—32 percent in 2004. The share of net worth accounted for by home equity fell as low as 27 percent in 2001 as the stock market boomed, then rebounded as financial assets declined in value. Mortgages account for most household debt—75 percent in 2004.

■ Credit cards are a small share of household debt, accounting for just 3 percent of the total in 2004, a figure that has barely changed over the years.

The net worth of the average household is growing

(median household net worth, 1989 to 2004, in 2004 dollars)

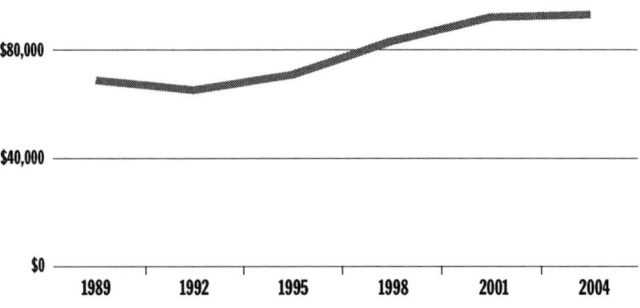

Table 10.1 Net Worth of Households by Age of Householder, 1989 to 2004

(median net worth of households by age of householder, 1989 to 2004; percent change, for selected years; in 2004 dollars)

	2004	2001	1998	1995	1992	1989	percent change 2001–04	percent change 1989–04
Total households	**$93,100**	**$92,200**	**$83,100**	**$70,800**	**$65,200**	**$68,800**	**1.0%**	**35.3%**
Under age 35	14,200	12,500	10,600	14,800	12,000	11,400	13.6	24.6
Aged 35 to 44	69,400	82,600	73,500	64,200	58,700	82,700	–16.0	–16.1
Aged 45 to 54	144,700	141,600	122,500	114,500	103,100	144,800	2.2	–0.1
Aged 55 to 64	248,700	197,400	148,200	141,900	150,200	143,500	26.0	73.3
Aged 65 to 74	190,100	189,400	169,800	136,600	130,000	112,400	0.4	69.1
Aged 75 or older	163,100	165,400	145,600	114,500	114,500	106,200	–1.4	53.6

Source: Federal Reserve Board, Survey of Consumer Finances, SCF Chartbook, Internet site http://www.federalreserve.gov/pubs/oss/oss2/2004/scf2004home.html; calculations by New Strategist

Table 10.2 Net Worth of Households by Race and Hispanic Origin of Householder, 1989 to 2004

(median net worth of households by race and Hispanic origin of householder, 1989 to 2004; percent change for selected years; in 2004 dollars)

	2004	2001	1998	1995	1992	1989	percent change 2001–04	percent change 1989–04
Total households	**$93,100**	**$91,700**	**$83,100**	**$70,800**	**$65,200**	**$68,800**	**1.5%**	**35.3%**
White, non-Hispanic	140,700	130,200	111,000	94,300	91,900	104,200	8.1	35.0
Nonwhite or Hispanic	24,800	19,100	19,300	19,500	15,800	9,800	29.8	153.1

Source: Federal Reserve Board, Survey of Consumer Finances, SCF Chartbook, Internet site http://www.federalreserve.gov/pubs/oss/oss2/2004/scf2004home.html; calculations by New Strategist

Table 10.3 Distribution of Household Assets and Debts by Type, 1989 to 2004

(percent distribution of household assets and debts by type, 1989 to 2004; percentage point change for selected years)

	2004	2001	1998	1995	1992	1989	percentage point change 2001–04	percentage point change 1989–04
TOTAL ASSETS	100.0%	100.0%	100.0%	100.0%	100.0%	100.0%	–	–
Financial assets, total	**35.7**	**42.0**	**40.7**	**36.7**	**31.5**	**30.4**	**–6.3**	**5.3**
Retirement accounts	11.4	11.9	11.2	10.3	8.0	6.5	–0.5	4.9
Stocks	6.3	9.1	9.2	5.7	5.2	4.6	–2.8	1.7
Mutual funds	5.2	5.1	5.0	4.7	2.4	1.6	0.1	3.6
Transaction accounts	4.7	4.8	4.6	5.1	5.5	5.8	–0.1	–1.1
Other managed assets	2.9	4.5	3.5	2.2	1.7	2.0	–1.6	0.9
Bonds	1.9	1.9	1.8	2.3	2.6	3.1	0.0	–1.2
Certificates of deposit	1.3	1.3	1.8	2.1	2.6	3.1	0.0	–1.8
Cash value of life insurance	1.1	2.2	2.6	2.6	1.9	1.8	–1.1	–0.7
Savings bonds	0.2	0.3	0.3	0.5	0.3	0.5	–0.1	–0.3
Other	0.7	0.8	0.7	1.2	1.2	1.5	–0.1	–0.8
Nonfinancial assets, total	**64.3**	**58.0**	**59.3**	**63.3**	**68.5**	**69.6**	**6.3**	**–5.3**
Primary residence	32.3	27.1	27.9	30.1	32.2	31.9	5.2	0.4
Business equity	16.7	17.0	16.9	17.2	18.0	18.7	–0.3	–2.0
Other residential real estate	6.4	4.7	5.0	5.1	5.8	5.6	1.7	0.8
Equity in nonresidential property	4.7	4.8	4.6	5.0	7.5	7.7	–0.1	–3.0
Vehicles	3.3	3.4	3.9	4.5	3.9	3.9	–0.1	–0.6
Other	1.0	0.9	1.0	1.5	1.1	1.7	0.1	–0.7
TOTAL DEBT	100.0%	100.0%	100.0%	100.0%	100.0%	100.0%	–	–
Home-secured debt	75.2	75.1	71.4	73.1	72.5	69.4	0.1	5.8
Installment loans	11.0	12.3	13.1	12.0	11.3	16.6	–1.3	–5.6
Other residential property	8.5	6.4	7.5	7.6	10.0	7.6	2.1	0.9
Credit card balances	3.0	3.4	3.9	3.9	3.2	2.8	–0.4	0.2
Other lines of credit	0.7	0.5	0.3	0.6	0.7	1.4	0.2	–0.7
Other	1.6	2.3	3.7	2.9	2.3	2.2	–0.7	–0.6

Note: "–" means not applicable.
Source: Federal Reserve Board, "Recent Changes in U.S. Family Finances: Evidence from the 2001 and 2004 Survey of Consumer Finances," Federal Reserve Bulletin, February 2006, Internet site http://www.federalreserve.gov/pubs/oss/oss2/2004/scf 2004home.html; and "Recent Changes in U.S. Family Finances: Results from the 1998 Survey of Consumer Finances," Federal Reserve Bulletin, January 2000, Internet site http://www.federalreserve.gov/pubs/oss/oss2/98/scf98home.html; calculations by New Strategist

Most Households Own Financial Assets

But the value of those assets fell between 2001 and 2004.

Ninety-four percent of households own financial assets, which range from transaction accounts (checking and saving) to stocks, retirement accounts, and life insurance. The median value of the financial assets owned by the average household stood at a modest $23,000 in 2004, down a substantial 23 percent since 2001 after adjusting for inflation. The recession of 2001 and the stock market decline were behind the falling value of financial assets.

Despite the decline in household financial assets between 2001 and 2004, their median value was 39 percent higher in 2004 than in 1995, after adjusting for inflation. Householders aged 55 to 64 saw a doubling in the value of their financial assets during those years.

Nearly half of households owned stock (either directly or indirectly through mutual funds and retirement accounts) in 2004, but the figure was down from the peak of 52 percent in 2001. The value of the stock owned by the average household fell 34 percent during those years, after adjusting for inflation. Despite the recent decline, the median value of the stock owned by the average household increased 35 percent between 1995 and 2004.

■ Householders aged 55 to 64 saw the value of their financial assets rise 25 percent between 2001 and 2004 as fewer opted for early retirement.

Stock values are down

(median value of stock holdings for households owning stock, 1995 to 2004; in 2004 dollars)

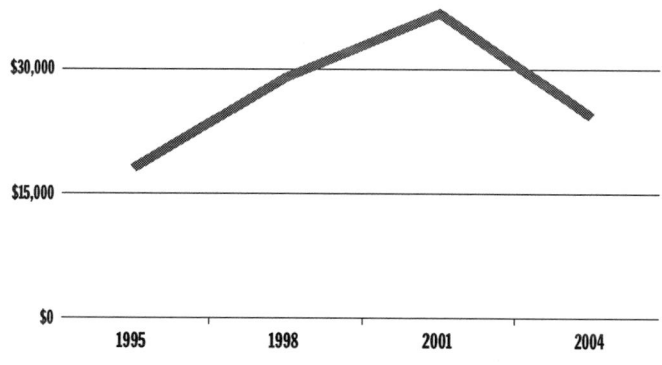

Table 10.4 Financial Assets of Households by Age of Householder, 1989 to 2004

(percentage of households owning any financial asset and median value of financial assets for owners, by age of householder, 1989 to 2004; percentage point change in ownership and percent change in value for selected years; in 2004 dollars)

	2004	2001	1998	1995	1992	1989	percentage point change 2001–04	1989–04
Percent owning any financial asset								
Total households	**93.8%**	**93.4%**	**93.1%**	**91.2%**	**90.3%**	**88.9%**	**0.4**	**4.9**
Under age 35	90.1	89.7	88.8	87.0	85.8	84.8	0.4	5.4
Aged 35 to 44	93.6	93.5	93.3	92.2	91.0	90.4	0.1	3.2
Aged 45 to 54	93.6	94.7	95.3	93.0	92.5	90.8	–1.1	2.8
Aged 55 to 64	95.2	95.2	95.6	91.2	92.5	87.7	0.0	7.5
Aged 65 to 74	96.5	94.6	95.6	93.0	91.2	92.6	1.9	3.9
Aged 75 or older	97.6	95.4	92.1	94.2	92.1	91.4	2.2	6.3

	2004	2001	1998	1995	1992	1989	percent change 2001–04	1989–04
Median value of financial assets								
Total households	**$23,000**	**$30,000**	**$26,000**	**$19,000**	**$15,200**	**$16,500**	**–23.3%**	**39.4%**
Under age 35	5,200	6,600	5,200	6,600	4,900	4,000	–21.2	30.0
Aged 35 to 44	19,000	28,600	26,500	16,700	13,200	20,600	–33.6	–7.8
Aged 45 to 54	38,600	48,000	4,300	33,500	25,200	26,700	–19.6	44.6
Aged 55 to 64	78,000	62,300	52,900	40,000	37,600	37,900	25.2	105.8
Aged 65 to 74	36,100	54,700	53,100	26,000	33,600	27,900	–34.0	29.4
Aged 75 or older	38,800	45,300	42,500	28,200	27,700	43,200	–14.3	–10.2

Source: Federal Reserve Board, Survey of Consumer Finances, SCF Chartbook, Internet site http://www.federalreserve.gov/pubs/oss/oss2/2004/scf2004home.html; calculations by New Strategist

Table 10.5 Financial Assets of Households by Race and Hispanic Origin of Householder, 1989 to 2004

(percentage of households owning financial assets and median value of assets for owners, by race and Hispanic origin of householder, 1989 to 2004; percentage point change in ownership and percent change in value of asset for selected years; in 2004 dollars)

	2004	2001	1998	1995	1992	1989	percentage point change 2001–04	percentage point change 1989–04
Percent owning any financial asset								
Total households	**93.8%**	**93.4%**	**93.1%**	**91.2%**	**90.3%**	**88.9%**	**0.4**	**4.9**
White, non-Hispanic	97.2	96.7	96.5	95.0	95.5	95.2	0.5	2.0
Nonwhite or Hispanic	85.0	83.3	81.6	78.1	74.1	70.2	1.7	14.8

	2004	2001	1998	1995	1992	1989	percent change 2001–04	percent change 1989–04
Median value of financial assets								
Total households	**$23,000**	**$30,000**	**$26,000**	**$19,000**	**$15,200**	**$16,500**	**–23.3%**	**39.4%**
White, non-Hispanic	36,000	42,000	35,000	22,900	20,400	23,200	–14.3	55.2
Nonwhite or Hispanic	5,000	7,700	7,600	6,900	4,000	3,000	–35.1	66.7

Source: Federal Reserve Board, Survey of Consumer Finances, SCF Chartbook, Internet site http://www.federalreserve.gov/pubs/oss/oss2/2004/scf2004home.html; calculations by New Strategist

Table 10.6 Stock Ownership of Households by Age of Householder, 1995 to 2004

(percent of households owning stock directly or indirectly, median value of stock holdings for owners, and stock holdings as a percent of financial assets, by age of householder, 1995 to 2004; percentage point change in ownership and share, and percent change in value of holdings for selected years; in 2004 dollars)

	2004	2001	1998	1995	percentage point change 2001–04	1995–04
Percent owning stock						
Total households	**48.6%**	**51.9%**	**48.9%**	**40.4%**	**–3.3**	**8.2**
Under age 35	38.8	48.9	40.8	36.6	–10.1	2.2
Aged 35 to 44	52.3	59.5	56.7	46.4	–7.2	5.9
Aged 45 to 54	54.4	59.2	58.6	48.9	–4.8	5.5
Aged 55 to 64	61.6	57.1	55.9	40.0	4.5	21.6
Aged 65 to 74	45.8	39.2	42.7	34.4	6.6	11.4
Aged 75 or older	34.8	34.2	29.4	27.9	0.6	6.9

	2004	2001	1998	1995	percent change 2001–04	1995–04
Median value for owners						
Total households	**$24,300**	**$36,700**	**$29,000**	**$18,000**	**–33.8%**	**35.0%**
Under age 35	5,200	7,500	8,100	6,300	–30.7	–17.5
Aged 35 to 44	12,700	29,300	23,200	12,300	–56.7	3.3
Aged 45 to 54	30,600	53,300	44,100	31,900	–42.6	–4.1
Aged 55 to 64	59,500	86,500	54,500	38,200	–31.2	55.8
Aged 65 to 74	75,000	159,800	64,900	41,900	–53.1	79.0
Aged 75 or older	85,900	127,800	69,600	24,600	–32.8	249.2

	2004	2001	1998	1995	percentage point change 2001–04	1995–04
Stock holdings as share of financial assets						
Total households	**47.4%**	**56.0%**	**54.0%**	**40.1%**	**–8.6**	**7.3**
Under age 35	30.0	52.5	44.9	27.2	–22.5	2.8
Aged 35 to 44	47.7	57.3	55.0	39.5	–9.6	8.2
Aged 45 to 54	46.8	59.1	55.7	43.1	–12.3	3.7
Aged 55 to 64	51.1	56.2	58.4	44.5	–5.1	6.6
Aged 65 to 74	51.1	55.2	51.3	35.8	–4.1	15.3
Aged 75 or older	39.1	51.4	48.7	39.8	–12.3	–0.7

Note: Indirect holdings are stocks in mutual funds, retirement accounts, and other managed assets.
Source: Federal Reserve Board, "Recent Changes in U.S. Family Finances: Evidence from the 2001 and 2004 Survey of Consumer Finances," Federal Reserve Bulletin, February 23, 2006, Internet site http://www.federalreserve.gov/pubs/bulletin/default.htm; calculations by New Strategist

Nonfinancial Assets Are Most Important

For the average household, the value of its nonfinancial assets is more than six times greater than the value of its financial assets.

The median value of the nonfinancial assets owned by the average household stood at $147,800 in 2004, a much greater share than the $23,000 median in financial assets. Between 2001 and 2004, the value of nonfinancial assets grew 22 percent, after adjusting for inflation, thanks to rising housing prices. Since 1989, the median value of the nonfinancial assets owned by the average household has grown by 49 percent.

For the average household, the home is its most important nonfinancial asset and accounts for the largest share of net worth. Consequently, the value of the nonfinancial assets owned by households varies greatly by age and race—as does homeownership. Older householders are most likely to own a home, which is why the value of nonfinancial assets peaks in the 55-to-64 age group at $226,300.

■ The rising homeownership rate was the only factor that boosted net worth between 2001 and 2004.

The value of nonfinancial assets peaks in the 55-to-64 age group

(median value of nonfinancial assets, by age of householder, 2004)

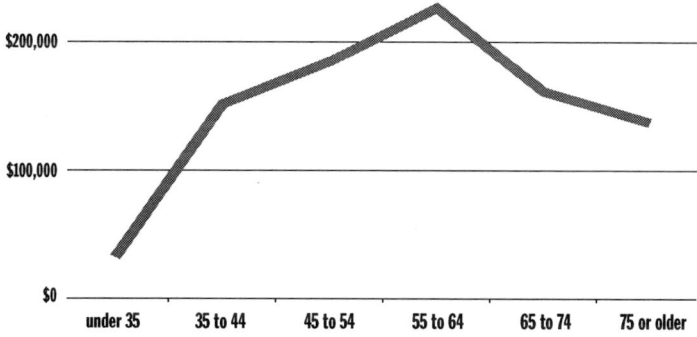

Table 10.7 Nonfinancial Assets of Households by Age of Householder, 1989 to 2004

(percentage of households owning any nonfinancial asset and median value of nonfinancial assets for owners, by age of householder, 1989 to 2004; percentage point change in ownership and percent change in value for selected years; in 2004 dollars)

	2004	2001	1998	1995	1992	1989	percentage point change 2001–04	percentage point change 1989–04
Percent owning any nonfinancial asset								
Total households	**92.5%**	**90.7%**	**89.9%**	**90.9%**	**90.8%**	**89.3%**	**1.8**	**3.2**
Under age 35	88.6	83.0	83.3	87.1	85.6	83.9	5.5	4.6
Aged 35 to 44	93.0	93.2	92.1	90.6	92.3	91.8	–0.2	1.1
Aged 45 to 54	94.7	95.2	92.9	93.6	94.4	93.2	–0.5	1.6
Aged 55 to 64	92.6	95.4	93.8	93.9	92.7	91.2	–2.8	1.4
Aged 65 to 74	95.6	91.6	92.0	92.6	91.6	92.7	4.0	3.0
Aged 75 or older	92.5	86.4	87.2	89.9	91.3	85.4	6.1	7.1

	2004	2001	1998	1995	1992	1989	percent change 2001–04	percent change 1989–04
Median value of nonfinancial assets								
Total households	**$147,800**	**$120,900**	**$113,300**	**$102,300**	**$91,000**	**$99,000**	**22.2%**	**49.3%**
Under age 35	32,300	31,700	26,300	27,100	22,900	25,100	1.9	28.7
Aged 35 to 44	151,300	125,500	119,900	118,500	108,600	123,600	20.6	22.4
Aged 45 to 54	184,500	150,800	147,000	139,100	124,400	158,200	22.3	16.6
Aged 55 to 64	226,300	157,500	147,100	133,000	140,300	137,700	43.7	64.3
Aged 65 to 74	161,100	158,900	127,400	116,800	104,000	93,600	1.4	72.1
Aged 75 or older	137,100	130,600	111,400	97,300	91,900	75,800	5.0	80.9

Source: Federal Reserve Board, Survey of Consumer Finances, SCF Chartbook, Internet site http://www.federalreserve.gov/pubs/ oss/oss2/2004/scf2004home.html; calculations by New Strategist

Table 10.8 Nonfinancial Assets of Households by Race and Hispanic Origin of Householder, 1989 to 2004

(percentage of households owning any nonfinancial asset and median value of nonfinancial assets for owners, by race and Hispanic origin of householder, 1989 to 2004; percentage point change in ownership and percent change in value for selected years; in 2004 dollars)

	2004	2001	1998	1995	1992	1989	percentage point change 2001–04	1989–04
Percent owning any nonfinancial asset								
Total households	**92.5%**	**90.7%**	**89.9%**	**90.9%**	**90.8%**	**89.3%**	**1.8**	**3.2**
White, non-Hispanic	95.8	94.7	93.9	95.1	95.0	94.1	1.1	1.7
Nonwhite or Hispanic	84.0	78.4	76.7	76.3	77.9	74.8	5.6	9.1

	2004	2001	1998	1995	1992	1989	percent change 2001–04	1989–04
Median value of nonfinancial assets								
Total households	**$147,800**	**$120,900**	**$113,300**	**$102,300**	**$91,000**	**$99,000**	**22.2%**	**49.3%**
White, non-Hispanic	164,800	141,400	125,000	115,300	105,400	110,000	16.5	49.8
Nonwhite or Hispanic	64,100	62,800	61,400	42,900	46,000	41,700	2.1	53.7

Source: Federal Reserve Board, Survey of Consumer Finances, SCF Chartbook, Internet site http://www.federalreserve.gov/pubs/oss/oss2/2004/scf2004home.html; calculations by New Strategist

Most Households Are in Debt

More than three out of four households owe money, up by 4 percentage points since 1989.

Seventy-six percent of households have debt, owing a median of $55,300 in 2004. The median amount of debt owed by the average debtor household increased by a substantial 34 percent between 2001 and 2004, after adjusting for inflation. Since 1989, median household debt has more than doubled.

Middle-aged householders are most likely to be in debt, but the biggest increase in the percentage of households with debt has occurred among the oldest householders. The percentage of households in debt peaks at 88 to 89 percent among householders aged 35 to 54, then drops with age to a low of 40 percent among householders aged 75 or older. But among householders aged 75 or older, the share with debt rose by 19 percentage points between 1989 and 2004, a larger increase than in any other age group.

■ Most households are cautious about taking on debt, with mortgages accounting for the largest share of debt by far. As people pay off their mortgages, net worth rises.

The average household with debt owes $55,300

(median amount of debt for households with debt, 1980 to 2004; in 2004 dollars)

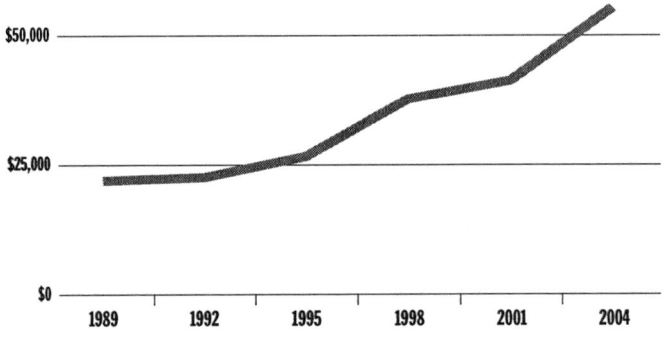

Table 10.9 Debt of Households by Age of Householder, 1989 to 2004

(percentage of households with debt and median amount of debt for debtors, by age of householder, 1989 to 2004; percentage point change in households with debt and percent change in amount of debt for selected years; in 2004 dollars)

	2004	2001	1998	1995	1992	1989	percentage point change 2001–04	percentage point change 1989–04
Percent with any debt								
Total households	**76.4%**	**75.1%**	**74.1%**	**74.5%**	**73.2%**	**72.3%**	**1.3**	**4.1**
Under age 35	79.8	82.7	81.2	83.5	81.5	80.0	–2.9	–0.2
Aged 35 to 44	88.6	88.6	87.6	87.0	86.3	88.6	–0.1	0.0
Aged 45 to 54	88.4	84.6	87.0	86.3	85.4	85.3	3.8	3.2
Aged 55 to 64	76.3	75.4	76.4	73.7	70.1	70.8	0.9	5.6
Aged 65 to 74	58.8	56.8	51.4	53.4	51.4	49.6	1.9	9.1
Aged 75 or older	40.3	29.2	24.6	28.4	31.6	21.0	11.1	19.4

	2004	2001	1998	1995	1992	1989	percent change 2001–04	percent change 1989–04
Median amount of debt								
Total households	**$55,300**	**$41,300**	**$37,700**	**$26,600**	**$22,600**	**$22,000**	**33.9%**	**151.4%**
Under age 35	33,600	26,500	22,300	18,500	13,700	16,700	26.8	101.2
Aged 35 to 44	87,200	65,500	64,500	45,600	47,400	44,100	33.1	97.7
Aged 45 to 54	83,200	57,800	55,800	48,200	35,600	34,700	43.9	139.8
Aged 55 to 64	48,000	36,900	39,600	25,900	25,200	14,000	30.1	242.9
Aged 65 to 74	25,000	14,000	13,800	8,700	6,400	7,300	78.6	242.5
Aged 75 or older	15,400	5,300	9,300	2,300	3,100	4,100	190.6	275.6

Source: Federal Reserve Board, Survey of Consumer Finances, SCF Chartbook, Internet site http://www.federalreserve.gov/pubs/oss/oss2/2004/scf2004home.html; calculations by New Strategist

Table 10.10 Debt of Households by Race and Hispanic Origin of Householder, 1989 to 2004

(percentage of households with debt and median amount of debt for debtors, by race and Hispanic origin of householder, 1989 to 2004; percentage point change in households with debt and percent change in amount of debt for selected years; in 2004 dollars)

	2004	2001	1998	1995	1992	1989	percentage point change 2001–04	1989–04
Percent with any debt								
Total households	76.4%	75.1%	74.1%	74.5%	73.2%	72.3%	1.3	4.1
White, non-Hispanic	78.0	75.8	74.8	75.4	74.3	73.3	2.1	4.7
Nonwhite or Hispanic	72.5	73.0	71.5	71.6	70.1	69.4	–0.5	3.0

	2004	2001	1998	1995	1992	1989	percent change 2001–04	1989–04
Median amount of debt								
Total households	$55,300	$41,300	$37,700	$26,600	$22,600	$22,000	33.9%	151.4%
White, non-Hispanic	69,500	47,700	46,000	32,600	28,700	27,100	45.7	156.5
Nonwhite or Hispanic	30,500	21,300	18,000	13,000	9,300	10,500	43.2	190.5

Source: Federal Reserve Board, Survey of Consumer Finances, SCF Chartbook, Internet site http://www.federalreserve.gov/pubs/oss/oss2/2004/scf2004home.html; calculations by New Strategist

The Expected Age of Retirement Has Climbed

More workers are confident they will have enough money for a comfortable retirement.

Only 27 percent of workers are "very confident" in their ability to afford a comfortable retirement, according to the 2007 Retirement Confidence Survey. Although small, the share is higher than the 24 percent who felt "very confident" a decade earlier. The percentage of workers who are "not at all" confident in having enough money for retirement fell from 15 to 10 percent during those years.

The demise of early retirement may be behind these changes. Over the past decade, the age at which workers expect to retire has climbed. The percentage of workers who expect to retire at age 65 or older increased from 54 to 57 percent between 1997 and 2007. At the same time, the percentage of those who expect to retire before age 65 fell from 45 to 38 percent.

■ The percentage of workers who are confident that Social Security will provide them with benefits at least equal to those received by retirees today rose from 22 to 31 percent between 1997 and 2007.

Most workers are not planning on early retirement

(percent of workers who expect to retire at age 65 or older, 1997 and 2007)

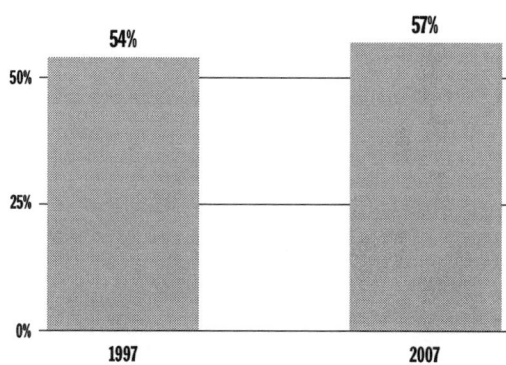

Table 10.11 Retirement Outlook, 1997 and 2007

(responses of workers aged 25 or older to selected questions about retirement, 1997 and 2007; percentage point change, 1997–2007)

	2007	1997	percentage point change
Confidence in having enough money to live comfortably in retirement			
Very confident	27%	24%	3
Somewhat confident	43	41	2
Not too confident	19	19	0
Not at all confident	10	15	–5
Confidence that the Social Security system will continue to provide benefits of at least equal value to the benefits received by retirees today			
Very confident	7	5	2
Somewhat confident	24	17	7
Not too confident	34	36	–2
Not at all confident	34	39	–5
Confidence that the Medicare system will continue to provide benefits of at least equal value to the benefits received by retirees today			
Very confident	6	3	3
Somewhat confident	30	21	9
Not too confident	33	37	–4
Not at all confident	28	34	–6
Expected age of retirement			
Before age 60	17	18	–1
Aged 60 to 64	21	27	–6
Age 65	27	29	–2
Aged 66 or older	24	17	7
Never retire	6	8	–2

Note: Figures may not sum to 100 because "don't know/refused" is not shown.
Source: 2007 Retirement Confidence Survey, Employee Benefit Research Institute, American Savings Education Council, and Mathew Greenwald & Associates, Internet site http://www.ebri.org/surveys/rcs/

Glossary

adjusted for inflation Income or a change in income that has been adjusted for the rise in the cost of living, or the consumer price index (CPI-U-RS).

American Community Survey The ACS is an ongoing nationwide survey of 250,000 households per month, providing detailed demographic data at the community level. Designed to replace the census long-form questionnaire, the ACS includes more than 60 questions that formerly appeared on the long form, such as language spoken at home, income, and education. ACS data are available for areas as small as census tracts.

American Housing Survey The AHS collects national and metropolitan-level data on the nation's housing, including apartments, single-family homes, and mobile homes. The nationally representative survey, with a sample of 55,000 homes, is conducted by the Census Bureau for the Department of Housing and Urban Development every other year.

American Indians In this book, American Indians include Alaska Natives (Eskimos and Aleuts) unless those groups are shown separately.

Asian The term "Asian" includes Native Hawaiians and other Pacific Islanders unless those groups are shown separately.

Baby Boom Americans born between 1946 and 1964.

Baby Bust Americans born between 1965 and 1976, also known as Generation X.

Behavioral Risk Factor Surveillance System The BRFSS is a collaborative project of the Centers for Disease Control and Prevention and U.S. states and territories. It is an ongoing data collection program designed to measure behavioral risk factors in the adult population aged 18 or older. All 50 states, three territories, and the District of Columbia take part in the survey, making the BRFSS the primary source of information on the health-related behaviors of Americans.

black The black racial category includes those who identified themselves as "black" or "African American."

Consumer Expenditure Survey The CEX is an ongoing study of the day-to-day spending of American households administered by the Bureau of Labor Statistics. The CEX includes an interview survey and a diary survey. The average spending figures shown in this book are the integrated data from both the diary and interview components of the survey. Two separate, nationally representative samples are used for the interview and diary surveys. For the interview survey, about 7,500 consumer units are interviewed on a rotating panel basis each quarter for five consecutive quarters. For the diary survey, 7,500 consumer units keep weekly diaries of spending for two consecutive weeks.

consumer unit *(on spending tables only)* For convenience, the term consumer unit and household are used interchangeably in the Spending chapter of this book, although consumer units are somewhat different from the Census Bureau's households. Consumer units are all related members of a household, or financially independent members of a household. A household may include more than one consumer unit.

Current Population Survey The CPS is a nationally representative survey of the civilian noninstitutional population aged 15 or older. It is taken monthly by the Census Bureau for the Bureau of Labor Statistics, collecting information from more than 50,000 households on employment and unemployment. In March of each year, the survey includes the Annual Social and Economic Supplement (formerly called the Annual Demographic Survey), which is the source of most national data on the characteristics of Americans, such as educational attainment, living arrangements, and incomes.

dual-earner couple A married couple in which both the husband and wife are in the labor force.

earnings A type of income, earnings is the amount of money a person receives from his or her job. *See also* Income.

employed All civilians who did any work as a paid employee or farmer/self-employed worker, or who worked 15 hours or more as an unpaid farm worker or in a family-owned business, during the reference period. All those who have jobs but who are temporarily absent from their jobs due to illness, bad weather, vacation, labor management dispute, or personal reasons are considered employed.

expenditure The transaction cost including excise and sales taxes of goods and services acquired during the survey period. The full cost of each purchase is recorded even though full payment may not have been made at the date of purchase. Average expenditure figures may be artificially low for infrequently purchased items such as cars because figures are calculated using all consumer units within a demographic segment rather than just purchasers. Expenditure estimates include money spent on gifts for others.

family A group of two or more people (one of whom is the householder) related by birth, marriage, or adoption and living in the same household.

family household A household maintained by a householder who lives with one or more people related to him or her by blood, marriage, or adoption.

female/male householder A woman or man who maintains a household without a spouse present. May head family or nonfamily households.

foreign-born population People who are not U.S. citizens at birth.

full-time employment Full-time is 35 or more hours of work per week during a majority of the weeks worked.

full-time, year-round Indicates 50 or more weeks of full-time employment during the previous calendar year.

General Social Survey The GSS is a biennial survey of the attitudes of Americans taken by the University of Chicago's National Opinion Research Center. NORC conducts the GSS through face-to-face interviews with an independently drawn, representative sample of 1,500 to 3,000 noninstitutionalized English-speaking people aged 18 or older who live in the United States.

Generation X Americans born between 1965 and 1976, also known as the baby-bust generation.

Hispanic Because Hispanic is an ethnic origin rather than a race, Hispanics may be of any race. While most Hispanics are white, there are black, Asian, American Indian, and even Native Hawaiian Hispanics.

household All the persons who occupy a housing unit. A household includes the related family members and all the unrelated persons, if any, such as lodgers, foster children, wards, or employees who share the housing unit. A person living alone is counted as a household. A group of unrelated people who share a housing unit as roommates or unmarried partners is also counted as a household.

Households do not include group quarters such as college dormitories, prisons, or nursing homes.

household, race/ethnicity of Households are categorized according to the race or ethnicity of the householder only.

householder The householder is the person (or one of the persons) in whose name the housing unit is owned or rented or, if there is no such person, any adult member. With married couples, the householder may be either the husband or wife. The householder is the reference person for the household.

householder, age of The age of the householder is used to categorize households into age groups such as those used in this book. Married couples, for example, are classified according to the age of either the husband or wife, depending on which one identified him or herself as the householder.

housing unit A housing unit is a house, an apartment, a group of rooms, or a single room occupied or intended for occupancy as separate living quarters. Separate living quarters are those in which the occupants do not live and eat with any other persons in the structure and that have direct access from the outside of the building or through a common hall that is used or intended for use by the occupants of another unit or by the general public. The occupants may be a single family, one person living alone, two or more families living together, or any other group of related or unrelated persons who share living arrangements.

Housing Vacancy Survey The HVS is a supplement to the Current Population Survey, providing quarterly and annual data on rental and homeowner vacancy rates, characteristics of units available for occupancy, and homeownership rates by age, household type, region, state, and metropolitan area. The Current Population Survey sample includes 51,000 occupied housing units and 9,000 vacant units.

housing value The respondent's estimate of how much his or her house and lot would sell for if it were for sale.

immigration The relatively permanent movement (change of residence) of people into the country of reference.

in-migration The relatively permanent movement (change of residence) of people into a subnational geographic entity, such as a region, division, state, metropolitan area, or county.

income Money received in the preceding calendar year by each person aged 15 or older from each of the following sources: 1) earnings from longest job (or self-employment); 2) earnings from jobs other than longest job; 3) unemployment compensation; 4) workers' compensation; 5) Social Security; 6) Supplemental Security income; 7) public assistance; 8) veterans' payments; 9) survivor benefits; 10) disability benefits; 11) retirement pensions; 12) interest; 13) dividends; 14) rents and royalties or estates and trusts; 15) educational assistance; 16) alimony; 17) child support; 18) financial assistance from outside the household, and other periodic income. Income is reported in several ways in this book. Household income is the combined income of all household members. Income of persons is all income accruing to a person from all sources. Earnings are the money a person receives from his or her job.

industry Refers to the industry in which a person worked longest in the preceding calendar year.

job tenure The length of time a person has been employed continuously by the same employer.

labor force The labor force tables in this book show the civilian labor force only. The labor force includes both the employed and the unemployed (people who are looking for work). People are counted as in the labor force if they were working or looking for work during the reference week in which the Census Bureau fields the Current Population Survey.

labor force participation rate The percent of the civilian noninstitutional population that is in the civilian labor force, which includes both the employed and the unemployed.

married couples with or without children under age 18 Refers to married couples with or without own children under age 18 living in the same household. Couples without children under age 18 may be parents of grown children who live elsewhere, or they could be childless couples.

median The median is the amount that divides the population or households into two equal portions: one below and one above the median. Medians can be calculated for income, age, and many other characteristics.

median income The amount that divides the income distribution into two equal groups, half having incomes above the median, half having incomes below the median. The medians for households or families are based on all households or families. The median for persons are based on all persons aged 15 or older with income.

metropolitan statistical area The general concept of a metropolitan area is a large population nucleus with adjacent communities having a high degree of social and economic integration with the core. The Office of Management and Budget defines the nation's metropolitan statistical areas. In general, they must include a city or urbanized area with 50,000 or more inhabitants and a total population of 100,000 or more. The county (or counties) that contains the largest city is the "central county" (counties), along with any adjacent counties that are socially and economically integrated with the central county (or counties). In New England, MSAs are defined in terms of cities and towns rather than counties.

Millennial generation Americans born between 1977 and 1994.

mobility status People are classified according to their mobility status on the basis of a comparison between their place of residence at the time of the March Current Population Survey and their place of residence in March of the previous year. Nonmovers are people living in the same house at the end of the period as at the beginning of the period. Movers are people living in a different house at the end of the period than at the beginning of the period. Movers from abroad are either citizens or aliens whose place of residence is outside the United States at the beginning of the period, that is, in an outlying area under the jurisdiction of the United States or in a foreign country. The mobility status of children is fully allocated from the mother if she is in the household; otherwise it is allocated from the householder.

National Ambulatory Medical Care Survey The NAMCS is an annual survey of visits to nonfederally employed office-based physicians who are primarily engaged in direct patient care. Data are collected from physicians rather than patients, with each physician assigned a one-week reporting period. During the week, the physician or office staff record a systematic random sample of visit characteristics.

National Compensation Survey The NCS, which is administered by the Bureau of Labor Statistics, examines the incidence and detailed provisions of selected employee benefit plans in small, medium, and large private establishments, and state and local governments. Each year BLS economists visit a representative sample of establishments across the country, asking questions about the establishment, its employees, and their benefits.

National Health and Nutrition Examination Survey The NHANES is a continuous survey of a representative sample of the U.S. civilian noninstitutionalized population. Respondents are interviewed at home about their health and nutrition, and the interview is followed up by a physical examination that measures such things as height and weight in mobile examination centers.

National Health Interview Survey The NHIS is a continuing nationwide sample survey of the civilian noninstitutional population of the U.S. conducted by the Census Bureau for the National Center for Health Statistics. In interviews each year, data are collected from more than 100,000 people about their illnesses, injuries, impairments, chronic and acute conditions, activity limitations, and use of health services.

National Hospital Ambulatory Medical Care Survey The NHAMCS, sponsored by the National Center for Health Statistics, is an annual national probability sample survey of visits to emergency departments and outpatient departments at non-Federal, short stay and general hospitals. Hospital staff collect data from patient records.

National Household Education Survey The NHES, sponsored by the National Center for Education Statistics, provides descriptive data on the educational activities of the U.S. population, including after-school care and adult education. The NHES is a system of telephone surveys of a representative sample of 45,000 to 60,000 households in the U.S.

Native Hawaiian and other Pacific Islander The 2000 census identified this group for the first time as a separate racial category from Asians. In most survey data, however, the population is included with Asians.

net migration Net migration is the result of subtracting out-migration from in-migration for an area. Another way to derive net migration is to subtract natural increase (births minus deaths) from total population change in an area.

nonfamily household A household maintained by a householder who lives alone or who lives with people to whom he or she is not related.

nonfamily householder A householder who lives alone or with nonrelatives.

non-Hispanic People who do not identify themselves as Hispanic are classified as non-Hispanic. Non-Hispanics may be of any race.

non-Hispanic white People who identify their race as white alone and who do not indicate an Hispanic origin.

nonmetropolitan area Counties that are not classified as metropolitan areas.

occupation Occupational classification is based on the kind of work a person did at his or her job during the previous calendar year. If a person changed jobs during the year, the data refer to the occupation of the job held the longest during that year.

occupied housing units A housing unit is classified as occupied if a person or group of people is living in it or if the occupants are only temporarily absent—on vacation, example. By definition, the count of occupied housing units is the same as the count of households.

outside principal cities The portion of a metropolitan county or counties that falls outside of the principal city or cities; generally regarded as the suburbs.

own children Own children are sons and daughters, including stepchildren and adopted children, of the householder. The totals include never-married children living away from home in college dormitories.

owner occupied A housing unit is "owner occupied" if the owner lives in the unit, even if it is mortgaged or not fully paid for. A cooperative or condominium unit is "owner occupied" only if the owner lives in it. All other occupied units are classified as "renter occupied."

part-time employment Part-time is less than 35 hours of work per week in a majority of the weeks worked during the year.

percent change The change (either positive or negative) in a measure that is expressed as a proportion of the starting measure. When median income changes from $20,000 to $25,000, for example, this is a 25 percent increase.

percentage point change The change (either positive or negative) in a value which is already expressed as a percentage. When a labor force participation rate changes from 70 percent of 75 percent, for example, this is a 5 percentage point increase.

poverty level The official income threshold below which families and people are classified as living in poverty. The threshold rises each year with inflation and varies depending on family size and age of householder.

principal cities The largest cities in a metropolitan area are called the principal cities. The balance of a metropolitan area outside the principal cities is regarded as the "suburbs."

proportion or share The value of a part expressed as a percentage of the whole. If there are 4 million people aged 25 and 3 million of them are white, then the white proportion is 75 percent.

race Race is self-reported and can be defined in three ways. The "race alone" population comprises people who identify themselves as only one race. The "race in combination" population comprises people who identify themselves as more than one race, such as white and black. The "race, alone or in combination" population includes both those who identify themselves as one race and those who identify themselves as more than one race.

regions The four major regions and nine census divisions of the United States are the state groupings as shown below:

Northeast:
• New England: Connecticut, Maine, Massachusetts, New Hampshire, Rhode Island, and Vermont
• Middle Atlantic: New Jersey, New York, and Pennsylvania

Midwest:
• East North Central: Illinois, Indiana, Michigan, Ohio, and Wisconsin
• West North Central: Iowa, Kansas, Minnesota, Missouri, Nebraska, North Dakota, and South Dakota

South:
• South Atlantic: Delaware, District of Columbia, Florida, Georgia, Maryland, North Carolina, South Carolina, Virginia, and West Virginia
• East South Central: Alabama, Kentucky, Mississippi, and Tennessee
• West South Central: Arkansas, Louisiana, Oklahoma, and Texas

West:
• Mountain: Arizona, Colorado, Idaho, Montana, Nevada, New Mexico, Utah, and Wyoming
• Pacific: Alaska, California, Hawaii, Oregon, and Washington

renter occupied *See* Owner occupied.

Retirement Confidence Survey The RCS, sponsored by the Employee Benefit Research Institute, the American Savings Education Council, and Mathew Greenwald & Associates, is an annual survey of a nationally representative sample of 1,000 people aged 25 or older. Respondents are asked a core set of questions that have been asked since 1996, measuring attitudes and behavior towards retirement. Additional questions are also asked about current retirement issues.

rounding Percentages are rounded to the nearest tenth of a percent; therefore, the percentages in a distribution do not always add exactly to 100.0 percent. The totals, however, are always shown as 100.0. Moreover, individual figures are rounded to the nearest thousand without being adjusted to group totals, which are independently rounded; percentages are based on the unrounded numbers.

self-employment A person is categorized as self-employed if he or she was self-employed in the job held longest during the reference period. Persons who report self-employment from a second job are excluded, but those who report wage-and-salary income from a second job are included. Unpaid workers in family businesses are excluded. Self-employment statistics include only nonagricultural workers and exclude people who work for themselves in incorporated business.

sex ratio The number of men per 100 women.

suburbs *See* Outside principal city.

Survey of Consumer Finances The Survey of Consumer Finances is a triennial survey taken by the Federal Reserve Board. It collects data on the assets, debts, and net worth of American households. For the 2004 survey, the Federal Reserve Board interviewed a representative sample of 4,522 households.

unemployed Unemployed people are those who, during the survey period, had no employment but were available and looking for work. Those who were laid off from their jobs and were waiting to be recalled are also classified as unemployed.

white The "white" racial category includes many Hispanics (who may be of any race) unless the term "non-Hispanic white" is used.

Bibliography

American Hospital Association
    Internet site http://www.aha.org/
    —*Hospital Statistics 2006*, Health Forum LLC, Internet site http://www.healthforum
    .com/healthforum_app/index.jsp

Bureau of Justice Statistics
    Internet site http://www.ojp.usdoj.gov/bjs/
    —Sourcebook of Criminal Justice Statistics Online, Internet site http://www.albany
    .edu/sourcebook/

Bureau of Labor Statistics
    Internet site http://www.bls.gov/
    —1984, 1990, 2000, and 2005 Consumer Expenditure Surveys, Internet site http://
    www.bls.gov/cex/home.htm
    —*Employee Benefits in Private Industry, March 2006 Summary*, National Compensation
    Survey, Internet site http://www.bls.gov/ncs/ebs/home.htm
    —Employee Benefits Survey, Internet site http://www.bls.gov/ncs/ebs/home.htm
    —Employee Tenure, Internet site http://www.bls.gov/news.release/tenure.toc.htm
    —*Employment and Earnings*, various issues
    —*Handbook of Labor Statistics*, Bulletin 2340, 1989
    —Labor Force Statistics from the Current Population Survey—Annual Averages,
    Household Data, Internet site http://www.bls.gov/cps/home.htm
    —*Monthly Labor Review*, "Industry output and employment projections to 2014," No-
    vember 2005, Internet site http://www.bls.gov/opub/mlr/2005/11/contents.htm
    —*Monthly Labor Review*, "Labor force projections to 2014: Retiring Boomers" Novem-
    ber 2005, Internet site http://www.bls.gov/opub/mlr/2005/11/contents.htm
    —*Monthly Labor Review*, "Occupational employment projections to 2014," November
    2005, Internet site http://www.bls.gov/opub/mlr/2005/11/contents.htm
    —Projected Labor Force Data, Internet site http://www.bls.gov/emp/emplab1.htm

Bureau of the Census
    Internet site http://www.census.gov/
    —2000 Census, Internet site http://www.census.gov/main/www/cen2000.html
    —2005 American Community Survey, Internet site http://www.census.gov/acs/
    www/
    —American Housing Survey for the United States in 2005, Internet site http://
    www.census.gov/hhes/www/housing/ahs/nationaldata.html
    —America's Families and Living Arrangements, Current Population Surveys,
    Internet site http://www.census.gov/population/www/socdemo/
    hh-fam.html
    —Census of Housing, Housing Characteristics in the U.S.—Tables, 60 Years of De-
    cennial Censuses, Internet site http://www.census.gov/hhes/www/housing/
    census/histcensushsg.html

—Censuses of Population and Housing, Journey-to-Work and Migration Statistics, Internet site http://www.census.gov/population/socdemo/journey/mode6790.txt

—Educational Attainment, Historical Tables, Current Population Survey Annual Social and Economic Supplements, Internet site http://www.census.gov/population/www/socdemo/educ-attn.html

—Families and Living Arrangements, Historical Time Series, Current Population Survey Annual Social and Economic Supplements, Internet site http://www.census.gov/population/www/socdemo/hh-fam.html

—*The Foreign Born Population: 2000*, Census 2000 Brief C2KBR-34, 2003

—Geographical Mobility/Migration, Historical Data, Current Population Survey Annual Social and Economic Supplements, Internet site http://www.census.gov/population/www/socdemo/migrate.html

—Historical Health Insurance Tables, Current Population Survey Annual Social and Economic Supplements, Internet site http://www.census.gov/hhes/www/hlthins/historic/index.html

—Historical Income Data, Current Population Survey Annual Social and Economic Supplements, Internet site http://www.census.gov/hhes/www/income/histinc/histinctb.html

—Historical Poverty Tables, Current Population Survey Annual Social and Economic Supplements, Internet site http://www.census.gov/hhes/www/poverty/histpov/histpovtb.html

—*Historical Statistics of the United States, Colonial Times to 1970*, Part 1, 1975

—Housing Vacancy Surveys, Internet site http://www.census.gov/hhes/www/housing/hvs/hvs.html

—*Income, Poverty, and Health Insurance Coverage in the United States: 2005*, Current Population Report, P60-231, 2006, Internet site http://www.census.gov/hhes/www/income/reports.html

—*Marital Status and Living Arrangements: March 1994*, Current Population Reports, P20-484, 1996

—Metropolitan and Micropolitan Statistical Area Estimates, Internet site, http://www.census.gov/population/www/estimates/CBSA-est2006-pop-chg.html

—*Metropolitan Areas and Cities*, 1990 Census Profile, No. 3, 1991

—National Population Estimates, Internet site http://www.census.gov/popest/national/index.html

—*Profile of the Foreign-born Population in the United States: 1997*, Current Population Reports, P23-195, 1999

—School Enrollment, Historical Tables, Current Population Survey Annual Social and Economic Supplements, Internet site http://www.census.gov/population/www/socdemo/school/.html

—Selected Historical Decennial Census Population and Housing Counts, Internet site http://www.census.gov/population/www/censusdata/hiscendata.html

—State Population Estimates, Internet site http://www.census.gov/popest/states/

—*Statistical Abstract of the United States: 1980, 1990, 1991*, and *1993* through *2007*, Internet site http://www.census.gov/statab/www/

—Voting and Registration, Historical Time Series Tables, Internet site http://www.census.gov/population/www/socdemo/voting.html

Centers for Disease Control and Prevention
    Internet site http://www.cdc.gov/
    —Behavioral Risk Factor Surveillance System, Prevalence Data, Internet site http://apps.nccd.cdc.gov/brfss/

Employee Benefit Research Institute, American Savings Education Council, and Mathew Greenwald & Associates
    Internet site http://www.ebri.org/
    —2007 Retirement Confidence Survey, Internet site http://www.ebri.org/surveys/rcs/

Federal Interagency Forum on Child and Family Statistics
    Internet site http://childstats.gov
    —*America's Children: Key National Indicators of Well-Being, 2007*, Appendix A: Detail Tables, Internet site http://childstats.gov/americaschildren/tables.asp

Federal Reserve Board
    Internet site http://www.federalreserve.gov/pubs/oss/oss2/scfindex.html
    —"Recent Changes in U.S. Family Finances: Evidence from the 2001 and 2004 Survey of Consumer Finances," *Federal Reserve Bulletin*, February 23, 2006, Internet site http://www.federalreserve.gov/pubs/oss/oss2/2004/scf2004home.html
    —"Recent Changes in U.S. Family Finances: Results from the 1998 Survey of Consumer Finances," *Federal Reserve Bulletin*, January 2000, Internet site http://www.federalreserve.gov/pubs/oss/oss2/98/scf98home.html
    —SCF Chartbook, Survey of Consumer Finances, Internet site http://www.federalreserve.gov/pubs/oss/oss2/2004/scf2004home.html

The Gallup Organization
    Internet site http://www.gallup.com
    —"Worry about Crime Remains at Last Year's Elevated Levels," October 19, 2006, Internet site http://www.gallup.com

Homeland Security
    Internet site http://www.dhs.gov/index.shtm
    —*2006 Yearbook of Immigration Statistics*, Internet site http://www.dhs.gov/ximgtn/statistics/publications/LPR06.shtm
    —"Estimates of the Unauthorized Immigrant Population Residing in the United States: January 2005," Internet site http://www.dhs.gov/ximgtn/statistics/publications/index.shtm

National Center for Education Statistics
    Internet site http://nces.ed.gov/
    —*The Condition of Education 2007*, Internet site http://nces.ed.gov/programs/coe/
    —*Digest of Education Statistics: 2006*, Internet site http://nces.ed.gov/programs/digest/
    —Projections of Education Statistics to 2015, Internet site http://nces.ed.gov/programs/projections/

National Center for Health Statistics

    Internet site http://www.cdc.gov/nchs/

    —*2004 National Hospital Discharge Survey*, Advance Data, No. 371, 2006, Internet site http://www.cdc.gov/nchs/about/major/hdasd/listpubs.htm

    —*Births: Final Data for 2000* through *2004*, National Vital Statistics Reports, Internet site http://www.cdc.gov/nchs/products/pubs/pubd/nvsr/nvsr.htm

    —Births: Preliminary Data for 2005, Health E-Stats, 2006, Internet site http://www.cdc.gov/nchs/products/pubs/pubd/hestats/prelimbirths05/prelimbirths05.htm

    —*Deaths: Final Data for 2004*, National Vital Statistics Reports, Vol. 55, No. 19, 2007, Internet site http://www.cdc.gov/nchs/deaths.htm

    —*Health, United States, 2001* and *2006*, Internet site http://www.cdc.gov/nchs/hus.htm

    —*Mean Body Weight, Height, and Body Mass Index, United States 1960–2002*, Advance Data, No. 347, 2004, Internet site http://www.cdc.gov/nchs/pressroom/04news/americans.htm

    —*Nonmarital Childbearing in the United States, 1940–99*, National Vital Statistics Reports, Vol. 48, No. 16, October 18, 2000, Internet site http://www.cdc.gov/nchs/births.htm

    —*Trends in Hospital Utilization: United States, 1988–92*, Vital and Health Statistics, Series 13, No. 124, 1996, Internet site http://www.cdc.gov/nchs/products/pubs/pubd/series/sr13/130-121/sr13_124.htm

University of California, Berkeley, Survey Documentation and Analysis, Computer-assisted Survey Methods Program

    Internet site http://sda.berkeley.edu/

    —General Social Surveys 1972–2004 Cumulative Data Files, Internet site http://sda.berkeley.edu/D3/GSS04/Docyr/gs04.htm

University of Michigan, Monitoring the Future Study

    Internet site http://monitoringthefuture.org/

    —Monitoring the Future Study, Data Tables and Figures, Internet site http://monitoringthefuture.org/data/data.html

Index

unemployed. *See* Labor force.
union representation, 317, 321
unmarried partners, 343, 348
utilities, fuels, public services, spending on
    as percent of household budget, 430–431
    by age of householder, 437–458
    by educational attainment, 492–504
    by household type, 466–478
    by race and Hispanic origin, 459–465
    by region, 479–491

vacation days, as an employee benefit, 318
vehicles, as nonfinancial asset, 508
vehicles, spending on
    as percent of household budget, 430–431
    by age of householder, 437–458
    by educational attainment, 492–504
    by household type, 466–478
    by race and Hispanic origin, 459–465
    by region, 479–491
vision care, as an employee benefit, 317–318
voting, 54, 60–61

wealth
    assets, financial, 506, 508–512
    assets, nonfinancial, 506, 508, 513–515
    debt, 506, 508, 516–518
    net worth, 506–507
    stock ownership, 506, 508–509, 512
weight status, 143–145
Whites. *See also* Whites, non-Hispanic.
    births to, 133–134, 137–138
    by age, 366
    by region, 381–382, 384
    by state, 392–395, 398–399
    cancer survival rate, 163, 165–166
    earnings, 228, 230–231
    educational attainment, 72, 76
    health status, 124
    homeownership, 185–188
    households of, 324, 329
    income, 220–221
    interracial marriage, 354, 356
    labor force, 254, 257–258, 268–269
    life expectancy, 171, 174
    living arrangements of children, 336, 340
    population, 364–366, 381–382, 384, 392–395,
      398–399
    poverty status, 234, 241–243, 247–252
    Scholastic Assessment Test (SAT) scores, 86
Whites, non-Hispanic. *See also* Whites.
    assets, 511, 515
    births to, 132–134, 137–139, 142
    by age, 367
    by region, 381, 383, 385

    by state, 391–393, 396–397, 400–401
    college enrollment, 98–99
    college enrollment rate, 87, 90
    day care use, 309
    debt, 518
    diabetes, 152
    earnings, 230–231
    educational attainment, 72, 76
    heart disease death rate, 161–162
    income, 208, 220–221
    interracial marriage, 354, 356
    labor force, 254, 258, 270
    net worth of households, 506–507
    population, 363–367, 379, 381, 383, 385,
      391–393, 396–397, 400–401
    poverty status, 241–244, 247–252
    voting, 61
widowhood, 352–353
women. *See also* Households, family,
      female-headed and People living alone.
    age at first marriage, 349, 351
    birth control use, 125–126
    births, 127–142
    blood pressure, high, 150–151
    by age, 362
    by occupation, 271–276, 287–293
    cancer, 163–165
    cholesterol, high, 152
    cigarette smoking by, 146–148
    college enrollment, 92–94
    college enrollment rate, 87–89
    death rate, 170
    degrees conferred, 102, 105–106, 108–109,
      111–112, 114–115, 117–118
    diabetes, 152
    drug use, prescription, 153
    earnings, 228–229, 231, 233
    educational attainment, 68–69, 71, 73, 75
    health status, 124
    heart disease death rate, 161–162
    income, 216–217, 219, 221, 224–225, 227
    job tenure, 312–314
    labor force, 254–256, 258–259, 262–264, 266–267,
      269–270, 301–308
    life expectancy, 171, 173
    living arrangements, 343, 345, 347
    marital status, 349–350, 352
    poverty status, 236
    Scholastic Assessment Test (SAT) scores, 84–85
    voting, 60
    weight status, 143–145
    wives earning more than husbands, 212, 215
    working, attitude toward, 33, 35
wood use, 198–199
work at home, 315–316